10/42

Jack S[illegible] '14
2523 [illegible]
Berkeley
Ph. Berk. 5633

# AN OUTLINE-HISTORY OF ENGLISH LITERATURE

## Volume I: TO DRYDEN

## *COLLEGE OUTLINE SERIES*

A. W. LITTLEFIELD, *General Editor*

---

|  |  |
|---|---|
| ACCOUNTING | BAUER-DARBY |
| ALGEBRA, College | MOORE |
| ANCIENT HISTORY | HYMA |
| ANCIENT, Medieval, Modern History | RICKARD-HYMA |
| BACTERIOLOGY, Principles of | BRYAN |
| BIOLOGY, General | ALEXANDER |
| BOTANY, General | FULLER |
| BUSINESS LAW | MARTIN-BABB |
| CHEMISTRY, First Year College | LEWIS |
| CHEMISTRY, Organic | DEGERING, et al |
| CORPORATION FINANCE | HAROLD |
| DOCUMENTED PAPERS, Writing | HUBBELL |
| ECONOMICS, Principles of | JAMES |
| EDUCATION, History of | THOMPSON |
| ENGLAND, History of | RICKARD |
| EUROPE, 1500-1848, History of | LITTLEFIELD |
| EUROPE, 1815-1940, History of | LITTLEFIELD |
| EXAMINATIONS, How To Write Better | HOOK |
| FRENCH REVIEW GRAMMAR | DU MONT |
| GEOLOGY, Principles of | FIELD |
| GERMAN GRAMMAR | GREENFIELD |
| GOVERNMENT, American | SAYRE |
| JOURNALISM, Survey of | MOTT, et al |
| LATIN AMERICA, History of | WILGUS-D'EÇA |
| LITERATURE, English, To Dryden | OTIS-NEEDLEMAN |
| LITERATURE, English, Since Milton | NEEDLEMAN-OTIS |
| MIDDLE AGES, 300-1500, History of | MOTT-DEE |
| NATURAL RESOURCES of United States | FIELD |
| PHILOSOPHY, Introduction to | RANDALL-BUCHLER |
| PHYSICS, First Year College | BENNETT |
| POLITICAL SCIENCE | JACOBSEN-LIPMAN |
| PSYCHOLOGY, Educational | PINTNER, et al |
| PSYCHOLOGY, General | FRYER-HENRY |
| SHAKESPEARE'S PLAYS, Outlines of | WATT, et al |
| SOCIOLOGY, Principles of | PARK, REUTER, et al |
| STATISTICAL METHODS | ARKIN-COLTON |
| STUDY, Best Methods of | SMITH-LITTLEFIELD |
| UNITED STATES, To 1865, History of | KROUT |
| UNITED STATES, Since 1865, History of | KROUT |
| WORLD, Since 1914, History of | LANDMAN |
| ZOOLOGY, General | ALEXANDER |

COLLEGE OUTLINE SERIES

# OUTLINE-HISTORY OF ENGLISH LITERATURE

## Volume 1: To Dryden

BY

WILLIAM BRADLEY OTIS
*Professor of English Language and Literature*
COLLEGE OF THE CITY OF NEW YORK

AND

MORRISS H. NEEDLEMAN

*Third Edition*

BARNES & NOBLE, Inc.

*New York*

Entered in Stationers Hall
London, England

First Edition, 1937
Revised Edition, 1938
Third Edition, 1939

*Printed in the United States of America
By De Pamphilis Press, Inc., New York, N.Y.*

# PREFACE

It is hoped that the OUTLINE-HISTORY will not be regarded as merely another summary of English literature. The OUTLINE-HISTORY covers the field, we believe, with an eclectic adequacy not attempted by any other manual. In matters of selection and interpretation the authors always have remembered the probable and the practical needs of both the undergraduate college student making his first long excursion into English literature and the majoring or even the graduate college student desiring a comprehensive handbook in compact form.

To make the volume primarily usable it has been found necessary to deviate from the conventional plan of most textbooks. The following are some of the departures:

1. The OUTLINE-HISTORY brings the treatment of the subject abreast of modern research and criticism. Where opinion contrary to that of the traditional is prevalent, the authors call attention to the fact by notes usually so specific in reference that the teacher or the student can check the statements made and correct any errors of judgment. While indicating where counsels are divided, an endeavor is made to avoid both antiquated opinions and crotchety modern preferences.

It is a cause for regret that we can not discharge completeley our indebtedness to earlier source-studies. Were one able to ferret out the borrowed ideas and to assign to each scholar his particular contribution to the field, such citation of authorities would still be prohibitive because of a number of considerations, chiefly the limitation of space. On the one hand, our general plan of stating matters of common knowledge without recording our indebtedness has meant that in not a few cases outstanding sources of information are mentioned only scantily, or not at all. But it is that very restriction that has made possible a fuller acknowledgment of our obligations in the more specialized instances.

2. The OUTLINE-HISTORY gives representation to all aspects of the field. For example, the diversified scope of the content provides for the allotment of considerable space to significant minor writers who too frequently have been neglected. A knowledge of these lesser contemporaries is essential to any real understanding of the temper and spirit of an age. In addition, more than cursory attention is accorded the earlier periods of our literature. The conviction that such material should be more generally accessible accounts for putting as much emphasis upon Chaucer and Spenser, for example, as upon Shakespeare and Milton. Even in its discussion of the fifteenth century in English literature, one usually dealt with fragmentarily or skipped altogether, the OUTLINE-HISTORY's fuller re-statement gives that period its long due.

If the OUTLINE-HISTORY should be considered over-minute in its analysis, it will at least have avoided in the main the mere tabulation of the names of authors and the titles of their works, and also the general barrenness of scrimped accounts and one-sided interpretations. College students might well be expected to approach the field of English literature from a mature point of view much in that spirit with which for many years they have been expected to approach the field of mathematics or physics or biology or chemistry.

3. The OUTLINE-HISTORY lends itself to immediate use for further study. Cross-references, footnotes, and other editorial aids have been utilized at strategic points so as to reduce to a minimum the necessity of directing students to other books. The footnotes themselves while stimulating the student's interest in specific literary problems are a concise, up-to-date bibliography. It should be apparent that the OUTLINE-HISTORY has been made, so far as space limitations would permit, a single unit, yet also a point of departure for supplementary readings and explorations.

4. The OUTLINE-HISTORY indicates foreign as well as native influences upon English literature. Occasionally, it is true, a textbook or two will indicate by a chart that, for example, Machiavelli wrote his *Prince* and Castiglione his *Cortegiano* at approximately the time More wrote his *Utopia.* But the OUTLINE-HISTORY makes the point of contact more immediate and more specific: thus, for example, it records the influence of Machiavelli's *Prince* upon Elyot's *The Boke named the Governour* and upon Spenser's *Veue of the Present State of Ireland,* and that of Castiglione's *Il Cortegiano* upon Spenser's *Fowre Hymnes* and Marlowe's *Hero and Leander.* As for Sir Thomas More's *Utopia,* the OUTLINE-HISTORY indicates the obligation to Amerigo Vespucci's account of his voyages, to Plato's *Republic,* St. Augustine's *De Civitate Dei* (upon which More once lectured), and Erasmus's *Institutio Principis Christiani.*

5. The OUTLINE-HISTORY has further departures from the usual textbook. A case in point is its attempt at correlation. Thus, in evaluating the most original portion of Anglo-Saxon poetry (*Deor, The Wife's Lament, The Husband's Message, The Ruin, The Wanderer,* and the like), the OUTLINE-HISTORY points out that those lyrical or elegiac poems anticipate the dramatic monologue, a form of which the ultimate master is Robert Browning; in outlining Chaucer's *Pardoner's Tale,* the OUTLINE-HISTORY states that one of the most recent analogues occurs in Kipling's *Second Jungle Book.* When examining William Godwin's *Enquiry concerning Political Justice, the* OUTLINE-HISTORY (Volume II) refers the student to various ideal commonwealths previously encountered, such as Bacon's *New Atlantis,* Hobbes's *Leviathan,* Bernard de Mandeville's *Fable of the Bees,* and also looks forward to Bulwer-Lytton's *The Coming Race,* Butler's *Erewhon,* Morris's *News from Nowhere,* H. G. Wells's *A Modern Utopia,* and Aldous Huxley's *Brave New World.*

While designed, therefore, primarily for the college undergraduate and the majoring or even the graduate student, it is felt that the OUTLINE-HISTORY is useful as well for all who do not have access to adequately equipped libraries or who may find it convenient to have in succinct form a representative discussion of English literature.

The OUTLINE-HISTORY doubtless will call for revision. All criticisms will be welcome. Suggestions that may improve the handbook's usefulness will be incorporated, if possible, in succeeding editions. Kindly address the authors in care of Barnes and Noble, Inc., New York City.

W. B. O. — M. H. N.

Acknowledgments

In the preparation of AN OUTLINE-HISTORY OF ENGLISH LITERATURE TO DRYDEN we have been assisted by many scholars, both friends and strangers, who have volunteered valuable suggestions for improving the manuscript. Our obligations to all of these can not, for lack of space, be specifically acknowledged here; but for generous aid we must express our special gratitude to Professor A. C. Baugh of the University of Pennsylvania; Dr. Alexander Boecker of Brooklyn, New York; Professor Haldeen Braddy of Sul Ross State Teachers College; Professor Carleton Brown of New York University; Professor Joseph George Cohen of Brooklyn College; Professor Emeritus Morris Raphael Cohen of The College of the City of New York; Professor R. D. Havens of The Johns Hopkins University; Professor Florence Hilbish of Cedar Crest College; Professor Karl J. Holzknecht of New York University; Professor T. H. Johnson of the Hackley School; Dr. Paul Klapper, President of Queens College; Professor Dawn Logan of Waynesburg College; Professor T. O. Mabbott of Hunter College; Professor Emeritus Lewis Freeman Mott of The College of the City of New York; Professor Vincent H. Ogburn of Leland Stanford University; Professor Charles G. Osgood of Princeton University; Professor J. J. Parry of the University of Illinois; Professor A. W. Secord of the University of Illinois; Dr. Samuel A. Tannenbaum, Editor of *The Shakespeare Association Bulletin;* Professor Homer A. Watt of New York University; and Professor Donald G. Whiteside of Brooklyn College. To Professors Charles F. Horne, Alfred D. Compton, Bird Stair, Arthur Dickson, and Ralph Gordon we must also acknowledge our indebtedness, as well as to Messrs. Donald A. Roberts, Maximilian G. Walten, Arthur K. Burt, Warren B. Austin, and John C. Thirlwall, Jr., all of the English department; also to Professors Samuel B. Heckman and J. Salwyn Shapiro, of The College of the City of New York. We owe a special debt of gratitude to the Honorable Francis J. Sinnott, Postmaster of Brooklyn, New York, and to Claire and Lee Howard, of Brooklyn, New York, without whose assistance the book would have been delayed considerably. For general guidance and detailed help in the preparation of the work we are deeply obligated to Mr. A. W. Littlefield, Editor of the COLLEGE OUTLINE SERIES.

W. B. O. — M. H. N.

## PRELIMINARY

### AN APPROACH TO THE COLLEGE SURVEY COURSE

English literature is a required study for all college students, yet there is a dearth of investigation as to the proper materials for teaching the subject at college levels. Even in the secondary school, where much emphasis has been placed upon subject-matter and educational procedures, the authorities are not agreed as to aims in the study of literature. Accordingly, the usual survey course in the college is narrow; it seems to lack the omnibus material that might lend itself to various points of view and methods.

A condition contributing much to the difficulty of determining the scope and methods of teaching the subject at the college level, is the ineffective articulation between the secondary school and the college. Frequently a more or less helter-skelter and shallow survey course of English literature has been required before students entered college and another such course often fails to stimulate a new enthusiasm. The partly known territory traversed may hold out no hope of discoveries because the instruction often falls below the level of college standards. In other courses, such as history and mathematics, the method is frequently imposed by the content, but this is less true, if true at all, of English literature. Whereas in the secondary school the recognized criterion in selecting reading material is the interests of the students, here in the college the cultivation of a taste for reading too commonly yields in importance to a more intensive study (usually through the over-worked lecture method) of literature as a "knowledge subject." This may not in itself be a discouraging approach, but tends to be made so by formalization. Moreover, what are social and political values to the student are lost when textbooks of literary history and consorting anthologies are dependent upon conventional and traditional ideas.

What, therefore, should be the educational procedures in the teaching of English literature to college students? If there is a consensus it is, first, that the main aim should be to relate the literature to life, vitalizing ideas and ideals, and integrating broad intellectual and philosophical connections. It is not good for literature, any more than it is for man, to be alone; and a periphery course, or preferably, an orientation course, can perform an important service. Second, a first college course should be designed in a fashion permitting adjustment to the needs of *all* students, both those who purpose to go no further than the first course and those who plan to go beyond. Third, the method in each case should grow out of both the problems of the subject and the nature of the student. The textbook itself should avoid undue stress on material apparently intended to yield entertainment suitable for adolescents rather than to provoke thinking on an adult level. If a choice is offered it should favor intellectually stimulating ideas rather than factual matter barren of ideas.

These main procedures have energized the growth of the OUTLINE-HISTORY until it has assumed the present proportions. Our convictions are that abstract account and dogmatic presentation deserve at the collegiate level a smaller place than they usually receive, and that divergent ideas are to be included for the purpose of putting before the students material that stimulates reflection and calls for solution of problems. To the suggestion that difficulties could be diminished by consigning the notes to an appendix, we would say that their neglect might thereby be encouraged. Moreover, it is not difficult, when advisable, to disregard the footnotes. If we have erred, we have preferred to do so on the side of fullness, for the reasons stated and also in the expectation that the instructor or the instructor and students will select the material to be studied.

Selective choice by the users of this handbook—that is the basis of the approach. It is obvious that the instructor or the instructor and students should have a large measure of freedom in planning and carrying on the course. The ideal approach would be to test the entering students and then group them according to their abilities and needs, as revealed by the placement tests, into first courses at differing levels of achievement. However, most classes include students of varying abilities. Containing more material than any specific survey course may require, the OUTLINE-HISTORY can be adapted to any class. It is expected that more or less of the material will be omitted. Specific minimal requirements should, however, be prescribed for each class. Some units will merit further consideration and some will be skimmed or even skipped in preparation for class. Specific study-guides with organizing questions might well include not alone the general assignment but also the supplementary work for successive levels. Some classes might even follow the procedure of the OUTLINE-HISTORY in basing apportionment of space, not upon conventional treatment elsewhere but upon the omnibus needs of a course planned to inform, interest, and stimulate varied groups of intellectually mature students. However, those who wish some minimal signposts may give heed to the works marked by an obelisk (†); those who wish to enrich the minimal requirements may make the reference notes the basis of additional work; and, finally, those who plan to do graduate work may follow up for themselves the various problems raised throughout the OUTLINE-HISTORY.

Selection, therefore, is imperative for the instructor, or the instructor and students together. This manual is not a substitute for thinking.

It must not supplant personal contact with the literature itself. Indiscriminate mastery of the material in the OUTLINE-HISTORY is not the desideratum. The student is not to work for the memorization of biographical facts, dates of literary works, or even critical judgments, except in a naturally subordinate degree. Were the OUTLINE-HISTORY not meant for heterogeneous classes of college students, its array of reference notes might be construed as exemplifying vivisection or over-annotation of literature, but in view of the specific purpose of the book the footnotes can be developed into a body of stimulating aids to the proper interpretation of the literature from which the OUTLINE-HISTORY itself has developed. Especial emphasis is to be placed upon the study of historical, intellectual, and aesthetic backgrounds of the literature, and upon the study of masterpieces rather than of literary types. By planning larger units designed for a more intensive study of individual authors and of specific works most representative of a particular period, the connections of literature with that period's social, political, and intellectual movements can be established effectively.

Whether in a first-year class where only two or three of Chaucer's Canterbury tales or of Shakespeare's plays may be assigned, or in a majoring class where a dozen or so may be required, or even in a graduate class where possibly all the tales or plays may be prescribed, the OUTLINE-HISTORY in each case provides a graduated editorial apparatus that can be utilized as an energizing guide to ideas and ideals according to the varying abilities and selective needs of a particular class or student. As a final caution may we again urge that in no case should the purpose of the college survey course be merely to supply aesthetic occupation or a like kind of relief after the work in other subjects in the curriculum; in all cases the instructor should keep in mind the needs, interests, purposes, capacities, or experiences of the students either as individuals, distinctive groups, or varied classes.

## TABLE OF CONTENTS

# AN OUTLINE-HISTORY OF ENGLISH LITERATURE

---

## Volume I: TO DRYDEN

## ON THE USE OF THIS HANDBOOK

### I

It is essential to read both the *Preface* (pages v-vii) and the *Preliminary* (pages vii-x) in order to comprehend the plan and scope of the OUTLINE-HISTORY OF ENGLISH LITERATURE, and to make full and proper use of it. The *Table of Contents* and the *Index* have their obvious uses, although it should be remembered that the latter does not include the *Supplementary List of Writers* (pp. I-XIII).

### II

The main text of this manual is set in ten-point type. The original intention of utilizing a reduced type to indicate the works of minor writers, the lesser works of major writers, and like matters, had to be abandoned when it was found that the contemplated frequent use of a smaller font would be a definite strain on the eyes. Unwilling, however, to forego entirely the plan of indicating subordination, it was decided not only to restrict the use of a reduced type but also to mark the more important works as indicated below.

### KEY TO SYMBOLS

† The dagger-mark or obelisk denotes the more important works.

* The asterisk indicates additional information alphabetically arranged in *Appendix B* (pages XIV-XXXII).

[1] The raised number refers to the note at the bottom of the page.

# INTRODUCTION

## THE FORMATION OF THE ENGLISH PEOPLE

### I. THE PRE-CELTIC INHABITANTS

**A. The Paleolithic Man**

Ages ago, when attached to the European continent, England was probably inhabited by the stunted Paleolithic man.

**B. The Neolithic Man**

Centuries passed; England took on its existing insular form; and there appeared the swarthy-complexioned Neolithic man or Iberian.[1]

### II. THE COMING OF THE CELTS

**A. Two Main Branches of the Celtic Race**

1. *Goidels* (*Gaels*). In west and north. Language, customs, and ethnic qualities were profoundly altered by contact with the aboriginal inhabitants. Survive in Ireland and West Scotland.

2. *Brythons* (*Britons* or *Cymri*). In southweast. Much less modified by external ethnic influences. Survive in Wales and Cornwall.

**B. Religion of the Celts: Druidism**

1. A hierarchy of gods resembling that of the pagan Greeks and Romans, but under different appellations. Worshipped a multitude of local deities.

2. The practice of human sacrifices; the belief in the transmigration of souls. Sanctified the oak (while reverencing the mistletoe when growing on the oak)—an emblem of the diuturnity of the Supreme Being.

**C. Celtic Influence upon English Literature**

1. Contributed to the language less than a dozen words; *e. g.*, *bannock, dun* (color), and river-names like *Avon* and *Thames*.

2. Contributed to the literature: (a) the *lais,* either lyrics or short verse romances (p. 46); and (b) *The Mabinogion*, a compilation of Welsh tales (p. 41).

### III. THE ROMAN OCCUPATION

**A. Invasions**

1. B. C. 55 and 54. Two invasions by Julius Caesar. Led to Roman Conquest and civilization.

---

1 This identification is little more than conjecture.

2. A. D. 43—84. Invasion by Aulus Plautius, under Emperor Claudius. Occupied the country south of the Severn and Avon. Successive governors (Ostorius Scapula, Aulus Didus, Veranius, Suetonius Paulinus, and particularly Cneius Julius Agricola) completed conquest by A. D. 84.

3. A. D. 401—410. Roman legions gradually withdrawn to protect Rome from barbarian attacks. Finally (410) Emperor Honorius renounced Rome's sovereignty over Britain.

### B. Roman Influence upon English Literature

1. Contributed to the language a small number of Latin words; *e. g., mile, street,* and the suffixes "-caster" or "-chester" and "-wich" or "-wick" in such names as Lancaster, Winchester, Greenwich, Berwick.

2. Contributed very little to the literature.

## IV. THE ANGLO-SAXON CONQUEST

### A. Invasions

1. A. D. 449. Withdrawal of the Romans left the Celts a prey to the barbarians. Upon the invitation, it is said, of Vortigern, a British (Celtic) chief, who wished assistance against the invasions of the Picts and Scots, a band of Jutes (from Jutland?) under Hengist and Horsa(?) dragged its boats up the beach at Ebbsfleet in the Isle of Thanet. At first the Jutes—a branch of the Teutonic race composed of three tribes, the other two being the Saxons and the Angles, and all three, according to prevailing opinion, living "somewhere on the Continent between Hamburg and the topmost point of the Jutish peninsula,"[1]—were loyal to their pledges; but, recognizing the helplessness of the Britons, soon took possession of the surrounding country. Settled in the southeast in Kent and on the Isle of Wight. Celts were absorbed, exterminated, or driven to the west and north, to Wales, Devonshire, and Cornwall.

2. A. D. 477. Saxons (from Schleswig?) under Ella marauded the shore west of Kent. Settled on the south and east coasts, in Sussex, Essex, and later in Wessex.

3. A. D. 547. Angles (from Holstein?) under Ida invaded the east and north. Settled north of the Humber. Founded the Kingdom of Bernicia (North Northumbria). From the Angles, who were the most numerous, the country became known as Angle-land, or England, the land of the Angles.

### B. Language

1. Language at first called *Englisc,* because the Angles were the ascendant tribe; afterward, when mixed with Norman, called *Saxon;* and, finally, *Anglo-Saxon.* Is a Low-German, West-Germanic, Indo-European language. Nearest relatives are Old Frisian and Low German

1 Langenfelt, Gösta, "Notes on the Anglo-Saxon Pioneers," *Englische Studien,* LXVI (1931-1932), p. 165 (pp. 161-244).

(*Plattdeutsch*). Many scholars (Freeman, Sweet, Cook) prefer to use the possibly ambiguous term *Old English* or *Oldest English* rather than *Anglo-Saxon*. Differs from later periods of English by reason of a relatively full inflectional system and of practically a unilingual vocabulary.

2. Four main dialects: (a) *Kentish*—spoken in the counties of Kent and the major part of Surrey (Jutes); (b) *West Saxon*—spoken in the rest of the territory south of the Thames (Saxons); (c) *Mercian* or *Midland*—spoken in the region between the Thames and the Humber (southern Angles); and (d) *Northumbrian*—spoken between the Humber in England and the Firth of Forth in Scotland (remaining Angles). While the surviving literature is almost all in West Saxon, the important dialect for to-day is the Mercian, from which more of modern English is derived.

### C. Religion of the Anglo-Saxons: Polytheism

1. Chief gods included Woden, Thor, Loki, Tiw (or Tiu). Memory of some gods preserved in the days of the week; *e. g.*, Tuesday (Tiw's or Tiu's day), Wednesday (Woden's day), Thursday (Thor's day), Saturday (Saturn's day).

2. Even the gods were subject to the decrees of the dread goddess Wyrd, or Fate. The "Wierd Sisters" of Shakespeare's *Macbeth* derive from the Wyrd, by whom the thread of destiny is spun.

### D. Advent of Christianity

1. Christianity, introduced by the Roman Occupation, had been practically wiped out by the Anglo-Saxons; but not before converted Celts had carried the Creed to Ireland (St. Patrick, *c.* 432—461) and to Scotland. Christian missionaries again reached England, this time from two directions. From Ireland came Aidan, who converted the North Anglians to a Celtic form of Christianity, with the seat of his episcopate at the island-promontory of Lindisfarne; and from Rome, sent by Pope Gregory the Great, came Augustine (597), who converted Kent, with the center at Canterbury.

2. Celtic and Roman churches differed on certain matters—*e. g.*, the form and shape of the tonsure, and the time of the celebration of Easter. Finally, at the Synod of Whitby (664), King Oswy gave his decision in favor of the Roman party. For the next nine centuries England submitted to papal domination.[1]

3. The re-introduction of Christianity exerted an important influence upon literature; *e. g.*, it not only contributed to the language many ecclesiastical terms, such as *alb, clerk, creed, martyr, verse,* but also stimulated contact with a richer culture and provided haven for literary composition as well as for the copying of manuscripts.

1 For some time after the Council of Whitby, however, Celtic Christianity not only survived, but was in the ascendant. See Meissner, J. L. G., *The Celtic Church in England* (1929).

**E. Anglo-Saxon Influence upon English Literature**

1. Made important contributions to the language. Vocabulary pertains to the common feelings and sights, to the simple modes and elementary arts of life, and to that which is essential to the construction of an English sentence—*e. g., man, sun, land, red, white, gold, silver; cat, horse, cow, sheep; go, eat, bark, bleat, love, hate, fear;* the verb "to be" in all its parts; and pronouns, prepositions, conjunctions, and articles.

2. Made many contributions to the literature. See subsequent pages.

## CHAPTER I

# THE ANGLO-SAXON PERIOD TO A. D. 1066

## *ANGLO-SAXON CHARACTERISTICS*

1. Stern, barbarous life. Subjected by nature to rude turmoil.
2. Mixtures of savagery, sentiment, and nobility.
3. Religious feeling, its philosophy being instinct with fatalism.
4. Responsiveness to Nature. Particularly did love of the sea inspire their poetry: the sea is the *water-street,* the *swan-road,* the *whale-path;* the ship, the *foamy-necked floater,* the *wave-skimmer,* the *sea-stallion.*
5. Common sense, power of endurance, and seriousness of thought characterize the Anglo-Saxons, as against the elfish mockery, ironic introspection, emotional temperament, bold imagination, sensitive nature, rainbow-like fancy, and violent but mercurial feelings of the Celts. These two racial strains imbue Anglo-Saxon literature. (The third racial strain—the Norman—came later, contributing to the English people and their literature an easy suppleness and prismatic wit. See p. 22 *ff.*)

## *ANGLO-SAXON IDEALS*

1. Love of glory is the ruling motive of every noble life.
2. Allegiance to lord or king is the social virtue most extolled.
3. Reverence for womanhood. Higher than was usual even among more enlightened peoples.
4. Love of personal freedom. Did not conflict with the fidelity, even unto death, of thane to lord.
5. Open-handed hospitality of lord to thane.
6. Honoring of truth.
7. Repression of sentiment.

## I. THE AGE OF BEOWULF AND THE BEGINNINGS (to 828)

### General View of the Literature

The Age of Beowulf and the Beginnings, embracing the so-designated Bookless Age (to 597, when St. Augustine brought Christianity to the Anglo-Saxons) and the Age of Poetry in the North (to 828, when Egbert of Wessex became "King" of all England), has left as literary survivals only specimens of poetry, their origin being in the Teutonic legends of the scop and the gleeman. The scop was the shaper or the maker of the verses—above all, the poet. The gleeman, on the other hand, was the harper who chanted what the scop had composed —above all, the singer or reciter. Each, however, often combined the functions of both.

## *POETRY OF PAGAN OR HALF-PAGAN ORIGIN*

### Anglo-Saxon Epics

***Beowulf*†*** (probably *c.* A. D. 675—725).[1] Most important specimen of Anglo-Saxon literature is also the oldest surviving epic of any Teutonic people. In the Late West-Saxon dialect. Completed, perhaps, before the ninth century and sung, perhaps, by the Anglo-Saxons before their invasion of England, the composition was, according to the traditional theory, probably formed by the coalescent refashioning or redaction of short lays. Accounts for the mingling of pagan and biblical elements: the reflections are largely Christian (*e.g.*, the depiction of the bog-living monsters as the issue of Cain, the first murderer), while the ceremonies are mainly heathen (*e. g.*, the account of Beowulf's funeral).[2] Note that the scenes are descriptive of Denmark and South Sweden, not of England; that the participating figures are Danes, Geats, Franks, and Frisians, not Britons. Influence of Homer not improbable in the heroic boasting, the two voyages of Beowulf, and the close of the epic. Parallels to different parts of ***Beowulf*** have been discovered in the *Grettisaga,* the *Hrolfssaga,* the *Flores Saga Konungs ok Sona hans,* the sagas of *Samson the Fair* and of *Orm Storolfsson,* and in two ballads each from the Faroe Islands and from Sweden. Reminiscent not only of the Irish saga *The Feast of Bricriu* (p. 60) but particularly of a *Märchen* extant in some two hundred versions and named "The Bear's Son Tale."

*Narrative*

I. (a) Beowulf's victory over the cannibal-ogre Grendel in Hrothgar's mead-hall Heorot.

(b) Beowulf's slaying of Grendel's dam (mother) in her lair, a cave at the bottom of the sea.

---

1 *Beowulf* best exemplifies the characteristics and life-ideals of the Anglo-Saxons (p. 5).

2 Growing opposition to this older point of view must be noted. The traditional idea, says W. W. Lawrence, "that the Christian elements in *Beowulf* are interpolations in an originally heathen poem, is now, as has already been suggested, generally abandoned." [*Beowulf and Epic Traditions* (1928), p. 282.] While other recent interpretations may admit the Christian elements to be anachronistic, they generally emphasize the organic unity of the poem: see Malone, Kemp, "The Finn Episode in *Beowulf,*" *The Journal of English and Germanic Philology,* XXV (1926), pp. 157-172; Bryan, Frank, "Epithetic Compound Folk-Names in *Beowulf,*" *Studies in English Philology: A Miscellany in Honor of Frederick Klaeber,* edited by Malone, Kemp, and Ruud, Martin B. (1929), pp. 120-134; Du Bois, Arthur E., "The Unity of *Beowulf,*" *Publications of the Modern Language Association of America,* XLIX (1934), pp. 374-405.

† * **Explanation of symbols immediately precedes page one.**

II. (a) Beowulf's return in glory to his uncle, Hygelac, King of the Geats, whose son, Heardred, he succeeded to the throne.
(b) Beowulf's victory-in-death, fifty years later, over the Fire-Drake or Dragon.

*Other Characters*

1. **Aeschere.** Hrothgar's counsellor, carried off by Grendel's dam.

2. **Breca.** Beowulf's opponent in a swimming contest.

3. **Hnaef** and **Finn.** Their tale, the so-called *Finn Episode,* is recited by Hrothgar's minstrel during the feast that follows Beowulf's victory over Grendel. (See *Finnesburh,* p. 8.)

4. **Unferth.** Hrothgar's thyle or spokesman who first taunts Beowulf for his defeat by Breca in a swimming match, and later lends his sword to Beowulf when the latter goes in search of Grendel's dam.

5. **Wealhtheow.** Hrothgar's queen.

6. **Wiglaf.** The shield-bearer who supports Beowulf in the fight with the Fire-Drake.

*Historical Basis*[1]

Hygelac is to be identified with that Chochilaicus (Cochilaicus) who about A. D. 512 raided the lower Rhine, an expedition in which Beowulf, his nephew, distinguished himself. Chochilaicus, slain in battle with the Franks about A. D. 520, was succeeded to the throne by his son, Heardred.

*Mythological Basis*[2]

1. Beowulf is a sun-god who overcomes the hostile forces of the mist and the cold night, of winter and darkness, of the miasma of the swamps and the power of the sea.

2. Beowulf symbolizes Mankind fighting for existence against the forces of Brute Creation; or, the Spirit of Summer overthrowing the Dragon of Winter; or, Man eventually subverted by Nature.

3. Beowulf is a culture-hero. The blessings of a fixed abode can be made permanently impregnable by overcoming the dangers of the sea with boats and with dikes.

1 See Klaeber, Frederick, *Beowulf and the Fight at Finnesburgh* (1922), pp. XXIX-XLVIII.

2 Mythological interpretations of *Beowulf* are being discountenanced. R. W. Chambers, while conceding an element of truth in the theories of K. V. Müllenhoff as elaborated from J. M. Kemble, is inclined to side with W. W. Lawrence in an attack upon mythological readings. To quote R. W. Chambers: "It is one thing to believe that the ancestor-king Beow may be a weakened form of an ancient divinity, a mere name surviving from the figure of an old corn-god Beow; it is quite another to assume, as Müllenhoff did, that what we are told about Beowulf was originally told about Beow *and that therefore we are justified in giving a mythological meaning to it.*" See Chambers, R. W., *Beowulf* (1932), p. 88.

4. Epic is a possible amalgamation of the historical story of Beowulf, a human fighter of prowess, with the Teutonic myth of Beowa, the slayer of the water demon and the dragon.

*Structure and Form*

For verse structure, see p. 10 *f*. Because the authorship is unknown, ***Beowulf*** is called a Popular (Racial, National, Folk) epic. Characteristics of the popular epic are:

1. Familiar traditions of a people.
2. Long, dignified narrative poem.
3. Momentous actions of an heroic character.
4. Sustained majestic verse.
5. Exalted or supernatural personages of the past; or, characters of noble birth. If at rare intervals one of low rank is introduced, that person's name goes unmentioned.

**Style and Characteristics of "Beowulf"**

| SUGGESTED MERITS | SUGGESTED DEFECTS[1] |
|---|---|
| 1. Broad study of character. | 1. No minute characterization. |
| 2. Many clear scenes and stirring episodes reveal a graphic pictorial power. | 2. Multitude of episodes and, generally, unvisualized scenes engender a lack of proportion and of unity. |
| 3. Repetition frequently effective in its simple-minded intensity. Note the marked feature of understatement. | 3. Repetition often overdone; *e. g.*, that of the dragon combat weakens the total effect. |
| 4. Stately speeches. | 4. Long speeches. |
| 5. Restrained tone, melancholy vein, profound earnestness. | 5. Absence of emotion or of delicate feeling. |
| 6. Subjective outlook on life and heroic sentiment, without the objective and sensuous features of the *Edda* and with a degree of refinement in social life higher than that of the *Nibelungenlied*. | 6. Extensive moralizing (although often gnomic) in its re-creation of a whole civilization tends to retard the progress of the tale. |
| 7. Swift direction. Massive simplicity. Sustained narrative, yet method is descriptive. | 7. Occasional confusion. Neither subtle nor varied. Not as clear as it is dramatic, yet method is expository. |

8. Includes examples of *flytings* (mocking word-combats between some pair of warriors), and of kennings or *kenningar* (periphrastic expressions or parallel descriptive phrases or compounds). Note, also, the general absence of the simile in Anglo-Saxon literature: even in the lengthy *Beowulf* there are only five or six similes, not one of them Homeric.

***Finnesburh**** (*Finnsburh*). Fifty-line fragment of epic cast. Note that a woman is the central figure. Vigor of narrative. Another part (*Hnaef and Finn*) of same story alluded to episodically in *Beowulf* (p. 7); in the latter, inspired by pity, the episode is told retrospectively and elegiacally; in the former, inspired by the lust of battle, told briskly and pointedly.

---

1 By *defects* the *Outline-History* means the absence of those qualities that seem essential to completeness or perfection of the specific work under discussion. While the critical opinions rendered are, in most cases, standard, yet an attempt is made to avoid repeating the occasional mistakes of well-known critics: one such, for example, deriving his opinion from a groundless assumption, notes, as a defect in ***Beowulf***, the absence of a love-interest.

† * Explanation of symbols immediately precedes page one.

***Widsith.***†* "The Song of the Far-Traveller" (Wide-Journey, Far-Path, or Far-Wanderer) is an autobiographical travel-book of about 143 lines, glorifying the professional singer and his royal patrons. Sadly retrospective in its descriptive cataloguing of what has been called the stock-in-trade of Anglo-Saxon bards. Small poetical value, but great archeological interest: probably begun in the fourth century and completed possibly as early as the seventh, it is perhaps the oldest poem in any modern language. Accounts for chronological inconsistencies.

***Waldere**** (*Waldhere*). Two epic fragments, 32 lines and 31 lines respectively. First gives Hildegund's (Hildegyth's) heartening of Waldere; second, a dialogue between the latter and Guthhere. Christian allusions. (Story found also in the German epic, the *Nibelungenlied.*)

#### Lyrical or Elegiac Poems

Most original portion of Anglo-Saxon poetry anticipates the dramatic monologue, a form of which the ultimate master is Robert Browning (1812—1889).

***Deor***† (*Deor's Lament* or *Deor's Complaint*). First English lyric. About 42 lines. Deor, a bard at the court of the Heodenings, bewails his eclipse by Heorrenda, a rival scop. One of the only two examples in Anglo-Saxon of strophic structure and the use of the refrain. (The other is *Wulf and Eadwacer.*) Recurring fatalistic burden—

"This man overcame, and so may I"

—is the chief reason for its occasional and possibly far-fetched classification as a ballad. Energized by melancholy emotion. Has been called by W. W. Lawrence, "a veritable *Consolatione Philosophiae* of minstrelsy."

***Wulf and Eadwacer.*** Enigmatical. A woman is speaking: she wishes to see her banished lover Wulf; she taunts a certain Eadwacer. Note strophic structure and refrain.

***The Wife's Lament***† (*The Maiden's Complaint*). Traditional interpretation: A supposedly-faithless and therefore banished wife plaintively laments her estranged husband. Probably the first love-poem in English.

***The Husband's Message*** † (*The Lover's Message*). On a tablet of wood an absent lover has inscribed a message asking his maiden or wife to set sail at the first note of the cuckoo for a home built by him in the south. Possibly a sequel to *The Wife's Lament.* Distinguished from all others by an absence of melancholy.

***The Ruin.*** Series of laments over the lichened remains and crumbling towers of a sacked Roman stronghold in Britain, possibly Bath. Poetic feeling, differentiated by its concern over a place and not over a person.

---

**† * Explanation of symbols immediately precedes page one.**

***The Seafarer*** (8th century). Lure of the deep, despite its attendant hardships, has a greater charm than a permanent home on the shore. Original but obscure poem of about 124 lines. Is it a sailor's monologue? Or a dialogue between an old salt and a youth who wants to go to sea? Is its pious Christian conclusion the important point—as a sailor despises comfort on dry land, so man ought to spurn earthly nothingness for heavenly happiness? Ending is probably an addition.

***The Wanderer.***†* Lyric or elegy, not to be mistaken for the epic *Widsith* (p. 9). Heathen tone, Celtic grace, wistful sadness. Notable absence of kennings. Its 115 lines or so constitute the longest and probably the most perfect in form of Anglo-Saxon poems of sentiment.

### Riddles, Charms, and Gnomic Verses

***The Riddles.***† Often attributed to Cynwulf (p. 13). Based mainly on Latin originals, being enigmatical descriptions of objects that are to be solved. Obscure, but ingeniously developed; prolix, but imaginative and picturesque. Riddles on everything—*Hurricane, Shield, Storm-Spirit on Land, Nightingale, Bible Manuscript, Bull's Horn, Anchor.* Of some 95 extant, all are probably Christian; best are those dealing with the sea. (See *Epistola ad Acircium,* p. 15.)

***Charms.***[1] Magical songs for curing disease, or incantations to some superior power, in prose and verse, in English and dog-Latin. Pagan, but Christianized. Example: *Nigon Wyrta Galdor,* "an incantation of the Nine Plants," for dressing a wound.

***Gnomic Verse.*** Sententious sayings, wise saws, sage counsels, often proverbial, mainly pagan. Found in *Beowulf* (p. 6), in *The Exeter Book* (p. 20), and the like. Examples: "Wyrd goeth ever as she is bound"; "Better is it for every man that he should avenge his friend than that he should greatly mourn"; "Far countries are seemliest sought by a man sure of himself."[2]

## STRUCTURE OF ANGLO-SAXON VERSIFICATION

### A. General Features

1. EMPHATIC STRESS. Number of stresses, not number of syllables, is important. Normally, there should be four stressed syllables in each line, and at least three of these syllables should be alliterated.

---

1 Felix Grendon has listed some of the general characteristics of the charms as being the appeal to a superior spirit, the exorcist's boast of power, ceremonial directions to both patient and exorcist, the statement of time for the performance of rites, and the like. Included among the charms are "Against a Dwarf," "For Diarrhoea," "For Loss of Cattle," "Against a Swarm of Bees," "For Headache." His point of view is essentially that of the folk-lorist. [See Grendon, Felix, "The Anglo-Saxon Charms," *The Journal of American Folk-Lore,* XXII (1909), pp. 105-237.]

2 See Williams, B. C., *Gnomic Poetry in Anglo-Saxon* (1914).

† * Explanation of symbols immediately precedes page one.

2. ALLITERATION. Repetition of the same letter or sound, usually the initial sound, in succeeding words, especially in accented syllables of verse. Usually the alliteration is upon a single consonant. Consonantal alliteration is most frequent; but when the alliteration is upon vowels, any vowel may alliterate with any other vowel. In other words, has a kind of initial rime (correspondence in sound at the beginning of words, at the initial letters). Almost no instances of terminal or end rime (correspondence in sound at the ends of words): the obscure *Riming Poem* is probably the only instance in the period "of the consistent use of end-rime and alliteration" in the same poem.

3. VERSE IS UNRIMED.

4. LINES ARE USUALLY END-STOPPED (HAVE DISTINCT PAUSES AT THE END).

5. RHYTHM, THOUGH NOT IRREGULAR, IS FREE.

### B. Specific Features

1. STRUCTURE.

(a) Each line(verse)is divided into two parts(hemistichs or staves).

(b) Each half has two strongly accented syllables or beats.

(c) A pause (caesura, cesura), or a slight break made to accentuate the beat of the rhythm, separates each part.

(d) At least one of the stressed syllables in the first half-line must alliterate with the first accented syllable in the second half-line, the latter syllable being known as the *rime-giver.* The final or fourth beat is permitted to rime with the accented syllable not riming with the *rime-giver,* but with the latter must not rime—occasionally, this rule is violated.[1]

(e) The number of unaccented syllables varies.

2. PARALLELISM. The casting of ideas into similar form or the repetition of an idea by means of other epithets or phrases (common in the Old Testament) frequently, but not always, results in cumulative emphasis.

3. HARP ACCOMPANIMENT. Probably a twang on the harp at the strongly accented syllables energized the movement of the rhythm and intensified the power of the chanted verse.

4. STYLE. Omission of explanatory detail and a tendency to abrupt directness result in swiftness of movement and of narrative. There is, however, a tendency toward monotony of language, meters, and style. Prevalence of compound words (see *Anglo-Saxon Characteristics,* 4, p. 5), of pronouns in place of nouns, and of metaphors; rarity of similes (see *Beowulf,* "Style and Characteristics," 8, p. 8).

---

1 Tersely, "the only metrical pattern in Anglo-Saxon verse is the two stresses to the line, with light syllables variously placed," says Baum, P. F., "The Character of Anglo-Saxon Verse," *Modern Philology,* XXVIII (1930), p. 155 (pp. 143-156).

## POETRY OF CHRISTIAN ORIGIN

### Caedmon and His School

**Caedmon,** *fl.* 670, first known poet of England: hence, called the "Father of English Song." Bede's *Historia Ecclesiastica,* Book IV, Chap. 24, (see page 16 of the *Outline-History*) records[1] how one night Caedmon, a neatherd lacking the gift of song, had fled from a feast where all were required to improvise and sing; and, in a vision, received the divine inspiration. Resulted in the

***Hymn of Caedmon.*** Nine lines in praise of the Creator, half of which are composed of kennings for "God." Only authentic fragment of his work.

*Anonymous Poems Formerly Attributed to Caedmon*

***Christ and Satan*** (probably *c.* 790—830). Composed of three poems. I—"The Laments of the Fallen Angels" (*ll.* 1—365), connected apparently with *Guthlac B* (p. 14). II—"Descent into Hell, Resurrection, and Ascension" (*ll.* 366—666), paralleled frequently in *Beowulf, Daniel, Genesis A, Christ, Andreas,* and elsewhere (pp. 8, 12, 13, 14). III—"Temptation of Christ by Satan" (*ll.* 667—733), incomplete and generally original. Homiletic tendency, plaintive tone. Has been assigned anywhere from the year 680—975.

***Daniel.*** Fairly close paraphrase of the Vulgate version of Daniel, Chaps. I—V. Colorless, if lucid, attempt to inculcate moral virtues. Balanced phrases. Noted for a beautiful simile.

***Exodus*****†** (probably earlier than *Beowulf*). Free paraphrase of the passage of the Israelites through the Red Sea and the destruction of Pharaoh's host (Exodus XIII, 17—XIV, 31 and Exodus XV, 1—21). Teutonic martial gusto revealed in embroidered, vivid epithets. Probably by Aldhelm or one of his school (p. 15). Avitus's poem, *De Transitu Maris Rubri,* probably is not one of its sources.[2]

***Genesis.*****†** Two poems. *Genesis A* (early 8th century) paraphrases the fall of the angels (*ll.* 1—234) and later continues until it ends with the story of Isaac and the ram (*ll.* 852—2,735). *Genesis B* (early 9th century or later) paraphrases the hiatus (*ll.* 235—851). The latter is a fine poetic passage, differing markedly from the dull *A* in metrical and linguistic style.[3] Note similarity, in point of imagina-

---

1 Similar stories are found in the poetry and dream-lore of all peoples. See Pound Louise, "Caedmon's Dream Song," *Studies in English Philology: A Miscellany in Honor of Frederick Klaeber,* edited by Malone, Kemp and Ruud, Martin B. (1929), pp. 232-239.

2 Moore. Samuel, "On the Sources of the Old-English *Exodus,*" *Modern Philology* IX (1911), pp. 83-108.

3 Eduard Siever was the first to recognize that *Genesis B* differs from *Genesis A* (*Der Heliand und die Angelsächsische Genesis,* 1875).

**† * Explanation of symbols immediately precedes page one.**

tion, to Milton's *Paradise Lost.* Each is an epic on an identical theme, each proceeds similarly, and each conceives of Satan as excelling in brightness of person before the Fall. Again, whereas this author's hell is "devoid of light and full of flame," Milton's flames, emitting no light, make "darkness visible."[1]

***Judith.*** Paraphrase of the story of Judith as told in the Apocrypha. Composed conjecturally in honor of Aethelflaed, the Lady of the Mercians. To deliver her native town the Jewish maiden of Bethulia slays Holofernes, leader of the Assyrians. Dramatic epic fragment of some 350 lines often vigorous as well as musical, but also made leaden-footed by kennings. Has been assigned anywhere from the eighth to the tenth century.

***The Paraphrase.*** Composed of the *Genesis,* the *Exodus* and the *Daniel.* (See foregoing notes, p. 12.)

### Cynwulf[2] and the Cynwulfian Poems

**Cynwulf,** *fl.* early 9th century, greatest Anglo-Saxon poet, excepting the unknown composer of *Beowulf.* Probably a Northumbrian ecclesiastic and scholar, although his work is extant only in the West-Saxon dialect. More lyrical and personal than Caedmon and the so-called Caedmonian poems (p. 12 *f.*); but as prolix, and as neglectful of the architectonics of the whole.

#### *Poems by Cynwulf*

(Signed by runic characters corresponding to the letters that compose his name)

***Christ.*†** Didactic poem of some 1,650 lines derived from Latin sources, especially the *Roman Breviary,* Gregory the Great's *Ascension Homily,* and the alphabetic hymn beginning "Apparebit repentina dies magna Domini," quoted by Bede in his *De Arte Metrica.* Deals triptych-like with life of Christ—"The Advent" (Nativity), "The Ascension" (signed part), and "The Last Judgment" (Doomsday). Faulty planning, obscure thought, limping narrative compensated by masterly details, lyrical verse, and imaginative passages. Structural relationship particularly influenced by the Great Antiphons of Advent, called the *O's of Advent.* Third part influenced the *Muspilli* (*c.* 870).

---

1 Gurteen, S. H., *The Epic of the Fall of Man* (1896), pp. 128-165. For a dissenting point of view, see Disraeli, Isaac, *Amenities of Literature* (1881), pp. 49-64.

2 We are following Kenneth Sisam's lead in spelling the name *Cynwulf* instead of, as traditionally, *Cynewulf.* See the "Sir Israel Gollancz Memorial Lecture," *Proceedings of the British Academy,* XVIII (1932), p. 305 *f.* (pp. 303-331).

† * Explanation of symbols immediately precedes page one.

***Elene.*†*** His masterpiece. Ultimate source in the *Legenda Aurea,* and in the *Vita Quiriaci* contained in the *Acta Sanctorum;* direct source possibly, according to C. F. Brown, derived from the Irish.[1] Conversion of the Emperor signified the transmutation of the cross from a symbol of ignominy to a symbol of glory. Tasteless narration overbalanced by smoothly-dovetailed narrative, imaginative descriptions, poetic feeling for nature, and high religious purpose. Note internal rimes in its fourteen cantos. Shows influence of *Beowulf* (p. 6). Passage describing Judgment Day (vv. 1,277—1,320) similar to one in Alcuin's *De Fide Sanctae et Individuae Trinitatis.*

***Fata Apostolorum.*** "The Fates of the Apostles" is insignificant as poetry. Possibly an epilogue to *Andreas* (p. 14).

***Juliana.**** Based upon the Latin prose version of St. Juliana in the *Acta Sanctorum.* Unpoetic, unemotional; tendency to wordy speeches. (Two hiatuses in text.)

### *Unsigned Poems Attributed to Cynwulf*

***Andreas.*†*** Based on a Greek story. Explosive descriptions of man's titanic struggle with the tempest. Wealth of incident in its 1,722 lines, yet less prolix than most Anglo-Saxon poems. "Though it glitters with barbaric splendor of phrase . . . ., it fails to subordinate the particular scene to the general plan as do *Juliana, Elene,* or *Guthlac's Death.*"[2] Phraseology and content influenced by *Beowulf*: not only has it been called the Christian *Beowulf* but also the Christian *Odyssey.*

***The Dream of the Rood.*†*** Probably the noblest and most imaginative of all Anglo-Saxon poems. Only dream-poem extant before the Conquest. Broodingly emotional, lyrically passionate, intensely imaginative, deeply religious. About 150 lines of alliterative verse, probably influenced by the hymn, *Pange lingua.* Portions of it are inscribed in runes on the Ruthwell Cross in Dumfries.

***Guthlac.**** First part or *A* anemic and confused. Second or *B* (which may be the work of an independent author) has moments of strength and charm. Some 1,353 lines. *B,* and possibly *A,* based upon a Latin work of Felix of Croyland. *Guthlac A* is a "poetic vision"; *Guthlac B,* a religious biography.[3]

***The Phoenix.*†** Based on the *De Ave Phoenice,* conventional elegiacs ascribed to Lactantius Firmianus (4th century). This fabulous

1 Brown, C. F., "Irish-Latin Influence in Cynewulfian Texts," *Englische Studien,* XL (1909), pp. 1-29.

2 Gerould, G. H., *Saints' Legends* (1916), p. 86.

3 Kurtz, B. P., "From St. Anthony to St. Guthlac," *University of Californ[ia] Publications in Modern Philology,* XII (1925-1926), p. 145 (pp. 105-146).

† * Explanation of symbols immediately precedes page one.

bird lives five hundred years or longer, is consumed in fire by its own act, and is reborn from its own ashes—originally a symbol of the cult of the rising sun, and here employed as a symbol of man's craving for eternal youth or of immortality and the resurrection.[1] Unlike most Anglo-Saxon poems, reveals an original delight in the beamy moods of nature —usually attributed to the Celtic temperament. Colorful enthusiasm, wild grace, delicate fancy, radiant description in its 677 lines. Unusual conclusion—first half of each of the terminating eleven lines is in English, the second half in Latin, the latter alliterating with the former.[2]

***The Old English Physiologus.*** Three poems extant of perhaps a fuller allegorical bestiary: *The Panther, The Whale,* (Asp-Turtle), and a fragment on *The Partridge.* An allegory is tacked to the description of the animal; thus, the Panther is the Lord God, the Whale is Satan. See *The Bestiaries,* p. 31. Also, see *The Phoenix,* p. 14.

## *ANGLO-SAXON WRITERS IN LATIN TO THE TIME OF ALFRED*

**Gildas,** *c.* 500—*c.* 570, the earliest native British historian. Surnamed by some Sapiens; by others, Badonicus.

***De Excidio et Conquestu Britanniae*** (*c.* 547). See p. 41.

**Nennius,** *fl.* 796, Welsh annalist.

***Historia Britonum*** (*c.* 796). See p. 41.

**Aldhelm** (or **Ealdhelm**), *c.* 640—709, first great English writer of Latin. Abbot of Malmesbury (675). Bishop of Sherborne (705).

***De Laudibus Virginitatis.*** Two separate versions, one in florid, metaphorical prose and another in hexameters, illustrating the merits of virginity and of virgins.

***Epistola ad Acircium.*** Acircius is Aldfrith, King of Northumbria. This "Letter to Acircius" includes a prose treatise on meter, but is more important for its five-score Latin riddles in verse. Some hexameters became the basis of the *Creation,* the longest of *The Riddles* (p. 10) in *The Exeter Book* (p. 20).

**Bede** (or **Beda,** or **Baeda**), 673—735, historian, greatest scholar of Anglo-Saxon period, often called "The Venerable Bede" and "The Father of English Learning." From the age of seven until his death, spent life in monasteries—chiefly at Jarrow, in Northumbria. Wrote about forty books, mainly theological but also historical and scientific. All books in Latin, except for a lost translation in English of the Gospel

1 Long before the birth of Christ, however, the idea of a resurrection was current: hence, the theme is a heritage from heathen nations. See Neinhauser, L. N., "The Legend of the Phoenix," *The Catholic Educational Review,* XIX (1921), pp. 129-141.

2 Smith, M. B., in *The Cambridge History of English Literature* (1920), I, p. 59. (Chap. IV, "Old English Christian Poetry," pp. 41-64.)

of St. John. Renowned for lovable piety, sober gentleness, and noble humility. Has been described by his contemporary, Boniface, the "Apostle of Germany," as the Candle sent by God for the spiritual illumination of the Church. Writings include homilies, Latin hymns, histories, a poem on Justin Martyr, one on the Day of Judgment, two lives of St. Cuthbert, and, among his theological treatises, primarily commentaries on the works of the four great Latin Fathers (Augustine, Ambrose, Gregory, Jerome). Anticipates the modern practice of duly crediting one's sources.

***De Natura Rerum.*** "Concerning the Nature of Things" is a treatise on physical science referring phenomena to natural causes.

***Historia Ecclesiastica Gentis Anglorum***† (completed 731). "Ecclesiastical History of the English Race" earns for him the title, "Father of English History." "The conversion and the struggle between the Roman and the Irish Church and final triumph of the former, are its principal themes," says Émile Legouis.[1] Five books (in Latin), drawing on Latin authors including Pliny, and on native writers including Gildas the Wise (p. 15) and possibly Nennius (p. 15), sketch the general history of Britain from the landing of Julius Caesar to the coming of St. Augustine; thence (596) more fully treat the progress of Christianity until 731. Tells two memorable stories: (a) Caedmon's divine gift of song (p. 12); and (b) the famous passage of the swallow, an elaborated image of human life (Bk. II, Chap. 13). The latter concerns the conversion of Northumbria in 633: man's life is likened to a sparrow that flies out of a whirlwind of rain and snow into a hall where men are feasting around the fire, tarries for a moment in the warmth and brightness, and flies out again into the dark winter—thus, the sparrow has been for a brief respite in light, "but what hath gone before or what will come after, we know not."

As history, is faithful and accurate; as literature, beautiful and valuable. Lucid, vivid, picturesque, well-proportioned, unaffected; wealth of anecdotes and character sketches. Without the ornateness of Boethius, the rambling of Orosius, or the rhetoric of Augustine (p. 18 *f*.).

***Bede's Death Song.*** In a letter from Cuthbert, Abbot of Jarrow, to Cuthwin, a friend, Bede is quoted as singing, in his last moments, a song of five lines.

**Alcuin (or Albinus, or Ealhwine),** *c.* 735—804, theologian; teacher and intimate adviser of Charlemagne. Abbot of Tours (796). Numerous liturgical and philosophical works. More personal though less artistic than Aldhelm (p. 15).

***Letters.*** Some 311 letters, valuable historical sources.

1 Legouis, Émile, and Cazamian, Louis, *A History of English Literature* (1926), I, p. 6.

† * Explanation of symbols immediately precedes page one.

***Poems.*** Most famous is that "On the Mutability of all Human Affairs," a Latin elegy on the Danish destruction of Lindisfarne.

***Vita Willibrordi.*** Two versions, one in homiletic prose and the second in hexameter verse, of the life of Willibrord (*c.* 658—739), Missionary in the Netherlands (691—739).

***On Grammar.*** Treatise in the form of a dialogue between a Saxon and a Frank with Alcuin.

## II. THE AGE OF PROSE IN THE SOUTH (828-1066)

### History

States of the Anglo-Saxon "heptarchy" acknowledge Egbert "King" of all England (*c.* 827—828).[1] Alfred the Great, checking the incursions of the Danes, makes peace with these Northmen (878). Aethelstan, King of England, defeats (937) a coalition of Irish, Scotch, and Welsh at Brunanburh (p. 19). Sweyn, King of the Danes, subjugates England (1013). Canute, the Dane, becomes King (1017). With Edward the Confessor (1042—1066) the Saxon line is restored to power; and, having been educated in Normandy, with him the *Norman Influence* (p. 22) is introduced even before the Battle of Hastings (1066), at which William of Normandy, a cousin of Edward, defeats Harold II (1066), Edward's brother-in-law whose claim to the throne William disputed.

### General View of the Literature

Wessex is not merely the political but also the literary and intellectual center. Unlike the poetry of the preceding period, the prose of this, while revealing no originality of thought or intensity of emotion in its earnestly practical or instructionally religious purpose, shows a marked contrast in its freedom from parallelisms, inversions, periphrases, and the almost surfeiting presence of metaphor and epithet. The poetry had been alliterative, somber, rugged; the prose had been loose in its compound-sentence structure, commonest in its simple-sentence arrangement, perhaps somewhat stiff and inflexible, but at its best generally direct and clear, forcible and occasionally rhythmical. Dramatic activity, stopped in the fifth and sixth centuries by the maraudings of the Northern barbarian and the attacks of the Christian ascetic, revived considerably: already in the tenth century, for example, a change had been made from the simple human tableaux of the fifth century to dialogue and action, while tropes, or interpolations of dramatic phrases, dialogue, music, and mimetic action, were introduced into the Latin service. To about the year 900 belongs the *Quem-Quaeritis* trope, the oldest extant antiphonal anthem or playlet in England, consisting of a dialogue in Latin between the three Marys and

1 The modern historian is inclined to reject the traditional theory that the Anglo-Saxons in England founded seven separate single kingdoms welded into one by Egbert, anachronistically called the first "King" of England when he was in reality only one of a succession of rulers who, having established hegemony over large territories, was given the venerable title of *Bretwalda.*

the Angel at the tomb of Christ on Easter morning (St. Mark, XVI, 1—7; St. Matthew, XXVIII, 1—7). For the Drama, see pp. 31, 52, 103 *ff*.

**Alfred the Great**, 848—901; King of Wessex, 871—901. Visits, as a youth, to Rome and to the court of Charles the Bald in France, gave him a cosmopolitan point of view. Treaty of Wedmore (878) gave him an opportunity to direct energies toward the administration of justice, the encouragement of learning, and the securing of aid from foreign scholars, the most important in the latter group being Asser, a Welsh cleric, whose *Life of King Alfred* (*c.* 894) is, until the year 889, a key to Alfred's possibly unsurpassed courtesy, wisdom, and nobility of character: hence, called "The Truth-Teller." Literary work consists mainly of translations, in which he was assisted by Asser, Bishop of Sherborne. Condensed the material, or expanded it by interpolating original matter.[1] While the language is occasionally long and involved, it is, on the whole, simple, direct, and unornamental. Not only did Alfred bring a considerable Latin element into English prose; he founded English prose.

***Cura Pastoralis.***† Translation of Pope Gregory's "Pastoral Care" or, in Alfred's words, the *Hierdebōc* or "Herdsman's Book." Handbook sent to every bishopric as a *vade mecum* to the clergy in their duties. Alfred's own preface, besides telling of his determination to revive learning, defends the use of the vernacular—thus bringing him the name, "Father of English Prose."

***Historia Universalis.***† "Universal History" or "History of the World" is a loose, rather uncritical translation of the *Historia adversus Paganos* by Paulus Orosius, a fifth-century Christian priest of Spanish birth, whose object was to refute the accusation that Christianity was responsible for the sack of Rome by the Goths in A. D. 410; *i.e.*, that the triumph of Christianity had provoked the ancient gods. Theme somewhat similar to the *De Civitate Dei*, written by St. Augustine to show that the Church preachings could not augment the world's misery. Alfred produced almost a new book by condensing seven books of 236 chapters to six books of 84 chapters and by adding original matter, such as geographical details about Germany, and also the reports of two seafarers, Ohthere (Ottar), a well-to-do Norwegian, and Wulfstan, of whom little is known.[2]

---

1 Potter, Simeon, "On the Relation of the Old English Bede to Werferth's Gregory and to Alfred's Translations," *Věstnik—Třída Folosoficko—Historicko—Jazykozpytná* (Královské České Společnosti Nauk; or, Mémoires de la Société Royale Des Sciences De Bohême), 1930-1931, pp. 55-71 (pp. 1-73).

2 Recent research tends to indicate that Wulfstan was probably an Angle or Englishman: see Craigie, W. A., "The Nationality of King Alfred's Wulfstan," *The Journal of English and Germanic Philology*, XXIV (1925), pp. 396-397; Malone, Kemp, "On King Alfred's Geographical Treatise," *Speculum*, VIII (1933), p. 68 (pp. 67-78).

† * **Explanation of symbols immediately precedes page one.**

***Historia Ecclesiastica Gentis Anglorum.*** Englished Bede's important history (p. 16). Made no additions; omitted many documents. Over-literal, un-English constructions not infrequent.

***De Consolatione Philosophiae.*** Free translation of "Concerning the Consolation of Philosophy" by (Anicius Manlius Severinus) Boethius (*c.* 480—*c.* 524). Philosophical dialogue between Boethius and his woman-guardian, written by this Roman patrician while in prison. Central doctrine sets forth the problem of Fate and Free Will, of fatalism and submission: "a golden volume," said Edward Gibbon, "not unworthy of the leisure of Plato or of Tully." Alfred's most original work: propels the lofty thoughts by vivid figures of speech. Prose-portion better than verse-portion. (Translated later by Chaucer; see p. 65).

***Blostman.*** First half of this "Blooms," or Anthology, based mainly on St. Augustine's *Soliloquia.* Latter half, derived from various sources, is Alfred's own work.

***Proverbs of Alfred.*** See p. 38.

***The Anglo-Saxon Chronicle.*** The *Chronicle* began before Alfred's time as casual jottings made by monks; but the systematic plan of registering national events in the language of the people is generally ascribed to Alfred. Four versions preserved in seven manuscripts. The six principal recensions are known as the Shorter Abingdon (to 977), the Kentish (to 1058), the Longer Abingdon (to 1066), the Winchester (to 1070), the Worcester (to 1079), and the Peterborough (to 1154). Of these the most important are the so-called *A-text* (the Winchester or Parker Chronicle) and the *E-text* (the Peterborough or Laud Chronicle). The entries, mostly bare and dry, occasionally become picturesque or spirited (see *Historical Battle-Poems,* p. 19). Most vivid portion is of the years 839—897. Terminated with an account of the accession of Henry II in 1154.

*The Anglo-Saxon Chronicle* is important for at least four reasons:

1. Most important source for the history of England up to the Norman Conquest.

2. Changes in the spelling of the language are exemplified: the Old English of the tenth century almost changes to a Middle English before the narrative comes to an end.

3—4. "From a historical point of view, the *Chronicle* was the first national continuous history of a western nation in its own language; from a literary point of view, it was the first great book in English prose."[1]

### *Historical Battle-Poems in The Anglo-Saxon Chronicle*

***The Battle of Brunanburh.***† Victory of Aethelstan, King of Wessex, (925—940) and his brother Eadmund over Constantine, King

---

1 Thomas, P. G., in *The Cambridge History of English Literature* (1920), I, p. 104. (Chap. VI, "Alfred and the Old English Prose of His Reign," pp. 88-107.)

† * Explanation of symbols immediately precedes page one.

of Alban or Scotland, and the latter's son-in-law Anlaf Sihtricsson (Olaf or Anlaf Cuaran) the Dane. Vigorous imagery, epic verse. Some 73 lines, recorded A. D. 937. Modernized by Alfred Tennyson (1809—1892).

***The Battle of Maldon*** (*Death of Byrhtnoth*). Heroic death of the ealdorman Byrhtnoth in the battle against the invading Danes under Olaf Tryggvason on the banks of the Pant or the Blackwater. Spirited 325 lines, recorded A. D. 991.

**Aelfric,** *c.* 955—*c.* 1023, called *Grammaticus* or the "Grammarian," the greatest prose writer of his time. Abbot of Eynsham. Among his many works are *Lives of Saints* (*c.* 997), sermons in alliterative rhythms[1]; *A Testimonie of Antiquity* (published 1566), a homily against transubstantiation; an old English version of *The Heptateuch,*[2] and the

***Homilae Catholicae***† (990—995). Some 80 "Catholic Sermons" on Church events, doctrine, and history. Picturesque, fervent, often alliterative, poetic prose; one preface in Latin, one in English. Direct exposition, flowing style. From the point of view of doctrine, even more valuable than his *Lives of Saints.*

***Colloquium.*** Latin dialogue intended as a manual of conversation. May be called the first English-Latin dictionary, because of its vocabulary arrangement.

## *IMPORTANT COLLECTIONS CONTAINING ANGLO-SAXON MANUSCRIPTS*

1. ***MS. Cotton Vitellius A xv*** (Cottonian MS.), British Museum. Contains *Beowulf, Judith,* and others.

2. ***The Exeter Book (Codex Exoniensis),*** Exeter Cathedral, Devonshire, England. Contains *Deor, Widsith, Christ, Juliana, The Ruin, The Seafarer, The Wanderer, The Phoenix,* gnomic verses, riddles, parts of an old *Physiologus, Soul and Body II,* and others.

3. ***The Junius Manuscript (Junius XI),*** Bodleian Library, Oxford. Contains *Genesis, Exodus, Daniel, Christ and Satan, Soul and Body I* (the latter a parallel to *Soul and Body II* in *The Exeter Book*).

4. ***The Vercelli Book (Vercelli Codex or Codex Vercellensis),*** Capitular Library, Vercelli, Italy. Contains *Andreas, The Dream of the Rood, Elene,* and others.

---

1 Whether the *Lives of Saints* and, particularly, the third series of *Homilae* are written in the form of prose or in that of verse is still a matter of discussion: see Gerould, G. H., "Abbott Aelfric's Rhythmic Prose," *Modern Philology* XXII (1924-1925), pp. 353-366; Bethrum, Dorothy, "The Form of Aelfric's *Lives of Saints,*" *Studies in Philology,* XXIX (1932), pp. 515—533.

2 Recently re-edited, after some 225 years, by Crawford, S. J., *The Old English Version of The Heptateuch, Aelfric's Treatise on the Old and New Testament and his Preface to Genesis* (1922).

† * Explanation of symbols immediately precedes page one.

## *ADDITIONAL AUTHORS OR WORKS*

| AUTHOR | WORK or WORKS | COMMENT |
|---|---|---|
| **ANEURIN** (or **ANEIRIN**), c. 600, Welsh bard. Called "Aneurin of the Flowing Muse" or "of the Golden Word." Probably the son of Gildas (p. 15). | **Y Gododin** | Fragmentary song-cycle, attributed to Aneurin, of Welsh chieftains who fell at the battle of Cattraeth. Large part consists of short elegies. Unusually direct, terse, vigorous. Chief poem of **The Book of Aneurin** (p. 41). |
| **EADFRITH**, Bishop of Lindisfarne (698-721). | **Lindisfarne Gospels** (ante 700). | Prose. North Northumbrian gloss added by one Aldred (c. 950), a priest. |
| **FAERMAN**, a priest of Harwood, and **OWUN**. | **Rushworth Gospels** (8th century). | Prose. Interlineation by one Leeds (fl. 950). So-called because once owned by John Rushworth. |
| **AETHELWOLD** (or **ETHELWALD**), c. 908-984. Bishop of Winchester (963). | **Regula Sancta Benedicte.** | Rules of Benedictine convents. |
| **BYRHTFERTH**, fl. 1000, Monk of Ramsey. | **Handboc.** | Homiletic Manual recently edited for the first time from MS. Ashmole 328 in the Bodleian library. (Crawford, S. J., editor, 1929.) |
| **AELFRIC**, fl. 1000, probably of the monastery of Bath. | **"West-Saxon" Gospels.** | Prose. This Aelfric is not to be confused with the "Grammarian" (p. 20). |
| **WULFSTAN**, d. 1023. Archbishop of York and of Worcester. | a) **Sermo Lupi ad Anglos (1014).** | a) Powerfully describes the moral breakdown of English society and castigates its evils. |
| | b) **Homilies.** | b) More concrete but less poetic than Aelfric (p. 20). |
| | **Blickling Homilies.** | Nineteen prose legends. MS. located at Blickling Hall, near Aylsham, Norfolk. |
| | **Apollonius of Tyre.** | First romance (p. 39). Reappears in **Confessio Amantis** (p. 54) and in **Pericles** (p. 219). |
| | **Alexander's Letter to Aristotle.** | Spurious. Particularly valuable to the lexicographer. |
| | a) **Wonders of the East.**<br>b) **Life of St. Christopher.** | Prose found, with the unique Anglo-Saxon prose version of **Alexander's Letter**, in **MS. Cotton Vitellius Axv** (p. 20). |

CHAPTER II

# THE ANGLO-NORMAN PERIOD

(1066—1340)

## THE NORMAN CONQUEST

The Battle of Hastings (Senlac) in 1066 dates the time from which for the following three centuries French culture dominated the English language and literature. However, even before the triumph of Duke William of Normandy over Harold II, the French influence had been mirrored in the sympathies of Edward the Confessor, who had spent his youth at the court of Normandy, and who as King had welcomed French-speaking courtiers and ecclesiastics. As early as Edward the Confessor's day the clothing of the court had been cut after the Norman taste, and the handwriting of the Normans had been adopted for use in all charters.

## RESULTS OF THE NORMAN CONQUEST

### A. Political

1. The fusion into one people and the growth of a unified national feeling were accelerated; *e. g.*, by breaking up earldoms such as Mercia and Wessex.

2. The King's court became the vital center of English government; *e. g.*, duty to the King became paramount, primarily through the feudal-tenure doctrine that all land is a grant from the Crown, and not from one's immediate lord, thereby endowing the Sovereign with a direct power hitherto unavailable.

3. The Conquest destroyed insular narrowness by bringing closer England's relation with Continental affairs, commercial, political, and religious. (See p. 23 *f.*)

4. The Norman began a change, which later became complete, in the English machinery of government. Introduction of the justiciar, for instance, made possible the Grand Inquest or Survey of all the real estate of England—the property-listing known as the *Domesday* (or *Doomsday*) *Book* (1085—1086), compiled by order of William the Conqueror. Also, the Anglo-Saxon *witenagemot* was superseded by a *curia regis,* the beginning of the House of Lords.

### B. Social and Cultural

1. With the Norman there came into England the most cultured ways of Continental Europe. Besides a passion for method and order, and a genius for administering affairs, the Norman possessed an intellectual suppleness and a mobile spirit, a self-controlled but vigorous aggressiveness, an ardent zest for refined life and living, the latter being exemplified by a gusto for light-hearted song, rich clothing, beautiful manuscripts, and graceful forms of architecture. Yet so completely were the races fused that within one hundred years it was not possible to differentiate between one of Norman and one of English birth.

2. The body of customs and ideals known as chivalry, linked as it was with feudal obligations, was introduced by the Normans. The knightly code, the romantic interest in women, a religious exaltation bordering on erotic mysticism, and a mingled tenderness and reverence paid to the Virgin Mary are reflected in the literature[1]—in *The Five Joys of Mary, Orisoun to Our Lady* (p. 38), *The Ancren Riwle* (p. 28), the *Luve Ron* (pp. 26, 29).

3. A new relationship began to exist among the Church, the Government, and the People. The Norman Catholic Church, more closely connected with Rome, brought the English Catholic Church nearer to the central power of the Papacy (*e. g.*, by gradually establishing Norman priests in the churches). However, no longer in temporal but only in ecclesiastical cases could Bishops now exercise jurisdiction.

4. The Crusades (1095—1272) introduced new tastes and desires, established the codes of knighthood and chivalry, and stimulated the contact of England with the Continent and the Orient. They also fostered the popularity of the Medieval Romance (p. 39 *ff.*).

5. The Norman introduced a style of architecture superior to that prevailing in England. Romanesque architecture, locally called Norman to distinguish it from Saxon, is characterized by round-headed arches and horizontal lines; but in the twelfth century Gothic architecture arose, characterized by pointed arches and vertical lines. Some great Gothic cathedrals of England: Rochester, *c.* 1077; Durham, *c.* 1093; Lincoln, 1123—1147; Canterbury, 1175; Winchester, *c.* 1325.

6. The founding and the rise of the Universities of Oxford and Cambridge resulted in a broadening of the intellectual horizon. Their influence helped fix the East Midland as the literary dialect. Of this period probably the chief English scholar, as well as the most brilliant representative of the Franciscans at Oxford, was Roger Bacon (*c.* 1214—1294), "The Admirable Doctor" (p. 36).

---

1 Not a few aspects of the cultus of the Virgin are paralleled in ancient and Oriental (non-Christian) religions.

## GENERAL VIEW OF THE LITERATURE AND LANGUAGE

### A. Literature

1. CHARACTER OF WRITINGS. After the Conquest the literature, while frequently prosaic and utilitarian, is varied in interest and extensive in range. The didactic work is mainly in Latin; the brilliant, characteristically in Anglo-Norman; and the informational, only scantily in the vernacular. Most valuable are the Latin histories or chronicles. Little of importance was written in English, except for the *Chronicle* and occasional works that were prevailingly of a religious tone [see *Social and Cultural,* (2) and (4), p. 23]. The feudal system, an aristocratic form of government, promoted the growth of the romance of chivalry; the church system promoted the beginnings and the development of the drama; and the guild system, dependent upon the common people, possibly promoted the spread of the popular ballad. In this period, poetry is, as a general rule, of greater consequence than prose.

2. MOOD OF WRITINGS. The Anglo-Saxon note of instinctive melancholy changed to that of animal hopefulness reflected from the French.

3. FORM OF METER. A compromise was affected between Anglo-Saxon poetry, based on alliteration and regular stress, with a varying number of syllables, and Anglo-French verse, dependent on rime or assonance, with a fixed number of syllables. Anglo-Saxon regularity of accent, and, as a subordinate device, the use of alliteration, were fused with Anglo-French end rime, identical line length, and a fixed number of syllables.

### B. Language

1. NUMBER OF LANGUAGES. For the following three hundred years three tongues were spoken in England: Norman-French, the official language of the Conquerors (*i. e.,* of polite society); Latin, the learned language of the clergy; and English, the tongue of the great mass of the people.

2. PERIOD OF MIDDLE ENGLISH. Three periods may be distinguished: (a) Middle English of the First Period (1100—1250), often called Early Middle English; (b) Middle English of the Second Period (1250—1400); (c) Middle English of the Third Period (1400—1500), often called Late Middle English. In the words of James Hadley and George Lyman Kittredge: "It must be remembered, however, that the process of change was gradual and incessant: the language did not remain fixed for a time, and then on a sudden leap to a new position."[1] Chief dialect-groups were: (a) *Northern* (O. E. *Northumbrian*); (b) *Midland* or *Mercian* (comprising *East-Midland* and *West-Midland*); (c) Southern (comprising *South-Eastern,* formerly *Kentish,* and *South-Western,* formerly *West-Saxon*).

---

1 *Webster's New International Dictionary,* Second Edition (1934), p. LXXXV.

3. Growth of Vocabulary. After 1300, French terms of warfare and chivalry, art and luxury, science and law, began to enter the English language. Also, the English vocabulary was given a *bilingual* character; thus, nouns, adjectives, and verbs often go in pairs—*e. g., home, domicile; bold, courageous; be, exist.* Likewise, prefixes and suffixes made an entrance; *e. g., -age* in *cottage, -hood* in *knighthood.*

4. Simplification of Grammar and Syntax. Grammatical gender was discarded, prepositions were introduced, order of words gradually approached that of modern English. Tendency to drop inflectional endings was accelerated. Most of the survivals of the system of inflection are in the pronoun, as in *who, whose, whom; they, their, them; he, his, him.* Also, strong (irregular) verbs became weak (regular).

5. Development of Spelling. A French orthographic basis was utilized; thus, *w* and *th* made their appearance, the old English *y* was discarded in favor of the French *u,* and *cw* was superseded by *qu.*

## *RELIGIOUS WORKS*

**Orm** (or **Ormin**), *fl. c.* 1185, probably a monk of the order of Augustinian Canons.

*Ormulum*† (c. 1200). "Orm's little book" is a metrical translation and paraphrase of some forty Gospels read at Mass, each interpreted by a verse-homily, and many based on Bede, Gregory, Josephus, Isidore, and others. Of little poetical value are its 20,000 short, wearisome, prolix, laborious lines. Only thirty-one of its 242 homilies (contemplated or finished) are extant.

### *Value in Philology*

a) Illuminates the evolution of the language; *e. g.,* his protracted homily is almost pure English, with less than a dozen French words.

b) Orients one to the pronunciation of the English of his time; *e. g.,* his orthographic device of doubling a consonant after a vowel *pronounced* short is a source of information on quantities of sound in Middle English: where the consonant appears as single, the preceding vowel is immediately recognizable as long (*wrohhte,* wrought; *brinngenn,* bring; *nemmnedd,* named; *unnderrstanndenn,* understand).[1]

c) Is our first phonetician; *e. g.,* he separated the various sounds of the letter *g,* and invented a new symbol for one of them.

### *Value in Prosody*

a) Adapted the Latin *septenarius* by versifying in lines alternately of eight and seven syllables; the meter is the iambic septenarius.

---

1 "Orm doubles a consonant after a short vowel, *except* when the vowel is in an open syllable: . . . ." See Sisam, Kenneth, "MSS. Bodley 340 and 342: Aelfric's *Catholic Homilies,*" *The Review of English Studies,* IX (1933), p. 4 (pp. 1-12).

† * **Explanation of symbols immediately precedes page one.**

b) Introduced into English verse the *regular* appearance of lines of fifteen syllables without intentional rime and with only accidental use of alliteration.

**Thomas de Hales,** *fl. c.* 1270, a Franciscan brother or Minorite in the reign of Henry III. Reflects faithfully the mystic spirit of the age (p. 23).

***Luve Ron (Luv Ron, Love Rune).*†*** Tells of the rapture of marriage with the Heavenly Bridegroom. Frequently conceded to be the most beautiful and devout of the religious lyrics extant from the Conquest to Chaucer. Stanza beginning "Hwer is Paris and Heleyne" shows the *ubi sunt* motive.[1] Twenty-six eight-line stanzas. Melodious simplicity, passionate longing.

**Robert Mannyng of Brunne,** *c.* 1260—1340, Gilbertine canon. Deliberately wrote for the "lewd" (unlearned).

***Handlyng Synne*†** (1303—1338). Series of metrical homilies of 12,632 lines is an amplified adaptation of the Anglo-Norman *Manuel des Péchiéz* (Manual of Sin) of William of Waddington. Stories (including the famous tale of the dancers of Colbek) spice the poem, the main body of which deals with the Ten Commandments, the Seven Deadly Sins (Pride, earliest of all, Anger, Envy, the chief sin of Englishmen, Sloth, Covetousness, Gluttony, Lechery), the Seven Sacraments, and the Twelve Spiritual Graces. Disapproves of women's use of powder and elaborate clothing; condemns tournaments and popular amusements; inveighs against the Miracle Play (p. 103 *ff.*) when performed outside the Church; and, above all, gibbets, like Langland after him (p. 56), the tyranny or rapacity or immorality of landlords, judges, merchants, robber knights, priests, and the like.

*Style*

Simple, quite charming, somewhat satiric are the eight-syllable iambic couplets. Vigorous are the passages on the Sins. (See *The Ancren Riwle,* p. 28.)

*Linguistic Importance*

By utilizing a few of the obsolescent Teutonic words and inflections, and by introducing many French words into the text (of the first five hundred, more than one hundred and fifty are of French origin), it takes its position as a landmark in transition from early to later Middle English.

*Story of Inglande* (finished 1338). Metrical chronicle. First half follows Wace's *Brut* (p. 45) in octosyllabic verse; second, the Anglo-Norman Pierre de Langtoft's *Chronicle,* in riming alexandrines and middle rimes. Latter part more interesting, possibly because more contemporaneous.

---

1 For the *ubi sunt* motivation in Anglo-Saxon literature, see Williams, B. C., *Gnomic Poetry in Anglo-Saxon* (1914), p. 45.

† * **Explanation of symbols immediately precedes page one.**

**Richard Rolle of Hampole,** *c.* 1300—1349, first prominent devotional mystic. Born probably at Thornton-le-Dale in the North Riding of Yorkshire, near Pickering. Quit Oxford at the age of nineteen, put on a hermit's garb, and spent his last years at Hampole, in the south of Yorkshire, near a Cistercian nunnery. After his death, was honored as a saint. Recently he has been described as "a typical *bhakta.*"[1] (Chief source for the facts of his life is *The Office of St. Richard Hermit,* an anonymous fourteenth-century compilation.) His works, both Latin and English, are generally instinct with emotion, sanely and sweetly reasonable, and inspired by the love of God. Wrote a number of epigrams, scriptural paraphrases and commentaries, sacred minor poems, short prose pieces,[2] canticles in praise of Christ and of the Virgin. Lyrics include "A Song of Mercy," "The Nature of Love," "A Song of Love-Longing to Jesus," "Thy Joy be in the Love of Jesus"; and epistles, the *Ego dormio et cor meum vigilat,* ("I sleep and my heart wakes"), the *Form of Living,* and the *Commentary on the Psalter,* the latter two having been written for a disciple, the anchoress Margaret Kirkby. Work most frequently associated with the name of Rolle is:

***The Pricke of Conscience.***† Almost certainly not by Rolle.[3] Didactic poem in seven books (9,544 lines), the purpose of which is to prick the reader's conscience into doing good works. As in *The Ancren Riwle* (p. 28), so here, it is said, the spiritual, not the formal, side of religion shines throughout; but it is also turgid, long, pedantic. Of comparatively advanced technical skill, with the stolidly devotional lines cast in the general form of the octosyllabic couplet (although it ranges up to a dozen syllables). Last important religious poem before Langland's *Vision* (p. 56).

## *ANONYMOUS RELIGIOUS WORKS*

***Poema Morale*** (*c.* 1170). "Moral Ode" on this transient life urges the doing of holy things. Discourse of almost 400 lines somewhat reminiscent of both Anglo-Saxon religious and gnomic poems, as subjective but less imaginatively-phrased. First important poem in English in which "end rime" appears, rimed throughout in couplets. Introduces into English the swinging fourteener line, the septenarius or trochaic tetrameter catalectic of Latin poets (the *Ormulum,* p. 25, uses the same metre, except that it does not rime). Examples of gnomic qualities[4]:

1 Elwin, Verrier, *Richard Rolle* (1930), p. 7.

2 Schneider, J. P., *The Prose Style of Richard Rolle: A Dissertation* (1906).

3 Frequenty attributed to Rolle but now generally recognized as the work of another. See Allen, H. E., "The Authorship of the *Prick of Conscience," Studies in English and Comparative Literature,* Radcliffe College Monographs, No. 15 (1910), pp. 115-170; Deanesly, Margaret, *The Incendium Amoris of Richard Rolle of Hampole* (1915), p. VII *f.* Allen, H. E., *Writings Ascribed to Richard Rolle, Hermit* (1927), pp. 372-397; Comper, F. M. M., *The Life of Richard Rolle* (1928) p. VIII *f.*; Heseltine, G. C., *Selected Works of Richard Rolle, Hermit* (1930), p. XXV.

4 *Old English Homilies.* translation by Morris, Richard (1868), pp. 158-160, lines 4 and 17.

† * Explanation of symbols immediately precedes page one.

"Thah ich bo a wintre ald to yung ich em on rede."
(Though I be old in years, too young am I in wisdom.)
"Erghe we beoth to done god · *and* to ufele al to thriste."
(Slow are we to do good, and all too bold to do evil.)

***The Ancren Riwle,*** or ***Regula Inclusarum*****†** **(*****c.*** **1237).** "The Rule of Anchoresses or of Recluses" is a prose manual of religious counsel prepared in eight divisions or "deals" for three sisters who live as nuns in a house at Tarrant in Dorsetshire. Ascribed traditionally[1] either to Richard Poore, Bishop of Salisbury (1217—1229), and of Durham (1229—1237), or to Simon of Ghent, Bishop of Salisbury (1297—1315). Sometimes involved, yet the best continuous prose between its century and Malory's *Morte d'Arthur* (p. 92). Graced by apt theological quotations, touches of humor, simplicity and coherence of style, knowledge of feminine character, and a religious tenderness and mysticism breathing forth the genuine spirit of religion.

Devotional *vade mecum* gives many rules for living: the keeping of no beast, except one cat; the maintenance of silence at meals; the speaking to no man often or long; the prohibition of drawing blood from oneself with holly twigs; the distrust of dreams; the daily reading of *The Ancren Riwle.* Furthermore, the Seven Deadly Sins, a subject dear to many theologians (*e. g.*, see p. 26), are represented as the lion Pride, the unicorn Wrath, the serpent Envy, the boar Sloth, the fox Covetousness, the swine Gluttony, the scorpion Lechery, each of these having many whelps.

***Cursor Mundi*****†** **(*****c.*** **1300).** "The Course (Surveyor, or Overrunner) of the World" is a scriptural poem. Decrying that so many waste their time by reading empty romances, emphasizes in the prologue that a story at least equally interesting is that from the Deliberations of the Trinity and the Creation of the World to the Day of Judgment and the Life to Come. Prologue definitely states, too, that the poem will be written in English, the speech of the English nation. Sources include the Vulgate, the Apocryphal Gospels, Robert Grosseteste's *Chasteau d'Amour,* Peter Comestor's *Historia Scholastica,* and French and Latin writers. The four-stressed line and the rimed couplet are its staples. Well-proportioned, flowing; enlivened by quaint divagations, attractive traditional stories, and popular fragments of hagiology. Work influenced the York and Wakefield plays (p. 104). Influenced by Herman of Valenciennes's *Bible.*[2]

1 See, however, Chambers, R. W., "Recent Research upon the *Ancren Riwle," The Review of English Studies,* I (1925), pp. 4-23.

2 Borland, Lois. "Herman's *Bible* and the *Cursor Mundi," Studies in Philology,* xxx (1933), pp. 427-444.

† * Explanation of symbols immediately precedes page one.

## *LYRICS, SONGS, AND POEMS*

### A. Sacred and Secular

1. Revelatory of Religious Exaltation

a) ***Luve Ron.***†* Personal mysticism. See p. 26.

b) ***Winter Wakeneth All My Care.*** Treats of the transitoriness "Of this worldes joie, how hit goth al to noht."

c) ***A Song on the Passion.*** Charming with its "Somer is comen and winter gon."

d) ***When I See Blossoms Spring.*** Gracefully subjective.

2. Revelatory of Love and Nature. In general, most important is the body of subjective secular lyrics and songs—they voice with grace and melody a delight in love and laughter; they express a fresh observation of, and an emotional sympathy with, the sunshine and the verdant earth.

a) ***Canute Song*** or ***The Song of Canute*** (*c.* 1166). Early boat-song, often called a ballad fragment, composed by King Canute or Cnut (1016—1035) and recorded by a monk of Ely. Occasional rime and assonance.

b) ***The Cuckoo-Song***† (first half of 13th century). Probably the earliest extant English lyric. Note refrain. With the vowel sound ***u*** pulsing throughout, song reveals a fresh delight in awakening Spring. Music to which it is sung is the *Reading Rota*: "six male voices singing a double canon with ground bass."[1]

c) ***Alysoun***† (*c.* 1300). Dreamily fresh and heartily human love-lyric of four stanzas, each with a four-line refrain.

d) ***Lenten ys come with love to toune***† (*c.* 1300). Sings of Spring (Lent) with charm and originality.

e) **My deth I love, my lyf I hate.** (*c.* 1300). Acceptable love-dialogue of lady and clerk.

### B. Political and Satiric

1. Revelatory of Popular Discontent

a) ***Song Against the King of Almaigne.*** Levelled directly at Richard, Earl of Cornwall (1209—1272), King of the Romans, and brother of Henry III. Abhorred by the people for his desertion of Simon de Montfort.

b) ***Song on the Flemish Insurrection.*** Expresses the popular hatred against France. Composed after the Flemish victory over Robert of Artois at Courtrai ("Battle of the Spurs") in 1302.

---

1 *The Foundations of Poetry,* published by The British Broadcasting Corporation (1928), p. 151.

† * Explanation of symbols immediately precedes page one.

c) **Laurence Minot,** *fl.* 1333—1352, poet, patriot, and probably a soldier. Extant war-songs concerned with the victories of Edward III's battles, ranging from that of Halidon Hill (1333) to the taking of Guines (1352). Eleven militantly jingoistic battle-poems, of no high imaginative quality, but metrically varied and spiritedly written.

2. Revelatory of Social Unrest

a) ***Song of the Husbandman.*** Denounces the groaning burden of taxation resulting from the foreign wars undertaken by Edward I.

b) ***A Song Against the Retinues of the People.*** Inveighs particularly against the expensive ostentation of dress.

c) ***The Fox and the Wolf***† (late 13th century). Comic satire characteristically symbolical of the "Reynard the Fox" tales, wherein Reynard represents the man preying upon society and escaping by his cunning.

d) ***The Land of Cokaygne***† (early 14th century). Fabliau (p. 32) of 190 lines ostensibly representing Cokaygne or "Cake-Land" as a fabulous abode of idleness; in reality, coarsely and satirically attacking the self-indulgence of the monks.

## *OTHER TYPES OF LITERATURE*

### A. The Debate (The French "Débat," the German "Streitgedicht")

The debate as a literary type is variously describable as a wordy mock quarrel, a strife, a contention, a controversial dialogue, a dispute between two or more disputants—thus, there are debates between death and life, summer and winter, wine and water, crusader and non-crusader, winner and waster.

***The Owl and the Nightingale***† (*c.* 1210). Debate or flyting of some 1,795 lines in short couplets. Attributable to either Nicholas of Guildford (*fl.* 1210) or to John of Guildford (*fl.* 1225). Influenced by Marie de France's *Laustic* (p. 46), Alexander Neckam's *De Natura Rerum,* and some general sources. It has been noted that the *contentio* or *disputoison* follows the formal procedure of contemporaneous lawsuits. Variously interpreted: *e. g.,* the nightingale represents "the melody, the sweetness, the grace, the beautiful in life," while the owl represents "the serious view of life"[1]; the contest is "between 'crabbed age and youth,' between gravity and gayety"[2]; and the like. Easy charm of rime, simple imagery, learned allusions from the proverbs of King Alfred (pp. 19, 38), lively dialogue, unity of effect; understanding of human feelings, life-like drawing of character, love of nature. Not

1 Saintsbury, George, *A Short History of English Literature* (1924), p. 60.

2 *The Owl and the Nightingale,* edited by Wells, J. E. (1907), p. xli.

†* Explanation of symbols immediately precedes page one.

only the best example before the fourteenth century of skilful handling of short (octosyllabic) rimed couplets but also "the greatest poem of medieval England before the days of Chaucer and the *Pearl*."[1] (Chaucer, p. 62; *The Pearl*, p. 59).

***Debate of the Body and the Soul*†*** (second half of 13th century). Probably the oldest of religious dialogues, reminiscent of the Anglo-Saxon *Soul and Body I* and *Soul and Body II* (p. 20), is often valued as the most beautiful theological poem of its period. Notable for skilful lyrical phrasing.

**B. The Drama**

The audience grew so large that the performance had to be moved out of the confines of the Church into the roomier spaces of the Churchyard, where often, it has been observed, the freshest graves became the choicest seats. From the churchyard the evergrowing audience compelled the moving into the market-place, where laymen replaced clerics as performers, and English superseded Latin as the language of the plays. Into the hands of the laity, however, the Church had bequeathed certain stock furniture—biblical subjects, spectacle, action, dialogue, and characters like Herod and the Devil. Further impetus had been given to the development of the drama by the order (1210) of Pope Innocent III for the drama to be performed outside the Church; and by the institution (1264) by Pope Urban IV of the festival of *Corpus Christi*.

To this period belong the Miracle play (a dramatization of incidents in the life of a saint) and the Mystery play (a dramatization of a scene from the Bible): although in England the term "Mystery play" does service for both. The earliest Miracle recorded in England by name is the *Ludus de Sancta Katharina* (*c.* 1110), relating the life of St. Katharine; the oldest of English miracle plays is perhaps[2] *The Harrowing of Hell* (thirteenth century); the best serious English Miracle play is the Brome *Abraham and Isaac*. See pp. 105, 106.

**C. The Bestiaries**

Purpose of the *Bestiary*, a name applied to a class of allegorical works or collections of pseudo-classical lore and natural history popular from the fifth to the fifteenth century, was to symbolize spiritual truths rather than to serve as a handbook of natural history. Under the guise of animals, real or fabled, human beings are satirized and morals are drawn: the romance of Reynard the Fox (*Roman de Reynart*) is the best example of this type of animal-fable (see *The Fox and the Wolf*, p. 30). The Bestiaries influenced literature down to the days of Shakespeare. Without a knowledge of these medieval books, passages

---

1 Tupper, Frederick, "The Date and Historical Background of *The Owl and the Nightingale*," *Speculum*, XLIX (1934), p. 425 (pp. 406-425).

2 There has been much discussion as to whether or no *The Harrowing of Hell* is a drama. J. O. Halliwell declared it "the earliest existing dramatic composition in the English language"; but many do not regard the piece as intended for dramatic representation. Consult page 105.

† * Explanation of symbols immediately precedes page one.

in Shakespeare might be obscure; *e. g.*, the references to crocodile tears in *Othello*, IV, 1, *l.* 256 *f.* and to the turtle-dove in *Henry VI, Part I*, II, 2, *l.* 30. Remember that the Bestiaries or Animal Stories are developments of the Physiologi (p. 15).

### D. The Satire

A satire is a literary composition, frequently in verse, in which public or private abuses, follies or corruptions are held up to reprobation, ridicule, or scorn. Attacks on the Church and the revolt of the middle-class against the romantic idealization of women are the staples of medieval satire. Examples are *The Fox and the Wolf* and *The Land of Cokaygne* (p. 30). Also see pp. 87, 97, 240.

### E. The Fabliau

The *fabliau* is a short and pointed tale, bourgeois in its coloring, frequently in octosyllabic verse, usually anonymous, generally realistic, scandalizing, comic, ironical, naughty, and sometimes frankly coarse. The *fabliaux* reveal the manners of the day, from those of the king to the serf, attacking the knavery of the monks and satirizing particularly the moral pretensions of women, the latter attitude being a reaction to the cult of idealizing women. With its dialogue and compressed plot, rapid and skilful telling, and style made subservient to the climax, the *fabliau* is really the precursor of the short-story. Examples are the Chaucerian tales told by the Miller, Reeve, Shipman, and Friar (pp. 72, 73, 74), and *Dame Siriz* (p. 38).

### F. The Exemplum

The *exempla,* dealing most commonly with stories of the Virgin or of the Saints, are told for the purpose of inculcating a moral or a religious principle; *e. g.*, Chaucer's *The Physician's Tale* and *The Pardoner's Tale* (p. 74). In essence the *exemplum* is an illustrative and anecdotal sermon; and as such the *exempla* were collected in preachers' handbooks. "The purposes served by exempla may be summed up as follows: (1) to furnish a concrete illustration of the result of obeying or disobeying some religious or moral law; (2) to give proof or confirmation of the truth of an assertion; (3) to arouse fear in the sinful or to stimulate the zeal of the godly; (4) to make clear the meaning of some abstruse statement; (5) to revive languid listeners, evoke interest or laughter; (6) to eke out a scant sermon by 'farsing' it with tales."[1]

### G. The "Miraculum"

The *miracula* tell of miracles performed by saints; *e. g.*, Chaucer's *The Prioress's Tale* (p. 73).

---

1 Mosher, J. A., *The Exemplum in the Early Religious and Didactic Literature of England* (1911), p. 8.

## *ADDITIONAL AUTHORS OR WORKS*

| AUTHOR | WORK or WORKS | COMMENT |
|---|---|---|
| **LANFRANC**, c. 1005-1089, theological lecturer. Born in Italy. Archbishop of Canterbury (1070—1089). | **De Corpore et Sanguine Domini** (post 1097). | Amateurish polemical tract in the Berengarian controversy over the Real Presence, or Transubstantiation. (Bérenger de Tours's **De Sacra Coena.**) |
| **ST. ANSELM**, c. 1033-1109, often called the father of scholasticism. Italian by birth. Archbishop of Canterbury (1093—1109). | a) **Cur Deus Homo** (1098). | a) "Why God Man" is important in Christian, particularly Catholic, theology. The Redeemer is **homo-Deus.** |
| | b) **Proslogium,** or **Fides Quaerens Intellectum.** | b) Treatise on "Faith Seeking Intellect." Ontological proof of God's existence. Arguments criticized by Descartes, Spinoza, Kant, Hegel, Locke, and others. |
| **EADMER** or **EDMER**, c. 1060-c. 1124 chronicler. Monk of Canterbury. Appointed, but not consecrated, to the Archbishopric of St. Andrews. | a) **Historia Novorum.** | a) "History of Recent Occurrences" of England (1066-1122) is a successful, well-proportioned Latin chronicle. |
| | b) **Vita Anselmi.** | b) "Life of St. Anselm" is a dependable biography of his friend. |
| **ORDERICUS VITALIS**, 1075-c. 1143, Anglo-Norman chronicler. Monk of St. Evroult in Normandy. | **Historia Ecclesiastica.** | "Ecclesiastical History" from A. D. 1 down to 1141. Thirteen books, originally begun as the annals of St. Evroult. Best in its contemporaneous accounts. |
| **FLORENCE OF WORCESTER**, d. c. 1118, chronicler. Monk of Worcester. | **Chronicon ex Chronicis.** | From the Creation down to 1117. Based, until 1030, upon work of Irish monk, Marianus Scotus (fl. 1080). Accurate if uninspired. Continuation until 1141 by John of Worcester (fl. 1150). |
| **SIMEON OF DURHAM**, d. post 1129, conscientious chronicler. | a) **Historia ecclesiae Dunelmensis.** | a) Extends to the year 1096. |
| | b) **Historia regum Anglorum et Dacorum.** | b) Important is the treatment of the years 1119-1129. |
| **HENRY OF HUNTINGDON**, c. 1080—1155, chronicler. Archbishop of Huntingdon (c. 1110). | **Historia Anglorum** (c. 1130) | Earlier part, until 1127, embroidered by many fancies. Fifth edition of compilation carries work down to 1154. |
| **RICHARD OF HEXHAM**, fl. 1141, chronicler. Prior of Hexham. | a) **Brevis Annotatio.** | a) Brief history of his church (674-1138). Based on Bede and Simeon of Durham (pp. 15, 33). |
| | b) **Historia de gestis regis Stephani ....** | b) Important for the beginning of Stephen's reign, and for the battle of Standard. |

| AUTHOR | WORK or WORKS | COMMENT |
|---|---|---|
| **BENOIT DE SAINTE-MORE** (or **SAINTE-MAURE**), 12th century French trouvère and chronicler. Born in Sainte-More in Touraine. | a) **Roman de Troie** (c. 1165). | a) "Romance of Troy" based on the apocryphal works of Dictys Cretensis and Dares Phrygius (p. 66). Introduces the episode of Troilus and Briseida, the basis of Chaucer's **Troilus and Criseyde** and Shakespeare's **Troilus and Cressida** (pp. 66, 201). |
| | b) **Le Roman d'Eneas.** | b) Continuation of the **Roman de Troie.** |
| **GIRALDUS CAMBRENSIS**, or **GERALD DE BARRI**, c. 1146—c. 1220, Welsh chronicler. Archdeacon of Brecon (1175-1203). Had a turbulently romantic career. Excellent classical scholar. Unpedantic; keen observation, humor. | a) **Topographia Hibernica.** | a) "Topography of Ireland" gives a biased account of its natural history and inhabitants. |
| | b) **Expugnatio Hibernica.** | b) "Conquest of Ireland" (1169-1185) reveals his partisan spirit. |
| | c) **Itinerarium Kambriae.** | c) "Itinerary of Wales" and |
| | d) **Descriptio Kambriae.** | d) "Description of Wales" are of importance. Also entertaining. |
| | e) **Gemma Ecclesiastica.** | e) Vivid indictment of the ignorance of the Welsh clergy. |
| | f) **De Rebus a se Gestis.** | f) Autobiography. |
| **JOHN OF SALISBURY**, c. 1120-1180, scholar, philosopher, theologian, jurist, historian, diplomatist. Bishop of Chartres (1176). Secretary to Thomas à Becket, Archbishop of Canterbury, and witnessed the latter's martyrdom (1159). Most learned and cultured man of his age. | a) **Polycraticus, sive De Nugis Curialium et Vestigiis Philosophorum** (1159). | a) "The Statesman's Book, or Concerning the Toys of Courtiers and the Traditions of the Philosophers" discusses in eight books the vanities of the court, an ideal government, and miscellaneous philosophical questions. Is "the earliest elaborate medieval treatise on politics."[1] |
| | b) **Metalogicon.** | b) "A Defense of Logic" is a four-book treatise on grammar as well as logic. Censures formal scholasticism, defends school studies, blends Aristotle with Augustine. |
| | c) **Entheticus de Dogmate Philosophorum.** | c) Elegiac poem of some 1,850 lines in praise of Becket. Theme as in **Polycraticus.** |
| | d) **"Letters."** | d) Some 300 of them, valuable for literary qualities and as a source of contemporaneous history. |

1 Dickinson, John, "The Medieval Conception of Kingship and Some of its Limitations, as Developed in the *Policraticus* of John of Salisbury," *Speculum,* I (1926), p. 308 (pp. 308-337). See also Dickinson, John, *The Statesman's Book* (1927).

| AUTHOR | WORK or WORKS | COMMENT |
|---|---|---|
| **GODRIC**, d. 1170, hermit. | **Hymn to the Virgin.** | First introduces into English "a regular composition in feet." |
| **WILLIAM OF NEWBURGH** (or **GUILIELMUS PARVUS**), c. 1135-c. 1200, chronicler. Canon of the Augustinian Priory of Newburgh, Yorkshire. | **Historia Rerum Anglicarum.** | Five books in Latin, in covering the period 1066-1198, emphasize the reigns of **Stephen** (1135-1154) and Henry II (1154-1189). Undertaken at the request of the abbot of Rievaux. Sources include Henry of Huntingdon and Jordan **Fantosme.** Clear, temperate, impartial, critical; statements, however, frequently inaccurate. Has been described as "the father of historical criticism." |
| **NIGEL WIREKER** fl. c. 1190, satirist. Precentor of Christ Church priory, Canterbury. | a) **Speculum Stultorum; or, A Mirror of Fools.** | a) Latin elegiac poem, through the comic Odyssey of the ass Brunellus or Burnellus, satirizes particularly the religious orders. Mentioned in Chaucer's **The Nun's Priest's Tale** (p. 74). |
| | b) **Contra Curiales et Officiales Clericos.** | b) Attacks the vices of his fellow ecclesiastics. |
| **RICHARD OF DEVIZES**, fl. 1191, chronicler. Monk. | **Chronicon de rebus gestis Ricardi primi.** | "History of Richard I" is a vivid narrative of events in England and in the Holy Land during the Crusade. |
| **ALEXANDER OF HALES** (or **ALEXANDER HALENSIS**), c. 1175-1245, scholastic theologian. Known as **Doctor Irrefragabilis.** Often considered as the author of scholastic theology. | **Summa Universa Theologiae.** | Defends the prerogatives of the papacy by subtle deductions, instead of by appeals to tradition. Anticipates some theories of the Franciscan school. Only authentic work, yet probably not entirely his own. |
| | **Paternoster** (12th century). | Earliest extant English poem consistent in its use of the short riming couplet. |
| **JOSELYN DE BRAKELOND** (or **JOCELIN DE BRAKLONDE**), fl. 1200, chronicler. Monk of Bury St. Edmunds. Chaplain to Samson of Tottington. | **Chronica.** | History of his abbey (1173-1202). Frequent minutiae. Character of Monk Samson influenced Carlyle's **Past and Present** (Bk. II, "The Ancient Monk"). |
| | **Bestiary** (c. 1200-1250). | Morals or doctrines drawn from descriptions or stories about animals (see p. 21). |

| AUTHOR | WORK or WORKS | COMMENT |
| --- | --- | --- |
| **MATTHEW PARIS**, c. 1200-1259, greatest English historian of the Middle Ages. Monk of St. Albans. Practical man of affairs. | a) **Chronica Majora**, or **Historia Major**. | a) "Larger Chronicle" or "Greater History" — from the Creation down to 1259—continues the **Flores Historiarum** of Roger of Wendover. Vigorous, accurate, thorough, critical survey of the affairs of England and Europe. |
| | b) **Historia Anglorum**, or **Historia Minor**. | b) An abridgment of the preceding chronicle, with some additions, from 1067 to 1253. |
| **ROGER BACON**, c. 1214-1294, scholar, philosopher, scientist, mystic. Studied at Oxford and Paris. Of the Franciscan Order. Imprisoned several times. (e. g., 1277-1292). Probably invented the microscope and the telescope; if he did not invent gunpowder, he at least suggested its use in war. Has been hailed as the Founder of Modern Philosophy, the True Forerunner of Modern Science; yet is frequently ultra-medieval.[1] See p. 23. | a) **Opus Majus** (1267). | a) First comparative history of world religions. Urges the reform of Christian education in order to establish the Roman Catholic Church as the supreme civilizing and ennobling agency. |
| | b) **Opus Minus** (1267). | b) A summary of his main work. |
| | c) **Opus Tertium** (1267). | c) A preamble to his chief work. |
| | d) **"The Voynich MS."** | d) So-called because discovered (1912) by W. M. Voynich. Conclusions of W. R. Newbold, who has deciphered the manuscript declared to be one of "the most important documents in the whole history of scientific thought," have been rejected by J. M. Manly as "entirely baseless."[2] |
| **GUIDO DELLE COLONNE** (or **GUIDO DA COLONNA**), 13th century, Sicilian author. A judge at Messina. | **Historia Trojana** (c. 1287). | Servile translation into Latin prose of **Roman de Troie**, by Benoit de Sainte-More (page 34). Source of plots for many English, French, and Italian works. |
| **ROBERT OF GLOUCESTER**, fl. 1260-1300, metrical chronicler. | **"Chronicle"** (c. 1300). | From Troy's destruction down to 1272. Helped by others. Rimed jogging couplets. Primarily a compilation from other sources; e.g., Geoffrey of Monmouth. Two-fold importance—as an adaptation of the two half-lines of Anglo-Saxon poetry, and as an example of the transition stage of the language before Chaucer. |

1 Little, A. G., "Roger Bacon," Annual Lecture on a Master Mind, *Proceedings of the British Academy,* XIV (1928), p. 284 (pp. 265-296).

2 Newbold, W. R., *The Cipher of Roger Bacon* (1928), edited by Kent, R. G.; Manly, J. M., "Roger Bacon and the Voynich MS," *Speculum,* VI (1931), p. 347 (pp. 345-391). See also Leonard, J. N., Chap. V, "The Doctor Mirabilis," *Crusaders of Chemistry* (1930), p. 48 *f.* (pp. 17-60).

| AUTHOR | WORK or WORKS | COMMENT |
|---|---|---|
| **JOHN DUNS SCOTUS** (or **JOANNES SCOTUS DUNS**), c. 1265-1308, Great British medieval philosopher. Called **Doctor Subtilis.** Of the Franciscan Order. Banished (1303) for opposing the anti-papal policy of Philip IV. | a) **Opus Oxoniense.** | a) Commentary on the **Sententia** of Peter Lombard. |
| | b) **De Modus Significandi sive Grammatica Speculativa.** | b) Philosophic grammar. |
| | c) **De Rerum Principio.** | c) On metaphysics. |
| | | **General Estimate.** A realist in philosophy. Supreme function of mind is will. Supported doctrine of the Immaculate Conception. Influenced by Ibn Gabirol (c. 1020-c. 1070), also known as Avicebron. Adherents called Scotists until 16th century, then Dunsmen or Dunces (originating the word **dunce**). |
| **RICHARD AUNGERVILLE** (or **RICHARD DE BURY**), 1281-1345, diplomat, statesman. Born at Bury St. Edmunds. Bishop of Durham (1333). Lord High Chancellor of England (1334). | **Philobiblon** (1345). | Latin autobiographical prose eulogy by the first English bibliophile. Tells how he collected his library, and gives rules for administering the affairs of the library he practically founded. "And because it principally treats of the Love of Books," concludes its Prologue, "it hath pleased us, after the fashion of the ancient Latins, fondly to name it by a Greek word **Philobiblon.**" |
| **DAN MICHEL OF NORTHGATE**, fl. 1340, translator. (Dan means Dominus or Master.) | **Ayenbite of Inwit** (c. 1340). | "The Again-Biting of the Inner Wit" or "The Remorse of Conscience" is translated from French moral treatise, **Le Somme des vices et des vertues** (1279) by Frere Lorens (Laurentius Gallus), in turn based on **Le mirour du monde** (c. 1250). Of high linguistic value, being an excellent dated specimen of the Kentish (southern) dialect of the 14th century. |
| | **Gesta Romanorum** (c. 1295). | "The Deeds of the Romans" is a collection of Latin sermonizing anecdotes and legends. Includes pieces of Oriental and European origin. Sourcebook; e. g., for Chaucer's **The Man of Law's Tale,** Shakespeare's **King Lear** and **Merchant of Venice.** |

| AUTHOR | WORK or WORKS | COMMENT |
|---|---|---|
| | **Proverbs of Alfred** (c. 1200). | Attributed to King Alfred (p. 19). Influenced literature; e. g., see **The Owl and the Nightingale** (p. 30). |
| | **Proverbs of Hendyng** (c. 1300). | Gnomic example: "Burnt child fire dreadeth." Six-line stanzas. |
| **ADAM DAVY,** 14th century. | **Five Dreams about Edward II** (c. 1310). | Obscure vision-poem in octosyllabic couplets. |
| | **The Tale of Gamelyn** (c. 1350). | Verse romance in couplets. Source of pseudo-Chaucerian "Cook's Tale of Gamelyn" (p. 72), Lodge's **Rosalynde** (p. 139), and Shakespeare's **As You Like It** (p. 197). |
| | **Squyr of Lowe Degre** (14th century). | Metrical romance. The Squire finally marries the princess of Hungary. |
| | **Libeaus Desconus,** or **Le Beaus Desconus.** (14th century). | Tail-rime romance in which Guinglain, Gawain's bastard son, is hero. Referred to in Chaucer's **Rime of Sir Thopas** (p. 73). |
| | **Orisoun to Our Lady.** | A vision, representative of the passion of worship for the Holy Virgin (see p. 23). |
| | **Life of St. Dunstan.** | A saint's legend. How the Abbot of Glastonbury ensnares the Devil. |
| | **Life of St. Brendan.** | A saint's legend. An Irish abbot's trip to and from the paradisiacal Land of Behest. |
| | **Dame Siriz, or The Weeping "Biche."** | Metrical tale of Eastern origin in short lines. Margery, a burgher's wife, is frightened by a witch into yielding to the advances of a clerk. |
| | **John the Reeve.** | Theme same as in **Rauf Coilyear** (immediately below). |
| | **Rauf Coilyear.** | A rough but hospitable charcoal-burner unwittingly entertains the King. Rimed poem. See p. 39. |

## Chapter III

# THE ANGLO-NORMAN PERIOD: THE MEDIEVAL ROMANCE

### GENERAL VIEW OF THE MEDIEVAL ROMANCE

The Medieval Romance, derived in English from, generally, a Latin or French original, prospered for about three hundred years (1200—1500) as the most significant division of literature. Its essential feature—(1) the Lack of Verisimilitude, *i.e.,* the lack of general resemblance to truth or reality—is shown by (a) an exaggeration of the vices of human nature, and an idealization of the virtues; and (b) an idolatry of adventures more or less remote from ordinary life, a passion for the strange, the marvelous, the impossible, or the improbable. Other features are (2) an emphasis upon supreme devotion to a fair lady, and a sentimental woman-worship arising from the Virgin cult; (3) scenes laid in the past, with the manners and morals representing some aspect or aspects of the contemporary ideal of Chivalry; (4) the presence, in one form or another, of a Quest; (5) the appearance of either a religious or a supernatural element, or both; (6) the analysis of characters in a typical, not in an individualized, manner; and (7) a *naïveté* of form (*e. g.,* a frequent lack of consecutiveness).

### THE THREE "MATTERS"

The subject-matters of Medieval Romance are drawn from the common stock of three main storehouses, epitomized somewhat inaccurately by Jehan Bodel's *Chanson des Saisnes* (13th century) as being "The Matter of France," "The Matter of Rome the Great" (or Classical Antiquity), and "The Matter of Britain."

#### A. The Matter of France

1. The Carolingian cycle centers around Charlemagne and his Twelve Paladins. Oldest and most notable of the *chansons de geste* (Old French epic poems written originally in assonant verse generally of ten or twelve syllables) is the *Chanson de Roland* (11th—12th century).

2. The Carolingian romances in English are, among others, *Sir Ferumbras, Sir Otuel, Roland and Vernagu, The Sowdone of Babylon, The Siege of Milan, Rauf Coilyear.* (The last-named is a Scotch romance; see p. 38.)

### B. The Matter of Rome

Imperial Rome, representing the greatest city of the ancient world, yielded stories from all Classical Antiquity. Main sources of medieval Trojan legends were Dictys Cretensis, Dares Phrygius, Benoît de Sainte-More, and Guido delle Colonne (see pp. 34, 36, 66).

1. The exploits of Alexander the Great; *e. g., Kyng Alisaunder* (13th century).

2. The tales of Ilium or Troy; *e. g., The Geste Hystoriale of the Destruction of Troy,* first English version of the Troy story, an alliterative poem translated from Guido delle Colonne's work.

3. The romances of Thebes, based on the *Thebaid* of Statius; *e. g.,* Chaucer's *The Knight's Tale* (p. 72), Lydgate's *Troy-Book* (p. 84).

4. Miscellaneous sources are located, primarily, in Byzantine romances; *e. g.* the influence of the Orient is seen in *Cligès* by Chrestien de Troyes (p. 47), *Flores and Blancheflour, Sir Isumbras, William of Palerne* (p. 61), *The Seven Sages of Rome.* Possibly of Oriental (perhaps of Greek or Latin) origin is the tail-rime romance, *Amis and Amiloun.**

### C. The Matter of Britain

1. The most significant division in this "matter," as well as of all the "matters," is the body of legendary material nucleated by King Arthur and the Knights of the Round Table. Important characters are Guinevere (there was no fairer or more faithless wife), Sir Lancelot (there was no braver or more amorous knight), Sir Kay (there was no more faithful knight), Sir Galahad (there was no purer soul), and Tristram and Iseult (there was no truer pair of lovers). In addition, separate cycles of romance grouped themselves about the figures of Tristram and Iseult, Lancelot, Merlin, Gawain, and about the Quest of the Holy Grail. Among the many separate Arthurian romances are *Arthour and Merlin, Morte d'Arthure, Sir Tristram, Awntyrs* (Adventures) *of Arthur at the Tarn Wadling,* and, eclipsing all, *Sir Gawayne and the Grene Knight* (p. 60).

2. Forming another important portion in this "matter" is a body of semi-historical legendary tales, dealing in the main with native English heroes—Horn, Havelock, and others (p. 48 *f.*). See Note 1, p. 48.

3. A third group, English or Breton in origin, are lays or poems based on lays; *e. g., Lanval** by Marie de France (p. 46). Other examples are *Sir Orfeo, Emare, Sir Degare, Le Fraisne* (p. 46) and Chaucer's *The Franklin's Tale* (p. 75).

---

† * Explanation of symbols immediately precedes page one.

## THE MATTER OF BRITAIN: THE ARTHURIAN LEGEND

### A. Origins of the Arthurian Tradition

**Gildas.** See p. 15.

***De Excidio et Conquestu Britanniae*** (*c.* 547). "Concerning the Destruction and Conquest of Britain" is the authority for the history of Britain from the time of the Roman invasions down to his own day. Although covering the whole period of the Arthurian story without referring to Arthur, yet is the first to mention the overwhelming defeat of the Saxons by the British at Mount Badon. Supplies the figure of Ambrosius Aurelianus as the one who for the first time checked the Saxons.

*Welsh Annals and Folklore Tales*

***The Book of Aneurin.*** Aneurin or Aneirin, *c.* 600, mentions Arthur once. See p. 21.

***Historia Britonum*** (*c.* 796). By **Nennius** (p. 15). "History of the Britons" makes, according to some, the first historical mention of Arthur by name. Describes him as the continuously victorious *dux bellorum* against the Saxons in a dozen enumerated battles, the twelfth being that of Mount Badon (Chap. LXI). Ambrosius appears in a subordinate position, but as one invested with magical powers.

***Annales Cambriae*** (*c.* 955). Welsh annals placing the battle of Mount Badon in the year 516; and that of Camlan in 537. First to allude to the death of Modred at Camlan, at which battle Arthur died.

***The Black Book of Caermarthen*** (12th century). Mentions Arthur at least five times.

***The Book of Taliessin*** (14th century). Mentions Arthur at least twice. (Author, however, possibly belongs to the sixth century.)

***The Red Book of Hergest*** (15th century). Makes only one reference to Arthur.[1] MS. contains *The Mabinogion* (plural of Welsh *mabinogi,* from *mabinog,* a bard's apprentice; means "instruction for a bard's apprentice" or "tales for young people" or "youthful career").

***The Mabinogion.***† Title given by Lady Charlotte Guest to a collection of prose tales, published 1838—1849. "Mabinogion," however, strictly applicable to only four of the translated tales: *Pwyll, Prince of Dyfed; Branwen, Daughter of Llyr; Manawyddan, son of Llyr;* and *Math, son of Mathonwy.* Four of the stories are part of *The Red Book of Hergest;* but not one refers to Arthur. However, the collection includes five tales dealing with Arthur: three of French, and two of British, origin. The French romances are not independent of three Welsh stories by Chrestien de Troyes (p. 47): his *Perceval* (*Conte del Graal*)

---

1 Dr. John Jay Parry, in a letter, points out that the statement about Arthur is true only of the oldest poetry contained in *The Red Book of Hergest.*

† * Explanation of symbols immediately precedes page one.

becomes *Peredur, the Son of Evrawc; Erec* (*Erec and Enide*) becomes *Geraint* or *Geraint and Enid;* and *Chevalier au Lion* (*Yvain*) becomes *Owen* or *The Lady of the Fountain.* The two drawn from British sources are *The Dream of Rhonabwy* and *Kilhwch and Olwen, or the Twrch Trwyth.** In the last-named tenth-century romance, or fairy tale, Arthur is invested with magical powers.

*Influence of Welsh Elements*

Welsh heroes, as well as other subjects, re-appear in the Arthurian legend with a metamorphosis of their original superhuman qualities. The Welsh Peredur* becomes Perceval; Kai,* Kay; Bedwyr,* Bedivere; Myrrdhin* (Myrrdin), Merlin. Even the Welsh form *Caledvwlch,* resembling the Irish legendary sword Caladbolg, becomes Caliburn (Excalibur). Climaxing all, the central incident of *Sir Gawayne and the Grene Knight* (p. 60) is derived from an adventure in the saga called *Fled Bricrend.*

**Walter Map (or Mapes),** *c.* 1137—*c.* 1209, a Welshman. Archdeacon of Oxford (1197). Also, see p. 47.

***Lancelot.*** French prose version formerly attributed to Map.[1] Included material on the Grail, and on the death of Arthur.

***La Queste del Saint Graal.*** Second French-prose part of *Lancelot.* Makes the Grail a vessel used at the Last Supper: Lancelot fails in the Quest, but Galahad achieves it.

***De Nugis Curialium*** (*c.* 1180—1193). "Of Courtiers' Trifles" is a Latin prose collection of anecdotes, reflections, and folk-lore tales. Satirizes the monks as well as the courtiers.

***"Goliardic Verses."*** So-called because they are satirical Latin poems and unfrocked profanities against Golias. Attributed to Map.

"Meum est propositum in taberna mori." Famous drinking-song.

### B. Development of the Arthurian Legend in England

**William of Malmesbury,** *c.* 1090—*c.* 1143, Anglo-Latin chronicler. First a monk and then librarian at Malmesbury Abbey. Best of the twelfth-century historians. Vivid, graceful.

***De Gestis Regum Anglorum.*** "History of the Kings of England" (A. D. 449—1127) includes two passages about Arthur the great chieftain (Bk. I).

***Historia Novella.*** Sequel carries the history down to 1142.

***Vita Wulfstani.*** Recently "printed in full for the first time."[2]

---

1 Although Map may have written an Anglo-French poem which was the germ of the Lancelot legend, he is generally no longer credited with the authorship of *Lancelot du Lac,* the Arthurian prose romance which includes *The Quest of the Holy Grail* and *The Death of Arthur.*

2 *The Vita Wulfstani of William of Malmesbury,* edited by Darlington, R. R. (1928)

† * **Explanation of symbols immediately precedes page one.**

**Geoffrey of Monmouth,** *c.* 1100—1155, historian-romancer. Born at Monmouth, Wales. Studied at Oxford. Probably obtained the arch deaconry of Llandaff (*c.* 1140). Subsequently promoted to the See of St. Asaph (*c.* 1151).

***Vita Merlini.*** While some do, others do not attribute the poem to him. Celtic influences apparent, as are those of Isidore of Seville's *Origines,* and possibly Apuleius's *God of Socrates* and Solinus's *De Rerum Mirabilia.*[1]

***Historia Regum Britanniae*** † (1135—1138). "History of the Kings of Britain" is an ornate Latin prose work drawing on Bede and Nennius, on the Welsh tale of the *Dream of Maxen Wledig,* and probably on Orosius, Livy, and Virgil. Avowal of reliance upon an ancient Cymric history furnished him by a certain Walter, Archdeacon of Oxford (Walter Calenius? Archdeacon Gaulter?) brought contemporary accusations that Geoffrey had manufactured the source, filling in the historical hiatuses with figments of a riotous imagination. Whether or not he made "the little finger of his Arthur bigger than the back of Alexander the Great" (William of Newburgh's *Historia Rerum Anglicarum*), Geoffrey's imperishable romancing makes the work the most significant product of the age, and makes him the popularizer of the Arthurian tradition quite faithful to the form known to-day. (See *Arthurian Framework.**) Probably Geoffrey deliberately created Arthur as "the exemplar of chivalry, the *courtois* British counterpart of the French Charlemagne."[2]

Introductory chapter states that the author will narrate "the actions of all the British kings, from Brutus, the first of them, down to Cadwallader, the son of Cadwallo." Of the dozen books the first three, which bring the record down to the time of Caesar's invasion, are less important from the point of view of his romanticizing than the next three, where details in the history of the Romans and the Saxons in Britain up to the time of King Arthur are embellished by the products of his fancy. The prophecies of Merlin, who appears in the seventeenth chapter of Book VI, are found in Book VII; but actually Book VII incorporates the *Prophecies of Merlin,* which Geoffrey had written previous to his *Historia.* Although Book VIII introduces Uther Pendragon as the father of Arthur, it is not until Book IX that Arthur the hero begins his reign; and then throughout Books X and XI holds complete sway. Book XII ends with the death of Cadwallader (689).

---

1 Parry, J. J., The *"Vita Merlini,"* University of Illinois Studies in Language and Literature, No. 3 (1925).

2 Nitze, W. A., and Dargan, E. P., *A History of French Literature* (1922), p. 41. See, also, Bruce, J. D., *The Evolution of Arthurian Romance* (1923), I, p. 23.

† * **Explanation of symbols immediately precedes page one.**

*Influence of Geoffrey on English Literature*

**A. Some Characters or Elements Added to the Arthuriad**

1. **Modred (Mordred).** Traitorous nephew (in some versions, the son by incestuous union) of King Arthur, and killed by the latter in battle.

2. **Uther Pendragon.** Father of Arthur by an adulterous union with Igerna (Igraine, Igerne, Ygerne), wife of Gorlois, Duke of Tintagil, or Tintagel, in Cornwall.

3. **Merlin.** Nennius's Ambrosius, who foretold the defeat of the Saxons by the Britons, becomes transformed into the romantic necromancer Merlin—perhaps originally a Welsh god, and subsequently a bard called Myrrdhin.*

4. States that Arthur was carried to the island of Avalon for the healing of his wounds.

5. Fixes Arthur's capital at Urbs Legionum (The City of Legions, or Caerleon on the Usk).

**B. Some Legendary Names and Tales**

1. Story of King Leir and his three daughters furnishes the plot for Shakespeare's *King Lear* (p. 211).

2. Account of Cymbeline provides the material for Shakespeare's *Cymbeline* (p. 220).

3. Name of Sabrina, virgin daughter of Locrine and Estrildis, is immortalized in Fletcher's *Faithful Shepherdess* (p. 241) and in Milton's *A Mask Presented at Ludlow-Castle,* or *Comus* (p. 279).

4. Legend of Ferrex and Porrex, sons of Gorboduc, forms the basis of *Gorboduc,* or *Ferrex and Porrex* (p. 121).

5. Succession of characters in English history influenced William Baldwin and George Ferrers's *A Mirror for Magistrates* (1559), William Warner's *Albion's England* (1586), and Michael Drayton's *Poly-Olbion* (1622). See p. 147.

**Geoffrey Gaimar,** *fl.* 1140, Anglo-Norman trouvère, and historiographer.

***L'Estorie des Engles*** (*c.* 1147). Undertaken for Constance, wife of Ralf fitz Gilbert. First part (now lost) is, except for the history of the Trojan War, a translation of Geoffrey of Monmouth's version into Anglo-Norman octosyllabic verse. Second part (still extant), drawn from other historical sources, carries on the history to the death of William Rufus (1087). Sometimes credited with having given the first suggestion for the legend of the Round Table.

**Robert Wace of Jersey,** *c.* 1100—*c.* 1184, Anglo-Norman chronicler. Born in Jersey (he himself says, in Guernsey). Canon of Bayeux. Called "Maistre Wace."

† * Explanation of symbols immediately precedes page one.

***Geste des Bretons,*** or ***Roman de Brut*****†** **(1155).** Free paraphrase of Geoffrey of Monmouth into Norman-French octosyllabic couplets. Courtly sentiment and spirit of Carolingian epics make the tone less impersonal and more flowingly colorful than that of Geoffrey of Monmouth.

*Elements Added by Wace to the Arthuriad*

1. Tranforms Arthur into the flower of chivalry.

2. Refers, probably for the first time, to the Round Table, although the legend was probably known to, but not utilized by, Geoffrey of Monmouth. By representing total equality through its circular shape, the form of the table prevents disturbances as to matters of precedence among the knights.

3. Introduces important statements; *e. g.,* the anticipated return of Arthur from Avalon.

4. Alludes to the forest of Brocéliande and its wonders.

5. Combines the tradition that Guinevere is of Cornish birth with Geoffrey of Monmouth's statement that she is a Roman lady.

**Layamon** (or **Laweman),** *fl.* **1200,** priest connected with the church at Ernley on the west bank of the Severn (Areley Regis, Worcestershire).

***Brut*****†** (*c.* 1205). First long poem of value in the vernacular of the period. Avows that, as source-books, "He took the English book that Saint Bede made; another he took, in Latin, that Saint Albin made, and the fair Austin who brought baptism in hither; the third book he took, laid there in the midst, that a French clerk made, who was named Wace, who well could write . . . ." Apparently, however, based in the main upon Wace's version of Geoffrey of Monmouth; or even, possibly, upon the lost riming chronicle of Gaimar. Originality lies in amplification of old, and introduction of new, material; *e. g.,* he doubles Wace's 15,300 lines to 32,241 (*A-text*), and invents lively speeches and original scenes, notably when Arthur is told of Modred's treachery. Note that (a) Layamon records for the first time in English the immortal stories of Lear, Cymbeline, Sabrina, and others; and that (b) Layamon, writing in English, yet exerted little, if any, influence upon the development of the Arthuriad.

*Some Legendary Embroideries*

1. Introduces the fairy element; *e. g.,* three elves appear at Arthur's birth; two queens in a magic boat remove him, when mortally wounded, to Avalon to be healed of his wounds.

2. Gives a fuller and more circumstantial account of the founding of the Round Table; *e. g.,* concerning its origin and purpose.

---

† * **Explanation of symbols immediately precedes page one.**

3. Makes Arthur's sword and lance of magic origin.

4. Saxonizes Arthur, who had almost become French or Anglo-Norman in character, into a mighty English monarch.

*Structure*

1. Style. Generally of no high poetic value. However, does reveal a leisurely pace, except where battles are described, simple metaphors, frequent repetition of "same or similar phrases,"[1] spirited rhythm, subjective tone, and a vividness and realism more telling than in Wace's version.

2. Vocabulary. Almost wholly Saxon. Important philologically as a monumental structure of early Middle English, varying estimates placing the number of French words in the *A-text* at approximately less than one hundred. Also illuminates the transition stage of the language.

3. Meter. Intermixes the Anglo-Saxon alliterative line of two short sections and the octosyllabic couplets employed by Wace. The alliteration is often broken down, assonance occasionally appears, and simple rimes are introduced.

## C. French Arthurian Poets

**Marie De France,** *fl.* 1154—1189, Norman lady-poet and fabulist (*e. g.,* her *Ysopet* comprises 103 fables) who wrote in French but lived in England probably in the reign of Henry II. Her *lais* (1167—1184)—chivalric romances in octosyllabic couplets, or brief poems (originally musical) derived from Celtic folk-lore and Breton (Armorican) sources and also from Byzantine, Classical, and Biblical legends—may be divided into three groups[2]: (a) realistic—*e. g., Eliduc, Equitan, Les Dous Amanz;* (b) anecdotal—*e. g., Chievrefueil, Laustic;* and (c) supernatural—*e. g., Guigemar, Guingamor, Lanval, Le Fraisne, Yonec.* Occasionally passionate, always delightfully deft and sentimental, and keenly analytical of human love. Also, see p. 1.

***Lanval**** (*c.* 1175). *Lai* connected with early Arthurian tradition. Basis of the English fairy tale *Sir Launfal,* by Thomas Chestre.

***The Honeysuckle (Le Chievrefueil*** or ***Gotelef).*** Incident in the love of Tristram and Iseult, reminiscent of the Anglo-Saxon *The Husband's Message* (p. 9): Tristan carves a code-message on a hazel twig and sends it to the Queen.

---

1 Tatlock, J. S. P., "Epic Formulas, Especially in Layamon," *Publications of the Modern Language Association of America,* XXXVIII (1923), pp. 494-529.

2 Damon, S. F., "Marie de France, Psychologist of Courtly Love," *Publications of the Modern Language Association of America,* XLIV (1929), pp. 968-996.

† * Explanation of symbols immediately precedes page one.

**Chrestien** (or **Chrétien**) **de Troyes,** *c.* 1140—*c.* 1191, Provençal romancer. Probably born in Troyes. Developed fluent, dignified, well-plotted, and entertaining stories as part of the Arthurian tradition, which he heightened by a chivalric tone. First to marshal the tales into a cycle. Introduced the figure of Lancelot (in *Erec and Énide*); also, the first suggestion of Lancelot's amour with Guinevere (in *Le Chevalier de la Charette*); and the first literary presentation of the story of Perceval (in his unfinished *Perceval le Gallois*). "Chrestien de Troyes was the real creator of Arthurian Romance."[1] See *The Mabinogion* (p. 41).

### D. Anglo-Norman and English Arthurian Romances

**Robert de Borron,** *c.* 1170—*c.* 1212, French romancer. Gautier de Montbeliard was the patron of this Anglo-Norman knight, who "wrote in an East-French dialect and not in Anglo-Norman."[2] Trilogy consists of:

***Grand Saint Graal.*** Prose recension forms basis of metrical romance *Joseph of Arimathea.* First attached a sacred Christian character to the Grail as part of the Arthuriad. (The Grail was originally a heathen talisman.)

***Merlin.*** The Necromancer is made the central figure.

***Perceval.*** Tells of the Quest of the Grail.

**Walter Map (or Mapes).** (See p. 42.) Formerly credited with having given to the cycle its religious and moral character: Lancelot's sin prevents him from achieving the Quest; and also with having made the Arthur legend inseparable from the Holy Grail. See Note 1, p. 42.

### E. World Influence of Arthurian Legend

The Arthurian tradition has assumed a prominent place in world literature through such names as, respectively, the Anglo-Norman and Norman Beroul and Thomas (Thomas de Bretagne); through the Italian, Rusticano of Pisa; through the Germans, Hartmann von Aue, Eilhart von Oberge, Wolfram von Eschenbach, Gottfried von Strassburg, and Walther von der Vogelweide; through the Frenchman, Joseph Bédier; through the Americans, J. R. Lowell and E. A. Robinson. In later English literature the legends appear in the works of Malory (p. 92) Spenser (p. 124), Dryden, Tennyson, Swinburne, Arnold, Masefield, and other writers.

---

1 Lewis, C. B., *Classical Mythology and Arthurian Romance,* p. 305 (1932).

2 Nitze, W. A., "On the Chronology of the Graïl Romances," *The Manly Anniversary Studies in Language and Literature* (The University of Chicago Press, 1923), p. 311 (pp. 300-314).

## *THE MATTER OF BRITAIN: THE NATIVE ENGLISH HEROES*[1]

The most important metrical romances based on the "matter" of England, rather than upon the legends of the Britons, recount in rambling fashion and with spiritless characterization the heroic or supernatural adventures of royal or noble characters, drawn from popular tradition or historical documents. The tales, founded usually on Norman versions of English or Scandinavian themes, generally have come back into English through a French intermediary.

***King Horn*†*** (*c.* 1250). Earliest extant English metrical romance, based on an Anglo-French *chanson de geste.* Not even the unfledged tale and the defective construction of the 1,548 verses can obscure the homely virility of the simple short rimed couplets and the interest in a conventional story containing the stock fixtures of timed arrivals and conquered hardships.

***Havelok the Dane*†*** (*c.* 1310). Verse romance based upon two Norman-French poems, in turn dependent upon an Anglo-Saxon source. Although unpolished and bluff, through its better characterization, hearty figurative language, and more circumstantial descriptive details, improves on its much shorter French version. The elements of the marvelous and of the love interest are less dominant than in *King Horn.* Some 3,001 lines, in octosyllabic couplets. Its bragging is reminiscent of Anglo-Saxon poetry. Definitely influenced by Gaimar (p. 44).

*Historical Element*

a) Similarity exists between the lay of Havelok and the tale of Hamlet (Amleth) as told by Saxo Grammaticus, Danish chronicler. Parallels also exist between the Hamlet-story and *King Horn* and *Sir Bevis of Hampton* (see p. 49).

b) Havelok might be identifiable as the exiled Anlaf Curran, son of Sihtric, King of Northumbria (925): Cuaran or Cuheran is Havelok's name as a kitchen-churl, and the name Havelok (Habloc, Abloec, Abloyc) may correspond in Celtic to Anlaf or Olaf. See *The Battle of Brunanburh,* p. 19.

c) Marriage of Havelok and Goldborough is symbolical of the union of Denmark and England.

***Guy of Warwick*†*** (English version, 14th century). Encounter with Colbrand, possibly an historical fact, with other feats are told in Drayton's *Poly-Olbion* (p. 147). Reveals the ancillary and alliterative phrases, as well as the stereotyped epithets, of tail-rime

1 It is necessary to emphasize that the stories of native English origin which appeared first in Anglo-French poems are actually distinct from what is commonly meant by the Matter of Britain. Other stories, too, can not be classified under the three "matters."

† * Explanation of symbols immediately precedes page one.

romances. Conventional characterization. Approaches closer than *Sir Bevis of Hampton* (p. 49) to the ideals of chivalry: first part is warlike, second part is religious.

**Sir Bevis of Hampton (or Hamtoun)†*** (*c.* 1300). Sometimes paralleled with Shakespeare's *Hamlet* (p. 204); *e. g.*, Bevis's mission to King Brademond of Damascus with a sealed letter demanding his own death is likened to that part where Hamlet is sent off on a mission to England under the escort of two courtiers who have in their possession a letter demanding Hamlet's death. (See *Havelok the Dane*, "Historical Element," p. 48.) Bevis's adventures recounted in Drayton's *Poly-Olbion* (p. 147). Conventional, except for its character analysis of Josian and possibly of Ascopart. Atmosphere confused by a multitude of characters, rapid change of scene, and hotchpotch of incident. Seven-eighths in short riming couplets; only the beginning 474 lines are in *rime couée.*

***Athelston*** (*c.* 1400). Tail-rime romance which mirrors some important events of English political history. Effectively and compactly constructed.[1]

---

1 As a corrective to the high praise frequently bestowed upon the romance, see Trounce, A. McI., *Athelston* (Publications of the Philological Society), XI (1933).

† * Explanation of symbols immediately precedes page one.

Chapter IV

# THE AGE OF CHAUCER
## (1340 — 1400)

**Political and Social Background**

a) ***The Beginning of the Hundred Years' War*** (1337—1453). The so-called Hundred Years' War originated in the Conquest of 1066 that made the Duke of Normandy, the French vassal, King of England. Precipitated primarily by commercial rivalry between France and England, it included the decisive English victories at Sluys (1340), which gave England command of the seas for three decades, at Crécy (1346), and at Calais (1347), which gave England possession of the seaport fortress until 1558. Nine years after the Peace of Brétigny (1360) had terminated the first stage of the war, the conflict was renewed. Finally, dismayed by a series of misfortunes and defeats, the English arranged a truce (1396) which lasted until 1415. (For a continuation of the War, see p. 82.)

b) ***Richard II's Misrule and Deposition.*** Richard had raised money by forced loans, and lavished it on his minions; had coerced the judges, failed to keep his promise to the peasants, antagonized the nobles by banishing or executing many of them, and had in other ways given proof of misgovernment. Finally the Lancastrians, led by Henry of Bolingbroke, forcibly acquired the crown (1399).

c) ***The Black Death.*** This Oriental plague, which ravaged Asia and Europe in the 14th century, wasted England for some three hundred years, particularly during 1348—1349, 1361—1362, and 1368—1369. Great economic and social changes resulted from the pestilence; by causing a scarcity of labor, wages doubled or trebled, and conditions of the working classes improved; to compel workers to serve when called upon, and to keep wages down to the level prevailing in 1347, the Statute of Laborers was enacted (1351). The Black Death quickened the fall of the feudal system, built up the towns and cities, and even fostered radical thought.

d) ***The Peasants' Revolt of 1381 (Tyler's Rebellion).*** Discontented with the strong arm of the ruling classes, the corruption of the clergy, and the harassing taxation of the government, the people stormed London, led by Wat Tyler, Jack Straw, and John Ball, the latter preaching his theory of democracy and socialism from the famous text:

"When Adam delved, and Eve span,
Who was then the gentleman?"

When the boy-king, Richard II, granted the insurrectionists their requests, such as the removal of the capitation tax, which was the immediate cause of the popular uprising, the total abolition of slavery for themselves and their children, and the liberty of buying and selling in all fairs and markets, the insurgents, chiefly from Essex and Hertfordshire, withdrew from the capital. Wat Tyler and his men of Kent, however, were among those who refused to disperse; and only Tyler's death broke the spirit and the ranks of the remaining bodies of insurgents. Although the King annulled the charters of manumission granted to the rebels, yet the social upheaval led to the virtual repeal of the Statute of Laborers, and the final abolition of villeinage.

e) ***The Lollard Movement.*** John Wyclif (p. 52) and his followers, called Lollards, taught what they believed to be the true Christianity, contending against the papal viceregency of Christ and accepting only those teachings of the Church that found sanction in the Bible, to which they appealed as the supreme authority. The orthodox assailed this position, proscribed the Wyclif translation of the Scriptures (p. 53), imprisoned or even burned his votaries; but nothing could cut short the preachings of Lollardy, which continued until the Reformation and finally became merged with Protestantism. Thus, a century and a half after Wyclif and his "poor preachers" had fought courageously for religious freedom, the political and social force of their ideas triumphed. (The literary monument of Lollardy is Langland's *Vision*, p. 56.)

f) ***Feudalism.*** The middle-classes were rich and prospering; the deputies of the people were increasing in strength; the feudal relation was becoming outgrown. What accelerated the decline and final extinction of the feudal system was the foreign wars: first, the victories of the English at Crécy and Agincourt, attributable primarily to the bowmen, indicated the equality of yeoman archers with mailed knights; second, and more important, the Kings, to obtain the support of the Parliament, and of the towns, which supplied the largest share of the expenses of such wars, granted redress of grievances, extension of liberties, and important privileges.

g) ***The English Church.*** The feeling was growing that the men of religious orders were less intent upon the teachings of the Gospel than upon worldly gratification. Popular opinion doubted the infallibility of the Pope, resented his decretals, and believed that the papacy was a political tool of France.

### General View of the Literature

Ranged beside Geoffrey Chaucer, who towers above all the other writers of this period, are men who have some claim to attention: Barbour, the first Scottish poet of merit; Gower, who gave to his works the stamp of "correctness" of prosody; Wyclif, who superintended the first complete English translation of the Bible; Langland, the poet and prophet of essentially modern social reforms who led in the revival of alliterative poetry; and the nameless author or authors of *Sir Gawayne and the Grene Knight* and *Pearl*. To the drama already in vogue as Scripture and Saints' plays was added the Morality, a dramatized allegory in which, generally, the Vices contend with Virtues, the characters being personified abstractions such as Justice, Reason, Mercy, Gluttony, Lust, Death, or typical figures like Youth and Everyman. Before long the Morality, originally serious in nature, took on broad farcical elements. (See p. 103 *ff*.) In general, poetry was more popular and more frequently written than prose.

**John Wyclif** (also spelt a score of other ways), *c*. 1324—1384, religious reformer, translator of the Bible.[1] Early years are a blank, for, like Chaucer, there is not to be found in all his writings even one reference to the place of his birth, to his parentage, or to his early life. Popular teacher at Oxford; Master of Balliol College, Oxford (1360). Vicar of Fillingham in Lincolnshire (1361—1369), of Ludgershall near Oxford (1369—1374), and of Lutterworth in Leicestershire (1374—1384). In an age of social agitation, of labor troubles, of change in the art of war, of radicalism and imperialism in Church and State, Wyclif stood worthily for religious and political freedom. Scorn of hypocrisy and greed, and moral courage and spiritual insight prompted him to oppose the hierarchical control of the State while at the same time advocating the doctrines of a Church strictly subordinate to the State. Militancy in reform, theology, and controversy brought upon him the ban of Pope Gregory IX, and later the condemnation by an ecclesiastical court. His popular writings, particularly the translation of the Bible, gained him the distinction of being, according to many, the founder of English prose (see, however, p. 18); his political, theological, and evangelical activities, the distinction of being the real originator of European Protestantism.[2] (Wyclif's followers were known as *Lollards*. See p. 51.)

***Determinatio quaedam de Domino*** (1366 or 1374). Tract champions national rights as against foreign aggression by urging that the papal claim for tribute and arrears (since 1333) as a feudal acknowledgment deserved no consideration, for no power, not even the spiritual as represented by the Pope, could exercise control over an independent country.

***De Dominio Divino***. "On the Lordship of God" expounds the doctrine that all authority is founded on grace. Bases its argument on "dominion" (p. 53).

***De Civili Dominio***. "On Civil Lordship" gives an elaborate scholastic argument for the secularization of Church property.

---

1 Workman, H. B., *John Wyclif*, (Two Volumes, 1926).

2 Workman, H. B., *The Dawn of the Reformation* (1901), Vol. I, Chap. IV, pp. 151-223; Cadman, S. P., *The Three Religious Leaders of Oxford and Their Movements* (1916), pp. 3-172.

***The Wyclif Bible*†** (Early Version, *c.* 1382—1384; Later Version, *c.* 1389). Earliest complete rendering of the Holy Scriptures into English, including the apocryphal and the canonical books. Translated from the Latin Vulgate of St. Jerome (A. D. 383—405). Undoubtedly Wyclif's zeal, inspiration, and direction instituted this translation. He himself probably rendered only a part of the Old Testament, and the Gospels of Saint Matthew and Saint Mark of the New, the rest being done under his direction by others. Valuable contribution to the growing standard of English prose, doing for it what Chaucer did for poetry. Pioneering made possible the *Authorized Version* (p. 149).

### *Style*

In his tracts and sermons (including, also, *The Ten Commandments, Ave Maria, The Church and her Members, Wedded Men and Wives, The Seven Werkys of Mercy; De officio regis, De eucharista, Trialogus, De ecclesia, De potestate Papae,* and the unfinished *Opus evangelicum*) Wyclif is sincere, imperious, and vituperative, with little distinction of style, the literary interest being chiefly historical. In his translation of the Bible also he shows a lack of elegance, being crude and imperfect but rugged and direct. Obscurities in the latter are definitely attributable to his desire, and that of his chief coadjutor Nicholas of Hereford, to be scrupulously faithful to St. Jerome's Latin work. Later, John Purvey smoothed out the harsh literalness.

### *Ideas*

Throughout his writings Wyclif appeals to Scripture as the primary and supreme authority in all matters of controversy, insistent that the power of the Pope is simply ministerial, and that not even the Pope can absolve or excommunicate for all eternity. He censures the corruption of the lawyers, opposes the exemption of ecclesiastical persons from lay control, demands the cessation of the practice of employing the clergy in secular business, denies the orthodox doctrine of transubstantiation, fights against the creed of Nominalism, rejects the alleged infallibility of the Church of Rome, defends the concepts of socialism, and, holding the theory of "dominion" that all things belong to God, and all men hold of him directly, even argues in favor of communism. For sufficient reason, therefore, is Wyclif called "the Morning Star of the Reformation."

**John Gower,** *c.* 1325—1408, poet. Came of a good Kentish family and was a man of independent means. Owned land in Kent, Norfolk, and Multon. Although not in holy orders, held the living of Great Braxted in Essex (1390—1397). When past the age of seventy, he married Agnes Groundolf within his lodgings in the Priory of St. Mary Overy, Southwark — probably his second marriage (1398).

---

† * Explanation of symbols immediately precedes page one.

Blindness came to him in 1400, the year of Chaucer's death. To commemorate his liberal contributions to the re-building of the Priory, the brethren, burying the poet in the north aisle of the nave of the Cathedral Church of St. Savior, Southwark, carved on the tomb his figure in effigy, the recumbent head being pillowed on his three chief volumes—the *Speculum Meditantis* (in French), the *Vox Clamantis* (in Latin), and the *Confessio Amantis* (in English).

However, the most famous items concerning the personal life of Gower are indissolubly linked with Chaucer. The former was one of the two to whom Chaucer, when leaving for Lombardy in May, 1378, gave a general power of attorney; and was one of the two to whom Chaucer dedicated his *Troilus and Criseyde* (Bk. V, *l.* 1856). Another matter inextricably connected with the two is the probable break in their friendship, inferred from the subsequent omission of Gower's tribute to Chaucer, put into the mouth of Venus (*Confessio Amantis,* Bk. VIII, *ll.* 2941—2957) but appearing only in the first edition.

***Speculum Meditantis*** or ***Mirour de l'Omme*** (1376—1379). Devotional, utilitarian poem of some 30,000 lines in French, thought to be lost, was re-discovered (1895) by G. C. Macaulay among recent additions to the University Library at Cambridge, disguised under the alternative title of *Mirour de l'Omme.* Sermon on the immorality of the age is medieval in its conception, doctrine, and erudition. Although not entirely unpoetical, yet on the whole falls flat through its dull execution and long-winded moralizing. Correct prosody, its twelve-line octosyllabics riming *aabaabbbabba.*

***Vox Clamantis**** (*post* 1381). "The Voice of One Crying" (in the Wilderness) is a dream-allegory in which the adventures symbolize the Peasants' Rising of 1381, and the death of Wat Tyler. Three-fold classification of society—clerk, soldier, and ploughman—is followed by Ruskin in his *Fors Clavigera,* Letter XV. Seven books, each with a prologue. Latinity of its elegiac verse is poor, the movement is generally tedious; the value of the poem lies in its exposure of social corruption and in its criticism of contemporaneous manners. Doubtless, its didacticism obtained for Gower the epithet "moral" (*i. e.,* sententious) applied to him by Chaucer (*Troilus and Criseyde,* Bk. V, *l.* 1856).

***Confessio Amantis*†*** (completed 1390; revised 1393). Prologue to "The Confession of a Lover," a poem of eight books, arraigns the dishonesty of the trades and the corruption of the Church. Mainly in short octosyllabic couplets. At Gower's worst, the 33,000 lines are prosy, digressive, and austerely fatiguing. At his best, the poem, allegorical in form and realistic in content, shows a talent, even if no genius, for story-telling which is always lucid, occasionally powerful and dramatic; *e. g.,* "The Trump of Death" (Bk. I., under *Surquidry or Presumption*), the "Tale of Rosiphelee" (Bk. IV, under *Idleness*),

† * Explanation of symbols immediately precedes page one.

the "Tale of Jason and Medea" (Bk. V., under *False Witness and Perjury*).[1] On the whole, graceful and fluent, unartificial and often picturesque. First English poem to be translated into other languages.

***Cinkante Balades.*** Collection of fifty-one Norman-French love-ballades, addressed to Henry IV. Conventional sentiments graced by more poetic feeling than is usual in unimpassioned Gower.

***Cronica Tripertita.*** Three books, in Latin leonine hexameters, give a condemnatory and biased account of the last years (1386—1399) of the reign of Richard II.

***Traitié*** (*c.* 1397). Series of 18 French ballades with envoys presents the nature and nobility of the married state and the evil of inconstancy. An anti-climax to the *Cinkante Balades.*

***In Praise of Peace*** (*c.* 1399). Seven-line pentameter English verses, riming *ababbcc,* point out the ephemeral nature of fame in arms and urge Henry IV, to whom addressed, to cherish peace. Charming.

*Estimate*

At all times extremely regular, yet Gower's laborious "correctness" is distinguished by fluency, distinct ease of style, pleasant melody, and good craftsmanship. Not unlike Langland, Gower dealt with social evils and their remedies; but he lacked the poet of Malvern's intensity of purpose and imagination. Not unlike Chaucer, Gower used (but creakingly) the machinery of a medieval dream-poem (*e. g.,* in his *Confessio Amantis*); but he did not approach the other's humor and pathos, narrative and dramatic power, realism and originality. Both were alike in their deficiency of lyric passion and intense human feelings; but Gower reveals a want of sympathy. In the ultimate analysis, Chaucer's assimilated greater learning, particularly in the sciences, may be contrasted with Gower's superficial knowledge; while the latter is more of a steady moralist, the former is superlatively more of a poet.[2] However, the work of Gower, to-day considered as flat and monotonous, is a monument of English and has a definite philological importance.

**John Barbour,** *c.* 1316—*c.* 1396, Scottish poet, historian. Archdeacon of Aberdeen (1357).

***The Brus***† (1375—1378). Patriotic epic romance, modelled on the *Thebaid* of Statius, chronicles the fortunes and adventures of King Robert the Bruce and his companion, Sir James of Douglas, in freeing Scotland from English domination. Plain, flowing, pithy, spirited style

1 Macaulay, G. C., *The Complete Works of John Gower* (1901), Vol. II, pp. 91-97, pp. 335-340; Vol. III, pp. 37-62.

2 Curry, W. C., *Chaucer and the Medieval Sciences* (1926); Fox, G. G., "The Medieval Sciences in the Works of John Gower," *Princeton Studies in English,* No. 6 (1931); Street, Ethel, "John Gower," *London Mercury,* XXIV (1931), p. 239 *f.* (pp. 230-242).

† * Explanation of symbols immediately precedes page one.

of its twenty books, over 13,000 lines, in octosyllabic couplets. Excellent description of the King's flight across the moor, and of the Battle of Bannockburn. Quotable passage is that beginning with (Bk. I, *l.* 225): "A! fredome is a nobill thing!"

***The Buik of Alexander.*** Translation from two French poems.

***Siege of Troy.*** Two fragments in octosyllabic verse translated from the Latin of Guido delle Colonne (p. 36).

## *THE REVIVAL OF ALLITERATIVE VERSE*

**William Langland,** *c.* 1332—*c.* 1400, poet, dreamer, prophet. Born probably at Ledbury, although Cleobury Mortimer in Shropshire is generally given as his place of birth.[1] Probably educated at the monastery of Great Malvern. Went to London. With his wife Kitte and his daughter Calote, resided for many years in Cornhill. Died in about 1400, the year of Chaucer's death. (Chief facts about his life are supplied by *The Vision of William concerning Piers the Plowman,* the masterpiece generally attributed to Langland.)

***Mum and the Sothsegger*** (1399—1400).[2] Includes "Richard the Redeles," or "A Poem on the Depositions of Richard II." That the work is by the author of *Piers Plowman* has been completely exploded, writes Dr. Carleton Brown.

***The Vision of William concerning Piers the Plowman,***† and its sequel *Vita de Do-Wel, Do-Bet, et Do-Best secundum Wit et Resoun.* In Latin called *Visio Willelmi de Petro Plowman.* Whole poem is properly named *Liber de Petro Plowman.*[3] The three versions of the poem:

1. *A-text* (*c.* 1362). First and shortest text contains the vision of Piers the Plowman (in a Prologue and eight Passus or cantos); and the Vision of Do-wel, Do-bet, and Do-best (in a Prologue and three Passus).

2. *B-text* (*c.* 1377). Expands the allegory. While the Vision of Piers Plowman consists of a Prologue and only seven Passus, yet this is of greater length because of a Prologue and six Passus of Do-wel, a Prologue and three Passus of Do-bet, and a Prologue and one Passus of Do-best. Generally considered the best version.

3. *C-text* (*c.* 1393—1399). New recension of the *B-text.* Longest version, and more deeply mystical.

### *The Question of Authorship*

Literary scholarship is still endeavoring to settle the question of single or composite authorship of the poem. J. M. Manly believes the

---

1 Bright, A. H., *New Light on 'Piers Plowman'* (1928).

2 *Mum and the Sothsegger,* edited by Day, Mabel and Steele, Robert (1936).

3 Skeat, W. W., *The Vision of Piers the Plowman* (1931), p. xi.

† * Explanation of symbols immediately precedes page one.

work to be by no fewer than five authors—the *A-text* is the work (a) of the man who breaks off the poem at Passus VIII, *l.* 131, (b) of the one who continues it to Passus XII, *l.* 55, and (c) of John But, Passus XII, *ll.* 55—117; while (d) and (e), the *B-* and *C-* revisions he believes to be by two different authors. Among those who consider the poem to be the work of one man are W. W. Skeat, J. J. Jusserand, and R. W. Chambers.[1]

*Meter, Style, and Discussion*

Written in the irregular alliterative long line, with all the limitations and defects of such a style. The liquid smoothness, significance, and style of Chaucer is absent. Langland is not a skilled metrist. *The Vision of William concerning Piers the Plowman* and Chaucer's *Canterbury Tales* are the greatest two literary poems produced in England during the Middle Ages. The great difference between the two writers is Langland's insularity as contrasted with Chaucer's cosmopolitanism (Jusserand). The latter, for example, is apparently unconcerned with the political unrest of the age, while the former's phrases were so apt that they were used as electrifying watchwords in the Peasants' Revolt. Moreover, while both possess a gift of satire and a sense of individuality, Langland is markedly deficient in Chaucer's abundant humor and well-proportioned narrative skill.

A growing maturity is apparent in the successive versions. The slight shallowness of the *A-text* disappears from the interesting *B-text,* as youth gives way to middle-age; then the variously changed *C-text* yields to the expatiating, almost prolix, attitude of old age. While the structure is complicated, while the narration is sprawling, and while the purpose of the poem is submerged in a sea of allegory, yet the work is noteworthy for its intense sincerity, vitalized personification, dramatic dialogue, tremendous realism, and imaginative vigour. Viewed in the whole, its disjointedness and digression are blacked out by a largeness of unity. For some effective passages, see the picture of the power of feudal custom, *B-text,* Passus VI, *ll.* 1—58; and the vignettes of medieval village life, *B-Text,* Passus V, *ll.* 94—119, Passus XVII, *ll.* 315—326.

With the whip of a satirist-preacher, the poet lashes the corruptions of Society. He praises poverty, but does not forget the shortcomings of the poor; he rebukes the workman who shirks his work, calls to task the women who put on their backs better clothes than they can afford, and denounces those who marry for money. The merchants are charged with cheating; the clergy, with seeking money, ease, and sloth, while neglecting the care of souls; the political officials, with being friends of Lady Meed (*i. e., Reward;* but here in the sense of *Bribery*). The rich who are wasteful and dishonest will suffer in the next world; the poor who have recourse to confession and contrition

1 There is not an iota of evidence that the ***Vision*** **was written by Langland, asserts** Oscar Cargill, who hazards the suggestion that the work may have been written even by William de la Rokele. See "The Langland Myth," ***Publications of the Modern Language Association of America,*** **L (1935), pp. 36-56.**

will be happy in heaven. Langland teaches that successive generations must pay in years of poverty for military victories, supports the Commons, and urges the King to make his decisions after consulting Reason and Conscience. This mystic does more than arraign the individuals who practise abuses in the Church and State; in the very tumult of his imagination, which sees visions and makes prophecies, he sights the remedies. Thus, for example, the cure for evil in the State abides in the Platonic conception of having each class perform its fitting function. At all times Langland's panacea is: Learn to love.

Within this magnificent allegory the poet embodies, as did Bunyan, personal, including spiritual, experiences; also, satirical pictures of contemporary life, sacred ethical truths, and a message of universal application. As an example of effective allegory, there is the picture of the famine of that time, represented by Hunger's battle with Wastor. Another example is the political fable of the rats and the cat (which does not appear in the *A-text*): the cat represents Edward II in the last year of his reign, while the rats and mice represent respectively the great and less important people of London. To reenforce the moral lessons taught, the author utilizes the theological and ethical literature of the age, including many Vulgate quotations (about 45 whole-line quotations in the *A-text*, about 300 in the *B-text*, and about 275 in the *C-text*).[1] The structure has a macaronic content; Latin words and passages abound throughout.[2] The whole poem is notable for its simple and tolerant piety, a piety that harmonizes with the three-fold conception of Piers Plowman: according to Skeat, first, the ideal honest man, second, Saint Peter, the Apostle, and last, the Incarnate Jesus. (This point of view is substantially that of Jusserand: "Piers Plowman personifies now the honest man of the people, now the Pope, now Christ."[3])

To the antiquary, the philologist, the historian, and the sociologist Langland's work has first-rank value; but to the *littérateur* it is "barely second-rate," in the words of Émile Legouis. The sixth centenary of this idealist and reformer, whose work pictures the social, political, and religious life of the fourteenth century, was passed in 1932, a year of crisis containing problems similar to those that Langland's age faced.

***MS. Cotton Nero A.x.*** (*c.* 1390.) In a vellum manuscript known as *Cotton Nero A.x.* are preserved four alliterative poems, generally conjectured to be by the same author[4]: *The Pearl, Cleanness* or *Purity, Patience,* and *Sir Gawayne and the Grene Knight.*

---

1 Adams, M. R., "The Use of the Vulgate in *Piers Plowman,*" *Studies in Philology,* XXIV (1927), pp. 556-566.

2 Sullivan, Carmeline (*Sister*), *The Latin Insertions and the Macaronic Verse in Piers Plowman* (1932).

3 Jusserand, J. J., *Piers Plowman* (1894), p. 155.

4 Menner, R. J., *Purity* (Yale Studies in English, LXI, 1920,, pp. XI-XIX; Gollancz, Sir Israel, *Pearl* (1921), pp. XL-XLVI; Chapman, C. O., "The Authorship of the *Pearl,*" *Publications of the Modern Language Association of America,* LXVII (1932), pp. 346 353.

***The Pearl*†*** (*c.* 1370). Elegy, not seldom theological and didactic, laments the death of a girl-child (probably the poet's) Margaret, describing her as the transfigured and happy Queen of Heaven.[1] Dream-allegory of mystical and devotional pathos, characterized by emotional appeal and lofty imagination, embodies the "Augustinian doctrine of grace as the basis of heavenly reward." Dream-motive, traces of personification, and beautiful descriptive passages obviously indebted to the *Roman de la Rose,* and to the vision of the New Jerusalem in the Apocalypse. Twelve-line octosyllabic stanzas, with alliteration, rime, and a refrain; riming *ababababbcbc.* Consists of 101 stanzas in 20 sections of five (excepting section 15, containing six) stanzas, with the last or main word or phrase of one stanza recurring as a refrain in the first line of the following stanza.[2] Its 1,212 lines are in the main charmingly stylistic, metrically elaborate, gracefully alliterative. Occasionally resembles Boccaccio's Latin eclogue, *Olympia.* Indebted to the Bible. Sir Israel Gollancz describes the poet of *Pearl* as one who "With one hand, as it were, toward Langland, and one toward Chaucer, he, in a sense, more truly than Chaucer, is the herald of the Elizabethan poets; . . . ."[3]

***Cleanness*** or ***Purity.*†** (1360—1400). So-called after its title word. Alliterative, unrimed poem inculcates the worship of purity and the joys of lawful love, through the medium of Scriptural stories[4]—the Parable of the Marriage Feast, the Fall of the Angels, the Deluge, the Destruction of Sodom and Gomorrah, the plunder of Jerusalem by Nebuchadnezzar, and the Fall of Belshazzar. Main source is the Vulgate text.[5] Effective descriptions of the Flood and Belshazzar's Feast.

***Patience*†** (1360—1400). Versified story of the Prophet Jonah illustrates the nobility of Patience and the necessity for practicing it. Opening word furnishes title. Companion piece to *Cleanness.* Vigorous, picturesque, realistic; occasionally tender. Unwitting gleams of humor. Alliterative, unrimed.

---

1 For re-interpretations of the poem, see Garrett, R. M., "The Pearl: An Interpretation," *University of Washington Publications in English,* IV, No. 1 (1918), pp. 1-45; Fletcher, J. B., "The Allegory of The Pearl," *The Journal of English and Germanic Philology,* XX (1921), pp. 1-21; Greene, W. K., "The Pearl: A New Interpretation," *Publications of the Modern Language Association of America,* XL (1925), pp. 814-827; Madeleva, M. (*Sister*), *Pearl: A Study in Spiritual Dryness* (1925); Cargill, Oscar, and Schlauch, Margaret, "*The Pearl* and Its Jeweler," *Publications of the Modern Language Association of America,* XLIII (1928), pp. 105-123.

2 Mitchell, S. W., *Pearl* (1906), p. 6 *f.;* Gollancz, Sir Israel, *Pearl* (1918), second page.

3 Gollancz, Sir Israel, "The Middle Ages in the Lineage of English Poetry," *Medieval Contributions to Modern Civilization,* edited by Hearnshaw, F. J. C. (1921), p. 181 (pp. 174-189).

4 Gollancz, Sir Israel, *Cleanness* (1921), pp. XV-XIX.

5 Menner, R. J., *Purity* (Yale Studies in English, LXI, 1920), p. XXXIX; Gollancz, Sir Israel, *Cleanness* (1921), p. XIX.

† * **Explanation of symbols immediately precedes page one.**

***Sir Gawayne and the Grene Knight*†*** (*c.* 1370). Verse-romance of 2,530 lines unites two old folk tales, derived ultimately from Celtic legend: the themes of the Beheading and the Wooing (*e. g.*, the oldest case of the beheading theme is found in the Irish saga of *Fled Bricrend* or *Bricriu's Feast* belonging to the Cuchulain cycle; while the test of chastity has many parallels.[1])

Alliterative verse varies in stanzaic form from less than twenty lines to more than forty, each stanza being concluded by a "bob" of five short lines riming *ababa*.[2] Originality lies less in its material than in the feature of its construction: only a single adventure vitally uniting two tales is recounted. The few minor incidents that are introduced are properly subordinated. Careful construction, masterly storytelling. Colorful, brilliant, and delicate descriptive details harmonize with a humor and vividness, a directness and mystery, and a freshness and originality.

*General Character of Sir Gawain*

Gawain appears in many other romances. His principal single adventure occurs in *Sir Gawayne and the Grene Knight.* Another interesting experience is found in the early medieval romance, *The Marriage of Sir Gawain,* a story retold by Chaucer in *The Wife of Bath's Tale* (p. 74). While in *Sir Gawayne and the Grene Knight* Gawain is pictured, except for one human lapse, as an ideal knightly hero, as the flower of courtesy, yet this characterization of him is true only in the earlier stages of Arthurian story, particularly in *The Mabinogion* (p. 41). In later versions his character shows deterioration: *e. g.*, Malory's *Morte d'Arthur* describes him as a "destroyer of good knights," and Tennyson's *Idylls of the King,* as loose, treacherous, "Light . . . . in life and light in death."

| **Sir Gawayne and the Grene Knight** | **Beowulf (p. 6).** |
|---|---|
| 1. Our first great romance before Spenser (p. 124). | 1. Our first national epic before Spenser (p. 124). |
| 2. Sophisticated and chivalrous in its emotion. | 2. Primitive and simple-minded in its stern courage. |
| 3. Presence of a love story. | 3. Absence of a love story. |
| 4. Delicate description of landscape, sympathetic understanding of human feeling. | 4. Broad description of landscape, rough-hewn understanding of human feeling. |
| 5. While ostensibly a combat with an enchanter, yet important parts are concerned with the hunting scenes.[3] | 5. While ostensibly a combat with a monster, yet significant portions are concerned with sea (and other nature) scenes. See p. 6*ff* |

1 Kittredge, G. L., *A Study of Gawain and the Green Knight* (1916); Brown, A. C. L., "The Irish Element in King Arthur and the Grail," *Medieval Studies in Memory of Gertrude Schoepperle Loomis* (Paris, and New York. 1927), p. 96 (pp. 95-111); Buchanan, Alice, "The Irish Framework of *Gawain and the Green Knight,*" *Publications of the Modern Language Association of America,* XLVII(1932), pp. 315-338.

2 Andrew, S. O., *Sir Gawain and the Green Knight* (1931), p. XIII *f.*

3 Savage, H. L., "The Significance of the Hunting Scenes in Sir Gawain and the Green Knight," *The Journal of English and Germanic Philology,* XXVII (1928), pp. 1-15.

† * Explanation of symbols immediately precedes page one.

## *ADDITIONAL AUTHORS OR WORKS*

| AUTHOR | WORK or WORKS | COMMENT |
|---|---|---|
| **NICHOLAS TRIVET,** c. 1258-c. 1328, historian. Dominican friar. Wrote many theological and Latin works. | **Annales Sex Regum Angliae qui a Comitibus Andegavensibus Originem Traxerunt.** | Chronicle of English history (1136-1307). Particularly valuable for the reign of Edward I. Source of Chaucer's **Man of Law's Tale** (p. 72). |
| | **William of Palerne** (c. 1355). | English romance. Part of **The Revival of Alliterative Verse** (p. 56). Exemplifies the belief in lycanthropy. |
| **RANULPH HIGDEN,** c. 1299-c. 1364, chronicler. Cheshire monk. | **Polychronicon.** | A general Latin-prose history in seven books. Continuation carried on by other pens. Important for its description of contemporaneous social conditions. |
| **JOHN OF FORDUN,** d. 1384, Scotch chronicler. Secular priest. | **Chronica Gentis Scotorum.**<br>(With its continuation, properly called **Scotichronicon.**) | First attempt to write a continuous history of Scotland. Only last two of the five books have historical value. Continuation from 1153 to 1437 by Walter Bower, c. 1385-1449, Scottish abbot. |
| **THOMAS USK,** d.—1388, author. Under-sheriff of London (1387). | **Testament of Love** (1384-1385).[1] | Allegorical prose work. Formerly attributed to Chaucer. Dull, elaborate; yet, some say, with it begins modern English prose.[2] |
| **JOHN OF TREVISA,** c. 1326-c. 1412, translator.[3] Fellow of Exeter (1362-1369) and Queens (1369-1379). Was expelled. Vicar of Berkeley. | a) **Polychronicon** (1387) | a) Translated Higden's Latin history of seven books (see above). Freely rendered into racy English: described, however, by Émile Legouis as "awkward prose." (Caxton, in an eighth book, carried history down to 1460.) |
| | b) **De Proprietatibus Rerum** (completed 1398). | b) Translated the medieval encyclopedia in nineteen books by Bartholomaeus Anglicus (Bartholomew de Glanville). Used by Spenser, Marlowe, Massinger, Jonson. |
| **ANDREW OF WYNTOUN,** c. 1350-c. 1420, Scottish chronicler. Canon regular of St. Andrews, and prior of St. Serf's Inch in Lochleven. | **Orygynale Cronykil.** | Long history of Scotland (from the Creation down to 1406). Octosyllabic couplet. Later books of the nine are important. Gives the story of Macbeth and the witches, Malcolm, and Macduff. Slight as poetry; valuable in philology as a specimen of Old Scots. |

1 Bressie, Ramona, "The Date of Thomas Usk's *Testament of Love,*" *Modern Philology,* XXVI (1928), pp. 17-29.

2 "We may perhaps say that modern English prose begins with the *Testament of Love* of Thomas Usk (*c.* 1388)." *The Encyclopedia Britannica,* Fourteenth Edition, XVIII (1929), p. 592.

3 See *Dialogus inter Militem Et Clericum,* edited by Perry, A. J. (1925).

## Chapter V

# THE AGE OF CHAUCER: GEOFFREY CHAUCER

**Geoffrey Chaucer,** *c.* 1340—1400, first great English poet. Geoffrey Chaucer the poet is traditionally accepted as being identical with the Geoffrey Chaucer described in public records as page, soldier, squire, court officer, magistrate, member of Parliament, and ambassador. Salient point is that in the whole significant record not a single item is concerned with Geoffrey Chaucer as a poet.

### THE LIFE OF CHAUCER[1]

#### A. Early Life: Until 1372

Son of John Chaucer, London vintner, and Agnes, daughter of James de Copton, niece and heir of Hamo de Copton. Probably born nearer the year 1345 than the commonly accepted date of 1340. In the service of Elizabeth, Countess of Ulster, wife of Lionel, Duke of Clarence, third son of Edward III (1357). While serving in the English army in France, taken prisoner near Rheims (1359—1360); but liberated (1360) upon the payment of a ransom to which the King subscribed £16. Yeoman or esquire in Edward III's household. Appointed as one of three commissioners to discuss with the Genoese the establishment in England of a port of entry where the Genoese might have special facilities for trade (November 12, 1372: his first Italian journey). For her services to his wife Constance, the Duke of Lancaster in August, 1372, granted Philippa, Chaucer's wife, ten pounds a year as an annuity. (Traditionally it has been conjectured that John of Gaunt, Duke of Lancaster, bestowed favors upon Chaucer and Philippa because the latter, the daughter of Sir Payne Roet, was also the sister of Katherine, widow of Sir Hugh Swynford, and, later, first the mistress and then the third wife of John of Gaunt. However, Russell Krauss has endeavored to show that while Thomas Chaucer was the son of Philippa Chaucer, Thomas's father was more likely John of Gaunt than Geoffrey Chaucer.[2])

---

1 Bulk of facts concerning Chaucer's life is available in *The Chaucer Society Publications: Life-Records of Chaucer,* I (1875), edited by Selby, W. D.; II (1876), edited by Furnivall, F. J.; III (1886), edited by Bond, E. A. and Selby, W. D.; and particularly IV (1900), edited by Kirk, R. E. G.

2 Krauss, Russell, *Chaucerian Problems: Especially the Petherton Forestership and the Question of Thomas Chaucer: a Dissertation* (1932). See, however, Manly, J. M., "Three Recent Chaucer Studies," *The Review of English Studies,* x (1934), pp. 262-267 (pp. 257-273).

### B. Middle Life: 1373—1385

Appointed Comptroller of the Customs and Subsidies of Wools, Hides, and Wool-fells in the port of London, and also Comptroller of the Petty Customs of Wines (1374). Went abroad on the King's secret affairs in the retinue of Sir John de Burley (1376). Probably went on a mission to Flanders with Sir Thomas Percy (1377); and later sent on an embassy to France, probably in connection with the peace negotiations between that country and England (1377). Comptroller of the Customs (1377). Probably in France in connection with a proposed marriage of Richard and a French princess (1378). Sent with Sir Edward de Berkeley to Bernabò Visconti, Lord of Milan, and to Bernabò's son-in-law, Sir John de Hawkwood, regarding certain business touching the King's War (1378). Deed of release (May 1, 1380) by Cecily Chaumpaigne to Geoffrey Chaucer respecting her *raptus,* probably referring to a case of abduction, and not to an act of physical rape. (W. W. Skeat has intimated that the "Little Lewis" of *A Treatise on the Astrolabe,* p. 69, was the son of Chaucer by Cecily.) Deeds of release (June 30 and July 2, 1380) by Richard Goodchild and John Grove to Chaucer, and by Cecily Chaumpaigne to them. (Seemingly indicates that the offenders against the woman were Goodchild and Grove.) Comptroller of the Petty Customs (1382).

### C. Last Years: 1385—1400

Appointed by the King a Justice of the peace for Kent (1385). One of the two knights of the Shire for Kent (1386). Loses (December, 1386) both his Comptrollerships. (At this time his patron, John of Gaunt, is absent in Spain, and the Duke of Gloucester has political supremacy.) At Chaucer's request, his two pensions of 20 marks each are turned over to a John Scalby. (Seems to indicate that Chaucer was in financial straits.) With John of Gaunt again in England, and King Richard in full control of the government, Chaucer is appointed Clerk of the King's Works at various palaces (1389—1390). Held the subforestership post of North Petherton Park in Somerset (1391). Granted a fresh annuity of £20 (1394). Henry IV, immediately after his accession, confirms the grant of an annuity of £20 and bestows upon Chaucer a new pension of 40 marks (1399). Death of Chaucer (1400). Buried in Westminster Abbey, in that part now known as Poets' Corner.

## CHRONOLOGICAL OUTLINE OF CHAUCER'S WORKS

It is customary to divide the works of Chaucer into three periods —that of French Influence (until 1372), of Italian Influence (1372—1385), and of English Influence (1385—1400). These convenient divisions, however, are not to be accepted too rigidly; *e. g.,* while *The*

*House of Fame* is placed in the Italian period, (one reason being the clear influence of Dante's *Divina Commedia*), yet it is in reality a transitional work, showing as it does also the French influence. Moreover, the chronology of Chaucer's writings is mostly conjectural, the dates being determined through various sources (*e. g.*, Chaucer's own lists of his works in the Introduction to *The Man of Law's Tale*, in the palinode at the end of *The Parson's Tale*, and in the Prologue to *The Legend of Good Women*), and through the characteristics of his style and the evidence of his power (*e. g.*, the poems of his early period are generally beautiful, but sentimental, with an excess of decorative description, and no rich humorous vein; while the stanzaic form of his early works is transformed into the decasyllabic couplets of his later ones).

## PERIOD OF FRENCH INFLUENCE: UNTIL 1372

### A. Major Poems

***The Romaunt of the Rose.**** Of the three fragments (*A-ll.* 1—1705; *B-ll.* 1706—5810; *C-ll.* 5811—7696), the general opinion is that *A* probably is, *B* is not, and *C* may be by Chaucer. Translation in octosyllabic couplets from the French *Roman de la Rose* influenced Chaucer's subsequent work; *e. g.*, contributed the stock features[1] of the dream-vision (a dream-setting, Maytime, when the birds twitter and the flowers perfume the air, the personification of allegorical figures, a helpful guide) to *The Book of the Duchess, The House of Fame, The Parliament of Fowls, the Legend of Good Women,* and other works.

First part of French original, by Guillaume de Lorris (*fl.* 1230), is an idealization of women and chivalrous love, or the laws of "courtoisie"; second, by Jean Clopinel, better known as Jean de Meun or de Meung (*c.* 1250—*c.* 1305), is, fabliau-like, a mocking, free-thinking attack on the conventional morality, follies, and shortcomings of the time (*e. g.*, Meun satirizes the deceptive arts and vices of women, and the so-called celibacy of the monastic orders).

***The Book of the Duchess*****†*** (1369: only absolutely datable work). Dream-allegory traditionally accepted as a lament over the death, on September 12, 1369, of Blanche, Duchess of Lancaster, first wife of John of Gaunt. Long-spun speeches and philosophical attitudinizings in 1,334 octosyllabic couplets are examples of his deficiency in directness, proportion, naturalness, and maturity. However, gives evidence of some charm and realism, of skilful dialogue, occasional pathos, introspective imagination, and definite originality. Influenced by Ovid's *Metamorphoses,* Froissart's *Le Paradys d'Amour,* and Guillaume de Machault's (or de Machaut's) *Le Jugement du Roy de Behaingne,* the

1 Sypherd, W. O., "Studies in Chaucer's *Hous of Fame*," *Chaucer Society, Second Series,* No. 39 (1907 for the Issue of 1904), p. 5*f*.

† * Explanation of symbols immediately precedes page one.

*Dit de la Fontaine Amoreuse, Le Jugement du Roy de Navarre,* the *Remède de Fortune,* the *Dit dou Lyon,* the *Lay de Confort.* F. N. Robinson agrees with G. L. Kittredge that "Here, for the first time, whether in French or English, we find the standard French conventions —the love-vision, and the lover's lament—turned to the uses of a personal elegy."[1] According to W. H. Schofield, "Chaucer's portrait of Blanche is the first life-like portrait in English literature of an actual English lady"[2]; but even for this portrait Chaucer is indebted to other sources. (In another connection, G. K. Chesterton has found in the Prioress of *The Canterbury Tales* "the first faint outline of the English lady."[3])

### B. Minor Poems

***Chaucer's ABC*** (*c.* 1369). Pious prayer to the Virgin Mary, paraphrased from Guillaume de Deguilleville's *Le Pèlerinage de la Vie Humaine* (*c.* 1330). Each of the stanzas, of which the first is the best, advances successively through all the letters of the alphabet (twenty-three in that day's English). Iambic pentameter, *ababbcbc.*

***A Complaint to His Lady.*** Plaintive lay or formal lament about a long and hopeless love. Introduces into English poetry *terza rima,* (riming *aba, bcb, cdc,* and so on); and is among the first to use the ten-line stanza, *aabaabcddc.*

***The Complaint unto Pity.*** Sweetly the poet complains allegorically that there is no hope of fulfillment of his love-dream.[4] Probably the first appearance in English of the seven-line stanza riming *ababbcc* —later designated as the *rime royal* (p. 88.)

## PERIOD OF ITALIAN INFLUENCE[5]: 1372—1385

### A. Prose

***Boece*** (1373—1385). Prose translation of Boethius's *De Consolatione Philosophiae,* earlier Englished by Alfred (p. 18). Each "metrum," as well as each "prosa," is translated into a structurally diffuse, involved, and Latinized prose. Influenced Chaucer's philosophy[6]; *e. g.,* the nature

---

1 Kittredge, G. L., *Chaucer and His Poetry* (1915), p. 54; Robinson, F. N., *The Complete Works of Geoffrey Chaucer* (1933), p. 315. The point is disputed by Rosenthal, C. L., "A Possible Source of Chaucer's *Booke of the Duchesse—Li Regret de Guillaume* by Jehan de la Mote," *Modern Language Notes,* XLVIII (1933), pp. 511-514.

2 Schofield, W. H., *Chivalry in English Literature* (1912), p. 18.

3 Chesterton, G. K., *Chaucer* (1932), p. 199.

4 Cowling, G. H., *Chaucer* (1927), p. 104 *f.*

5 Praz, Mario, "Chaucer and the Great Italian Writers of the Trecento," *The Monthly Criterion,* VI (1927), pp. 18-39, 131-157.

6 Jefferson, B. L., *Chaucer and the Consolation of Philosophy of Boethius* (1917).

of capricious Fortune (Bk. II) is revealed in *The House of Fame* (Bk. III), while the discussion of predestination (Bk. V) is embodied so permeatingly in *Troilus and Criseyde* that W. C. Curry considers the latter work based fundamentally on the theory of predeterminism.

### B. Major Poems

***The House of Fame*†* (1379—1384). Love-vision[1] probably symbolizes the approaching union of Richard II and Anne of Bohemia. Another reading is that Chaucer, suspecting John of Gaunt of having had illicit relations with Philippa (Chaucer's wife), makes a covert attack upon Lancaster for appearing in public (1378) with his mistress, Catherine Swynford.[2] Cast in the structural form of a French allegorical vision and in the meter of the octosyllabic couplet. 2,158 lines. Influenced by Dante's *Divine Comedy,* Nicole de Margival's *La Panthere d'Amours,* Froissart's *Paradys d'Amours,* and particularly by the *Jugement du Roy de Behainge.* Despite its defects (*e. g.,* a lack of proportion, and an abruptness of ending[3]), note, *inter alia,* the bland conversational gifts of the eagle, and the dramatic description of the commotion in the House of Rumor. (Examples of style: Digressions, *ll.* 2,059 *ff.;* bookishness, *ll.* 972—990; fancy, *ll.* 762—822; irony, *ll.* 2,059 *ff.;* humor, *ll.* 621, 1,349, 1,414; imaginative thought, *ll.* 1,148—1,164; revelatory attitude of Chaucer toward his own art, *ll.* 614 *ff.*)

***Troilus and Criseyde*†* (1372—1384). Chaucer's best example of sustained narrative frequently recognized as the first great poem in English. Protracted conversations, languid soliloquies, deficient action; yet in occasional superb stretches he never excelled himself in his mastery of the rime-royal stanza, in his characteristic naturalness, dialogue, ready humor, understanding of incident and situation, and sympathetic penetration into the emotions (see especially Bks. II and III). Throughout, Chaucer is guided by the system of Courtly Love and of Medievalization.[4] While Chaucer's incidental borrowings come from Ovid, Statius, Boethius, Dante, and Petrarch, his main immediate source is Boccaccio's *Il Filostrato,* which had considerably advanced the potential versions of Dictys Cretensis, Dares Phrygius, Benoît de Sainte-More, and Guido delle Colonne (pp. 34, 36) by impregnating the story

---

1 Sypherd, W. O., "Studies in Chaucer's *Hous of Fame*" (1907, for the Issue of 1904).

2 Riedel, F. C., "The Meaning of Chaucer's House of Fame," *The Journal of English and Germanic Philology,* XXVII (1928), pp. 441-469.

3 Manly, J. M., "What Is Chaucer's *Hous of Fame?*" *Anniversary Papers by Colleagues and Pupils of George Lyman Kittredge* (Ginn and Company, 1913), p. 76 *f.* (pp. 73-81).

4 Dodd, W. G., *Courtly Love in Chaucer and Gower* (1913) pp. 129-208; Lewis, C. S., "What Chaucer Really Did to *Il Filostrato,*" *Essays and Studies by Members of The English Association,* XVII (1932), pp. 56-75.

† * Explanation of symbols immediately precedes page one.

with intense feeling, by changing the name of Briseida to Griseida, or Criseida, and by creating the figure of Pandarus.[1]

*Characterization in Boccaccio and in Chaucer*

1. In Boccaccio, the emotions of Criseyde are consistently simple and sensual; in Chaucer, debatingly complex and less sensual. (In Shakespeare's retelling, p. 201, Cressida is the deliberate wanton. Also, see Henryson's sympathetic continuation, p. 88.)

2. In Boccaccio, Pandarus is a young dissolute gallant, cousin to Criseyde and companion to Troilus; in Chaucer, Pandarus is an old uncle, the wise, loquacious, racy, morally-blunt commentator on life. "He is the dominating personage of Chaucer's poem . . . ." (Root)

3. In Boccaccio, emphasis is placed upon passion; in Chaucer, upon character. Chaucer reveals a greater charity toward the character of Criseyde; he ennobles and sentimentalizes the character of Troilus. Some point out that the Englishman has made Criseyde the central figure; but she is the "artistic center" of the story while Troilus is its nucleating figure.

***The Parliament of Fowls*†*** (1377—1382). Probably honors the betrothal of Richard II to Anne of Bohemia, while the other two princelings are Frederick of Meissen and Charles VI of France. A second interpretation identifies the formel eagle with Marie, daughter of Charles V of France, while the three eagles are Richard, the Margrave of Meissen, and William of Bavaria; while a third traces the allegory to Philippa of Lancaster, oldest daughter of John of Gaunt, wooed by Richard II, John of Blois, and William of Hainault.[2]

Besides the personal, there may be a social allegory. Classification of the birds into groups may represent the different castes: the birds of prey, or the nobility; the worm-fowl, or the bourgeoisie; the seed-fowl, either the clergy or the agricultural class; and the water-fowl, or the mercantile class. Speeches of the lower classes then interpretable as voicing the social discontent culminating in the Peasants' Revolt (1381).[3]

---

1 Young, Karl, *The Origin and Development of the Story of Troilus and Criseyde* (1908, for the Issue of 1904); Root, R. K., *The Book of Troilus and Criseyde* (1926), pp. XX-XLVII; De Sèlincourt, E., *Oxford Lectures on Poetry* (1934), pp. 50-52 (Chap. III, pp. 50-77).

2 Braddy, Haldeen, "*The Parlement of Foules*: A New Proposal," *Publications of the Modern Language Association of America,* XLVI (1931), pp. 1007-1019.

3 Patrick, David, "The Satire in Chaucer's *Parliament of Birds,*" *Philological Quarterly,* IX (1930), pp. 61-65.

† * Explanation of symbols immediately precedes page one.

The promise of the very first half dozen lines of pure poetry, beginning with the quotable

"The lyf so short, the craft so long to lerne,
Th'assay so hard, so sharp the conqueryng,"

is fulfilled throughout the 699 lines in rime royal. Overbalancing the medieval conventionalities—*e. g.*, the reading of a book (*ll.* 17—84), the oncoming sleep and the resulting dream (*ll.* 95 *ff.*), the supernatural guide (*ll.* 96 *ff.*), the abstractions (*ll.* 211—228), the classical digressions (*ll.* 113—119), the list of trees (*ll.* 176—182) and of lovers (*ll.* 283—292)—are a freshness and originality enhanced by apt proverbial expressions[1] (*ll.* 140, 299, 574, 595), lively dialogue (*ll.* 532 *ff.*), melodious verse (the roundel, *ll.* 680—692), realistic humor (*ll.* 610—616), and rich imagery (*ll.* 148—150).

***The Legend of Good Women.*** (*c.* 1384—*c.* 1386). Of some twenty contemplated lives of faithful woman-followers of the God of Love, he wrote nine (the last unfinished): Cleopatra (*source,* Boccaccio), Thisbe (*source,* Ovid), Dido (*source,* Virgil), Hypsipyle and Medea (*sources,* Ovid, Guido delle Colonne), Lucretia (*source,* Ovid), Ariadne (*sources,* Ovid, Plutarch, Boccaccio), Philomela (*source,* Ovid), Phyllis (*source,* Ovid), Hypermnestra (*source,* Ovid). Dream-poem of 2,723 lines is probably the first to introduce into English the ten-syllable riming couplet, later called "riding rime" or "heroic couplet."

The *Prologue* (extant in two forms) is more picturesque, more full of a fresh love of springtide, and more felicitous in expressing poetic feeling than the legends themselves. Significance of the possibly allegorical compliment to Queen Anne in the form of the panegyrized daisy (showing participation in the symbolic cult of the Marguerite or daisy), or the celebration of the Queen in the second guise of Alceste (the God of Love might then be identical with King Richard), yields to the primary importance of the *Prologue's* self-portraiture: thus, Chaucer's library contained sixty books; furthermore, besides an enumeration of his known and extant works, the *Prologue* mentions a *Life of Saint Cecilia,* apparently preserved in *The Second Nun's Tale; The Love of Palamon and Arcite in Thebes,* apparently an earlier and possibly an identical version of *The Knight's Tale; Origen Upon the Magdalene,* and the *Wretched Engendering of Mankind,*[2] two lost translations; and many missing "balades, roundels, virelayes." While the legends are drawn largely from Ovid, the *Prologue* has its sources mainly in Eustache Deschamps (*c.* 1340—*c.* 1406) and Jean Froissart (*c.* 1337—*c.* 1410). In connection with Chaucer's favorite sentence, "But pite renneth soone in gentil herte," see its recurrence in ***The Knight's Tale***

1 Whiting, B. J., *Chaucer's Use of Proverbs* (1934).
2 Brown, Carleton, "Chaucer's *Wretched Engendring*," ***Publications of the Modern Language Association of America,*** L (1935), pp. 997-1011.

(*l.* 1,761), *The Man of Law's Tale* (*l.* 660), *The Merchant's Tale* (*l.* 1,986), *The Squire's Tale* (*l.* 479).

As for the legends proper, which are in a way introductory to *The Canterbury Tales,* they are dispatched in a monotonously thematic and perfunctory manner. However, that of Cleopatra is concise; of Thisbe, fresh and appealing; of Dido, simple and charming. Notable purple passage occurs in the legend of Ariadne (*ll.* 2,185—2,196).

### C. Minor Poems

***The Complaint of Mars*** (1373—1379). Treats delicately of love. Probably based upon Ovid's *Metamorphoses* (IV, *ll.* 170—189). Variously interpreted as treating (1) of a conjunction of Mars and Venus; or (2) of some court *liaison—e. g.,* an intrigue between Lady Isabel of York (Venus) and John Holland, Earl of Huntingdon (Mars); or of the seduction by John Holland of John of Gaunt's daughter Elizabeth. In both Chaucer's seven-line stanza (*ll.* 1—154), and the nine-line stanza riming *aabaabbcc* (*ll.* 155—298).

***Chaucer's Words unto Adam, His own Scriveyn*** (*post* 1380). Addresses his careless copyist or scribe in amiable yet somewhat pointed raillery. *Troilus* stanza.

***Rosemounde*** (*post* 1380). Courtly ballade to an unknown lady. Gracefully, humorously mock-sentimental. Rime-scheme, *ababbcbc.*

***Womanly Noblesse,*** or ***The Ballad that Chaucer Made*** (*post* 1380). Conventionally-treated sentiments. Involved rime scheme.

***Anelida and Arcite*** (1383—1384).* Chaucer's most complicated metrical work, an arrangement of various stanzas, with strophe and answering antistrophe. May be an allegorical commentary on some court episode.[1] Style generally imitative. Influenced by Ovid's *Heroides.*[2]

## PERIOD OF ENGLISH INFLUENCE: 1385—1400

### A. Prose

***A Treatise on the Astrolabe*** (1391). Unfinished prose exposition addressed to the ten-year-old "Lyte Lowys my sone," and called by Chaucer *Bread and Milk for Children.* Is a key to technical lines elsewhere in Chaucer. While adapted primarily from the eighth-century Arabian Messahala's *Compositio et Operatio Astrolabii,* the introduction is Chaucer's. R. T. Gunther (who dates the work as of 1387) de-

1 Tupper, Frederick, "Chaucer's Tale of Ireland," *Publications of the Modern Language Association of America,* XXXVI (1921), pp. 186-222.

2 Shannon, E. F., "The Source of Chaucer's *Anelida and Arcite,*" *Publications of the Modern Language Association of America,* XXVII (1912), pp. 461-485.

† * Explanation of symbols immediately precedes page one.

clares Chaucer to be "our greatest astronomer-poet," one who has given us the earliest extant work in English "upon an elaborate scientific instrument."[1]

*Tale of Melibee.* See CHART, *The Canterbury Tales,* "Second Day" (p. 73).

*The Parson's Tale.* See CHART, *The Canterbury Tales,* "Fourth Day" (p. 76).

**B. Major Poem**

*The Canterbury Tales*† (1387—1400)

1. LITERARY ORIGIN AND PARALLELS.[2] Literary form of enclosing a number of tales within one narrative is Oriental in origin; *e. g., The Seven Wise Masters, The Thousand and One Nights, Panchatantra, Fables of Bidpay.* Other familiar parallels are: Ovid's *Metamorphoses,* Peter Alphonsus's *The Disciplina Clericalis,* Boccaccio's *Decameron* and *Ameto,* Giovanni Sercambi's *Novelle,*[3] Gower's *Confessio Amantis* (p. 54).

2. PLAN. A company of some thirty persons (twenty-nine, according to the *Prologue, l.* 24; thirty, by actual count[4]), while lying at the Tabard Inn in Southwark on the eve of a three-to-four day pilgrimage to the shrine of Thomas à Becket at Canterbury, accept the offer of Henry Bailly to show them the way. They also approve the Host's suggestion that, to while away the journey, each pilgrim shall tell two tales on the sixty-mile ride to Canterbury and two on the way back (A—*ll.* 790 *ff.*); and the best *raconteur* is to be given a supper by the rest on the return to the Tabard. Only twenty-four of the contemplated 120 tales are told by twenty-three pilgrims—or the contemplated 124 tales, if in the party is included the Canon's Yeoman, who later overtakes the assemblage.

3. ADVANTAGES OF THE PLAN. (a) *A Real Fellowship.* Various representative classes of society, cemented by a common religious purpose and meeting on a certain equality, are brought together. Despite the clearly marked distinctions of rank, no one rank shows a slavish submission to another. While giving little notice to the humbler classes of society, yet in Chaucer's representative parliament of social and industrial England is observable the great English spirit—a natural respect of man for his fellow. (Some of the pilgrims may be real

1 Gunther, R. T., *Chaucer and Messahala on the Astrolabe* (1929), p. v.

2 Praz, Mario, "Chaucer and the Great Italian Writers of the Trecento," *The Monthly Criterion,* VI (1927), pp. 143-150 (pp. 131-157).

3 See particularly Young, Karl, "The Plan of the Canterbury Tales," *Anniversary Papers by Colleagues and Pupils of George Lyman Kittredge* (Ginn and Company, 1913), pp. 405-417.

4 Brown, Carleton, "The Squire and the Number of the Canterbury Pilgrims," *Modern Language Notes,* XLIX (1934), p. 218 *f.*, p. 222 (pp. 216-222).

† * Explanation of symbols immediately precedes page one.

persons; *e. g.*, the Shipman may be identical with Peter Risshenden, master of the vessel *Magdaleyne* in 1391, and the Sergeant of the Law, with Thomas Pynchbek.[1]). (b) *Flexibility.* Monotony is less likely to occur. The different characters introduced throw into relief every type of tale, set off by each narrator's personality; while the whole series is given a dramatic unity by the pervading personality of the Host, a master of ceremonies who senses every situation instantly.

4. Probable Order of the Tales. The *Tales* have come down in a series of nine (or ten) detached groups, usually lettered A, B1 (and B2), C, D, E, F, G, H, I. In other words, the arrangement of the order of the tales, in most editions, is not by Chaucer, but by those editing the fragments. The commonly-accepted tabulation of the tales is given in the chart (pp. 72—76).

## THE "PROLOGUE"

The sketches of the various pilgrims contained in the *Prologue* are regarded as the most graphic picture extant of typical figures of fourteenth-century England, a series of almost perfect character sketches ranging from the high-born Knight to the lowly Plowman. So well drawn, however, is this procession that the pilgrims are individuals as well as types. Revealed in the *Prologue* are Chaucer's selective descriptive power, vivid portrayal of personality, subtle shafts of humor and satire—all his general qualities save that of story-telling (see *General Characteristics of Chaucer,* p. 78). To quote J. L. Lowes:

"Persons of every sort and condition represented in the Prologue had been intimately known to Chaucer through years crowded with experience and observation. What the portraits actually do, all conjecture aside, is to strike the delicate balance between the *character,* in the technical, Theophrastian sense of the word, and the *individual*—a balance which preserves at once the typical qualities of the one and the human idiosyncrasies of the other.

" . . . . The Prologue gives us the *tellers*—statically, in their potentialities. But as the cavalcade moves on, the static becomes dynamic . . . . And in the links between the tales Chaucer has made the most original of all his contributions. The tales are not isolated entities. They stand in intimate relation to all that Chaucer has revealed about the tellers, and also to the give and take of dialogue which in the linking narrative leads up to them and follows them. The *Canterbury Tales,* even though their plan remains a splendid torso only, are an organic whole, and that whole is essentially dramatic. 'Dialogue and action, gesture, costume and scenery, as in real life'—all are there. Long before Balzac, Chaucer conceived and exhibited the Human Comedy."[2]

---

1 Manly, J. M., *Some New Light on Chaucer* (1926), pp. 169-181, 131-157.

2 Lowes, J. L., *Geoffrey Chaucer and the Development of His Genius* (1934), pp. 201-204.

## FIRST DAY, APRIL 17—LONDON TO DARTFORD

| TALE TOLD BY | TYPE AND SOURCE | STYLE AND COMMENT |
|---|---|---|
| **Knight.*** Ideal figure, noble in port and manners, devoted to loyalty and honor, generosity, courtesy, and humility. | Chivalric romance (of Palamon and Arcite). Shortened adaptation of Boccaccio's **Le Teseide.** Influenced by Statius's **Thebaid,** and Boethius. | Longest tale and traditionally considered his best. Chief charms lie in its highly-wrought beauty of tapestry, and thoroughly-informed romanticism of tone. Superior to original in burning movement, vivid situation, individualizing characterization, effective narrative. Possibly over-abundant in detail. Many anachronisms (e. g., two ancient Theban gentlemen pictured in a medieval tournament). |
| **Miller.*** Loud talker, noted wrestler, teller of ribald stories. Burly of figure, wart on nose, red of beard. | Fabliau (of the carpenter John, his wife Alison, and her lover Nicholas). Source unknown; but the separate jests have their parallels. | Directed at the Reeve, who had been a carpenter. Direct, dramatic; inventive comic power. Masterly unity of setting and action. But naughty. See the fabliau, (p. 32). |
| **Reeve.*** Slender, choleric, hair cut short in front. No man could catch him in arrears. As deceitful as the Miller. | Fabliau (of how two Cambridge students got the better of the cheating Miller of Trompington). Source unknown. Numerous analogues; e. g., Boccaccio's **Decameron** (IX. 6) and Jean de Bove's **De Gombert et des Deux Clers.**[1] | Retaliates at the expense of the Miller. Licentious, clever. Excellent characterization, skilful narrative. Reveals the essential characteristics of the fabliau (p. 32). Often considered even more salacious than **The Miller's Tale.** |
| **Cook.*** Expert. Knew all the flavoring powders, and good ale. | Unfinished; but promises to be a fabliau. Source unknown. | Tale followed in some manuscripts by what is probably the spurious **Tale of Gamelyn,*** probably meant for **The Yeoman's Tale.** |

## SECOND DAY, APRIL 18—DARTFORD TO ROCHESTER

| TALE TOLD BY | TYPE AND SOURCE | STYLE AND COMMENT |
|---|---|---|
| **Man of Law.*** Knew by heart all the cases and decisions. Could convey the property as though it were held in absolute possession. | Virtue story (of Constance). Immediate source of this wide-spread folk-tale of the Wife who symbolizes Resignation or Fortitude is Nicholas Trivet's often so-called **Anglo-Norman Chronicle** (c. 1335). See p. 61. | Moralizing reflections, legendary character.[2] Constance almost personifies "Christianity itself." Improbable narrative often considered inappropriate to the character and vocation of the teller. |

1 See also Dempster, Germaine, "On the Source of the *Reve's Tale,*" *The Journal of English and Germanic Philology,* XXIX (1930), pp. 473-488.

2 Schlauch, Margaret, *Chaucer's Constance and Accused Queens* (1927).

† * Explanation of symbols immediately precedes page one.

| TALE TOLD BY | TYPE AND SOURCE | STYLE AND COMMENT |
|---|---|---|
| **Shipman.***<br><br>Skilful mariner. Rough, jovial, sunburned. Quite conscienceless: had stolen many a draught while the supercargo was asleep. | Fabliau (of a merchant, his wife, and the monk John).<br><br>Source unknown. Probably Chaucer obtained the matter from some French fabliau. Similar stories elsewhere; e. g., in Boccaccio's Decameron (VIII, 1).[1] | Happily conceived, carefully executed. More delicate, yet more immoral, than the tales of the Miller and the Reeve. Feminine phraseology in the use of pronouns seemingly indicates that the tale was originally written for a woman-pilgrim, probably the **Wife of Bath.**[2] |
| **Prioress.***[3]<br><br>Of noble birth. Coy, amiable, tender of heart. Fond of pretty clothes. Had little refinements and affectations. | Legend ("miracle of the Virgin"); or exemplum. Concerns the "litel clergeon."<br><br>Source indefinite. Many versions exist[4]; **e. g., Hugh of Lincoln.** | Touchingly told with exquisite taste. Simplicity of plot, faultlessness of technique. Chaucer's poetry is never loftier. See also the exemplum (p. 32). |
| **Chaucer.** | | |
| a) **Rime of Sir Thopas.*** | a) Unfinished verse satire (of the metrical romance).<br><br>No one source.[5] | a) Unerring burlesque of the absurdities of the romances (p. 39), and possibly of Flemish knight-errantry. Diffuse. |
| b) **Tale of Melibee.***<br><br>Chaucer is described by the Host as riding ever with his stare upon the ground, exchanging pleasantries with no one. Has a figure of generous proportions. | b) Prose romance (of the world, the flesh, and the devil).<br><br>Immediate source is Jean de Meun's or Renaud de Louens's **Livre de Melibè et de Dame Prudence,** in turn abridged from Albertano da Brescia's **Liber Consolationis et Concilii.** | b) Possibly its "bathos, forced allegory, spiritless and interminable moralizing," will alienate the modern reader. Ker also states that it "is perhaps the worst example that could be found of all the intellectual and literary vices of the Middle Ages."[6] Possibly the tale was intended for the Man of Law.[7] (One of the two prose tales in the collection; see **The Parson's Tale.**) |
| **Monk.***<br><br>Bald, fond of riding and hunting, jovial. Full fat, in good physical condition, loving a fat swan "best of any roost." | Series of exempla (of men "yfallen out of high degree").<br><br>Main sources are Boccaccio's **De Casibus Virorum et Feminarum Illustrium,** and the **Roman de la Rose.** Incidental sources are the Scriptures, Greek, Roman, and Spanish history or mythology. | Uninteresting, tedious. For the characteristics of the exemplum, see p. 32. Eight-line stanzas riming ababbcbc (hence called the "Monk's Tale Stanza": by adding a final c alexandrine the **Spenserian Stanza** is formed. See p. 136). |

1 Spargo, J. W., "Chaucer's Shipman's Tale: The Lover's Gift Regained," *The Folklore Fellows, FF Communications,* XXXII, No. 91 (1930).

2 Tupper, Frederick, "The Bearings of the Shipman's Prologue," *The Journal of English and Germanic Philology,* XXXIII (1934), pp. 356-358 (pp. 352-371).

3 Madeleva, M. (*Sister*), *Chaucer's Nuns and Other Essays* (1925), pp. 3-42.

4 Brown, Carleton, "A Study of the Miracle of Our Lady," *Chaucer Society, Second Series,* No. 45 (1910, for the Issue of 1906). See Chap. VI, pp. 107-136.

5 Magoun, F. P., Jr., "The Source of Chaucer's *Rime of Sir Thopas,*" *Publications of the Modern Language Association of America,* XLII (1927), pp. 833-844.

6 Ker, W. P., in *English Prose,* edited by Craik, Henry (1893), Vol. I, p. 40 (pp. 39-43).

7 Tupper, Frederick, "The Bearings of the Shipman's Prologue," *The Journal of English and Germanic Philology.* XXXIII (1934), pp. 353-356 (pp. 352-371).

† * Explanation of symbols immediately precedes page one.

| TALE TOLD BY | TYPE AND SOURCE | STYLE AND COMMENT |
|---|---|---|
| **Nun's Priest.*** He is not described in the **Prologue.** It has been inferred that he might well be of powerful physique, sanguine complexion, and keen eyes. | Beast fable (of Dan Russell the Fox and Master Chaunticleer the Cock); or exemplum; or mock-heroic poem. Ultimate source is the French **Roman de Renart** (see p. 30), and the German **Reinecke Fuchs.** | First important mock-heroic in English. Mature in its vivacious dialogue, genial and quizzical humor, well-motivated action, ironical pathos, acute observation. Learned digressions heighten effect. Characterization more important than slight plot. |

## THIRD DAY, APRIL 19—ROCHESTER TO OSPRINGE

| | | |
|---|---|---|
| **Physician.*1** Well-dressed; but moderate in expenditure. Knew the hours astrologically propitious for giving medicine. "For gold in phisik is a cordial. Therefore he loved gold in special." | Tragic story (of Appius and Virginia); or **exemplum.** Source is an old Roman tale; **e. g.,** found in Livy's **History** (Bk. III), and in the **Roman de la Rose** (*11,* 5,589 **ff.**). | Not even "a long digression on the character and education of young girls" (F. N. Robinson) can halt the progress of this simple tale. Sometimes considered not particularly befitting the character of the Doctor. **General Characteristics of Chaucer, p. 78.** |
| **Pardoner. *** Flaxen-haired, beardless face, glaring eyes. Treble-voiced seller of Papal indulgence. Kittredge once called the Pardoner the one lost soul among the pilgrims. (See also **prologue, D-*1*,** 162 **ff.**). | **Exemplum,** or medieval illustrative sermon (of Death and the Three Revellers). Immediate source of Eastern tale unknown. Oldest version in the Hindoo collection called **Vedabbha Jàtaka;** a recent analogue in Kipling's **Second Jungle Book** ("The King's Ankus"). | Has been called the best short narrative poem in the language. Matchless for its dialogue, characterization, atmosphere, and swift crescendo. Deeply poetic, approaching in its spirit the fatalism and terror of Greek tragedy. Heroic couplet. See **Characteristics of Chaucer, p. 78.** |
| **Wife of Bath.*** Prosperous clothmaker. Had married five husbands. Brawny, gat-toothed, red of face, partly deaf. Coarse-spoken but good-natured. | Arthurian fairy tale inculcating a lay sermon (of "What thyng is it that wommen most desiren?"). Source unknown. Many parallels of the version of the Loathly Lady exist.[2] | Of greater importance than the tale is its Prologue, brilliant in its exposition. Satire (p. 79), verve, raciness, penetrating humor. Utter frankness about marriage and virginity. Paradoxically the tale itself is told gracefully, not coarsely. |
| **Friar.*** Expert in gossip and flattery. Preferred the worldly pleasure of women and taverns. Hypocritical. | Fabliau (of a Summoner carried off by the Devil). Immediate source is possibly the Latin collection **Promptuarian Exemplorum.** | Attempts to discredit the Summoner. Skilful characterization, comic irony. For pungent dialogue see that between the two travellers. **Rimed couplets.** |

1 Curry, W. C., *Chaucer and the Medieval Sciences* (1926), pp. 3-36; Nicholls, A. G., "Medicine in Chaucer's Day," *The Dalhousie Review,* XII (1932), pp. 218-230.

2 Maynadier, G. H., *The Wife of Bath's Tale* (1901).

† * **Explanation of symbols immediately precedes page one.**

| TALE TOLD BY | TYPE AND SOURCE | STYLE AND COMMENT |
|---|---|---|
| **Summoner.*** Cherubed and pimpled face. Close-set eyes. Repulsive conduct. Fleeced whomever he could. | Fabliau (of the Friar and the invalid Thomas); or popular anecdote. Exact origin unknown. Possibly suggested by the **Tale of the Priest's Bladder**, by Jakes de Basiu. | Purposes to expose the Friar. Direct discourse and psychological observation heighten the characterization and vitalize the realistic talk of the coarse farce. J. L. Lowes has declared the picture of the Friar to be Chaucer's greatest portrait within a tale. According to G. H. Cowling, the most weakly constructed of all his tales. |
| X **Clerk.*** Lean of figure, sober of bearing. Preferred books to rich robes. A philosopher, "Yet hadde he but litel gold in cofre." "And gladly wolde he lerne and gladly teche." | Virtue story (of Patient Griselda and the Marquis of Saluces), symbolical of Patience and Obedience. Source is Petrarch's **De Obedientia ac Fide Uxoria Mythologia**, rendered into Latin from Boccaccio's **Decameron** (X, 10). | Lack of "energetic compression," to quote a critic, is more than compensated by the narrative treating sympathetically and with beauty the trials and tribulations of the heroine. Her character, however, is ridiculous in the eyes of the modern woman. |
| **Merchant.*** Forked beard. Flemish beaver hat. Rich, powerful. Always talking about increasing his profits, keeping the sea guarded at all costs. | Fabliau (of Baron January, his wife May, and her lover Damyan). Source unknown; but the basic **Märchen** (folk tale or fairy story) frequently goes by the name of the "Pear-Tree Episode." | Dramatic satire on married life, delightful in its telling but almost bitter in its attitude. January's cuckoldom is poetically just, "a sort of crude morality." |

## FOURTH DAY, APRIL 20—OSPRINGE TO CANTERBURY

| TALE TOLD BY | TYPE AND SOURCE | STYLE AND COMMENT |
|---|---|---|
| **Squire.*** Aspirant to knighthood. Medieval dandy: curled locks; could sing and play the flute. | Unfinished typical romance (of King Cambuscan and the wondrous gifts). Source unknown. Close analogue in the romance of **Cléomadès** by Adenès le Roi. | Reveals many characteristics of the romance (p. 39). Heroic couplet. Only other unfinished tales are **The Cook's Tale** and Chaucer's **Rime of Sir Thopas**. |
| **Franklin.***[1] White-bearded as is the daisy, sanguine-complexioned. Disciple of Epicurus. Possibly identical with a Sir John Bussy. | **Lai**, or short romantic tale (of Arveragus, his wife Dorigen, and Squire Aurelius). Source, according to Chaucer, is a lost Breton lay; but source seems to be Boccaccio's **Decameron** and **Filocolo.** | The spirit of courtly love and the supernatural features breathe romance into this idealized character-story. Felicitously told, beautifully descriptive, outstandingly dramatic.[2] For the **lai**, see p. 46. |

1 Gerould, G. H., "The Social Status of Chaucer's Franklin," *Publications of the Modern Language Association of America,* XLI (1926), pp. 262-279.

2 Hart, W. M., "The Franklin's Tale," *Haverford Essays* (Haverford, Pa., 1909), pp. 185-207 (pp. 185-234).

† * Explanation of symbols immediately precedes page one.

| TALE TOLD BY | TYPE AND SOURCE | STYLE AND COMMENT |
|---|---|---|
| **Second Nun.*** Probably to be identified with "Another Nonne," "chapeleyne" to the Prioress (A—*l.* 163 *f.*). | Saint's legend (of St. Cecilia). Source is the **Legenda Aurea** ("Golden Legend") of Jacopo da Varagine. | Its genuine dignity and piety prompt many to stamp Chaucer as sympathetically and basically devotional. Seven-line stanza. |
| **Canon's Yeoman.*** The Canon and his Yeoman overtake the pilgrims at Boghton under Blee. The Yeoman is garrulous. | Contemporaneous tale exploding the impostures of alchemy. Source unknown; but conjecturally the anecdote might be the result of a personal experience of Chaucer. | Straightforward, interesting. Maturity of style, command of rhythm. Effective is the description of the scene when the crucible is broken. Note the Yeoman's veering feelings toward his master. Heroic couplet. |
| **Manciple.*** As steward to a college or an inn of court he outwits all his learned masters. | Fable (of why the Crow is black). Source is Ovid's story of Apollo and Coronis (**Metamorphoses,** II, *11,* 531-632). | Digressions and exempla (see p. 32); yet short and simple. Sometimes considered a tale not appropriate to the Manciple. |
| **Parson.*** Ideal portrait of a poor but generous parish priest, rich in holy thought and work. Faithful, diligent. Wycliffite in the shepherding of his flock. Taught "Cristes lore," but "first he folwed it himselve." | Prose sermon (on Penitence, with emphasis upon the Seven Sins). Source unknown; but main parts derived from Frère Lorens's **Somme des Vices et des Vertus** and Raymond de Pennaforte's **Summa Casum Poenitentiae** (Bk. III). | Longest tale in the collection and also the most boring. Lifeless in style and swamped by wearying sermonizing. (Only other prose tale in the series is Chaucer's **Tale of Melibee**; see under "Second Day"). |

## CHAUCER'S RETRACTION

Immediately after the Parson's tale follows the *Retractation,* in which Chaucer repudiates certain of his works. The palinode is probably authentic.

---

† * Explanation of symbols immediately precedes page one.

## C. Minor Poems

*Five Ballades (1386—1398): Influenced by Boethius*

***The Former Age (Aetas Prima).*** Theme is the old idea of the earthly paradise of man's primeval state. Charming. Eight lines, *ababbcbc.*

***Fortune.*** Appeal for patronage from either the King or from John of Gaunt. Consists of three ballades (each has three stanzas, riming *ababbcbc*) and an envoy.

***Lak of Stedfastnesse.*** Evocative in its feeling of the probable state of that period (*c.* 1386—*c.* 1390) of England of which the ballade treats. Envoy addressed to King Richard. Meter same as that of *Truth.*

***Gentilesse (Moral Balade of Chaucer).*** Nobility, says Chaucer, depends on righteousness or character: it is not an appanage of birth, for no man can "Bequethe his heir his vertuous noblesse" (*l.* 17). Three seven-line stanzas.

***Truth (Balade de Bon Conseyl).*** Distinctively Chaucerian in spirit. Three stanzas and an envoy, all in the seven-line stanza. According to Rickert, might well have been addressed to Sir Philip (de) la Vache (1346—1408). Includes: "Flee fro the prees, and dwel with sothfastnesse" (*l.* 1: "Flee from the crowd, and dwell with truth"); "Hold the heye wey, and lat thy gost thee lede" (*l.* 20: "Hold the highway, and let your spirit lead you"); and the familiar refrain, "And trouthe thee shal delivere, it is no drede" (*ll.* 7, 14, 22, 28: "And truth shall make you free, doubt it not").

## D. Later Minor Poems

***The Complaint of Venus*** (1392—1393). A translation from three French poems by Otes de Granson (*d.* 1397). Possibly refers to Isabel of York (see *The Complaint of Mars,* p. 69). Three ballades, each riming *ababbcbc,* and an envoy, riming *aabaabbaab.*

***L'Envoy de Chaucer à Scogan*** (1393). Slyly humorous epistle seems to ask for the favor of either Henry Scogan (*c.* 1361—1407) or possibly his elder brother John (*d.* 1391). Six stanzas and an envoy, all in the seven-line stanza.

***L'Envoy de Chaucer à Bukton*** (1393—1396). Playfully indicates the disadvantages of (approaching) wedlock; *e. g.,* experience will teach that it were better to be taken prisoner in Friesland than later to fall into the trap of marriage (*ll.* 22—24). Refers either to Sir Robert Bukton, of Gooseweld in Suffolk (*d.* 1408) or to Sir Peter Bukton, of Holdernesse in Yorkshire (1350—1414). Three stanzas and an envoy of eight lines each, riming *ababbcbc.*

*The Complaint of Chaucer to His Empty Purse* (1399—1400). Frankly genial, comically begging. Was probably written with Richard II in mind; but the Envoy is addressed to Henry IV. Written either before or immediately after the latter's coronation on September 30, 1399, it had its desired effect: on October 3, 1399, the new Sovereign doubled Chaucer's former pension of twenty marks. Three seven-line stanzas; their envoy rimes *aabba.*

### E. Minor Poems of Doubtful Authorship

There are some half dozen poems ascribed more or less hesitatingly to Chaucer—*Against Women Inconstant, A Balade of Complaint, Balade of the Plough, Proverbs, Balade of the Reeve, Complaynt d'Amours, Merciles Beaute.* Of these the last-named is most characteristically Chaucerian, with its clever metrical style, jaunty substance, and animated spirit; its rime-scheme is *abbabababbabb.*

## GENERAL CHARACTERISTICS OF CHAUCER[1]

(See also pp. 55 and 57.)

Love of Nature. Never does his wholly objective attitude draw any sermons from Nature. He is "the poet of the lusty spring," says H. A. Beers; and also the poet through whose pages blows a "fresh vernal air." However, R. K. Root points out that "when we speak of Chaucer's love of nature, we must be careful not to confuse this with the love of nature which marks more modern poets. Nowhere in his works is there any suggestion that he cared for the wilder beauty of mountains and rocks and surging seas . . . . What Chaucer, and the men of the Middle Ages in general, loved in nature was the peaceful and the gentle, the beneficent to human life." Summarily, Chaucer's readiness of descriptive power, sensitiveness to external aspects, and sense of literary proportion build up vari-colored pictures.

Dramatic Method. Has a sureness of dramatic instinct that is genius. Cases in point are the *Prologues* to the individual tales told by the Miller, the Manciple, and the Wife of Bath; but above and throughout all the tales towers the sustained character of the Host. Note, too, the poet's sense of dramatic irony[2]; *e. g., The Miller's Tale* (A—*ll.* 3,679—3,680), *The Reeve's Tale* (A—*ll.* 4,122—4,126), *The Wife of Bath's Tale* (D—*l.* 1,085 *f.*), *The Friar's Tale* (D—*ll.* 1,636—1,638), *The Merchant's Tale* (E—*l.* 2,160), *The Pardoner's Tale* (C—*l.* 772).

Comic Art. (a) *Good Humor.* A hearty laugh rings through the tales—the only exception being in *The Prioress's Tale,* where, in the interest of dramatic self-restraint, Chaucer's "unexpected and unpredictable" good humor does not play "round the horizon like heat-

1 Spurgeon, C. F. E., "Five Hundred Years of Chaucer Criticism and Allusion (1357-1900)," *Chaucer Society, Second Series,* No. 56, Index Volume. See pp. 17-20.

2 Dempster, Germaine, "Dramatic Irony in Chaucer," *Stanford University Publications, Language and Literature,* IV, No. 3 (1932).

lightning," although there is an unwitting suggestion of it in possibly one line. A concentrated triumph occurs in the quotable *Prologue* (for example, *l.* 443 *f.*), where even the Prioress is described in a humorous vein (*e. g., ll.* 128—131). There is humor, too, in having himself, the great poet of all the other immortal tales, tell the two that are possibly the dullest in the collection. (b) *Satire.* A keen sense of the ridiculous keeps Chaucer from wounding people too deeply with the power of his pungent but smiling satire. To the criticism that his satire is directed against women (*e. g.,* in the Wife of Bath's confession in the Prologue to her story) can be opposed the tales told by the Man of Law and the Clerk. (c) *Coarseness.* Keen but genial, richly protean in their ready wit, gracefully superabundant in their humorous and satirical flashes, the *Tales* generally have a delicate and unaffected humor. However, sometimes indulging in the bold naturalness of his time, Chaucer gives us a broad jest, boisterous horse-play, or robust laughter, but, always, this directness of utterance is in thorough keeping with the salty character of the teller of the tale or with the gross character of the tale itself.[1]

Command of Pathos. His genuine pathos, consistently untouched by a maudlin sentimentality, is thoroughly contagious and manly. As T. H. Ward has put it, "'Routhe' indeed, pity for inevitable sorrow, is a note of Chaucer's mind which for ever distinguishes him from Boccaccio, and marks him out as the true forerunner of the poet of *Hamlet* and *Othello.*"

Liquid Smoothness of Verse. Critics have described the music of his verse as being melodious, varied, flexible, smooth, graceful, unerring, and even golden-tongued; (*e. g.,* the roundel or triolet that concludes *The Parliament of Fowls*—see p. 67). His is "an exquisite ear for music," says W. W. Skeat; and to read the tale and verse says Stopford Brooke, "is like listening in a meadow full of sunshine to a clear stream rippling over its bed of pebbles."

Imagery. Amazing is the brightness and variety of his imagery, whether he describes a woman (*e. g., The Miller's Tale,* Alison, A—*ll.* 3,223 *ff.*) or a man (*e. g., The Miller's Tale, Absolon* A—*ll.* 3,314 *ff.*) or an animal (*e. g., The Nun's Priest's Tale,* B—*ll.* 2,850 *ff.*) The delicacy of his sense for selecting characteristic and suggestive detail is reproduced in his remarkable talent for description; (*e. g.,* in the description of the chamber of Nicholas, with its *Almagest,* astrolabe, clothes-press, and gay psaltery (*The Miller's Tale,* A—*ll.* 3,208—3,217), and in the description of the friar who softly and immediately makes himself at home in the house of Thomas (*The Summoner's Tale,* D—*ll.* 1,775—1,777). For his skill in creating atmosphere and tone, see the

1 Stapleton, C. R., "Chaucer the Catholic," *The Catholic World,* CXXVII (1928), pp. 183-193; Stewart, G. R., Jr., "The Moral Chaucer," *Essays in Criticism* (University of California Press, 1929) pp. 91-109.

opening of *The Pardoner's Tale,* (*ll.* 661 *ff.*); for beauty and appropriateness of phrase, see *The Knight's Tale* (A—*ll.* 1,975—1,980); for superb mastery of dialogue, see the entire Prologue to *The Miller's Tale.* (For further discussion of merits and defects, see pp. 55, 57.)

CHIEF VERSE FORMS. (a) Possibly borrowing it from Guillaume de Machault, Chaucer introduced into English the seven-line (decasyllabic) stanza, riming *ababbcc,* and later called the *rime royal* (also called *Troilus verse, Cressid verse,* the *Chaucer stanza*). Examples: *The Parliament of Fowls, Troilus and Criseyde, The Clerk's Tale, The Prioress's Tale, The Man of Law's Tale, The Complaint unto Pity.* (b) Chaucer introduced the eight-line (decasyllabic) stanza, riming *ababbcbc.* Examples: *Chaucer's ABC, The Former Age, The Monk's Tale.* (The addition to this stanza of the final alexandrine riming *c* becomes the famous Spenserian stanza. See p. 136.) (c) By adapting probably Eustache Deschamps's ten-syllable line to English, Chaucer introduced the ten-syllable couplet (the five-beat line, in stanza or couplet, making it an iambic pentameter). Called also the *heroic couplet.* Examples: *The Legend of Good Women, The Knight's Tale,* and most of *The Canterbury Tales.* (d) Chaucer also (1) introduced *terza rima* in a section of *A Complaint to His Lady* (p. 65); (2) struck off a fine burlesque example of *rime couée* in the *Rime of Sir Thopas;* and (3) popularized French forms, such as the *roundel* (*Merciles Beaute,* p. 78; conclusion of *The Parliament of Fowls,* p. 67), and the ballade (*Rosemounde,* p. 69; *Truth,* p. 77).

## CHAUCER THROUGH THE AGES

From his own age to this Chaucer has been a moving force. His contemporaries (Gower, Lydgate, Hoccleve) acknowledged his genius, which during the fifteenth and sixteenth centuries helped discipline the work of the so-called Scottish Chaucerians (p. 88). Toward the latter part of the sixteenth century, however, Chaucer began to be regarded as a poet whose language was intricate and obsolete, and whose versification and style were imperfect and barbarous. It was not until Dryden modernized several of Chaucer's poems in *Fables* (1700) that interest in the poet of *The Canterbury Tales* rose from the low ebb of its tide in the seventeenth century. But even Dryden, who recognized the greatness of Chaucer, declared in his preface to the *Fables* that the verse of Chaucer is not harmonious; and it was not until Thomas Tyrwhitt's edition of *The Canterbury Tales* in 1775 that the belief in Chaucer's irregularity of meter was shattered, for scholarly study pointed out the importance of ordinarily pronouncing the numerous final *-e's* in Chaucer. Since Tyrwhitt's prefatory essay the delightful importance of Chaucer has again made itself felt. Chaucer certainly does not lack eminent eulogists. J. R. Lowell has described the poet as being the most natural of the great English poets, who "keeps his feeling free and unspoiled by his knowledge of books and affairs."

This artlessness is the very essence of Chaucer's character; and has been described by J. C. Robertson as placing "the kind heart above the coronet and faithfulness over the claims of high descent. Nobility of soul had ever his warmest admiration, without regard to the rank of life in which it was revealed." To T. H. Ward, Chaucer "is the first great painter of character, because he is the first great observer of it among European writers."

The practical yet poetic personality of the man seems to shine through all his writing. His varied public life brought him into unforced and healthful contact with human nature and the world, contributing to the spirit of his writing an illuminating realism, a penetrating psychology, a catholic sympathy, and an objective charity unparalleled by any but the greatest writers. It is true that he often is garrulous and dawdling; that he more frequently re-echoes than transcends the philosophy of Boethius, Dante, and others; that he, medieval-like, parades his learning; that he is not a truly lyrical poet; true that, being the poet of the eye and not of the spirit, he is neither strong in genuine passion, nor profound in thought, nor sustained in imagination and idealism: all epitomized by Matthew Arnold's charge that Chaucer was incapable of "high seriousness," an accusation frequently opposed by other Chaucerians. But Chaucer is invariably sincere, conversationally direct, and abundantly dramatic. A complete mastery of the essential elements of the short-story is his—flow of diction and freedom from artifice, faultless technical details and lightness of touch, and, finally, a graphic style, which propels the story in a rapid and effective manner.

Chapter VI

# THE FIFTEENTH CENTURY

## POLITICAL AND SOCIAL BACKGROUND

### Europe of the Fifteenth Century

a) ***A Period of General Unrest.*** (1) James I (p. 88), set at liberty by the English, became King of Scotland (1426); but was assassinated (1437). (2) Fall of Constantinople registered the end of the Byzantine or Eastern Empire and the final cessation of the disturbing forces of the ancient civilization (1453). (3) Fall of Granada, counterbalancing somewhat the loss of Constantinople a half century earlier, marked the end of Moslem sway in Spain (1492). (4) Franco-Italian wars, waged for twenty-five years between France and Spain, broke out (1494).

b) ***The Reformation.*** (1) The prestige of the Papal name, and the authority of the Church in general, received a crushing blow through the struggle of three Popes for the tiara (1409). (2) John Huss, a Bohemian Wycliffite, was condemned for heresy and burned (1415). (3) In Spain, upon receipt of a bull from Sixtus IV of Rome, the Inquisition was reorganized (1478). See p. 110 *ff*.

c) ***The Revival of Classical Learning.*** (1) Invention of printing (1438—1450). (2) Exodus of Greek scholars from Constantinople (1452). (3) Chief Italian humanists include Francesco Petrarch (1304—1374), Giovanni Boccaccio (*c.* 1313—1375), Poggio Bracciolini (1380—1459), Aeneas Sylvius (1405—1464; Pius II, 1458—1464), Lorenzo de' Medici (1449—1492). See p. 110 *ff*.

### England of the Fifteenth Century

a) *Renewal of the Hundred Years' War* (p. 50). In 1415 Henry V invaded and conquered France. On May 21, 1420—five years after the English victory at Agincourt (1415)—the Treaty of Troyes recognized Henry V as the immediate Regent of France, and as successor to the crown on the death of Charles VI. Both kings died in 1422; the French supported Charles VII as against Henry VI as the King of France; and the war was resumed. Within a score of years France recaptured much of the ground she had lost. Among her famous victories were those in which Joan of Arc participated. Finally, in 1453, the year in which Constantinople fell, the Hundred Years' War was terminated by England's defeat at Castillon. Of all her Continental conquests only Calais remained to England, and then only to 1558. Other results in England included the end of feudalism, the emergence of a strong national state, and the development of manufacturing.[1]

b) ***The Wars of the Roses*** (1455—1485). The thirty-year struggle between the houses of Lancaster (*red rose*) and York (*white rose*) for the succession to the throne broke out (1455). Its conclusion (1485) gave England the *Tudor* line of kings, brought an end to feudalism, and laid the foundation of England's greatness and prosperity.

c) ***The Jack Cade Rebellion.*** Jack Cade, a native of Ireland, playing somewhat the same part as Wat Tyler in 1381 (p. 50), as a protest against maladministration led an insurrection of some 15,000 men against London (1450). The rebellion was finally suppressed.

d) ***Reigns of Henry IV*** (1399—1413), ***Henry V*** (1413—1422), ***Henry VI*** (1422—1461; restored, October, 1470—May, 1471), ***Edward IV*** (1461—1483), ***Richard III*** (1483—1485), ***Henry VII*** (1485—1509). (1) The *De Haeretico comburendo* (burning of heretics), against the Lollards, was the first English statute putting a death penalty on religious offenses (1401). (2) Henry IV defeated the Percys at Shrewsbury (1403). (3) Henry V persecuted the Lollards (1413) and finally eliminated them. (4) Henry VI, previously captured and thrown into the Tower of London (1465), was murdered (1471). (5) Edward IV died (1483). (6) Edward V was deposed (1483), and finally murdered in the tower (1483). (7) Richard III was defeated and slain at Bosworth (1485). (8) Henry Tudor, Duke of Richmond, became Henry VII (1485).

### General View of the Literature

The fifteenth century is traditionally described as the "barren" period of English literature. For this decline in literary activity some of the causes have been indicated: the chief ones being the political confusion of the wars, civil and foreign, which not only absorbed the attention of those who could give possible writers support but also killed many of the nobles who had previously been patrons of the arts; and the early impulses of the Reformation and the Revival of Learning, which turned scholars to the study of the classics rather than to the creation of a native literature. However, this apparently starved century is not unimportant in the historical development of the literature. It introduced the eclogue, continued the development of the carol, became the especial springtide of the ballad, inspired one or two translations of the Bible (see p. 148), revealed Scottish poets of more vitality than the English followers of Chaucer, and saw the increasing popularity of the drama. Admittedly, on the other hand,

---

1 For France the War, while resulting in the wasting of farm lands, the destruction of towns, and an enormous loss of man power, also decimated the nobility and marked the growth of a strong middle class.

the prose, chiefly in Latin yet also showing the growing importance of English, is obviously didactic or controversial; the poetry, giving way for the next three centuries to an Italian influence rather than a French influence dominant from the Norman Conquest to Chaucer, is mainly imitative and uninspired. Rather than regard the century as one of barrenness and dearth, consider it as one of healthful fallow and germination.

## *ENGLISH FOLLOWERS OF CHAUCER*

**John Lydgate,** *c.* 1370—*c.* 1450, poet. Born probably at the village of Lydgate (in Suffolk) which gives him his name. Monk of Bury St. Edmunds. Chief works of most prolific follower of Chaucer and most voluminous verse-writer between the periods of Chaucer and Spenser, are translations and compilations. Drawled-out style, not too logically connected; homiletic, flat. Once considered Chaucer's equal, but resembles the master only in versatility; has been called the English Virgil; at his best is interesting because of his love of rural life. Possibly not as metrically halting and incompetent as traditionally described. His works include beast fables (*e. g., The Horse, the Sheep, and the Goose, The Churl and the Bird*); saints' lives (*e. g., The Life of Saint Margaret*); popular poems (*e. g., A Ditty of Women's Horns, Ballade of the Midsummer Rose, Mumming at Hertford, Bycorne and Chichevache*).

***The Damage and Destruccyon in Realmes*** or ***The Serpent of Division***† (*c.* 1400). His only prose tract. Among the first political pamphlets in English history; also, the most comprehensive discussion of Julius Caesar in Middle English literature. Written at the request of Duke Humphrey of Gloucester to show the dangers of strife. Clear, smooth.

***Reson and Sensuallyte*** (1406—1408). Almost doubles the linage of its source, the early French love-romance *Les Èchecs amoureux*. Characteristic defects, as well as hackneyed and excessive reduplication of expressions, pleonasms, padding, and loose syntax. Almost 7,050 lines in couplets. Unfinished.

***Troy-Book***† (1412—1420). Undertaken at the request of Prince Henry, afterwards Henry V; founded on Guido delle Colonne's *Historia Trojana* (p. 36). Practically all of its wordy 30,117 lines are in ten-syllable couplets. Five books, the fourth being the most prolix and least interesting, and the third containing the best-known passage, a long tribute to Chaucer. Notable are the love story of Jason and Medea (I), and Agamemnon's words of comfort to Menelaus (II).

---

† * Explanation of symbols immediately precedes page one.

***Siege of Thebes*** (1420—1422). Anachronistically representing himself as having been invited to join Chaucer's pilgrims on their return journey, Lydgate on the first day out tells the first tale, an amplification of that told by the Knight (p. 72). Includes a Prologue modelled on Chaucer's, the foundation of Thebes, the struggle between the brothers Ethiocles and Polymetes for supremacy, and the siege and destruction of Troy. Shorter, less tedious than usual; (4,716 lines). Paraphrases Lawrence de Premierfait's *Des Cas des Nobles* French *Roman de Thebes* (1150), but also Statius's *Thebaid,* Boccaccio's *Teseide,* Chaucer, and the Bible.

***Fall of Princes*** (1431—1439). Written at the request of Humphrey, Duke of Gloucester. His most tedious and longest work (about 36,365 lines). Paraphrases Lawrence de Premierfait's *Des Cas des Nobles Hommes et Femmes,* prose version founded on the same Italian source as Chaucer's *Monk's Tale* (p. 73). Nine books, in both the rime-royal stanza, and the eight-line stanza riming *ababbcbc.* Of philological importance (like the *Troy-Book*), many French words being documented here for the first time. Imitated in *A Mirror for Magistrates* (folio, 1554) by George Ferrers and William Baldwin.

***The Daunce of Machabree*** (*ante* 1433).[1] Employed to write the verses for a painted mural dance at St. Paul's, London, Lydgate translated these verses at the Holy Innocents (1424) at Paris. Introduced into England the Dance of Death (*dance macabre*) motive, a term used to describe allegorical compositions in art or literature that have for their subject the inevitability of death. Study of anatomy during the Renaissance brought in the Skeleton, thereby taking the place of the male character. Origin of term is unknown.

***Temple of Glas.*** A long, dull, allegorical love poem modelled upon Chaucer's *House of Fame* (p. 66)—*e. g.,* The Temple of Glass, the depiction on the walls of famous lovers, the court of Venus. In both the heroic couplet and the seven-line stanza. Possibly associated with the betrothal of Judge William Paston with Agnes Berry, in 1420 (see p. 98).

***London Lickpenny.***† Lively humorous satire, possibly not by Lydgate, of a penniless countryman who is driven from one court of Westminster to another in his search for justice. Picture of London street life.

***The Court of Sapience.*** Poem attributed to Lydgate. Influenced Hawes's *Passetyme of Pleasure* (p. 97).

***The Complaint of the Black Knight.*** Once ascribed to Chaucer. Pleasant pictures. About 680 lines.

---

1 *The Dance of Death,* edited by Warren, Florence (1931).

† * Explanation of symbols immediately precedes page one.

***The Child Jesus to Mary the Rose.*** Fourteen lines of "Catholic verse" discovered by H. N. MacCracken.

X **Thomas Hoccleve** (or **Occleve**), *c.* 1368—*c.* 1450, poet. For more than twenty years a clerk in the Privy Seal Office, London (spread over a period of thirty-five years); teacher, philosopher, reformer, self-described rake. Verse, chiefly religious, in sprawling rime royal or couplets; but less dreary than Lydgate's. Best narrator among the English Chaucerians. Works include a verse-remonstrance to Sir John Oldcastle; and the personal *Dialog with a Friend.*

***De Regimine Principum*†** (1411—1412). Treatise on the duty of a ruler, addressed to Henry, Prince of Wales, (later Henry V), in rime royal. Draws upon the *Secreta Secretorum,* the psuedo-epistle of Aristotle; the *Game of chess moralized by Jacques de Cessoles;* and the *De Regimine Principum* ("The Regement of Princes") of Aegidius Romanus (Aegidius de Colonna). Tedious homilies contain, however, some personal details, particularly in the dialogue between the poet and a beggar. Points out that two kinds of justice, one for the rich and another for the poor, prevail; feels that wars waste the wealth of the country; urges the conclusion between France and England of "peace, that precious jewel." Memorable for its eulogy of Chaucer, and for containing the best portrait of the master extant. (Also called *The Gouvernail of Princes.*)

***Le Male Règle de T. Hoccleve*** (1406). Compunctious, autobiographical poem of penitence, confessing to various youthful dissipations: for twenty years he led a fast life, drinking to excess, daring to kiss girls at the Paul's Head Tavern, but going no further because of cowardice. Often overtipped the boatmen because his vanity was tickled when they called him "Master."

***Ars Sciendi Mori.*** Mature the art of learning to die by always having within you the fear of God. Excellent poetical piece, translated and amplified from Chap. II, Bk. II of Heinrich Suso's *Horologium Sapientiae* (1334).[1]

***Letter to Cupid.*** Poetical tale in honor of women. Translated from *L'Epistre au Dieu d'Amours* of Christine de Pisan.

***The Mother of God*** (or *Ad beatam Virginem*). Subjective poem in twenty seven-line stanzas. Once ascribed to Chaucer.

***The Emperor Jereslaus' Wife.*** Source of moralized tale is in the *Gesta Romanorum* (p. 37).

***Jonathas.*** Source in the *Gesta Romanorum* (p. 37). Macabre-like shadows.

---

1 Kurtz, B. P., "The Relation of Occleve's *Lerne to Die* to Its Sources," *Publications of the Modern Language Association of America,* XL (1925), pp. 252-275.

† * Explanation of symbols immediately precedes page one.

**John Skelton,** *c.* 1460—1529, "poet-laureate," satirist.[1] Tutor (probably) to Prince Henry. Parson of Diss in Norfolk (1504). Most original and vivacious English Chaucerian. Wrote doggerel almost with genius. Metrical ease attributable to either his structural adaptation of the Low Latin hymns or to his introduction of Martial d'Auvergne's pattern of the short line: "Skeltonical" verse is a staccato, voluble, now scrambling, now shuffling, often slipshod, octosyllabic couplet, usually six-syllable lines varying in length and riming together in continuous succession two, three, four, and sometimes as many as seven times. (Analagous to the *fatras* or *fatrasies* of the French, the *frottola* of the Italian, and to Trevisa's occasional employment of the short line when following Higden's Latin original. See p. 61.)

***The Bouge of Court***† (*c.* 1509). The poet plunges overboard to escape from the machinations of the Seven Vices masquerading as passengers. Original allegorical poem in rime royal imaginatively satirizing the precariousness of court favor during the time of Henry VIII. Scheme of poem influenced by Barclay's *Shyp of Folys* (p. 97). In Chaucer's seven-line stanza.

***Garlande of Laurell*** ( 1523). Stilted self-laudatory allegorical poem, mainly in rime royal. Competent lyrics in praise of Margaret Hussey and Isabel Pennell.

***Colyn Cloute***† (1519—1524). A vagabond satirically indicts ecclesiastical duplicity and immorality. Veils an attack on Cardinal Wolsey. Influenced Spenser (p. 124).

***Why come ye nat to Courte?***† (1521—1523). Unreserved and jeering satire on Cardinal Wolsey, whose dominating position prevented the poet from receiving preferment.

***The Tunnynge of Elynour Rummyng.***† Vigorous, humorous, coarse syncopation of the drunken orgies participated in by the mixed company who drink the ale brewed by the slut, Elinor Rumming. ("Tunnynge" means "brewing.")

***The Boke of Phyllyp Sparowe.***† Jane Scroop poetizes a lament on her pet bird killed by Gib, the family cat, and Skelton follows with a song in honor of the bird's owner. Sportive 1,400 lines, described by Coleridge as "an exquisite and original poem." Probably inspired by an eighteen-line poem of Catullus. Note its macaronics.

***Speke, Parrot*** (1517—1518). Somewhat obscure versifying attack on Cardinal Wolsey.[2] Based on *The Green Lover* (parrot) by Jean Lemaire de Belges (Bavay). In Chaucer's seven-line stanza.

1 *The Complete Works of John Skelton,* edited by Henderson, Philip (1931); Nelson, William, *John Skelton, Laureate* (1939).

2 Berdan, J. M., "Speke, Parrot: An Interpretation of Skelton's Satire," *Modern Language Notes,* xxx (1915), pp. 140-144.

† * Explanation of symbols immediately precedes page one.

***Magnyfycence*†** (1515—1523). Morality play (p. 103 *ff;* p. 106), in which Mankind is rescued from the Vices by Good Hope, Perseverance, and others: but "the outcome of the conflict presented involved the safety of a kingdom rather than the salvation of a soul."[1] Prompted by personal satire. Poor characterization, stronger personifications. Chiefly in a long line of four stresses divided after the second stress by a caesura. Makes him one of our first dramatists known to us by name.

## *SCOTTISH FOLLOWERS OF CHAUCER*

**James I.** of Scotland (1394—1437; King of Scotland, 1406—1437). Merchant ship *Maryenknight,* in which the eleven-year-old prince had embarked for France in 1406, was seized by Norfolk pirates and James was carried to London. For eighteen years he was detained a prisoner despite truce, but was well treated and educated. By the terms of a treaty, he was released upon the payment by Scotland of a huge sum of money, and upon its agreeing to his marriage on February 2, 1424, with Lady Jane Beaufort, daughter of John Beaufort, Earl of Somerset, and niece of Richard II. (D. G. Rossetti's ballad, *The King's Tragedy,* 1881, narrates the King's tragic career.)

***The Kingis Quair*†*** (1423). In "The King's Quire" (or Book) familiarity with Chaucer is apparent—*e. g.,* the prince's first sight of Jane is similar to Palamon's and Arcite's first sight of Emily (see *The Knight's Tale,** p. 72); James's concluding address to his book (st. 194) has its counterpart in *Troilus and Criseyde* (Book V, *l.* 1,786). Tender, modest, earnest tone of the *cour d'amour* type of allegory; delicate in its delineation of love's dawning. Written in Chaucer's seven-line pentameter stanza, riming *ababbcc,* henceforth called "rime royal" in honor, it is said, of King James.

***Ballad of Good Counsel.*** Three stanzas in rime royal imitative of Chaucer's *Truth* (p. 77), repeating, as in the latter, the last line in each stanza.

**Robert Henryson,** *c.* 1425—*c.* 1506, Scottish poet. A schoolmaster probably connected with the grammar school of the Benedictine Abbey in Dunfermline.

***The Testament of Cresseid*†*** (1593). Powerful dramatic sequel to Chaucer's *Troilus and Criseyde* (p. 66). Silent interview is authentic psychology. H. J. C. Grierson has declared the 616 lines in rime royal to be "perhaps the most original poem that Scotland has produced."[2]

---

1 Swain, Barbara, *Fools and Folly* (1932), p. 162.

2 Grierson, H. J. C., "Robert Henryson," *The Modern Scot,* IV (1934), p. 299 (pp. 294-303).

† * Explanation of symbols immediately precedes page one.

***Morall Fabilles of Esope.***† Not always brief, yet consistently fresh, humorous, grave, and even original. Less suggestive of the French fabulist La Fontaine (1621—1695) than of the Russian Krylov (1768—1844) in their terseness, expressiveness, and vividness. Influenced by the versions of Anonymus and Lydgate (p. 84). The *moralitas* attached to each of the thirteen fables does not detract from the charm of incident, dialogue, and imagery. Rime royal. *The Taill of the Uponlondis Mouss and the Burges Mouss* (Town and Country Mouse) is a sustained analysis of two social institutions. *The Taill of the Schir Chanteclir and the Fox* is borrowed from Chaucer's *Nun's Priest's Tale* (p. 74.)

***Robene and Makyne.*** Earliest pastoral poem in the language. Pleasing, humorous, terse *débat* (p. 30). Influenced probably by the *pastourelles.*

***Orpheus and Eurydice.*** A *moralitas* concludes this feebly told, long allegorical narrative. Boethian philosophy. Mainly in rime royal.

**William Dunbar,** *c.* 1460—*c.* 1530, Scottish poet. An East Lothian educated at the University of St. Andrews; M.A., 1479. Franciscan friar. Wandering preacher. King's messenger. Poet-laureate. Many kinds of poems—allegorical, amatory, comic, laudatory, satirical, precatory, moral, religious. Conventional elements (*e. g.,* garden scene, abstract personifications); generally not lyrical; but also variety of meters, effortless technique, startlingly appropriate figures of speech, dexterous versatility, vitriolic satire, gross materialism, and Rabelaisian mirth. Called the Chaucer of Scotland: like his master, at times indecent; unlike his master, a grim shadow replaces the smile of Chaucer.

***The Thrissil and the Rois***† (1503). Political allegory of twenty-seven stanzas in rime royal celebrating the marriage of James IV (the Thistle) to Margaret Tudor (the red and white Rose of York and Lancaster). Lofty prothalamium, excellent description, rich imagery, metrical felicity.

***The Dance of the Sevin Deidly Synnis***†(1503—1508). Mahound (the Devil) has the Seven Deadly Sins perform a *danse macabre* (p. 85). Vivid portraits of Anger, Envy, and Highlanders in Hell. Strong vocabulary, rapid swing of lines, weird sublimity of imagination. Profoundly moral allegoric satire intensely original in the power of its unrelieved grotesquery.

***The Goldyn Targe***†* (1508). Conventional machinery of the allegory redeemed by poetic vigor, directness, bright glows, sensuous imagery, musical verse. Descriptive felicity of poem's opening.

---

†* Explanation of symbols immediately precedes page one.

***Lament for the Makaris.*** Enumeration of a score of poets eminent from the earlier half of fifteenth century down to the reign of James V gives poem an historical value. Lifeblood of poignant threnody concentrated in the macaronic, plangent but tolling repetend, *Timor mortis conturbat me*—"the fear of death distresses me." High level of pathos, unwearying cadence of faultless music. Uses the *kyrielle* (four-line verses riming in couplets with a refrain).

***The Twa Mariit Wemen and the Wedo.***† Two married women and a widow, in particularizing their marriage-experiences, out-Chaucer the Wife of Bath by their coarseness, ribald imagining, unpleasant realism.[1] Both alliterative and blank verse.

**Gawain (Gawin or Gavin) Douglas,** *c.* 1474—1522, Scottish poet. Bishop of Dunkeld (*c.* 1516). Most scholarly of the Scottish Chaucerians, but the least vigorous.

***The Palice of Honour*** (1501). Chaucerian verse allegory, suggestive of *The House of Fame* (p. 66). Well-conceived, pompous. Stanzas rime *aabaabbab.*

***King Hart*** (first printed, 1786). More original but listless allegory of eight-line stanzas in which Queen Pleasaunce courts the Heart (*i. e.,* Human Nature).

***Eneidos*** (completed July 22, 1513). First verse translation of the *Aeneid* into any English dialect. Vigor and vision; but an absence of the Virgilian music and spiritual dignity. In heroic couplets, except for the varied metrical forms of the thirteen original prologues (the translation includes the thirteenth book by Mapheus Vegius), some of the other meters being the five-line stanza *aabba,* the rime royal, the octave *ababbcbc.* Seventh prologue suggestive of Thomson's *Seasons* (1726) in its independent description of Winter; the twelfth, famous for its description of May—all sometimes being considered, possibly without reason, as anticipatory of the spirit of the Renaissance.

**Sir David Lyndsay,** *c.* 1490—*c.* 1555, Scottish poet. Lyon King of Arms (1529), ambassador, Parliamentary representative. "The poet of the Scottish Reformation," Morley has called him, "but . . . . far more social than doctrinal."

***The Dreme*** (1528). Overhauls the abuses of the country, ending with a sound exhortation to the King. Chaucerian allegory in rime royal. Satiric, somewhat biographical. Warton has praised the rich style of its prologue.

---

1 Rutter, G. M., "The Wife of Bath," *Studies in English* (Western Reserve University Bulletin), New Series, xxxiv, No. 13 (1931), p. 61 *f.* (pp. 60-64).

† * Explanation of symbols immediately precedes page one.

***The Testament and Complaynt of our Soverane Lordis Papyngo*** (1530). The King's popinjay complains of state and particularly of ecclesiastical corruptions. Satire, chiefly in rime royal.

***Ane Pleasant Satyre of the Thrie Estaitis, in Commendatioun of Vertew and Vituperatioun of Vyce*****†*** (1540). Long political Morality play (p. 103 *ff.*; p. 106), in humorous billingsgate and in various meters. Acutely satirizes the Church. Only complete Scottish morality play that is now extant.

***The Tragedie of the Cardinal*** (1547). Poem on the death of Cardinal Beaton. Reminiscent of Chaucer's *Monk's Tale* (p. 73). Octosyllabic couplets.

***The Testament of Squyer William Meldrum*** (*c.* 1549). Hearty Chaucerian verbal romanticizing, in generally smooth octosyllabic couplets, of the exploits of the Squire. Gleams of humor.

***The Monarche*** (1553). Dramatic dialogue between Experience and a Courtier. Tells "of the Miserabyll Estait of the World" from the Fall of Man down to Doomsday. His longest poem (some 6,333 lines).

## *OTHER WRITERS OF THE PERIOD*

**"Sir John Mandeville"** (*c.* 1300—*c.* 1372).[1] According to the book (see below), Sir John Mandeville was born at St. Albans, England (1300), started on his extensive travels (1322), and settled in Liége (1357) under the name of Jehan de Bourgogne, otherwise Jean à la Barbe, a Liége physician. There he wrote the book, and there he died (1372), being buried in the church of Guillemins.

***The Voiage and Travaile of Sir John Maundeville, Knight.*****†*** (English translation, 1449). Probably the hoaxing creation of Jean d'Outremeuse (1338—1400), chronicler and poet of Liége. Five centuries later it was discovered that "Sir John Mandeville" was as nonexistent as the apocryphal marvels that the book describes; and that the travels are pilferings from other sources, the greater part of the material having been appropriated from the narratives of Friar Odoric of Pordenone (1330), William of Boldensele (1336), Albert of Aix, John of Carpini, Haiton of Armenia, Vincent of Beauvais, William of Tripoli, and Jacques of Vitry. Some of the many manuscripts claim that the book was written originally in Latin, while others say in English; but evidence points to the French version (1357—1371),[2] as the first, and from it translations have been made into English, Irish, Italian, Latin, Dutch, Bohemian, and German.

1 Chronologically, however, "Sir John Mandeville" belongs to *The Age of Chaucer* (p. 50).

2 The work was "composed between 1365 and the early part of 1371," says Steiner, Arpad, "The Date of Composition of *Mandeville's Travels*," *Speculum*, IX (1934), p. 147 (pp. 144-147).

† * Explanation of symbols immediately precedes page one.

The English versions, creatively imaginative and not merely slavish, avoid the polyloquent and homiletic prose of the period, and are limpid and direct, flowing and graphic. Verisimilitude is achieved through various means, particularly through a concreteness of statement (*e. g.*, by giving not only the year but also the very day of the author's death, as of November 12, 1372) and through the artifice of attributing to others some of the wondrous stories told (*e. g.*, by parenthesizing statements by "Men say . . . ," which is analogous to the cautious newspaper reporter who says, "It is alleged . . . ."). For more than four centuries this verisimilitude contributed greatly to making the work acceptable as genuine, although in the eighteenth century Joseph Addison already (*The Tatler*, No. 254, November 23, 1710) speaks of "Sir John Mandeville" as having "distinguished himself by the copiousness of his invention." Refreshing style and sheer *naïveté* of the compilation mark it as the first notable specimen of prose used primarily for the purpose of entertainment. For a fine example of the author's art, read the description of the Great Chan of Cathay and his court.

X **Sir Thomas Malory,** *c.* 1395—1471, translator-compiler, romancer. According to G. L. Kittredge, Malory may be identical with a Sir Thomas Malory, Knight, of Winwick in Northamptshire and Newbold Revell (Fenny Newbold) in Warwickshire.[1] Saw extensive military service in France while in the retinue of Richard Beauchamp, Earl of Warwick, the "King-maker." Represented Warwickshire in Parliament (1445). Imprisoned for participation in the Wars of the Roses. Died in prison, into which he had again been thrown for twenty years (except for short intervals of liberty) after he had been adjudged guilty of charges of robbery, insurrection, and, most serious of all, of violence on two occasions upon Joan, wife of Hugh Smyth of Monks Kirby—the latter accusation being, possibly, a case of ***raptus,*** such as occurred in Chaucer's life (p. 63).[2]

X ***Morte d'Arthur*†** (completed in prison between March, 1469, and March, 1470; printed by Caxton, 1485). *Rifacimento* or remaking of the mass of Arthurian legends (see pp. 41 *ff.*) is the greatest prose achievement of its century. Avowedly translated from Old French sources; but also draws upon English sources and makes some original contributions. Concerned primarily with (1) King Arthur and his Knights, and (2) the Achieving of the Sangreal. For the first time Arthur becomes the

---

1 Kittredge, G. L., "Who Was Sir Thomas Malory?" (Harvard) *Studies and Notes in Philology and Literature,* v (1896; issued 1897), pp. 85-106.

2 Baugh, A. C., "Documenting Sir Thomas Malory," *Speculum,* VIII (1933), pp. 3-29.

† * **Explanation of symbols immediately precedes page one.**

central figure. While Caxton (p. 95), who divided the work into twenty-one books, introduces Malory as being morally edifying as well as entertaining, Ascham (p. 116), forgetful of the ingredients of "noble chivalry, courtesy, humanity, friendliness," and overlooking Caxton's exhortation, in the preface, to "Do after the good and leave the evil," has criticized Malory for "open manslaughter and bold bawdry."

Epitomizes the literature of an epoch when the age of chivalry and feudalism was swiftly disappearing: the *Morte d'Arthur,* in the words of W. H. Schofield, is: "a work of retrospect, tinged with sadness for the passing of the good old days; a work of idealism, troubled with knowledge of miserable facts daily divulged; a work of patriotism, written when the land was being wasted by civil strife; a work of encouragement to the right-minded, and of warning to the evil-minded, among men of that class in which the author lived and moved."[1]

Despite such defects as looseness of grammar, repetition of stereotyped phrases, and inconsistencies of plot, the *Morte d'Arthur* throughout is direct, vivid, and homogeneous. Herbert Read[2] notes that Malory's "stark" realism embodied in a manly prose has too often been sentimentalized by editors: important, indeed, for Malory has been immortalized by his style no less than by his material. Some of the epithets applied to his poetical prose: simple, sensuous, resonant, muscular, quaint, colorful, elevated yet essentially artless, straightforward yet leisurely, pliant and skilful in dialogue, noble and passionate in spirit, instinct with chivalrous feeling and genuine human sympathy. Influenced (1) many English poets (*e. g.,* Spenser, Tennyson), and (2) the development of a flexible prose style in English. Memorable passages: the death scene of the Fair Maid of Astolat, the last meeting of Lancelot and Guinevere, the passing of Arthur.

**John Capgrave,** 1393—1464, historian, theologian. Augustinian friar. Many Latin sermons, tracts, and commentaries.

***Nova Legenda Angliae.*** First memorable collection of lives of English saints. Compiled from the work of John of Tinmouth (Tynemouth).

***A Chronicle of England from the Creation to the Year A. D. 1417.*** Colorless but business-like history-fiction, dedicated to Henry IV. In English. Unfinished.

***De Illustribus Henricis*** (*c.* 1450). Latin. Lives of twenty-four men (emperors, kings, celebrities) who bear the name of Henry. Characteristically feeble, but logically arranged as are all his works.

---

1 Schofield, W. H., *Chivalry in English Literature* (1912), p. 87 (pp. 75-123).
2 Read, Herbert, *The Sense of Glory* (1929), pp. 34-56.

**Sir John Fortescue,** *c.* 1394—*c.* 1476, earliest English constitutional theorist. Chief Justice of the King's Bench (1442). Author of syllogistic Latin works.

***De Natura Legis Naturae*** (1461—1463). Latin eulogy upon the laws of England attempts in the form of an argument to establish the right of Henry VI to the throne. Fortescue founds the law of nature upon the rule that "whatsoever ye would that men should do to you, do ye even so to them." Main arguments, protracted and not too readable, derive from the theories of St. Thomas Aquinas and of Aegidius.

***De Laudibus Legum Angliae*** (1471). "The Praise of the Laws England" is a Latin treatise distinguishing absolute from constitutional monarchy (France from England), "in commendation" of the latter. Form is a dialogue between an old Chancellor (Fortescue) and a young Prince (Edward, eldest son of Henry VI).[1] Famous description of the Inns of Court. (For his theories, see his *Monarchia.*)

***Monarchia, or the Difference between an Absolute and a Limited Monarchy*†** (*c.* 1471; printed 1714; later called *The Governance of England*). To St. Thomas's theory of *dominium regale* ("royal [*i. e.,* absolute] monarchy") and *dominium politicum* ("politic monarchy") Fortescue in nervous English suggests *dominium politicum et regale* (both "politic and royal monarchy"), under which a country is ruled by laws to which its people has given assent. Conception of a true limited monarchy is probably original with Fortescue, according to Sir Frederic Pollock.

**Reginald Pecock,** *c.* 1395—1460, religious writer. Bishop of St. Asaph (1444) and of Chichester (1450).

***The Donet*** (*c.* 1440). Introduction to the main truths of Christian religion, in the form of a dialogue between a father and son, is, avowedly, a complement and summary of his next work.

***The Reule of Crysten Religioun*** (*c.* 1443). First of a series of treatises intended to furnish a rule of religion and life.

***The Poor Man's Mirror*** (*c.* 1443—*c.* 1449). In dialogue form.

***The Repressor of Over Much Blaming of the Clergy*†** (*c.* 1449; published 1456). Defends Catholicism against Lollardy: vindicates, first in a general and then in a special discussion, eleven particulars raised by the Lollards; *e. g.,* the use of images, the holding of landed possessions by the clergy, the costliness of ecclesiastical decora-

1 Lévy-Ulmann, Henri, *The English Legal Tradition,* translated by Mitchell, M. and revised by Goadby, F. M. (1935), p. xxxii, p. 161.

† * Explanation of symbols immediately precedes page one.

tions, the taking of oaths. Attitude of appealing to Wycliffites through reason and natural law, instead of burning them, branded him as a heretic. His employment of subordinate clauses is more artful than Wyclif's; his complex sentence-structure, more mature than Mandeville's: his prose is a prose of reason. Possible preference for an English, rather than a Latin, vocabulary, in which he even coined words; freedom from dialectal features; essentially opinionative, cogent, if awkward and repetitious, English—all point to him as the first eminent writer to employ the vernacular in argument, and as important as Wyclif in the development of literary prose.[1]

***The Follower to the Donet*** (*c.* 1453—1454). In the same form as *The Donet.* Explains further the medieval European ideas of moral and intellectual virtues.

***The Book of Faith*** (*c.* 1456). Daring in its denial of the right of the Church to expound Holy Writ. Part of his general attempt to bring the Lollards into the Church.

**William Caxton** *c.* 1422—1491, first English printer; translator. In Bruges (1441—1470). Acted as governor of a chartered association of English merchants trading in the Low Countries (1465—1469). In the service of Margaret, Duchess of Burgundy, sister of Edward IV (1471—1476). Returned to England (1476). Established a press at Westminster (1476—1491).[2] Issued more than fourscore individual books, among them *The Canterbury Tales, Confessio Amantis,* and *Morte d'Arthur;* he himself translated more than twenty works. Caxton's prefaces, particularly the one to the *Morte d'Arthur* (p. 92), and the epilogues, are of great interest, being at different times simple or clumsy or ornate, but consistently personal, frequently humorous, and always spontaneous.[3] He merits acknowledgment as one foreshadowing "that love for classical antiquity which was to become the literary passion of the succeeding generation," and as "the first of the arbiters of English literary taste."

***The Recuyell of the Historyes of Troye*** (1474). First book printed in English and issued probably at Bruges. Caxton himself had previously (1469—1471) translated part of Raoul de Fèvre's *Le Receuil des Histoires de Troye* under the encouragement of the Duchess Margaret.

---

1 But see Krapp, G. P., *The Rise of English Literary Prose* (1915), pp. 73-75.

2 Not 1477, as hitherto believed. See Note 1 on page 96.

3 Byles, A. T. P., "William Caxton as a Man of Letters," *The Library,* Fourth Series, xv, No. 1 (1934), pp. 1-25.

***The Dictes or Sayengs of the Philosophres*** (November 18, 1477). First dated book printed in England,[1] and issued from the Westminster press, is Lord Rivers's translation of Guillaume de Tigonville's *Dits Moraulx des Philosophes.* The omission by the Earl of some matter about women made a gap which Caxton filled by introducing the opinion of Socrates about women.

**Blind Harry (or Henry the Minstrel),** *fl.* 1470—1492, Scottish poet. (Possibly never a minstrel and possibly never blind.[2])

***The Acts and Deeds of the Illustrious and Valiant Champion, Sir William Wallace, Knight of Ellerslie*†;** generally known as *The Wallace* (*ante* 1488). Purports to be based on a lost Latin work of the Chaplain, John Blair; but neither the man nor his work has been traced. Eleven uninspired books of more than 11,000 lines, mainly in heroic couplets, sometimes revealing fine narrative and descriptive passages, unvaryingly reflecting the revengeful and jingoistic spirit of the author. (Some do not attribute the poem to Blind Harry.)

**Sir John Bourchier, Lord Berners,** *c.* 1467 — 1533, translator. Chancellor of the Exchequer (1516).

***Froissarts Cronycles*†** (1523—1525).[3] Englished Froissart's work covering period 1326—1400, in a manner charming, vivid, and faithful to the spirit of the original, yet personal. Includes an excellent account of the times of Edward III. Prologue somewhat anticipatory of the euphuistic style (p. 151). Source book for William Morris's *The Dream of John Ball,* and other works.

***The Boke of Huon de Bordeaux*** **(*c.* 1534).** Prolixity of original *chanson de geste* reproduced. Utilized by Shakespeare in the fairy scenes of *A Midsummer-Night's Dream* (p. 188).

***The Golden Boke of Marcus Aurelius*** (1532). Translated from a French version of Guevara's historical romance, *El Relox de Principes* ("The Dial for Princes"). Influenced the development of Euphuism (p. 151).

---

1 The first dated book in England had been preceded, it was generally believed, by other types of printed matter; but only recently was proof of this found. In 1928 Mr. S. C. Ratcliffe (Ratcliff) discovered an *Indulgence* of some 360 words, dated in Westminster on December 13, 1476, and printed in blank for John Sant, Abbot of Abingdon, presumably the author. This important historical document is the earliest extant piece of printing done in England; hence, printing in that country began in 1476, not in 1477. See Pollard, A. W., "An Indulgence of 1476," *The Times* (London), Tuesday, February 7, 1928, p. 15, col. 6; p. 16, col. 1.

2 Schofield, W. H., *Mythical Bards and The Life of William Wallace* (1920).

3 *Froissarts Cronycles,* published by Basil Blackwell, Oxford (1927-1928, Eight Books in Two Volumes).

† * Explanation of symbols immediately precedes page one.

***The Castell of Love*** (1540). Probably translated from the Spanish with the aid of his knowledge of French.[1]

**Alexander Barclay,** *c.* 1475—1552, (probably Scottish) poet, prose writer, scholar. First a Benedictine, then a Franciscan, monk.

***The Shyp of Folys of the Worlde*†** (1509).[2] Translation and adaptation of probably Jacob Locher's Latin version of Sebastian Brandt's *Narrenschif* (Swabian dialect, 1494). Satirical portraits of many kinds of men and their follies (note that the figures are not abstractions); pictures of manners and customs of the day; censure of various evils and corruptions. Principal meter of the listless 14,000 lines is rime royal. Doubles the length of original.

***The Eclogues*†** (*c.* 1513). First eclogues in the English language. Of the five, the first three are translated from *De Curialium Miseriis Epistola* of Aeneas Sylvius (Pope Pius II, 1458—1464); the fourth and fifth are free paraphrases mainly of the fifth and sixth eclogues by Mantuan (1448—1516), a Carmelite monk. Vigorous, proverb-ridden, satiric. Heroic couplets.

**Stephen Hawes,** *c.* 1474—*c.* 1530, idealistic court poet. Follower of Chaucer and Lydgate, and even more tedious than the latter. Scholastic, moral, didactic, chivalric-romantic. Frequent use of the magic numeral seven, meaningless phrases, elaborate diction, halting lines. Links the love allegory of Chaucer to the moral allegory of Spenser (pp. 62, 124).

***The Exemple of Vertu*** (1504). Moral allegory of life in which Youth is tempted by Lust, Avarice, and Pride, but finally marries Cleanness. Rime royal.

***The Passetyme of Pleasure, or the Histoirie of Graunde Amour and la Bel Pucel, conteining the Knowledge of the Seven Sciences and the Course of Man's Life in this Worlde*†** (1506). Details the adventures to which Graunde Amour (the Perfect Lover) is exposed before he can win La Belle Pucel (the Pure Beauty); their happy marriage, and his death. Allegory of the life of man, with the appearance of such abstractions as Law, Avarice, Contrition, Death, Mercy, Fame, and the Virtues. Forty-six chapters of about 5,800 lines, mainly in a lax rime-royal stanza, but also in the iambic pentameter riming couplet of *The Canterbury Tales.* Prolix, uninspired; the characters are bloodless; yet the work is "an historic landmark in the evolution of English literature."[3] Possibly influenced by Martianus Capella's *Marriage of Mercury and Philology.* Notable couplet (*l.* 5,479 *f.*):

> "For though the day be never so longe,
> At last the belles ringeth to evensonge."

1 Crane, W. G., "Lord Berners's Translation of Diego de San Pedro's *Cárcel de Amor,*" *Publications of the Modern Language Association of America,* XLIX (1934), pp. 1032-1035.
2 Swain, Barbara, *Fools and Folly* (1932). Chap. VII, pp. 114-134.
3 *The Pastime of Pleasure,* edited by Mead, W. E. (1928), p. CXIII (pp. XIII—CXIII).
† * Explanation of symbols immediately precedes page one.

## THE PASTON LETTERS (1422—1509)

***The Paston Letters***† is a collection of about 1,100 letters and other documents mostly written by or to members of the well-to-do Paston Family of Paston in Norfolk. Straightforward prose, but not strictly literature; rather an illuminating storehouse of English social history—the complex manners, morals, business methods, and domestic conditions of the upper middle classes of fifteenth century England; and especially of the troublous times during the Wars of the Roses, showing how undisturbed by war was the greater part of England. Through these letters can be reconstructed such matters as the medieval methods of marriage-making, the relation between parents and children, the contents of the medieval house, the life at a university, the conceptions of justice, the place of religion, the breakdown of feudalism. Invaluable source for historical novels; *e. g.*, the account of Robert Ledham (1452) was drawn upon by R. L. Stevenson for character names and other details in *The Black Arrow* (1888).

## ANONYMOUS POETRY

***The Cuckoo and the Nightingale*** (*c.* 1403). Delicate three-hundred-line debate, partly under obligation to Chaucer's *The Parliament of Fowls* and the "Prologue" to *The Legend of Good Women.* Five ten-syllable lines riming *abbba.* Now attributed to Sir Thomas Clanvowe, *fl.* 14th—15th century. (Called also *The Book of Cupid God of Love.*)

***The Flower and the Leaf.*** Chaucerian dream-allegory of 600 lines in rime royal, in which the poet develops the subject of the green flower (either the life of happy-go-luckyism or of love) and of the white leaf (either the life of gravity or of honor). Elfin, graceful. Probably by a woman-poet. Honored by John Keats (1795—1821).

***The Nut-Browne Maid.***†* Hybrid carol-ballad (see pp. 101, 103). Complicated rime scheme, alternating refrain (the *stychomythia*), tender, dramatic.

***Quia Amore Langueo***[1]† (*c.* 1430). Has been declared by Sir Henry Newbolt to be "the first and greatest religious lyric in English." Source is probably Canticles, VII, 11—13.

***The Pilgrim's Sea Voyage.*** Regarded as the earliest sea song in the language.

---

1 *Quia Amore Langueo,* edited by Webb, H. D. and Webb, H. G. (Carodoc, Bedford Park, 1902).

† * Explanation of symbols immediately precedes page one.

## *ADDITIONAL AUTHORS OR WORKS*

| AUTHOR | WORK or WORKS | COMMENT |
|---|---|---|
| **DAME JULIANA BERNERS** (or **BERNES** or **BARNES**), b. c. 1388, possibly the world's first woman sports writer. Said to be the daughter of Sir James Berners of Essex, beheaded in 1388. Probably prioress of Sopwell nunnery near St. Albans. | **The Treatyses Pertynynge to Hawkynge, Huntynge and Fysshynge with an Angle** (1486). Later (1496) called **The Boke of St. Albans.** | First known volume in English on the art of fishing. Treatises on that sport and on hunting are attributed to her. Accurate observations on fishing. Influenced by Nicholas Upton (1441), and by a work on **Venerie de Twety.** |
| **SIR RICHARD HOLLAND,** fl. 1450, Scottish author. Rector of Halkirk, and later of Abbreochy. | **The Buke of the Howlat** (c. 1450). | Original allegorical poem of some 1,000 lines influenced by Chaucer's **Parliament of Fowls.** Characterization of birdlife executed with simplicity and understanding. Alliteration and final rimes. |
| **WALTER KENNEDY,** c. 1460-c. 1508, Scottish poet. University examiner. | **The Flyting of Dunbar and Kennedie** (c. 1508). | Scurrilous poem is a débat between Dunbar and Kennedy. |
| **ROBERT FABYAN,** d. 1513, chronicler, Alderman of London. | **The New Chronicles of England and France** (1516). | Extends from the arrival of Brutus until the battle of Bosworth (1485). Unscholarly, uncritical, valueless except as a chronicle of London life after the reign of Richard I. Influenced Holinshed. Later continued down to 1588. |
| **HECTOR BOECE** (or **BOYCE** or **BOETHIUS**), c. 1465-c. 1536, Scottish canon, historian, humanist. Professor of philosophy at the Collège Montaigu, Paris (c. 1492-c. 1498). Principal of the University of Aberdeen (1505). | **Scotorum Historiae a prima gentis origine cum aliarum et rerum et gentium illustratione non vulgari** (1527). | Much of its seventeen books is fiction-romance, zealous in its praise of Scotland. Through the intermediary of Holinshed's **Chronicles** (p. 147), Boece's account of Macbeth and Duncan influenced Shakespeare. Commendable Latin prose style. |
| **JOHN COLET,** c. 1467-1519. Chief Christian humanist of day. Studied at Paris and Italy (1493-1496). Friend of Erasmus. Dean of St. Paul's School. Lectured on the New Testament at Oxford (1496-1504.) See also p. 112. | **Daily Devotions.**<br><br>**Epistolae ad Erasmum.**<br><br>**Exposition of St. Paul's First Epistle to the Corinthians.**<br><br>**Latin Grammar.** | His works are made important by their urging of reform in the Church. Liberal religious opinions. Influenced More and Erasmus. His **Latin Grammar,** the syntax of which was supplied by W. Lily, ultimately developed into the **Eton Latin Grammar.** |
| **HUGH LATIMER,** c. 1485-1555, popular preacher, reformer. Bishop of Worcester (1535-1539). Found guilty of heresy, and burned. (Trial and execution described in Foxe's **Actes and Monuments.** See p. 117.) | **"Sermons."** | One of his most famous is his "Sermon of the Plough." In general, he is simple, colloquial, pithy, quaint, and particularly graphic and humorous. Urges the necessity and the work of reformation. |
| **ANDREW BOORDE** (or **BORDE**), c. 1490-1549, traveler, physician. Suffrager bishop of Chichester (c. 1521). | a) **Handbook of Europe.**<br><br>b) **Fyrst Boke of the Introduction of Knowledge** (c. 1547). | a) First continental guidebook.<br><br>b) Includes the earliest printed specimen of the Gypsy language. |

## Chapter VII

# THE FIFTEENTH CENTURY: POPULAR LITERATURE

## *THE TRADITIONAL BALLAD*

### Origin

The popular ballad, an anonymous story handed down by oral transmission among generations of the folk, can not be dated: when a date is affixed, it indicates when the ballad was written down, not when it originated. It is generally recognized that during the fifteenth century the ballad received its greatest impulse.[1] Note that the ballad, fundamentally the song of the common people, developed coetaneously with the metrical romance (p. 39 *ff*., 48), fundamentally the poetry of the upper classes; while the latter is aristocratic in origin and sprawls in a more or less involved fashion over a number of adventures, the former is plebeian in origin and concentrates in simple style over one situation. From the several discussions as to the origin and composition of some 305 ballads extant in over a thousand versions, two main theories emerge:

### Theories of Ballad-Making

(a) The Communal or the Co-operative Folk-Intelligence Theory. Holds, substantially, that the ballads were composed by the community as a whole, in which each singer, as part of a dancing and choral group, contributed impromptu to the simple but incremental story being told. Chief exponents of the so-called Communal Theory are F. B. Gummere, Andrew Lang, G. L. Kittredge, and W. M. Hart. (Ballad-making is still going on in many parts of the world; *e. g.*, among the negroes of the South, and among the trappers in the far north-east of Canada.[2])

(b) The Literary (Artistic) or Individual Theory. Maintains that the ballads are the work of bards who derived the material from more "literary" work, especially from the metrical romances (p. 48). Among the upholders of this theory espousing the ballads as "degenerate romances" are Sir Walter Scott, Bishop Thomas Percy, Joseph Ritson, W. J. Courthope, T. F. Henderson, Sir Walter Raleigh, G. G. Smith, and Louise Pound. F. J. Child, while explaining the communal theory, nevertheless appears to lean toward the literary point of view.

---

1 Scholars are rejecting the view that the ballad's greatest development occurred particularly during the thirteenth and fourteenth centuries. Most ballads in their existing form belong to a later age; they were more probably fashioned in the sixteenth century.

2 Pound, Louise, "New-World Analogues of the English and Scottish Popular Ballads," *The Mid-West Quarterly*, III (1916), pp. 171-187.

**Definition**

The ballad, originally a dance-song, is a short-story told in song or verse, or "a song that tells a story," "simple in plot and metrical structure, divided into stanzas," told impersonally or with connotative and dramatic objectivity, ascribed to and circulated by oral tradition among people culturally homogeneous.

**Classification**

(a) Ballads of the Greenwood. Primarily comedies. The Robin Hood cycle, often called a popular epic, is one of the largest and richest collections of ballad poetry that remains (the cycle covers more than a hundred pages in the Student's Cambridge Edition of *English and Scottish Popular Ballads*). Examples: *A Geste of Robyn Hode* ("several ballads rhapsodized into a short epic"), *Robin Hood and the Monk, Robin Hood and Guy of Gisborne.** Among the traditional outlaw's comrades were Little John, Will Scarlet, Friar Tuck, Allan-a-Dale, Maid Marian. (Three other noted outlaws are celebrated in the ballad, *Adam Bell, Clim of the Clough, and William of Cloudesly.*)

(b) Ballads of History. Examples: *Chevy Chase** (praised by Joseph Addison in his *Spectator,* numbers 70 and 74, May 21 and 25, 1711), *Sir Patrick Spens** ("may or may not be historical"; also called a *funeral* ballad), *The Battle of Otterburn,* The Hunting of the Cheviot* (probably founded upon the same event as *The Battle of Otterburn*), *Young Waters** (only possibly historical), *Hugh of Lincoln* (for one version of tale see that told by Chaucer's Prioress, p. 73).

(c) Ballads of Love. Examples: *Child Waters,* Glasgerion,* King Estmere,* Helen of Kirkconnell.**

(d) Ballads of Humor. Examples: *The Crafty Farmer, The Gardener, Get up and Bar the Door.**

(e) Ballads of Domestic Tragedy. Examples: *Edward,* The Douglas Tragedy,* Babylon; or, the Bonnie Banks o Fordie,* Lord Thomas and Fair Annet,* The Two Sisters,* The Cruel Brother.**

(f) Ballads of the Supernatural. Examples: *Thomas Rymer,* *The Wife of Usher's Well,* Tam Lin,* Kemp Owyne,* Riddles Wisely Expounded, Fair Margaret and Sweet William, Clerk Saunders, Sweet William's Ghost.*

(g) Ballads of the Domestic Border. Examples: *Captain Car, or Edom o Gordon* (also classifiable as an *historical* ballad); *Bonnie George Campbell.**

(h) Ballads of Art. Example: *The Nut-Browne Maid** (p. 98). Strictly, however, in the *Art Ballad* the authorship is known, *e. g., The Rime of the Ancient Mariner* by S. T. Coleridge (1772—1834).

(i) Ballads Derived from Epic Material. Example: *King Orfeo.*

---

† * **Explanation of symbols immediately precedes page one.**

**Characteristics**

(a) Its impersonality and objectivity: "the fundamental characteristic of popular ballads is . . . . the absence of subjectivity and self-consciousness." Does not moralize or preach.

(b) Simple repetition and its apposite, structural or incremental repetition ("incremental" or cumulative because each singer contributed an impromptu line of verse, couplet, or stanza—if the Communal Theory is acceptable).

(c) Centralization upon a single episode enhanced by swift, simple, emotional, graphic narration. Note how *actable* most ballads are, a sort of one-act play. (*Robin Hood and the Friar,* a folk-play [p. 103], is a dramatization of an old English ballad.)

(d) Use of dialogue. Often the story is hinted at rather than told in full.

(e) General absence of figures of speech.

(f) Appearance of a refrain, even if sometimes meaningless; possibly "the most conclusive evidence . . . . of the derivation of ballads from choral song."

(g) Frequency of parallelism in phrase and idea.

(h) Stereotyped epithets (often effective) as well as concrete diction.

(i) Use of mystical numbers or their combinations.

(j) Anonymity of authorship. Definitiveness of text impossible: local, not cultural; oral, not literary.

**Metrical Form**

Employs the so-called "ballad" or "common" measure—a four-line stanza (generally riming *abcb*) written in alternating lines of iambic tetrameter and iambic trimeter (*i.e.,* the first and third lines, sometimes riming together, have four iambic feet, while the second and fourth lines, always riming together, have three iambic feet). Often irregular in meter and defective in rime. G. H. Gerould has noted that the couplet with seven stresses to the line "is the commonest metrical form of our ballads"; while "only less common than the line of seven stresses is the line of four." However, G. R. Stewart, Jr., points out that in the ballad "the seven stresses of its line tend to be alternately strong and weak: . . . . In other words the ballad line consists not of seven simple, but of four complex units. The structure, therefore, can best be termed *dipodic,* and the units *dipods.*"[1]

---

1 Gerould, G. H., *The Ballad of Tradition* (1932), p. 126; Stewart, G. R., Jr., "The Meter of the Popular Ballad," *Publications of the Modern Language Association of America,* XL (1925), p. 935 (pp. 933-962).

## *THE CAROL*

The carol, a song of religious praise or devotion, and sometimes of joy or exultation, probably originated in the folk song and pagan festival. (The ballad is connected in its origin with the *carole* or round dance: the cheerfulness of the carol is attributable in some measure to its French origin.) Examples: "I sing of a maiden"; "Wherefore should I hang up my bow"; "Mary mother, I am thy child"; "Adam lay ibounden." (Christmas carols are called *noels.*)

## *THE DRAMA*

(See also pp. 17, 31, 52.)

### Origin

Within the early Christian Church, in its religious functions and in its dramatizations of the liturgy, are found the germs of the English drama. In the neumes,[1] parts of the Testament were embellished by means of an elaborated tone; in the chants, one section of the Choir (or a single voice) was answered by another section (or all the other voices); in the tropes (originally, alternating chants) the antiphonal structure served to introduce the Introit to the Third Mass. From this point it was but a step to the spoken dialogue and the pageant. These early "plays" were always in Latin, with the subjects invariably drawn from the Scriptures and the performances invariably given in the Church. (Also containing dramatic elements of contributory influence were the traditional games, festivals, and folk-plays—the St. George and the Dragon mummeries, the Sword and the May-pole dances, the Hock Tide festival, the Morris or Ploughboy dances, the Robin Hood plays, and the like, many of these having originated in pre-Christian religious ceremonies.[2])

### Miracle Play

Out of the liturgical drama, particularly the *Quem-Quaeritis* trope (p. 17), there evolved by degrees the Miracle plays, based on either or both Scriptural subjects and episodical sequences from the life of a saint. (In France, but not in England, a distinction is made between a Miracle play and a Mystery play: the latter, properly, represents events taken from the Bible; the former, strictly speaking, deals with incidents in the life of a saint.) The eventual development of the tropes, or additions to the liturgical chant of the Medieval Church, into the Miracle plays resulted in the introduction of songs of lamentation, of new characters, and of traces in the use of the vernacular interpolated in the performances still chanted (almost never spoken) in Latin. Contemporaneously, the subject-matter began to expand beyond merely biblical or apocryphal scenes; the performance not only moved out of the Church into the churchyard, but also crossed the square into the tavern yard; the actors, previously priests, boys, and occasionally nuns, began to obtain the assistance of lay talent. Plays grew into cycles

1 Kirwan, Patrick, *The Dawn of English Drama* (1920), p. 10.
2 Chambers, E. K., *The English Folk Play* (1932).

which serially told the story from the Creation to the Day of Judgment; annual dramatic performances, lasting three or four days, were instituted; and finally the presentation of the collective pageant was taken over by the town guilds, each of which made itself responsible for an episode in the connected cycle. Of these composite cycles, presented at least once a year in the principal cities of England, four in Middle English, differing much in their style and treatment, and one in the native Cymric dialect (the last-named group of pageants is often not counted as a major cycle), have come down in a fairly complete form (besides fragments preserved from other cycles).

### MAJOR CYCLES OF THE "MIRACLE PLAY"

*The Cornish Cycle* (1300—1400). Consists of 50 episodes so arranged into three parts (*Origo Mundi* or "The Origin of the World," *Passio Domini Nostri,* or "The Passion of Christ," *Resurrexio Domini Nostri,* or "The Resurrection of Christ") that each, having an independent unity, could occupy a separate day in the presentation. The only one of the major cycles not composed of distinct pageants. Also represents, except for an epic poem on the Passion of Christ, the extant remains of the ancient Cymric language.

*The Chester Cycle* (1475—1500; but originated, according to many, as early as 1328). Its 25 plays mix the didactic pronouncement of the York cycle with the rustic humor of the Wakefield. Evidence of deliberate cultivation of style and high religious tone suggests that this cycle is of a later date; but possibly the general opinion is that its composition belongs to about the year 1328. Some even attribute it to Higden (p. 61). Less dramatic than the York and Wakefield cycles. Not remarkable as poetry. Possibly influenced by the *Cursor Mundi* (p. 28). Dramatic parallels in the *Mystère du Viel Testament* and in Greban's *Passion.*

*The York Cycle* (1350—1440). Only 48 of the original 54 pageants are extant. General soberness of tone. Probably the most representative of all the cycles. Anticipates in a manner the chronicle play.[1] Takes its name from the city where performed.

*The Wakefield Cycle* (*c.* 1450). Some 32 plays, not all complete. Elements of jocularity, even of vulgarity, and a sense of dramatic value have crowded out the ingredients of religion (present in the York cycle) and the potentialities for pathos. Apparently adapted from a (lost) group of old York plays; but opinion is divided: some believe that the York cycle borrowed from the Wakefield, or the latter from the former; others, that a common source accounts for similarities. Frequently called the *Towneley* cycle because the Towneley family at Towneley Hall in Lancashire once owned it.

Within the cycle is a group so well defined that probably one author composed its four plays.[2] Original characterization and deliberate

1 MacKinnon, Effie, "Notes on the Dramatic Structure of the York Cycle," *Studies in Philology,* XXVIII (1931), pp. 433-449.
2 Carey, Millicent, *The Wakefield Group in the Towneley Cycle* (1930).

humor mark the *Mactacio Abel,* the story of Cain and Abel; effective character depiction occurs in the *Processus Noe,* the story of Noah and the Flood; keener characterization and higher comedy than in the *Prima Pastorum* ("The First Shepherds' Play") dovetail in the *Secunda Pastorum** ("The Second Shepherds' Play"). Superior to all others are these four plays in their homely realism, almost horse-play sense of humor, energetic action, vivid characterization, well-motivated plot, free and wide range of sources, and sure, if crude, sense of technical structure and dramatic power. The author of this group of plays might be called the first English dramatist; (but see pages 88 and 108).

***Ludus Coventriae,*** or ***The Plaie called Corpus Christi*** (*c.* 1468)[1]. Forty-two plays, according to J. O. Halliwell; forty-three, according to E. K. Chambers. Reflects the liturgical drama more closely than the other cycles: its New Testament plays in particular are puritanically doctrinal and humorless, relying often on hymns and paraphrases of Scripture.

### SPECIMENS OF THE "MIRACLE PLAY"

***Ludus de Sancta Katharina*** (*c.* 1110). Earliest miracle play of record performed in England. Probably in Latin or in French. Not extant. (See p. 31.)

***Le Mystère d'Adam*** (*c.* 1150). Incomplete Anglo-Norman semiliturgical drama. Earliest extant play written almost completely in the vernacular. Well-handled characterization, humorous element; spoken rather than sung. Occasional deviation from its Biblical source and relative elaborateness of scenic devices, action, and composition mark the *Adam* as transitional between the liturgical play and the secularized play.

***The Harrowing of Hell*** (*c.* 1250). Perhaps the earliest English miracle[2] play that survives. Describes the *Descensus Christi ad Infernos.* Frequent alliteration of its rimed octosyllabic couplets. (See p. 31.)

1 Professor A. C. Baugh, in a letter, points out that the *Ludus Coventriae* is not a Corpus Christi cycle, for, as the prologue states, the performance was given on Sunday, whereas Corpus Christi Day was always Thursday. The title of the cycle, he continues, was given by James, an early librarian, probably as a conclusion hastily reached through the circumstance that Coventry was in James's day most famous for its old miracle plays.

Such is the consensus to-day. On the strength of an inscription by Richard James, Sir Robert Cotton's librarian who in 1629 had acquired the original manuscript from Robert Hegge, the *Ludus Coventriae* was ascribed, either mistakenly or generically, to Coventry. While the title has been retained since, the *Ludus Coventriae* is not to be confused with the *Coventry Plays,* a civic cycle consisting of two surviving pieces, *The Shearmen and Tailors' Pageant* and *The Weaver's Pageant,* both of which were given annually, on Corpus Christi Day. On the other hand, the conclusion of the prologue of the *Ludus Coventriae* does seem to indicate that the performances were in the hands of a strolling company, and that the plays were acted not by the Grey Friars but rather by craft-guilds. Consult *Ludus Coventriae or The Plaie called Corpus Christi,* edited by Block, K. S. (1922).

2 Dr. Carleton Brown reminds us in a letter that "recent scholars, while recognizing the dramatic character of the dialogue, . . . are far from regarding it as the text of a miracle play." It must not be mistaken for an early miracle play; it was not intended for dramatic representation: see Chambers, E. K., *The Medieval Stage* (1925), Vol. I, p. 81; Vol. II, p. 74.

***Mary Magdalene*** (*c.* 1500). Third of a series of four plays belonging to the so-called *Digby Mysteries*. Combines the elements of the Miracle and of the Morality: scenes from the life of Christ mark it as a Miracle; abstract personages (Flesh, Luxuriance) mark it as a Morality (p. 106). Has been admired for its variety of action. First in English to employ allegorical machinery.

***Noah and the Flood.*** In the *Chester Cycle*. Unsophisticated details about animals and humorous items are mingled with religious history. Version of story occurs in other cycles, the most vivacious being in the Wakefield series.

***Secunda Pastorum.***†* The *Wakefield Cycle* has two versions, this being called *The "Second" Shepherds' Play*. Best Miracle play simultaneously recognized as the first English farce. A play within a play, yet slender in plot. Original in its realistic characterization and dialogue, effective in its comedy, sure in its dramatic treatment of situations. Version of story in other cycles. (See p. 105.)

The Brome ***Abraham and Isaac***† (15th century). Non-cyclical. Manuscript preserved at Brome Manor in Suffolk. Notable for arousing rational emotion and creating melodramatic suspense within its short compass. Absence of secular or native elements. Unrivalled in pathos by any early religious drama. "In the whole range of the Scripture cycles there are only two writers who display any noteworthy sense of dramatic effect—the unknown genius who wrote the "Secunda Pastorum" and a few other pageants of the Townley series, and the equally unknown master of stage-craft who transformed the placid pathos of the Chester Abraham and Isaac into the dynamic scenes of the Brome play."[1]

### Morality Play

The Morality play probably did not originate much earlier than the fourteenth century, and did not become common until the fifteenth. Some 30 examples are extant.

"The Middle Ages had an appetite for allegory quite as vigorous as the liking for legend; and after the saintly legends had been set on the stage as miracle-plays, allegory was also cast into dialogue, and we have the moral plays. The 'morality' was a medieval forerunner of our modern novel-with-a-purpose, as unconvincingly didactic as it is inevitably dull. The morality may even be defined as an attempt to dramatize a sermon, whereas the mystery is simply a dramatization of the text."[2]

---

1 Manly, J. M., "The Miracle Play in Medieval England," *Essays by Divers Hands* (Transactions of the Royal Society of Literature of the United Kingdom), VII (1927), p. 140 (pp. 133-153).

2 Matthews, Brander, "The Medieval Drama," *Modern Philology*, I (1903), p. 91 *f.* (pp. 71-94).

† * Explanation of symbols immediately precedes page one.

| MIRACLE PLAY | VS. | MORALITY PLAY |
|---|---|---|
| 1. **Definition:** Dramatization of episodes in the Bible or of events in the life of a saint or of a martyr. Origin in the religious rites of the Church. See p. 103 ff. | | 1. **Definition:** Dramatization of personified abstractions, generally of Vice warring against Virtue. Possible origins of the Virtues and Vices in St. Paul's Epistle to the Ephesians, in the **Psychomachia**, the **Hamartigenia**, the **Antichristus**; in the **débat** (p. 30) and the **Danse Macabre** (p. 85). |
| 2. Characters of real or supposedly real existence vitally set among the tragic and comic realities of life. | | 2. Characters of personified virtues, vices, mental attributes, and the like, or of universalized types, set in a framework of allegory. |
| 3. Incidents restricted to Biblical stories and sacred personages. Presumably factual. | | 3. Incidents drawn from many sources. Ostensibly fiction. |
| 4. **Theme:** Inevitable punishment engendered by revolt against Divine Guidance. Purpose was to teach obedience to God. | | 4. **Theme:** (Primarily) the struggle for the possession of the Soul, or Mankind, between Vice and Virtue. Purpose was to impart a lesson for guidance through life. |
| 5. Development of character-types. See item 7 below. | | 5. Development of character depiction. See item 7 below. |
| 6. Pointing of the moral always consciously done. | | 6. Pointing of the moral generally not consciously executed. |
| 7. Advancement of the drama through the introduction of the use of the vernacular and through the development within the cycles of a sense of dramatic structure. Bequeathed such character-types as the Devil; Herod, the first comic character on the modern stage; Noah's wife, the first scold. | | 7. Advancement of the drama through the introduction of new characters and through the stimulation of original plot-making. System of characterization evident even to the day of Sheridan (1751-1816). Development of the Vice (whose aliases included Fraud, Ambidexter, Sin, and others) later blended in the character of the stage villain and the stage clown. |
| 8. Performance generally given by lay actors. | | 8. Performances generally given by semi-professional actors. |

## UNIVERSAL MORALITY PLAYS

*Concerned with the discussion of moral problems common to all humanity.*

*The Pride of Life* (early 15th century). Fragmentary: the prologue indicates the argument. Central motive is "The Summons of Death."

*The Castle of Perseverance*† (*c.* 1415). Traditionally accepted as the earliest extant full-scope English Morality. Also the most typical in its struggle between Sin and Holiness for the soul of Mankind and in its medieval ecclesiastical teaching and spirit: exemplifies all three prominent themes known as "The Conflict of the Vices and Virtues," "The Debate of the Four Daughters of God," (Mercy, Truth, Peace, and Righteousness), and "The Summons of Death." Prolix,

†* Explanation of symbols immediately precedes page one.

tedious, graceless, sometimes obscure; but breadth of motive. Mainly in stanzas of thirteen lines riming *abababababaccca,* eleven of the lines having four (the ninth and thirteenth having three) accents. Note, in the prologue for vexillaries, the space left for the name of the place of performance. A Macro Morality: so-called because found with two other plays (*see below*) in the collection of Cox Macro (1683—1767), antiquary, physician, cleric.

***Mind, Will, and Understanding,*** or ***Wisdom*** (*c.* 1460). Dull, protracted, didactic, actionless; fair command of rhythm and good sense of structure. Sometimes entitled *A Morality of Wisdom who is Christ.* A Macro play: see *The Castle of Perseverance* (p. 107).

***Mankind*** (*c.* 1470). Third Macro play, probably adapted from the anonymous poem, *Mercy Passeth Righteousness,* does not possess the good rimes of *Mind, Wit, and Understanding.* However, in its comparative avoidance of pointing a moral and in its dramatic make-up lie the foreshadowing of the Interlude (p. 109).

***Mundus et Infans,*** or ***The World and the Child*** (printed 1522). Interesting for its language and boasting speeches. Preference for alliteration does not obscure the actionless clearness of the theme, as it did in *The Castle of Perseverance.*

***Everyman***† (printed *c.* 1529). Finest of the Moralities. So closely parallels the Dutch play, *Elckerlijk,* attributed to a Petrus Dorlandus, that the English Morality is often regarded as a translation. Plot derived from an old Buddhist parable. Generally in rimed couplets. Not without humor. Frequently revived even in the twentieth century.

***Magnyfycence*** (1515—1523). By **John Skelton** (p. 87 *f.*).

***Ane Pleasant Satyre of the Thrie Estaitis*** (1540). By **Sir David Lyndsay** (p. 90 *f.*).

## LIMITED MORALITY PLAYS

*Concerned with the discussion of moral problems generally less common to universal humanity.*

***Nature***† (*c.* 1495). By **Henry Medwall** (*fl.* 1490), chaplain, playwright; *protégé* of Cardinal Morton. Separation of the play into two parts (containing twenty-two characters) seemingly indicative of the Interlude-type of play (p. 109). Competent versifying, true-to-life dialogue, humorous realism. First morality without a devil.

***Fulgens & Lucres***† (*c.* 1497). By **Henry Medwall** (see preceding play). Probably the earliest known purely secular English

† * Explanation of symbols immediately precedes page one.

play.[1] Double plot: source of serious plot is *De Vera Nobilitate* ("Concerning True Nobility,") a Latin *declamatio* by Bonaccorso of Pistoja (1428); the comic sub-plot is Medwall's. Also divided into two parts, but has only seven characters. "Important document in the history of humanism."[2]

***Hyckescorner*** (possibly late 15th or early 16th century). Imagination and Free Will show Man the Path to Irreligion. Frequently classed as an Interlude (with morality elements).

**Interlude**

With its characters not infrequently as allegorical as in the Morality, and with its comic elements even more pronounced, the Interlude is not always distinguishable from the Morality. A working definition might be that the Interlude is a short play or diverting entertainment designed for presentation either between the acts of the Miracle or the Morality plays or for performance in the intervals at banquets, *fêtes,* or other important festivities. In the restricted sense of a brief, semi-dramatic comedy—where the characters, generally of the humble type, are real, where the actors are limited in number to a handful, and where the humor is farcical or even coarse—it is, according to J. A. Symonds, "the creation of John Heywood." See p. 122.

---

1 *Fulgens & Lucres,* edited by Boas, F. S. and Reed, A. W. (1926). See also Reed, A. W., "Fulgens and Lucres," *The Times* (London), Thursday, April 3, 1919, p. 178, col. 2*f*.

2 Baskervill, C. R., "Conventional Features of Medwall's *Fulgens and Lucres,*" *Modern Philology,* XXIV (1926-1927), p. 419 (pp. 419-442).

## Chapter VIII

# THE RENAISSANCE: THE BEGINNINGS

### MEANING AND SIGNIFICANCE

The term *Renaissance* means, literally and etymologically, a rebirth; without implying previous death, the term is traditionally[1] applied to the intellectual movement that embraced the reawakening of scholarship, the recovery of the ancient learning, the rise of the spirit of religious and scientific inquiry, and, summarily, the self-emancipation of the individual from the thralldom of institutions. By subverting feudalism, the intellectual tyranny of scholasticism, and of the church in secular matters, the transition from medieval to modern methods of study and thought occurred. (More properly, however, *Renaissance* is applied to the revival of Art resulting from the rediscovery and imitation of classical models.)

---

1 Many scholars are now beginning to view the period of the Renaissance as reactionary and even decadent. They contend that the term is a misnomer.
"The ideal of the humanists was in the past; they looked backward not forward; they derided or opposed all progressive or emancipating forces in their own age except those for which some analogy could be found in antiquity."

—Smith, Preserved, *A History of Modern Culture* (1930), I, p. 7 *f*.

"Beneath the surface of brilliant social culture lurked gross appetites and savage passions, unrestrained by mediaeval piety, untutored by modern experience. Italian society exhibited an almost unexampled spectacle of literary, artistic and courtly refinement crossed by brutalities of lust, treasons, poisonings, assassinations, violence. A succession of worldly pontiffs brought the Church into flagrant discord with the principles of Christianity. Steeped in pagan learning, desirous of imitating the manners of the ancients, thinking and feeling in harmony with Ovid and Theocritus, and at the same time rendered cynical by the corruption of papal Rome, the educated classes lost their grasp upon morality . . . . The Christian virtues were scorned by the foremost actors and the ablest thinkers of the time, while the antique virtues were themes for rhetoric rather than moving springs of conduct . . . . At the height of the Renaissance the five great Powers in the peninsula formed a confederation of independent but mutually attractive and repellent states. Equilibrium was maintained by diplomacy, in which the humanists played a foremost part, casting a network of intrigue over the nation which helped in no small measure to stimulate intelligence and create a common medium of culture, but which accustomed statesmen to believe that everything could be achieved by wire-pulling. Wars were conducted on a showy system by means of mercenaries, who played a safe game in the field and developed a system of bloodless campaigns."

—Symonds, J. A., "The Revival of Learning in Italy," p. 128 (pp. 125-128), article on *The Renaissance* (pp. 122-135) in *The Encyclopaedia Britannica* (Fourteenth Edition), XIX (1930). See also Preserved Smith's attached conclusion to the same article, p. 134. (Note 2, page 112 of the *Outline-History*.)

The most famous two names associated with the beginnings of the movement are Petrarch (1304—1374) and Boccaccio (1313—1375)[1]; the former Italian wrote poetry filled with the new classical spirit, discovered two previously unknown orations of Cicero, and constructed the first modern map of Italy; the latter wrote a book of tales also filled with the modern spirit, was the first western scholar to read Homer in the original, and prepared the first dictionaries of classical geography and mythology. From Italy the movement spread through Germany, Spain, France, the Netherlands, England, Scotland.

## INFLUENCES LEADING TO THE RENAISSANCE

### Humanism

Strictly applies to the revival of interest in the classic literature of Greece and Rome. It put emphasis upon the worldliness of this life, not upon the other-worldliness of the life to come; it aimed to recapture an appreciation of classical antiquity by using the *litterae humaniores,* or humane studies, as a rule of life for modern use: its fundamental precept was the law of measure, the *Est modus in rebus* ("There is a measure in things") of Horace or, better still, the *Quam sit satis* ("What may be enough" or "Nothing too much") of Seneca. Pagan in its revulsion from medieval mysticism and symbolism, in its rebellion against the bondage of intellectual and ecclesiastical authority, it aimed at liberating the free human personality.

### Rise of Geographical Discovery

Great era of exploration included Bartholomeu Diaz (1487), Columbus (1492), Vasco da Gama (1497—1499), the Cabots (1497 and 1498), Fernando Magellan (1519—1521), Hernando Cortez (1519—1521), and Francisco Pizarro (1533).[2]

### Invention of Printing

The contemporaneous discovery of the art of printing by movable type (1438—1450), as well as new methods of manufacturing paper, coming so opportunely, disseminated the new learning over Europe. For the first time it made the *littérateur* independent of patrons.[3]

### The Copernican System

Nikolaus Copernicus (1473—1543), Polish astronomer, published his *De Revolutionibus Orbium,* the first work to draw distinct attention

---

1 Note their dates of birth and death. While the Renaissance is generally regarded as the period of history dating from 1453, the Fall of Constantinople, to 1603, the death of Queen Elizabeth, the Renaissance really began at least a century earlier.

2 See Thompson, J. W., "Exploration and Discovery during the Renaissance," pp. 5-42, *The Civilization of the Renaissance* (1929), edited by Thompson, J. W., Rowley, George, Schevill, Ferdinand, and Sarton, George. See also Hudson, W. H., "The Age of Discovery and Invention," (Chap. II, pp. 15-29), in *The Story of the Renaissance* (1924).

3 Binns, L. E., *The History of the Decline and Fall of the Medieval Papacy* (1934), p. 268.

to the fact that the earth and other planets move round the sun as a center. He upset traditional theology and science, for his theory made the earth merely " a restless midge hurtling through space," and man but "an atom in the scheme of things."[1]

### Fall of Constantinople

Constantinople was captured by the Turks in 1453; many Greek scholars, among whom were Demetrius Chalcondyles, Constantine Lascaris, and Andreas Joannes Lascaris, found shelter in Italy. It is a mistake, however, to believe that the revival of the study of Greek in the West dated from the Fall, for at least a half dozen Greek scholars had come to Italy before that date.

### The Revolt Against Authority: The Reformation[2]

The Reformation was a logical result of the questioning spirit of the Renaissance, which bored into the dogmatic and repressive practices of the Church. Chief issue was the denial of the authority of a universal church and a reliance on the dictates of the individual conscience. Among the leaders were Luther, Calvin, Knox, and Huss. (In 1529 the reformers in Germany presented a protest—hence the name *Protestant*—to the Diet of Spires.)

## THE RENAISSANCE IN ENGLAND

### The Oxford Group

Thomas Linacre (*c.* 1460—1524) and William Grocyn (*c.* 1446—1519), returning from Florence, introduced the "New Learning" at Oxford. A few years later John Colet (see p. 99), an Oxford graduate like the others, also studied in Florence; upon returning, he was among the first to introduce the new studies into the English secondary school. But little impression was made by this new learning, imported in the closing years of the fifteenth century. They were helped in their task

---

1 Berdan, J. M., *Early Tudor Poetry* (1920), p. 24.

2 Frederick Nietzsche's view, that, the Reformation was a reactionary movement against the Italian Renaissance, is now quite generally accepted. Preserved Smith calls attention to the scholarly consensus "that the spirit of the Renaissance was largely secular and that of the Reformation intensely religious, that the former was tolerant and often indifferent and sceptical and that the latter was usually intolerant, devout, and sometimes superstitious, that the humanists were aristocratic and the Reformers democratic in method, and that Puritanism proved hostile to and often destructive of the artistic and pleasure-seeking interests of the Renaissance. In criticism of this view, however, it has been contended that the Renaissance was not, any more than the Reformation, consciously progressive; rather did both movements find their ideal in the past, the one in the golden age of Rome and the other in the primitive age of Christianity. It has been further shown that the humanists did little to emancipate the reason from authority; they were closely bound by their own authorities in the classical poets and orators, and could only attack the schoolmen on the basis of the ancient pagans as the Reformers attacked them from the standpoint of the ancient Fathers. In conclusion one may say that neither movement was a conscious appeal to reason or an intentional step forward and away from the past, but that each accomplished, undesignedly, a great work of emancipation and that each created new cultural values."

—*The Encyclopaedia Britannica* (Fourteenth Edition), XIX (1930), p. 134. See Note 1, page 110 of the *Outline-History.*

by Desiderius Erasmus (*c.* 1465—1536), the great Dutch humanist, who taught Greek at Cambridge (1511—1514). About this time, too, John Colet, now Dean of St. Paul's Church, endowed the cathedral school of St. Paul's in London (1510), the first school in England expressly devoted to the "New Learning." But the most important of the English humanists was Sir Thomas More (p. 113).

### The English Reformation

The foundations of the English national church had been laid before the reign of Henry VIII; *e. g.*, in the utterances of Wyclif (p. 52), and from time to time in the assertions of English statesmen for a free National Church. Then came the nominal struggle over the divorce of Henry VIII from Catherine of Aragon. In 1533 Cranmer (p. 149), Archbishop of Canterbury, pronounced null and void this marriage, disregarding the decision of Pope Clement VII; in 1534, England renounced the sovereignty of the Pope, and the Parliament passed the Act of Supremacy declaring the King and his successors to be the protectors and the only supreme heads of the English Church; and, finally, in 1535, Henry VIII was formally proclaimed the supreme head of the English Church. Four years later (1539) the Parliament passed the Six Articles, described by Foxe (p. 117) as the "whip with six strings" and reaffirming the main principles in Catholic doctrine; ten years later, declared the Act of Uniformity in public worship and adopted the Book of Common Prayer (1549). The Forty-two Articles, set forth in 1553, were subsequently revised: thirty-eight were adopted in 1563, and the thirty-ninth in 1571. For three and a half centuries the Thirty-nine Articles continued in force. Finally, upon the succession of Mary Tudor, daughter of Henry VIII and Catherine of Aragon, Catholicism was revived, and until her death Protestants were mercilessly persecuted.

## *EDUCATIONAL AND RELIGIOUS WORKS*

**Sir Thomas More,** 1478—1535, author, scholar, judge, politician, ambassador, statesman. Son of a barrister who later rose to be a justice of the court of King's Bench. In the household of Cardinal Morton, Archbishop of Canterbury (1489). At Oxford, where he was possibly a pupil of Colet, Grocyn, and Linacre (*c.* 1492). Entered at New Inn, London (*c.* 1494); at Lincoln's Inn (1496). Beginning of friendship with Erasmus (*c.* 1497). For a few years disciplined himself according to the regime of the Carthusian monk (1499—1503), but finally chose the worldly in preference to the ascetic life. Member of Parliament (1504). Marriage (1505) with Jane Colt (Cult, Colte) of Newhall, in Essex, who gave him three daughters and one son. Visited (1508) by Erasmus at Bucklersbury, where at his host's suggestion the Dutch humanist wrote the satire *Encomium Moriae* ("The Praise of Folly"). Became bencher of Lincoln's Inn (1509). Under-sheriff of London (1510). A month or two after the death of Jane, he married Alice Middleton, a widow with one daughter (*c.* 1511). Ambassador to Flanders (1515). Privy Councilor (1518). Knighted (1521). Subtreasurer to the King (1521). Speaker of House of Commons (1523). Chancellor of the Duchy of Lancaster (1525). Appointed, against his own wish, to the office of Lord Chancellor, succeeding Wolsey (1529). First layman to hold that office. Resigned the Great Seal, in disapproval of Henry's projected divorce from Catherine of Aragon (1532). While willing to swear political fidelity to the King by subscribing to the new Act of Supremacy, More refused to take oath that would impugn the Pope's spiritual authority and affirm the justice of the King's divorce. Committed to the Tower (April 17, 1534). Beheaded for high treason (July 7, 1535). More was always pious; so much so, in fact, that it led him to be merciless in his persecution of heretics.[1] He "literally laid down his life to prevent an old Church from being eradicated and supplanted by a new one."[2] Was canonized by Pius XI in 1935.

His Latin writings reveal a copiousness and scholarship flavored by elegance, wit, and personal touches. In the vernacular he writes in the middle style--his English is moderate, direct, unpoetic; vigorous, dignified, sanely sensible, playful, almost nervous; also redundant and occasionally affected by Latin idiom. While his spiritual earnestness is apparent, also he is frequently prejudiced, abusive, and scurrilous.

• ***Utopia***† (Latin, 1515—1516; Englished freely by Ralph Robynson, 1551). Political essay-romance in two books describes an imaginary commonwealth—its ideals of political and social order, of education, of religion, of statecraft, all approximating perfection. Book I is more sober, factual, and polemical, but less romantic, than Book II: both, however, are based essentially on the idea of community of goods, and on the philosophy of sacrificing the individual to the common good.[3] Fertile inventio ı, practical imagination, wittily-phrased satire poignant in its sympathetic message. "Certainly as an artist, More was the master of Defoe and Swift and neither excelled him in 'the art of feigning.' "[4] Influenced by Amerigo Vespucci's account of his voyages, by Plato's *Republic,* St. Augustine's *De Civitate Dei,* Erasmus's *Institutio Principis Christiani.*[5]

---

1 That he preached tolerance in his Utopia, but persecuted reformers in England, is the traditional view. See, however, Gairdner, James, *The English Church in the Sixteenth Century from the Accession of Henry VIII to the Death of Mary* (1903), pp. 130-132; Chambers, R. W., "The Saga and the Myth of Sir Thomas More," *Proceedings of the British Academy,* XII (1926), pp. 189-196 (pp. 179-225).

2 Daly, J. J., *A Cheerful Ascetic and Other Essays* (1931), "Sir Thomas More: Saint and Humorist," p. 41 (pp. 41-52).

3 Kautsky, Karl, *Thomas More and his Utopia* (Translated by Stenning, H. J., 1927).

4 *Sir Thomas More's Utopia* (1904; reprinted 1927), edited by Collins, Churton, Preface, p. III, Introduction, p. XLI.

5 Sherwin, P. F., "Some Sources of More's Utopia," *Bulletin of the University of New Mexico,* Whole No. 88, I, No. 3 (1917).

† • Explanation of symbols immediately precedes page one.

In More's Utopia (meaning "No place" in Greek) the modern point of view is frequently anticipated; *e. g.*, that concerning penology, religious toleration, and the socialization of the curriculum. Specifically, streets were twenty feet wide, and every house had a garden; pre-marital investigations were the order of the day (*e. g.*, men and women contemplating matrimony exhibit their naked bodies to one another); opposition to organized war was emphasized (*e. g.*, the Utopians carried arms only to defend themselves or to assist others against oppression).

Other ideal commonwealths are described in Bacon's *New Atlantis* (1626), Campanella's *Civitas Solis* (*c.* 1630), Hobbes's *Leviathan* (1651), Harrington's *Oceana* (1656), Bulwer-Lytton's *The Coming Race* (1871), Bellamy's *Looking Backward* (1888), William Morris's *News from Nowhere* (1891), W. D. Howells's *A Traveler from Altruria* (1894), H. G. Wells's *A Modern Utopia* (1905) and *The World Set Free* (1914).

*English Writings of Sir Thomas More*[1]

***The Lyfe of John Picus, Earle of Mirandula*** (1510). Translation from the original Latin. Important because the man influenced More.

***Historie of Richard the Third*** (*c.* 1516; correctly printed, 1557).[2] First modern historical narrative in English. Colloquial, witty, dignified, restrained prose; dramatic dialogue. Probably based on a Latin work by Cardinal Morton, to whom even this English version is not infrequently attributed. Like his *Utopia,* it attacks the non-moral statecraft of his day.

***Supplycacyon of Soulys*** (1529). Answer in two parts to Simon Fish's *A Supplication for the Beggars* (an attack upon the clerics, their pluralism, nepotism, and simony) defends the laws for the punishment of heretics. (Simon Fish was one among many who attacked the clergy as an *imperium in imperio,* not only as a body privileged locally but also as one truckling to a foreign lord, the Pope.)

***An Apologye of Syr Thomas More*** (1533). Defends his own practice of polemics and his own actions that often aroused criticism. Less scurrilous and more moderate in tone than usual.

***A Dyaloge of Comfort against Tribulacion*** (1533). Written in prison. Nowhere else is his personal note so dominant.

1 *The English Works of Sir Thomas More,* edited by Campbell, W. E., Reed, A. W., Chambers, R. W., and Doyle-Davidson, W. A. G. (Volume II, 1927; Volume I, 1931); Doyle-Davidson, W. A. G., "The Earlier English Works of Sir Thomas More," *English Studies* (Amsterdam), XVII (1935), pp. 4-70.

2 Pollard, A. F., "The Making of Sir Thomas More's *Richard III,*" *Historical Essays in Honour of James Tait,* edited by Edwards, J. G., Galbraith, V. H., and Jacob, E. F. (1933), pp. 223-238.

**Sir Thomas Elyot,** *c.* 1490—1546, author, member of Parliament, diplomat, Greek scholar, Erasmian. Wrote Platonic dialogues, translated numerous classical works.

***The Boke named the Governour*** (1531). Earliest English treatise on moral philosophy and on the theory of education. Principal design to outline the ideal education necessary for a gentleman who hoped to hold office at the Court. Favors a monarchy in preference to either an aristocracy or a democracy. Part of detailed course includes Latin and Greek, and participation in the sports of wrestling and riding. Ethics much like that of Francesco Patrizzi's *De Regno et regis institutione;* derived to some extent from Machiavelli's *Prince* (1513), and Castiglione's *Il Cortegiano* (1518); influenced by Plato and Xenophon. Famous story of "Titus and Gysippus" (Bk. II, Chap. XII) less likely derived from Boccaccio's *Decameron* (X, 8) than from Petrus Alphonsus's *Disciplina Clericalus*: story probably influenced Lyly's *Euphues* (p. 150). Clear style, wealth of anecdote and allusion, stately elocution, practical approach; occasionally tedious. Obtained for author his appointment as ambassador to Charles V.

***The Castel of Health*** (1534). Popular work on medicine written in English by a layman for laymen; unprecedented occurrence aroused protest from the medical fraternity. Based on the Greek Galen and other ancient writers.

***The Dictionary of Syr T. Eliot, knight*** (1538, 1545). First complete Latin-English dictionary. Basis of Thomas Cooper's *Thesaurus.*

***The Doctrine of Princes*** (1534). Valuable contribution to the study of political science and a contributory influence to the euphuistic style before being given its permanent stamp by Lyly (p. 150).

**Roger Ascham,** 1515—1568, classical author, pioneer in the English language, "first English exemplar of polished epistolary correspondence." First Greek lecturer on the Socratic dialogues at Cambridge. Tutor to Princess Elizabeth, to whom as Queen he was later Latin Secretary. First great writer in the vernacular on practical education: catholicity of spirit, geniality of wit; thoroughly English in his love of labor and in his regard for children. Memorable for having anathematized *The Canterbury Tales* and the *Morte d'Arthur* (pp. 70, 92).

***Toxophilus*** (1545). Patriotic treatise, in Platonic dialogue form between Philologus (a lover of learning) and Toxophilus (a lover of archery), in defense of the art of shooting in times of peace as well as of war, and in advocacy of physical training in education. Valuable for technical details of archery, even to the specification as to the species of goose from the wing of which the best feathers are to be plucked for the shaft. His attack on gambling shows, according to

Andrew Lang, "a rather unholy knowledge of all the tricks of the dice-board." Preface urges the use of English in scholarly writing, thereby anticipating the final victory of the vernacular over Latin. Clarity of prose; more Latinized than idiomatic.

*The Scholemaster* (1570). First important English treatise on education. Two chapters; one, a general discussion of pedagogy; the other, the ready way of learning Latin. Urges that patience, gentleness, and love are a better inducement to learning than a beating (the olive branch versus the birch rod); discards the use of foreign terms; and, crowning all, presents in the second chapter the double translation method of teaching Latin. Straightforward, if graceless, prose; sparing utilization of "alliteration's artful aid" and of antithetic clauses, the excessive use of which later weighted down the works of Lyly. Wide reading exemplified by references to about 250 different men in its some 50,000 words.[1]

**John Foxe,** 1516—1587, pamphleteer, prebendary of Salisbury, martyrologist. Preached famous sermon, "On Christ Crucified" (1570). Numerous controversial and other works.

*Actes and Monuments of these Latter and Perilous Times* (first English edition, 1563). Popularly known as *The Book of Martyrs.* History of the Christian martyrs of all ages, particularly of the Protestant martyrs of Mary's reign. Scholarly vocabulary, vivid and occasionally eloquent style, dramatic dialogues. So often distorted that it is neither history nor literature, but rather propaganda against Catholicism.

**Thomas Wilson,** *c.* 1525—1581, Dean of Durham, Member of Parliament, Master in the Court of Requests, Ambassador to the Netherlands, Secretary of State in 1579. Frequently called Sir Thomas Wilson, although he was never knighted.

*The Arte of Rhetorique* (1553). First modern treatise on English composition; the ideas on the subject derived from Latin rhetoricians (Bks. I—II from Quintilian, Bk. III from Cicero as well as Quintilian). Derides "any strange or inkhorn terms," pleads for a simple prose style that avoids affectations and Latinisms. Sane criticism in an anecdotal, and in a clear, somewhat florid[2] style. It has been noted that, as in all his other works, so even here is definite proof of his support of the Reformation.

---

1 Patterson, Herbert, "The Humanism of Roger Ascham," *The Pedagogical Seminary,* XXII (1915), pp. 546-551.

2 Craig, Hardin, "Shakespeare and Wilson's *Arte of Rhetorique,* An Inquiry into the Criteria for Determining Sources," *Studies in Philology,* XXVIII (1931), pp. 86-98.

**Richard Hooker,** *c.* 1554—1600, savant, philosophical theologian, divine. Deputy professor of Hebrew at Oxford. Held the living of St. Mary's at Drayton-Beauchamp, Buckinghamshire (1584). Master of the Temple (1585—1591). Rector of Bascombe, Wiltshire (1591); and of Bishopsbourne, Kent (1595). Sometimes considered as having introduced the ornament of figures into English prose; certainly emphasized the "periodic style."

*Of the Laws of Ecclesiastical Polity* (completed 1593; published Bks. I—IV, 1594; V, 1597; VI, VIII, 1648; VII, 1662). Scholarly, reasoned defense of the Anglican Church as against the Presbyterian. Extensive learning, breadth of vision, cogent argument, and an essential moderation of tone definitely free from rancor. Self-restraint, balance; choice and learned vocabulary heighten homely and quiet power; logical transitions prevent a break in swinging, often soaring, always carefully constructed and musically rich, order of majestic sentences. Occasional appearance of coined words and Latinized construction. Hooker is as ponderous as Pecock (p. 94), as precise and full in expressing complex attitudes and subtle doctrines; but in pursuing expository argument similar to that used by Pecock against the Lollards, Hooker weaves subordinate phrases generally entertaining in their luxuriance, and is more eloquent and majestic. (Of the last four books, often challenged as unauthentic, the eighth, on political science, has been the subject of most controversy.)

## *THE NEW POETRY*

**Sir Thomas Wyatt the Elder,** *c.* 1503—1542, poet, courtier, ambassador, alleged lover of Queen Anne Boleyn; died of a fever. A derivative genius: influenced by Clément Marot in his lyric poems, by Luigi Alamanni in his three Horatian satires in *terza rima* (possibly his most famous is *Of the Mean and Sure Estate*), by Pietro Aretino in his versions of the Penitential Psalms in both *ottava rima* (*abababcc*) and *terza rima,* by Serafino d'Aquilano in his thirty-one epigrams in *ottava rima,* and, most important, by Petrarch and Jacopo Sannazaro in his sonnet-patterns. Some ninety-six poems.[1]

Wyatt's *"Sonnets."* With Henry Howard, Earl of Surrey, Wyatt introduced the sonnet into English; but because the patterns were derived from Petrarch and Sannazaro through Saint-Gelais and other French poets, Wyatt is more French than English, Gallic in his insouciance. Conventional Petrarchan love-themes embellished by conceits and woven with antics are redeemed by a melancholy and sweet-

1 Wyatt's "characteristic principles" have been "falsified" or "obliterated" as they appear in *Tottel's Miscellany* and in most general anthologies. See Shephard, O. H., "Sir Thomas Wyatt." *Papers of the Manchester Literary Club,* LVI (1930), pp. 30-52.

ness, touches of grace and beauty, deeper earnestness of passion than Surrey, and a spontaneous, virile, and intense lyricism. Petrarch's rime-arrangement is generally either *abba abba cdcdcd* or *abba abba cdecde;* but Wyatt often departs from the set rime-scheme of fourteen iambic pentameter lines by ending his sonnets with a final couplet, a very uncommon, if not inadmissible, variation in Italian; thus, the rime-scheme of the majority of his sonnets is *abba abba cddc ee.* Examples of his sonnets: *The Lover Compareth His State to a Ship in Perilous Storm Tossed on the Sea; A Renouncing of Love; The Lover Having Dreamed of Enjoying of His Love, Complaineth that the Dream Is not Either Longer or Truer.*

**Henry Howard, Earl of Surrey,** *c.* 1516—1547, poet, courtier, soldier, envoy; executed for treason. Sonnets, lyrics, elegies, translations, paraphrases of the Psalms (VIII, LV, LXXIII, LXXXVIII) and of Ecclesiastes (Bks. I—IV). Memorable for elegiac tribute, *A Praise of Sir Thomas Wyat the elder, for his excellent learning;* and for the lines on the death of the Duke of Richmond (1546). More fluent, spontaneously sweet, light-hearted, and excitable than Wyatt; quicker eye for external nature, less imitative and more dramatic. Wyatt remodeled the iambic pentameter line, and introduced the "poulter's measure"; Surrey not only popularized the latter and established the later so-called Shakespearean sonnet, but also introduced blank verse. (The "poulter's measure," the common time of the hymn book, was a favorite: the couplet consisted of an Alexandrine, or line of twelve syllables, followed by one of fourteen: poulterers give between twelve and fourteen for a dozen.)

Surrey's *"Sonnets."* Co-founder with Wyatt of the English sonnet; but Surrey modified the Petrarchan form by substituting three alternately riming quatrains, and a concluding independently-rimed couplet to epitomize the thought: thus (prevailingly), *abab cdcd efef gg* (the first example of the so-called English or Shakespearean rim scheme). Conventional, possibly insincere, subjects; artificial diction. Many of his love-poems addressed to "Geraldine," or Elizabeth Fitzgerald, youngest daughter of the ninth earl of Kildare (see under Nash, p. 143). Examples of his sonnets: *Description of Spring, wherein Each Thing Renews Save Only the Lover; Description and Praise of His Love Geraldine; Complaint of a Lover Rebuked; Complaint of a Lover Disdained; A Complaint by Night of the Lover Not Beloved.*

***Certain Bokes of Virgiles Aeneis turned into English meter*** (1557). Translation of Books II and IV introduced blank verse into English. Influenced by the texts of Nicolo Luburnio (1534), Cardinal Ippolito de' Medici (1539), and Gawain Douglas (p. 90). Homely virility, spirited succinctness, picturesque fidelity.

**Richard Tottel,** *d.* 1594, printer, stationer.

***Songes and Sonnettes, written by the ryght honorable Lorde Henry Howarde, late Earle of Surrey, and others*** (1557). Commonly goes by the name of *Tottel's Miscellany.* First printed anthology of English lyrics. Tottel probably assisted in the compiling by Nicholas Grimald (1519—1562), a poet who contributed to the miscellany. Only important poets included are Wyatt (p. 118) and Surrey (p. 119), the latter undoubtedly singled out for mention on the title-page because of his high rank. Historically important collection of 271 poems, published on June 5, 1557, dates the beginnings of modern English poetry.

*Tottel's Miscellany* set the vogue for similar collections. Among the best are *The Paradyse of Daynty Devices* (1576), a generally moralizing collection gathered by Richard Edwards (*c.* 1523—1566) and published posthumously; *A Gorgious Gallery of Gallant Inventions* (1578); *A Handefull of Pleasant Delights* (1591); *Brittons Bowre of Delights* (1591); *The Phoenix Nest* (1593); *The Arbor of Amorous Deuises* (*c.* 1594); *England's Parnassus* (1600); *A Poetical Rhapsody* (1602), compiled by Francis Davison (*fl.* 1602) and his brother Walter. *The Passionate Pilgrim* (1599), contains Marlowe's "Come Live with me and be my Love," and five pieces by Shakespeare; *The Phoenix and the Turtle* (p. 163) contains thirteen four-line stanzas attributed to Shakespeare. The best collection is *England's Helicon* (1600), which includes the work of Spenser, Marlowe, Ralegh, Lodge, Greene, Sidney, and other poets.

## THE NEW DRAMA

**John Bale,** 1495—1563, author. Bishop of Ossory (1552). Wrote mysteries and miracle plays.

***Kynge Johan*** (*c.* 1540—1548). If not the first English historical play, it does mark the transition between the Morality (or possibly the Interlude) and the historical play proper. Reveals a Protestant bias: practically an adaptation of the old play of *Antichrist.* Characters include: Dissimulation (Simon of Swynsett), Private Wealth (Cardinal Pandulph?), Usurped Power (the Pope?).

**Nicholas Udall,** *c.* 1505—1556, schoolmaster, translator, playwright. Educated at Winchester College (1517); at Corpus Christi, Oxford (1520). Arrested (1526) for possession of Tindale's New Testament (p. 148). M. A. (1534). Magister Informator (head-master) of Eton (1534—1541). Master of Westminster School (1555). Translated two books of Erasmus's Apophthegmes; collaborated upon translation of Erasmus's *Paraphrases* of the Gospels.

***Ralph Roister Doister*****†*** (*c.* 1553; printed *c.* 1566). Generally considered the earliest extant "regular" comedy in the language. Regular plot divided into five acts and a number of scenes observes the unities

† * Explanation of symbols immediately precedes page one.

of action, time, and place. Characters and incidents modelled upon Roman comedy; but with original departures in plot, incidents, and dialogue. Character-parallels in Plautus, and especially in Terence's *Eunuchus.* Roister Doister is Plautus's *Miles gloriosus,* possibly blended with Terence's portrait of Thraso; Merygreeke is the typical parasite. While unsubtly depicted, yet the characters are more individualized than their conventional counterparts. Raciness of language enhanced by the short, rough, riming jingles. Parallel to prologue appears in Wilson's *Arte of Rhetorique*[1] (p. 117).

**William Stevenson,** *d.* 1575, playwright. Fellow of Christ's College, Cambridge (1559—1561; possibly also 1551—1554). Ordained deacon in London (1552). Prebendary of Durham (1561).

***Gammer Gurton's Needle*†*** (1556; printed 1575).[2] Second English comedy in verse. Only extant vernacular University comedy. Loose doggerel, effective construction, broad realism; indigenous dialogue, lifelike characters, abundant humor. Opens second act with famous Elizabethan song the refrain of which is, "Backe, and syde go bare, go bare." Influenced by classical Latin comedy. Larger element of more truly English local realism than in *Ralph Roister Doister* (p. 120).

**Thomas Sackville,** *c.* 1536—1608, dramatist, poet, ambassador; first Earl of Dorset, Baron Buckhurst. Dignified poetry, master of the rime royal stanza, grand style, elegiac spirit.

***Gorboduc,*** or ***Ferrex and Porrex*†*** (1561—1562). First English tragedy and the first play written in blank verse. Written with Thomas Norton. Wooden Senecan tragedy, while not strictly observing the unities of time and place, follows Senecan practices; *e. g.,* the use of protracted declamations of chorus at the end of each act, (more reminiscent of the Morality than of Seneca) the use of messengers, and the division into five acts. Immediate source possibly Grafton's *Chronicle* (1556); but see Geoffrey of Monmouth for ultimate source (p. 43).

***Induction*†** (1563). Contributed to *A Mirror for Magistrates.* Only work of merit in the collection is by Sackville. *Induction* consists of seventy-nine stanzas in rime royal. Influenced by Dante. Hallam speaks of it as a noble poem uniting the school of Chaucer and Lydgate to that of Spenser's *Faerie Queene;* Sidney Lee calls it the greatest English poem between Chaucer and Spenser. Note, however, the overwrought and hollow rhetoric of emotion.

---

1 Were it not for Wilson's added reference in the third edition of his *Arte of Logique,* the first textbook on the subject in English, *Ralph Roister Doister* might have remained an anonymous play. See Reed, A. W., "Nicholas Udall and Thomas Wilson," *The Review of English Studies,* I (1925), p. 278 (pp. 275-283).

2 Authorship of play is in dispute. Has also been attributed to John Still, *c.* 1543-1608, Bishop of Bath and Wells in 1593; and to Dr. John Bridges, Bishop of Oxford, possibly a coadjutor.

† * Explanation of symbols immediately precedes page one.

*The Complaint of Henry, Duke of Buckingham* (1563). Second contribution to *A Mirror for Magistrates.* Notable three stanzas beginning with "Midnight was come, and every vital thing."

**John Heywood,** *c.* 1497—*c.* 1580, dramatist, epigrammatist.[1] Master of a choir-school at the Court. As a writer of the Interlude (p. 109), he bridges the gap between the abstractions and homiletic purposes of the old Moralities and the *Comédie Humaine* of the modern drama.

*The Play of Love** (*c.* 1518). A double *débat* (p. 30), generally wearying rather than entertaining.

*The Play of the Wether** (*c.* 1521). Dramatic. Plot of less consequence than the dialogue. *Merry-Report,* the fool, is essentially a Vice (see p. 107).

*The Pardoner and the Frere* (*c.* 1521). Slight plot of comedy, possibly by Heywood, satirizes the hangers-on of the Church. Simple structure; but given to horseplay in dialogue. For sources, see *The Four P's* (on this page).

*Johan, Tyb his Wife, and Sir Jhan the preest* (1533). Effective farce, attributed to Heywood, about a henpecked husband and a priest-paramour. Most dramatic work may also be the first English "triangle" play. Source possibly the French *Farce nouvelle tresbonne et fort ioyeuse de Pernet qui va au vin.*[2]

*A Dialogue concerning Witty and Witless** (printed 1562). Influenced by Erasmus's *Encomium Moriae* ("The Praise of Folly").

*The Four P's*†* (printed 1569). Interlude-play. Broad, native humor; witty doggerel verse. Part-debate, it is somewhat long-winded; part-romance, it paradoxically lacks action. Satirizes the corrupt practices of the Roman Communion. Source probably a French *sottie,* the *Farce nouvelle d'un Pardonneur, d'un Triacleur, et d'une Tavernière,* and Chaucer's *Canterbury Tales.* Play has been doubtfully assigned to William Cornyshe (or Cornish), the master of the Chapel Royal.[3]

*John Heywoodes workes.* Includes ballads, a dialogue containing effectual proverbs in the English tongue concerning marriages, and four collections totaling about six hundred proverbs.

**George Gascoigne,** *c.* 1527—1577, courtier, soldier, member of Parliament. Versatile in literature; pioneer in the use of blank verse; forerunner of Lyly. Devotional treatises, penitential pamphlets, translations, sonnets. Moralizing yet immoral poet.

---

1 Bolwell, R. W., *The Life and Works of John Heywood* (1921).

2 Young, Karl, "The Influence of French Farce upon the Plays of John Heywood," *Modern Philology,* II (1904-1905), pp. 97-124.

3 Wallace, C. W., *The Evolution of the English Drama up to Shakespeare* (1912), pp. 51-53, 80-83." See also Reed, A. W., *Early Tudor Drama* (1926), pp. 94-96.

† * **Explanation of symbols immediately precedes page one.**

***The Supposes*** (1566). Earliest extant comedy in English prose. In general, this sense-adaptation of Ariosto's *Gli Suppositi* (prose), and *I Suppositi* (verse), introduced into English the romantic domestic comedy of intrigue. Sentimental under-plot of Bianca and her lovers in Shakespeare's *Taming of the Shrew* (p. 192) apparently stems from this prose comedy. Sportive, vigorous, varied and comic plot. Frequent alliteration and incidental antithetic structure are its anticipatory traces of Euphuism (p. 151). "It conducts a romantic intrigue in a realistic fashion through a world of actualities."

***Jocasta*** (1566). Second earliest English tragedy in blank verse is a close paraphrase of Ludovico Dolce's *Giocasta* (1549), an Italian adaptation of probably a Latin version of Euripides's *Phoenissae.* Possibly the first English translation of Greek tragedy. Witty, conversational dialogue; patched-up blank verse, not infrequent grossness. (Co translator is Francis Kinwelmersh, responsible for Acts I and IV.)

***Certayne Notes of Instruction Concerning the Making of Verse or Rhyme in English*** (1575). Earliest wholly critical essay on English prosody. Generally sound: be sparing of poetical license and alliteration; use words in their accustomed order, without unnatural stress in the line; avoid commonplaces; abstain from Latin inversions. Describes the "poulter's measure"—the twelve and fourteener-lines in which he excelled.

***Steele Glas*** (1576). Generally regarded as the earliest regular blank verse satire. The crystal mirrors then in vogue flattered rather than reflected the truth: by holding up the old-fashioned metal mirror, Gascoigne purposed to reveal the vices of contemporaneous manners.

***A Lover's Lullaby.*** Famous lyric.

## Chapter IX

# THE BEGINNINGS OF THE RENAISSANCE
# EDMUND SPENSER

**Edmund Spenser,** *c.* 1552—1599, poet. Elder son of John Spenser, probably a journeyman in the art of cloth-making. His mother's Christian name was Elizabeth. Connected with "An house of auncient fame," the Spencers of Althorp in Northamptonshire. Edmund was educated at the Merchant Taylor's School, of which Richard Mulcaster was headmaster from 1561 to 1586. Proceeded as a sizar to Pembroke Hall, Cambridge (1569); B. A., 1573; M. A., 1576. At Cambridge became close friend of Gabriel Harvey, through whom he probably obtained a place in the household of Robert Dudley, Earl of Leicester, Queen Elizabeth's favorite (1578). He had already been secretary to Dr. John Young, Bishop of Rochester. Together with Sir Philip Sidney, nephew of the Earl, he was a member of the *Areopagus,*[1] a *cénacle* that attempted to make over English versification by substituting for rime and accentual meter the Greek and Latin system based on exact quantity of syllables. Appointed private secretary to Lord Grey of Wilton, the newly-designated Lord Deputy of Ireland (1580). Thenceforth lived mostly in Ireland. Mainly in Dublin (1582—1586). Appointed Clerk of the Chancery for the Faculties in Dublin (1581), succeeding Ludowick Bryskett, author of *A Discourse of Civil Life, Containing the Ethic Part of Moral Friendship,* important as a memorial to their friendship. Deputy to Bryskett in the clerkship of the Council of Munster (1585), whom he succeeded as clerk (1589). Leased Kilcolman Castle in the County of Cork (1586). Living at Kilcolman Castle (1589), in which year he was visited by Sir Walter Ralegh. Under the latter's prompting Spenser accompanied him to London, bearing the first three books of *The Faerie Queene,* published in 1590. Although awarded a pension of £50, Spenser was disappointed in his hopes of substantial recognition at court. After an absence of nearly two years, he returned to Ireland (1591). Kilcolman Castle with its 3,000 acres was legally transferred to him (1591). Married one Eliza-

1 According to E. F. Pope, "doubtless a counterpart of the *Accadèmia della Nuova Poesia* and of the *Academie de Poésie et de Musique.*" See her article, "The Critical Background of the Spenserian Stanza," *Modern Philology,* XXIV (1926-1927), p. 33 (pp. 31-53). Possibly, however, the Areopagus was a largely fictitious organization. See Faverty, F. E., "A Note on the Areopagus," *Philological Quarterly,* v (1926), pp. 278-280.

beth (June 11, 1594),[1] probably Elizabeth Boyle, related to the first Earl of Cork. To London with three more books of *The Faerie Queene* (1595). Again he did not gain the political advancement he was seeking. Returned to Ireland (1597—1598.) In the course of Tyrone's Rebellion, Kilcolman Castle was burned to the ground (October, 1598). Fled with wife and four children to Cork. (Lost books of *The Faerie Queene* probably were burned in castle.) Left Cork for London (December, 1598). Died suddenly at a London inn (January 16, 1599), probably in distress if not in abject want.[2] Buried, at the expense of the Earl of Essex, near Chaucer in Westminster Abbey.

***The Shepheardes Calender*****†** (1579).[3] Series of *Aeglogai* (goatherd's tales; eclogues) called a calendar because there was one for each month of the year. Dedicated to "Maister Philip Sydney," published under the anonym "Immerito," and accompanied by prose notes to the poem as a whole and to the eclogues severally, the latter being supplied by "E. K.," probably Edward Kirke, a Cambridge colleague. General theme is the unrequited love of Colin Clout (Spenser applied the name, appropriated from Skelton's poem, to himself) for Rosalind; but the eclogues, put into the mouths of shepherds, are also a means by which references are made to political conditions, religious abuses, and eulogies of friends and patrons. Theme may be conventional and rhythm rough, nature-description may be merely decorative and thought quite unoriginal; but his deliberate use of rustic and archaic words anticipates *The Faerie Queene,* while, out-topping all, the easy vigor, graceful utterance, effective fantasy, and general technical mastery mark "the first unequivocal appearance of lyric genius in Elizabethan song,"[4] the appearance of a rhythm greater than Chaucer's and a virtuosity Renaissance-like in its poetic scope.

In various meters (*e. g.,* heroic couplet, ballad measure, elegiac quatrains, eight-line stanzas, unrimed sestina) tells[5] the religious allegory of the Oak and the Brier (February), sings the extravagant praises of Elizabeth (April), dialogues about true religion (May), laments Rosalind's spurning of Colin's love in favor of Menalcas (January, June; also, November, December). Influenced by Bion (March), Theocritus (August), Mantuan (July, October), and particularly by

1 This traditional date is still doubtful. See Hyde, Douglas, "Spenser's Marriage," *The Review of English Studies,* VII (1931), pp. 271-290; Carpenter. F. I., "The Marriages of Spenser," *Modern Philology,* XXII (1924), p. 97 *f.;* Welply, W. H., in *Notes and Queries,* CXLI (1932), p. 169 (pp. 165-169), p. 182 *f.* (pp. 182-187).

2 Critics, disregarding Ben Jonson's statement (quoted by Drummond) that Spenser died "for lack of bread," have generally theorized that Spenser's friends might not have heard of his condition until too late. But see Heffner, Ray, "Did Spenser Die in Poverty?" *Modern Language Notes,* XLVIII (1931), pp. 221-226.

3 *The Shepherd's Calendar,* edited by Renwick, W. L., (1930), pp. 163-222.

4 Erskine, John, *The Elizabethan Lyric* (1931), p. 106 *f.*

5 Greg, W. W., *Pastoral Poetry and Pastoral Drama* (1918), pp. 84-90.

† * Explanation of symbols immediately precedes page one.

Clément Marot's *Complainete de ma Dame de Savoye* (the November dirge) and his *Eglogue au Roy soubs les noms de Pan et Robin* (the December elegy or complaint).

Characters include Hobbinol (Harvey), Algrind (Archbishop Grindal), Roffyn (Dr. Young), Eliza (Queen Elizabeth), Lobbin (Leicester? Lord Robb?), Tityrus (Chaucer or Virgil). Critics have disagreed upon the identity of Rosalind. She has been identified variously as Rose Linde, Eliza Horden, Rose Dyneley, Rose Daniel (sister of Samuel Daniel), Elisa Nord (Elizabeth North, only daughter of Sir Thomas North—see pp. 145, 147); while others, scouting the idea that "Rosalind" is an anagram, believe her to be a creation of Spenser.

***Complaints Containing Sundrie Small Poemes of the Worlds Vanitie*** (1591).[1] Volume of miscellaneous verse, the general themes being the mutability of fortune or the vanity of human wishes. Collection of minor poems published, as the bookseller Ponsonby states, because of the success of the first part (Bks. I—III) of *The Faerie Queene*. "The Printer to the Gentle Reader" has an autobiographical importance, listing, as it does, additional works by Spenser, not one of which has come down to us: *Ecclesiastes, Canticum canticorum; A senights slumber, The hell of lovers,* his *Purgatorie* (translations); *The dying Pellican, The howers of the Lord, The sacrifice of a sinner, The seven Psalms* (pamphlets).[2] The *Complaints* volume includes:

(a) *The Ruines of Time.* Macedoine-like poem in rime royal on the Chaucerian and Lydgatian theme of how the mighty are fallen, blended with the Widsithian theme of how the poets confer immortality by their songs. Uninspired and slovenly-constructed lines (*e. g., ll.* 239—280) redeemed by occasional beautiful ones (*e. g., ll.* 400—406). Noted for its satire on Burghley; and, particularly, for the necrological passage on the Earl of Leicester, who, with Sidney and Sir Francis Walsingham, is the inspiration of the poem. Influenced by Joachim du Bellay's *Antiquités de Rome,* and other parts by Horace, Ovid, Propertius, and Theocritus.

(b) *The Teares of the Muses.* Laments the decay of the Arts, in not too pleasant a tone.[3] Poetic theories definitely allied with the doctrine of the *Pléiade*. Rhetorical. Has been interpreted as an attack upon Burghley. "Willy" has been identified as Shakespeare, Thomas Wilson, Sir Philip Sidney, George Gascoigne, John Lyly, the Earl of Oxford, and Spenser himself.[4] Dedicated to Alice (Lady Strange), daughter of Sir John Spencer, before whom Milton's *Comus* (p. 279)

---

1 Stein, Harold, *Studies in Spenser's Complaints* (1934).

2 Recently, one of Spenser's "lost" translations was made available by Padelford, F. M., *The Axiochus of Plato* (1934).

3 *The Complete Poetical Works of Edmund Spenser,* edited by Dodge, R. E. N. (1908), p. 70.

4 Ward, B. M., " 'Willy' and the 'Gentle Spirit' in Spenser's 'Tears of the Muses,' " in *The Seventeenth Earl of Oxford* (1928), Appendix D, pp. 359-369.

was presented about two-score years later. Title probably suggested by Gabriel Harvey's *Smithus, vel musarum lachrymae pro obitu T. Smith.*

(c) *Prosopopoia: or Mother Hubberds Tale.*[1] Most vital poem in volume was originally two separate poems. Satirical apologue[2] of the ape who purloins the royal cloak and sceptre from the sleeping lion (Elizabeth), and then shares the spoils of government with the fox until Jove sends Mercury (Lord Leicester) to awaken the lion. Probably a warning against the much-discussed proposal of marriage between Queen Elizabeth and the Duc d'Alençon—a proposal bitterly opposed by Leicester and possibly favored by Burghley. (The ape in many cases represents Jehan de Simier, Duc d'Alençon's Master of Robes; the fox may represent Burghley.) Occasional crudity of style; but predominantly well-managed, amusing, concise, proverbial, epigrammatic. Polemic, neatly phrased in unhurried decasyllabic couplets, stems from Spenser's life-activities, and not from a perusal of books. One of the first to use the heroic couplet in English for a satirical purpose.

Political poem includes an attack upon the simony of the "worldly-minded"[3] clergy, a discussion of labor, the court, and the administration, and, digressing from the satire on the corrupt courtiers, includes (*l.* 117 *ff.*) a portrait of a perfect courtier, probably Sidney. Influenced by the *Speculum Stultorum* (p. 35), by Chaucer,[4] by Calvin's *Institutes of the Christian Religion,* and particularly by *Reynard the Fox.*[5] Sidney, it is to be noted, suffered temporary banishment from Court for opposing the proposed marriage of the Queen; Spenser, it is said, suffered exile in Ireland because he had incurred the disfavor of Burghley and possibly the displeasure of Leicester.

(d) *Virgils Gnat.* Fairly accurate translation-paraphrase[6] in *ottava rima* of the Latin *Culex,* an epyllion or little epic poem probably by an imitator of Virgil. May represent a sequel to *Prosopopoia*—the sleeping shepherd may be Leicester, the gnat may be Spenser.[7] Excellent descriptive power and frequent brilliant lines in this adoxographic[8] poem.

---

1 Greenlaw, E. A., *Studies in Spenser's Historical Allegory* (1932), pp. 108-132.

2 Greenlaw, E. A., "Spenser and the Earl of Leicester," *Publications of the Modern Language Association of America,* XXV; New Series, XVIII (1910), pp. 545-557 (pp. 545-561).

3 Padelford, F. M., "Spenser and the Puritan Propaganda," *Modern Philology,* XI (1913-1914), pp. 102-106 (pp. 85-106).

4 Russell, I. W., "Biblical Echoes in *Mother Hubberds Tale,*" *Modern Language Notes,* XLIV (1929), pp. 162-164.

5 Greenlaw, E. A., "The Sources of 'Mother Hubberds Tale,'" *Modern Philology,* II (1904-1905), pp. 417-432 (pp. 411-432); Allen, Percy, *Anne Cecil, Elizabeth, & Oxford* (1934), Chap. VIII, pp. 158-178.

6 Emerson, O. F., "Spenser's Virgils Gnat," *The Journal of English and Germanic Philology,* XVII (1918), pp. 94-118.

7 Greenlaw, E. A., "Spenser and the Earl of Leicester," *Publications of the Modern Language Association of America,* XXV; New Series, XVIII (1910), pp. 557-559 (pp. 545-561).

8 Pease, A. S., "Things Without Honor," *Classical Philology,* XXI (1926), pp. 27-42.

(e) *Ruines of Rome: by Bellay.* Generally attributed to Spenser. Slipshod Englishing of thirty-three sonnets of du Bellay's *Antiquités de Rome* on the theme of the mutability of life's offerings. Except for the Envoy (original with Spenser), the rime scheme is *abab cdcd*. Reveals influence of the *Pléiade.*

(f) *Muiopotmos: or The Fate of the Butterfly.*† Clarion the butterfly is caught in the web spun by Aragnol the spider. Delicate charm of this *jeu d'esprit;* impressionistic description in this mock-heroic allegory or fable. Dedicated to Elizabeth (Lady Carey). Spenser's most original poem has been interpreted in a variety of ways. Is it an allegory of the life and death of Sidney?[1] Is it Leicester the butterfly versus Burghley the spider; or Sidney versus the Earl of Oxford[2]; or Ralegh versus Essex[3]; or Spenser versus his mistress?[4] Is it a parable of the poet and the politician, the one dedicated to beauty, the other to pragmatism: perhaps derived from a personal experience?[5]

(g) *Visions of the Worlds Vanitie.* General theme of this emblem-book is to show how the fortune of the great may be marred by that of the small.[6] Knotty style, unflowing rhythm. Spenserian sonnet form.

(h) *The Visions of Bellay.*[7] Middling translation of Joachim du Bellay's *Songe: ou Vision sur le mesme subject*, a series of Italian sonnets appended to the French Ovid's *Antiquités de Rome.* End-stopped blank verse. All except four sonnets (Nos. VI, VIII, XIII, XIV) appeared originally in the *Theatre .... for Worldings* (1569) by Jonker Jan van der Noot, Flemish poet.

(i) *The Visions of Petrarch, formerly translated.*[8] Translation of Clément Marot's twelve-line French version of the sixth canzone of Petrarch's *Morte di Madonna Laura.* Appeared in van der Noot's *Theatre .... for Worldlings,* where they are called Epigrams.

***Daphnaïda*** (1591). Conventional elegy on the death of Douglas Howard, daughter of Lord Byndon (Henry, Lord Howard) and wife

1 Lemmi, C. W., "The Allegorical Meaning of Spenser's *Muiopotmos,*" *Publications of the Modern Language Association of America,* XLV (1930), pp. 732-748.

2 Hulbert, V. B., "A New Interpretation of Spenser's *Muiopotmos,*" *Studies in Philology,* XXV (1928), pp. 138-148 (pp. 128-148).

3 Lyons, J. M., "Spenser's *Muiopotmos* as an Allegory," *Publications of the Modern Language Association of America,* XXXI; New Series, XXIV (1916), pp. 90-113.

4 Long, P. W., "Spenser's 'Muiopotmos,'" *The Modern Language Reivew,* IX (1914), pp. 457-462.

5 Grierson, H. J. C., "Spenser's 'Muiopotmos,'" *The Modern Language Review,* XVII (1922), p. 411 (pp. 409-411).

6 Fletcher, J. B., "Spenser's Earliest Translations," *The Journal of English and Germanic Philology,* XIII (1914), p. 307 (pp. 305-309).

7 Friedland, L. S., "Spenser's Earliest Translations," *The Journal of English and Germanic Philology,* XII (1913), pp. 449-470.

8 *Ibid.*

† * Explanation of symbols immediately precedes page one.

of Sir Arthur Gorges.[1] Influenced less by the pastoral tradition than by Chaucer's *Book of the Duchess* (p. 64)[2]. Empty rhetoric of emotion redeemed by beautiful cadence of stanzas, riming *ababcbc,* and by such passages as the description of evening (*ll.* 22 *ff.*) and of the shepherds' dance (*ll.* 303 *ff.*). Stanza employed is basically the rime royal.

***Colin Clouts Come Home Againe***† (1595). Allegorical pastoral records Ralegh's visit to Kilcolman in 1589 and Spenser's impressions of Cynthia's (*i. e.,* Elizabeth's) court upon his return to it under Ralegh's guidance. Beneath the charming autobiographical interest and the familiar style are some accents of satire. Deficient in balance and proportion. Among a dozen contemporary poets mentioned are Samuel Daniel, Ralegh, and Sidney. Reminiscent of parts of *The Faerie Queene.*

*Key to Some Characters*: Shepherd of the Ocean (Ralegh); Cynthia (Elizabeth); Amyntas (Ferdinando, Earl of Derby); Stella (Lady Rich); Theana (Anne Russell, wife of Ambrose Dudley, Earl of Warwick); Marian (Margaret, Countess of Cumberland); Urania (Mary, Countess of Pembroke); Alcyon (Sir Arthur Gorges); Amaryllis, Charillis, and Phyllis (Alice, Anne, and Elizabeth Spencer, respectively, all daughters of Sir John Spencer of Althorp).

***Astrophel***† (1586; published 1595). Pastoral elegy to the memory of Sidney, friend and patron who fell at the battle of Zutphen (p. 139). Alliterative and rhetorical six-line stanzas not infrequently felicitous, but almost always frigid. Indebted to Bion's *Lament for Adonis.*[3]

***The Doleful Lay of Clorinda*** (1586). Lamentation on Sidney's death. Frequently had been attributed to the Countess of Pembroke, Sidney's sister.[4]

***Amoretti***† (1591—1595). Sonnet-sequence recounts Spenser's courtship of one Elizabeth (Elizabeth Boyle? Elizabeth Pease? Elizabeth Carey?[5]). Now conventional, now original. Characteristically Spenserian in its soft-flowing, liquid, musical sound, in its rich beauty of

---

1 Sandison, H. E., "Arthur Gorges, Spenser's Alcyon and Raleigh's Friend," *Publications of the Modern Language Association of America,* XLIII (1928), pp. 645-674.

2 Nadal, T. W., "Spenser's *Daphnaïda,* and Chaucer's *Book of the Duchess,*" *Publications of the Modern Language Association of America,* XXIII; New Series, XVI (1908), pp. 646-661.

3 Shafer, Robert, "Spenser's *Astrophel,*" *Modern Language Notes,* XXVIII (1913), pp. 224-226.

4 For the confirmation of Ernest de Sèlincourt's suggestion that the *Lay* is by Spenser, see Long, P. W., "Spenseriana: The Lay of Clorinda," *Modern Language Notes,* XXXI (1916), pp. 79-82; Osgood, C. G., "The 'Doleful Lay of Clorinda,'" *Modern Language Notes,* XXXV (1920), pp. 90-96.

5 Long, P. W., "Spenser and Lady Carey," *The Modern Language Review,* III (1907-1908), pp. 257-267. For a re-examination of Spenser's "literary relations with Lady Elizabeth Carey," consult Strathmann, E. A., "Lady Carey and Spenser," *ELH: A Journal of English Literary History,* II (1935), pp. 33-57.

† * Explanation of symbols immediately precedes page one.

language, and in its pure, if somewhat diffused, atmosphere of epithalamic love. Many of the eighty-nine sonnets (although the last is not properly a sonnet) are in a kind of Spenserian stanza, *ababbcbccdcdee;* others are in three linked quatrains and a concluding couplet. Influence of Petrarch, Tasso, and Desportes.[1] Among the best sonnets are: "Lyke as a ship that through the Ocean wyde," (No. XXIV); "Most glorious Lord of lyfe that on this day," (No. LXVIII); "Fresh spring the herald of loues mighty king," (No. LXX); "One day I wrote her name upon the strand," (No. LXXV); "Men call you fayre, and you doe credit it," (No. LXXIX). Note the sensuousness of "Fayre bosome fraught with vertues richest treasure," (No. LXXVI); and "Was it a dreame, or did I see it playne," (No. LXXVII).

***Epithalamion*†** (1591—1595). Nuptial hymn, modelled upon the Catullan form, influenced by the Italian or Provençal *canzone,* and indebted to Chaucer's *Parliament of Fowls,* yet in an independent fashion celebrates Spenser's own wedding. Colorfully melodic, appealingly pictorial, beautifully sustained, exuberantly personal, passionately modest: has been described as "the contained tremor of an intimately personal emotion" (Murry). Each of the twenty-three stanzas (followed finally by an envoy) is terminated by a refrain, the last line of which is an alexandrine. Narrative, descriptive, pageant, and lyric elements harmonized into possibly the most beautiful peal of bridal music in the language.

***Prothalamion*†** (1596). Spousal song in honor of the marriage, at Essex House, of Lady Elizabeth Somerset to Master Henry Gilford, and of Lady Katherine Somerset to Master William Peter, in August, 1596. Double marriage of the daughters of Edward Somerset, Earl of Worcester, prompts Spenser to lyricize in the *canzone* manner,[2] as mellifluously and beautifully as in the *Epithalamion,* while less naturally and more gayly. Probably influenced by Leland's *Cygnea Cantio* (1545) and W. Vallans's *A Tale of Two Swannes* (entered in Stationers' Register, 1590).

***Fowre Hymnes*** (1596).[3] Hymns in honor of Love, of Beauty, of Heavenly Love, and of Heavenly Beauty. Influenced by Italian or Christian Platonism and also by Hebrew lore. The sensual and neo-Platonic love of the first two complements the pure and mystical love of the last two: has a unity of theme.[4] Parallels have been found

---

1 Scott J. G., "The Sources of Spenser's 'Amoretti,'" *The Modern Language Review,* XXII (1927), pp. 189-195.

2 Erskine, John, *The Elizabethan Lyric* (1931), pp. 196, 295.

3 Erskine, John, *The Elizabethan Lyric* (1931), pp. 193-195; Padelford, F. M., "Spenser's *Fowre Hymnes*: A Resurvey," *Studies in Philology,* XXIX (1932), pp. 207-232.

4 Greenlaw, Edwin, (A.), in a review of three books, *Modern Language Notes,* XLV (1930), pp. 326-328 (pp. 320-328); Bennett, J. W., "The Theme of Spenser's *Fowre Hymnes,*" *Studies in Philology,* XXVII (1931), pp. 18-57.

† * Explanation of symbols immediately precedes page one.

in Plato's *Symposium* and *Phaedrus,* Ficino's *Commentarium in Convivium,* Bruno's *De gl'Heroici Furori,* and Castiglione's *Il Cortegiano.*[1] Probably influenced also by Pico della Mirandola's *Commento,* Girolamo Benivieni's *Canzone dello Amore celeste e divino,* and Pietro Bembo's *Gl' Asolani.*[2] More certain is the influence of Calvin's *Institutes,* and, according to C. G. Osgood, the Hebrew Books of Wisdom.[3]

***A Veue of the Present State of Ireland*** (*c.* 1596; published 1633). Prose dialogue between Eudoxus and Irenaeus, the latter being Spenser himself. Well-knit topical development advocates a "firm government" or a "repressive government," depending upon one's point of view: but Spenser is definitely one-sided and almost ferocious in his support of Lord Gray's reign-of-terror policy.[4] Influenced by Machiavelli,[5] by Jean Bodin's *Six Livres de la République* and, as in *The Shepheardes Calender,* by Aristotle's *Politics* and *Ethics.*

***Briefe Note of Ireland.*** Official report to the Queen on the Tyrone rebellion specifies certain methods for crushing the rebels.

***Letters*** (entered on the Stationers' Register, 1580).[6] Two letters from Spenser to Gabriel Harvey.

## *The Faerie Queene*† (1589—1596)

### The Plan

Prefixed to the 1590 edition is a letter by Spenser to Sir Walter Ralegh, in which the former explains that the "generall end" or purpose of the work "is to fashion a gentleman or noble person in vertuous and gentle discipline." The plan as sketched called for a twelve-day feast held by Gloriana, Queen of Fairyland, on each day of which a stranger, appearing and asking for help against a giant, tyrant, or dragon, is assigned a knight. The twelve contemplated books, each divided into twelve cantos, were to tell each of the adventures of one knight; each knight was to represent one of the twelve (thirteen?[7]) virtues of Aristotle opposed to which was one of the twelve vices. All the virtues were to be shown combined in the central figure, Prince

1 Elton, Oliver, "Giordano Bruno in England," *Modern Essays* (1907), p. 28 *f.* (Chap. II, pp. 1-36); *Daphnaïda and Other Poems,* edited by Renwick, W. L. (1930), p. 209 (pp. 209-224). A point of view is also presented by Saurat, Denis, *Literature and Occult Tradition* (1930), Chap. v, pp. 163-238.

2 Fletcher, J. B., "Benivieni's 'Ode of Love' and Spenser's 'Fowre Hymnes,'" *Modern Philology,* VIII (1910-1911), pp. 545-560; Renwick, W. L., *Edmund Spenser* (1925), p. 164.

3 That is, the Hebrew personification of Wisdom as found in the Book of Proverbs, Job, and the apocryphal books of Wisdom, Sirach, and Baruch. Furthermore, Denis Saurat has directed attention to the Schekhina or Matrona of the *Cabala* as possibly the true prototype of the Sapience of the Fourth Hymn.

4 Henley, Pauline, *Spenser in Ireland* (1928), p. 181.

5 Greenlaw, E. A., "The Influence of Machiavelli on Spenser," *Modern Philology,* VII (1909-1910), pp. 187-193 (pp. 187-202); Henley, Pauline, *Spenser in Ireland* (1928), p. 180.

6 Greenlaw, E. A., "Spenser and the Earl of Leicester," *Publications of the Modern Language Association of America,* XXV; New Series, XVIII (1910), pp. 535-538 (pp. 535-561); Jones, H. S. V., *A Spenser Handbook* (1930), pp. 388-393.

7 Jones, H. S. V., "The *Faerie Queene* and the Mediaeval Aristotelian Tradition," *The Journal of English and Germanic Philology,* XXV (1926), pp. 283-298.

† * Explanation of symbols immediately precedes page one.

Arthur, the Ideal Knight symbolizing Magnificence (*i. e.,* Magnanimity or Highmindedness or Manliness or Gentlemanliness), who appears at the crucial moment in every book. Not only is there present (1) an allegory of the virtues and vices, but also (2) an allegory of the times and people, and (3) a story of romance and adventure in which both character and action may have a double meaning. Only six of the planned twelve books were completed, and possibly a part of the seventh. It has been noted, however, that Spenser's design is not executed as planned.[1]

### The Allegory

1. MORAL. The characters represent various virtues and their contrary vices at war in the soul, which strives for perfection.

2. RELIGIOUS. The representation seems to be the struggle of the English Reformed Church, the Church of England, the Church of Rome, with Atheism and Paganism.

3. POLITICAL-HISTORICAL. The main theme is to glorify the State in the "most excellent and glorious person of our soveraine the Queene, and her kingdom in Faery land." Queen Elizabeth is variously represented, as are many contemporary Elizabethans and other figures.

### Chief Events

1. The Huguenot massacre of St. Bartholomew's Eve.
2. The defeat of the Spaniards in the Netherlands.
3. The execution of Mary, Queen of Scots.
4. The administration of Ireland under Lord Grey of Wilton.
5. The recantation of Henri IV of France.

### Some Immediate Influences on Spenser in Writing "The Faerie Queene"

a) CLASSICAL. (1) Virgil's pastorals, (2) Homer's *Iliad* and *Odyssey,* (3) Aristotle's philosophical works, (4) Plato's writings, (5) *La Pléiade,* (6) Natale Conti's *Mythologia,* and (7) Boccaccio's *De Genealogia Deorum.*

b) ROMANTIC. Epics of chivalry such as (1) Ariosto's *Orlando Furioso,* (2) Tasso's *Gerusalemme Liberata,* (3) Montalvo's *Amadis of Gaul,* and (4) Malory's *Morte d'Arthur* (p. 92).

c) ALLEGORICAL. (1) Dante's *Divina Commedia,* (2) *Roman de la Rose* (p. 64), (3) *Pricke of Conscience* (p. 27), (4) *Vision of William concerning Piers the Plowman* (p. 56), (5) Chaucer's *Parliament of Fowls* (p. 67), and (6) Sackville's *Induction* (p. 121).

### Book 1. The Legend of the Red Cross Knight, or of Holiness

a) STORY. Georgos, the knight, accompanies Una, and succeeds in slaying the Dragon, which is besieging the castle of Una's father.

---

1 Does Spenser's plot fit into his outlined plan? See Draper, J. W., "The Narrative Technique of the *Faerie Queene,*" *Publications of the Modern Language Association of America,* XXXIX (1924), pp. 310-324; Blair, Laurence, "The Plot of the *Faerie Queene,*" *Publications of the Modern Language Association of America,* XLVII (1932), pp. 81-88

b) Allegory.[1] The Red Cross Knight (St. George, the "patron" or champion of Christian Holiness, representing the Anglican Church) guided by Una (Truth, or the True Religion) overcomes the Dragon (Error). Is "a detailed statement of the Calvinistic doctrine of Salvation."[2]

c) Style. Best book, only the tenth canto being, possibly, somewhat dull. Richness of contrasts exemplified by Canto I; tenderness, by Canto III; purple patch, by Canto XI; quiet *dénouement,* by Canto XII. General rapidity of movement. Sources include *The Legend of St. George; Libeaus Desconus, or the Fair Unknown* (p. 38); *Bevis of Hampton* (p. 49); *Guy of Warwick* (p. 48); *Sabra and the Seven Champions; Huon de Bordeaux* (p. 96); and other works.[3] Essentially corresponds to *The Pilgrimage of the Life of Man* by Guillaume de Guileville.[4]

### Book II. The Legend of Sir Guyon, or of Temperance

a) Story. Sir Guyon visits the cave of Mammon, captures the enchantress Acrasia, and devastates her Bower of Bliss. In these adventures he is saved by Prince Arthur, who dispatches Cymochles and Pyrocles, two brothers, and delivers Alma.

b) Allegory. Sir Guyon (Temperance, or the Golden Mean) protects Alma (the Spirit or Virgin Soul, queen of Body Castle and the House of Temperance) from Acrasia (Intemperance).

c) Style. More abstract than Book I; political allegory less prominent and more obscure. Pregnant with elaborate detail; *e. g.,* the Cave of Mammon (Canto VII), the Bower of Bliss (Canto XII). Third canto influenced Shakespeare's *Much Ado About Nothing.* Influenced by Tasso's *Gerusalemme Liberata,* Ariosto's *Orlando Furioso,* Claudian's *Rape of Proserpine,* Virgil, and Homer. Particularly influenced by Aristotle.

---

1 For the moral and spiritual allegory, see: Ruskin, John, *Stones of Venice* (1853), Vol. II, Chap. VIII, and Vol. III, pp. 205-209; Church, R. W., *Spenser* (1879), pp. 124 *f.*, 163; Padelford, F. M., "The Spiritual Allegory of the *Faerie Queene,* Book One," *The Journal of English and Germanic Philology,* XXII (1923), pp. 1-17; Osgood, C. G., "Spenser and the Enchanted Glass," *John Hopkins Alumni Magazine,* XIX (1930), pp. 8-31; Heffner, Ray, "Spenser's Allegory in Book I of the *Faerie Queene,*" *Studies in Philology,* XXVII (1930), p. 161 (pp. 142-161); Jones, H. S. V., "Magnanimity in Spenser's Legend of Holiness," *Studies in Philology,* XXIX (1932), pp. 200-206.
For the historical allegory, see: Buck, P. M., Jr., "On the Political Allegory in the Faerie Queene," *Nebraska Studies,* XI (1911), pp. 159-192; Padelford, F. M., *The Political and Ecclesiastical Allegory of the First Book of the Faerie Queene* (1911); Heffner, Ray, "Spenser's Allegory in Book I of the *Faerie Queene,*" *Studies in Philology,* XXVIII (1930), pp. 142-161; Greenlaw, Edwin A., *Studies in Spenser's Historical Allegory* (1932), pp. 1-100.

2 Padelford, F. M., "Spenser and the Theology of Calvin," *Modern Philology,* XII (1914), pp. 1-18; Buyssens, E., "Calvinism in the Faerie Queene, of Spenser," *Revue Belge de Philologie Et D' Histoire,* V (1926), p. 37 (pp. 37-69; pp. 381-400).

3 *The Works of Edmund Spenser* (1932), I, pp. 379-421, edited by Greenlaw, Edwin A., Osgood, C. G., and Padelford, F. M.

4 Padelford, F. M., "Spenser and *The Pilgrimage of the Life of Man,*" *Studies in Philology,* XXVIII (1931), pp. 211-218.

**Book III. The Legend of Britomart, or of Chastity**

a) STORY. Britomart rescues Amoret from the magician Busirane.

b) ALLEGORY. Emphasizes the ideal of Chastity, or of Love without Lust: Britomart (Chastity) saves Amoret (Feminine Loveliness and Wifely Devotion) from Busirane (Unlawful Love).

c) STYLE. Political allegory even more vague than in preceding book. Of looser construction than Books I and II: a string of stories rather than one dovetailing allegory. Noted for elaborate description: *e. g.,* the Garden of Adonis (Canto VI), the House of Busirane (Canto XI), the Masque of Cupid (Canto XII). Influenced by *Second Report* (1594), *Amadis of Gaul,* and the *Arthur of Little Britain.*

**Book IV. The Legend of Cambel and Triamond, or of Friendship**

a) STORY. How only Amoret is able to keep the girdle clasped about her waist; how Britomart is revealed as the maiden-knight; how Timias is rescued by Prince Arthur from the Blatant Beast; but particularly how Spenser completes Chaucer's *The Squire's Tale* (p. 75).

b) ALLEGORY. While Book III celebrates the love between different sexes, Book IV symbolizes the swearing of eternal friendship and love between like sexes.[1]

c) STYLE. Generally held to be meandering, formless, and wordy. Best descriptions are of the Temple of Venus (Canto X) and of the nuptials of the Thames and Medway (Canto XI); in the latter canto, Spenser's frequent use of "classical allusions and classical proper names"[2] is notable; while in the former, the vision of Scudamour has been pronounced by W. B. Yeats to be "the finest invention in Spenser." Influenced by Ariosto, *Amis and Amiloun*[3] (p. 40), Chaucer's *Knight's Tale* (p. 72), the *Aeneid,* and possibly not only by Giraldi Cinthio's *Tre Dialoghi della Vita Civile*[4] but also by Alonzo Pietro's continuation of Montemayor's *Diana.*[5]

**Book V. The Legend of Sir Artegal, or of Justice**

a) STORY. Sir Artegal metes out Justice: to the ruffian Sanglier, to the charlatan who is in possession of false scales, to the sneaking Braggadocchio, to the twin brothers, to Guyle. Prince Arthur rescues Belge from Geryoneo; Sir Artegal rescues Irena from Grantorto.

b) ALLEGORY. Justice, crushed to earth, shall rise again.

---

1 Smith, C. G., (1) "Spenser's Theory of Friendship," *Publications of the Modern Language Association of America,* XLIX (1934), pp. 490-500; (2) "Spenser's Theory of Friendship: An Elizabethan Commonplace," *Studies in Philology,* XXXII (1935), pp. 158-169; (3) "Sententious Theory in Spenser's Legend of Friendship," *ELH: A Journal of English Literary History, II* (1935), pp. 165-191.

2 Draper, J. W., "Classical Coinage in the *Faerie Queene,*" *Publications of the Modern Language Association of America,* XLVII (1932), pp. 97-108.

3 Ayres, H. M., "*The Faerie Queene* and *Amis and Amiloun,*" *Modern Language Notes,* XXIII (1908), pp. 177-180.

4 Erskine, John, "The Virtue of Friendship in the *Faerie Queene,*" *Publications of the Modern Language Association of America,* XXX; New Series, XXIII (1915), pp. 837-843 (831-850).

5 Harrison, T. P., Jr., "*The Faerie Queene* and the *Diana,*" *Philological Quarterly,* IX (1930), pp. 51-60.

c) Style. Not as poetic in its allegory as the other books; but political allegory clearer.[1] As in the following book, so here there is an "uncanny naturalness both of narrative and versification."[2] Brilliant description of Radigund and of the duel. Influenced by Aristotle's *Nicomachean Ethics* and chiefly by Ariosto's *Orlando Furioso.*

**Book VI. The Legend of Sir Calidore, or of Courtesy**

a) Story. Sir Calidore finally overtakes and chains the Blatant Beast; (but the latter, while in the keeping of Queen Gloriana, soon breaks its bonds).

b) Allegory. Courtesy subverts Scandal.

c) Style. Occasionally prolix; but tender, sad, and into it "enters a warm fragrance of reality" (Murry). Influenced by Sannazaro's *Arcadia* and Montemayor's *Diana.*

**Book VII. Two Cantos of Mutabilitie: The Legend of Constance** (*Unfinished*)

a) Story. Fragment on mutability: the two cantos remaining are the sixth and the seventh.

b) Allegory. The dangers to a State inherent in all changes.

c) Style. Delightful description, tender melancholy. Done with gusto. Influenced by Ovid, Lucretius,[3] and Aristotle.

## GENERAL STYLE[4]

| SUGGESTED MERITS | SUGGESTED DEFECTS |
|---|---|
| 1. Supreme in his vision world of poetic fluency, ornate imagination, rich imagery, and lofty idealism. | 1. While noble in intention, yet often ineffectual in communication. Profusion of pictures not seldom defeats purpose. |
| 2. Recognized as master of luxuriant color and verbal music, he is possibly the most sensuous of poets. | 2. While known as the poets' poet, he is often neither lyrical nor sublime. |
| 3. Blended classic structure and romantic ideas, nationalistic feeling and idealistic thought, Renaissance-like sensuous pleasure and the spirit of the Reformation. | 3. While remarkable in spiritual unity, he is deficient in constructive power or technical unity. Style frequently involved, diffuse, loose, and unfinished. Allegory complicated by pagan mythology. |
| 4. Experimented with the language and enriched it (see item 5); used archaisms and outlandish provincialisms, neologisms and pinchbeck words. | 4. Made impenetrable by rank overgrowth of archaic eccentricities and verbal legerdemain. Affected and cloying language resulted from self-imposed strictures. |

1 Jones, H. S. V., *A Spenser Handbook* (1930), pp. 261-270.

2 Brooke, Tucker, "Stanza-Connection in the *Fairy Queen,*" *Modern Language Notes,* xxxvii (1922), p. 227 (pp. 223-227).

3 Greenlaw, E. A., "Spenser and Lucretius," *Studies in Philology,* xviii (1920), pp. 439-464; Cummings, W. P., "The Influence of Ovid's *Metamorphoses* on Spenser's 'Mutabilitie' Canto," *Studies in Philology,* xxviii (1930), pp. 241-256.

4 Most stimulating is the essay by Notcutt, H. C., "The *Faerie Queene* and Its Critics," *Essays and Studies by Members of The English Association,* xii (1926), pp. 63-85.

5. Invented the consummate Spenserian meter, a stanza consisting of eight decasyllabic lines and an Alexandrine, riming **ababbcbcc**.[1] Influenced many poets; *e. g.*, Drayton, Browne, Giles and Phineas Fletcher, Wither, Milton, Prior, Pope, Gay, Thomson, Wordsworth, Keats.

5. Characteristically Elizabethan, he reveals an excessive flattery of the Queen.

6. Compared with Chaucer, Spenser shows a lack of humor, a want of dramatic constructive power, a deficiency in realism, a monotony of characterization and description.

---

1 Mackail, J. W., *The Springs of Helicon* (1909), pp. 119-127; Jones, H. S. V., *A Spenser Handbook* (1930), pp. 142-145. The stanza's closest parallel in Italian is the eight-line madrigal, itself a derivative of the *terza rima*, says Pope, E. F., "The Critical Background of the Spenserian Stanza," *Modern Philology*, XXIV (1926-1927), pp. 31-53.

## Chapter X

# THE RENAISSANCE: THE AGE OF ELIZABETH

## HISTORICAL AND SOCIAL BACKGROUND

### Religious Conditions

Religious intolerance was acute, but Queen Elizabeth so steered her course that her administration left the English Church upon a firm foundation. During her reign she became the champion of European Protestantism.

### Economic Conditions

Critical was the problem of extensive unemployment and increased pauperism. By a proclamation of 1560 the stabilization of coinage and thereby of prices was achieved; by the Statute of Apprentices in 1563, which aimed to conserve man-power, and by the passing in 1601 of the first of a series of regular Poor Laws, labor conditions for six-score years afterwards were affected. With piracy and war came prosperity. General standards of housing conditions were raised; for example, tin spoons and pewter platters replaced wooden ones, while window and glass, even chimneys, were introduced. The Queen herself set an example for improvements in apparel by the extravagance of her dress and the splendor of her court. All these changes created a wider public for the literature of the period.

### Domestic and Foreign Policy

The maintenance of England's security and the prevention of foreign interference was the Queen's foreign policy, and with the aid of Cecil and Walsingham peace was maintained for twenty-five years. Despite its assistance to the Protestants in Scotland, France, and the Low Countries, England avoided open war. Under Martin Frobisher, John Davis, William Baffin, John Hawkins, Francis Drake, and Sir Walter Ralegh, the foundations of the British navy were laid and Britain's colonial enterprise was furthered. The destruction of the *Invincible Armada* crippled Spain's naval power, saved English Protestantism, and marked the rise of English sea-power. While the national life was to be vitiated by the deterioration in tone of the court of both James I and Charles I, during whose reigns there was no unity, but division (p. 249 *ff*.), yet by the time Elizabeth's reign had ended, by her policy of keeping France and Spain in check for thirty years, England had become independent of all European powers.

## GENERAL VIEW OF THE LITERATURE

### Ideal of Gloriana

The court and the courtier were the centers of national life; display and adulation the ideals of personal and public life. Despite the Queen's almost insatiable desire for fulsome praise of her person and her sovereignty—a desire to which the writers of the age catered—the period of her reign produced many of the permanent contributions to English letters. An integral part of the golden age in English literature, as well as in English politics, is this hero-worship of Elizabeth.

### Poetry, Prose, and Drama

Prose, while showing the extravagant love of decoration, was rapidly developing into the flexibility it shows to-day; the poetry, only less important than the drama, frequently achieved original beauty and exuberance. Before the close of the period, the essential fecundity and seriousness of the drama had declined into melodramatic plots and gross indecency; but above all is the reign of Elizabeth to be identified with the consummate age of the English drama.

### Scottish Literature

With this period Scottish literature disappeared, not to show itself again until the latter part of the eighteenth century.

**George Puttenham,** *c.* 1530—*c.* 1590. Educated at Oxford. Travelled in Spain, France, and Italy.

*The Arte of English Poesie* (1589). A review of ancient and contemporaneous poetry, chiefly in their formal aspect. First part on Poets and Poesy; second, on Proportion; third, on Ornament. Published anonymously. Ascribed also to his brother Richard.[1]

**Stephen Gosson,** 1554—1624, satirist, critic, playwright, poet, miscellaneous writer. Educated at Corpus Christi College, Oxford (1572—1576). Rector of Great Wigborough (1591) and of St. Botolph's, Bishopsgate (1600).

*School of Abuse* (1579). Critical treatise virulent in its attack on the theatre. Herds together "Poets, Pipers, Players, Jesters and such like Caterpillars of a Commonwealth," and attacks the poets as being the "fathers of lies" and the theatre as having "robbed Greece of gluttony, Italy of wantonness, Spain of pride, France of deceit, and Dutchland of quaffing." Unauthorized dedication to Sir Philip Sidney evoked from the latter his *Defence of Poesie* (p. 139), wherein it was declared that a play could be a vehicle for moral instruction as readily as any other form of poetry. (Also, see Lodge, p. 139.)

---

1 Possibly by neither George nor Richard Puttenham. See Ward, B. M., "The Authorship of the *Arte of English Poesie*: A Suggestion," *The Review of English Studies*, I (1925), pp. 284-308.

***Pleasant Quippes for Upstart Newfangled Gentlewomen*** (1595). Coarse, satiric poem, particularly on woman's mode of dress in time of Elizabeth. Rimes *ababcc.*

**Thomas Lodge,** *c.* 1557—1625, dramatist, romance-writer, excellent lyricist and sonneteer, pamphleteer, translator, University Wit. Son of Sir Thomas Lodge. Educated at Trinity College, Oxford. Entered Lincoln's Inn (1578). Turned from law to literature. Collaborated with Greene (*e. g., A Looking-Glass for London and England*). Best imitator of Lyly's style. Will probably live by his songs.

***A Defence of Poetry, Music, and Stage Plays*** (*c.* 1580). Controversial reply to Gosson (p. 138) written in headlong, yet disciplined, prose. Weightily pedantic but not without force.

***Marius and Sylla; or, The Wounds of Civil War*** (*c.* 1588). Some psychological insight in this Marlowesque drama. Creaky, rhetorical style of verse.

***Rosalynde, Euphues Golden Legacie*** (1590). Euphuistic pastoral prose-romance, interspersed with sonnets and eclogues, is based on the fourteenth-century *Tale of Gamelyn* (p. 38). Famous as inspiring Shakespeare's *As You Like It*: in the latter work, Celia is Lodge's Alinda; Orlando, his Rosader; Oliver, his Saladyne; while the name of Rosalind is retained. Imperishable lyric is "Rosalynde's Madrigal":

> "Love in my bosom like a bee
> Doth suck his sweet."

**Sir Philip Sidney,** 1554—1586, poet, pastoral romancer, scholar, soldier, diplomat; the ideal Elizabethan courtier, the reincarnation of Castiglione's courtier. Son of the high-born Sir Henry Sidney. Educated at Shrewsbury and Christ Church, Oxford. Travelled widely in France, Austria, Geneva, Venice, and Padua (1572—1575). Married Lady Frances Walsingham (1583); but the great love of his life is commemorated by a sonnet-sequence addressed to Lady Penelope Devereux, whom he met in 1576. Member of the *Areopagus,* English literary academy having for its chief purpose the naturalizing of the classical meters into English verse.[1] Ardent Protestant, he assisted the Dutch against the Spaniards, falling mortally wounded at Zutphen (1586); immortal is the story of his passing a cup of water to another wounded soldier, and saying, "Thy necessity is greater than mine."

***The Defence of Poesie*****†** (written *c.* 1580; published 1595). Prose essay answered Gosson's *School of Abuse* (p. 138). Critical discussion of the state of English poetry. Indebted to Minturno, Scaliger, and Castelvetro. Praises Chaucer, deplores the lack of classical decorum inherent in the mixture of tragedy with comedy in the same play, laments the follies and affectations of the current English style. Crowning all, points out that all literature of an idealistic nature is embrace-

1 See page 124, Note 1.

† * Explanation of symbols immediately precedes page one.

able under the head of poetry. Musical prose, quiet humor (rarely mocking in tone), controlled sentence-usage: the idiomatic talk of a great man, sweet of temper, serene of spirit, gentle while hearty, diplomatic while critical. (Also called *Apologie for Poetrie.*)

***The Countesse of Pembrokes Arcadia*†** (1590). First long prose-verse pastoral romance in English, written for the entertainment of his sister, the Countess of Pembroke, marks probably the beginning of the love plot and female characters in fiction. Leisurely movement, wealth of episode, complicated plot, novel similes, lack of unity, affected and prolix style, frequent interspersing of verse (about fourscore pieces, many of them being metrical experiments). Work, sometimes cloying and Guevaristic, mingles the brocading characteristics of a Greek romance, Italian *novella,* medieval romance, and Renaissance pastoral.

Aristotelian philosophy, Renaissance-like stoicism; over his conception of Nature presides a god of Reason. Influenced by Jacopo Sannazaro's *Arcadia* (1504), Jorge de Montemayor's *Diana Enamorada* (1542—1559), and Heliodorus's *Aethiopica.* Political ideas determined probably by Phillipe de Mornay's (or Languet's) *Vindiciae contra Tyrannos* (1579) and Hotman's *Franco-Gallia* (1573).[1] In turn, influenced others: Bellaria in Beaumont and Fletcher's *Philaster* (p. 244) is identical with Zelmane; sub-plot of Gloucester and his sons in Shakespeare's *King Lear* (p. 211) is from the incident of the blind King of Paphlagonia (Bk. II); title of Richardson's *Pamela* is taken from it.

Sonnets in ***Arcadia:*** "O stealing time the subject of delaie"; "Locke up, faire liddes, the treasure of my harte"; "My true love hath my hart, and I have his."

***Astrophel and Stella*†** (1591). Sequence of 108 sonnets, inspired by Penelope Devereux,[2] daughter of Lord Essex, who, after her divorce from Lord Rich, married Charles Blount, Earl of Devonshire. ("Stella" or "Star" is Penelope; Astrophel or "Star-Lover" is Sir Philip.) As a sonnet-sequence, generally immature in thought; typical of age in rampant use of rime, alliteration, word-melody, and conceits; but poetically executed, revealing the sensually-ideal flashes of real if exaggerated passion that the genuine intrigue developed. Mostly adheres to the Petrarchan form, particularly in the octave (occasionally *abababab* is substituted for *abbaabba*); but in the less regular sestet he frequently uses four lines, riming alternately, followed by a couplet (*cdcdee*). Memorable: "With how sad steps ô Moone thou clim'st the skyes" (XXXI); "Come Sleepe, ô Sleepe, the certaine knot of peace" (XXXIX); "Having this day, my horse, my hand, my Launce" (XLI);

---

1 Briggs, W. D., (1) "Political Ideas in Sidney's *Arcadia,*" *Studies in Philology,* XXVIII (1931). pp. 137-161; (2) "Sidney's Political Ideas," *Studies in Philology,* XXIX (1932), pp. 534-542.

2 Accepted interpretation is unreliable, according to Purcell, J. M., *Sidney's Stella* (1934). See also Hudson, H. H., "Penelope Devereux as Sidney's Stella," *The Huntington Library Bulletin,* Number 7 (1935), pp. 89-129.

† * Explanation of symbols immediately precedes page one.

"No more my deere, no more these counsels try" (LXIV); "When farre spent night perswades each mortal eie" (XCIX).

**Sir Walter Ralegh** (commonly but incorrectly spelled **Raleigh**), *c.* 1552—1618,[1] historian, poet, political essayist, courtier, musician, chemist, soldier, navigator, explorer, member of Parliament. Educated at Oriel College, Oxford (1568). Served in the Huguenot army (1569). Captain of a company of foot in Munster (1580), where he believed, as Spenser did, in the suppression of the Irish rebels by force. At Court (1581) as a protégé of Leicester. Knighted (1584). Lieutenant of Cornwall (1585). Captain of the Queen's Guard (1587). Three attempts to colonize Virginia (1584—1587). Visited Spenser in Ireland (1589). Forfeited the Queen's favor by seducing Elizabeth Throckmorton, one of her maids-of-honor. Upon his release after a brief commitment to the Tower (1592), he married (if he had not already married) the same Elizabeth Throckmorton. Undertaking an expedition in search of the mythical El Dorado, he sailed into Guiana, exploring the Orinoco. By this time he was extremely unpopular in England, because of his arrogance and religious scepticism.[2] Governor of Jersey (1600). Accused of complicity in a plot against James I (1603). By an unfair trial he was condemned to death, but was committed to perpetual imprisonment (1603—1616). His gallant bearing at the trial brought him back into popular favor. Released from the Tower (1616) expressly to head an expedition to the Orinoco to locate a gold mine asserted by Ralegh to exist there, the only stipulation being that he in no way encroach upon Spanish territory. In the course of the search, while Ralegh was at Trinidad ill with fever, part of his expedition came into conflict with the Spanish settlement of San Tomás, during which Sir Walter's son was killed. Failure of expedition. Probably to placate Gondomar, the Spanish ambassador upon whose demand Ralegh had been arrested upon the latter's return to England, the Englishman, condemned to die on the old sentence, was executed on October 29, 1618. Some say there is authentic warrant for the story of the cloak (as told in Sir Walter Scott's *Kenilworth* in 1821); and also for his answer, when asked while his head was on the block to turn his face east: "What matter how the head lies, so the heart be right."

### Prose

***A Report of the Truth of the Fight about the Isle of Açores, this last summer, betwixt the Revenge, one of her Majesties Shippes, and an Armada of the King of Spaine*** (1591). Animated prose epic of Sir Richard Grenville's encounter at the Azores with the Spanish fleet. Basis of Alfred Tennyson's war-ballad, *The Revenge* (1880).

---

1 Although 1552 is traditionally given as Ralegh's date of birth, there is important evidence pointing to 1554.

2 Buckley, G. T., *Atheism in the English Renaissance* (1932), Chap. XI, "The Atheism of Sir Walter Raleigh," pp. 137-152.

***The Discovery of the large, rich, and bewtiful Empire of Guiana*** (1596).[1] Account of his first expedition. Vivid if loose prose, vigorous movement, effective descriptions of natural scenery, accuracy of geographical observations. Some apocryphal stories. Territorial expansion was the purpose of the Guiana project. Shakespeare's *Othello* probably indebted to it for some details.

***The History of the World***† (written in prison 1604—1614; published 1614). Only one volume completed, the torso covering early history until B. C. 130. Purpose is to show, according to the preface, how God judges the wicked. Originally composed for young Prince Henry, whose father finally had Sir Walter beheaded. Confused, poorly-balanced; of little if any value as history. Unerudite erudition and easy scholarship. Prompt quotations and metrical translations[2] from Virgil, Plato, Lactantius Charron, Marius Victor, Euripides, and other writers. Memorable for some somber passages infused by grandeur of thought, sonority of rhythm, magic of emotion.[3] As an example even superior to his opening lines on the attributes of God is his apostrophe to Death, one of the most majestic organ-notes in English literature:

> "O eloquent, just and mighty death, whom none could advise, thou hast persuaded; what none hath presumed, thou hast done; and whom all the world hath flattered, thou hast cast out of the world and despised: thou hast drawn together all the extravagant greatness, all the pride, cruelty and ambition of man, and covered all over with two narrow words: *Hic jacet.*"[4]

**Poetry**

***A Vision upon this Conceipt of the Faery Queene.*** "Methought I saw the grave where Laura lay" is a brisk, almost epigrammatic sonnet appended to Spenser's *Faerie Queene* (Bks. I—III).

***The Lie.*** Bitter, worldly-wise satire.

***Fayne Would I: But I Dare Not.*** Intellectual appeal.

***The Nimphs Reply to the Sheepheard.*** Cynical answer to Marlowe's *The Passionate Shepherd to his Love* (p. 158). Generally attributed to Ralegh.

***The Passionate Mans Pilgrimage.***† Suffuses a naked cry of disillusionment and resignation by a feeling of noble piety. Sometimes considered as anticipating the mystical poetry of the seventeenth century. His best poem, according to Edmund Gosse; superior to any poem in the language in purity of thought and line, says Chidsey. (Both this and *The Lie* were probably written in prison.)

---

1 For a stimulating and somewhat iconoclastic approach to Sir Walter Ralegh, see *The Discoveries of the large and bewtiful Empire of Guiana,* edited by Harlow, V. T. (1928), pp. xv-xliii.

2 *The Poems of Sir Walter Ralegh,* edited by Latham, A. M. C. (1929), pp. 50-63.

3 Stebbing, William, *Sir Walter Ralegh* (1891).

4 Quoted from *The Pageant of English Prose,* edited by Leonard, R. M. (1912), p. 523.

† * Explanation of symbols immediately precedes page one.

***The 11th: And Last Booke of the Ocean to Scinthia.***[1] Fragment is a continuation of ten preceding books. Chiefly in quatrains. "The Shepherd of the Ocean" (Ralegh) pays homage to Cynthia (Queen Elizabeth) while bewailing his misfortunes.

***Even such is Time.*** Found in his Bible, these nine lines were probably written on the night before his execution.

*Estimate.* He writes in an enthusiastic prose which often becomes so meandering as to be difficult to trail; but his style is strong, his statements logical. Unlike his prose, his poetry, concise and aphoristic, is never difficult to follow, except possibly in the fragment addressed to "Scinthia"; but occasionally, while revealing his half-ironical and sophisticated-eloquent approach to love and living, he yields to the addiction of his age to the use of conceits. George Puttenham's *Arte of English Poesie* (p. 138) describes Ralegh's "vayne" of poetry as "most loftie, insolent, and passionate." In all his writings there is a distinct lack of humor. Frequently this seriousness took him afield into writing essays on political subjects; *e. g., The Prerogative of Parliaments* (1628) and *The Cabinet Council* (1658).

**Thomas Nash (or Nashe),** 1567—1601, satirist, poet, pamphleteer, playwright, early progenitor of the novel, University Wit. Educated at St. John's College, Cambridge. Settled in London (*c.* 1588) after touring France and Italy. Took part as "Pasquil" in the Martin Marprelate controversy. Anticipated Defoe and Smollett, linking the two to the *picaresque* fiction of Spain. (See, also, p. 158.)

***Summer's Last Will and Testament*** (1600). Satirical masque in celebration of the harvest festival. Weak in plot and character. Influenced by Robert Copland's *The Hye Way to the Spyttel Hous* (*ante* 1547), a very full catalogue of knaves of sixteenth-century England. Country-fresh songs: "Autumn hath all Summer's fruitful treasure"; and

> "Spring the sweet spring, is the year's pleasant king;
> Then blooms each thing, the maids dance in a ring."

***Pierce Penilesse, His Supplication to the Divell*** (1592). Prose satire based on the theme of the Seven Deadly Sins. Partly leveled at the participators in the Martin Marprelate controversy and against the astrologer Richard Harvey, brother of Gabriel Harvey; and, more important, against a society that permitted its creative members to starve while others batten. Rambling, digressive; yet so popular that it was translated into the French.

***Christs Teares over Jerusalem*** (1593). Allegorical pamphlet, applying Christ's prophecy of the fall of Jerusalem as a warning to

---

1 For choosing this title instead of *The 21st: And Last Book of the Ocean to Scinthia,* see Latham, A. M. C., "Sir Walter Ralegh's *Cynthia,*" *The Review of English Studies,* IV (1928) pp. 129-134.

loose-living London, wittily, satirically, and sometimes lyrically pictures the vices and abuses of the time. Lack of wholeheartedness probably accounts for a less extravagant style and a more sober denunciation.

***The Unfortunate Traveller, or The Life of Jack Wilton*** † (1594). First English historical novel, first English picaresque tale or novel of adventure. Somewhat incoherent plot interrupted by protractedly turgid and irrelevantly moralizing passages is held together by the journalistic variety of interest, riotous vigor of narrative, good-humored audacity of satire, concrete realism, impassioned if not truculent pamphleteering style, tabloid-like in its bantering and telling raciness, and an almost triumphant gaiety.

Probably prompted by the Spanish picaresque romance, *Lazarillo de Tormes.* Characteristics of the *picaresque* or *rogue* novel include practical joking, interest in travel, and the supplanting of chivalrous heroes, romantic love, and supernatural occurrences by scamps and their realistic adventures. (His tabloid-like tone and interest are revealed by his descriptions of the sweating sickness, the magic of Cornelius Agrippa, vivisection; particularly notorious is the alleged connection of Surrey with Geraldine, given definite form by one part of Nash's romantic farrago. See p. 119.)

**Thomas Campion,** *c.* 1566—1619, lyricist, masque-writer, lutenist, composer, physician, a pioneer in the art of literary criticism.

***Poemata*** (1595). Admirable Latin verse reveals autobiographical details. Practise gave him dexterity in verse (*e. g.,* in all his work he frequently versifies the same thought in both English and Latin).

***Observations in the Art of English Poesie*** (1602). Tilts against the artificiality of rime in poetry, pleading for the abandonment of rime in favor of the adoption into English of the (unrimed) classical meters; *i. e.,* "metres classified according to the terminology of Greek and Latin poetry, which he sought to make, and believed to be, imitations of classical quantitative verse."[1] Attempted to do in England what Claudio Tolemei's *Versi e Regoli della Nuovo Poesia* was doing in Italy. "Rose-cheeked Laura, come" is his best attempt at a rimeless lyric.

***A Booke of Ayres*** (1601); ***Two Bookes of Ayres*** (1612); ***The Third and Fourth Booke of Ayres*** (1617). Songbooks reveal fresh feeling, pleasantly euphuistic phrasing, light fancy; fluidity of rhythm, mastery of complicated meters and of musical notation. Magically melodic lyrics: "Hark, all you ladies that do sleep"; "There is a Garden in her face"; "When thou must home to shades of underground"; and the devotional hymn:

> "Never weather-beaten Sail more willing bent to shore,
> Never tired Pilgrim's limbs affected slumber more."

---

1 *Campion's Works,* edited by Vivian, Percival (1909), p. LX.

† * Explanation of symbols immediately precedes page one.

**Samuel Daniel,** 1562—1619, sonneteer, historian, epistle-writer, masque-writer, poet-laureate. Son of a music-master. Three years at Magdalen College, Oxford (1579—1582). Master of the Queen's Revels (1603—1615). Gentleman-extraordinary and Groom of the Chamber to Queen Anne. Absence of vital movement, passion, and imagination; presence of moral earnestness, correct English, and a self-controlled style. Influenced by Spenser.

***Delia*** (1592). Sonnet-cycle (fifty in number) indebted to Tasso, du Bellay, Desportes. "Delia" is probably Mary, Countess of Pembroke, or Elizabeth Carey, daughter of Sir George Carey. General form is that of three quatrains followed by a couplet (*ababbcbccdcdee*). Happy phrasing wedded to silvery lyricism. "When men shall find thy flower, thy glory pass"; "I must not grieve my Love, whose eyes would read"; "Let others sing of Knights and Paladines"; "Care-charmer Sleep, son of the sable Night."

***The Complaint of Rosamund*** (1592). Companion-piece to *Delia*. Mistress of Henry II fluently but unanimatedly soliloquizes over her transgressions and her lost beauty. Pathos. In the *Troilus* stanza. Prefixed by a prose epistle to Mary, Countess of Pembroke.

"Sweet, silent rhetoric of persuading eyes,
Dumb eloquence, whose power doth move the blood
More than the words of wisdom of the wise."

***Cleopatra*** (1594). Rimed tragedy after the Senecan fashion.

***History of the Civil Wars between the Two Houses of York and Lancaster***† (1595—1609). Eight-book poem of 900 skilfully-handled stanzas in *ottava rima* concerned chiefly with the Wars of the Roses. Pure language, philosophical passages; heavy moralizing, unpoetic imagination.

***Musophilus, or Defence of All Learning*** (*c.* 1599). Weightily didactic and sustained poetic dialogue, in six- and eight-line stanzas. The idealist Musophilus defends the Muses against the materialistic Philocosmus.

***A Defence of Rime***† (1602). Courteous, triumphant refutation of Campion's attack on rime (p. 144). Qualities of prose style probably excel those of any contemporaneous writer.

***Epistles*** (1603). Demonstrates some of his most felicitous phrasing and seasoned reflective powers. Best is to Lady Margaret, Countess of Cumberland. Epistle to Lucy, Countess of Bedford, uses *terza rima;* but it is possibly a mistake to believe that this rare form in English poetry makes its first appearance in Samuel Daniel.[1]

---

1 "The epistle to Lucy, Countess of Bedford, is remarkable among those as being composed in genuine *terza rima,* till then not used in English." *The Encyclopedia Britannica,* Fourteenth Edition, VII (1929), p. 31 (p. 30 *f.*). See Chaucer's *A Complaint to His Lady* (p. 65) and Wyatt's satires (p. 118).

† * Explanation of symbols immediately precedes page one.

***Philotas*** (1605). Blank-verse Senecan tragedy founded on Plutarch's version. Aroused some political opposition.

**Michael Drayton,** 1563—1631, painstaking voluminous versifier whose music occasionally kindles to a strange and sheer Spenserian fire. Buried in Westminster Abbey. Elegies and epistles are similar to those by Daniel (p. 145), who is more graceful and delicate but less vitalizing and varied.

***The Harmony of the Church*** (1591). Tame metrical paraphrases of scriptural passages in jogging fourteen-syllable verse. Traces of Euphuism. Mysteriously confiscated by public order of Archbishop Whitgift.

***Idea, the Shepherd's Garland*** (1593). Nine eclogues in the tradition of Spenser, with a homely tone substituted for the master's archaisms. Sugared verse and awkward inversions dim the Elizabethan glow. Heroine's name borrowed indirectly from Plato through *L'Idée* (1579), by the French sonneteer-physician, Claude de Pontoux.

***Idea's Mirror*** (1594). Sonnet-sequence in Shakespearean and Petrarchan form. Its 51 "amours" or sonnets influenced by Claude de Pontoux's collection, *L'Idée.* In general, dramatic and versatile, but pseudo-passionate and indelicate. Drayton has been described by Henry Morley as one who "lived to the age of eighty-eight, and died a bachelor." "Idea" is probably Anne, younger daughter of his patron Sir Henry Goodere of Polesworth, who married Sir Henry Reinsford in 1596; or possibly Lucy, Countess of Bedford. "Idea" means the Platonic conception of beauty. Memorable: "Dear, why should you command me to my rest" (XLI); "Since there's no help, come let us kiss and part" (LXI), asserted by Rossetti to be "almost the best in the language, if not quite."

***England's Heroicall Epistles*** (1597). Historical figures exchange imaginary letters in verse. (*Cf.* Walter Savage Landor's *Imaginary Conversations,* 1824—1853.)

***The Barons' Wars*** (1603). War-song in *ottava rima,* generally lacking life and movement, is an account of the barons against Edward II. Designed to emphasize the evils of civil strife. (Originally published in 1596 as *Mortimeriados,* in the seven-line stanza of Chaucer's *Troilus and Criseyde.*)

***Poems Lyrick and Pastorall*** (1606). Includes the harp-stirring "Ode to the Virginian Voyage," in essence a metrical paraphrase of some parts of Hakluyt (p. 148)[1]; and the swinging "Ballad of Agincourt," regarded as the most spirited of martial lyrics, even if it is thin in substance.

---

1 Adams, J. Q., "Michael Drayton's *To the Virginian Voyage,*" *Modern Language Notes,* XXXIII (1918), pp. 405-408.

***The Poly-Olbion*** † (1613—1622). Principal work. Bulky, careful, erudite, zealously patriotic poem celebrates chief topographical features of England. Interspersed with tales, catalogues of British saints, and the like. Indebted to Geoffrey of Monmouth (p. 43).[1] Frequently flat and tedious; but also abounding in passages of true poetic fire, particularly in its pastoral descriptions. Twelve-syllable (Alexandrine) rimed couplets.

***Nimphidia, the Court of Faery*** (1637). Mock-heroic fantasia. Ingenious fancy, delicate beauty. Perhaps the gem of delightful fairy-poems in language. Probably suggested by Chaucer's *Rime of Sir Thopas* (p. 73). Inspired Herrick.

**Raphael Holinshed,** *d. c.* 1580, chronicler whose chief title to fame is that his work was a source-book for Elizabethan dramatists.

***Chronicles of England, Scotland, and Ireland*** (1578). Most famous Elizabethan chronicle. Known by Holinshed's name, but compiled with the assistance of such men as William Harrison, Edward Campion, and Richard Stanyhurst. Memorable as the chief quarry for the plots of Shakespeare's historical plays, for *Macbeth, King Lear,* and for the legendary history in *Cymbeline.* Clear, often spirited, style excels that of most chroniclers.

**Sir Thomas North,** *c.* 1535—*c.* 1601, scholar, translator. Knighted (1591). Pensioned by Queen Elizabeth (1601).

***The Diall of Princes, with the famous booke of Marcus Aurelius*** (1557). Translation through a French intermediary of Antonio de Guevara's *Libro de Emperador Marco cõ rélox de principes* . . . . First full version of Spaniard's plea for moderation in politics. Not infrequently regarded heretofore as of direct assistance in introducing some elements of Euphuism; for the Spaniard's work is noted for its alliteration, allusiveness, affectation, vivacity, and learning. (See Lord Berners, p. 96.)

***Lives of the Noble Grecians and Romans*** (1579). Generally called Plutarch's *Lives* or North's *Plutarch.* Most famous Elizabethan translation. Also the best. With additions from other authors, North translated Jacques Amyot's French version of the original Greek into idiomatic prose—vivid, dramatic, powerful, noble. Strongly reenforced the classical influence in England; was quarried for historical, critical, and ethical examples; above all, rich source book for Shakespeare (*Julius Caesar, Coriolanus, Antony and Cleopatra*) who often changed North's phraseology but little.[2]

---

1 Gourvitch, I., "Drayton's Debt to Geoffrey of Monmouth," *The Review of English Studies*, IV (1928), pp. 394-403.

2 Matthiessen, F. O., *Translation, An Elizabethan Art* (1931), Chap. III, pp. 95-98 (pp. 54-102); Murry, J. M., *Countries of the Mind* (1931), Second Series, Chap. VI "North's Plutarch," pp. 92-94 (pp. 78-96).

† * Explanation of symbols immediately precedes page one.

X **Richard Hakluyt,** *c.* 1552—1616, geographer, imperialist. Chaplain to Edward Stafford (1583—1588). Archdeacon of Westminster (1603). Has been called England's "national Homer."[1]

***The Principal Navigations, Voyages, Traffiques, and Discoveries of the English Nation, made by Sea or over Land, within the Compass of these 1500 years*****†** (1598—1600). Among some 517 bald, vigorous, and faithful accounts, chronicles in a spirit of national pride the narratives of such men as Sir Humphrey Gilbert, Sir John Hawkins, Thomas Cavendish, Sir Francis Drake, and Ralegh. Written in confutation of the Frenchman's estimate of an Englishman as one who was insular and spiritless, the work is important not only as a literature of enthusiasm but also as historical material effective from the point of view of empire-building. Warner's *Albion's England* includes many extracts taken from Hakluyt[2]; Kingsley's *Westward Ho!* is based on Hakluyt. (Samuel Purchas, *c.* 1575—1626, a rector, in 1625, continued the work in *Hakluytus Posthumus or Purchas his Pilgrimes.*)

## *ENGLISH TRANSLATIONS AND TRANSLATORS OF THE BIBLE*

For earlier translators, see Caedmon (p. 12), Aldhelm (p. 15), Bede (p. 15), Alcuin (p. 16), Alfred (p. 18), Aelfric (p. 20) Eadfrith (p. 21), Faerman (p. 21), Rolle of Hampole (p. 27).

### Fourteenth Century

**John Wyclif.** First complete version in English. See p. 53.

### Sixteenth Century

**(a) William Tindale,** *c.* 1484—1536, scholar, reformer, a leader of the Protestant Reformation, martyr. First to translate the New Testament from the Greek text (1525). Translated the Pentateuch (*c.* 1531) and the book of Jonah (1535). Rhythmic, crisp prose and a suffused mastery of the English idiom helped fix the style and tone of the *Authorized Version* (p. 149); accurate, scholarly, generally clear. Annotated the text. Combined translations published in *Matthew's Bible.*

**(b) Miles Coverdale,** 1488—1568. Bishop of Exeter (1551). First complete translation of the Bible printed in the English language (1535), adapted from the Latin and German-Swiss. *Coverdale's Bible* includes Tindale's work on the Old Testament. Main basis of *Matthew's Bible.* Notable for the rhythmical beauty of the Psalter in the English Prayer Book. Also superintended the issue of *The Great Bible* (1539)

---

1 Dodds, T. L., "Hakluyt and Voyages of Discovery in Tudor Times," *Proceedings of the Literary and Philosophical Society of Liverpool,* LXII (1912), p. 5 (p. 1-31).

2 Cawley, R. R., "Warner and the Voyagers," *Modern Philology,* XX (1922), pp. 113-147.

† * Explanation of symbols immediately precedes page one.

and edited *Cranmer's Bible* (1540). Less scholarly than Tindale. (*Coverdale's Bible* sometimes called the "Bug Bible" because of the translation of Psalms, XCI, 5.) See also *The Great Bible* (p. 149).

(c) **John Rogers,** *c.* 1500—1555, London rector, first of the Marian martyrs. Issued the so-called *Matthew's Bible* (1537) under the pseudonym of Thomas Matthew. Pronouncedly Protestant version included Tindale's New Testament and Old Testament as far as the end of 2 Chronicles. Marginal notes formed the earliest English commentary on the Scriptures.

(d) **Richard Taverner,** *c.* 1505—1575, prepared the *Taverner's Bible* (1539), a revision of the *Matthew's.*

(e) ***The Great Bible*** (1539). Coverdale's revision of his own Bible of 1535, collated with Tindale's and Matthew's. Sometimes called (Thomas) "Cromwell's Bible" at whose direction it was undertaken. Its Psalms are still retained in the Prayer-book.

(f) **Thomas Cranmer,** 1489—1556, Archbishop of Canterbury burned at the stake as a heretic. *Cranmer's Bible* is so-called because he wrote a preface to Coverdale's second edition of *The Great Bible* in 1540.

(g) ***The Geneva Bible*** (1560). Undertaken by the English exiles at Geneva during the persecutions under Mary. First in Roman type instead of black letters, first in which the chapters are divided into verses, first in which italics are used for explanatory words and phrases. (Sometimes called the "Breeches Bible," in allusion to Genesis, III, 7: "They sewed fig leaves together and made themselves breeches.")

(h) ***The Bishops' Bible*** (1568). This revision of the *Great Bible* is the basis of the *Authorized Version.* To it most of the Anglican bishops contributed. Instigated to counteract the popularity of the Calvinistic *Geneva Bible.* Translation promoted by Matthew Parker, 1504—1575, Archbishop of Canterbury; hence, sometimes called "Matthew Parker's Bible."

### Seventeenth Century

(a) ***The Douai*** or ***Douai-Rheims Version*** (1582—1609). Romanist translation of the New Testament (1582) at Rheims; of the Old Testament (1609) at Douai.

(b) ***The Authorized Version***† (1611).[1] Most famous of all English translations, executed by a body of forty-seven scholars and divines supported in the undertaking by James I (hence, frequently called

1 Of the succeeding versions only one or two need be mentioned. The *Revised New Testament* (1881) and the *Revised Old Testament* (1885) were executed by British and American committees. Recently James Moffatt published his version of the New Testament (1922) and the Old Testament (1924)—the so-called *Moffat Bible.*

† * Explanation of symbols immediately precedes page one.

*King James' Bible*). *The Bishops' Bible* of 1568 is the basis; but other previous translations also used.[1] Homely but dignified phrase wedded to a noble sonority. Exercised a commanding influence on English literature, to which T. H. Huxley testifies:

"Consider this historical fact, that, for three centuries, this book has been woven into all that is noblest and best in English history; consider that it has become the national epic of Great Britain; and that it is as familiar to noble and simple, from John O'Groat's to Land's End, as Tasso and Dante once were to the Italians; consider that it is written in the noblest and purest of English, and that it abounds in exquisite beauties of literary form; and, finally, consider that it forbids the veriest hind, who never left his native village, to be ignorant of the existence of other countries and other civilizations, and of a great past stretching back to the furthest limits of the oldest nations in the world."

## *THE PREDECESSORS OF SHAKESPEARE IN THE DRAMA*

**John Lyly,** *c.* 1553—1606, romance writer or rudimentary novelist, dramatist, court poet, University Wit. Educated at Magdalen College, Oxford, and at Cambridge. Member of Parliament (1589—1601). Supported the bishops in the Martin Marprelate controversy; *e. g.*, through his tract called *Pappe with an Hatchet, alias a figge for my Godsonne.*

***Euphues, or the Anatomy of Wit*** (1578). ***Euphues and his England***†* (1580). Prose romance in two parts, the first dovetailing the parable of the Prodigal Son with the legend of Two Friends (*Decameron,* X, 8), the second loosely joining three stories but in a more imaginative way. Not seldom regarded as the first novel of psychology, and the first novel of manners. Slender plot apparently exists for the purpose of discoursing upon such matters as love and youthful folly, woman and constancy, friendship and education, irreligion and immorality. Triangle-plot. Conventional characters. Owes both the title and the substance to Ascham's *Scholemaster* (p. 117). Influenced by such Italian authors as Boccaccio, Petrarch, Alciati, Sannazaro, Tasso, Guarini,[2] and by Thomas Lupton, and Gascoigne.

---

1 Tindale's translation influenced the *Authorized Version* probably as much as any. Gardiner, J. H., *The Bible as English Literature,* (1906), pp. 325-327; Pollard, A. W., *The New Testament Translated by William Tindale 1525* (1926), p. xxi; Ware, Lois, "The Peculiar Excellence of William Tindale's Translation of the Gospels," *Studies in English, The University of Texas Bulletin,* Number 12 (1932), pp. 56-76; Wild, L. H., "An Observation upon Tindale's Linguistic Genius," *The Macdonald Presentation Volume* (Princeton University Press, 1933), pp. 457-470.

2 Jeffery, V. M., *John Lyly and the Italian Renaissance* (1928); *Euphues: The Anatomy of Wit; Euphues and His England,* edited by Croll, M. W., and Clemens, Harry (1916).

†* Explanation of symbols immediately precedes page one.

Its style has given the term *Euphuism*[1] to rhetorical writing; but its chief characteristics correspond to similar tendencies in Antonio de Guevara and Marini, and in the Englishmen Lord Berners, Fisher, George Pettie, Elyot, North, and More. Distinctions of its style are (1) skilful sentence-building, (2) word-and-clause antithesis, (3) parallelism of all kinds, and (4) rhythm and harmony. However, *Euphuism* is known primarily for its vices: (1) incessant parallelism of sentence-structure, (2) a debauch of multiple word-plays and alliteration, (3) profuse use of artificially balanced phrases and periodic sentences, with the perpetual introduction of proverbs,[2] (4) excessive use of labored and fantastic similes, comparisons, and far-fetched allusions from mythology and the "unnatural natural history" of the *physiologi,* lapidary, and bestiary, and (5) a pervading effort after excessive elegance of language: ambiguous phrases, subtle similes, tortured conceits, pedantic exfoliations and affectations.

***The Woman in the Moone**** (*c.* 1584; published 1597). Only play in (blank) verse. Satirizes women. Elizabeth likened to Pandora. Poetic in conception. A music drama but without Lyly's usual wit.

***Alexander and Campaspe*†*** (1584). Euphuistic prose comedy, based on an historic anecdote. Neatness of epigram, wit of dialogue, ingenuity of thought. Many characters. Lyrics: "What bird so sings yet so does wail"; and particularly

"Cupid and my Campaspe play'd
At cards for kisses: Cupid paid."

***Sapho and Phao**** (1584). Prose court-allegory, based on a pseudo-classical myth. Sapho is Elizabeth, Phao is the Duke d'Alençon.

***Endimion, the Man in the Moone*** (*c.* 1588). Allegorical prose-play. Frequently said to concern Elizabeth (Cynthia, the Moon or the Chaste Huntress), Mary Stuart or Lady Sheffield (Tellus), James of Scotland or Leicester (Endimion), the Earl of Sussex or Sir Philip Sidney (Eumenides), the Countess of Shrewsbury (Dipsas), and others. Contemporary criticism inclined to reject traditional reading. First to introduce fairies into the English drama. Characters: Sir Tophas and his page Epiton.

***Midas*** (1592). Skilful prose court-allegory. Parable of Philip II's (Midas's) effrontery in attempting to rival England (Lesbos). Lyric: "My Daphne's hair is twisted gold."

---

1 An advanced discussion of "The Sources of Euphuistic Rhetoric" is given in *Euphues: The Anatomy of Wit; Euphues and His England,* edited by Croll, M. W., and Clemens, Harry (1916), pp. 15-64.

2 Tilley, M. P., *Elizabethan Proverb Lore in Lyly's "Euphues" and in Pettie's "Petite Pallace"* (1926).

† * Explanation of symbols immediately precedes page one.

*General Estimate.* With a vivid imagination and a sense of form which respectively played upon and made coherent his careful diction, Lyly helped mould English prose. His distinctions are an equable style, neat phraseology, ready rhythm, and ever-present opulence. Only his excesses have been disparaged; his dialogue, for example, has been satirized in the speeches of Shakespeare's Don Adriano de Armado, Jonson's Puntarvolo, Scott's Sir Piercie Shafton. Influenced Greene, Lodge, and Sidney. As a playwright, Lyly is considered the creator of essentially high comedy. Stilted talk, little plot, and anemic although sometimes happy characterization are seesawed by pretty fancies and delightful songs,[1] smart-talk prose dialogue and personal and current-event allusions, fair motivating action and love-story suspense, subtle comedy and saucy wit instead of buffoonery and knockabout humor. Court-comedies gave hints to other playwrights and to Shakespeare by their virtuoso treatment of prose, their dainty lyrics and music (his Anacreontics are the best produced by sixteenth-century England), and their romantic masques.

**Thomas Kyd,** *c.* 1557—*c.* 1594, dramatist, translator, last of the University Wits (although possibly not a University man). Educated at Merchant Taylors' School, London. Best work shows good construction of plot, simplicity, effective stage situations, development of character. Historic, rather than artistic, pioneering influenced other dramatists.

***The Spanish Tragedy*****†*** (*ante* 1600; possibly *c.* 1589). Non-religious drama, most popular of plays in its own time, introduced the type known as "the tragedy of blood," to which *Titus Andronicus* (p. 178) belongs. *Hamlet* itself is said to be a refinement based upon the *Ur-Hamlet,* ascribed to Kyd. (The *Ur-Hamlet,* through its German prefix meaning "primordial," is used to describe a conjectured Hamlet-play no longer available.)

Play, in frequently ranting as well as tame blank verse, of horror piled, Seneca-like, upon horror, of murder, unbridled frenzy, bloodshed, and sudden death. (Other Senecan influences apparent in the chorus, the ghost, the declamation, and the frequent balanced speeches or stichomythy.) Large tragical conception, not wholly without pathos, reveals how the interaction of episode and developing story bears upon the crystallization of beefy character, although, essentially, Hieronimo is paroxysmally rhetorical and Bel-imperia merely a plot-personage. Style

1 Lyly's authorship of the songs in his plays has been challenged. In defense of Lyly, see Lawrence, W. J., "The Problem of Lyly's Songs," *The Times* (London), Literary Supplement, December 20, 1923, cols. 1-3; Bond, R. W., "Addendum on *Lyly's Songs,*" *The Review of Reviews,* VII (1931), pp. 442-447. In opposition to this stand, see Greg, W. W., "The Authorship of the Songs in Lyly's Plays." *Modern Language Review,* I (1905), pp. 43-52; Moore, J. R., "The Songs in Lyly's Plays," *Publications of the Modern Language Association of America,* XLII (1927), pp. 622-640.

† * Explanation of symbols immediately precedes page one.

parodied by Shakespeare in the play-scene before the King in *Hamlet;* and, as in the latter, there is a ghost, a play within a play (contained in Henry Wotton's collection of five stories, published in 1578 as *Courtlie Controuversie of Cupids Cautels*), and, at the curtain's fall, corpses dripping blood upon the stage. (Hamlet, however, is different in that it is the story of the revenge of a son for the murder of his father.)

***Arden of Feversham**** (1592). Has been attributed to Kyd, or to an imitator, or even to Shakespeare himself. First extant example of the domestic tragedy is founded on a murder committed in 1551. Vivid, dramatic.

***Pompey the Great, his Faire Corneliaes Tragedy*** (1595). Senecan tragedy in blank verse based on a French work by Robert Garnier.

**Robert Greene,** *c.* 1558—1592, dramatist, lyric poet, novelist, satirist, "conny-catching" pamphleteer, University Wit. Educated at Cambridge. Possibly travelled abroad rather extensively (1578—1583). Founder of English pastoral comedy. Prolific: more than two dozen novels, about two-score prose tracts interspersed with songs, broadsides, romances,[1] plays. Concentrated energy vies with diffused euphuism; comic humor with malicious wit; fluent versification with weighted classical ornament; idyllic impressions of country life with seamy depictions of town-cutpurses. Generally indistinct characterization redeemed by delicate drawing of English maidenhood: the first to delineate women in the manner of Shakespeare: called by Nash "the Homer of women." Moreover, his Nano, Miles, and Slipper are the prototypes of Shakespeare's Launce, Touchstone, and Launcelot. Among his real women are Bellaria and Fawnia, in *Pandosto;* Margaret, in *Friar Bacon and Friar Bungay;* Sephestia, in *Menaphon;* Ida and Queen Dorothea, in *The Scottish Historie of James the Fourth.* Introduced the heroine disguised as a page. Practice of interspersing his blank verse with rimed couplets, and of giving a kind of organic unity to the sober and humorous elements in plays, taught Shakespeare the trick. Fresh lyrics (besides those mentioned below) are: "Fair is my love, for April's in her face"; "Ah, what is love? It is a pretty thing" (*The Mourning Garment*); "Sweet are the thoughts that savour of content" (*Farewell to Folly*).

***Pandosto, or Dorastus and Fawnia*** (1588). Pastoral prose romance based on a Polish tale, and in turn the source of the whole plot of Shakespeare's *Winter's Tale* (p. 221). Fawnia, Dorastus, and Bellaria are respectively Shakespeare's Perdita, Florizel, and Hermione.

---

1 Tynan, J. L., "The Influence of Greene on Shakespeare's Early Romance," *Publications of the Modern Language Association of America,* XXVII; New Series, XX (1912), pp. 246-264.

† * Explanation of symbols immediately precedes page one.

Euphuistic, moralizing; influenced by Sidney's *Arcadia*. Song: "Ah! were she pitiful as she is fair."

***Menaphon*** (1589). Prose-verse romance. One source probably William Warner's *Albion's England* (Bk. IV, Chap. XX).[1] Arcadian songs: "Weep not, my wanton, smile upon my knee"; "Like to Diana in her summer weed."

***Friar Bacon and Friar Bungay*†*** (1589). Verse-prose romance on white-magic supposedly written in emulation of Marlowe's *Faustus*,[2] a play on black-magic (p. 157). Love-story probably original, while the plot proper is derived from the tale, *The Famous Historie of Friar Bacon* (late 16th century?). Magic scenes reminiscent of the older morality play; pastoral descriptions are almost a new departure; pictures of life as dramatic as those in Shakespeare's *Merry Wives of Windsor* (p. 194). Prince Edward and Margaret are immediate prototypes of Shakespeare's Prince Hal and Perdita.

***The Scottish Historie of James the Fourth*†** (*c.* 1591). English pseudo-history chronicle play. Imaginary account based on the first novel of the third decade of Giraldi Cinthio's *Hecatommithi*. Lady Ida, with whom the King has fallen in love, and Queen Dorothea, who symbolizes the Griselda unable to suspect the King of plotting her death, redeem an otherwise languid play; see, for example, the touching reconciliation at the close. Most perfect in technique of all his plays.

***A Groatsworth of Wit bought with a Million of Repentance*** (1592). Fluent, vigorous autobiographical prose document memorable for its possible allusion to Shakespeare. Before concluding with the fable of the grasshopper and the ant, Greene admonishes such boon-playwrights as Marlowe and Lodge to give up writing plays, "for there is an upstart Crow, beautified with our feathers, that with his Tygers hart wrapt in a Players hyde, supposes he is . . . . an absolute Ioannes fac totum, is in his owne conceit the onely Shake-scene in a countrey." Parody of Shakespeare's line, "O tiger's heart wrapt in a woman's hide!" (*Henry VI, Part III, Act I, 4, l. 137*), and apparent pun in "Shake-scene" appear to be a depreciative allusion to the great master.[3]

***Orlando Furioso*** (1596). Adapted from Sir John Harrington's translation of Ariosto's poem. Occasionally effective.

1 Adams, J. Q., Jr. "Greene's 'Menaphon' and 'The Thracian Wonder,'" *Modern Philology*, III, No. 3 (1906), pp. 317-325.

2 More than a few scholars, by dating Marlowe's *Faustus* as of 1592, say that Marlowe wrote it to compete with Greene's play. (In another connection, Greene's *Alphonsus of Aragon*, *c.* 1587, has been described as "Tamburlaine emasculated.")

3 The traditional interpretation of the "tiger's heart" passage may be fallacious: it is almost certainly not an accusation of plagiarism. Consult Smart, J. S., *Shakespeare: Truth and Tradition* (1928), pp. 191-201; Gaw, Allison, "The Origin and Development of 1 Henry VI," *University of Southern California Studies*, First Series, Number 1 (1926); and White, H. O., *Plagiarism and Imitation During the English Renaissance* (1935), p. 100 *ff*.

† * Explanation of symbols immediately precedes page one.

**George Peele,** *c.* 1558—*c.* 1597, dramatist, lyricist, pageant-composer, miscellaneous verse writer, University Wit. Educated at Christ's Hospital, London, and Pembroke and Christ College, Oxford. Flowery diction, poetic beauty, dignified pathos. Lyrics sweeter and daintier than Lyly's. Blank verse often rises to a grandeur possibly unattained by any poet before Shakespeare. But lacks construction and vitality. Knowledge of Greek and wide knowledge of folk-lore apparent in his work.

***The Arraignment of Paris*†*** (*c.* 1582). Court pastoral masque-play. Ultimate award of the apple to the nymph Eliza is obviously flattery of Queen Elizabeth, before whom the five-act play was acted by the Children of the Chapel Royal. Most alive character of all his plays is Oenone. Innovates the combination of mythological and pastoral elements. Absence of varied and subtle characterization almost forgotten because of charming nature-descriptions, pleasant songs, delicate verse in a harmonizing variety of meters skilfully commanded. Genuine dramatic sense. Influenced by Spenser's *Shepheardes Calender,* Greene's *Orlando Furioso,* the folk-tales *Childe Rowland* and *The Three Heads of the Well,* and by Anello Paulilli's *Il Giuditio di Paride.*[1]

***Polyhymnia*** (1590). Poem, sung before the Queen at Westminster, celebrates Sir Henry Lee's retirement from the office of Queen's Champion on November 17, 1590. "A Farewell to Arms," beautiful tribute to the Queen (quoted in Thackeray's *The Newcomes*):

> "His golden locks Time hath to silver turned;
> O Time too swift, O swiftness never ceasing!"

***Edward the First*** (1593). Early historical play, crude yet an advance in the chronicle-type, helps usher in the historical plays of Shakespeare. Lyrical, tender.

***The Battle of Alcazar*** (1594). Verse-play in which the historical English adventurer Thomas Stucley (*c.* 1525—1578) appears. Source is an anonymous pamphlet. Much indifferent poetry. Imitates Greene and Marlowe.

***The Old Wives' Tale*†*** (acted *c.* 1591; published 1595). Prose-play which for the first time in English satirizes the romantic dramas of the day. Conventional devices and construction; original sources and purpose. Notable induction. Topical characters; *e. g.,* Huanebango is Gabriel Harvey. Influenced, if it did not inspire, Milton's ***Comus*** (p. 279). Title later used by Arnold Bennett (1867—1931).

---

1 Is Paulilli the source of *The Arraignment of Paris?* See Jeffery, V. M., "Italian and Engish Pastoral Drama of the Renaissance: (II) The Source of Peele's 'Arraignment of Paris,' " *Modern Language Review* (1924), pp. 175-187.

† * **Explanation of symbols immediately precedes page one.**

***The Love of David and Fair Bethsabe*** (1599). Only extant Elizabethan play with a wholly scriptural subject; a poetic paraphrase in beautiful blank verse of 2 Samuel XI—XX. Ornamental and sonorous diction, colorful passages; slow-moving, prettily rhetorical, frigidly decorative. Has a Greek chorus. Influenced Milton's *Paradise Lost* (p. 286). (Similar drama written by Racine ninety years later in *Esther,* 1689.)

**An Eclogue Gratulatory.** Addressed to Robert, Earl of Essex.

**Christopher Marlowe,** 1564—1593, Shakespeare's greatest predecessor, father of English tragedy. Born in the same year as Shakespeare. Son of a Canterbury shoemaker. Entered King's School, Canterbury (1579). At Corpus Christi College, Cambridge (1581). B. A. (*c.* 1583). M. A. (*c.* 1587). University Wit associated as a dramatist in London with the Lord Admiral's and Strange's companies. Warrant issued by Privy Council for his arrest (1593), possibly because of his reputed unorthodoxy in religion, or possibly because of his association as an agent in the secret service. Before the case of the twenty-nine-year-old dramatist could be considered, he was stabbed to death, it is said, in a sordid brawl at the house, or tavern, of the widow Eleanor Bull, in Deptford.[1] (Marlowe possibly had a hand in the Shakespearean plays *Henry VI, Richard III,* and *Titus Andronicus.* See pp. 175-179.)

**Plays**

***Tamburlaine the Great*†*** (*c.* 1587—1588). Heroic epic in dramatic form divided into two parts, each of five acts. Humor not genuine; poetry rhetorical, plot and characters static, dramatic structure poor; but rhetoric gorgeous, dialogue effective, diction electrifying, blank verse resonant, and poetry frequently lyrical, even epical. Traditionally considered the instaurator of dramatic blank verse—see his prologue-manifesto. From among the two-score available sources, he probably leaned most on Ariosto's *Orlando Furioso,* Ortelius's *Theatrum Orbis Terrarum* (1570) Petrus Perondinus's *Magni Tamerlanis Scythiarum Imperatoris Vita* (1553), and particularly Pedro Mexía's *Silva de Varia Lectíon* (1543).[2] Prose parts and short lines may not be by Marlowe.[3]

---

1 It is frequently said that Marlowe met a violent death at the hands of Francis Archer, a "bawdy" serving-man; but other conjectures have been made. Did Marlowe, supping with Nicholas Skeres, cutpurse, Robert Poley, *agent provocateur,* and Francis Ffrezer (Ingram Ffrysar), servant to Sir Thomas Walsingham, receive Ffrezer's dagger-thrust because of the poet's service as a secret political agent? Consult Hotson, J. L., *The Death of Christopher Marlowe* (1925). Was Marlowe murdered at the instigation of Sir Walter Ralegh, traditionally regarded as Kit's personal friend? See Tannenbaum, S. A., *The Assassination of Christopher Marlowe* (1928). For a simple summary-analysis of the mysterious death, refer to Slater, Gilbert, *Seven Shakespeares* (1931), Chap. VII, pp. 117-149.

2 Seaton, Ethel, "Fresh Sources for Marlowe," *The Review of English Studies,* V (1929), pp. 385-401; *Tamburlaine the Great,* edited by Ellis-Fermor, U. M. (1930), pp. 17-61.

3 Van Dam, B. A. P., "Marlowe's Tamburlaine," *English Studies* (Amsterdam), XVI (1934), pp. 1-17, 49-51.

† * Explanation of symbols immediately precedes page one.

***The Tragical History of Doctor Faustus*†*** (*c.* 1588—1592). Tragedy in blank verse and vivid prose; but only the blank verse, particularly magnificent in the first two acts, is conclusively Marlowe's.[1] By its scenes of dramatic intensity and power the play compensates for the lack of proportion and looseness of technique, defects less apparent in his other three great plays. Based on a medieval legend attached to a real Dr. Faustus, a sixteenth-century necromancer; the legend, found in the German *Volksbuch,* was used, for example, by Calderon in *El Magico Prodigioso,* and by Goethe in *Faust.*[2] Immediate source probably an inaccurate translation (possibly P. F. Ghent's in 1592) of Johann Spies's *Faustbuch,* or *Historia von D. Johann Fausten, dem weitbeschreuyen Zauberer und Schwartzkunstler* (1587)—*i. e.,* "The History of Dr. Johann Faust, the widely-known master-conjuror of the Black Art." The cheap, coarse, incongruous humor may not be Marlowe's[3]; nor, for that matter, the vivid prose. Note the final soliloquy and terrible climax of one who, lusting for the infinite, has sold his human soul to gain it.[4] Famous: "Was this the face that launch'd a thousand ships?"

***The Jew of Malta*†*** (*c.* 1592). Drama in blank verse of a hero-villain is a melodrama, or even a farce,[5] rather than a tragedy. Source unknown. Improbable plot, capitalizing on anti-Semitic prejudice, gives Marlowe ample opportunity to reveal his best character-portrayal. Tragic interest, superb opening scenes, and grandeur of the first two acts are generally regarded as slumping sharply in the succeeding acts. In technique an advance upon *Dr. Faustus,* without the latter's imaginative beauty. While superseded by Shakespeare's more human *Merchant of Venice,* yet Marlowe's first act is probably a better picture of the Jew.[6]

***Edward II*†*** (1593). First Elizabethan historical drama, similar in theme to Shakespeare's *Richard II* (p. 179), who also imitated Marlowe in *Richard III* (p. 177). While not his best from the point of view of lyricism or imagination, it is probably his supreme effort from the point of view of sympathy, tragic beauty, organized technique,

---

1 Simpson, Percy, "The 1604 Text of Marlowe's 'Doctor Faustus.'" *Essays and Studies by Members of The English Association,* VII (1921), pp. 143-155.

2 Traditional criticism believes that Marlowe's work differs greatly in general conception from Goethe's *Faust.* But see Heller, Otto, "Faust and Faustus: A Study of Goethe's Relation to Marlowe," *Washington University Studies,* New Series, Language and Literature, No. 2 (1931).

3 That the comic scenes are not Marlowe's is the point of view of Simpson, Percy, "Marlowe's Tragical History of Doctor Faustus," *Essays and Studies by Members of The English Association,* XIV (1929), pp. 20-34.

4 "The overtone reflects the faith of the age—Catholicism," says Sister Mary Genevieve, "The Tragical History of Doctor Faustus: An Exposition of Catholic Faith in Medieval Times," *The Catholic Educational Review,* XXXII (1934), p. 36 (pp. 34-36).

5 Eliot, T. S., *The Sacred Wood,* (1920), p. 84 (pp. 78-86).

6 Stockley, W. F. P., "The Jews of Marlowe and Shakespeare," *The Irish Ecclesiastical Record,* XLIV (1934), pp. 71-88 (pp. 67-88).

† * Explanation of symbols immediately precedes page one.

and ripe maturity: never is his style more evenly knit, or his structure more coherent, or his blank verse more controlled, or his incidents more selected, or his power more psychological. Uses Holinshed mainly (p. 147), but also the chronicles of Robert Fabyan and John Stow.

***The Massacre of Paris*** (1593). Poor fragment based on the massacre of St. Bartholomew.

***The Tragedy of Dido Queen of Carthage*** (1594). Unfinished tragedy in sensuous[1] blank verse shows an effective understanding of female character. (Completed by Thomas Nash, p. 143.) Primary source is the *Aeneid* (*Bks. I, II, IV*), "And he'll make me immortal with a kiss" (*Dido*), foreshadowed in "Sweet Helen, make me immortal with a kiss" (*Doctor Faustus*).[2]

**Poems**

***The Passionate Shepherd to His Love*****†** (*c.* 1588). Lyric, published in *The Passionate Pilgrim* and in *England's Helicon* (p. 120). Has its ultimate source in Theocritus's *Idyl XI* and more immediate source in Ovid's *Metamorphoses* (Bk. XIII). It has been asserted that the ninth line should read "Wher we will make a bedd of Roses" rather than the version found in most anthologies. Influenced English poetry.[3]

***Hero and Leander*****†** (1598). Unfinished paraphrase of Musaeus's *Hero and Leander* completed by Chapman (p. 233), the latter's continuation adding characteristic moral obscurities and metaphysical discussions to the former's Ovidian warmth,[4] sensuous (even sensual) imagery, and rich cadence. Occasional imperfect rimes and inverted syntax. Heroic couplets. Famous line (Sest. I, *l.* 176) quoted in *As You Like It* (III, 5, *l.* 82). Possibly influenced by Hoby's *The Courtier* and Tasso's poem on Hero and Leander. Nothing could be less Greek, says Émile Legouis, in the face of Swinburne's statement that the poem has Hellenic qualities.

"*Hero and Leander,* this unfinished tragedy, is purely pagan both in conception and in execution; . . . . This is a lyrical hymn in praise of a virgin's and a youth's nakedness. When Hero loses her virginity, and before his possession of her, these raptures of the flesh and the spirit, these dear and strange contrivances of the naked girl to hide her burning beauty from her lover's eyes, her blushing nakedness which

1 Parallels are said to exist between *Dido* and *Hero and Leander.* See Bradbrook, M. C., " 'Hero and Leander,' " *Scrutiny,* II (1933-1934), p. 61 *ff.* (pp. 59-64).

2 Praz, Mario, "Christopher Marlowe," *English Studies* (Amsterdam), XIII (1931), p. 215 (pp. 209-223).

3 Forsythe, R. S., "*The Passionate Shepherd;* and English Poetry," *Publications of the Modern Language Association of America,* XL (1925), pp. 692-742.

4 Bush, Douglas, "Notes on Marlowe's *Hero and Leander,*" *Publications of the Modern Language Association of America,* XLIV (1929), pp. 760-764.

† * Explanation of symbols immediately precedes page one.

takes colour from the dawn before the dawn arises: never, in the whole realm of poetry, as far as I know, have these lines been surpassed."[1]

***Ovid's Elegies*** (printed 1596). Translation of Ovid's *Amores,* done probably during his years at Cambridge, is mediocre.

***The First Book of Lucan*** (published 1600). Good, rhythmic line-for-line translation of Lucan's *Pharsalia* (Bk. I) into non-dramatic blank verse.

## GENERAL STYLE

### SUGGESTED MERITS

1. Innovated the drama based on one omnipotent theme—a titanic figure whose lust for the infinite (for universal dominion, as in **Tamburlaine**; for intellectual dominion, as in **Doctor Faustus**; for universal wealth, as in **The Jew of Malta**) foredooms him.

2. Gives full-throated voice to many characteristics of Elizabethan England—its elaboration of theatrical spectacles, its towering pride, unbridled enthusiasm for discovery, volcanic expression of passionate ambition and aspiration, boundless vistas opened to the human spirit.

3. Reveals passages of brilliant, sensuous description, impassioned lyrical vitality, impetuous outbursts of powerful diction, and passages of profound intellectual suggestiveness.

4. Established blank verse as the form of the Elizabethan tragedy and as the meter of the English drama. His blank verse, announced by the pretentious prologue-manifesto of **Tamburlaine**, was later perfected by Shakespeare, Milton, and Wordsworth. Our first great English dramatist, he paved the way to Shakespeare.[3]

### SUGGESTED DEFECTS

1. Shows a faulty dramatic construction, despite simplicity and centralization of theme. Deficient in individualization of character—his main characters are supermen, his gentle characters, weaklings; no woman is a heroine, all women are lay figures.

2. Presents lurid themes, full of blustering declamation and violent bloodshed. Deficient in humor. While a pioneer of our romantic drama, he is totally or almost totally wanting in benevolent quality: his passion for destruction has been described as **"molochiste."**[2]

3. Deteriorates frequently into bombast, and falls frequently into bathos. Lack of restraint conduces to a continual intensity that must of itself weaken the breathtaking sweep and rush of his resonant verse.

---

1 Symons, Arthur, "A Note on the Genius of Marlowe," *The English Review,* XXXVI (1923), p. 312 *f.* (pp. 306-316).

2 Praz, Mario, "Christopher Marlowe," *English Studies* (Amsterdam), XIII (1931), p. 213 (pp. 209-223).

3 Murphy, Doreen, "Shakespeare's Debt to His Predecessors," *The Irish Monthly,* LXII (1934), pp. 501-507 (pp. 496-507, 552-558).

## Chapter XI

# THE RENAISSANCE: THE AGE OF ELIZABETH

## WILLIAM SHAKESPEARE

**William Shakespeare, Shakspeare, or Shakspere,**[1] 1564—1616. player, poet, dramatist. William Shakespeare, eldest son and third child of John Shakespeare and Mary Arden,[2] was baptized on April 26, 1564: it is, therefore, generally assumed that William was born on or about April 23, 1564. Probably attended the King's New School of Stratford-on-Avon (*c.* 1571—*c.* 1577). If he ever attended that free grammar school, he left it about 1577, possibly because his father was in financial straits. License issued for William Shakespeare's marriage to Anne Whately of Temple Grafton on November 27, 1582; marriage bond issued to William Shakespeare and Anne Hathwey of Stratford on November 28, 1582.[3] Thus, at eighteen he had married a woman of twenty-six. A daughter, Susanna, was baptized only six months later, on May 26,

---

1 Out of 400 authorities consulted for their spelling of Shakespeare's name, about 300 of them spell it *Shakespeare,* about 75 of them spell it *Shakspeare,* and about 25 of them spell it *Shakspere.* Although the *Outline-History* spells the name as the majority do, it is not at all unlikely that some day the name will be spelled *Shakspere.* There are, according to S. A. Tannenbaum, seven known signatures of the Poet of Avon (the "Deposition" signature, the "Warranty-Deed" or "Guildhall" signature, the "Mortgage-Deed" or "British Museum" signature, the three signatures occurring in the poet's will, and the signature adorning what was originally the fly-leaf of a copy of Florio's translation of Montaigne's *Essayes,* which Shakespeare is said to have owned or borrowed from a friend of his). According to S. A. Tannenbaum, Shakespeare spelled his name *Shakspere.* It is significant that the Columbia University Press announced, in the fall of 1934, that thereafter in all its publications it would spell the name *Shakspere,* without the first "e" and the second "a." In 1937, however, Harvard University officially inserted the "e" and "a."

2 The versatility of his genius has been attributed to the possible fact that William Shakespeare was possibly French on his father's side, and Saxon on his mother's side. See Adams, J. Q., "A Norman Origin for Shakespeare," *The Sewanee Review,* XXIX (1921), pp. 386-391. See, also pp. 5, 22 *ff.* of the *Outline-History.* Much has been made of Shakespeare's "universality," one recent critic, for example, pointing out Shakespeare's numerous familiar quotations and even slang expressions as "another proof of his universality." But F. E. Schelling and R. G. Shahani have asserted that Shakespeare is not essentially universally minded. Consult Marquardt, F. S., "Shakspere and American Slang," *American Speech,* IV (1929), pp. 118-122; Schelling, F. E., "The Significance of Shakespeare," *The Barnwell Bulletin,* VI (1929), No. 31; Shahani, R. G., *Shakespeare Through Eastern Eyes* (1932).

3 Are Anne Hathwey and Anne Whately identical? The question is debatable.

1583, thereby revealing the reason for their hurried marriage. Hamnet and Judith, twins, were baptized on February 2, 1585. Probably Shakespeare left his family soon after the birth of the twins. It is thought that he arrived in London about 1587 or 1588. There is no record of what occurred to Shakespeare between the baptism of the twins (1585) and Greene's indictment in *A Groatsworth of Wit* (1592—see p. 154). Appearance of Henry Chettle's *Kinde-Hartes Dreame* (Stationers' Register, December 8, 1592), in which he apologized for Greene's attack. Member of the Lord Chamberlain's Company of Players (1594—1595). Burial of his son Hamnet (August 11, 1596). Assessed for taxes as a resident of St. Helen's Parish, Bishopsgate, from which he removed his lodging to the Surrey side of the Thames. Applied to the College of Heralds for a grant of arms to his father (1596).[1] According to an old court-record, William Shakespeare is alleged to have taken part in a quarrel between Francis Langley, builder of the Swan theatre, and William Wayte, stepson of William Gardiner, Justice of the Peace in Surrey. Purchased New Place, possibly the largest house in Stratford, for £60 (1597), and in succeeding years made other purchases of landed property. Probably established his wife and daughters at New Place. Listed as an important holder of corn and malt in Stratford (1598). A principal actor in Jonson's *Every Man in his Humour* (1598). Francis Meres's *Palladis Tamia, Wit's Treasury* (1598), a kind of manual of English literature from Chaucer's day to Shakespeare's, lists twelve plays by William Shakespeare. Part-owner of the Globe theatre (1599). Coat-of-arms, applied for in 1596, now confirmed and extended by the Heralds' College to John Shakespeare (1599). Certain occurrences may have clouded Shakespeare's life; *e.g.*, the execution of Essex and the sentencing of Southampton to life-imprisonment (1600), the rise of the Children of the Chapel (1600), the death of John Shakespeare (1601), and the so-called "War of the Theatres" (1601). Bought 107 acres of freehold land in Old Stratford (1602). A principal actor in Jonson's *Sejanus his Fall* (1603). For £400 he purchased a large interest in an unexpired term of the Great Tithes of Stratford and adjacent villages (1605). Susanna, his daughter, marries John Hall (1607), to whom one child, Elizabeth, is born (February, 1608). Mary, Shakespeare's mother, dies (1608). Suit against John Aldenbrooke of Stratford (1608—1609). Shakespeare extends his purchase of land (1610). Retires to Stratford (*c.* 1610—*c.* 1612), where, except for visits to

1 A critic has stated that either William Shakespeare or his father John applied for the Heraldic honor in 1596 and possibly obtained it; the second application, in 1599, was for permission to impale the arms of the Ardens with those of Shakespeare, and this was refused. See, for example, Tannenbaum, S. A., *Was William Shakspere a "Gentleman"?* (1909). J. Q. Adams states that since John Shakespeare was still alive, William Shakespeare, when making his application to the College of Heralds in 1596, had to enter the application in his father's name. Three years later the College of Heralds gave him formal permission to quarter his arms with the ancient arms of the Ardens of Wilmecote.

London, he lived until his death. Had previously lodged at the house of Christopher Mountjoy, and is called (1612) to testify in the Belott-Mountjoy dowry case. Purchased a home in Blackfriars for £140, and mortgaged it the next day for £60 (1613). Judith married Thomas Quiney without a special license (1616), and "a decree of excommunication was issued against them." Made changes in his will, leaving most of his estate to Susanna (March, 1616). Died on April 23, 1616, and was buried in the chancel of Stratford church.[1] (William Shakespeare left no direct descendants. His wife Anne died in 1623; the last of the three unmarried sons of Judith and Thomas Quiney, in 1639; Elizabeth, the childless daughter of Susanna and John Hall, in 1670.)

## POETRY

### A. The Poems

***Venus and Adonis***† (1593). In the traditional story the handsome youth responds to the blandishments of Venus; in the Shakespearean account Adonis is not only indifferent to Venus but actually rejects her love. The new version is generally attributed to the strong likelihood that Shakespeare deliberately combined (or unwittingly confused) the elements of two tales in Ovid's *Metamorphoses*—the Adonis-Venus fable (X, *ll.* 503—579) and the wooing of Hermaphroditus by Salmacis (IV, *ll.* 285—588).[2] Suggestions for the change may also have come from Spenser's *Faerie Queene* (III, 1, xxxiii-xxxiv), from a song in Robert Greene's *Never too Late,* and from Marlowe's *Hero and Leander.* Other influences have been suggested: Ludovico Dolce's *La Favola d'Adone* (1545), Metello Giovanni Tarchagnota's *L'Adone* (1550), Girolamo Parabasco's *La Favola d'Adone* (*ante* 1557), Étienne Jodelle's "Ode de la Chasse" in his *Oeuvres et Mélanges Poëtiques* (1574), Lodge's *Scyllas Metamorphosis* (generally entitled *Glaucus and Scilla*), and other parts of Ovid's *Metamorphoses.*

It is an erotic piece, the story of which is told with a coherence lacking in Lodge's *Scyllas Metamorphosis* and with a lovely grace un-

---

1 For documentary evidence concerning Shakespeare's life, consult Brooke, Tucker, *Shakespeare of Stratford* (1926), and Chambers, E. K., *William Shakespeare,* II (1930).

2 Dürnhöfer, Max, in his *Shakespeares "Venus and Adonis" im Verhältnis zu Ovids Metamorphosen und Constables Schäfergesang* (1890), contends that Shakespeare used the Latin original rather than a translation of Ovid. The question has not been settled conclusively. It is possible, however, that Shakespeare knew Ovid in the original as well as in Golding's translation (1567).

† * Explanation of symbols immediately precedes page one.

like the conventional and fashionable erotic poetry of the time, for it should be recognized that Shakespeare's theme and treatment are essentially a product of the Renaissance.[1] Memorable for its charming landscape and eloquent set speeches. Written in iambic pentameter riming *ababcc*. Dedicated to Henry Wriothesley, Earl of Southampton.

***Lucrece*** (1594). Retells an old story found in works preceding by centuries even Fiorentino's *Il Pecorone,* Bandello's *Novelle,* Gower's *Confessio Amantis,* Lydgate's *Fall of Princes,* Painter's *Palace of Pleasure,* and old ballads. One or two hints may have been found in Virgil, Ovid's *Tristia,* Watson's *Hecatompathia,* and Giles Fletcher's *Licia,* but Shakespeare seems to have drawn particularly upon Chaucer's *Legend of Good Women* (p. 68), even more upon Ovid's *Fasti,* and, especially for ideas and passages, upon Livy's prose.

Despite the theme, Shakespeare tells the tale in a manner remarkably free from the eroticism in *Venus and Adonis.* Its rhetorical outbursts, conceits, long tirades, and set speeches are tedious, but frequently the lyrical and felicitous Shakespeare is evident. It is thought that Daniel's *Complaint of Rosamund* (p. 145) influenced not only the choice of the iambic pentameter riming *ababbcc* (rime royal) but also the very tone of the poem. Again addressed to Henry Wriothesley, Earl of Southampton.

***The Passionate Pilgrim*** (1599). Of the twenty poems (published by William Jaggard, and attributed on the title-page to William Shakespeare), only five have been generally accepted as Shakespeare's. These are: No. I (really Sonnet CXXXVIII), No. II (really Sonnet CXLIV), No. III (from *Love's Labour's Lost,* IV, 3, *ll.* 60—73), No. V (from *Love's Labour's Lost,* IV, 2, *ll.* 109—122); and (of the second section preceded by a second title page called *The Sonnets to Sundry Notes*), No. V (from *Love's Labour's Lost,* IV, 3, *ll.* 101—120). The other pieces have been ascribed with more or less certainty to such poets as Richard Barnfield, Bartholomew Griffin, and Marlowe.

***The Phoenix and the Turtle*** (1601). To his poem, *Loves Martyr or Rosalins Complaint* (1601), Robert Chester added, as he says, new compositions by several modern writers including Marston, Chapman, and Jonson. In that appendix to Chester's work all retold the allegory, but only Shakespeare gave a different treatment to the theme, possibly because Shakespeare was unaware of the meaning of Chester's poem (J. Q. Adams), or because Shakespeare was merely acceding to Chester's

1 An attempt has been made to show that poet-friends of Shakespeare are responsible for occasional stanzas in *Venus and Adonis.* See Forrest, H. T. S., *The Original Venus & Adonis* (1930). The same author has attempted to ascribe the *Sonnets* (p. 164) to four other poets (Barnes, Warner, Daniel, Donne) besides Shakespeare. See his *The Five Authors of 'Shake-Spears Sonnets'* (1923).

request for a contribution (Carleton Brown), or possibly because the poem had not been written specifically for Chester's appendix (Lee). Probably influenced by Chaucer, Matthew Royden's elegy on Sir Philip Sidney, and the emblem-writing conventions of the Renaissance.[1] Thirteen quatrains riming *abba,* concluded by a "Threnos" consisting of five three-line stanzas, each stanza having a single rime. (See p. 120.)

***A Lover's Complaint*** (1609). Elegiac poem written in the same meter as *Lucrece* (p. 163) and having a kind of Spenserian pictorial quality and tenderness. But bungling rhythm, non-Shakespearean Latinisms, and peculiar syntax lead most critics either to question or to reject the authenticity of this artificial lamentation.[2] J. M. Robertson has assigned the piece to Chapman.[3] Recently J. A. Fort has asserted that about the year 1596 or 1597 the poem was sent to the Earl of Southampton during his liaison with Lady Elizabeth Vernon.[4]

### B. The Sonnets† (Published 1609)

DATE. The *Sonnets* may date from as early as 1592 and as late as 1603, but the bulk of them seems to have been written between 1593 and 1598[5]. At least four methods have been employed to help determine the date of the *Sonnets*: (1) By attempting to apply lines in the sonnets to public events of contemporary interest; (2) By attempting to correlate references in the *Sonnets* with the controversy concerning Southampton, Pembroke, and the Dark Lady; (3) By attempting to establish relationships between certain passages in the *Sonnets* and lines by other authors; (4) By attempting to gauge the style; *e.g.,* the repetition of a word or phrase (Dr. Herman Isaac's suggestion, 1884).

ARRANGEMENT OF THE "SONNETS." The general opinion seems to be that Nos. I—CXXVI are substantially the sequence in which the *Sonnets* were originally written. Among the groups apparently in their proper order are Nos. I—XVII, XXXIII—XLII, LXIII—LXV, LXXVIII—LXXXVI, CVIII—CXXIV. Not only has it been shown that the Quarto arrangement is not Shakespeare's, but also that the arrangement is neither according to chronology nor subject.[6]

---

1 Fairchild, A. H. R., "The Phoenix and Turtle: A Critical and Historical Interpretation," *Englische Studien,* XXXIII—XXXIV (1903-1904), pp. 337-384.

2 Mackail, J. W., "*A Lover's Complaint,*" *Essays and Studies by Members of The English Association,* III (1912), pp. 51-70.

3 Robertson, J. M., *Shakespeare and Chapman* (1917), pp. 9-95.

4 Fort, J. A., *The Two Dated Sonnets of Shakespeare* (1924).

5 No. CIV was written about April, 1596, and No. CVII, about November, 1598, according to Fort, J. A., *The Two Dated Sonnets of Shakespeare* (1924).

6 Alden, R. M., "The Quarto Arrangement of Shakespeare's Sonnets," in *Anniversary Papers by Colleagues and Pupils of George Lyman Kittredge* (Ginn and Company, 1913), pp. 279—288.

† * Explanation of symbols immediately precedes page one.

AUTOBIOGRAPHICAL VALUE. To such critics as Halliwell-Phillipps and Lee, the *Sonnets,* for all their occasional beauties, are conventional and imitative literary exercises which do not record Shakespeare's own experiences; but to others such as Brandes and Acheson the *Sonnets* are intimate personal confessions. Whether or not Shakespeare "with this key . . . . unlocked his heart" (Wordsworth), certain questions have always been asked and debated[1]:

1. *Who Was "W.H."?* "W. H." has been identified by different critics as William Hall (Lee); William Hughes (Malone, Tyrwhitt, Butler[2]); William, Lord Herbert, Earl of Pembroke (this identification has been practically abandoned); Sir William Harvey, the third husband of Southampton's mother (C. C. Stopes); and Henry Wriothesley, Earl of Southampton (G. H. Rendall).

2. *Who Was the "Dark Lady"?* Among those who have been nominated are Elizabeth Vernon (Massey); Mary Fitton (Tyler, J. R. Strong); Mistress Davenant (Acheson); and Elizabeth Trentham (Percy Allen).

3. *Who Was the "Rival Poet"?* The most important choices seem to be Drayton (Wyndham), Chapman (Minto), and Spenser (Montmorency).[3]

***The Technique of Shakespeare's "Sonnets."*** In the Petrarchan sonnet-form there is a break in sense between octave and sestet (see under Wyatt and Surrey, p. 118 *ff.*). In the English or Shakespearean sonnet-form, although the pause between octave and sestet is present, the structure consists rather of three quatrains riming *abab, cdcd, efef,* and clenches with its distinctive feature, the final couplet (*gg*). Occasionally, however, Shakespeare makes the Petrarchan break in thought between the octave and sestet; *e.g.,* Nos. XXI, XXII, LXXII, LXXVI.

***Shakespeare's "Sonnets" as Literature.*** Many of Shakespeare's 154 sonnets are marred by Platonic conceits and an excess of emotion, but others have a greater content and value. Frequently Shakespeare attains perfect expression of lofty thought,[4] and a sensuous phraseology that penetrates. Among the best are: Nos. XV, XVIII, XXV, XXIX, XXX, XXXII, XXXIII, LIV, LV, LXIV, LXV, LXVI, LXXI, LXXIII, XCVII, CIV, CVI, CVII, CIX, CX, CXI, CXIX, CXXIX, CXXX, CXLVI.

1 Robertson, J. M., *The Problems of Shakespeare's Sonnets* (1926), pp. 9-106.

2 Butler, Samuel, *Shakespeare's Sonnets Reconsidered* (1899; new edition, 1927).

3 Was the "Rival Poet" Chaucer? See Ord, Herbert, *Chaucer & the Rival Poet* (1921).

4 Shakespeare's ethics, says Cardinal Gasquet, "are irreproachable . . . . Indeed, one of the most beautiful and accurate expressions of the Christian life to be found in any lay writer occurs in Sonnet CXLVI." Quoted from Gasquet, (F. A. Card.), "Shakespeare," in *A Book of Homage to Shakespeare,* edited by Gollancz, Israel (1916), p. 26 (pp. 25-27).

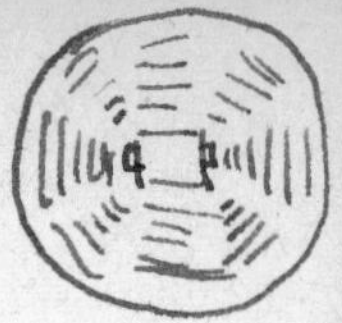

## SHAKESPEARE'S THEATRE[1]

"The Elizabethan playhouse for which Shakespeare wrote had little in common with the theatre of to-day. To the modern playgoer, familiar with the seating arrangements and the picture-frame stage of the present, Shakespeare's playhouse would seem more like a stadium than a theatre. His theatre was a circular or polygonal wooden structure of galleries surrounding an open court into the middle of which projected a covered platform. About this platform most of the audience stood, rather than sat, though some of the more affluent found seats in the galleries or even on the stage itself. Most of the action of an Elizabethan play took place upon the platform, which had no front curtain and was backed on each side by the "tiring-house" or actors' dressing-rooms, so constructed as to give the illusion of a house fronting a street, for which the platform often stood. In the center of this back wall and between the entrance doors were two annexes to the platform which could be brought into use when necessary—an inner stage for propertied interiors, such as studies, tents, caves, cells, or shops; and directly above this alcove, an upper stage for scenes requiring elevation. Both the inner and the upper stages were fitted with traverse curtains which could be closed when the annexes were not in use, and which created the illusion of a tapestried wall when the platform represented a hall in a castle.

"Naturally, painted scenery and properties in the modern sense were used only sparingly in the theatre of Shakespeare's day, the object being not so much completely to realize a setting as to suggest or symbolize it. Little in the way of artificial lighting was possible, yet spectacular effects of no mean kind were obtained by the pageantry of mass scenes and by rich costumes, for which actors were famous from early times.

"To many readers of Shakespeare who do not take the trouble to understand his stage, the conditions under which he and his contemporaries worked seem not only primitive but decidedly limiting to the playwright as well. Yet, taken as a whole, Shakespeare's theatre was adequate for his needs and a far more resourceful and flexible place than is sometimes supposed. Change of scene could be effected quickly without loss of continuity, and consequently the action of a play could be rapid and continuous. Drama under such conditions was essentially a narrative art, play-construction was looser than it is to-day, and as a result the technique of the average Elizabethan play was more

1 Reprinted, by permission of the publisher, from Watt, H. A., Holzknecht, K. J., and Ross, Raymond, *Outlines of Shakespeare's Plays* (1934), pp. 6-10 (pp. 5-10). For a discussion of Shakespeare's company and theatre, some of the best books are: Thorndike. A. H., *Shakespeare's Theatre* (1916); Adams, J. Q., *Shakespearean Theatres* (1917); Baldwin, T. W., *The Organization and Personnel of the Shakespearean Company* (1927); Lawrence, W. J., *The Physical Conditions of the Elizabethan Public Playhouse* (1927); Chambers, E. K., *The Elizabethan Stage* (Four Volumes, 1932).

like that of the movie than that of the modern drama. On the other hand, the absence of a front curtain, painted scenery, and artificial lighting made certain modern stage effects impossible. Hence, there is little attempt at local color in the average Elizabethan play and a disarming informality about the precise location or time of every scene. The producer simply used the built-in scenery at his disposal in combinations that pleased him. His stage was a setting—no more—and he permitted the audience to concentrate its attention upon the play. Whenever place or time mattered, some references to them could be introduced into the dialogue, and if special atmosphere or dramatic effects were needed, they could be created by the poet's pen. Hence, it is to the Elizabethan stage that we are indebted in great measure for the exquisite descriptive poetry of Shakespeare. Such conditions, moreover, encouraged a greater imaginative cooperation on the part of the audience in the production of a play, and this active participation was further increased by the informality of the platform stage. With such intimacy, soliloquies, asides, and long set speeches are natural and not absurd as they are in the modern theatre. These are but a few of the ways in which the physical conditions of the theatre and the characteristics of the Elizabethan drama explain one another, yet they should make clear that Elizabethan theatrical conditions begot a whole code of conventions which Shakespeare accepted—just as he would accept those of the modern theatre, were he writing today. On his stage he was a king of infinite space, though to our eyes he may seem to have been bounded by a nutshell.

" . . . . All of the women's parts in plays were acted by boys, whose lithe figures and unchanged voices made them suitable for their rôles. They were not rank amateurs, but the apprentices to the individual actors in the company, and, as the understudies and potential successors of their masters, were as well trained as many an actress to-day. Indeed, some private theatre companies which grew up around the royal singing schools, were composed entirely of boys and enjoyed immense popularity with the court and the London social set. As a result of this ladder-like organization, producing plays for an Elizabethan troupe must have been more like writing for a team of actors than for a modern company. At least it is pleasant to think of Shakespeare's plays as having been tailor-made for a troupe of stagers who had worked together for a period of years and whose physical, mental, and professional peculiarities he knew perfectly and made dramatic capital of."

## THE SEQUENCE OF SHAKESPEARE'S PLAYS[1]

"Obviously, if the reader wishes to observe the development of Shakespeare's style and the growth of his powers as an artist, the most

1 Reprinted, by permission of the publisher, from Watt, H. A., Holzknecht, K. J., and Ross, Raymond, *Outlines of Shakespeare's Plays* (1934), pp. 11-13.

satisfactory order in which to read his plays would be that in which they were composed. Yet, important as the matter is, the arrangement of Shakespeare's work in chronological order is one of the most difficult of scholarly problems. In many cases it is quite impossible to determine the order of succession, many of the dates usually assigned to plays are conjectural, and those who know most about Shakespeare are the least willing to suggest a definite order or to be dogmatic concerning the exact year in which an individual play was written. In the case of a modern author, information to answer questions of this kind is readily accessible; in Shakespeare's case it is almost wholly lacking. The traditional order of the First Folio, which classifies the plays as Comedies, Histories, and Tragedies, and places *The Tempest* first and *Cymbeline* last, is still adhered to in many modern editions, but scholars universally reject this arrangement as having no chronological basis. The character of the evidence upon which they attempt a rearrangement will be clear from a few examples. The sources of information are six in number:

### (a) Records of Performance:

These are few in number and usually furnish a date *before* which a play was composed, without any information as to how long before. Thus, an account of the revels of the law students at Gray's Inn on December 28, 1594, mentions a performance of *The Comedy of Errors;* one John Manningham, a student at the Middle Temple, in his diary mentions seeing *Twelfth Night* there on February 2, 1602; a foreign visitor to London, Thomas Platter, records in his diary seeing *Julius Caesar* on September 21, 1599; the first edition of *Love's Labor's Lost* (1598) mentions a performance at court the previous Christmas; and an account of the burning of the Globe Theatre June 29, 1613, refers to *Henry VIII* as a new play.

### (b) Literary Allusions:

Of these the most important is Francis Meres' praise of Shakespeare in *Palladis Tamia* (1598) and his specific mention of twelve plays then written: *The Two Gentlemen of Verona, The Comedy of Errors, Love's Labor's Lost, Love's Labor's Won* (unidentified), *A Midsummer Night's Dream, The Merchant of Venice, Richard II, Richard III, Henry IV, King John, Titus Andronicus,* and *Romeo and Juliet.* There is also an allusion to Talbot, a character in *1 Henry VI,* in Thomas Nashe's *Pierce Pennilesse* (1592); a quotation from *Julius Caesar* in Jonson's *Every Man Out of His Humor* (1599); and a note about *Hamlet,* made by Gabriel Harvey sometime between 1598 and 1601. Like the notices of performances, these allusions are usually indefinite and furnish only a terminal date.

### (c) References in the Plays to Datable Historical Events:

Shakespeare, again, is sparing in "topical allusions," and passages thought to refer to current events or controversies require caution on the part of the interpreter. Yet, the chorus before the fifth act of *Henry V* contains a clear allusion to the campaign of the Earl of Essex in Ireland, and fixes the date of the performance at which that prologue was used between March 27 and September 28, 1599. There are also allusions in *Hamlet* to the revival of the boy actors (1599); in *Macbeth,* to the house of Stuart; and perhaps, in *A Midsummer Night's Dream,* to the baptism ceremonies of Prince Henry of Scotland (1594).

### (*d*) *Links between Plays themselves*:

The most marked of these is the continuity of *Richard II, 1 and 2 Henry IV,* and the author's promise at the end of the last-named play of continuing the story in *Henry V,* which establish the chronological sequence of four plays. The pointed allusion of Robin Goodfellow in *A Midsummer Night's Dream* that this time "naught shall go ill, Jack shall have Jill," likewise seems to be a link with *Love's Labor's Lost,* which "doth not end like an old play, Jack hath not Jill." If so, it establishes the order of composition, though not a definite date.

### (*e*) *Dates of Publication:*

Dates on title pages or dates of registration in the books of the Stationers' Company are less valuable than might at first be supposed, because in Shakespeare's time plays were almost never written for publication, and those which "escaped into print" usually did so after their popularity on the stage had declined. Yet, for several of Shakespeare's plays no other reliable information exists, among them *Richard III* (1597), *Romeo and Juliet* (1597), *Richard II* (1597), *1 Henry IV* (1598), *Much Ado* (1600), and *The Merry Wives* (1602). *Antony and Cleopatra* was entered for publication in 1608 and *As You Like It* in 1600, though neither appeared in print before 1623; *Troilus and Cressida* was registered in 1603, though no edition earlier than 1609 is known. The date of licensing or of publication, therefore, at least gives a terminal date, and is sometimes a valuable clue.

### (*f*) *Variations of Style and Versification:*

This is the least reliable type of evidence, and great caution must be exercised in drawing inferences from it. The assumption is that as Shakespeare grew in experience, his style of writing reflected his intellectual development, his character study deepened, his taste improved, and his technique became more and more individual. Especially singled out have been the variations of Shakespeare's blank verse and its growth from a stereotyped to a flexible medium. Certain broad features of Shakespeare's development as an artist are of course recognizable, but obviously also, a detailed literary and psychological analysis is possible only *after* the proper order of the plays has been established, and not *before*. Subject matter and mood, too, determine to a large extent the style of writing, and allowance must also be made for experiment or for passing influences. Yet, taken as a whole, this "internal evidence," when tactfully and objectively used, is valuable, if only as a check upon other evidence. In the case of some plays, notably *The Taming of the Shrew, All's Well, Coriolanus, Cymbeline,* and *Timon of Athens,* little or no other evidence exists as to the date of composition.

"If, therefore, the absolute chronology of Shakespeare's plays is far from certain, students have found it necessary to establish at least a working order."

# SHAKESPEARE'S DEVELOPMENT AS A DRAMATIST[1]

## FIRST PERIOD

### A. Experimental Comedy

### *The Comedy of Errors*† (c. 1589)

Source. (1) The plot was directly or indirectly[2] borrowed from the *Menaechmi* ("The Two Menaechmuses") of Plautus. (2) Act III, Scene I has been found to bear resemblances to the *Amphitruo* of Plautus. (3) Possibly Shakespeare's play was the re-casting of an older one, tentatively identified as *The Historie of Error* (1576—1577). (4) The "threatened execution .... was modelled upon the actual execution of William Hartley at Hollywell,"[3] on October 5, 1588.

Adaptation of the Source. Shakespeare's experiment in dramatic archaeology improves upon Plautus. He reduced the number of characters from nine to six (dropping out, for example, Plautus's parasite),

1 Did the works attributed to Shakespeare come from the traditional Stratfordian author, or from an aristocrat, or from a group of Elizabethan playwrights or aristocrats? Some say that William Shakespeare seems to have been used as a pseudonym of the leader of a group, and that William Shakespeare is not identical with William Shakespere. On the theory of "an Orchestra playing a great symphony" or "a noun of multitude," in F. E. Schelling's words, these men question if William Shakespeare "ever had a name and was not rather a trust or a syndicate." Many have been suggested, individually or in connection with others, as the author or authors of the plays. The so-called *Shakespeare-Bacon Controversy,* probably started by Herbert Lawrence's *The Life and Adventure of Common Sense* (1769), has put forth Bacon as the author, possibly as the editor of a group, for a longer period than any other individual. Among those who have attacked the theory that Bacon, because of his style, could not have written the plays are Batchelor, H. C., *Francis Bacon Wrote Shakespeare* (1912), Hookham, George, *Will o' the Wisp* (1922), and Lawrence, B. E., *Notes on the Authorship of the Shakespeare Plays and Poems* (1925). See also p. 271, Note 2. Another important group of critics put forth the theory that the Earl of Oxford wrote the plays. Read Looney, J. T., *Shakespeare Identified in Edward de Vere, Seventeenth Earl of Oxford* (1920), who originated the theory; Ward, B. R., " 'Mr. W. H.' and 'Our Ever-Living Poet,' " *The National Review,* LXXX (1922), pp. 81-93; Ward, B. R., "Edward de Vere and William Shakespere," *The National Review,* LXXX (1922), pp. 266-276; Ward, B. M., *The Seventeenth Earl of Oxford* (1928); Allen, Percy, *The Case for Edward de Vere as "Shakespeare"* (1930); Rendall, G. H., *Shakespeare Sonnets and Edward de Vere* (1930); Allen, Percy, *The Oxford-Shakespeare Case Corroborated* (1931); Douglas, M. W., *The Earl of Oxford as "Shakespeare"* (1931); Clark, E. T., *Hidden Allusions in Shakespeare's Plays* (1931); Allen, Percy, *The Life Story of Edward de Vere as "William Shakespeare"* (1932); Phillips, Gerald. *The Tragic Story of "Shakespeare"* (1932); Allen, Percy and Allen, Ernest, *A Reply to John Drinkwater* (1933); Holland, H. H., *Shakespeare, Oxford and Elizabethan Times* (1933). Others who have been suggested as the author or as a member of the group are Sir Walter Ralegh, Lord Paget, Lord Buckhurst, the Third Earl of Southampton, the Fifth Earl of Derby, the Sixth Earl of Derby, the Fifth Earl of Rutland, and not only Marlowe but even, for the sweet passages, the Countess of Pembroke. Consult Greenwood, G. G., (1) *The Shakespeare Problem Re-Stated* (1908); (2) *In Re Shakespeare, Beeching and Greenwood* (1909); (3) *Is there a Shakespeare Problem?* (1916); (4) *Shakespeare and a Tertium Quid* (1923)—who, although he attacks the orthodox position, is essentially a pure agnostic in the controversy. Consult, also, Connes, George, *The Shakespearean Mystery* (1927), who examines various arguments in favor of different claimants and sums up in favor of the Stratfordian tradition, as does Brooke, Tucker (C. F.), *Shakespeare of Stratford* (1926), p. 140 *ff.*

2 Neither the *Menaechmi* nor the *Amphitruo* was available in translation when Shakespeare wrote this play. It is thought that he either read the plays in the original Latin or learned their story in some indirect way.

3 Baldwin, T. W., *William Shakespeare Adapts a Hanging* (1931), p. 141.

† * Explanation of symbols immediately precedes page one.

added the characters of Solinus and Luce, and created the characters of Aegeon and Aemilia, thereby dignifying the theme; out-Plautused Plautus by inventing the two Dromios (probably suggested to him by the *Amphitruo*), who redouble the complexity of the intrigue and correspondingly heighten the farce, and romanticized the plot by contributing the love-scenes between Antipholus of Syracuse and Luciana, and a romantic background spun out by the tale of *Apollonius of Tyre.* Shakespeare bettered the dialogue (but see under *Style*), broadened the humor, and both modified and amplified the Plautine models.

Style. The thinness of the characterization, in which only Adriana stands out somewhat from the others, may be explained away by the necessity of making the characters unindividualized so that the cases of mistaken identity are possible (eighteen important cases have been tabulated). While there are some poetic passages, the play has almost no poetic beauty, nor wit nor drama. The dialogue is not infrequently wordy, even irrelevant; the blank verse is Marlovian, while some of the dialogue uses doggerel fourteen-syllable lines, and these, with the presence of corrupt Latin epithets, suggest that the play is a re-writing of pre-Shakespearean material. Certainly nowhere else is his style so artificial. However, Shakespeare's adaptation of classical comedy to his stage is technically interesting (e. g., the frequent use of the simple-line dialogue, or the *stichomythia*). Loud-mouthed fun, well-constructed management of the complicated plot, swift action of the intrigue, adept use of the improbable. Shakespeare's skill in exposition is exemplified by the ninety-five word appeal of Aegeon (I, 1, *ll.* 37—96, 99—121, 125—140), and his genius for construction by the play's final scene. Note: (1) This is Shakespeare's only complete farce. (2) It is his only play in which situation and incident so transcend character. (3) Only in this (probably his first) play, and in *The Tempest* (probably his last play) are observed, so it is said, all the unities of time, place, and action. (4) Unlike all his other plays, this one has no nucleating philosophical idea.

## *The Two Gentlemen of Verona* (c. 1591)

Source. (1) The story of Julia and Proteus is generally recognized as derived directly or indirectly from the story of Don Felix and Felismena in the second book of Jorge de Montemayor's *Diana Enamorado* (1542).[1] (2) A group of critics point out that the structural similarities between Montemayor's and Shakespeare's versions are commonplaces of Italian comedy, and therefore attribute Shakespeare's work to some Italianate play. (This school also applies its theory to *Love's Labour's Lost.*) Some of these indicate the *Flavio Tradito,* an

1 An English version was not available until translated by Bartholomew Young in 1598. It is a question whether Shakespeare knew the work in the original or in any foreign version. See also Note 2 to *The Comedy of Errors* (p. 170).

Italian comedy found in Flamino Scala's collection of scenarios of the *commedia dell'arte* published in 1611. (3) A third school believes that the play may be a revision of an old lost play, *The History of Felix and Philiomena* (1584—1585), based also on Montemayor. (4) Other suggested sources and influences include: (a) *Tragoedia von Julio und Hyppolita,* found in *Englische Camoedien und Tragoedien,* a collection published in 1620; (b) Brooke's *Romeus and Juliet* (1562); (c) Barnaby Rich's "History of Apolonius and Silla" included in his *Riche his Farewell to Militarie Profession* (1581); (d) Munday's *The Two Italian Gentlemen* (1584).

Native Influence. To Lyly (p. 150) Shakespeare was indebted for the play's symmetrical balancing of structure. But, more important, it was Greene (p. 153) from whom Shakespeare borrowed the formula of romantic comedy, with its conception of central female characters and of romantic love episodes. Greene probably helped Shakespeare mold a blank verse more regular and pleasant than that in *The Comedy of Errors* (p. 170).

Characterization. Obvious and feeble is the paired grouping of the characters, although the latter are somewhat better differentiated than in *The Comedy of Errors.* Of the major characters, Julia is most sharply outlined, anticipating Viola and Imogen; of the minor, Eglamour is, in John Masefield's simple words, "the most beautiful." The wit of Speed is barely tolerable; the humor of Launce has potentialities for fun, particularly in the scenes with his dog Crab. (Eglamour, and the clowns, are Shakespeare's own characters.)

### *Valentine's Renunciation of Silvia*

Several explanations have been given of the crucial statement, "All that was mine in Silvia I give thee" (V, 4, *l.* 83). (a) Valentine wishes to prove that he believes Proteus worthy of Julia. (b) It is, in Lamb's phrase, "a sudden flight of heroism." (c) The line is deliberately ambiguous, its purpose being to motivate the *dénouement.* (d) The mood is identical with that in which the *Sonnets* were written, especially No. XL and No. XLII. (e) Shakespeare's rapid, clumsy solution is attributable to the Elizabethan practise of huddling up the conclusion; like his audience he was interested less in the drama than in the story, and he subordinated the problem of character to a "musical comedy" or hugger-mugger ending. (f) It exemplifies the Renaissance canon of evaluating friendship between man and man as of greater importance than that between the two sexes: part and parcel of the conventions of medieval romance and Elizabethan courtly love. (g) Possibly Shakespeare's original solution, found to be ineffective on the stage, was finally rewritten by another. (h) The ending is "in keeping with the general tone of the play and with Shakspere's practice elsewhere."[1]

STYLE. Shakespeare is still in the experimental stage. The love-story is slight and protractedly dull, the language is often insipid, the characters are not too expertly balanced, the structure is loose, and the comic scenes, although frequent, do not bear upon the plot. Less effective on the stage than his preceding play, yet much can be said for this light Italianate comedy. The emotion is more authentic. The blank verse is more careful, the diction so melodious that some think it too honey-sweet, the poetic and the dramatic passages are more frequent, and the characters are becoming inevitably dovetailed into the plot. Famous song: "Who is Silvia"?

Note the beginning of his plot- and stage-devices in this, his first romantic comedy dealing principally with the theme of love: (1) a central female character masquerading as a boy; (2) the openings for dramatic irony afforded by disguises; (3) the forest scene and outlaws; (4) low comedy provided in the persons of servants; (5) symmetrical arrangement of characters; (6) the impossible solution; (7) feeble punning and unrestrained, even tedious, quibbling; (8) a romantic story of love and intrigue for a main plot relieved by the low comedy of a sub-plot. Yet this comedy (says O. J. Campbell) is important less for its new forms of dramatic ingenuity than it is for "the emotional deepening of elements taken bodily from a drama which was at once comedy of intrigue and high complicated farce."[2] (Concerning the problem of the frequently considered unpsychological *dénouement,* see under *Valentine's Renunciation of Silvia,* p. 172.)

## *Love's Labour's Lost* (1590—1594; probably 1593)

SOURCES. Shakespeare's first invention of a dramatic plot is definitely topical.[3] Moth, previously identified as La Motte, French ambassador, is more likely identical with Nash; Holofernes, once tentatively believed to be a caricature of the translator Florio, is better considered a stock character of French and Italian comedy (his name, for example, appears in Rabelais's *Gargantua* as a tutor of Gargantua); while the "Academe" may be a satire of the "School of Night" probably connected with Chapman. Some of the characters have names of men prominent in London's current talk (1589—1594) about French political personages: Ferdinand is said to be Henri IV (Henry of Navarre); Biron, Charles de Gontaut, Baron de Biron; Longaville, Henri d'Orléans,

---

1 For this rationalistic conclusion consult Thaler, Alwin, *Shakspere's Silences* (1929), Chap. I, "Shakspere's Silences," pp. 16-18 (pp. 3-63); and also the Epilogue: "On Shakspere's Epilogues," pp. 257-259.

2 Campbell, O. J., "*The Two Gentlemen of Verona* and Italian Comedy," in *Studies in Shakespeare, Milton and Donne* (The Macmillan Company, 1925), p. 54 (pp. 49-63).

3 All critics agree upon this point; *e. g.,* Allen, Percy, *Shakespeare and Chapman as Topical Dramatists* (1929).

Duke of Longueville, Governor of Picardy; Dumain may be the Duke du Maine, or de Mayenne, brother to the Duke of Guise (but in actual history a political opponent of Henri IV and two of his generals, the Maréchal Biron and the Duc de Longueville).[1] Also with some basis in history is the visit of the Princess of France to Navarre. Either in 1578 at Nerac or in 1586 at St. Bris, Catherine de' Medici, Queen-Mother of France, accompanied by a group of ladies-in-waiting, whose allure, it was hoped, would affect negotiations, met Henri of Navarre for diplomatic purposes: her daughter, Marguerita, subsequently became the wife of Henri. What also has influenced the early dating of the play[2] is the masque of the Muscovites in the last act, for in 1582—1583 a Russian embassy at Elizabeth's court brought ridicule upon itself by its representations for the marriage of Czar Izan to one among the kinswomen of Elizabeth.

NATIVE INFLUENCE. Lyly is the most prominent influence in this court comedy. Don Armado the coxcomb and Moth the "handful of wit" have been recognized as a second edition of Lyly's Sir Tophas and Epiton in *Endimion* (p. 151); but their similarities might as easily stem from the traditions of the *capitano*. Undoubtedly, however, while Lyly served as a model for Shakespeare's word-fence and wit-combats[3] (in which, as in Lyly, the subjects of conversation are love, learning, women, and marriage), and as a model for Shakespeare's grouping of characters and obvious symmetry of structure, the latter allied himself against the current affectations. Particularly is Shakespeare indebted to Lyly for the introduction of songs (no other play has so many lyrics) and for the emphasis upon witty prose "talk" or dialogue at the expense of plot and characterization.

CHARACTERIZATION. In this play, where the characterization is superficial, the most alive are Rosaline and Biron, who point to the Beatrice and Benedick of *Much Ado About Nothing* (p. 195). Don Armado's companions are thought to resemble type-figures in Italian comedy. "The courtiers are the brilliant and witty euphuists, Armado

---

1 The language and manners, even the scenes, are French, not English, and the plot is a thinly-masked study of court life under Henri of Navarre, who afterwards became Henri Quatre of France, says Lefranc, Abel, *Sous le Masque de William Shakespeare* (Two volumes, 1919). He denies Shakespeare's authorship, and attempts to build up a case for the Earl of Derby as the writer of *Love's Labour's Lost.* Not a few believe that the play is so learned, academic, and scholastic that it can not possibly be attributed to Shakespeare. J. Dover Wilson's explanation that Shakespeare accepted personal service as a member of the Earl of Southampton's household and accompanied the Earl to Italy, has been attacked on the ground that after an eight-year investigation C. C. Stopes found nothing to link Shakespeare with Southampton.

2 This is inconclusive, according to Taylor, Rupert, *The Date of Love's Labour's Lost* (1932), in which he gives the revolutionary date of the play as 1596. But see also Sorensen, Fred, "'The Masque of the Muscovites' in *Love's Labour's Lost,*" *Modern Language Notes,* L (1935), pp. 499-501.

3 It might prove illuminating to examine the proverbs in *Love's Labour's Lost.* Consult Tilley, M. P., *Elizabethan Proverb Lore in Lyly's "Euphues" and in Pettie's "Petite Palace"* (1926), pp. 411-414 (of the index).

is the gongorist, Holofernes the disgorger of scholastic pedantries, Costard the canny lout whose misprisions of the Queen's English are all to his own bodily profit."[1]

Style. This bold study of English country life, in which is enmeshed the political talk of the day, contains a sound philosophical idea: in Dowden's words, "a dramatic plea on behalf of nature and of common sense against all that is unreal and affected . . . . the superiority of life, as a means of education, over books."[2] Directed by this philosophy, it is almost inevitable, therefore, that his experiment evolves into one of dialogue rather than of incident. His first original play is an onslaught upon pedantry and academic culture; in the burlesque features much of their topical nature probably escapes us,[3] but what is not lost to us is the play's good-humored satire of mere word-wit and current social follies. Especially delightful are the dialogue, illustrative of the features of Lyly's style (p. 151), and the poetry, illustrated by the lyric winding-up provided in the last scene by "When daisies pied and violets blue" and "When icicles hang by the wall." On the stage, where not a single change of scene is necessary, the freshness of the atmosphere is nevertheless unaccountably present.

Why did Hazlitt like this play least? Its rime, doggerel, and end-stopped blank verse are abundant, its quips and conceits are often labored, its topical nature results in occasional obscurity; its story is not dramatic, its characters are not excitingly interesting. Its mechanical symmetry is obvious, its detail faulty, its structure immature, while only by the eavesdropping scene is its almost complete lack of life and movement belied.

### B. Early Chronicle Plays

## *Henry VI, Parts I—III* (*c.* 1592)

*Part I* (*c.* 1592).[4] The main source of *Part I* is Holinshed's *Chronicles* (p. 147). Four theories[5] as to authorship have been suggested: (a) Shakespeare wrote practically no part of *I* (Malone, Dowden, Furnivall); (b) Shakespeare collaborated with others (White, Ingram); (c) Shakespeare is its sole author (Samuel Johnson, Knight, Schlegel, Ulrici, Brandl, Courthope); (d) Shakespeare made some additions (Ward, Gollancz, Schelling) or contributed some scenes (Herford, Lee,

1 Charlton, H. B., "A Midsummer Night's Dream," *Bulletin of The John Rylands Library,* XVII (1933), p. 47 (pp. 46-66).

2 Dowden, Edward, *Shakspere* (1888), p. 63.

3 While Sir Edmund Chambers believes that the plays contain but few topical allusions, J. Dover Wilson denies that the plays contain a deliberate avoidance of topical allusions.

4 According to Tucker Brooke, *Part I* should be assigned to the year 1599. It is, for example, quite certain that the best scene of *Part I* (see Act II) was written later, possibly in 1598—1599.

5 Gaw, Allison, "The Origin and Development of 1 Henry VI," *University of Southern California Studies,* First Series, Number 1 (1926).

Rolfe) or revised some playwright's earlier work (Coleridge, Gervinus, Halliwell-Phillipps, Gray). Theory "d" is most generally favored, the original play probably having been written by either Marlowe, or Greene, or, most likely, Peele. The real hero of this prologue-part to *Henry VI, Parts II and III,* is Talbot. Critics are loath to accept as Shakespeare's the unfeeling portrait, or possibly the historical misrepresentation, of Joan of Arc's character as that of an evil witch and a strumpet.[1] Note the anachronisms.

*Part II* (c. 1592). While the ultimate source is Hall and Holinshed, the only direct source, aside for an episode dependent upon Sir Thomas More, is *The First Part of the Contention betwixt the two famous Houses of Yorke and Lancaster* (1594). The most likely author of *The First Part of the Contention* is Marlowe,[2] who may have been assisted by such writers as Peele, Greene, and Shakespeare. Unlike the other two parts, *Part II* is not a battle-play. It is said that in the Jack Cade scenes, Shakespeare gives us his earliest use of the crowd as a theatrical device. The dominating character of *Part II* is Margaret.

*Part III* (*c.* 1592). This play is founded on the earlier *The True Tragedie of Richard Duke of Yorke* (1595).[3] Gloucester and, again, Margaret are the principals.

General Discussion. It is commonly recognized that the three-part panoramic play reveals little of Shakespeare's hand. *Part I* may be a revision of Peele's *Henry VI* (1592); *Parts II* and *III* may be Marlowe's work, assisted possibly by Peele; or if Parts *II* and *III* are by Shakespeare, then the latter worked under the direct influence of Marlowe. Consider the three parts primarily as revisions of three older plays, worked upon by Marlowe, Peele, or Shakespeare—revisions probably prompting Greene's accusation of plagiarism (possibly an improper interpretation—see p. 154).

In *Henry VI* the common people are almost as negligible as in the epic (p. 8); the three or four women who appear are attention-calling by their vehemence of speech, the point of view is openly partisan, or even chauvinistic. As in his other *Henry* plays, so here the style is

1 Joan of Arc's declaration that she is *enceinte* is not the only occasion when Shakespeare offends against taste, according to critics, who point to Hero's marriage to Claudio, Valentino's renunciation of Silvia, Posthumus's wager about Imogen's chastity, and the like.

2 Brooke, C. F. T., "The Authorship of the Second and Third Parts of King Henry VI," *Translations of the Connecticut Academy of Arts and Sciences,* XVII (1912-1913), pp. 141-211.

3 For a discussion of the relation of the *Contention* and the *True Tragedy,* consult Doran, Madeleine, "Henry VI, Parts II and III," *University of Iowa Studies,* IV, No. 4 (1928); Alexander, Peter, *Shakespeare's Henry VI and Richard III* (1929); Greer, C. A., "The Relation of Richard III to the *True Tragedy of Richard Duke of York* and the *Third Part of Henry VI,*" *Studies in Philology,* XLVII (1932), pp. 543-550; Greer, C. A., "The York and Lancaster Quarto-Folio Sequence," *Publications of the Modern Language Association of America,* XLVIII (1933), pp. 655-704.

wordy, the verse protractedly rhetorical, the technique formless, with scene straggling after scene. In no other play attributed to Shakespeare is action so subordinated to the moral idea.

### *Richard III*† (c. 1594)

Source. Shakespeare is indebted primarily to Holinshed's *Chronicles*[1] and to Hall's *The Union of the two noble and illustre famelies of Lancaster and Yorke* (1550): the ultimate source of both is More's *Historie of Richard the Third* (p. 115). Polydore Vergil's *Anglicae Historiae* also contributed some matter to Hall's *Chronicle.* Shakespeare's play, while perhaps echoing unimportant items from the anonymous *The True Tragedie of Richard III, with the conjunction and joining of the two noble houses, Lancaster and Yorke* (*ante* 1588; published 1594), owed nothing or practically nothing to Dr. Thomas Legge's *Richardus Tertius* (1579).

Native Influence. One school states that this chronicle play may be assigned almost completely to Marlowe on the basis of style, vocabulary, and general characteristics (J. M. Robertson); another, that it is at certain spots a revision by Shakespeare of a (now lost) *Richard III* by Marlowe (S. S. Ashbaugh); a third, that the play was written entirely by Shakespeare (Lee). If Marlowe had no hand in *Richard III,* it certainly shows his influence: (a) it is decidedly a one-man play; (b) the characterization of the central figure is static, not progressive; (c) the tone is less frequently dramatic than it is lyrical or epical; (d) the prose and lyrical experiments appearing in Shakespeare's early plays are here absent, while blank verse is used almost exclusively; (e) Marlowe's formula (of subject-matter, of the protagonist, of the "mighty line," of plotting) is best exemplified by *Richard III.*

Characterization. Richard is the Marlovian monster-protagonist, a Shakespearean abnormality frequently regarded as falling only below Iago as a self-conscious and self-avowed arch-villain. Imperious of will and obtrusive in hypocrisy, he makes a puppet of the worldly Buckingham, who, with blunt-spoken Hastings, is a strong minor character. Next to Richard, Queen Margaret is most important: the "flinty, rough, remorseless" "she-Wolf of France" of *Henry VI, Part III,* has been humbled into a hag who as a kind of Greek chorus speaks horrible prophecies: she is the embodiment of Richard's avenging Nemesis.

Style. Poetic as the opening soliloquy may be, it is probably a serious defect in characterization.[2] This sequel to *Henry VI, Part III* has been labeled as crude in the free dramatization of its sources,

---

1 Probably the second or 1587 edition, for in that edition there is some matter unobtainable from the first; *e. g.* Shakespeare repeats a mistake made only in the second edition. See, also, p. 179, Note 1.

2 That is, the soliloquy may be a defect from the modern point of view. In Shakespeare's day, however, the "crude" dramatic technique accomplished much through the soliloquy.

† * Explanation of symbols immediately precedes page one.

Marlovian in its blank verse, Senecan in its choral lamentations. Dramatic possibilities are said to be sacrificed to single-line dialogue (*stichomythia*), declamatory verse, swollen figurative language, and stagey, melodramatic action. Whether weak in the unities, as one school contends, or compact in structure, as most critics agree, this continuation of *Henry VI, Part III* is recognized for its rattling strength on the stage rather than for its study-room revelations of poetry. By the introduction of the Nemesis that consummates Richard's fall, Shakespeare departs from Marlowe.

### C. Early Tragedy

## *Titus Andronicus* (c. 1593)

Source. No direct source has been found. (a) The German play, *Eine sehr Klägliche Tragoedia von Tito Andonico und der hoffertigen Kayserim, darinnem denckwürdige actiones zubefinden,* for a time assumed to be the source, is probably a loose translation of Shakespeare's play. (b) "The lamentable and tragical history of Titus Andronicus," a ballad available in Percy's *Reliques* (1765), was formerly considered as the source. (c) Shakespeare's theme, a blend of diverse elements from several sources, is possibly reminiscent of the poem, *A Lamentable Ballad of the Tragicall End of a Gallant Lord and of his Beautiful Lady, . . . .* (c. 1570). (d) The play entered by the illiterate Henslowe on January 24, 1594, under the title of *titus & ondronicus,* might be by Peele; it is probably identical with *Titus and Vespacia,* entered previously by Henslowe on April 11, 1591.

Authorship. The patent barbarity of theme, the apparent crudity of workmanship, and the bloody succession of unrelieved horrors place the tragedy among Shakespeare's doubtful plays, despite the external evidence that *Titus Andronicus* was published as a Quarto (1594), was mentioned by Meres's *Palladis Tamia* (1598) among Shakespeare's dozen plays, and was included in the First Folio (1623). There are four main theories of authorship. (a) Shakespeare had no hand in *Titus Andronicus* (Coleridge, Hallam, Dyce, Gervinus, Fleay, Robertson). (b) Shakespeare is the author of the tragedy, probably an early experiment written under the influence of predecessors (Collier, Knight, Appleton, Morgan, Crawford, Courthope, Raleigh, Saintsbury, McCallum, and, except for occasional modifications, practically all German critics, including Horn, Schlegel, Delius, Ulrici, Brandl, Creizenach, Schröer). (c) Shakespeare either put very little into the play (Furnivall, Herford, Hudson, Rolfe), or touched up, more or less perfunctorily, an older play (majority of present-day American and English critics). Kyd, Marlowe, or Greene has been suggested as the possible author of the earlier work, but Peele is most generally assumed to be that playwright (see under *Source,* "d").

NATIVE INFLUENCE. *Titus Andronicus* belongs to the same type of play as Kyd's *Spanish Tragedy* (p. 152) and also Shakespeare's *Hamlet* (p. 204). Titus is modelled after Kyd's Hieronimo. In both of Shakespeare's Kydian dramas of revenge, Nemesis triumphs, taking vengeance upon innocent and guilty alike.

CHARACTERIZATION. Character-portrayal is so inconsistent and indefinite as to be negligible. Only Aaron the Moor has aroused some interesting discussion, which generally regards him as influenced by Marlowe's conception of Tamburlaine and Barabas, and as an early edition of Shakespeare's Richard III, Shylock, Edmund, and even Iago.

STYLE. This Senecan tragedy presents one bloodily-revolting incident after another, and when the Kydian machinery (of a father's revenge, a supposedly mad hero, of repellent intrigue and unnatural horrors) has come to a stop, fourteen out of the twenty-two characters have met with violence. The lack of consistency apparent in the broad strokes of characterization is likewise seen in the melodramatic plot-structure, a garish olla-podrida. A few poetic or pseudo-poetic passages do crop up, but more frequently the verse is pedestrian, rhetorical, regular, and somewhat Marlovian. It includes classical allusions and occasional Latin quotations. The anachronistic arrangement, ugly language, and straggling workmanship, the false tragedy of its repulsive horrors, and the absence of unity and of poetic imagery, have led critics either to deny Shakespeare's authorship or to rate the work as his worst.

## SECOND PERIOD

### A. Middle Chronicle Plays

### *Richard II*† (c. 1595)

SOURCE. *Richard II* is faithful to Holinshed's *Chronicles,*[1] while the specific information about Mowbray's life was found in Stow's *Chronicles* or *Annales.* Certain changes were made to correspond with Daniel's *Civil Wars.* Shakespeare might also have used an old play.

NATIVE INFLUENCE. That this chronicle play shows the influence of Marlowe is held by most critics, who point particularly to the identical theme of *Edward II* (p. 157). Striking freedom from his predecessor is apparent in Shakespeare's better craftsmanship: the historical period covered is shorter (April 29, 1398—March, 1400), the blank verse deserts the Marlovian rhetoric for a more fluent meter, and the interpretation of the protagonist is subtler.

CHARACTERIZATION. Vividly and also poetically imagined is his conception of a king unmanned, not by an external power, but by a self-

---

1 Those interested in evaluating Shakespeare's treatment of his source are referred, as a basis for research, to *Holinshed's "Chronicles"*, edited by Wallace, R. S., and Hansen, Alan (1917) pp. 1-79. Read, also, Chambrun, Clara Longworth de, "The Book Shakespeare Used," *Scribner's Magazine,* C (1936), pp. 28-34.

† * Explanation of symbols immediately precedes page one.

indulging sentimentalism, mental and moral vacillation, and aesthetic blindness to realities. Bolingbroke, with his icy sense for fact, is the foil to Richard II: Henry is not a man of mere words but calculating and politic, strong where Richard II is weak in the practical qualities of a ruler. The better-outlined minor characters are Mowbray, a foil to Bolingbroke, John of Gaunt, "time-honored Lancaster," and the Duke of York, well-meaning but indecisive time-server. Shakespeare is becoming master of theatric-psychologic truth in the delineation of his *dramatis personae.*

STYLE. *Richard II,* as Brooke has stated, falls below *Richard III* in passion of movement and rhetoric, in dramatic power and gloom of fate, and rises above that play in kindly humanity and lovely poetry. While following Holinshed closely, the chronicle play invents some incidents for dramatic purposes. As the play continues, our sympathies turn from Bolingbroke, the maker of puppets, to Richard II, the poet of dreams. On the stage this chronicle's weaknesses include commonplace couplets among the frequent rimes, plays on words, inflation of figurative language for its own sake (even the gardeners speak poetry), slight action, especially the halting movement of the beginning, and the thinness of objective reality. What is memorable is the lyrical quality, profuse eloquence, effective pathos, and subtler characterization. Most famous: John of Gaunt's apostrophe to England.

### *King John* (c. 1596)

SOURCE. The play constitutes a recast of an earlier two-sectioned and separately-entitled play, *The Troublesome Raigne of John King of England* and *The Second Part of the Troublesome Raigne of King John* (1591; both parts, 1611). It is not certain that Shakespeare also drew directly upon Holinshed or Hall for some information.

INFLUENCE. That the older two-part play was written by Shakespeare in imitation of Marlowe's *Tamburlaine* (p. 156) is the opinion of some critics (Tieck, Steevens, Ulrici), but that its author was probably Peele, who depended primarily upon Holinshed, is the more general opinion. Shakespeare is by far the stronger and subtler of the two playwrights: (a) His general clarity is pronounced, although he is occasionally less explicit (*e.g.,* in his explanation of Faulconbridge's anger at the arranged marriage between Lewis the Dauphin and the Lady Blanch). (b) While Shakespeare usually is faithful to his source in scenes, characters, plan, and historical matter, he sometimes deviates for dramatic gain (*e.g.,* in his touching representation of Arthur as a child[1]). (c)

---

1 It has been observed that no child character in any play by Shakespeare has any important part, although the children are treated with understanding.
"By the bye," asks Schelling, F. E., in his *Shakespeare and "Demi-Science"* (1927), p. 187 (pp. 181-193), "is there anyone who can tell me why it is that Shakespeare's heroines are, so many of them, orphans, or at least motherless?" This "absence of motherhood" and "the preponderance of fathers" are discussed by Quiller-Couch, Sir Arthur, "Paternity in Shakespeare," *Proceedings of the British Academy,* XVIII (1932), pp. 93-110.

Shakespeare copies some weakness of the pre-Shakespearean play (*e.g.*, John is not the hero in either work), but makes at least one notable excision by omitting the coarse if amusing scenes reflecting upon the morals of nuns and friars. (d) Although still re-echoing the patriotic tone of the earlier play, Shakespeare has considerably modified its ultra-Protestant propaganda. (e) He compressed the ten acts of the two plays into the five acts of one, and possibly introduced one new scene into Act IV. (f) By a process of modification and expansion Shakespeare has made more human and more noble the characters found in or suggested by the earlier work. (g) Finally, Shakespeare has introduced his own dialogue and frequently has given us splendid verse.

Characterization. Except for the picture of Faulconbridge, declared by Blunden to be Shakespeare's most gallant, loyal, and chivalrous gentleman, little about the other characters is of major interest. If there is a central figure, it is either the Bastard in the capacity of a kind of Chorus to the play enunciating the ideals of true patriotism and national interests, or England herself. Faulconbridge, sometimes looked upon as a sort of predecessor to Falstaff, is Shakespeare's own creation, developed out of the blurred outline of the older play. The interpretation of John, a tragedy of hereditary incompetence, is of basic historical truth, the opening scenes alone belying somewhat his despicable character. Among the other fuller-bodied portrayals, Arthur, Hubert, and Pandulph yield in importance to Constance, a sentimental Shakespearean woman whose poetic speech is in keeping with her character.

Style. As a work of poetry, *Richard II* shows a better organic unity; as a work of stagecraft, *Richard III* goes better in the theatre—in fact, the episodical structure of *King John* results, it has been said, in neither a chronicle play nor a tragedy nor a history play. No hero gives the plot a needed coherence. Not a little rhetoric and doggerel appear in the dialogue, among the rather regular Marlovian blank verse where there is neither evidence of prose nor of frequent rime (although a larger amount of rime than one would expect in 1596). There are few vitalized characters, and too little of a detached point of view to subdue the Anti-Romish and Anti-French spirit. These inequalities are somewhat levelled by a workmanlike compression, despite the slowly-developed action, and by an emotional rhythm, despite the sentimentality apparent even in the dramatic scene between Hubert and Arthur. Shakespeare triumphs most in his characters, whose imaginative developments from hints in the older play are essentially original creations even though they are earlier types of innocence and guilt and patriotism.

***King John*** is cited frequently on two counts—as proof of Shakespeare's patriotism and of his non-Catholicism. His so-called failure to mention or utilize the granting of the Magna Charta during John's reign has been explained in various ways, *e.g.*, as evidence of Shakespeare's stand as a monarchist, as a case of political discretion upon his part (why does Shakespeare not use the important figure of the Duke of Gloucester in *Richard II?*) and as an instance where Shakespeare, following his source, did not find that incident in it. There is evidence connecting this play politically with the Earl of Southampton's insurrection against the Queen (February 7, 1601).

### *Henry IV, Parts I—II*† (c. 1598)

Source. For the serious matter of both parts Shakespeare went to Holinshed's *Chronicles* (1587 edition), and possibly for some material to Hall's *The Union of the two noble and illustre famelies of Lancaster and Yorke* (1550), Elyot's *Governour* (p. 116), Stow's *Chronicles* or *Annales* and Daniel's *Civil Wars* (p. 145). For his comic plot Shakespeare probably found suggestions in the slight Chronicle play, *The Famous Victories of Henry V, containing the honorable battle of Agincourt* (acted 1588; licensed 1594), or possibly, according to Pollard and J. Dover Wilson, Shakespeare drew upon a still older play upon which that crude chronicle play might have been based.

Characterization. With his "indirect crook'd ways" King Henry IV is consistent with the subtle Bolingbroke of *Richard II.* Even more than as a contrast to the "passive, pivotal figure" of the King, the hot-headed, blunt, unselfish, manly Hotspur is presented as a foil to Prince Hal, whose madcap nature develops into a practical efficiency never part of Hotspur's worth. Out from the minor characters stand Glendower, an imaginative dreamer, Mistress Quickly, of "infinite loquacity and accommodating morality," and Justice Shallow. Out-topping all is Falstaff,[1] he of the unmalicious lie, irrepressible wit, and amoral sense: the Gluttony of the Interlude metamorphosed into a distinct personality. E. de Sèlincourt has declared that only Chaucer's Pandarus may be compared to Shakespeare's greatest comic creation "for brilliance of conception and execution." Few deny the accusation that Falstaff "was a filthy old ruffian, physically repulsive, disorderly in garb, in habits, in morals; in fact, . . . . a liar, a sot, a coward, and a whoremonger," but nevertheless almost all conclude that Falstaff is "essentially a poetic creation; . . . . a thing of beauty."[2]

Style. Through the complementary actions and characters of Falstaff and Prince Henry, Shakespeare gains a dramatic unity of the serious and the comic in *Part I,* a unity lessened considerably in *Part II* by the Prince's repudiation of his erstwhile companion. About half of the scenes in each part are devoted to Falstaff, and through this

1 Falstaff was originally called Sir John Oldcastle. Out of deference to Lord Cobham, the Lord Chamberlain who was descended from Sir John, Shakespeare renamed the irresponsible knight. Recently it has been suggested that the original of Falstaff was Robert Greene: see Maxwell, Baldwin, "The Original of Sir John Falstaff—Believe It or Not," *Studies in Philology,* XXVII (1930), pp. 230-232.

2 Thus Wilson, J. D., *The Essential Shakespeare* (1932), pp. 87, 88.

† * Explanation of symbols immediately precedes page one.

comic element Prince Hal's not too admirable nature is expressed. The Prince's rejection of Falstaff has been labelled by some as unnecessarily cruel, by others as inevitable for dramatic purposes, and by a third group as a political necessity, for each part is specifically political.[1]

As in *King John,* Shakespeare in *Henry IV* for dramatic purposes makes effective departures from his source. Marlowe's influence is no longer in evidence. Shakespeare's commingling of the serious and the comic is, of course, in the tradition of an older type of chronicle play, but his contribution is the effective blend as in *Part I.* It is true that the plots of both parts are slight, and that no central action dominates; this structural weakness is pronounced in *Part II* where the fusion of the grave and the gay is poorer, and the historical action is slow-moving and less unified. In both parts, however, his free use of verse and prose, and the changes from one to the other, are done with a sinewy ease. Finally, it is the tableaux-representation and epic looseness of events marching toward no determined end that induce most critics to agree upon the lack of unity of plot-structure of each part.[2]

### *Henry V*† (c. 1599)

SOURCE. From Holinshed's *Chronicles* and the play entitled *The Famous Victories of Henry IV*—the same sources of *Henry IV* (p. 182) —Shakespeare took his material.

CHARACTERIZATION. Except for Henry V, Shakespeare is not specially happy in his character-delineation. Caricature is strong in the depiction of the Frenchmen, although King Charles and the Dauphin have substantial possibilities. Jamy and Macmorris are recognized as Jonsonian humour-types, while Bardolph, the scamp-corporal, and Nym, the pretender to military brevity, are both easily surpassed by the sketch of honest, talkative, pedantic Fluellen who outbullies and dramatically exposes the swaggering Pistol. Henry V is a problem—Hazlitt detested him, Ruskin believed him to be Shakespeare's only substantial hero. Does Henry V represent Shakespeare's ideal of kingship, not a commonplace but a great man, of high courage and practical commonsense? (Rolfe, Dowden, Hardin Craig, Parrot.) Or is the King the cad of his younger days, an ill-bred egoist of obtrusive morality and calculating nature (Bradley, Masefield, Yeats, Stoll), one whose conception of patriotism is definitely nationalistic, essentially empty, even jingoistic?

---

1 Fortescue, Sir John William, in his many-volumed *A History of the British Army* (1899—1930), rates Shakespeare's characterization of Falstaff, Pistol, Bardolph, Nym, Parolles, and the like, as an important source not only for the history of the Elizabethan soldier, but also for the military history of the sixteenth century. (See Vol. I, 1899, p. 140.)

2 But see Law, R. A., "Structural Unity in the Two Parts of *Henry the Fourth,*" *Studies in Philology,* XXIV (1927), pp. 223-242.

† * Explanation of symbols immediately precedes page one.

STYLE. Now that Falstaff's death has been memorably reported (II, 3), the portrayal of Nym, Pistol, and Fluellen is further developed. The comic scenes, however, fall below those in *Henry IV;* without the presence of the fat knight, not even Katherine's broken English (entertaining to the immature and of questionable taste) can contribute much to whatever amusing qualities are present. There are isolated bursts of eloquent poetry; in general, the play exemplifies the splendid declamatory quality of the Elizabethan drama. Like the preceding play, *Henry V* is a series of tableaux—a compound of embassies and expeditions, sieges and battles, their loose epic construction further emphasized by occasional effective scenes, expository Prologues, and a tame conclusion. Only in its rhetorically patriotic passages can it stand beside *Henry IV,* particularly the latter play's magnificent soliloquies of *Part II;* as already indicated, *Henry V* lacks the climacteric power of *Henry IV, Part I,* and the variety of humor of *Henry IV, Part II.* The unities of time and place are violated; a unity of effect is obtained through its nationalistic fervor, and a moral unity through the contrast between Henry V and his foil, the Dauphin. Shakespeare's utilization of the Chorus is the most interesting feature of this national epic in dramatic form.[1] Outside of its solemn phraseology and lyrical cast of language there are other dramatic values: (a) The Chorus bridges over the gaps of time. (b) It interprets matter that can not be presented dramatically, in apologetic explanation of the limitations of Shakespeare's stage. (c) It makes deliberate appeals to the imagination of the audience. (d) This is Shakespeare's only play in which the Chorus materially furthers the progress of the story. If the central idea of *Henry IV, Part I,* represents Rebellion, and that of *Henry IV, Part II,* represents Peace, then that of *Henry V* represents Nationality.

### *Henry VI, Part I.* (See *Henry VI,* under "First Period".)

## B. Middle Tragedy

### *Romeo and Juliet*† (c. 1596)

SOURCE. The most direct influence upon Shakespeare's version was Arthur Brooke's English poem, *The Tragicall Historye of Romeus and Juliet* (1562), and a prose re-telling of the same story in Painter's *Palace of Pleasure* (1567).[2] Earlier versions of the story's elements have been located elsewhere, from the fifth-century Greek romance *Ephesiaca* to the much developed story as told by several Italian authors, including Masuccio di Salerno's *Novellina* (1476) and Luiga da Porto's *Istoria*

1 The play may be ironic. See Gould, Gerald, "A New Reading of *Henry V,*" *The English Review,* XXIX (1919), pp. 42-56.

2 It is unlikely that the story is based on historical fact. For example, the "powerful families of Montague and Capulet . . . . never resided in Verona, and in fact never existed at all," says Moore, O. H., "The Origins of the Legend of Romeo and Juliet in Italy," *Speculum,* v (1930), p. 264 (pp. 264-277).

† * Explanation of symbols immediately precedes page one.

*novellamente ritrovata dei due nobili amanti* (*c.* 1530). However, it was Bandello's *Giulietta e Romeo* (1554) that was expanded in *Histoires Tragiques* (1559), a French translation of Boaistuau (or Boisteau) and François de Belleforest, upon whom Brooke in turn based the first extant English version of the tragic story, followed with reasonable fidelity yet so expanded and altered that Brooke is undoubtedly Shakespeare's mainstay. It has been suggested that a 1630 play by Jacob Struijs may be an adaptation of a lost play giving an English version of the Romeo-Juliet story before Brooke's work.

Adaptation of the Source. Shakespeare's *Romeo and Juliet* is generally considered a rewritten Shakespearean play,[1] for it contains, for example, his earlier characteristics of puns, exasperating conceits, and rimed couplets. Although Shakespeare depends in many ways upon Brooke, he also makes effective alterations; thus, he introduces the Romeo-Paris duel, abbreviates the action from five to four days, gives the household of the Capulets a tone that is as much Elizabethan as Italian, enlarges the part of Mercutio, and triumphs in his realistic creation of the Nurse.

Characterization. An inherent if not too obvious symmetrical arrangement accentuates the contrasts. Mercutio, he of the broad (to some, smutty) wit, high spirits, and galvanic temperament, provides the high comedy; not only do his impetuosity and cynicism serve as a foil to the sentimental Romeo but as a contrast to the peace-making Benvolio, in turn a foil to the fiery Tybalt. The Nurse, she of the familiar (indecent but not prurient) talk and cockney-like animal nature, provides the low comedy; her naturalism not only emphasizes the reserve of Lady Capulet and the ideal passion of Juliet but is essentially a foil to the Friar as an adviser. Friar Lawrence himself is a Franciscan of shrewd judgment; by those who consider the lovers destroyed by their own characters, he is frequently regarded as Shakespeare's spokesman.

Two answers have been given to the question, "What is Shakespeare's philosophy in this tragedy?" The very nature and more or less conscious motives of Romeo and Juliet bring about their doom, says one group, sure that Shakespeare believed in Indeterminism and in the biblical-Christian conception of Free Will. To the other extremists Shakespeare is the poet of the fatalistic beliefs inherent in Renaissance paganism; by the theory of destiny this school can account, for example, for the many accidents of circumstance befalling the star-crossed lovers. Probably Shakespeare's experimental hand had all it could do in steering a wavering course between both philosophies: it is as easy

1 But see Van Dam, B. A. B., "Did Shakespeare Revise *Romeo and Juliet?*" *Anglia*, LI (1927), pp. 39-62.

to see him with to-day's eyes as a poet of necessity as it is to see him as a poet of free will. View *Romeo and Juliet* as both a tragedy of character and of accident.

STYLE. Abundance of rime and of prose-word quibbles, much in the style of *Love's Labour's Lost,* are considered faults probably retained from Shakespeare's earlier version (1592?) of the tale of Romeo and Juliet. More important structural defects are the digressions, the protracted melodramatic speeches, the over-worked trick-preparations for the tragic conclusion, and the super-emphasis upon a series of accidents rather than upon turns of character. A few profess to see the low comedy as a fault. Shakespeare's first tragedy written under no markedly discernible influence is highly rated for its careful motivation of dramatic actions set out with minute exactness, and for its masterly stagecraft. Especial recognition has been accorded to its poetry, much of it in a rare blank verse begotten of a lyric mood or of a precipitate passion. Note: (1) No other tragedy has either its lightheartedness or its lyrical atmosphere. (2) It is the first tragedy in English literature motivated by the theme of romantic love. (3) When compared with Shakespeare's later work, it is found built "on an elementary order of tragic experience," unlike, for example, the lust in *Anthony and Cleopatra* of an elderly sophisticate for a coquette whose infinite variety custom can not stale; yet it is generally recognized as the consummate tragedy of ideal love "brought to a tragic doom without a hint of inner severance."[1] (4) Competent critics believe that the play should be acted with a minimum of sentiment and a maximum of deadly seriousness. (5) The Marxist regards "the struggle of the lovers against their social environment" as "the struggle of bourgeois humanism against feudalism" (A. A. Smirnov).

### *Julius Caesar*† (c. 1599)

SOURCE. In the main Shakespeare's material is a dramatization of incidents in the individual lives of Caesar, Brutus, and Antony as found in North's *Plutarch* (p. 147). *Julius Caesar* may be an old play rewritten only by Shakespeare,[2] or an old play by Marlowe, revised by Shakespeare and completed by Beaumont.[3] Possibly Shakespeare was influenced by earlier English dramatizations (now lost) of the same theme. Efforts have been made to indicate other origins; *e. g.,* his possible indebtedness to Orlando Pescetti's *Il Cesare* (1594).

ADAPTATION OF THE SOURCE. Of the three Roman plays (*Julius Caesar, Antony and Cleopatra, Coriolanus*) his first is the least faithful

---

1 Herford, C. H., (1) "The Normality of Shakespeare Illustrated in his Treatment of Love and Marriage," *The English Association,* Pamphlet No. 47 (1920); (2) *Shakespeare's Treatment of Love and Marriage* (1921). p. 25 (pp. 2-43). See also Murry, J. M., *Countries of the Mind, First Series* (1931), "Shakespeare and Love," p. 1-17.

2 Parrott, T. M., "Marlowe, Beaumont, and *Julius Caesar,*" *Modern Language Notes,* XLIV (1929), pp. 69-77.

3 Wells, William, *The Authorship of "Julius Caesar"* (1923).

† * Explanation of symbols immediately precedes page one.

to the source. Yet the phraseology is sometimes North's own words put into verse-order, and the incidents are with few exceptions taken from Plutarch. Shakespeare's selection and excision of material is commendable; it has been estimated that he used about one-sixth of the available matter. Departures from the historical portrait of Julius Caesar are generally attributed to the traditional representation fostered by the non-extant earlier English plays on the same subject and emphasized by the Renaissance stage. Note that Antony's famous oration appears to be wholly Shakespeare's.

Characterization. How account for Shakespeare's parody of Julius Caesar as boastful, superstitious, and physically infirm? Earlier plays on the same theme and the sixteenth-century stage traditions may be the explanation. Another view holds that to justify the conspiracy it was a dramatic necessity to depress the character of Caesar and to heighten that of Brutus and Cassius. A third group emphasizes that Julius Caesar, if not the hero of the tragedy, is the protagonist whose spirit irrevocably destines the outcome; therefore Shakespeare is intent on showing the ultimate triumph of Imperialism over Republicanism.

A contrast to the littleness of Caesar is the pure idealism of Brutus, if not the protagonist then the true tragic hero of the play. Too hopelessly visionary in action, his philosophical Republicanism is at the other end of the highly practical Caesarism. Brutus imagines in others the unselfish sense of honor that is his own. His love for Cassius is sincere, his gentleness for the sleeping boy is touching, his relation with his noble-minded wife is beautiful. As a foil to Brutus the Stoic, Shakespeare presents Cassius the Epicurean. The latter is not a political schemer, but a man of admirable qualities. Despite a practical and direct political idealism, personal friendship influences him to yield to Brutus's moral idealism. Fanatical hatred of tyranny in the abstract rather than the subsidiary stratum of personal jealousy moved him to conspire against Caesar. It has been pointed out that of the conspirators only Cassius can not bring himself to accept Caesar's hospitality just before plunging a dagger into the latter's body. Finally, it may be unwise to regard Antony, the foil to unpractical Brutus, as an unscrupulous politician, loyal only to Caesar. An analysis of the fuller portrait in *Antony and Cleopatra* (p. 216) helps fix the opinion that Antony may not be an opportunist and a demagogue.

Style. Disregard of the unities of time and place, use of violent deeds, deviation from the historical picture of Julius Caesar as a great despot, and distribution of emphasis upon several figures are definite evidences of Shakespeare's romantic treatment of a classical theme. Some even believe that the play is called *Julius Caesar* instead of *Marcus Brutus* in order to lure the public into the theatre. One view is that Caesar's death and the retribution following it split the tragedy into two parts, a serious fault of construction; but that assertion is generally held to be untenable for two reasons. First, the murder is the play's crisis, and the revenge (death of Brutus and Cassius) exacted for it is the play's catastrophe; secondly, the spirit of Caesar hovers over the action and defeats the conspirators. The simplicity of plot structure brings out the perfect organic unity. No sub-plot interferes. Dignity and restraint are sustained by appropriate language—the blank verse is grave, even sonorous, and the diction is simple, almost classical. *Julius Caesar* is much more than an advance upon the external conflicts presented in *Romeo and Juliet;* Brutus is Shakespeare's first triumph in the depiction of a mind's inner struggle.

### C. **High Romantic Comedy** ("Early")

### *A Midsummer-Night's Dream*† (c. 1595)

Source. No direct source of this comedy is known. Some of the characters and minor incidents may have come from floating resemblances in Chaucer's *Knight's Tale* and the life of Theseus in North's *Plutarch* (Theseus and Hippolyta); Chaucer's tale of Thisbe in his *Legend of Good Women,* probably Golding's translation of Ovid's *Metamorphoses,* and Thomas Moffett's *The Silk-wormes and their Flies*[1] (Pyramus and Thisbe); Chaucer's *Wife of Bath's Tale,* Berners's *Huon de Bordeaux,* Lyly's *Endimion,* and Greene's *James the Fourth* (fairy element and action); Chaucer's *Merchant's Tale* and Montemayor's *Diana Enamorada* (the device of the "love-juice" or the pansy's philtre). The conception of Puck is derived from English folk-lore, particularly from the fairy songs about Robin Goodfellow[2]; and that of Bottom and the fairies from the commingling of elements found in medieval romances, Warwickshire countryside traditions, and personal observation and imagination.

Characterization. The persons are slightly sketched; most of them are puppets wire-pulled by the situation and stagified by the acts of magic. Hippolyta and the quartet of lovers are bloodlessly imagined; the brunette Hermia and the blonde Helena are sketched by conventionally artificial contrast, as transparently colorless and unindividualized as their lovers, Lysander and Demetrius. Most interesting are Egeus, who anticipates the repetitive Polonius; Theseus, less a Greek soldier-lover than a romanticized typical English gentleman; Puck, whose traditional evil traits Shakespeare modified to a dramatic point of miniature perfection; and Bottom and his supporters, whose clowning makes the play Shakespeare's first comic masterpiece. Observe how the very style sets apart the characters; *e.g.,* the rustics speak in prose, the King in blank verse.

---

1 Farrand, M. L., "An Additional Source for *A Midsummer-Night's Dream,*" *Studies in Philology,* XXVII (1930), pp. 233-243.

2 *The Sources and Analogues of 'A Midsummer-Night's Dream,'* compiled by Sidgwick, Frank (1908), pp. 81-121, 144-148.

† * Explanation of symbols immediately precedes page one.

Style. Shakespeare's first fairy play (the only other is *The Tempest*) is probably his first masterpiece, despite the assertions frequently made that it is more a masque than a play, despite the abundance of puns, conceits, and classical allusions, despite the immaturity of its blank verse delightfully blended with rime, despite the emphasis upon incident rather than upon character, and despite the anachronistic scrambling of classical figures of a pre-Homeric Athens and medieval fairies and realistic sixteenth-century Warwickshire rustics. Through the use of puns and conceits, the symmetrical arrangement of characters, and the fusion of fairy mythology and low peasant life, this court comedy suggests the work of Lyly. Like the latter, too, Shakespeare introduces into his aristocratic comedy a marriage-masque, possibly as part of the festivities attending the wedding of William, Sixth Earl of Derby, to Elizabeth de Vere at Greenwich on January 24, 1595.[1]

The plot[2] of this high romantic comedy is a triple interlocking of (1) the main story, the sentimental-romantic blunders of the Athenian quartet of lovers (Theseus and Hippolyta provide the background or the enveloping action), (2) the sub-plot, the grotesque-buffoon actions of the Athenian mechanicals, and (3) the linking-chain, the complicating factors of the fairy element. The low comedy action lampoons the current *bourgeois* entertainments; note, for example, that Bottom is a burlesque of a principal who wishes to play three or four parts at once, that the interlude is a sort of anti-masque satirizing the love-elements in other acts of the same play, and also the extravagances of current classical tragedy. Yet the expert polymathic plot-craft and pretty unified tone yield the place of honor to the romantic beauty of the lyrical passages and exquisite songs (*e. g.*, "Over hill, over dale"; "'You spotted snakes with double tongue'"; "Now the hungry lion roars"), to the imaginative insight into a fairy world where the characters are depicted with unfailing consistency and whose songs are fairy-like, to a splitting "feast of frolic and fun," and, above all, to the controlling unity of the comic idea.[3]

## *The Merchant of Venice*† (c. 1596—1597)

Source. (1) The Bond-story is of Eastern origin, its archetype reaching at least as far back as the *Mahabharata.* Pound-of-Flesh ingredients have been located in the *Dolopathos,* or *The King and the*

1 Lefranc, Abel, *La Réalité dans "Le Songe d'une Nuit d'Eté"* (1920).

2 The play, according to a recent hypothesis, includes not only a satire on the idiosyncrasies of King James but primarily much political propaganda for the Earl of Hertford's or the Suffolk heir. Consult Rickert, Edith, "Political Propaganda and Satire in *A Midsummer-Night's Dream,*" *Modern Philology,* XXI (1923-1924), pp. 53-87, 132-154.

3 Max Reinhardt has made a more or less memorable screen production of *A Midsummer-Night's Dream* (1935).

†* Explanation of symbols immediately precedes page one.

*Seven Sages* (*c.* 1200),[1] the *Cursor Mundi* (p. 28), the *Gesta Romanorum* (p. 37), the old ballad of *Gernutus, the Jew of Venice* (available in Percy's *Reliques*), and in "Declamation 95" of Sylvain's *Orator*. All or almost all European literatures contain the Jew-story itself. For the Bond-Story, however, Shakespeare was indebted most to the first tale of the fourth day of Ser Giovanni Fiorentino's *Il Pecorone* ("The Blockhead" or "The Gaby"), fifty tales collected about 1378 and printed in 1558. (2) The Casket-Story is found in St. John of Damascus's *Barlaam and Josaphat* (*c.* 800), the *Decameron,* the *Gesta Romanorum,* and in Gower's *Confessio Amantis.* (3) Besides the two main plots of the bond and the caskets, there are, according to Moulton, two others: (a) The elopement of Jessica and Lorenzo is considered as being original, or is attributed to the fourteenth *novella* of Masuccio di Salerno.[2] (b) The ring-episode is also regarded as Shakespeare's invention, or stems from Ser Giovanni's *Il Pecorone.* (4) It would appear that native influences played an important part. Probably *The Iew,* mentioned by Gosson's *School of Abuse* (p. 138) as among the few moral plays, and acted at the Bull Inn, represents an older play or heavy interlude (no longer extant) upon which Shakespeare's version is based. It is also generally recognized that Marlowe's conception of Barabas and Abigail influenced Shakespeare's Shylock and Jessica. Munday's *Zelauto* (1580) may also have been a part-source. Finally, few have disagreed with Lee's theory that the original of Shylock is Dr. Roderigo Lopez, Portuguese-Jewish physician to Queen Elizabeth hanged in June, 1594, for alleged treason against the Queen's life. It appears that the Earl of Essex was Lopez's main accuser, and it is not improbable that Shakespeare's political ideas were influenced by the Earl.

Characterization.[3] More significant than the advance in craftsmanship is Shakespeare's developing power in character analysis. Of the minor people, Salanio and Salerio are essentially parasites; Gratiano, live foil to Antonio, is talkative and mercurial; Gobbo, an invented character, is a better clown than Launce. Much in the tradition of *Romeo and Juliet* is the romantic love of Lorenzo and Jessica, although the latter's traits may leave an unfavorable impression. Portia, somewhat gloomy when she is not sparkling in talk, and somewhat catlike in her playing with Shylock and even Bassanio, is traditionally regarded as an ideal compound of intellect and romance; creatively apart from the siren of the source *novella,* she is merry-hearted, sensible, virtu-

1 For a discussion of the version in the *Dolopathos,* consult Cardozo, J. L., *The Contemporary Jew in The Elizabethan Drama* (1925). For a Danish and two Icelandic versions of the Pound-of-Flesh story, and analogues of the motif of "The Three Lovers," see Schlauch, Margaret, "The Pound of Flesh Story in the North," *The Journal of English and Germanic Philology,* XXX (1931), pp. 348-360.

2 "The theme of a Jewish maiden loved by a Christian is common to a large number of exempla," says Brown, B. D., "Medieval Protoytpes of Lorenzo and Jessica," *Modern Language Notes,* XLIV (1929), pp. 227-232.

3 A critical survey of the characters is available in Small, S. A., *Shakespearean Character Interpretation: The Merchant of Venice* (1927).

ous, a noble-minded and queenly Renaissance lady. The modern subjective approach, un-Elizabethan in its attitude toward the commercialized preparations for the marriage, rates Bassanio as "a fortune-hunter and a wastrel, who, when he has squandered his inheritance and his borrowings, resolves to retrieve his estate by marrying a rich woman."[1] The historical point of view is also essential to an understanding of the unassertive Antonio, labelled by E. K. Chambers as "melancholy." One school feels he is unimportant to the action; the second, that he and Shylock are the protagonists of the main plot: if Antonio represents the religious bigotry of Belmont or of Christianity, then Shylock (even if forced by external circumstances) represents the religious bigotry of the Ghetto or of Judaism.

The critical problem of Shylock's character overshadows any single element of the play.[2] Shakespeare, either as an Elizabethan with the political and racial prejudices of his day or as a good business man, presents the typical or traditional Jew expected by his audience, an audience that indulges in the popular pastime of Jew-baiting. These critics point to the wave of Anti-Semitism in the England of about 1594, opportunely seized upon by Shakespeare as a time for drawing Shylock as a medieval ogre. A dissenting circle of critics insists that *The Merchant of Venice* is a satire on religious bigotry and a plea for toleration. Shakespeare's purpose, says the second group, is to picture a subjective individual, not a type, a Jew desperately put to making a living in a Christian community. However presented on the stage, whether in Elizabethan fashion as a Jew-baitable monster craving the blood of Christians[3] or as a sentimentalized-philosophical human being, Shylock nucleates our sympathy possibly better than do the Christian Venetians.

STYLE. From the standpoint of style little can be said in disparagement. Puns are numerous and classical allusions often unnatural; the soliloquies may be long and trite; the humor is sometimes coarse; the minor characters are not always well discriminated, and, particularly, the court scene has been criticized as seemingly different from English practice and English legal procedure, as "an historical anamorphism."[4] Yet *The Merchant of Venice* is an important example of tragi-comedy.

---

1 Ervine, St. John, "The Realistic Test in Drama," *Yale Review*, XI (1922), p. 289 (pp. 285-303).

2 Walley, H. R., "Shakespeare's Portrayal of Shylock," in *Essays in Dramatic Literature* (The Parrott Presentation Volume), edited by Craig, Hardin (1935), pp. 213-242. See also, "Shakespeare in Tel Aviv," editorial in the *Jewish Frontier*, August, 1936, p. 6.

3 Some deny that Shylock is a Jew. See Packard, Maurice, *Shylock Not a Jew* (1919); Friedlander, Gerald, *Shakespeare and the Jew* (1921), Chap. I, "Shakespeare and the Jew," pp. 1-28.

4 Quoted from Silverman, Maurice, "Shylock—Shakespeare's Enigma," *The Reflex*, IV (April, 1929), pp. 60-69. Mr. Silverman's general summary is useful. Consult also Griston, H. J., *Shaking the Dust from Shakespeare* (1924), in which the author contends that the tragi-comedy reveals the legal, historical, and geographical facts of the fourth century, not, as the traditional opinion has it, of the fourteenth or fifteenth or sixteenth century.

Shakespeare harmonizes the main plot of the semi-tragic bond-story with the romantic casket-story, into both of which are dovetailed the two subordinate episodes of the Lorenzo-Jessica courtship and of the ring.[1] To an important group of critics the main plot is the story of the caskets; to these the Fifth Act is not an anti-climax but a significant *dénouement*. As already stated, his maturing full-bodiedness of characterization is equal even to his organic plot-structure. Finally the blank verse is gravely dramatic if not magically lyrical, and the expressed thoughts are detachedly lofty.

### D. Low Romantic Comedy

## *The Taming of the Shrew* (c. 1593—1599)

Source. The older and more current view is that the anonymous *The Taming of A Shrew* (1594) was Shakespeare's basic source; but some have believed that both plays have a common original and one or two are inclining to the opinion that *The Taming of A Shrew* is a textual adaptation of Shakespeare's farce. In either case the Bianca-Lucentio sub-plot and its artifices were supplied by Ariosto's *Gli Suppositi* (prose), and his *I Suppositi* (verse, 1579), almost certainly by way of Gascoigne (p. 122). Furthermore, the Induction has been traced as far back as "The Sleeper Awakened," an Arabian Night tale in which Abou Hassan is the prototype of Christopher Sly. Some critics look upon *The Taming of the Shrew,* rather than upon *All's Well That Ends Well* (p. 200), as possibly identical with the *Love's Labour's Wonne* listed by Meres.

Authorship. Warburton holds that Shakespeare rewrote the dialogue and contributed scenes; Steevens, that Shakespeare has a part in practically every scene, especially in the shrew-taming plot; White, Fleay, and Parrott, that the inferior underplot belongs to a collaborator, while practically everything of importance is Shakespeare's; Charlotte Potter, and Quiller-Couch and J. Dover Wilson, that Shakespeare wrote the whole play.

Adaptation of the Source. As close in plot as in title are Shakespeare's play and *The Taming of A Shrew.* Each has a similar Induction; but the absence of an Epilogue in Shakespeare explaining what happened to Sly after the play had been performed, leaves the impression that the play is incomplete. But Shakespeare's artistry is much the greater: the lovers are less conventional, the romantic sentiments less

---

1 Interesting approaches to the realism of *The Merchant of Venice* are Ervine, St. John, "The Realistic Test in Drama," *Yale Review,* XI (1922), pp. 288-298 (pp. 285-303), and Kaiser, J. W., *Introduction to the Study and Interpretation of Drama* (Amsterdam, 1929), pp. 35-77.

frivolous, and, finally, Shakespeare does not permit the actor-onlookers to interrupt the performance more than once, and then in a delightful fashion.[1]

CHARACTERIZATION. To declare, as one critic does, that the natural characterization in this comedy is quite unrivalled is doubtless an exaggeration. Farce, seldom permitting the developmental treatment of character-rôles, gives not even Shakespeare any special opportunities for truthful delineations of life. Only three persons are of some account —Biondello, whose infrequent capers are effectively sustained; Katherina, whose concluding speech almost strips from her character the label "an automaton"; and Petruccio, a consummate liar and consummate horse-play actor.

STYLE. Never did Shakespeare's comic muse go to such preposterous lengths. The farce of the main or wife-taming plot has an extravagance of action that can be staged effectively today, to the open annoyance of the modern woman, and to the feigned delight of her escort.[2] Despite the skilful connection with the Petruccio-Katherine plot, the Lucentio-Bianca Italianate episodes have not been fused with Shakespeare's characteristic powers. Note, again, that the early disappearance of Sly creates the feeling that the curtain has not yet fallen on the play,[3] just as the concluding scene of the 1935 technicolor moving picture of *Becky Sharp,* leaves many with the impression that the end of the film is possibly over-abrupt.

The three divisions of the play are the humorous Induction (Sly), the comedy of character (Petruccio and Katherina), and the comedy of intrigue (Lucentio, Bianca, *et alii*). It is customary to attribute the uneven quality of the work to dual authorship or collaboration. Certainly there is evidence of neither Shakespeare's subtle portraiture nor poetic grasp. How to tame termagants seems to be a perennially popular theme, and Shakespeare uses many stock devices to broaden the buffoonery. Of the triptych-parts the most interesting is the Induction, praised by most critics not merely for its value to the comedy but especially for its "mood of memory of the country" (Masefield). This "subtle, quizzical, humane, philosophical piece of nonsense" (Chapman) has been declared (by J. Dover Wilson) to be an important document for historians of education.

---

1 For a "Comparison of the Plots in *The Taming of the Shrew, The Taming of a Shrew,* and *I Suppositi,*" see *The Taming of the Shrew,* edited by Boswell-Stone, W. G. (1908), pp. xv-xxv.

2 Recall the talking moving-picture version of *The Taming of the Shrew,* in which Douglas Fairbanks and Mary Pickford appeared (1929).

3 Is there an artistic explanation for the disappearance of Sly? Consult Kuhl, E. P., "Shakspere's Purpose in Dropping Sly," *Modern Language Notes,* xxxvi (1921), pp. 321-329.

### *The Merry Wives of Windsor* (c. 1599)[1]

Source. Shakespeare's own invention has given us this farce-comedy. Conjectures, however, have been made that he built upon suggestions in various works, especially upon "The Two Lovers of Pisa" in Tarlton's *Newes out of Purgatorie* (1590), a version of Straparola's *Filenio* in Painter's *Palace of Pleasure,* and *The Jealous Comedy* (1593), probably a typical Italianate play.[2] Hints may also have been derived from Plautus's *Casina,*[3] Fiorentino's *Il Pecorone,* Straparola's *Piacevoli Notti,* and "The Fishwife's Tale of Brentford" in *Westward for Smelts* published by Kinde Kit of Kingston.

Native Influence. Possibly Lyly influenced the satyr-hobgoblin-fairy scenes of the Fifth Act. More definite is the importance of Jonson's work in the field of "humours" and of realistic satire. Superficial in its horseplay-amusement and fast-paced in its plot of intrigue, this comedy of manners is Shakespeare's only complete work treating of middle-class country society.

Characterization. Shakespeare's lone bourgeois comedy of contemporaneous manners introduces merely slight sketches of bourgeois figures. Hazlitt did not err in deciding that only Slender has individuality. Sir Hugh Evans and Dr. Caius, although essentially characters belonging to the Jonsonian "humour" school, are each more personable than either Nym or Master Ford, two other Jonsonian representations. Mrs. Quickly is a worn-out edition of her previous self. So is Falstaff, if one compares him with the Falstaff already made memorable; but the general agreement seems to be that the Falstaff of *The Merry Wives of Windsor* is not to be identified as the Falstaff of *Henry IV* and *Henry V,* but is rather to be regarded as a second fat knight called by the same name. It is said that some of the characters must be as topical as some of the allusions; but it is inconclusive that Dr. Caius is the Dr. Caius of Caius College, Cambridge, or that Slender is William Wayte, stepson of William Gardiner, or that Shallow is either Sir Thomas Lucy or Justice William Gardiner[4], or that this second Falstaff is the Sir John Fastolfe of *Henry VI, Part I.*[5]

1 Possibly 1597, dated thus by means of the Garter Feast celebrated at Westminster Palace on St. George's Day, April 23, 1597. Consult Hotson, Leslie, *Shakespeare Versus Shallow* (1931), p. 113.

2 Campbell, O. J., "The Italianate Background of *The Merry Wives of Windsor,*" in *Essays and Studies in English and Comparative Literature* by Members of The English Department of the University of Michigan (University of Michigan Press, 1932), pp. 81-117.

3 Forsythe, R. S., "A Plautine Source of *The Merry Wives of Windsor,*" *Modern Philology,* xviii (1920), pp. 57-77.

4 Hotson, Leslie, (1) "A Great Shakespeare Discovery," *Atlantic Monthly,* cxlviii (1931), pp. 419-436; (2) *Shakespeare Versus Shallow* (1931).

5 Baldwin, T. W., *The Organization and Personnel of the Shakesperean Company* (1927), p. 235.

STYLE. Dashed off in a fortnight, so the story goes, at the express order of Queen Elizabeth who wished to see Falstaff in love, *The Merry Wives of Windsor* shows a hasty construction. Loose ends and inconsistencies are evident, dramatic bits are cut short, scenes are loosely joined, the time-element is sometimes confused, and incidents, not characters, are emphasized. Only one-tenth of the play is in verse, all of it with little or no distinction; while the nine-tenths in prose is of no special significance except for the Falstaffian exuberance of language. The intrigues following upon each other have abortions along the way; yet it is remarkable how intelligibly Shakespeare connects the main plot (of Falstaff vs. the Wives, of Master Ford vs. Falstaff, and of the Wives vs. Falstaff) with the secondary plot (of Anne Page and her three suitors). Critics have noted that about midway this written-to-order comedy slumps in briskness, and never do its unassimilated scenes catch up with the sprightly beginning. Whether considered as written against time, or as, possibly, a hasty reworking of some Italianate source-comedy, *The Merry Wives of Windsor* bears witness to Shakespeare's farcical skill (much of the horseplay might be considered less superficial were critics able to recognize the topical nature of the allusions), and to his creation of the English atmosphere. Like *The Taming of the Shrew,* this farce comedy is definitely playable.

### E. High Romantic Comedy ("Later")

## *Much Ado About Nothing*† (c. 1599)

SOURCE. Mateo Bandello's story (1554) of Signor Timbreo di Cardona (Claudio, in Shakespeare) and Fenicia (Hero), daughter of Messer Lionato de' Lionati, came to Shakespeare more or less directly through Belleforest's *Histoires Tragiques* (1582). It is likely that the trick disguise of Margaret was appropriated from Ariosto's *Orlando Furioso* (V) and Spenser's *Faerie Queene* (II, 3). Original with Shakespeare is the low comedy of Dogberry and Verges; also, the subsidiary plot of Benedick and Beatrice, some of whose passages may be reminiscent of Castiglione's *Il Cortegiano.* Attempts have been made to establish connections with Duke Heinrich Julius of Braunschweig's *Vincentius Ladiszlaus* and especially with Jacob Ayrer's *Die Schöne Phaenicia* (*c.* 1595). *Much Ado About Nothing* may be identical with the comedy entitled *Benedicite and Betteris,* or with the *Love's Labour's Wonne* included in Meres's list.

CHARACTERIZATION. Don John[1] is usually regarded as an early draft of Iago, but without the latter's interesting villainy and important role; Friar Francis, as faintly reminiscent of Friar Lawrence. The pro-

---

1 How true to life are Shakespeare's criminal types? Consult Goll, Augustus, *Criminal Types in Shakespeare* (1909); Stoll, E. E., "Criminals in Shakespeare and in Science," *Modern Philology,* x (1912-1913), pp. 55-80; and White, E. J., Shakespeare's Criminal Types," *The American Law Review,* LII (1918) pp. 347-370.

† * Explanation of symbols immediately precedes page one.

to types of Don Pedro, of pleasant temper and superficial, and of Leonato, of well-meaning wit and revered, are found in Bandello, as are also those of Claudio and Hero. The latter's maidenly reserve is a foil to Beatrice's assertive talkativeness. By no means is Hero as great a disappointment as her lover; Claudio's shallow (and possibly plot-ridden) treatment of her and his possessive rather than loving sense of her weaken our sympathy even though he is more of a man when the play concludes than when it starts. Shakespeare's triumphs are his original characters. While stock Elizabethan figures, there is nothing quite like Verges, the clodpated oaf who "will be talking," and Dogberry, the consequential officer of the law—two neatly struck-off predecessors of today's malapropian, muddle-headed, and blundering Jacks-in-office. All recognize that the chief charm of the play is attributable to Shakespeare's second pair of creations, the poniard-speaking Beatrice and the misogynistic-rallying Benedick, corruscating in their wit and humor—in fact, the protagonists of *Much Ado About Nothing*.[1]

STYLE. The first of Shakespeare's three "Joyous Comedies" has recognized qualities. Note the excellence of the prose, the brilliance of the raillery, even the virility of the dialogue. Also marked is the deft characterization, and the lightness of the poetry (lighter and less frequent than in most of his other comedies). Not episodical but essential in the foiling of the counteraction is the low satire on country constables, a comic episode subtly worked into the humorous interest of the subsidiary plot and the near-tragedy of the main plot. Despite its main source the tone is more English than Italian, and the progression of the tale more masterly.

1 Shakespeare's theatre was conditioned by his audience. Robert Bridges has pointed out that Shakespeare made concessions "to the most vulgar stratum of his audience," and that too readily Shakespeare's "offences of the first rank are sometimes overlook'd and pardon'd." He has condemned Shakespeare's "bad jokes and obscenities," his "mere foolish verbal trifles," and his "brutality . . . . essentially an error of manners, an unnecessary rudeness," and feels, for example, that the "coarse terms in which Claudio repudiates Hero enfeeble the plot of *Much Ado*." Shakespeare certainly catered to the populace; for example, in his history plays he consistently exploited the "genealogical interest of his spirited cavalier audience in the martial and glorious doings of their ancestors" (R. B. Sharpe). Frequently, however, Shakespeare's revisions as determined by his audience seem to have enhanced the value of the play. To quote Hardin Craig: "The most favorable situation so far suggested for such current revisions is that in which a particular part of the play was found to give such pleasure to the audience that this particular part was exploited by amplification, frequently at the expense of other less interesting parts of the play. This hypothesis lies at the basis of the supposed revision of *Much Ado About Nothing*, where the witty dialogue between Beatrix and Benedict are thought to have grown at the expense of the Italian story of Claudio and Hero [Hardin Craig's reference at this point is to *Much Ado About Nothing*, edited by Arthur Quiller-Couch and J. Dover Wilson, 1923, pp. XII-XIII 104-107], and of *1 and 2 Henry IV*, where the part of the mighty Sir John Falstaff is thought to have risen in dimensions at the expense of a good deal of no doubt excellent dramatization of serious history from Holinshed." [Hardin Craig's reference at this point is to Morgan, A. E., *Some Problems of Shakespeare's "Henry the Fourth"* (1924).] Consult Bridges, Robert, *Collected Essays Papers* &c. (1927), I, "The Influence of the Audience on Shakespeare's Drama," pp. 1-29; Sharpe, R. B., "'We Band of Brothers,'" *Studies in Philology*, XXVI (1929), pp. 166-176; Craig, Hardin, "Shakespeare's Revisions," *The Johns Hopkins Alumni Magazine*, XIX (1930-1931), pp. 331-348.

## *As You Line It*† (c. 1600)

SOURCE. What is not original in this comedy is adapted from Lodge's *Rosalynde* (p. 139), founded in turn on the *Tale of Gamelyn* (p. 38). Of more or less direct influence were the Robin Hood ballads and plays (pp. 101, 103).

ADAPTATION OF THE SOURCE.[1] Except for minor changes and omissions, Shakespeare follows the main outlines of Lodge's *Rosalynde.* The conventional pastoral elements, particularly the element of atmosphere, is pronouncedly less stereotyped than the source, and also shows the influence of Lyly's idyllic hand. The action is compressed; the motive in Shakespeare is greed, not jealousy. Audrey, Touchstone, and Jaques, as well as Amiens and William, are Shakespeare's creations. To Lodge's pastoral romance, Shakespeare's main contributions were dramatic characters and the spirit of high comedy.

CHARACTERIZATION. If not as challenging, Rosalind's wit is as nimble and sparkling as Beatrice's. Rosalind's tender mockery of love is permeated by youthful womanliness and stingless gaiety, and is modern and volatile in its approach. Of course Orlando is modest and noble, but he is also a conventional example of heroic young manhood. Celia is a foil to Rosalind, and her departures from a conventional nature arise usually from her love for Rosalind; according to some critics, her marriage with the unworthy Oliver violates the consistency of the portrait for which Shakespeare originally prepared the reader.

While Rosalind is the centre of the comedy, it is Jaques the malcontent who is the chief interest of the play. Different siftings of this Jonsonian humour character have not yet separated the mixture of his reality and affectation. Recognize Jaques at various moments as the vaporing rather than acting moralist, as the misanthropic, even superficial, rather than vicious or contemplative cynic, and as the sentimental rather than stony philosopher satirizing the follies of mankind. (See *The Malcontent,* p. 240.) Touchstone, like Jaques, appears to be a character apart from the plot and action; his part was probably created not for the purpose of furthering the play, but probably for the purpose of giving employment to the actor Armin. Yet this loyal and honest court fool is among Shakespeare's best professional wits; his wooing of Audrey is a burlesque of romantic love, and his skeptical philosophy is a lampoon of Jaques's humorous melancholy.[2] Adam stands alone as an ideal figure of devotion, pathetically if not poetically imagined.

---

1 For a critical analysis of Shakespeare's use of Lodge's romance we recommend Romig, E. D., "'As You Like It'; Shakespeare's Use of his Source, Lodge's 'Rosalynde.'" *The University of Colorado Studies,* XVI, No. 4 (1929), pp. 300-322.

2 A stimulating analysis of Touchstone's character is available in Priestley, J. B., *The English Comic Characters* (1925), pp. 20-42. So are his discussions of Bottom (pp. 1-19) and, particularly, of Falstaff (pp. 69-105).

†* **Explanation of symbols immediately precedes page one.**

Finally, the realistic naturalness of William and Audrey is a contrast to the sentimental artificiality of the Arcadians, Silvius and Phebe.

STYLE. The beginning of this high romantic comedy is as weak as the ending is huddled, the plotting is as careless as the construction is loose, the action is as feeble as the heightened dramatic conflicts are few[1]. But *As You Like It* is memorable for its fresh pastoral element and woodland atmosphere, for its independent character creations and effective poetry, for its bright humor and lucid wit. The main plot of romantic love (Orlando and Rosalind) is threaded by four subsidiary episodes—pseudo-pastoral (Silvius and Phebe), parody and low comedy (Touchstone and Audrey), and, finally, the huddling-up scenes (two episodes, that of Oliver and Celia; and that of Duke Senior and Frederick, usurped and usurper). Perfectly expressive is the language, whether in prose or dialogue, blank verse or lyric. Throughout Shakespeare's plays his songs function in several ways; note the effectiveness of "Under the greenwood tree," "Blow, blow, thou winter wind," and "It was a lover and his lass." Shakespeare's songs "heighten the dominant mood of a scene; they dally with it, or relax it; they give atmosphere; they help to supply the lack of scenery (notably in *As You Like It*); they further the action, or tide over pauses in it; they lend variety to a popular show."[2]

## *Twelfth Night: or, What You Will*† (c. 1601)

SOURCE. "The Historie of Apolonius and Silla" in Barnaby Rich's *Riche in Farewell to Militarie Profession* (1581) was probably Shakespeare's immediate source.[3] Rich probably took the story from Bandello's *Novelle* (1554) or Cinthio's *Hecatommithi* (1565) or Belleforest's *Histoires Tragiques* (1570). However the elements of the tale have been found in older, but probably not the oldest, sources; *e.g.*, resemblances

1 The so-called *Ipse-Vere* cipher (Act V, Scene I) is supposed by some to contain a most striking repudiation of Shakespeare as the author of the plays.

2 Roberts, W. W., "Music in Shakespeare," *Bulletin of The John Rylands Library*, VII (1922-1923), p. 486 (pp. 480-493). Edmund Gosse has said that Shakespeare created and introduced into English literature the Dramatic Song, and J. R. Moore has declared Shakespeare virtually the first Elizabethan who systematically employs the song for dramatic purposes. Augustus Ralli, however, believes that the attempts made to assign a dramatic value to the songs have met with but partial success, despite the assertions of such critics as Gosse, Moore, and also Noble, who has shown how Shakespeare's songs have become essential to the plays. Consult Moore, J. R., "The Function of the Songs in Shakespeare's Plays," in *Shakespeare Studies*, by Members of the Department of English of the University of Wisconsin (1916), pp. 78-102; Noble, Richard, "Shakespeare's Songs and Stage," in *Shakespeare and the Theatre* (1927), by *The Shakespeare Association* (London, 1925-1926), pp. 120-133. For the text of his principal songs, with notes and explanations, consult Noble, Richmond, *Shakespeare's Use of Song* (1923); for a list of Shakespeare's songs set to music, consult Williams, Loraine, "Published Shakespearean Music," *The Quarterly Journal of Speech*, XIX (1933), pp. 503-513.

3 Shakespeare may also have used Rich's story, "Of Two Brethren and Their Wives," according to Neilson, W. A., "The Variorum Twelfth Night," *The Atlantic Monthly*, LXXXIX (1902), pp. 715-718.

† * Explanation of symbols immediately precedes page one.

are more distinct in *Gl'Ingannati* or "The Deceived" (available in the volume called *Il Sacrificio, Commedia de Gl'Introvati,* 1537), than in either Nicolo Secchi's (or Secco's) *Gl'Inganni* or "The Cheats" (acted 1547, printed 1562) or in Curzio Gonzaga's *Gl'Inganni* (1604). No source is known for the secondary plot, that of which Malvolio is the center.

CHARACTERIZATION. Viola is a beautiful character, tactful, wistful, and sympathetic, truly womanly. She is the central character of the chief plot, but not the centre of interest. On the other hand, Olivia represents sentimentality rather than sentiment; she is "in love with grief" in much the same way that Orsino, the day-dreaming sentimentalist, is "in love with love." The persons of the subordinate plot are vividly drawn. Sir Toby may be a diluted Falstaff, but standing apart from the fat knight is bodied forth fully as a selfish, quaffing, sponging, yet genial and lovable old libertine whose marriage to Maria, the tease, is not likely to reform him. For complete insignificance, and for consummate imbecility, it would be difficult to better Shakespeare's study of Sir Andrew, dupe of Sir Toby and faint-hearted suitor. Feste, as is known, lacks Touchstone's personality, but is Shakespeare's most penetrating Elizabethan court jester. Finally, there is Malvolio, whose character has been adjectived as trustworthy, complacent, foppish, self-important, humorless, especially overweening and puritanical. While the main plot does not depend upon the steward, Malvolio has been declared by Symons to be the protagonist of the play—although that could not have been Shakespeare's purpose.

STYLE. Its capital construction when analyzed is found to build in some ways upon the plot devices and parallel episodes of his earlier plays, such as *The Comedy of Errors* (mistaken identity), *The Two Gentlemen of Verona* (the disguise), *Henry IV* (the Falstaffian character), *The Merchant of Venice* (friendship among men), *As You Like It* (a woman's love for a woman disguised as a man). The underplot of intrigue (the trick used is much like that in *Much Ado About Nothing*) is complicated smoothly with the complex love-affairs of the main plot—Orsino's love for Olivia, Olivia's love for Viola, Viola's love for Orsino. The language is figurative and the poetry is tender (famous lyric: "Come away, come away, death"); the satire is droll and the characters are natural creations on the same important footing as the plot and the background. This is Shakespeare's best high romantic comedy, supreme in its blend of mirth and beauty, romance, realism, and satire.

## THIRD PERIOD

### A. Problem Comedy

### *All's Well That Ends Well* (c. 1602—1603)

Source. The main plot is a version of a tale in Boccaccio's *Decameron* (III, 9), probably found by Shakespeare among William Painter's *contes* in his *Palace of Pleasure* (1566). By practically common consent *All's Well That Ends Well* is considered a recast of an earlier play, possibly, on the basis of internal evidence, identical with Shakespeare's *Love's Labour's Wonne* mentioned by Meres. If so, the play must be re-dated as belonging to 1598 or earlier.

Adaptation of the Source. Shakespeare's version has neither the directness nor the simple dignity of Boccaccio's. Lafeu, Lavache, and Parolles, character-contributions by Shakespeare, do not set off to advantage the general ineptness and unpleasantness of the main plot. Boccaccio's Bertrand, however, is a more consistent figure in Shakespeare.

Characterization. Lavache is foul-mouthed, a base wax figure thrown to the groundlings; Parolles, a lesser Falstaff,[1] is an "obnoxious" and "unsavory" *miles gloriosus,* described by S. A. Tannenbaum as "the nearest thing to a contemptible character in Shakspere." The Countess is Shakespeare's only pleasant creation; hers is an old age buttressed by a common-sense sophistication. Possibly Bertram is not the dastardly coward, liar, and profligate so commonly assumed. Even if in his day position and blood had not had its fundamental importance, certainly his first meeting with "the poorer born" Helena could not dispose him to accept her without a struggle.[2] Over the purposeful character of Helena many battles have been waged.[3] Hazlitt thinks her sweet, Masefield thinks her despicable: each represents a camp. To the Elizabethan the substitution in bed of one for another was not out of keeping with medieval tradition. Never before and never after did Shakespeare present a heroine who came of middle-class stock.

Style. *All's Well That Ends Well,* in which the nature of the plot[4] could have admitted a coarseness of tone that is generally absent, may be a satire on social distinctions. It is said to abound in wisdom. Deficient workmanship marks this problem comedy. Classical allusions and fifty-percent prose, verse-letters and abnormal rimed passages indicate that Shakespeare's revision of an earlier comedy (c. 1596) left un-

---

1 A convincing "No" to this frequent assertion is given by Krapp, G. P., "Parolles," an essay (pp. 291-300) in *Shaksperian Studies,* edited by Matthews, Brander, and Thorndike, A. H. (1916).

2 Arthur Acheson believes that Helena and Bertram are identical with Elizabeth Vernon and the Earl of Southampton.

3 Consult Lawrence, W. W., *Shakespeare's Problem Comedies* (1931), Chap. II, "All's Well That Ends Well," pp. 32-77.

4 The plot gave the main basis to Audrans's French operetta, *Gilles de Narbonne,* and to Felicien David's opera, *La Saphir.*

touched much of his juvenile work, although the thought-compacted and elliptical style of his later work (c. 1606) is also in evidence. Boccaccio's conclusion is as simple as Shakespeare's is unconvincing; the workmanship of Shakespeare's final scene is stagey. The humor is feeble, the romance totally aborted. Uneven is this "composite of archaic and illogical folk-tale situations" (W. W. Lawrence) which "aesthetic criticism has in vain striven to redeem from neglect due to insuperable ethical repugnance" (A. W. Ward). To-day, the idea upon which the theme is based is probably less shocking and possibly more interesting.

### *Troilus and Cressida* (c. 1602)

Source. For the love story of Troilus and Cressida, Shakespeare is most indebted to Chaucer's version (p. 66); for the camp-story of the Greek and Roman figures, to Caxton's *Recuyell of the Historyes of Troye* (p. 95)[1], possibly with Lydgate's *Troy-Book* (p. 84) at the side. Chapman's *Iliad* (p. 234) provided suggestions for the character of mud-slinging Thersites. Heywood's *Iron Age* (Part I) may have had an indirect influence. It is very possible that the Prologue and all of Act V excepting Scenes 4-6 may be by another hand. Regard the play from the subjective point of view, say such critics as Brooke and Chambers; but other critics, such as Lawrence and Tatlock, say that tradition fixed the character of Shakespeare's debased treatment of the theme.

Various Interpretations. Attempts have been made to read part of Shakespeare's life into this play. (1) *Troilus and Cressida* may be a caricature of the Jonson-Marston-Dekker "war of the theatres" (pp. 228, 235, 240). Ajax may be meant for Jonson; Thersites may be meant for Marston or Dekker (Fleay, Wyndham). (2) The travesty of the Homeric story-elements may be planned as an attack upon Chapman. Not only is Chapman usually identified as "the rival poet" of Shakespeare's *Sonnets* but is also usually regarded as having done most to oust Shakespeare from the favor of his patron through the translation of the *Iliad* (Furnivall, Gollancz). (3) Shakespeare's purpose is to depreciate medieval heroism and chivalry (Boas), or to satirize ancient Greek ideals as reflected in the Homeric poems (Ulrici) . (4) The play is another work arising out of Shakespeare's spirit of bitterness and disillusionment, and is a criticism of womanhood (Dowden, Brandes). (5) Shakespeare's satirical treatment of love and heroism was done in the vein popular at the time (Thorndike).

Characterization. Troilus is a naive, Romeo-like lover who wastes himself on Cressida, the loose and heartless coquette, one whose very name had become a synonym for harlotry. Their go-between is Pandarus, a rank sensualist. Thersites is a scamp "whose gall coins

1 Stein, Elizabeth, "Caxton' s*Recuyell* and Shakespeare's *Troilcs,*" *Modern Language Notes,* XLV (1930), pp. 144-146.

slanders like a mint," and who acts as a foul-mouthed Greek chorus, a part usually taken in the comedies by the fool. The other characters of any importance are the brave Hector, and the grave, thoughtful, shrewd Ulysses.

STYLE. So poorly developed are the potentialities of the theme that some critics consider *Troilus and Cressida* a scenario rather than a play. The long and undramatic draft has a Latinized vocabulary, sorry dialogue, scurrilous humor, and, particularly at the end, slipshod structure. A tone of over-cynicism and wantonness permeates the love-element. Shakespeare has not treated his subject with the insight necessary to leave behind an impression that is anything but pessimistic and unpleasant. Its two divisions show dissimilar styles: the love story reveals Shakespeare's early characteristics; the camp story, Shakespeare's later characteristics. This play of disillusionment is neither a comedy nor a tragedy[1]; nor, of course, has its Trojan background any value as history. Shakespeare's somber irony and scoffing cynicism have a rather modern appeal. *Troilus and Cressida* has been declared "a dramatic and poetic symbolism of a purely metaphysical problem: the dynamic opposition in the mind of two opposing faculties, intuition and intelligence, or faith and reason."[2]

### *Measure for Measure* (c. 1604)

SOURCE. George Whetstone's rimed two-plot play, the *History of Promos and Cassandra* (1578), was Shakespeare's immediate source. It is possible that Shakespeare knew Whetstone's prose version published in the latter's *Heptameron of Civil Discourses* (1582). The source of the main plot also suggested the subsidiary plot. Whetstone, in turn, had found the tale in the fifth story of the eighth decade of the *Hecatommithi* (1565) by Giovanni Battista Giraldi, called Cinthio. Yet the elements of the tale told by Cinthio's *Epitia* before its inclusion in his *Hecatommithi* are extant elsewhere.[3]

ADAPTATION OF THE SOURCE. In the Italian version Isabella sacrifices her honor. Whetstone, however, instead of having her brother executed, has him escape from prison. Shakespeare permits neither his Isabella to yield her virtue nor her brother to get out of the law's clutches. By introducing a new character, Mariana, and by repeating

---

1 Among those who tilt a lance against the interpretation denying the play's harmony of structure and unity of theme is Guha, P. K., "On Two Problems in Shakespeare," *Dacca University Bulletin*, No. IX (1926), "The Problem of Shakespeare's *Troilus and Cressida*," pp. 31-38 (pp. 23-41).

2 Knight, G. W., "The Metaphysic of 'Troilus and Cressida,'" *The Dublin Review*, CLXXXV (1929), p. 228 (pp. 228-242). See also his stimulating analysis in *The Wheel of Fire* (1930), pp. 51-80.

3 For a guide to some early versions of the *Measure for Measure* theme, consult Budd, F. E., "Material for a Study of the Sources of Shakespeare's 'Measure for Measure,'" *Revue de Littérature comparée*, XI (1931), pp. 711-736.

the trick of the substituted bed-fellow from *All's Well That Ends Well,* he helps unravel the tangle. Wretched as Whetstone's version is, Shakespeare's debt is clear in matters of character, dialogue, and action.

Characterization. Only three characters call for discussion. Vincentio, it is said, represents an earthly providence; yet he does, after all, evade responsibility by deputing his authority to another. Angelo is a man of abstinence; but even he, like not a few men of his type, goes the way of all flesh. Finally, the character of Isabella, the most important person, is inconsistent. She and her rigid chastity are the soul of the play, says one school. Dowden's description of Isabella's "white passion of purity" represents that opinion; but with a change of standards[1] other critics point out that her chastity lacks human feeling, and that her ready substitution of another virgin for herself in Angelo's embraces represents only a negative virtue.[2]

Style. Four intrigues (of the Duke versus Angelo, of Angelo versus Isabella, of Angelo versus Claudio, of the Duke and the substitution of Mariana) indicate Shakespeare's Elizabethan tendency to extreme plotting.[3] The "inrush of sensual passion" is intensified by the grim realism and bawdy humor of the underplot. Despite the effective trial scene of Act V, the conclusion of the play leaves behind frayed pieces of characterization and loose ends of action. Throughout one feels the lack of emotion. Although not as "painful" as it was to Coleridge, the main plot is generally considered unpleasant. Acts II and III have been praised for their poetic dialogue, and the craftsmanship of Acts I and II have been designated as perfect. Beautiful lyric: "Take, O, take those lips away." The play "is written in much the same key as Point Counter Point and others of Mr Aldous Huxley's novels. The hatred of sentimentalism and romance, the savage determination to tear aside all veils, to expose reality in its crudity and hideousness, the self-laceration, weariness, discord, cynicism and disgust of our modern

---

1 Consider Shakespeare in the light of his own age, says Durham, W. H., "Measure for Measure as Measure for Critics," *Essays in Criticism* (University of California Publications in English), I (1929), pp. 113-132. E. E. Stoll is the American protagonist of the historical method in approaching all Shakespearean problems. He has endeavored to expose the fallacies of the romantic critics and to reject the subjective portraitures of Shakespeare the man. His criticism is a provocative and important corrective to what Benedetto Croce has called *exclamatory* criticism, one that drowns Shakespeare "beneath a flood of superlatives." Iconolatrous scholars have too frequently sentimentalized Shakespeare; this is true even of Edward Dowden. Schücking and Stoll, both of whom believe that the interpretation of Shakespeare should proceed in the light of Shakespeare's era, would probably take issue, as a case in point, with Hubert Griffith's *Iconoclastes, or The Future of Shakespeare* (1927) in which he asserts (p. 48) that by modernizing Shakespeare (by using dinner jackets in *Hamlet,* for example) verisimilitude in Shakespeare's plays could be obtained. As an exemplification of approaching Shakespeare from the point of view of an Elizabethan, read Ellis, Oliver C. De C., "Shakespeare as a Scientist," *Papers of the Manchester Literary Club,* LIX (1933), pp. 81-118.

2 Read Lawrence, W. W., *Shakespeare's Problem Comedies* (1931), Chap. III, *Measure for Measure,* pp. 78-121.

3 Shakespeare's theme is followed, but not too faithfully, by Richard Wagner's opera comique, *Die Novize von Palermo* (1836); now called *Das Liebesverbot; oder, Die Novize von Palermo* ("The Ban on Love; or, the Novice of Palermo").

'literature of negation' all belonged to Shakespeare about 1603."[1] This gloomy comedy-tragedy of lust and chastity is more than an important moral study: it revolves about a question of social control with which economic and social legislation of today is still grappling.

### B. Late Tragedy

### X *Hamlet, Prince of Denmark*† (c. 1598—1604; probably c. 1600[2])

Source. In *The Annals of Ireland by the Four Masters* there appears, under the year 917, what may be the earliest reference to the name *Hamlet,* referred to also, three centuries later, in Snorri Sturlason's *Skaldskapar-mal,* or Gradus to the Northern Parnassus, a section of his *Prose Edda* (*c.* 1230).[3] The crude outline of the *Hamlet* story as it appears in Saxo Grammaticus's *Historia Danica* (*c.* 1200) is the basis of Belleforest's version in the fifth book of *Histoires Tragiques* (1570), and under the title of *The Hystorie of Hamblet* the Hamlet-theme was made available by Thomas Pavier in an English translation (1608). It is very likely that Shakespeare drew upon an earlier *Hamlet* by Kyd. This pre-Shakespearean play may have provided some of the material for the German play (dated October 27, 1710, and published in 1781) entitled *Der Bestrafte Brudermord: oder Prinz Hamlet aus Dänemark* ("Fratricide Punished, or Prince Hamlet of Denmark").

Characterization. Through the figure of the blockhead Osric, Shakespeare satirizes the dandified affectations of his day. Common opinion stigmatizes Rosencrantz and Guildenstern as false to their friend Hamlet and as fawning courtiers,[4] the foils to the disinterested Horatio, Hamlet's confidant. Laertes is as much a practical man of action as Fortinbras, and as a foil to Hamlet, his immorality and hot-headed unscrupulousness bear upon the action with an emphatic directness greater than does the character of the Prince of Norway. In Ophelia is sketched a woman who is sweet, timid, pathetic, even unsophisticated despite the indelicate song she sings while mad; she is not grossly insulted by Hamlet until he suspects her innocence. Her essential shallowness may arise from a dramatic necessity of subordinating the love-story to the main tragedy.

Neither Claudius nor Gertrude is wholly despicable. While licentious, Claudius loves the Queen; while not a coward, he uses poison to gain his shifty ends; while a subtle trickster, he is, except for his act of

---

1 Wilson, J. D., *The Essential Shakespeare* (1932), p. 117.

2 Lawrence, W. J., *Shakespeare's Workshop* (1928), pp. 98-109; Gray, H. D., "The Date of Hamlet," *The Journal of English and Germanic Philology,* XXXI (1932), pp. 55-61.

3 Gollancz, Sir Israel, *The Sources of "Hamlet"* (1926).

4 Rosencrantz and Guildenstern are not "perfidious," says Jha, Amaranatha, *Shakespearean Comedy and Other Studies* (1930), "Two Misjudged Characters in Shakespeare," pp. 122-134.

† * Explanation of symbols immediately precedes page one.

fratricide, a rather weak villain.[1] Gertrude, an adulteress in the old story, was not true to Hamlet's father, but neither was she, probably, privy to her husband's death. Shallow and weak-willed she was, but there is no denying her love for Hamlet. Toward her "Hamlet maintains throughout the greater part of the play a wounded reserve appropriate to the situation. He speaks of her with sarcasm, but addresses her with curt respect."[2]

Next to Hamlet, Polonius is probably most carefully pictured; yet concerning the Lord Chamberlain, possibly a satire on Lord Burghley, there is a wide divergence of opinion. He always orates to his children. His precepts are good but not moral. "Brevity is the soul of wit," he says—and then spoils the maxim by adding to it. Some recognize him as the incarnation of self-conceit and as a faithful time-server who considers spying a part of the high form of statecraft; others, as a worldly-wise official zealous in the discharge of his duties, but obsequious, loquacious, and over-confident, a good case, in Johnson's words, of "dotage encroaching upon wisdom."

It has been observed that the Ghost is the pivot on which everything turns. The treatment throughout is in accordance with Catholic doctrine.[3] But subordinating even the importance of the Ghost is the problematical character of Hamlet, a scholar and an idealist, cultured, intellectual, sincere, versatile, witty, unpretentious, one whose sensitive nature shrinks from bloody vengeance. Most discussion revolves about the question concerning Hamlet's delay in killing Claudius.[4]

1. *Theory of Internal Difficulties.* Older critics like Coleridge, Gervinus, Hugo, Dowden, Turck, Doring, Goethe, Lowell, Hazlitt, and others, explain Hamlet as a victim of procrastination, a sentimental creature brain-bound by moral scruples, an irresolute pessimist, a shattered idealist. The excess in Hamlet of a reflective habit of mind

---

1 Jones, H. M., "The King in Hamlet," *University of Texas Bulletin*, No. 1865: November 20, 1918, Comparative Literature Series No. 1, Vols. I—III (1918-1923).

2 Santayana, George, "Hamlet," *Life and Letters*, I (1928), p. 30 (pp. 17-38).

3 Bridge, Gerard, *Shakespeare's Catholicity in Hamlet* (1927); Butler, L. F., "Was Shakespeare a Catholic?" *The Irish Monthly*, LXII (1934), pp. 173-180. It is important to note that one may see in Shakespeare an idealist, because one may be an idealist; a second may see in him a realist, because a second may be a realist; others see in him a nature-lover, a scientist, or a philosopher, because they may be nature-lovers, scientists or philosophers. Likewise men will see in him a Catholic, or a Protestant, and the like. Many of the statements made are too ingenious to be anything but discounted. One of the best approaches to this aspect of Shakespeare is the article by Hunter, Mark, "Spiritual Values in Shakespeare," in *Speculum Religionis* (1929, Oxford, At the Clarendon Press), pp. 113-130.

4 It is difficult to agree with L. C. Knights and Tolstoy that it is futile to discuss at much length the character of one who has no character, but we believe, as do C. M. Lewis, E. E. Stoll, and A. J. A. Waldock, that it may be wiser to minimize the importance of Hamlet's delay. It might, as C. C. H. Williamson has suggested, even be possible to make out a case for Hamlet as a victim of necrophilism (graveyards, worms, the fight on Ophelia's coffin, and the like). But we have given the problem considerable space because it is one generally discussed. For further general information, refer to Cruikshank, A. B., *The True Character of Hamlet* (1918); Clutton-Brock, (Arthur), *Shakespeare's "Hamlet"* (1922); Conrad, B. R., "Hamlet's Delay—A Restatement of the Problem," *Publications of the Modern Language Association of America*, XLI (1926), pp. 680-687.

paralyzes his faculty for action. "Hamlet, the victim of introspection," Fitzmaurice-Kelly has declared, "is fleet in the sphere of ideas, benumbed when confronted with realities"; the play, says Schlegel, "is purposed to show that calculating consideration exhausts .... the power of action."

2. *Theory of External Difficulties.* Werder, Furness, Hudson, Rolfe, Corson, and others, reject the subjective theory and substitute an objective one. Their opinion is that Hamlet was confronted with a difficult or almost insurmountable task; for example, it is not a simple matter to murder a king surrounded by a Swiss bodyguard, nor could Hamlet, desiring public and not private revenge, execute his purpose until he had obtained sufficient evidence to arraign the King before the Danish people.

3. *Theory of Modern Critics.* The troubled conception of Hamlet reveals that Shakespeare is Hamlet (Taine), that Shakespeare's own mind is in a state of bafflement (T. S. Eliot), that Shakespeare is presenting two characters, an amalgam of Kyd's Hamlet and his own (Robertson). Bradley, however, bridges the subjective and the objective theories with his statement that Hamlet is the victim of psychic shock, anticipatory, for example, of Clutton-Brock's description of Hamlet as a case of mental shock and paralysis of the will. Stoll looks upon Hamlet as a man of action, but believes that the tragedy is a typical revenge play in which the central character delays in order to keep up the suspense of the audience. With Stoll critics like Schücking and Quiller-Couch urge that one should see the play from the Elizabethan point of view, not from any critical ideal based on contemporary thought. Finally, there are four main interpretations of Hamlet's "madness": (a) His is a feigned madness, say most literary critics (Johnson, Hallam, Schlegel). (b) His character is made up of feigned madness and real madness, says the pioneering J. C. Bucknill. (c) Shakespeare reveals his power to draw a real case of melancholic madness or of a psychoneurosis, state A. O. Kellogg, Ray, Brigham, Somerville, Lily Campbell, and Conolly. (d) A fourth school (Ernest Jones, Ella Sharp, N. J. Symons) put forth the theory of a sex neurosis, believing that Hamlet's character represents a consistent example of an unresolved Oedipus Complex.[1]

Guha has called attention to "that initial chilling of his passion of personal vengeance by a numbing sense of the depravity of human nature, and the resultant feeling of the futility of his task of revenge, which he interpreted as the impossible feat of curing a degenerate world.

---

1 An excellent article with an excellent bibliography is that by Edgar, I. I., "Shakespeare's Medical Knowledge with Particular Reference to his Delineation of Madness," *Annals of Medical History,* New Series, VI, (1934), pp. 150-168.

The spirit of personal revenge, having been thus cooled at its very inception, could never work itself up into that passionate fury which is necessary for a speedy action of murder."[1]

G. W. Knight describes Hamlet as a sick soul, to whom "the universe smells of mortality,"[2] and to whom "Nothing is worth while . . . . Hamlet looks inward and curses and hates himself for his inability to feel passionately about his father's murder, and then again he hates himself the more for his futile self-hatred."[3]

Another suggestion is that Hamlet voices the confused conditions of his own day. He delayed "because he was a man hesitating between two worlds—the medieval and the modern; because the motives which urged him to act had their origin in a medieval system of thought which his deepest self no longer accepted.

". . . . The idea that marriage with a deceased husband's brother constituted the mysterious sin of incest was a medieval idea, and so was the whole conception of the duty of private vengeance. Hamlet was living in a world dominated by these medieval ideas and he supposed that he accepted them; but he was also a thinker, and his deepest thoughts were modern thoughts.

"In the end, custom and the weight of current opinion drove him into a catastrophe which represents the triumph of the dying world, but Hamlet seemed criminally slow, even to himself, because Hamlet 'was ahead of his time.' He did not delay because he was mad or because his adventure had to fill five acts. He delayed because, like all men who have got beyond the system of thought current in their time, he was able neither to act as that system of thought supposed that he should nor, by his own effort, create the intellectual atmosphere in which he could function effectively. He was hesitating between the world which was dead and the world which was powerless to be born . . . . Shakespeare himself was living in an age just emerging from medievalism into the Renaissance."[4]

Style. Three minor defects are usually pointed out in this consummately-told tale. The account of Ophelia's death, for example, differs in Act IV and Act V, thus exemplifying one among a number of inconsistencies; the advice of Hamlet to the Players is among the matters not directly connected with the play[5]; and the soliloquy, "To

---

1 Guha, P. K., "On Two Problems in Shakespeare," *Dacca University Bulletin,* No. IX (1926), pp. 1-22.

2 Knight, G. W., "The Problem of Hamlet," *The Quest,* XXI (1929-1930), p. 424 (415-424).

3 *Ibid.,* p. 292 (pp. 283-293).

4 "Sweet Prince," editorial in *The Nation* (New York), CXL (1935), p. 730 (p. 729 *f.*).

5 A good example is the Polonius-Reynaldo episode at the beginning of Act II. To J. M. Robertson, the scene is "superfluous" and "irrelevant"; to J. D. Wilson, "absolutely vital to the whole structure of the play."

be, or not to be: that is the question," recalls Sonnet LXVI, thereby illustrating how Shakespeare may be voicing through Hamlet his own thoughts. But inconsistencies, personal utterances, and extraneous matter are unimportant when compared with the merits of the tragedy, not infrequently regarded as the world's greatest. To the Kydian or other pre-Shakespearean *Hamlet* are generally attributed the many melodramatic elements, such as the Senecan ghost, death by poison, a play within a play,[1] a suicide, an insurrection, a hand-to-hand fight in the grave, a fencing-match, and a general massacre. No play of Shakespeare's is as long. No play of his moves so slowly, yet this slowness is paced perfectly by the main theme,[2] a dramatic embodiment of the "sick soul" described by William James. To the Elizabethan the lunatic was a butt, and Ophelia's insanity and Hamlet's (real or assumed) madness must have provided some fun. The most important comic element, however, was afforded by the solecistical grave-diggers; the scene, one of the best examples of comic relief in any literature, deepens the gloom. *Hamlet* is a tragedy of thought and character,[3] splendidly motivated and solidly executed. "The mistaking of epical or constructive devices for dramatic or psychological, the misconception of the open-hearted purport of soliloquy and comment in the dramatic economy, and the substitution of modern moral notions for Shakespeare's own,—all these shortcomings are to be found in the ablest interpretations of Hamlet as in the feeblest."[4]

---

1 Lawrence, W. W., "The Play Scene in *Hamlet*," *The Journal of English and Germanic Philology*, XVIII (1919), pp. 1-22.

2 Edith Rickert considers *A Midsummer-Night's Dream* (p. 188) a piece of political propaganda: Lilian Winstanley believes that *Hamlet* and *King Lear* are political and historical in action, their purpose being to defeat the Catholic League, and to strengthen the position of James I, previously caricatured (according to Edith Rickert) in the person of Bottom. See Winstanley Lilian, (1) *Hamlet and the Scottish Succession* (1921) and (2) *King Lear* (1923). B. M. Ward, we believe, has been the first to emphasize that during the war years a Propaganda Department had been established by the Government in order to inculcate patriotism. Out of sixteen plays published before 1604, thirteen contain political and war propaganda, according to B. M. Ward. This critic has attempted "to show that the war-propaganda dramas were initiated by Queen Elizabeth as a deliberate piece of policy: that she created a secret service Department of State to carry this policy into effect: that she placed the Earl of Oxford at the head of this Department: that Oxford gathered round him a group of helpers: and that this group comprised on the one hand his son-in-law Lord Derby and his cousin Francis Bacon, and on the other hand "University Wits" and actors like Marlowe, Peele, and William Shakspere of Stratford, who formed a link between him and the theatres." Consult Ward, B. M., "Shakespeare and the Anglo-Spanish War, 1585-1604," *Revue Anglo-Américaine*, VI (1928-1929), pp. 297-311; VII (1929-1930), pp. 298-311.

Under such circumstances it has not been over-difficult for some men to present Oxford as the author of the plays attributed to Shakespeare. Lilian Winstanley believes that possibly Bacon was in charge of the Group of the old War Propaganda Department after the death of Oxford.

3 H. M. Jones has commended Kittredge's statement that "Hamlet is a family tragedy" as "probably the first profoundly original criticism of the play since Goethe's famous 'oak-tree in a costly vase.'" Were it not probably for a slip of memory, H. M. Jones would have remembered that it was Ruskin who expressed the belief that the name "Hamlet" is "connected in some way with *homely*, the entire tragedy turning on the betrayal of home duties."

4 Stoll, E. E., "Hamlet and Iago," in *Anniversary Papers by Colleagues and Pupils of George Lyman Kittredge* (Ginn and Company, 1913), pp. 270 (pp. 261-272). In this connection, for example, the churchyard scene might be an addition. See Schücking, L. L., "The Churchyard-Scene in Shakespeare's *Hamlet*, V. i An Afterthought?" *The Review of English Studies*, XI (1935), pp. 129-138.

## *Othello, The Moor of Venice*† (c. 1604)

SOURCE. Cinthio's *Il Moro di Venezia* ("The Moor of Venice"), the seventh tale of the third decade in his *Hecatommithi* (1565), is almost certainly the main source. The tale itself may be of Oriental origin; see, for example, "The Three Apples," in *The Thousand and One Nights*. Possibly of some influence were Ludovico Dolce's *Marianna* and Philemon Holland's translation of Pliny's *Natural History*. Two historical characters may have helped determine Shakespeare's conception of Othello: (1) Christofalo Moro was an heroic Lord-Lieutenant of Cyprus who in 1508 returned to Venice. The name "Othello" is of unknown origin; but while many critics believe that Othello was not a negro, others point out that "Moro" in Italian means "mulberry" or "blackamoor." (An account is available in *Ragguagli sulla Vita e sulle Opere di Marin Sanuto,* published by Rawdon Brown in 1837.) (2) San Pietro di Bastelica (or Sampiero) was an Italian soldier of fortune who, returning unexpectedly in 1563, with a handkerchief strangled his innocent wife for alleged intimacies with a lover.

ADAPTATION OF THE SOURCE. Out of Cinthio's sordid tale of sexual jealousy Shakespeare has created one of high tragedy. Not only the splendid opening act but particularly the swift conclusion is his own. Many revolting incidents of the original story are omitted. The tale no longer rambles, but moves with speed. Shakespeare is swift, not straggling; his incidents are realistic-romantic rather than brutal. Brabantio, Ludovico, Montano, the Duke, and the Clown are among Shakespeare's created characters. The main characters, however, as well as the chief events, have their prototypes in Cinthio, who merely calls them "the courtesan" (Bianca), "The Captain of the troop" (Cassio), "the Ensign" (Iago), "the Ensign's wife" (Emilia). Only "Disdemona" (Desdemona) is named. Note (1) how "the Moor" (Othello) is transformed from a barbarian into a noble soldier, and (2) how the villainous ensign is baptized with the Spanish name of "Iago," significant because of the possible suggestion to the Elizabethan of the cruelties committed by Spain in the Low Countries and Mexico.[1]

CHARACTERIZATION. Except for Iago, all the characters are drawn on simple lines. Cassio, whose weakness for wine and women sets at naught his honorable, frank, brave nature, is as easily duped by Iago as is Roderigo, who is foolish rather than despicable. Emilia is common, even vulgar, but her loyalty to Desdemona unwittingly (and, in another sense, ironically) exposes her husband Iago's villainy. To call Brabantio jealous and tyrannical is not completely fair when even many a modern father might hesitate before sanctioning intermarriage

1 Does this tragedy of Othello and Desdemona symbolize the tragedy of Italy in the grip of Spain? *"Othello" as the Tragedy of Italy* (1924) by Winstanley, Lilian, gives an affirmative answer.

† * Explanation of symbols immediately precedes page one.

between the white and black races. Only in the first act is the loving and gentle Desdemona reminiscent of Cordelia; the bewildering jealousy of her husband strips her of her previous independence and resoluteness, and reveals her as a pathetic figure.[1] As for Othello, simple in his moral outlook, trusting in his friendship, and swayed by a rigid sense of duty, think of him as possessed of a single-track mind.

Few will deny that the "honest Iago" is the greatest of Elizabethan Machiavels and possibly the greatest stage villain ever created. What evokes the spirit of evil in Iago has always been a much discussed question. Is Iago an ordinary villain, human in his feelings? Although taking a satanic delight in doing evil, does his motive, for example, spring from a wounded vanity? By no means, says one group. It agrees that Iago is human, but insists that he is fired by extraordinary motives. His is a thwarted nature whose subconscious mind is seeking satisfaction, through the carrying out, for example, of intellectual feats or diabolic intrigues. Another group considers Iago a seventeenth-century Machiavel. He delights in evil because it *is* evil. His is a malignity motiveless and Mephistophelian. All groups, however, would probably agree that Iago is subtle and ironic, egoistic and callous, completely calculating.

STYLE. While lacking the meditativeness and pathos of *Hamlet*, *Othello* appeals directly because of its modern setting and unsymbolistic approach. The greater part of this tragedy is in mature blank verse. Its dialogue is more to the point than in the preceding play, and its emotional passages go beyond those of *Hamlet*. *Othello* is a direct story of domestic tragedy, drawn on simple lines of continuously accelerating action from the opening words of the play to the final catastrophe. If not "the most perfect work of art in literature," *Othello* is undoubtedly Shakespeare's masterpiece of construction.[2] There is no secondary plot and practically no comedy. C. F. E. Spurgeon has found that its "main image is that of animals in action, preying upon one another."[3] The unity of tone and the unity of action are achieved

---

1 For a "disintegrating" interpretation of Desdemona's character, consult Draper, J. W., "Desdemona: A Compound of Two Cultures," *Revue de Littérature Comparée*, XIII (1933), pp. 337-351.

2 Both Tolstoy and Robert Bridges have charged that *Othello* has a weak mechanism.

3 Spurgeon, C. F. E., *Leading Motives in the Imagery of Shakespeare's Plays* (1930), p. 28. She believes that "recurrent images play a part in raising, developing, sustaining and repeating emotion in the tragedies." In *Romeo and Juliet*, "the dominating image is light," for "Shakespeare saw the story, in its swift and tragic beauty, as an almost blinding flash of light, suddenly ignited, and as swiftly quenched" (p. 7); in *Hamlet*, the dominating thought is "the idea of an ulcer or tumour, as descriptive of the unwholesome condition of Denmark morally" (p. 11), iterative imagery of "*rottenness*, disease, corruption, the result of *dirt*" (p. 13). C. F. E. Spurgeon, we understand, will soon publish a book on Shakespeare's imagery, in which, by selecting and classifying some 7,000 images in Shakespeare's plays, she arrives at a conclusion that " 'the image test is an unfailing test of authorship, which scholars might well apply to the doubtful Shakespeare plays, such as *Henry VIII*.' " Consult the *New York Herald Tribune*, Thursday, January 24, 1935, p. 15, col. 3. *Postscript*: Dr. Spurgeon's *Shakespeare's Imagery and What It Tells Us* has just been published (Fall, 1935).

through a tom-tom upon the dominant motive and the dominant character, and the very singleness of the action engenders a tragedy that is nowhere in Shakespeare more compact and swift, or more romantic and realistic.[1]

### *King Lear*† (c. 1605—1606)

Source. Although the earliest known version of the Lear legend seems to be in Geoffrey of Monmouth's *Historia* (p. 43), and although the tale had been retold in one form or another by such writers as Layamon, Robert of Gloucester, Fabyan, William Warner, and Spenser (pp. 45, 36, 99, 124), Shakespeare's immediate source of the central plot was Holinshed's *Chronicles* (Chaps. V and VI), and *The moste famous Chronicle historye of Leire kinge of England and his Three Daughters,* an old play entered on the Stationers' Register on May 14, 1594, but printed about 1605. The Gloucester sub-plot was probably derived from a tale in Sidney's *Arcadia* entitled *"The pitifull state, and story of the Paphlagonian unkinde kinge, and his kinde sonne, first related by the son, then by the blind father."* Minor elements may have come from one or two minor sources; *e.g.*, the names of fiends mentioned by Edgar in Act III, Scene 4, may have been supplied by Bishop Harsnett's *A Declaration of egregious Popish Impostures* (1603).

Adaptation of the Source. The pre-Shakespearean play was essentially a legend weakly touched up by conventional melodrama, sorry attempts at humor, and a rather pathetic "musical comedy" or "happy" conclusion. Shakespeare's main contributions are the storm-scenes, Lear's madness, the unexpected end, and, of course, a subsidiary plot which, while over-complicating the *dénouement,* heightens the interest and the credibility of the tale. Tersely, Shakespeare's play resembles the older one in plot, but has been metamorphosed from a legend into a stirring tragedy of old age.

Characterization. Most of the characters are extreme depictions, and, like Lear, less than human and more the embodiment of elemental forces miraculously conceived with a minuteness of reality.[2] Only as Lear's paternal wilfulness is slowly sapped does one begin to sympathize with the Lear already presented as headstrong, self-centered, and domineering. His is an intense spiritual agony, and it has been suggested

1 Impressionistic descriptions of *Othello* might profitably be compared with rationalistic descriptions. Consult, for example, Swinburne, A. C., *Three Plays of Shakespeare* (1909), pp. 27-56, and Stoll, E. E., "Othello: An Historical and Comparative Study," (The University of Minnesota), *Studies in Language and Literature,* Number 2 (March, 1915).

2 For the symbolism of the play, consult Winstanley, Lilian, *Macbeth, King Lear & Contemporary History* (1922). Among the historical events that influenced parts of *King Lear* are, according to the book's contention, the stories of the Darnley murder, of the St. Bartholomew massacre, of Coligny's death, of Bothwell, Lady Bothwell, and Mary, Queen of Scots.

† * Explanation of symbols immediately precedes page one.

that Lear might well be identified as a "scapegoat king."[1] Literary critics are not in agreement concerning Lear's sanity, but pathological psychologists label Lear a true example of senile dementia. Gloucester shows himself as credulous, hot-headed, and uncontrolled of temper as does Lear: upon two characters so much alike Nemesis descends in much the same fashion. Like her father, Cordelia is plain-spoken and obstinate, good-natured and spirited. Although she has no more than five-score lines and appears in no more than a half-dozen scenes, she is an essential part of the whole action.

The symbol of Religious Resignation in *King Lear* is Edgar, the most complex and unsatisfactory character. Lear's Fool, who with Cordelia and the outspoken Kent is faithful to the old King, functions as a kind of tragic Chorus indispensable to the action. Whether considered the incarnation of Lear's conscience or as a boy out of his wits, he is still Shakespeare's greatest fool, one who is not present to add mere comic relief to the tragedy. Edmund and Cornwall are as inhuman as Goneril and Regan; the latter of the two sisters executes the schemes initiated by the former. Like the "toad-spotted" Edmund, the villain of the play, and unlike the base-natured Duke of Cornwall, the Duke of Albany has a change of heart toward the end of *King Lear*.

STYLE. *King Lear* lacks both the coherence and the dramatic qualities of *Othello* and *Hamlet*. Extremes of plot, characters, setting, and style conjure up a monstrous image of filial ingratitude. The artistry is over-complex and even obscure; the setting is as confused as the time-sequence; the abstract yet flesh-and-blood figures are exaggerated symbols of wickedness or goodness; the buffoonery is not always relevant; the motivation not always apparent. Although the parallel action of Gloucester and his sons illuminates the main dramatic story,[2] the sub-plot crowds the stage with too many characters. Why must the audience see Gloucester's eyes ground out? why must Gloucester journey to the cliffs of Dover? why do Edgar and Kent retain their disguises? why do Cordelia and Lear die in the last act? are among the questions raised in indicating Shakespeare's imperfect, careless, or sensational construction.[3]

Of all the tragedies *King Lear* is the most complex in plot. It is also the most painful. The Father-and-Children (or Balzac's *Père-Goriot*) theme has been worked up into a grand tragedy in which speculation becomes rife concerning such ideas as Retribution or Man's impotence before Fate. To say with Bradley that *King Lear* is Shakespeare's greatest achievement but not his greatest drama is safe enough.

---

1 Davidson, S. A., "King Lear, Scapegoat," *Vassar Journal of Undergraduate Studies*, v (1931), pp. 117-136.

2 Crawford, A. W., *Hamlet, An Ideal Prince* (1916), Chap. v, "King Lear: A Tragedy of Despotism," p. 249 (pp. 247-288).

3 It is "not the height of perfection." See *Tolstoy on Art*, edited by Maude, Aylmer, (1924), pp. 397-429 (pp. 393-463).

It is much less tenable to repeat the critics who have repeated Lamb to the effect that *King Lear* is a sublime poem but an unstageable play. Finally, two characteristics are customarily noted: (1) the exalted poetic dialogue, and (2) the frequent references to the lower animals, and the comparison of man to them.

### *Macbeth*† (c. 1606)[1]

Source. Most of Shakespeare's material is supplied by Holinshed's *Chronicles* (p. 147), although the source-version seems to be at variance with some historical matter. (Compare Holinshed's version with that of John of Fordun, of Andrew of Wyntoun, and of Boece.) Possibly Reginald Scot's *Discourse of Witchcraft* (1584) and James I's essay on *Daemonologie* (1597) were also of service. J. M. Robertson believes there is evidence of a pre-Shakespearean *Macbeth,* just as there is of an earlier *Hamlet.*[2]

Adaptation of the Source. In Holinshed the weak Duncan is killed in battle by the blood-and-thunder Macbeth; in Shakespeare, the kind, wise Duncan is murdered in his sleep. But Shakespeare is probably still obligated to Holinshed, who tells elsewhere how Donwald goaded on by his wife murders King Duff in his sleep. A good example of direct indebtedness is the long, tedious dialogue between Macduff and Malcolm (Act IV), almost a literal transcription from Holinshed. It is generally recognized that the incident of the moving wood is found in the folk-lore of both Semitic and Indo-European peoples. Because James I (before whom the play was probably performed) claimed descent from Banquo, the latter is not connected by Shakespeare with the crime.[3] Original with Shakespeare are the first scene of the witches (Act I), the apparition-scene (Act III), and the sleep-walking of Lady Macbeth (Act V). As he had done in *King Lear* and *Othello,* so in *Macbeth* the master-poet speeds up the action. The most remarkable contribution, however, is, possibly, the supernatural atmosphere created as an indispensable part of the tragedy.

Characterization. Compared with the persons of Macbeth and Lady Macbeth, the others are dwarfed in stature. Strong contrasts to the usurping Macbeth are the figures of the gracious Duncan, the

1 Much internal evidence indicates that some year after the accession of James I (1603) saw the play's composition. Hitherto the date of composition had been fixed as not later than 1610, because Dr. Simon Forman's diary entitled *The Booke of Plaies and Notes thereof* states that he was present at a performance of *Macbeth* at the Globe on April 20, 1610. But Forman's account is a forgery by J. P. Collier, says J. Q. Adams. See *The Tragedy of Macbeth,* edited by Adams, J. Q., (1931), pp. 293-298.

2 J. Q. Adams believes, as J. M. Robertson does, that certain additions to the *Macbeth* in the Folio are by Middleton. Certain songs mentioned by title in *Macbeth* (III, 5; IV, 1) may be interpolations made from Middleton's *The Witch* (p. 238). See Robertson, J. M., *Literary Detection* (1931).

3 *Macbeth* has definite connections with the political situation of the time. Consult Winstanley, Lilian, *Macbeth, King Lear & Contemporary History* (1922); *The Tragedy of Macbeth,* edited by Adams, J. Q. (1931), pp. 242-247.

† * Explanation of symbols immediately precedes page one.

patriotic Malcolm, and the noble, impulsive, judicious Macduff. The perfect foil for Macbeth is Banquo, a loyal, honest soldier probably idealized out of respect to James I. To depict Lady Macbeth as an inhuman creature is as much a mistake as it is to imagine her a specimen of sweet, gentle womanhood. She, strong-willed and unscrupulous, is also hypersensitive; like her husband's, hers is a "vaulting ambition." Bradley has said (as have Stoll and Schücking) that her fainting-spell is real, and he believes that it is the first sign that her highly-strung feelings will dethrone a nature compelled by unslackening will to be ruthless.[1] There can be no dispute that it is the witches who represent the most malignant form of evil.[2] Tersely, Lady Macbeth "is only another force along with the other witches. The Witches and Lady Macbeth are positive forces, centering on Macbeth. All the other people are negatives."[3] Finally, what of Macbeth himself? It is commonly held that he is a man filled with "the milk of human kindness," but unable to keep to the narrow path. Shakespeare has made his unpleasant historical character even more villainous. Quiller-Couch has pointed out that the strong and hale Macbeth, a sworn soldier and a host, murders the old and enfeebled Duncan, his liege lord, and a guest within his gates. Gradually the writhings of his conscience are modified until he can murder with a premeditated delight and without any compunction. His personal bravery degenerates into the courage of a cornered animal: so mandatory and systematized are his delusions that they might be those of a paranoic.[4] Yet somehow or other Macbeth retains our sympathy.

Style. Were it not for *The Comedy of Errors* and *The Tempest, Macbeth* would be not only the shortest of Shakespeare's tragedies but also the shortest of all his plays. No Shakespearean tragedy is swifter in action or simpler in outline. There is a threefold action—(1) the outer action of "vaulting ambition" fighting and succumbing to the human forces of justice and social order; (2) the inner force of conscience bringing about the moral ruin of two souls; and (3) the action of the supernatural powers of Evil. *Macbeth's* simpler plot lacks the depth of *Othello.* Its emotional and concentrated speed stands out against the meditative and slow-moving *Hamlet.* Simple and intense is its poetry, violent and terrible is its language. The ghastliness of the

---

1 For a suggestive and stimulating conception regarding *Macbeth* as "a tragedy of result after the Greek fashion," rather than "a drama of development and result," refer to Tynan, J. L., "The Woman in the Case," *The Shakespeare Association Bulletin,* I, No. 2 (1925), pp. 3-6.

2 Tonge, Mildred "Black Magic and Miracles in Macbeth," *The Journal of English and Germanic Philology,* XXXI (1932), pp. 234-246; Curry, W. C., "The Demonic Metaphysics of Macbeth," *Studies in Philology,* XXX (1933), pp. 395-426. W. C. Curry's notes are a most useful bibliography on the subject of witchcraft as it relates to *Macbeth.*

3 Ross, Douglas, "The Craig-Shakespeare Macbeth," *The Drama,* XIX (1928), p. 69 (p. 68 *f.*)

4 For a Doctor's approach to the extensive use of madness in Shakespeare's tragedies, consult Somerville, H(enry), *Madness in Shakespearian Tragedy* (1929).

Porter scene[1] is unstomachable, say Coleridge, Quiller-Couch, J. D. Wilson, and Robertson, who for that or a like reason reject it as non-Shakespearean. Its irony is Sophoclean, say Hales, Brandes, and Bradley, who accept the scene. Not only in *Hamlet* but also in this tragedy does Shakespeare's treatment of sin seem to accord with Catholic teaching.[2]

*A Midsummer-Night's Dream, Hamlet,* and *The Tempest* are the other plays into which the Supernatural element enters; but it is in *Macbeth* that the Supernatural plays the largest part.[3] Macbeth is "the Apocalypse of Evil"—no worse evil could be found than to murder, as he does, a man who "is at once Macbeth's kinsman, king, and guest." The image of blood is constantly presented; the animal-symbolism is "for the most part of fierce, ugly, or ill-omened significance."[4] Shakespeare's effects in his greatest plays are accentuated by his use of darkness; and in *Macbeth* the actions usually take place in the night. "In *Romeo and Juliet,* . . . . the tragic action really starts under a moonlit balcony and ends in a vaulted tomb"; in *Hamlet,* the play "opens on the dark embattlements of Elsinore, with a colloquy in whispers, such as night constrains, between sentinels who report a ghost visiting their watch"; in *Othello,* Shakespeare "opens with a mutter of voices in a dark street, and ends by a bedside lit by one candle"; in *Lear,* "the total impression . . . . is of a dark heath upon which three or four men wander blindly, lit only at intervals by flashes from the dark elements."[5]

## *Timon of Athens* (c. 1605—c. 1607)

Source. The story of Timon in Painter's *Palace of Pleasure,* Lucian's dialogue called *Timon the Misanthrope,* and an old play on Timon (written about 1600, printed 1842), may have given Shakespeare some suggestions. It was, however, a parenthetical account in Plutarch's *Lives* that provided the most material.

Authorship. While some critics contend that Shakespeare imperfectly retouched an older drama, leaving inferior portions in the play, most critics believe that a lesser playwright completed a play left unfinished by Shakespeare. J. M. Robertson's theory is that the original draft was made by Chapman, and partly revised by Shakespeare; Parrott's, that *Timon of Athens* was written by Shakespeare, added to

1 Read Thomas de Quincey's essay "On the Knocking at the Gate in 'Macbeth.'"

2 Purdie, A. B., "Macbeth—A Study in Sin," *The Catholic World,* cx (1919), pp. 184-195.

3 Clark, Cumberland, *Shakespeare and the Supernatural* (1931).

4 Knight, G. W., "Macbeth and the Nature of Evil," *The Hibbert Journal,* xxviii (1929-1930), pp. 328-342.

5 Quiller-Couch, Arthur, "The Workmanship of 'Macbeth,'" *The Fortnightly Review,* xcvi, New Series; cii, Old Series; (1914), p. 816 (pp. 653-666, 815-832).

by Chapman, and revised by a third hand, perhaps Middleton.[1] If one can find a consensus, it is that much of the play is non-Shakespeare and whatever parts are by Shakespeare are concerned primarily with Timon.

CHARACTERIZATION. Of no genuine importance are the lesser roles, although they are drawn efficiently. Even the practical and compromising Alcibiades is not subtly dramatized as a foil to Timon (originally meant for Robert Devereaux, Second Earl of Essex?), whose misanthropic imprecations look back to the maniacal ravings of Lear. The only other person of consequence is Apemantus, the uncharitable, cynical philosopher.

STYLE. To Frank Harris *Timon of Athens* is a drama of Despair. It is a more or less psychological study of a generous soul "brought low by his own heart, undone by goodness," and ruined by public and private ingratitude. In meter, style, and temper, in theme, protagonist, and moral intensity, it is reminiscent, even if dilutedly, of *King Lear.* Timon's monologue (Act IV, Scene 1) is truly Shakespearean. Not even the weak plotting of the Timon-theme dovetailed by the Alcibiades-story can erase the evidence of a unity of purpose and a directness of structure. Effective poetry occurs only occasionally. Fleay has described the want of action as languid and wearisome. Several commentators have called attention to Timon's syphilitic megalomania, to his "extended tirades . . . . against sexual corruption," and to Shakespeare's understanding of the various manifestations and different phases of syphilis.[2] Patchy, disproportionate, and ineffective on the whole, *Timon of Athens* leaves behind a feeling of almost bitter pessimism.

## *Antony and Cleopatra*† (c. 1606—c. 1608)

SOURCE. Shakespeare is again obligated to Plutarch's *Lives,* from which he not only lifts whole passages but also, in many cases, the very arrangement and succession of the scenes.

CHARACTERIZATION. Octavia, a foil to Cleopatra, is, one might conjecture, virtuous to the point of frigidity; Octavius, foil to Antony, is self-controlled yet tenacious, direct yet calculating, but his efficiency as a soldier and statesman seems neither imaginative nor brilliant. Like most experienced soldiers, Enobarbus has few illusions; he is loyal, frank, coarse, and his dying from remorse reveals an innate nobleness. As a kind of ironic Chorus he has a prominence out of proportion to historical fact. Antony is neither a noble nor an unheroic figure. He is enslaved by lust. Rapid and realistic is his deteriora-

---

1 Robertson, J. M., *Shakespeare and Chapman* (1917), pp. 121-181; Parrott, T. M., "The Problem of Timon of Athens," *Shakespeare Association Papers,* No. 10 (1923) (*The Shakespeare Association,* 1923). A third theory is that represented by Wecter, Dixon, "Shakespeare's Purpose in *Timon of Athens,*" *Publications of the Modern Language Association of America,* XLIII (1928), pp. 701-721.

2 Packard, F. R., "References to Syphilis in the Plays of Shakespeare," *Annals of Medical History,* VI (1924), pp. 194-200.

† * Explanation of symbols immediately precedes page one.

tion; once or twice he appears to be putting Cleopatra behind him only to fall backwards into her arms. The Queen of Egypt's character is not altogether clear. She is a shameless coquette-harlot skilled in the arts of sensual love, yet "the only Shakespearean woman who dies heroically upon the stage" (Masefield), and possibly Shakespeare's subtlest woman.[1]

STYLE. The early action and the numerous scenes (there are forty-two) have been criticized, respectively, as slow-moving and loosely-connected. Indecision (?) had dethroned the man in *Hamlet,* rashness in *King Lear,* jealousy in *Othello.* What brings ruin upon Antony is lust. The construction of the tragedy could be bettered, but the speech is thought-packed and the poetry is naturally dramatic. *Antony and Cleopatra* is a spectacular canvas, full of contrasts and romantic elements, crowded with living characters, and turbulent with movement. If not, as G. W. Knight declares,[2] one of Shakespeare's two greatest tragedies, it is, with *Romeo and Juliet, Troilus and Cressida,* and *Othello,* one of Shakespeare's four great love poems.

### *Coriolanus* (c. 1608)

SOURCE. Except for one major departure, and for some minor adaptations, Shakespeare follows North's translation of Plutarch, even to a close correspondence in vocabulary, yet more freely than he did in *Antony and Cleopatra.* (For North's influence see particularly I, 4, *ll.* 55—60; III, I, *ll.* 63—138; IV, 5, *ll.* 71—107; V, 3, *ll.* 94—98.) According to Brooke, the fable of Menenius (I, 1) came probably from William Camden's *Remaines of a Greater Worke, Concerning Britain* (1605).

CHARACTERIZATION. Few disagree with Bradley's assertion that the weakest spot in the characterization is that of Aufidius; but it is perfectly possible for Aufidius either to be sincerely "struck with sorrow" after setting assassins upon Coriolanus or to be acting out his character of an opportunist and strategist. Sicinius and Brutus are typical demagogues; like Ibsen, it has been noted, Shakespeare seems to be siding with the ruling class. The most important roles are those of Menenius, Virgilia, Volumnia, and Coriolanus. Next to Coriolanus, the most striking character is Menenius, who is to all purposes Shakespeare's creation. Aristocratic like Coriolanus, and as unsympathetic with the people, he is amiable, witty, and certainly not as tactless: one feels, for example, that if Menenius had done all the talking (in III, 3), things would have turned out better. Gentle Virgilia, foil to Volumnia, has been declared by Murry to be the tragedy's only congenial character; while meagerly sketched she is suggestively and strik-

---

1 Guthrie, A. M. B., *Wordsworth and Tolstoi and Other Papers* (1922), "Milton and Shakespeare as Lovers," pp. 59-63 (pp. 37-73).

2 Knight, G. W., *Myth and Miracle* (1929).

ingly conceived.[1] A mother who put Rome before her children—such is Volumnia, a typical Roman matron, eloquent and noble. There is about the humorless Coriolanus, as there is about his mother, an uncommon grandeur and a towering pride, but neither one nor the other brings him ruin. He falls because he succumbs to a natural affection for his family.[2] From to-day's point of view there is generally nothing but contempt for one who is courteous only to his family and immediate class.

Shakespeare and the Common People. The characterization of the plebeians has stirred discussion. One school's contention that Shakespeare represented the mob as ignorant, treacherous, and contemptible because of the dramatic necessity of making Coriolanus the protagonist, is opposed by a second school's contention that, just as in *Julius Caesar,* Shakespeare, dependent upon the good will of his patrons, more or less sincerely shared the contempt of court nobles for the plebs. On the whole it appears that Shakespeare's sympathies leaned to the patrician rather than to the popular side (Hazlitt, Whitman, Crosby), although many raise objections (Gervinus, Dowden, Parrott).[3]

---

1 A splendid characterization is struck off by Murry, J. M., *Countries of the Mind, First Series* (1931), "A Neglected Heroine of Shakespeare's," pp. 18-32. See also Thaler, Alwin, *Shakspere's Silences* (1929), p. 25 *f.* (pp. 3-63).

2 Coriolanus might quite easily be explained as a typical "Oedipus." Consult, for example, Jones, Ernest, "The Oedipus-Complex as an explanation of Hamlet's mystery: A Study in Motive," *The American Journal of Psychology,* XXI (1910), pp. 72-113.

3 Frequently Shakespeare's *Coriolanus* and a number of his other plays have been used as a text to proclaim his hatred of democracy. Among those who have charged Shakespeare with an unsympathetic attitude toward the working classes, as essentially anti-democratic, and as catering to the nobility, are Crosby, Whitman, Frank Harris, Shaw, and Tolstoy. Even G. E. Woodberry has admitted "the fact that the world he [Shakespeare] saw, dealt with and knew was an aristocratic world." Others have refuted the view that Shakespeare prostituted his art to uphold the privileges of the aristocratic classes, that he regarded the common people as completely foolish and despicable, and that he brought "citizens" on the stage merely to ridicule them, insisting that the picture Shakespeare was presenting was honest and not one-sided. We have already noted what Robert Bridges condemned in Shakespeare (p. 196, Note 1), although that critic acknowledged "Shakespeare's dazzling skill in qualifying and harmonizing." Tolstoy has described the worship of Shakespeare as a cult, as a mental obsession, charging that Shakespeare's plays "violate the proper canons of theatrical morality" and religious essence. More recently, J. W. Krutch has stated that "Shaw's central criticism of Shakespeare—that his point of view was merely that of the man in the street—is based upon an accurate observation."

Consult Crosby, Ernest, *Shakespeare's Attitude toward the Working Classes* (1903); Bradley, A. C., "Coriolanus," (Second Annual Shakespeare Lecture), *Proceedings of The British Academy,* V (1911—1912), pp. 460—467 (pp. 457—473); Schelling, F. E., "The Common Folk of Shakespeare," *Proceedings of the American Phiolsophical Society,* LV (1916), pp. 471-480; *Tolstoy on Art,* edited by Maude, Aylmer (1924), Part XVIII, "Shakespeare and the Drama," pp. 393-463; Tolman, A. H., *Falstaff and Other Shakespearean Topics* (1925), "Is Shakespeare Aristocratic?" pp. 14-43; Harrison, R. C., "Walt Whitman and Shakespeare," *Publications of the Modern Language Association of America,* XLIV (1929), pp. 1201-1238; Priestley, J. B., "Shakespeare as a Man of Our Time," *The English Journal,* XVIII (1929), p. 809 (pp. 808-810; Furness, C. J., "Walt Whitman's Estimate of Shakespeare," *Harvard Studies and Notes in Philology and Literature,* XIV (1932), pp. 1-33; Wood. F. T., "Shakespeare and the Plebs," *Essays and Studies by Members of The English Association,* XVIII (1933), pp. 53-73; Tannenbaum, S. A., *Shaksperian Scraps and Other Elizabethan Fragments* (1933), Chap. X, "Shakspere's Caste Prejudices," pp. 153-176; Krutch, J. W., "The Meaning of the Modern Drama: II. The Shavian Dilemma," *The Nation* (New York), CXLI (1935), p. 292 (pp. 291-293). See, also, Smirnov, A. A., *Shakespeare: A Marxist Interpretation* (1936).

STYLE. The charge has properly been made that *Coriolanus* is at least in the beginning strongly akin to the chronicle play, with, for example, its single combats and pitched battles. Thereafter its construction is less loose. Occasionally a scene exposing Coriolanus's arrogant pride might be cut, or the execution of some actions on the stage might be substituted for the narration of those actions, thereby heightening the conflict. But generally the situations of this one-protagonist play are managed so that there is a constant accumulation of dramatic interest. It is not the first play in which Shakespeare contributed an Elizabethan tone to an un-Elizabethan story, or in which he mixes pagan and Christian elements, but it is practically the first play in which no character obtains our wholehearted sympathy. Yet, although the characters have type-traits, they are well-conceived. Murry has praised the tragedy's "economy, swiftness, solidity, astonishing clarity and pregnancy of language." There is unity of tone throughout. No character is permitted to clown—an unusual thing for Shakespeare. Note that rime has been practically abandoned, and that the imagery of the play is metallic. Finally, the political struggle between the patrician and the plebeian classes serves as a background for the heightened conflict within Coriolanus of his towering self-esteem and overmastering prejudices against the lower classes. According to one critic, *Coriolanus* turns upon a political situation based upon economic circumstances.[1]

## FOURTH PERIOD

### A. Early Romance

### *Pericles, Prince of Tyre* (c. 1607—1608)

SOURCE. In *Pericles* Shakespeare dramatizes an old story found by him both in Gower's *Confessio Amantis* and in Lawrence Twine's *Patterne of Paineful Adventures* (1576). Based ultimately upon a lost pagan Greek romance (*c.* 200—*c.* 400), the tale is found in a number of Latin works usually entitled *Historia Apollonii regis Tyrii* (*c.* 425), and also has been retold in the Latin *Pantheon* by Godfrey of Viterbo (12th century) and in the *Gesta Romanorum* (p. 37).

AUTHORSHIP. According to prevailing opinion, most of the last three acts, with the exception of the tetrameter Gower choruses, and some infrequent passages in the first two acts, are by Shakespeare. The brothel-scenes (Act V, Scenes 2, 5, 6), while generally attributed to another writer, are not unShakespearean. Different critics, believing that Shakespeare had one or more collaborators, have suggested such

1 Farnam, H. W., "Shakespeare as an Economist," *Yale Review*, II (1913), pp. 436-455. The article is stimulating, and is in accord with proletarian contentions and interpretations of literature. Other plays are discussed; *e.g.*, H. W. Farnam contends that what unhinges Timon's mind is an economic situation.

men as Thomas Heywood,[1] Dekker, Chapman, and Rowley. It appears most likely that George Wilkins, the author of the comedy called *The Miseries of Enforced Marriage* (1607) and the novel entitled *The Painful Adventures of Pericles, Prince of Tyre* (1608), may be responsible for those parts not by Shakespeare. Possibly Shakespeare rewrote primarily the last three acts of an old play, if not by Wilkins, then by another inferior writer.

STYLE. On the whole *Pericles* is a poor, unequal, and unreal play. The first two acts are inferior; the last three straggle along. Possibly the prologue-choruses and the dumb shows were retained from the source-play. Obvious is the lack of unity; *e.g.*, the Gower choruses seem to be inorganic additions[2] blocking the action of the tale, and the "Epilogue" is unShakespearean in its artificiality and didactism. Not a few critics, however, believe that *Pericles* anticipates in one or two respect the Shakespeare to come. Cerimon and Marina are early outlines of Prospero and Miranda; the storm-scene (III, 1) and the recognition-scene (V, 1) look forward to Shakespeare's later mastery. Finally, even the brothel-scenes, often rejected as too coarse to be Shakespeare's, are said to have touches of restrained realism.

## B. Late Romance

### *Cymbeline*† (1609—1610)

SOURCE. The Imogen—Posthumus—Iachimo part of this tragicomedy was derived from Boccaccio's *Decameron* (II, 9), in turn stemming from the French *Roman de la Violette*. The wager-story, however, is familiar in medieval literature.[3] Holinshed's *Chronicles* supplied the name of Cymbeline and that of other characters, and also the pseudo-political setting. Furthermore, floating hints suggest minor obligations to the fairy-tale of "Little Snow White" and to an account of Imogen's wanderings found in *Westward for Smelts* (1603), a collection of tales published by Kitt of Kingston. A critic has pointed out the possible importance of *Frederick of Jenner* (1518), an English translation of the analogue *Historie von vier Kaufmännern*, or *Four Merchants*. There is, also, a definite relationship between *Cymbeline* and Beaumont and Fletcher's *Philaster* (p. 244), but which influenced the other has not been determined; compare, for example, the characters of Imogen and Euphrasia. Possibly both *Cymbeline* and *Philaster* were merely typical plays of the time.

---

1 Gray, H. D., "Heywood's *Pericles*, Revised by Shakespeare," *Publications of the Modern Language Association of America*, XL (1925), pp. 507-529.

2 Garrett, R. M., "Gower in 'Pericles,'" *Jahrbuch der Deutschen Shakespeare—Gesellschaft*, XLVIII (1912), pp. 13-20.

3 Thrall, W. F., "*Cymbeline*, Boccaccio, and the Wager Story in England," *Studies in Philology*, XXVIII (1931), pp. 107-119.

† * Explanation of symbols immediately precedes page one.

CHARACTERIZATION. Almost all affirm that Imogen, the perfect wife, yet "more goddess-like than wife-like," is one of Shakespeare's most beautiful characters, graced by womanliness and intellect. Not only are the other figures sketchy, but they are essentially plot-ridden. Posthumus, than whom "A nobler sir ne'er lived 'twixt sky and ground," is a conventional tragic figure who makes a melodramatic wager with the immoral, crafty, somewhat Iago-like Iachimo, who, unlike Iago, redeems himself by a remorseful confession. As for the other characters, Cymbeline is dominated by the plotting Queen, whose only praiseworthy quality is her love for her son Cloten, an arrogant gull, foil to Posthumus.

STYLE. Cymbeline is a romantic tragi-comedy whose main problem is concerned with the wager-plot,[1] the plan to determine whether or not Imogen is "more fair, virtuous, chaste, constant, qualified, and less attemptable than any the rarest" of all ladies. W. W. Lawrence even considers it with Shakespeare's other problem plays (pp. 200—204), for that scholar has defined the "essential characteristic of a problem play" as one in which "a perplexing and distressing complication in human life is presented in a spirit of high seriousness," and has applied the term "problem play" to those works "which clearly do not fall into the category of tragedy, and yet are too serious and analytic to fit the commonly accepted conception of comedy."[2] Like most plays of the period, Shakespeare's *Cymbeline* caters to the tastes of his audience, gratifying them through spectacular incidents and sudden recognitions, through an intriguing wager and an unexpected repentance. The two plots are poorly blended; at some points the story of the King's sons takes precedence over the main plot; the ending has, according to Wendell, no fewer than twenty-four *dénouements*. Most critics contend either that the vision (V, 4) is below Shakespeare's standard or that it is probably by another playwright: Quiller-Couch has said outright that the masque is not only flat but also silly. Memorable are the beautiful song, "Hark! hark! the lark at heaven's gate sings," and the lovely dirge, "Fear no more the heat o' the sun," as well as the thought-laden blank verse.

## *The Winter's Tale*† (1610—1611)

SOURCE. This romance is a dramatization of Greene's *Pandosto* (p. 153). Shakespeare goes beyond changing the names of characters: he alters the original conclusion in which Leontes commits suicide,

1 For an analysis of the wager-plot, as well as that of Posthumus's character and motives, consult Lawrence, W. W., "The Wager in *Cymbeline*," *Publications of the Modern Language Association of America*, xxv (1920), pp. 391-431. The article is also available in the author's *Shakespeare's Problem Comedies* (1931), Chap. v, pp. 175-205.

2 Lawrence, W. W., *Shakespeare's Problem Comedies* (1931), p. 4 *f*.

† * Explanation of symbols immediately precedes page one.

invents the theatrically-effective statue-scene, and creates such characters as Antigonus, Paulina, and Autolycus.[1] It is thought that Jonson's masque of *Oberon* (p. 231) may have influenced the dance of the twelve satyrs (Act IV).

CHARACTERIZATION. Shakespeare's depiction is more subtle than Greene's, yet it is in general less an advance upon the characters in previous plays than a light re-embodiment of those people. Hermione, who suggests Queen Katherine of *Henry VIII,* is noble, forbearing in adversity, queen-like; Perdita is charming, gentle, princess-like. Leontes, unlike Othello, is obsessed by a rootless jealousy. Most delightful is Autolycus, a scamp and ballad-mongerer, who confesses that he, like his father before him, "was likewise a snapper-up of unconsidered trifles." Emilia, Mopsa, Doreas, and the Clown are also Shakespeare's inventions.

STYLE. In both *Pericles* and *The Winter's Tale,* "the hero loses his wife and daughter just after the birth of his child; in both the idea of a child's helplessness is synchronized with a sea-storm of the usual Shakespearean kind; in both the wife and child are miraculously restored after a long passage of years."[2] In both there are strange emotional appeals and spectacular effects, such as, in *The Winter's Tale,* the grotesque dance of the twelve satyrs and the animated statue-scene; in both the plot is poorly constructed and is lacking in organic unity. The first three acts are tragic; the last two are romantic—and a gap of sixteen years separates them. There are many anachronisms. Possibly the greatest piece of absurdity in this episodic play is having a ship land on the mythical coast of Bohemia. "Another thing that the sea-gulls have commented upon as one of Shakespeare's absurdities is . . . . the instruction, 'Exit, pursued by a bear.' . . . . But up to this time there has been no bear in the play and no reason for there being a bear."[3] Despite these imperfections, *The Winter's Tale* is often rated Shakespeare's greatest tragi-comedy. The character-portrayal, particularly that of Hermione, Paulina, and Autolycus, is effective: the Queen is as charming as her daughter's flower-pictures; Pauline, as trustworthy as Camillo; and Autolycus, as rascally as any rogue in literature. Critics are not agreed on the effectiveness of the recognition-scene in the last act: Quiller-Couch represents a school that believes Shakespeare scamped an opportunity for heightening the effectiveness of the play; Gervinus, that Shakespeare made an effective stroke by not showing the scene on the stage. But by almost common consent three scenes are achievements: Act IV, Scene 2, for its superb dramatic technique; Act IV, Scene 4, for its poetry; and Act V, Scene 3, in which music is used as a point of emotional tension, much in the same way as in *The Merchant*

1 The similarities and changes are discussed by Dewar, Robert, " 'The Winter's Tale' and its Source," *Discovery,* II (1921), pp. 40-46.

2 Knight, G. W., *Myth and Miracle* (1929), p. 11.

3 Morley, Christopher, *Shakespeare and Hawaii* (1933), p. 18.

of *Venice* when the lovers appear. *The Winter's Tale* is a realistic-romantic tragi-comedy possessing the sweetness of English country sights and revels, folks and customs.

### *The Tempest*† (c. 1611)

Source. No one source has been agreed upon. (1) Contemporaneous accounts of the wreck of Sir George Somers's flagship *Sea Adventure* off the Bermudas in July, 1609, may have influenced Shakespeare's conception. Two narratives particularly are cited: Silvester Jourdan's *A Discovery of the Barmudas, otherwise called the Ile of Divels* (1610), and William Strachey's *A True Reportory of the Wracke, and Redemption of Sir Thomas Gates Knight; upon and from the Ilands of Bermudas* .... (1610).[1] (2) *The Die Schöne Sidea,* part of the *Opus Theatricum* (1618) by Jacob Ayrer, a notary of Nuremberg (*d.* 1605), has certain resemblances to *The Tempest.* It is as unlikely that the German version is Shakespeare's source as it is likely that Ayrer's work is based on the English version. The *Die Schöne Sidea* is probably an analogue, possibly based on a pre-Shakespearean account of *The Tempest;* it may go back to the same source (now lost) from which Shakespeare took his materials or to an analogue related to the one Shakespeare had used. (3) Resemblances to Shakespeare's main plot have been found in the fourth chapter of *Las Noches de Invierno* (1609), a collection of Spanish stories by Antonio de Esclava. (4) Another suggested source is the Spanish romance of chivalry, *Espejo de Príncipes y Caballeros* (1562, and continuations), Englished into a nine-volume work entitled *The Mirrour of Princely Deeds and of Knighthood* (1578—1601).[2] (5) A fifth group holds that the Caliban sub-plot levied basic tribute from Italian scenari, pointing, for example, to parallels in *La Nave* and *Li Tre Satiri.*[3] (A collection of *commedia dell'arte* scenarios was made by Basilio Locatelli, about 1620.) (6) Shakespeare took suggestions from various other sources; *e.g.*, Gonzalo's description of an ideal commonwealth (II, 1, *ll.* 147 *ff.*) is derived from Florio's translation of Michel de Montaigne's *Essayes* (1603, Bk. I., Chap. XXX, *Des Caniballes* or "Of the Cannibals"), an account that verges upon a kind of philosophical anarchism.[4] Other hints may have come from Thomas's *History of Italy,* Eden's *History of Travaile,* James I's *Daemonologie,* Scot's *Discovery of Witchcraft,* Sterling's *Darius,* and Hakluyt's *Principall Navigations.*

1 Gayley, C. M., *Shakespeare and the Founders of Liberty in America* (1917), pp. 40-69.

2 Perott, Joseph de, "The Probable Source of the Plot of Shakespeare's Tempest," *Publications of the Clark University Library,* I (1905), pp. 209-216.

3 Gray, H. D., "The Sources of *The Tempest,*" *Modern Language Notes,* xxxv (1920), pp. 321-330.

4 Farnam, H. W., *Shakespeare's Economics* (1931), pp. 132-136. For Montaigne's influence, see Taylor, G. C., *Shakspere's Debt to Montaigne* (1925).

†* Explanation of symbols immediately precedes page one.

CHARACTERIZATION. No character is subtly portrayed. Prospero, unlike Marlowe's Faustus, has used his power to achieve the highest wisdom. Under his white magic the other figures are practically personified abstractions of Loyalty (Gonzalo), Treachery (Alonzo, Sebastian, Antonio), the Higher Nature of Man (Ariel), the Lower Nature of Man (Caliban), and the like. A bloodless creature of innocence and sweetness is Miranda (Purity), a colorless wax-figure is Ferdinand (Perfect Lover), who exemplifies chivalric submission to one's fair lady. Ariel is a buoyant, restless spirit representing the upper elements of air and fire; Caliban, foil to Ariel, represents the lower elements of earth and water. In the latter Shakespeare has achieved one of his best creations; as Hazlitt once wrote, Caliban "is the essence of grossness, but there is not a particle of vulgarity in it."

THE QUESTION OF ALLEGORY. To one circle of scholars, *The Tempest* is " a pure fantasy without any dominant or controlling idea behind it" (Schücking, Stoll); to a second, "an allegory having some inner significance which transcends its immediate and obvious purpose as a stage play"[1] (Gervinus, Dowden). Some among those who have not resisted the temptation to read between the lines regard Ariel as genius or the lawless imagination, Caliban as a kind of primitive creature or as a barbarian ousted by civilized man,[2] Prospero as destiny itself or the future superman, and so on. One camp (Brandes, Churton Collins, Brooke, Chambers) identifies Prospero with Shakespeare himself bidding farewell to the stage (thereby making Ariel represent imagination; Caliban, the vulgar public; Miranda, drama; Ferdinand, Shakespeare's successor, Fletcher—see *Henry VIII,* p. 225); but another circle (Masefield, Lytton Strachey, Schücking, Stoll) discredits this theory.[3]

STYLE. This play of reconciliation and of peace is not without its imperfections. Not only have the character-outlines no particular merit but the very action is essentially undramatic, and, beyond the first two scenes, practically static. Before the second act begins, Prospero's known purpose automatically and undramatically disposes of the plot. Some have suggested that the fragment of a hymeneal masque in Act IV, Scene 1, may be an interpolation by Beaumont or Chapman: the play, in its present form probably a revision of a dramatic romance

---

1 Quoted from Still, Colin, *Shakespeare's Mystery Play* (1921), p. 236 (pp. 233-248).

2 In *Caliban upon Setebos; or, Natural Theology in the Island* (1864), Robert Browning gave the monster an interest in theology, and also through him satirized the anthropomorphic theology (probably having in mind Darwin's *Origin of Species,* 1859, and the subsequent debate between Samuel Wilberforce, Bishop of Oxford, and Thomas Huxley, on June 28, 1860). Browning's letter to Dr. F. J. Furnivall, on April 25, 1884, reveals his indebtedness to Shakespeare's Caliban. See *Letters of Robert Browning Collected by Thomas J. Wise,* edited by Hood, T. L. (1933), p. 228 *f.*

3 Again Stoll, E. E., attacks an "insidious biographical fallacy" in "The Tempest," *Publications of the Modern Language Association of America,* XLVII (1932), pp. 699-726.

originally written in 1611, was performed (1613) as part of the marriage-festivities in honor of Princess Elizabeth, daughter of James I, and the Elector Frederick of the Palatine. Yet *The Tempest* is a good "variety show": its four themes (Prospero-Antonio, Ferdinand-Miranda, Sebastian-Alonzo, Trinculo-Stephano-Caliban) easily absorb such novel elements as the shipwreck, the magic banquet, the pursuit of Caliban, a fine brute, and of Stephano and Trinculo, men who have lowered themselves to brutes, by Ariel and his fellow spirits in the form of hunting dogs. While the Epilogue is, as Stoll points out, a succession of "wire-drawn conceits," all agree that before a dozen lines of *The Tempest* have been spoken the whole atmosphere has been created. (According to J. D. Wilson, the wreck-scene is a revision.) *The Tempest* has the fairy-like elements of *A Midsummer-Night's Dream* (note Ariel's songs), but if less poetic is at least as effective on the stage. Shakespeare's late romance preserves the Aristotelian unities of time, place, and action[1]; many critics say that it is Shakespeare's only play in which he preserves the unities of time and place (see, however, *The Comedy of Errors*). The play is imaginative, original, poetically emotional. Shakespeare's craftsmanship has inextricably wedded exquisite poetry and serene wisdom.

### C. Other Plays

## *Henry VIII* (1613)

Source. Holinshed's *Chronicles* supplied most of the material for Acts I—IV, and Act V, Scene 5; Foxe's *Actes and Monuments,* for Act V, Scenes 1—4. Some details came from Hall's *Chronicle* and George Cavendish's *Life of Cardinal Wolsey.*

Authorship. Spedding's view of a divided authorship is generally accepted.[2] The common theory is that Shakespeare probably wrote Act I, 1, 2; II, 3, 4; III, 2, *ll.* 1—203 (to the exit of the King); and V, 1. The rest of the play, including probably Wolsey's farewell to greatness (II, 2, *ll.* 350—372), is by Fletcher (p. 241). While H. Dugdale Sykes and other critics accept the view of a joint authorship, they substitute the hand of Massinger for the so-called Shakespearean scenes.

Characterization. The figures are inconsistent and rather static in the development. Henry VIII is sketched in his historical character as proud and selfish, tyrannical and fickle, while Cardinal Wolsey is shown as a piously-scheming churchman, self-seeking, over-bearing, and arrogant. As a foil to Wolsey, Cranmer appears as an honest ecclesiastic-statesman. Most memorable is the portrayal of the pathetic, yet strong, noble Queen Katherine.

---

1 Conway, R. S., *New Studies of a Great Inheritance* (1921), Chap. viii, "The Classical Elements in Shakespeare's *Tempest,*" pp. 165-189.

2 Alexander, Peter, "Conjectural History or Shakespeare's *Henry VIII,*" *Essays and Studies by Members of The English Association,* xvi (1931; for 1930), pp. 99-119 (pp. 85-120).

STYLE. Usually the generally accepted fact that no one mind determined the play's course is given to account for the non-Shakespearean qualities of the blank verse, the inferiority of character-depiction, the weakness of plot-structure, and the almost total absence of dramatic unity. There is neither an organic relation among the scenes nor a central idea to bind them together. Even chronological succession is missing; note, for example, the anachronism of including the appearance of Cranmer before the Council (1544—1545) in a play covering the years 1520—1533. Much can be said for Schlegel's statement that the death of Katherine is the true conclusion of this chronicle, important for the ethical point turning upon the victory of Protestantism. *Henry VIII* is less a play than an historical pageant whose appeal on the stage depends upon a succession of spectacular scenes and events.

### *The Two Noble Kinsmen* (1613; published 1634)

This tragi-comedy is, except for some departures, a reasonably faithful dramatization of Chaucer's *Knight's Tale* (p. 72). The lofty poetry is usually ascribed to Shakespeare, while the weak characterization and imperfect construction are generally attributed to Fletcher (p. 241). Shakespeare's hand is particularly seen in most of Act I, 1; Act III, 1; and Act V, 1; (and Fletcher's, in II, 3—6; III, 3—6; IV, 1—2; V, 2). See page 242.

### *Sir Thomas More* (printed 1844)

A few years after Sir Edmund Tyllney, the official censor of the plays, had refused to license Anthony Munday's *Sir Thomas More,* a group of five writers revised the play and added new scenes. The manuscript is extant, and, on the basis of Shakespeare's handwriting as preserved in his six (or seven) signatures, such scholars as Pollard and Thompson have with more or less certainty identified the scene dealing with the climax of the riot (three pages of the manuscript play) as written (*c.* 1595—1596) by Shakespeare. Others, notably S. A. Tannenbaum, have attacked the theory.[1] The play yields in importance to no document concerning Sir Thomas More: it reveals what tender thoughts London had of Sir Thomas More about fifty years after his death.

---

1 Consult Simpson, Percy, "The Play of 'Sir Thomas More' and Shakespeare's Hand in It," *The Library*, Third Series, VII (1917), pp. 79-96; *Shakespeare's Hand in the Play of Sir Thomas More: papers by Pollard, A. W., Greg, W. W., Thompson, E. Maude, Wilson, J. Dover, and Chambers, R. W..* (1923); Schücking, L. L., "Shakespeare and *Sir Thomas More,*" *The Review of English Studies,* I (1925), pp. 40-59; Acheson, Arthur, *Shakespeare, Chapman, and "Sir Thomas More,"* (1931), Chap. VI, pp. 99-134. S. A. Tannenbaum does not believe that we have in *Sir Thomas More* a Shakespeare holograph. His method depends upon a knowledge of paleography and bibliotics, and frequently, S. A. Tannenbaum says, that method invalidates the bibliographic method. The "T. Goodal" notation may be a modern forgery by J. P. Collier. Consult Tannenbaum, S. A., (1) *Shakspere's Unquestioned Autographs and "The Addition" to "Sir Thomas Moore"* (1925); (2) *Problems in Shakspere's Penmanship* (1927), Chap.. X, "Folios 8 and 9 of *The Booke of Sir Thomas More,*" pp. 179-211; (3) *"The Booke of Sir Thomas Moore"* (1927); (4) "More about The Bookie of Sir Thomas Moore," *Publications of the Modern Language Association of America,* XLIII (1928), pp. 767-778; (5) *Shakspere and "Sir Thomas Moore"* (1929); (6) *Shaksperian Scraps and Other Elizabethan Fragments* (1933).

## Chapter XII

# THE RENAISSANCE: THE DECLINE[1]

**Benjamin Jonson ("Ben Jonson"),** *c.* 1573—1637, greatest of Shakespeare's dramatic contemporaries, lyric poet (elegies, epistles, Pindaric odes, epigrams, love-poems, epitaphs), translator (of the *Ars poetica*), "the first . . . . of English literary dictators." Educated at Westminster School under the great scholar William Camden. Worked for a while in the trade of his stepfather, a master-bricklayer. Probably volunteered against the Spaniards in the English Contingent in the Low Countries. Back in London by 1592. Married (*ante* 1593). Actor-playwright in Henslowe's company (1597). Killed a fellow-actor, Gabriel Spencer, in a duel, but escaped the gallows by pleading benefit of clergy (1598), becoming a Catholic during imprisonment, and receiving a brand on his left thumb. Temporarily imprisoned for his share in *Eastward Hoe* (p. 234). Abjured Catholicism (*c.* 1610). Virtually became poet-laureate when granted a pension and a butt of Canary wine by James I (1616). First English dramatist to publish collected edition of his own works (folio, 1616). Went to Scotland, where during a stay of a year and a half he was for one month the guest of Drummond of Hawthornden, who recorded the visit in the so-called *Conversations.*[2] M.A., Oxford (1619). Elected Chronologer of London (1628). Quarreled with Inigo Jones (1630), and lost patronage. Chance inscription made upon his tombstone: *O Rare Ben Jonson.*[3]

### Early Comedies — "Humours," Allegory, Satire

***Every Man in his Humour***†* (1598). Comedy of humours, by lashing the variously-exaggerated caprices of persons, discloses the vanity of society. Note alliance of Humour play with the Morality (p. 106 *ff.*). Structure could be stronger, action more developmental, and plot more full-bodied; yet his general technique is more original than any other Elizabethan. Has a to-the-point style, incisive expression, carefully-ordered pictures of English life and character. Classical sentiments and paraphrases taken from such men as Juvenal, Ovid, Seneca, Plautus,

---

1 For the introduction to the Renaissance Period, see p. 110 *ff.*

2 Are the *Conversations,* even if "poetically absolutely true" about Jonson [quoting Steegmüller, Francis (Steel, Byron, *pseud.*)], an eighteenth-century forgery? See Stainer, C. L., *Jonson and Drummond, Their Conversations* (1925).

3 Latin inscription reads, *Orare Ben Jonson* ("Pray for Ben Jonson"), says Steegmüller, Francis (Steel, Byron, *pseud.*), *O Rare Ben Jonson* (1927).

† * Explanation of symbols immediately precedes page one.

Terence, and Horace; characters and situations borrowed from conventional Roman comedy: (1) the deceived father and the wayward son; (2) the guileful servant or slave; (3) the braggart soldier (ancestor of the immortal Falstaff); (4) the gull; (5) the would-be poet; (6) the mistaken identity; and (7) the clandestine marriage. Principal sources of the father-son motive occur particularly in Plautus (*e. g., Mostellaria, Mercator, Truculentus*) and in Terence (*e. g., Andria, Adelphi, Heautontimoroumenos*). Not his greatest play, but his most influential: his theory of humours affected the work of Shakespeare, Chapman, Middleton, Massinger, Marston, Shirley, Beaumont and Fletcher, and the comic dramatists of the Restoration.

***Every Man out of his Humour*** (1599). Comedy satirizes absurd characters and fashions of the times. Not as brisk as its companion-play. Characters not alive. Reminiscent of Shakespeare.[1] Asper is Jonson himself.

***The Case is Altered*** (*ante* 1599; printed 1609). Comedy generally attributed to Jonson. Fuses the serious intrigue and farcical exposé of Plautus's *Captivi* and *Aulularia.* Satirizes Anthony Munday in the character of Antonio Balladino. Characteristic in its action and unity; elaborate in plot.

***Cynthia's Revels, or the Fountain of Self-Love*** (1601). Allegorical comedy satirizing court types is slight and somewhat obscure in plot. Weak in characterization. Influenced by classical writers (Juvenal, Lucian, Aristophanes, Virgil) and by Lyly's *Sapho and Phao, Endimion,* and *Midas* (p. 151). Lyrics: "Queen and huntress, chaste and fair"; "Still to be neat, still to be drest." *Key*: Cynthia (Queen Elizabeth), Actaeon (Essex?), Crites (Jonson?), Hedon (Dekker), Anaides (Marston).

***The Poetaster*** (1601). Comedy in which the characters directly attacked are contemporaries: Crispinus (Marston), Demetrius (Dekker), Tucca (a certain Captain Hannam). Horace is Jonson himself. In turn, Jonson was attacked by Dekker's *Satiromastix* (p. 235).[2] Acted, as was *Cynthia's Revels,* by the Children of Queen Elizabeth's Chapel. Satirical invective influenced by Ovid. Includes good comedy and critical poetry.

**Mature Comedy — Realism**

***Volpone, or The Fox*†*** (*c.* 1606). Comedy original in plot, even if stemming from the Roman satire of legacy-hunting (*captatio*) as exemplified by Juvenal, Petronius, and especially Lucian's *Terpsion*

---

1 Allen, Percy, *Shakespeare, Jonson, and Wilkins as Borrowers,* (1928), Chap. IV (pp. 43-97).

2 A summary of the "Dekker-Marston-Jonson Quarrel" is found in Small, R. A., *The Stage-Quarrel between Ben Jonson and the so-called Poetasters* (1899), pp. 126-132.

† * Explanation of symbols immediately precedes page one.

*and Pluto, Smylus and Polystrata,* and *Dialogues of the Dead.* The characters are directly influenced by Horace's works and Erasmus's *Encomium Moriae.* Universal satire on the baseness of human nature. Fast-paced dialogue, energetic characters, masterly dialogue, savage laughter, uncomfortable cynicism. Effective structure generally considered marred by the scenes concerning the Would-Bees.[1] *Key*: Volpone (the fox), Mosca (the fly), Voltore (the vulture), Corbaccio (the crow), Corvino (the raven); Sir Politick Would-Be (caricature of Sir Henry Wotton?). First mature play, succeeded by three others.

X ***Epicoene, or the Silent Woman*†*** (1609). Prose comedy provokes farcical mirth at the expense of mental eccentricity: theme, woven of two Greek practical jokes, hits at the noise-hating Morose, the pretending-to-knowledge Sir John Daw, the always-jabbering barber Cutbeard, and others. Close observation of the unities, strong construction, original treatment of a conventional intrigue, gaudy incident and expository dialogue, comic invention if trivial motive. Influenced by Plautus, Ovid, Juvenal, and Shakespeare's *Twelfth Night* (p. 198). Could be successfully produced to-day. (Dictionary-meaning of titular-word "epicene" epitomizes the *dénouement.*)

X ***The Alchemist*†*** (acted 1610; printed 1612). Comedy attacking human gullibility. Brilliant portraitures, consummate construction, observation of the unities of time and place. Influenced more or less directly by Plautus's *Mostellaria* and *Poenulus,* Erasmus's *De Alcumista,* and possibly even by Giordano Bruno's *Il Candelaio.* Best of his realistic plays.

X ***Bartholomew Fayre*†*** (1614). Farcical comedy slight in plot, light in character, defective in structure, episodic in action, frequently vulgar, yet rich in drollery, brilliantly realistic, varied in number of London characters. Two notable characters in this broadside against Puritan hypocrisy: Ursula; Rabbi Zeal-of-the-Land Busy. Lanthorn Leatherhead is a character in which Inigo Jones may have been ridiculed. With *The Alchemist* probably represents the highest achievement of the strict comedy of manners. His last great realistic and satirical comedy.

**Late Comedies—Allegory, Satire**

***The Devil is an Ass*** (1616). Allegorical comedy exposes social abuses, satirizing particularly the institution of the duello (private duel-

1 The adaptation of the play by the Theatre Guild (New York) in 1928 omits Jonson's original underplot of Sir Politick Would-be and Peregrine. This translation by Ruth Langner from the German of Stefan Zweig is "a very free conception of the context."

† * Explanation of symbols immediately precedes page one.

ling), of monopoly, and of witchcraft. Redeems a weakness in coherence by effective plot and fresh characters. Possibly contains personal satire; *e. g.*, Fitzdottrel may be either Sir Edward Coke or Justice Eitherside. Influenced by Dekker's *If it Be not good, the Divell is in't.*

***The Staple of News*** (1626). Comedy satirizing the abuse of riches through such characters as Lady Pecunia and Pennyboy, and the gullibility of the age through "The Staple of News," which disseminates apocryphal as well as authentic gossip. Cymbal might be Nathaniel Butter; Madrigal, either Jonson or George Wither. Sources include especially Aristophanes's *Plutus* and Lucian's *Timon;* also, Aristophanes's *Wasps,* Plautus's *Aulularia,* Chaucer's *House of Fame* (p. 66), the morality play called *The Contention between Liberality and Prodigality* (1602), and *The London Prodigal* (1605).[1]

***The New Inne*** (1629). Comedy deservedly unsuccessful, despite occasional eloquent parts. Influenced by Plato's *Symposium,* Beaumont and Fletcher's *The Widow,* and other writers.

***The Magnetic Lady, or Humours Reconcil'd*** (1632). Comedy scoring the follies of the day: such classes as the politician and money-lender, such moral defects as usury, fortune-hunting, and bribery. Action made heavy-gaited by the tedious descriptive speeches; but sound portraitures and coherent plot. Witty, satiric.

***A Tale of a Tub*** (1633). Comedy, defective only in unity, is otherwise a fresh, genuine, zestful transcript of life.

**Classical Tragedy**

***Sejanus his Fall*** (1603). Roman tragedy in which Shakespeare acted a part. Human treatment of his sources, yet kept within the frigid confines of historical tradition. Effective construction, despite departure from the unity of time and violation of Aristotelian dictum of creating no protagonist without a redeeming quality. Poor portraiture. As in *Epicoene* (p. 229), so here Jonson reveals a lack of sympathy and pity. Influenced by Suetonius, Juvenal, and Seneca, but primarily by Tacitus's *Annales* (IV, V) and Dion Cassius's *Roman History.*

***Catiline*** (1611). Roman tragedy based on the events of the year B. C. 63. Excellent construction overweighted by sterile movement, flat talk, and conscientious erudition. Senecan: a ghost, a depraved character, a chorus, a prologue. Companion-piece to *Sejanus* influenced

1 Stonex, A. B., "The Sources of Jonson's *The Staple of News,*" *Publications of the Modern Language Association of America,* XXX; New Series, XXIII (1915), pp. 821-830.

in plot particularly by Sallust's *Catilina;* in dialogue, by Lucan's *Pharsalia;* in choruses, by Petronius's *Satyricon.*[1]

### Court Masques and Entertainments[2]

Among the many masques and entertainments Jonson wrote are: *The Satyr* (1603); *The Penates* (1604); *Masque of Blackness* (1605); *Hymenaei* (1606); *Masque of Beauty* (1608); *Masque of Queens* (1609); *Oberon, the Faery Prince* (1611); *Love Freed from Ignorance and Folly* (1611); *Love Restored* (1612); *The Irish Masque* (1613); *Challenge at Tilt* (1613—1614); *Mercury vindicated from the Alchemists* (1615); *The Golden Age Restored* (1616); *Christmas his Masque* (1616); *Lovers made Men* (1617); *Vision of Delight* (1617); *Pleasure reconciled to Vertue* (1618); *News from the New World Discovered in the Moon* (1621); *Masque of Augurs* (1622); *Time Vindicated to Himself and to his Honours* (1623); *Neptune's Triumph for the Return of Albion* (1624); *The Fortunate Isles and their Union* (1625); *The Masque of Owls at Kenelworth* (1624); *Love's Triumph through Callipolis* (1613); *Chloridia* (1613); *Love's Welcome at Welbeck* (1633); *Love's Welcome at Bolsover* (1634); and—

***The Hue and Cry after Cupid*** (1608). Based upon a classical legend, Jonson's masque retains its original simplicity and imaginative quality. In elaborating this form of entertainment Jonson established or introduced an "antimasque" as a foil to the principal masque. (See also *The Gipsies Metamorphosed,* p. 231.) This masque was originally called *The Description of the Masque, . . . . at the Lord Viscount Haddington's Marriage.*

***The Gipsies Metamorphosed*** (1621; published 1640). Slight, spirited masque marred by the vulgar wit of the antimasque. Includes about ten songs.

### Pastoral Drama, Literary Criticism, and Grammar

***The Sad Shepherd, or, A Tale of Robin Hood*** (1641). Fragmentary pastoral drama departs from its conventional type by introducing an actual forest (Sherwood Forest) and real characters (Maid Marian, Robin Hood), even substituting for the typical satyr the witch Maudlin. Blends serious reflection with romantic spirit. Influenced by Theocritus.

---

1 Harris, L. H., "Local Color in Ben Jonson's *Catiline* and Historical Accuracy of the Play," *Classical Philology,* XIV (1919), pp. 273-283.

2 *Ben Jonson* (1925), edited by Herford, C. H., and Simpson, Percy, pp. 249-334 (critical introduction); *Ben Jonson* (1919), edited by Smith, G. G., pp. 128-184.

***Timber, or Discoveries made upon Man and Matter*** (1640). Collection of detached thoughts varying in length from one-sentence jottings to miniature essays on many subjects, moral, political, and literary. Unaffected diction, solid wisdom. Of the 137 sections perhaps a hundred lines are Jonson's own; the others are in general arid adaptations from Latin writers. Sources include Jacobus Pantanus's *Poeticarum institutionum libri tres* (1594) and Daniel Heinsius's *De tragoediae constitutione* (1611).[1] Commonplace book best in section on literary criticism, particularly famous for its characterization of Shakespeare.

***The English Grammar*** (1640). Draft shows influence of Sir Thomas Smith (1568), John Hart (1570), and Richard Mulcaster (1582); in punctuation, of Petrus Ramus's *Grammatica.*

### Non-Dramatic Poetry

***Epigrams*** (1616). Of the 133 pieces some are reflective or satiric or scurrilous. "He may with truth be called the founder of the English epigram."[2]

***The Forest*** (1616). Miscellaneous odes, epistles, and songs. Careful lyrics, but neither naturally elegiac nor inspired. Includes: "Come, my Celia, let us prove"; and "Drink to me only with thine eyes," a transcript from the Greek of Philostratus.

***Underwoods*** (1640). Collection of poems. Includes the valuable if uneven poem to the memory of Shakespeare. Later edition (1756) includes the epitaph on the Countess of Pembroke now generally attributed to William Browne (p. 253). Said to be the first to use the form of the Pindaric ode, with strophe, antistrophe, and epode. As in his other non-dramatic works, the decasyllabic rimed couplet is his chief measure.

### His Theory of the Drama

Jonson's classicism insisted on an adherence to the unities of time, place, and action, emphasizing a unity of tone and rejecting the admixture of comedy and tragedy. But possibly even more important was his Sidney-like manifesto (first appearing in the folio edition, 1616, of *Every Man in his Humour*) to give "Deeds and language such as men do use," to "show an image of the times," and to "sport with human follies, not their crimes."

---

1 Spingarn, J. E., "The Sources of Jonson's 'Discoveries,'" *Modern Philology,* II (1905), pp. 451-460.

2 Whipple, T. K., "Martial and the English Epigram from Sir Thomas Wyatt to Ben Jonson," *University of California Publications in Modern Philology,* x (1920-1925), p. 406 (pp. 384-414) [pp. 279-414].

## GENERAL STYLE

| SUGGESTED MERITS[1] | SUGGESTED DEFECTS[1] |
|---|---|
| 1. Strict comedies of manners anticipate Molière and the English Restoration theatre. | 1. His dramas, it is said, founded no school. |
| 2. Adapts to the life of his times the spirit of classical comedy.[2] | 2. While supporting by precept and example his classic ideals in the theatre, his characters often are taken from Latin comedy rather than English life. |
| 3. Theory of "humours"[3] influenced such men as Chapman, Beaumont and Fletcher, and Marston. | 3. Exaggeration of some one characteristic contributed to unreal portraiture. |
| 4. Moral earnestness influenced Massinger, Shirley, and other dramatists. | 4. Realism of later plays often degenerates into flat coarseness. |
| 5. In his masques, he reveals some imaginative beauty and fertile invention. | 5. In his poems, he shows scholarly accuracy of form rather than natural inspiration. |
| 6. In summary: premeditation of songs,[4] inventiveness of plot,[5] power of comic creation, logic of construction, local color and realism, immensity of learning, power of observation. | 6. In summary: deficiency of delicacy and passion, lack of warm sympathy, parade of classical allusions and quotations, absence of imaginative beauty in his compact verse.[6] |

**George Chapman,** *c.* 1559—1634, poet, dramatist; earliest and perhaps best translator of Homer (evoked Keats's immortal sonnet, *On First Looking into Chapman's Homer*). Probably educated at Oxford. Lost his position as server-in-ordinary to Prince Henry upon the latter's death in 1612. Patronized by Robert Carr, Earl of Somerset. In his plays, generally based on French history, he presents vividly felicitous figures, occasionally spirited action, romantically exalted moments, frequent resonant verse; also, a multiplicity of ideas and associations (the ethical thoughts of which are adapted from classical treatises), an excess of rhetoric, obscurities, and swollen similes, a weakness of characterization and plot, a lack of careful construction and dramatic instinct.

***The Shadow of Night*** (1594). Obscure but novel poem, consisting of a "Hymnus in Noctem" and a "Hymnus in Cynthiam," has been regarded as the spiritual father of the Metaphysical School (p. 254 *ff.*).[7] Influenced by Natale Conti's *Explications*.

---

1 Archer, William, *The Old Drama and the New* (1923), pp. 80-88 (defects); Stoll, E. E., *Poets and Playwrights* (1930), pp. 139-151 (merits).

2 Briggs, W. D., "Source-Material for Jonson's Plays," *Modern Language Notes,* XXXI (1916), pp. 193-205; Goldmark, R.I., *Studies in the Influence of the Classics on English Literature* (1918) pp. 1-40.

3 Baskerville, C. R., "English Elements in Jonson's Early Comedy," *Bulletin of the University of Texas, Humanistic Series,* No. 12, *Studies in English,* No. 1 (1911), pp. 34-75.

4 Lindey, E. S., "The Music in Ben Jonson's Plays," *Modern Language Notes,* XLIV (1929), pp. 86-92.

5 Knowlton, E. C., "The Plots of Ben Jonson," *Modern Language Notes,* XLIV (1929), pp. 77-86.

6 But see Walker, R. S., "Ben Jonson's Lyric Poetry," *The Criterion,* XIII (1934), pp. 430-448.

7 Williamson, George, *The Donne Tradition* (1930), Chap. II, "Chapman and Donne," pp. 58-74; also, pp. 254-257.

***Iliad*** (1598—1611). Fire and vehemence of vigorous, colorful translation in long riming lines of fourteen syllables sweep away the thought of its occasional harshness, obscurity, and lack of fidelity. Defects, according to Swinburne, are that it is "romantic, laborious, Elizabethan"; but, he continues, "no praise can be too warm or high for the power, the freshness, the indefatigable strength and inextinguishable fire which animate this exalted work." To Henry Morley, Chapman "wrestles for expression, makes bold use of homely phrases, dashes into Euphuism"; while to Saintsbury, "Chapman is far nearer Homer than any modern translator in any modern language."

***Hero and Leander.*** See p. 158.

***Eastward Hoe*** (1605). Comedy by Chapman, Marston, and Jonson. Quips, offending the impecunious Scotchmen upon whom King James was showering Court favors, temporarily brought the first two playwrights into prison, where Jonson soon voluntarily joined them.[1] Offending clauses were removed in the first publication of the play. The "Sir Petronel" sub-plot is derived from Masuccio Salernitano. Another source is Gascoigne's *Glass of Government.* Probably Jonson's general supervision blended Chapman's good-humor with Marston's bitter realism. (Baconians make frequent use of the comedy's allusions to *Hamlet.*)

***All Fools*****†*** (1605). Best comedy. Lively characters, dovetailing situations, ingenious plot, Jonsonian characters and cynicism. Mostly in verse. Influenced by Terence's plays, *Heautontimoroumenos, Adelphi,* and *Eunuchus.*

***The Gentleman Usher*****†** (1606). Tragi-comedy almost entirely in blank verse. Memorable characters: Strozza; and Bassiolo, the go-between for the young lovers, has been compared with Malvolio in *Twelfth Night* (p. 198). Serious, elevated tone; deficient construction, vague characterization, unmeritorious plot.

***Bussy D'Ambois*****†*** (1607). Intrigue, action, heightened style, as well as inarticulate bombast and inadequate characterization, mark this pseudo-historical tragedy. Influenced by Seneca. Possible sources of his material are Jacques Auguste de Thou's *Historiae sui Temporis,* Rosset's *Histoires tragiques,* and the memoirs of Brantôme and Marguérite de Valois.

***The Conspiracy and Tragedy of Charles, Duke of Byron*** (Two parts, 1608). Double melodrama on a single theme. Frequent passages of lofty thought and exalted poetry. Negligible development

1 According to another source, Marston was out of London at the time Jonson and Chapman were thrown into prison.

† * Explanation of symbols immediately precedes page one.

of character, surfeit of rant: essentially undramatic. Incidents derived probably from Edward Grimeston's *A General Inventory of the History of France,* a translation of Jean de Serres.

***The Revenge of Bussy D'Ambois*** (1613). Incomplete, ill-coordinated sequel. Likenesses in play (*e. g.,* the use of a ghost that urges vengeance) suggest Shakespeare's *Hamlet* (p. 204); also Clermont's irresolution and stoically philosophical cast of mind are paralleled by Hamlet's. Indebted to Grimeston's work, and to Pierre Matthieu's *Histoire de France.*

***Odyssey*** (1614—1615). Translation of Homer in heroic verse or riming ten-syllable lines.

***Caesar and Pompey: A Roman Tragedy*** (1631). Ethical reflection. Cato, the protagonist, commits suicide.

***The Tragedy of Chabot*** (1639). Sources include Étienne Pasquier's *Les Recherches de la France* (1621).

**Thomas Dekker,** *c.* 1570—*c.* 1641, dramatist, pamphleteer, lyricist. Often in debt, for which he was imprisoned (1613—1616). Wrote more than forty plays, alone or in collaboration with Drayton, Ford, Massinger, Middleton, Webster, and others. Rich imagination; combined vivid realism with tender pathos; understanding delineation of women[1]; direct dialogue. Plots ill-coordinated; blank verse often prosy; general execution of the intrigue uneven. Earthy intimacy and light-hearted gayety have made some pronounce him "the last of the Elizabethans."

***The Shoemaker's Holiday*****†*** (1600). Boisterous, breezy comedy; drawn partly from Deloney's prose tract, *The Gentle Craft* (1598). Unskilful characterization, weak plot. Interesting for its dramatic realism and overflowing spirits juxtaposed to a romantic treatment of the life of London working classes. Comic creation, Simon Eyre, is drawn from an actual Mayor of London; while a half-dozen other characters also have their basis in history.[2] Merry song: "Cold's the wind, and wet's the rain."

***Old Fortunatus*****†*** (1600). Poetic morality play, based on a legend in the German *Volksbuch* (1509) dramatized by Hans Sachs (1553), abounds in strong passages of rare beauty.

***Satiromastix, or the Untrussing of the Humorous Poet*** (1602). Comedy, through the character of Horace, ridicules Jonson's idiosyn-

1 Bradford, Gamaliel, "The Women in Dekker," *The Sewanee Review,* XXXIII (1925), pp. 284-290.

2 Chandler, W. K., "The Sources of the Characters in *The Shoemaker's Holiday,*" *Modern Philology,* XXVII (1929-1930), pp. 175-182.

†* Explanation of symbols immediately precedes page one.

crasies of dress and appearance, and his vain-glory. Dekker's answer to *The Poetaster* (p. 228), in which Jonson had satirized Dekker through the character of Demetrius Fannius.

***The Wonderfull Yeare*** (1603). Vividly photographs London lying sick with the plague of that year. Descriptive horrors relieved by amusing anecdotes. Daniel Defoe borrowed from it in his *Journal of the Plague Year* (1722).

***Patient Grissil*** (1598; printed 1603). Comedy in collaboration with Henry Chettle and William Haughton. Story of the patient wife told in Chaucer's *The Clerk's Tale* (p. 75). Memorable songs: "Golden slumbers kiss your eyes"; Balbulo's "Art thou poor, yet hast thou golden slumbers?"

***The Bachelor's Banquet*** (1603). Droll prose tract of fourteen chapters on the mistreatment of husbands by their wives. Attributed to Dekker. Is a translation of *Les quinze joyes de mariage.*

***The Honest Whore***†* (I, 1604; II, 1630). Powerful domestic drama, marred by coarseness and exaggeration but drawing characters from life. Most original character is Orlando Friscobaldo. Influenced Shakespeare. (Middleton may have had a hand in this play.)

***The Bel-Man of London*** (1608). Exposes life among vagabonds: "their conditions: their lawes amongst themselves: their degrees and orders: their meetings, and their manners of living (both men and women) . . . ."

***The Guls Hornebooke*** (1609). Ostensibly a guide to the young bloods about town; in reality a primer of directions in marked ironic strain and with a wealth of detail satirizing the various types of London gulls: describing, for example, the audible criticism by fops during the performance of a play. Genial satire reminiscent (particularly in its paraphrased beginning) of the *Grobianus* of Dedekind, German Latin satirist of sixteenth century. Valuable source of information on social manners and customs. (Today *grobian* means a rude, loutish person.)

**Thomas Middleton,** *c.* 1570—1627, dramatist, pamphleteer, pageant- and masque-writer. City-Chronologer of London (1620). Well-managed amusing intrigue, daring originality of expression, lively dialogue, good lyrics, human stories, photographic observation, lightly but capably-sketched characters, and, particularly in the tragedy, tensely vigorous scenes. But frequently poor blank verse, occasionally vulgar language and plots, little pathos and humor, coarse relief. Favorite situation is the turning of the tables upon individuals; *e. g., Michaelmas Turn* (1607), *A Trick to Catch the Old One* (1608). Primarily satirizes the ideals of the London middle-class. Works reveal decadent tendencies.

---

† * Explanation of symbols immediately precedes page one.

***Blurt, Master Constable*** (1602). Romantic play influenced by Shakespeare. Famous: "Love for such a cherry lip."

***A Trick to Catch the Old One*†*** (1608). Zestful farce. Easy dialogue, psychological touches. Compare with *Michaelmas Turn,* "a trick to catch the young one"; and with Massinger's *A New Way to Pay Old Debts* (p. 245).

***The Roaring Girl*†*** (1611). Comedy notable for presentation of London life.

***A Chaste Maid in Cheapside*** (1612). Realistic, satirical comedy; effective fun.

***Women beware Women*** (*c.* 1612; printed 1657). Tragedy of definite power. Defective in construction and in character-delineation; strong in vulgar scenes and situations. Plot derived from a contemporaneous novel, *Hyppolito and Isabella,* and the adventures of the Italian courtesan, Bianca Capello (1548—1587), and her paramour, Francesco de' Medici. Definitely decadent.

***A Fair Quarrel*** (1617). Comedy in which Rowley collaborated. Moral problem so soundly treated as to evoke the praise of Charles Lamb (1775—1834). But offensive under-plot.

***The Spanish Gypsy*** (1623).[1] Romantic tragi-comedy. Collaborator again is Rowley. Two closely-dovetailed plots influenced by Cervantes. In turn, influenced H. W. Longfellow's drama, *The Spanish Student* (1843).

***The Changeling*†*** (*c.* 1624; printed 1653). Powerful if sensational tragedy of blood. Intensely dramatic and psychological situations; human and permanent in their fundamental tragic scope but relieved by comic scenes. In a *non sequitur* and coarse secondary plot, Antonio is disguised as a changeling: hence the title of the play. Main plot derived from John Reynold's *The Triumphing of God's Revenge against the Crying and Execrable Sin of Murther* (1621). Influenced in one episode by Leonard Digges's translation of the Spanish novel of Céspedes, *Gerardo the Unfortunate Spaniard* (1622). Co-author is Rowley.

***A Game at Chesse*** (1624). Allegorical political drama suppressed by order of the Privy Council. Powerful topical satire concerns the White House and the Black House (England and Spain), and the popular aversion to the wooing of the Infanta Maria: "the whole Spanish business is ripped up to the quicke."[2] Dominating character is

---

1 The play was not written by Middleton and Rowley, according to Sykes, H. D., "John Ford, the author of 'The Spanish Gypsy,'" *The Modern Language Review,* XIX (1924), pp. 11-24.

2 Wagner, B. M., "New Allusions to *A Game at Chesse,*" *Publications of the Modern Language Association of America,* XLIV (1929), p. 828 (pp. 827-834).

† * Explanation of symbols immediately precedes page one.

Count Gondomar (Don Diego Sarmiento de Acuña); sweet creation is the figure of the White Queen's Pawn. *Key*: White King (James), White Knight (Charles), White Duke (Buckingham), White Bishop (Archbishop Abbot); Black King (Philip IV of Spain), Black Duke (Olivares, Spanish minister), Black Bishop (Father General of the Jesuits: the underplot exposes the methods of the Jesuits). Influenced by Rowley, Shakespeare, and particularly by the pamphleteers Thomas Scott and Thomas Robinson.

***The Witch*** (*ante* 1627; published 1778). Tragi-comedy. The witch Hecate is often compared with and differentiated from Shakespeare's witches in *Macbeth;* furthermore, stage catch-lines in *Macbeth* name two songs found in Middleton: while traditionally believed to have been original in *The Witch,* the interpolated songs were possibly taken from *Macbeth* (p. 213). Feeble, intricate plot.

**Thomas Heywood,** *c.* 1572—*c.* 1650, dramatist, pageant-writer, poet, translator, compiler. Resident member of Cambridge University. Member of the Lord Admiral's company (1598), and later of the Queen's Servants (at that time known as the Earl of Worcester's players). Like Dekker (p. 235), a dramatic journalist who loved London; but was more artistic if less lyrical. Over-enthusiastically described by Charles Lamb (1775—1834) as "a sort of *prose* Shakespere."[1] His works epitomize the bourgeois ideals of the age.

Preface to *The English Traveller* describes that tragi-comedy as one "being reserved amongst two hundred and twenty, in which I have had either an entire hand, or at the least a maine finger."[2] Among his poems are *Troia Britannicum, or Great Britain's Troy* (1609), in seventeen pleasant cantos, and *The Hierarchy of the Blessed Angels* (1635), in nine didactic books. His extant plays include *The Captives* (1634) and *A Challenge for Beautie* (1636), romantic comedies of adventure strong in characteristic qualities of effective construction and loyalty to English tradition; *The Late Lancashire Witches* (1634) and *The Wise-Woman of Hogsdon* (acted *c.* 1604; printed 1638), realistic comedies of manners in the latter of which the splendid technique is enriched by a social point of view, while in the former it is marred by low transcripts of life; *The Royall King and the Loyall Subject* (*c.* 1602; printed 1637) and *The Rape of Lucrece,* two romantic comedies, the first marred by coarseness, the second by untoward farce and inappropriate comic songs. Best-known allegorical play is *Loves*

---

1 *The Works of Charles and Mary Lamb,* edited by Lucas, E. V. (1903), Vol. I, p. 45.

2 Did Thomas Heywood write *Appius and Virginia?* See under John Webster, p. 245 *f.*; also, Brooke, Rupert, "The Authorship of the Later 'Appius and Virginia,'" *The Modern Language Review,* VII (1913), pp. 433-453. Who is the original author of Pericles? See Gray, H. D., "Heywood's *Pericles,* Revised by Shakespeare," *The Publications of the Modern Language Association of America,* XL (1925), pp. 507-529. See also p. 219 *f.*

*Maistresse, or The Queens Masque* (1640); while his dramatizations of classical stories include his "Four Ages": *The Golden Age* (1611), *The Silver Age* (1613), *The Brazen Age* (1613), and *The Iron Age* (1632, two parts).

## More Important Plays

**King Edward the Fourth** (two parts, 1600, 1605). Some vigor redeems an otherwise poorly constructed historical play. Includes a famous patriotic war-song.

***If You Know Not Me, You Know No Bodie,: or, The Troubles of Queene Elizabeth*** (I, II, 1605, 1606). Chronicle history inferior to its predecessor. Comic scenes in prose. Mainly in iambic pentameters. As in *King Edward the Fourth,* so here there are some poetic flashes.

***The Fayre Mayde of the Exchange*** (1607). If it is Heywood's, it is his most unpleasant play. Realistic comedy of manners with occasional islets of poetry. Lyric: "Ye little birds that sit and sing."

***A Woman Kilde with Kindnesse*****†*** (acted *c.* 1603; printed 1607). Domestic tragedy. Proverbial phrase of tragi-comedy's title given deeper meaning by quiet pathos, touching manliness, and human understanding. Simplicity of conception and directness of narrative compensate the imperfect craftsmanship revealed by the use of two plots. Main plot (sentimental in the good sense) influenced by a story in the *Heptameron* translated into Painter's *Palace of Pleasure;* sub-plot (sentimental in the poor sense) based on the 1611 Sienese *novella* of Bernardo Lapini, surnamed Illicini, translated into Geoffrey Fenton's *Tragicall Discourses* as well as into Painter's collection. Tone of primary plot and characters, however, is thoroughly English.

***The Foure Prentises of London*** (acted *c.* 1595; printed 1615). Mediocre romantic drama flattering to London citizens. Burlesqued in *The Knight of the Burning Pestle* (p. 243).

***The Fair Maid of the West, or A Girle Worth Gold*** (1631). Comedy of adventure in two parts, the first of which is breezy. Note the tavern-scenes. Patriotic feeling. Influenced D'Avenant's *Siege of Rhodes* (1656).[1]

***The English Traveller*** (1633). Romantic drama of domestic incident shows his characteristics of gallant simplicity, healthful reality, and genuine tragic effect. End similar to that of *A Woman Kilde with Kindnesse.* Comedy of sub-plot borrowed from Plautus's *Mostellaria.*[2]

---

1 Thaler, Alwin, "Thomas Heywood, D'Avenant, and *The Siege of Rhodes,*" *Publications of the Modern Language Association of America,* XXXIX (1924), pp. 624-641.

2 Gilbert, A. H., "Thomas Heywood's Debt to Plautus," *The Journal of English and Germanic Philology,* XII (1913), p. 596 *f.* (pp. 593-611).

† * **Explanation of symbols immediately precedes page one.**

*Fortune by Land and Sea* (acted *c.* 1607; printed 1655). Romantic comedy of adventure geared up by a realistic opening. Collaborator, William Rowley.

### GENERAL STYLE

| SUGGESTED MERITS | SUGGESTED DEFECTS |
|---|---|
| 1. Genuine sentiment and elevated moral tone. | 1. Absence of great poetry and philosophic insight. |
| 2. Command of humor without its satire. | 2. Tendency to broad farce. |
| 3. Faithful, sympathetic delineations of English home and life. | 3. Characters not as full-bodied as one would expect. |
| 4. Utterance is lucid, dialogue direct, scenes striking, stage situations dramatic. | 4. Incidents frequently strung together without technique; subplot usually loosely connected to main plot. |
| 5. Reflection of the patriotic spirit of his age. | 5. Zealous patriotism leads possibly to momentary deviation from the facts. |

**John Marston,** *c.* 1575—1634, dramatist, satirist. Educated at Brasenose College, Oxford (1592—1594). Ceased writing when he took orders: rector of Christ Church, Hampshire (1616—1631). Tombstone, according to story, inscribed with two words—*Oblivioni sacrum.* Collaborated with Dekker in *Satiromastix* (p. 235), with Chapman and Jonson in *Eastward Hoe* (p. 234). Is identical with Crispinus in Jonson's *Poetaster* (p. 228). Changed from early coarseness; but always lacks proportion, moderation, probability of plot, natural note. Violent, melodramatic, ranting, cynical.

*The Metamorphosis of Pygmalion's Image: And certain Satires* (1598).[1] Erotic, coarse, virulent, tergescently-worded satirical poem. Six-line stanzas, in same meter as Shakespeare's *Venus and Adonis* (p. 162). Ordered burned by Archbishop Whitgift.

*The History of Antonio and Mellida* (I, II—both printed, 1602). Tumescent blood tragedy of black revenge and ghost scenes reveal melodramatic, macabre influence of *The Spanish Tragedy.* Features ridiculed in Jonson's *Poetaster* (p. 228).

*The Malcontent*†* (*c.* 1600—*c.* 1604).[2] Tragi-comedy with some competent situations and interestingly-varied Jonsonian characters among its muddled obscurities. Utterances of Malevole reflect the bitter ironic strain of Marston's early verse-satire. Excellent portraiture of hero somewhat exaggerated when compared with Molière's misanthropic Alceste. Play similar to *Hamlet* (p. 204). Influenced Shakespeare's Jacques in *As You Like It* (p. 197).

---

1 Alden, R. M., "The Rise of Formal Satire in England" (Publications of the University of Pennsylvania), *Series in Philology, Literature and Archaeology,* VII, No. 2 (1899), pp. 129-148.

2 Stoll, E. E., "The Date of *The Malcontent*: A Rejoinder," *The Review of English Studies,* XI (1935), pp. 42-50.

† * Explanation of symbols immediately precedes page one.

**Francis Beaumont,** 1584—1616, dramatist. Son of Sir Francis Beaumont. Educated at Broadgate Hall (Pembroke College), Oxford (1597—1600). Member of the Inner Temple. Wrote commendatory verse for several of Jonson's plays. Died at the age of thirty-two. (*For his relationship with Fletcher, see* p. 243.)

***The Woman-Hater*** (1607). Second-rate mock-heroic comedy showing the "humour" influence of Jonson. Traditionally assigned to Beaumont alone.

**John Fletcher,** 1579—1625, dramatist. Son of the Dean of Peterborough, afterwards Bishop of London. Nephew of Giles Fletcher the elder, cousin of Giles and Phineas Fletcher (pp. 251, 252). Educated at Benet College, Cambridge. Died of the plague. Collaborated with many. Careless poet, poor characterization, slipshod writer, superficial though sweet verse. (*For the so-called Castor-and-Pollux relationship of Beaumont and Fletcher, see p.* 243.)

## *PROBABLY BY FLETCHER ALONE*

***The Faithful Shepherdess*** (printed *c.* 1609). Pastoral tragicomedy. Rich poetic passages frustrated by a tone iterative and unvarying. Gross humor introduced through the characters of the wantons Chloe and Alexis, and of the Sullen Shepherd. Influenced by Guarini's *Il Pastor Fido,* modelled in turn upon Tasso's *Aminta.*

***Wit without Money*** (written *c.* 1614; printed 1639). Original, effective comedy.

***Bonduca*** (*ante* March, 1619). Romantic tragedy based on the story of Boadicea as it appears in Holinshed. Central character is Caratach. Fervent rhetoric.

***Valentinian*** (1610—1614). Romantic tragedy based somewhat on historical fact. Lyrics: "Now the lusty spring is seen"; "Hear, ye ladies that despise."

***The Loyal Subject*** (acted 1618). Lively comedy. Is always plausible.

***The Mad Lover*** (acted *ante* 1619). Sprawling romantic comedy.

***The Humorous Lieutenant*** (acted *c.* 1619). Vivacious, romantic comedy.

***Women Pleased*** (*c.* 1620; printed 1647). Tragi-comedy not closely knit. Famous: "Tell me what is that only thing."

***The Wild-Goose Chase*** (1621; printed 1652). Successful romantic comedy—artificial, sparkling dialogue. Basis of Farquhar's ***The Inconstant*** (1702).

***The Woman's Prize*** (written *ante* 1625; printed 1647). Comedy. How Shakespeare's Petruccio is tamed (p. 192 *f*.).

***A Wife for a Month*** (acted 1624). Ineffective romantic drama.

***Rule a Wife and Have a Wife*** (acted 1624). Fletcher's comic masterpiece is coarse. The Perez-Estefania under-plot is derived from a novel in Cervantes's second volume of *Novelas Ejemplares* (1613).

***The Chances*** (*c.* 1620; printed 1647). Fletcher's best dialogue enhances the well-constructed plot of this coarse, sometimes farcical, comedy. Founded on a novel by Cervantes in his *Novelas Ejemplares* (1613). (Prologue and epilogue are almost certainly not by Fletcher.)

### PROBABLY BY FLETCHER AND MASSINGER

***Sir John van Olden Barnavelt*** (acted 1619). Historical tragedy.

***The Little French Lawyer*** (1619—1622). Comedy. Source of plot in Masuccio Salernitano's *Novellino* (1476).

***The Custom of the Country*** (1619—1622). Romantic drama with some indecent passages. Influenced by Cervantes.

***The Spanish Curate*** (1622). Comedy based on stories in a novel translated from the Spanish *Gerardo, the Unfortunate Spaniard* (1622) by Leonard Digges.

***The Beggar's Bush*** (*c.* 1622). Drama contains realistic pictures of thieves and their cant. (Possibly Beaumont had a hand in the play.)

***The Elder Brother*** (printed 1637). Drama probably not indebted to Calderón's comedy, *De una causa dos effectos.*

### PROBABLY BY FLETCHER AND JONSON

***The Bloody Brother, or Rollo, Duke of Normandy*** (*c.* 1616). Tragedy. "Drink to-day, and drown all sorrow." "Take, o take those lips away" and "Hide, o hide those hills of snow"—occurring, variously changed, in Shakespeare's *Measure for Measure* (p. 202).

### BY FLETCHER AND SHAKESPEARE

***The Two Noble Kinsmen*** (printed 1634). In the main, retells Chaucer's *Knight's Tale* (p. 72). Certain passages by Shakespeare.[1]

***Henry VIII*** (acted 1613). Historical drama. See page 225.

---

1 Both Fletcher and Shakespeare were assisted, according to traditional opinion, by Massinger. But see Cruickshank, A. H., *Massinger and "The Two Noble Kinsmen"* (1922). Also see p. 226 of the *Outline-History*.

***Julius Caesar.*** Conservative opinion holds that this tragedy is an old play re-written by Shakespeare alone.[1] See p. 186.

## BEAUMONT AND FLETCHER

Associated in an effective and intimate literary partnership in a series of drama. Works comprise fifty-two plays, a masque, and several minor poems.[2] Beaumont, the more thoughtful and tragic, is traditionally recognized as the superior in plot construction, dramatic technique, pathos, romantic characterization, unmannered verse; Fletcher, the more idyllic, as the superior in vivacity, lyric power, effusive observation, luxuriant fancy. Generally original plots with ingenious complications graced by naturalness of diction and spontaneity of action are never checkmated by the frequent character types and the foreign localities. Note the wide range of subject-matter, effective construction, simple versification, and character-creations. Their comedy, with its romantic pathos and passion, lightness and wit, fondness for prose and loose blank verse, straining for effect and lack of moral seriousness, demonstrates a decadent spirit and foreshadows the Restoration comedy.[3]

***The Knight of the Burning Pestle*** (written *c.* 1607—1608; printed 1613). Comedy-skit of the chivalric romance and of manners; *e. g.*, gives, most likely unwittingly, an excellent picture of an Elizabethan play-audience. Freshly burlesques excessive military valor, through the ludicrous, quixotic adventures of Ralph, the Grocer-Errant, on whose shield is depicted a burning Pestle. Real plot concerns Jasper's winning of Luce, in the face of her father's opposition and that of the rival Humphrey. Original music of thirteen among the forty songs is extant: most of them, sung by Merrythought, help directly in characterization or creating-intensifying the atmosphere. Rollicking drinking song: "For Jillian of Berry, she dwells on a hill."

***A King and No King*** (acted 1611). Romantic drama. It transpires that the love of Arbaces for his sister Panthea is not incestuous. Cutting in its satire, practical in its rollicking nature.

***The Maid's Tragedy*†*** (acted *c.* 1611). Effective characterization, excellent construction; brutal grossness. Exquisite song of Aspatia: "Lay a garland on my hearse."

---

1 The coinciding theory of E. H. C. Oliphant and William Wells is rejected by Parrott, T. M., "Marlowe Beaumont, and *Julius Caesar*," *Modern Language Notes*, XLIV (1929), pp. 69-77. Also, see p. 186 *ff*. of the *Outline-History*.

2 For the general characteristics of their romance, see Thorndike, A. H., *The Influence of Beaumont and Fletcher on Shakespeare* (1901), Chap. VII, pp. 109-132.

3 Sprague, A. C., *Beaumont and Fletcher on the Restoration Stage* (1926); Wilson, J. H., "The Influence of Beaumont and Fletcher on Restoration Drama," *Ohio University Studies* (1928).

† * Explanation of symbols immediately precedes page one.

***Philaster, or Love lies a-Bleeding*†* (acted *c.* 1608—1611; printed 1620). Romantic drama or tragi-comedy with an improbable plot, coarse in parts but less painfully so than in *The Maid's Tragedy.* Introduces the element of surprise. A parallel to Shakespeare's *Twelfth Night; e. g.,* Euphrasia is suggestive of Viola. Possibly the traditional view that Shakespeare was influenced by this play is not tenable.

**Philip Massinger,** 1583—1640, dramatist. Educated at St. Alban Hall, Oxford (1602—1606). Wrote about fifteen plays, and in conjunction with others (*e. g.,* Fletcher, Dekker), fully three dozen plays. Admirable blank verse, command of stagecraft, skilful manipulation (especially of the parallel or double plot), interesting variety of subject-matter, simplicity of language, naturalness, balanced moral judgment (although, not infrequently, indecent language), steady religious convictions. Absence of passion or of pathos, prosy rhetorical verse, grimly ironical humor, tendency to sensational plot and the drawing of a moral, aversion to the tragic end demanded by his story. Strong conception of character, according to Sir Walter Scott; unindividualized, one-sided characterization, according to S. T. Coleridge and Leslie Stephen. Some see in him the beginning signs of decadence; others, notably Émile Legouis, believe that his work "redeems his age from the charge of decadence."[1] (See, also, page 242.)

***The Unnatural Combat*** (*c.* 1621). Somber tragedy. Not strongly conceived. Structure traditionally believed to be awkward; theme traditionally believed to be similar to Shelley's *Cenci.*[2]

***The Maid of Honour*** (1622). Romantic drama. His most classical play in simplicity of plot, unity of action, and regularity of construction. Camiola is his best woman-portrait. Derived directly through Painter's *Palace of Pleasure,* and ultimately from Boccaccio's "Camiola and Rolande."

***The Duke of Milan*** (1623). Tragedy often impressive in its unrelieved gloom and horror. Complex plot. Superficial resemblance to Shakespeare's *Othello* (p. 209).

***The Bondman*** (1624). Application of a classical story to topical events and characters; *e. g.,* Guiso represents Buckingham.

***The Renegado*** (1624). Tragi-comedy. Catholic convictions apparent.

***The Roman Actor*** (1626). Competently-constructed tragedy based on the life of the Emperor Domitian. Exemplifies his method of a play within a play.

---

1 For Massinger's religious, philosophical, and social concepts and theories, see Spencer, B. T., "Philip Massinger," pp. 3-119, in *Seventeenth-Century Studies,* edited by Shafer, Robert (1933).

2 Telfer, R. S., *The Unnatural Combat* (1932).

† * Explanation of symbols immediately precedes page one.

***A New Way to Pay Old Debts***†* (*c.* 1626). Well-plotted study of a miser. Comedy reveals dramatic action masterly in its craftsmanship and unflagging in its interest; but also a poetry rhetorical in its tendencies. Sir Francis Michell is probably the prototype of Greedy, " a Hungry Justice of Peace"; Sir Giles Mompesson, of Sir Giles Overreach. If not based on, then influenced by Middleton's *A Trick to Catch the Old One* (p. 237).

***The Great Duke of Florence*** (1627). Delightful romantic comedy. Well-constructed plot, good humor.

***The Fatal Dowry*** (1632). Best tragedy; collaborator, Nathan Field (1587—1620). Effective funeral scene. (Theme is the basis of Nicholas Rowe's blank-verse tragedy, *The Fair Penitent,* in 1703.)

***The City Madam*** (1632). Vigorous comedy of manners reminiscent of *A New Way to Pay Old Debts.* Influenced by Jonson. Conclusion reveals his moralistic bent. Creation: Luke.

**John Webster,** *c.* 1580—*c.* 1625. Traditionally regarded as the greatest tragic dramatist after Shakespeare and equal in intensity to him. Frequent collaborator with others. Tragedies of horror founded on Italian *novelle.* Poignantly powerful beauty of phraseology, epigrammatic terseness, concentrated poetic language, imaginative intensity, command of the turbulent emotions of supernatural horror and compassion, tragic potency, Greek morality of retribution. Considered by Swinburne to be superior to Marlowe in dramatic subtlety of detail and conscientiousness of craftsmanship. Chief defects are an oxymoronic kind of prose, involved plotting, not infrequent static characterization; a lack of unity of action, and a lack of restraint that revoltingly crowds the scene with horror upon horror. But his pornography is endemic rather than deliberate.

***The White Divil, or Vittoria Corombona***†* (1612). Tragedy of blood, effective in its characterization and energetic in its spirit. Famous for the trial scene and for the dialogue with Brachiano. Flamineo has been described as "the pocket-Montaigne." Dirge of Cornelia over her son Marcello: "Call for the robin redbreast, and the wren." (Vittoria Accoramboni was murdered on December 22, 1585.)

***The Duchess of Malfi***†* (1612—1614). Somber tragedy based ultimately upon Bandello's twenty-sixth novel but directly upon Painter's *Palace of Pleasure* (XXIII). Highly dramatic and condensed moments, clear portraitures; loose plot, exaggerated horrors, and, in general, less poetic and less plausible than *The White Divil.* Duke Ferdinand speaks an immortal line: "Cover her face; mine eyes dazzle; she died young." Lyrics: "Hark, now everything is still"; "Arms and honour deck thy story."

†* Explanation of symbols immediately precedes page one.

***Appius and Virginia*** (*c.* 1620). Tragedy, taken from William Painter's *Palace of Pleasure,* relates the classical story of Virginia. Singleness of plot, coherence of structure, fair regularity of blank verse. Some remarkable passages. Play sometimes assigned to Thomas Heywood, at least as part-collaborator.[1] See p. 238.

**John Ford,** 1586—*c.* 1639, dramatist. Probably educated at Exeter College (1601). Entered the Middle Temple (1602). Collaborated with Webster, Rowley, and particularly with Dekker. Not seldom reveals a lyric spontaneity; sweet pathos; powerful and passionately intense in the depiction of the despairing or sin-laden soul; subtle in introspective analysis of women. Also, absence of genuine (and presence of insipid) humor; inadequate plot structure; erotic situations. Tendency towards decadence: strong propensity for the strangely fantastic and the forbidden theme, violence, horror.

***Fame's Memorial*** (1606). Long elegy on the death of Charles Blount, Lord Mountjoy and Earl of Devonshire, whom Lady Penelope, on being divorced, had married. Courageously takes "a losing side." Not unsympathetic.

***The Lover's Melancholy*** (1629). Romantic comedy generally dreary even if interesting by virtue of its study of melancholy and delicate emotions. Indebted to Burton (p. 271).

***'Tis Pity She's a Whore*****†*** (1633). Sensational but human, tender, psychological study of a guilty passion. Beauty of diction, vivid characterization, clear understanding of incestuous love.

***Love's Sacrifice*** (1633). Tragedy. Insane jealousy deals out death. Feeble, sentimental conclusion. Comic creation: Old Mauruccio. Reminiscent of *Othello* (p. 209).

***The Broken Heart*****†*** (1633). Tragedy. Impressive scenes, particularly the effective one in the last act. Triangle-play best of Ford's from point of view of plot and development of character, pathos and beauty of lines. Insight into the characterization of both women. Lacks vitality of movement. Crotolon is faintly reminiscent of Shakespeare's Polonius. Richard Crashaw in *Delights of the Muses* (p. 260):

> "Thou cheats't us, Ford: mak'st one seem two by art:
> What is Love's Sacrifice but the Broken Heart?"

---

1 Brooke, Rupert, (1) "The Authorship of the Later 'Appius and Virginia,'" *The Modern Language Review,* VII (1913), pp. 433-453, and also (2) *John Webster and the Elizabethan Drama* (1916), pp. 165-210; Clarke, A. M., "The Authorship of 'Appius and Virginia,'" *The Modern Language Review,* XVI (1921), pp. 1-17; Sykes, H. D., *Sidelights on Elizabethan Drama* (1924), Chap. V, pp. 108-139; Gray, H. D., "*Appius and Virginia*: By Webster and Heywood," *Studies in Philology,* XXIV (1927), pp. 275-289.

† * Explanation of symbols immediately precedes page one.

***The Chronicle History of Perkin Warbeck*****†*** (1634). Chronicle play. In addition to Ford's general characteristics, this historical tragedy, with its absence of erotic love-scenes, its regular versification, skilful construction, comparative freedom, and sympathetic drawing of Lady Gordon and Warbeck, has been regarded as the best historical drama, excepting the plays of Shakespeare. Materials drawn from Bacon's *History of Henry the Seventh* (1622) and Thomas Gainsford's *True and Wonderful History of Perkin Warbeck* (1618).

***The Witch of Edmonton*** (1658). Powerful domestic drama, founded on story of Elizabeth Sawyer, executed for witchcraft in 1621. Collaborators are Dekker and Rowley.

**James Shirley,** 1596—1666, dramatist. Educated at Oxford (1612) and at Cambridge (*ante* 1619). Took orders; but later became a Roman Catholic. Master of a grammar school. Soldier in the Royalist cause under the Duke of Newcastle. Reverted to teaching school. He died, on the same day as his second wife, from exposure in the Great Fire. Wrote about forty works—dramas, masques, poems, grammatical treatises. Generally simple, effective, even original plotting. Spontaneous dialogue, easy and correct versification, appropriate characters, genuine humor; strong moral purpose (note how virtue generally triumphs),[1] faultless construction of his tragedies, effective dramatic sense, endemic grossness. Characterization generally conventional, thin plots thinned out further by surprise-elements, ingenuity too labored, use of the passions of lust and revenge excessive, moral sense, while definitely didactic, also as emphatically callous, licentiousness frequent. Lyrics: "You virgins, that did late despair"; "The glories of our blood and state."

***The Maides Revenge*** (1626). Tragedy based on a story in Reynold's *Triumphing of God's Revenge against . . . . Murther.*

***Love's Crueltie*** (1631). Effective tragedy. Strong moral emphasized by stronger plot.

***The Traytor*** (1631). Romantic tragedy influenced by the assassination of Duke Alessandro de' Medici. Competent verse, characterization, construction. Efficacious comic relief. Source possibly Margaret of Navarre's *Heptameron.*

***Hyde Park*****†*** (1632). Comedy of manners notable, primarily, for its representation of London's fashionable life. Plot not well unified. Life-like characters.

***The Gamester*** (1633). Somewhat coarse, realistic comedy of manners. Main plot taken from Margaret of Navarre's *Heptameron.*

---

1 Radtke, S. J. (*Rev.*), *James Shirley: His Catholic Philosophy of Life* (1929).

† * Explanation of symbols immediately precedes page one.

***The Young Admiral*** (1633). Tragi-comedy. Good construction, generally inoffensive language, occasional genuine feeling. Possibly influenced by Lope de Vega's *Don Lope de Cardona.*

***The Lady of Pleasure*** (1635). Moral-immoral comedy of intrigue. Strong satire, vivacious repartee. Calculating character of Aretina anticipates Sheridan's Lady Teazle in *The School for Scandal* (1777).

***The Polititian*** (1639). Somber tragi-comedy weakly reminiscent of *Macbeth.* Love-elements properly subordinated.

***The Cardinall*†*** (1641). Romantic tragedy. Plot firmly-managed, characterization distinctly developmental, verse often beautiful.

## *CHARACTER-WRITING*

**Sir Thomas Overbury,** 1581—1613, poet, essayist. Courtier poisoned at the instigation of the notorious and "fatal" Frances Howard, Countess of Essex, whose marriage to Robert Carr (Earl of Somerset) he had opposed.[1] (See also John Donne, p. 254.)

***A Wife*** (1614). "Being a most exquisite and singular Poem of the choice of a Wife." In six-line stanzas Overbury pictures the virtues desirable in a married woman: Circumspect commonplace written, according to his father, to dissuade the Earl of Somerset from marrying the Countess of Essex.

***Characters*** (1614). Prose. Published as an appendix to *A Wife;* by Overbury and "other learned Gentlemen." Primarily a series of sketches of types; not infrequently some individualized portraits. Aphoristic vies with euphuistic style. "A Milkmaid," "An ignorant Glory-hunter," "A Mere Scholar," "A Braggadochio Welshman," "An Affectate Traveler." A phase of the evolution of the English essay, modelled after the work of Theophrastus, Greek philosopher (*d.* B. C. 287); but the twenty-one characters (of the first edition) reveal a wider range of theme, and exhibit less interest in Theophrastian simplicity and ethical traits than in cleverness and external facts.

(Other character-writers are Nicholas Breton, Joseph Hall, John Stephens, John Earle, and John Cleveland: consult the *Supplementary List of Writers,* pp. 293—295. See also Donne's *Juvenilia,* p. 256, and Thomas Fuller's works, p. 274.)

---

1 Whibley, Charles, *Essays in Biography* (1913) pp. 3-75; Roughead, William, "The Fatal Countess," *Juridical Review,* XXXIV (1922), pp. 226-267; Parry, E. A., *The Overbury Mystery* (1925).

† * Explanation of symbols immediately precedes page one.

## Chapter XIII

# THE AGE OF MILTON
(1616—1660)

## POLITICAL AND SOCIAL BACKGROUND

### Historical

***James I*** (1603—1625). When the Tudor dynasty was brought to a close by the death of Elizabeth in 1603, James VI of Scotland, the son of Mary Stuart, Protestant, and descendant of Henry VII of England, ascended the throne as James I. With the declining years of the Renaissance Queen had waned the patriotic unity of the country, and the wisdom necessary to cement the factions and to revive patriotic fervor was not possessed by the new King. The people resented the new taxes made necessary by the Monarch's lavish expenditures and resented the attempt at an alliance with Spain through the betrothal of the King's son Charles. Persecutions of the Catholics by Parliament and of the Puritans by James I led to the establishment at Plymouth (1620) of the first permanent English settlement in New England, and to the "Great Emigration" (1630) to Massachusetts. As the middle-class rose to power, it clashed with the Crown, who in turn dissolved three Parliaments (1604, 1614, 1621) over imposition of customs, money grants, and right of free speech. Continuously the defenders of popular privileges endeavored to check the King's prerogative, assigned to himself by his Theory of Divine Right.

***Charles I*** (1625—1649). At his accession Charles I was popular, but his deliberate deceitfulness and wrong-headed impulsiveness soon turned the people against him. Difficulties with Parliament were increased by his marriage with Princess Henrietta Maria of France, a Roman Catholic, and by his appointment of James's hated favorite Buckingham as Lord Chancellor. Public feeling became further embittered by the King's dissolution of three Parliaments convoked in four years. Finally Charles I was forced to concede the *Petition of Right* (1628), designed to prevent the abuse of royal prerogative by providing for no taxation without the consent of Parliament, no arbitrary billeting of soldiers on the citizenry, and no arbitrary imprisonment without trial.

Then Charles I dissolved Parliament and had some of the leading members imprisoned. For eleven years he governed without the Parliament, substituting in its place the Star Chamber and Court of High Commission. During these years Archbishop Laud's policy of punishing Puritans caused large emigrations to America, and his attempt to impose episcopacy upon Scotland provoked riots. Refused his demands for money, and urged to conclude a peace with Scotland, Charles I dissolved the "Short Parliament" (1640). The "Long Parliament," summoned by Charles I after his defeat at the hands of the Scots, impeached both Strafford and Laud, imprisoning the latter and executing the former. By compelling Charles I to confirm a bill by which Parliament was not to be dissolved without its own consent, the actual control of the kingdom was no longer in the hands of the King.

***Civil War*** (1642—1648). At first the Royalists (or Cavaliers, represented by the Court, the Church, the Catholics, and the northern gentry) were the victors; but the Parliamentary forces (Puritans or Roundheads, represented by the bulk of the middle classes, the merchants, artisans, London, and the southeast, who in contrast to the flowing locks of the Cavaliers cut short their hair), soon acquiring experience, defeated Prince Rupert (1644) and annihilated the royal army (1645). The King, surrendering to the Scottish army, was delivered to the English Parliament. Finally, after his escape from the residence assigned him, he was recaptured, tried, and sentenced to death for murder and treason (1649). Thus at last ended the struggle between Parliament and James I and his son Charles I.

***The Commonwealth*** (1649—1653). The country was declared a commonwealth, nominally a republic. When Scotland proclaimed Charles II King of Ireland, Scotland, and England, Cromwell immediately took steps to break Scotland's resistance, succeeding in his purpose by 1651. The place of the provisional Rump, expelled in 1653, was taken by the Nominated or "Barebone's" Parliament.

***The Protectorate*** (1653—1658). When the "Barebone's" Parliament was voted into dissolution, Cromwell, under an adopted written constitution, called the *Instrument of Government,* assumed the title of Lord Protector of England, Scotland, and Ireland. He became recognized for his strong foreign policy, which brought the Dutch War to a successful conclusion, and for a dictatorial home policy, which tolerated many sects, including the re-admission of the Jews, expelled since 1290. By 1658 the Protectorate had become virtually a monarchy. Upon Cromwell's death (1658) there succeeded a period of strife, under his son Richard. Finally the Parliament voted (1660) to restore the monarchy with Charles II as King.

**Social**

***Life and Temper of the Times.*** Horse-racing, bear-baiting, the sport of the cock-pit, and the theatrical performance were all condemned by the Puritans, who looked upon the Cavaliers as given to profane swearing and sensual excesses. To the King and his courtiers, on the other hand, the Puritan was a symbol of spiritual pride, hypocrisy, rebellion, and tyranny. But the typical Puritan was a person of high ideals, tolerant of differences of opinion; the spirit of the Puritan was a noble force: it inspired the Commonwealth to safeguard England's national ideals, it gave to the Pilgrim Fathers the courage to search for a land where they could worship in their own manner, it had as its spokesmen two of the greatest English writers—Milton (p. 277) and Bunyan (treated in the next volume). Progress should also be noted in several fields—in philosophy by Bacon (p. 268), in medical science by William Harvey, in mathematics by John Napier. While advances were made in the field of architecture by Inigo Jones, yet in general the fine arts obtained but small patronage. On the whole the nation was prosperous.

### General View of the Literature

Relaxing in vigor, this period is one of gradual transition from the exuberant gaiety and imaginative freedom of the Renaissance to that of artificial cheer, philosophic melancholy, and Puritan sobriety. Often political or religious, the prose is in general either simple and disputatious or florid and oratorical; despite its quaint affected mannerism, the prose displays a new freedom, copiousness, and power. The poetry is marked much less by its originality of thought and impetuosity of emotion than by a correctness of form and an intellectual play of fancy; while fashionably short, its greatest weaknesses are possibly an affected adulatory language for the charms of women and a triviality of subject matter. While the Civil Wars contributed to bringing about the collapse of the drama, now frequently marked by a studied indecency, it was the Puritan opposition that effected the closure of all theatres (1642). Not until eighteen years later were the dramatic performances legally permitted. Meanwhile the neo-classicism, fostered by Jonson, was making progress. In conclusion, although Milton is the only great representative in the field of blank verse, and the only writer of great versatility, he is, it must be noted, not altogether representative of his age, better called, were it not for its unwieldy title, the Age of the Cavalier and the Puritan.

## *THE SCHOOL OF SPENSER*

**Giles Fletcher** (the Younger), *c.* 1584—1623, poet. Educated at Westminster and Trinity College, Cambridge. Rector of Alderton in Suffolk. Less prolific than his brother Phineas (p. 252).

***A Canto upon the Death of Eliza*** (1603). Laments Elizabeth and welcomes James. Notable for its use of the modified form of Spenserian stanza. Appeared in *Sorowe's Joy,* a book of elegies on Queen Elizabeth.

***Christ's Victorie, and Triumph in Heaven, on Earth, over, and after Death*** (1610).[1] Theme, partly derived from Du Bartas's *Semaines,* nobly retells the Biblical story of Satan's temptation of Christ after the latter's forty days of fasting: the Temptation in the Desert, the Ascension, and Christ's final victory. Influenced by *The Faerie Queene,* particularly by the *Mutabilitie Cantos* (p. 135); Spenserian echo of language and likeness of imagery. Modified Spenserian stanza: a riming triplet concludes the first five of the eight-line stanzas, beginning *ababb.* Occasionally strained allegory, incongruous wit; but melodic if far-fetched similes, scattered passages of lyric beauty, and, in general, a work instinct with fresh imagery and religious fervor. Anticipates Milton's *Paradise Regain'd* (p. 288).

***The Reward of the Faithful*** (1623). Religious prose treatise.

**Phineas Fletcher,** 1582—1650, poet. Elder brother of Giles the Younger. Educated at Eton and King's College, Cambridge. Rector of Hilgay, Norfolk (1620). Clear, direct allegory. Fluent verse, possibly as colorful but never as sublime and natural in imagery as his brother's. With the latter he links Spenser to Milton, differing from the "poets' poet" by reason of an absence of archaism and the presence of greater religious feeling.

***Locustae*** (in Latin); ***The Locusts*** or ***Apollyonists***—parallel poem in English, freely paraphrased and expanded (1637).[2] Religious allegory in five cantos describes the fall of Lucifer and fiercely attacks the Jesuits. Forerunner of Milton's depiction of Satan's rebellion and downfall, and of the fallen angels' council: *Paradise Lost* (Bk. I).

***The Purple Island: or The Isle of Man*** (1633).[3] Cumbrous allegorical-spiritual poem on the human body: its irrigating veins and functioning organs are attacked by foes or various human vices, and are beaten off: the body is the purple island; the veins the streams, the bones the foundations. Second half is more poetical than the first, which is an elaborately worked-out conceit. Twelve cantos (724 stanzas of seven lines each) for the major part discursive, humorless, unimaginative, pedantic; occasionally distinguished in isolated passages by descriptions of rural scenery. Much elaborated from an allegory in *The Faerie Queene* (II, 9—11). Also influenced by du Bartas.

***Piscatory Eclogs*** (1633). Published with *The Purple Island.* Inspired by the Italian Sannazaro. Sweet versification echoes Spenser; effective description. Most important as a key to the life of the poet.

---

1 Cory, H. E., "Spenser, the School of the Fletchers, and Milton," *University of California Publications in Modern Philology,* II, No. 5 (1912), pp. 325-330 (pp. 311-373).

2 *Ibid.,* pp. 316-318.

3 *Ibid.,* pp. 318-325.

***Elissa*** (1633). Excellent written-to-order elegy on the death of Sir Antony Irby.

***Brittain's Ida.***[1] Almost satiating in its pretty luxuriousness. Once ascribed to Spenser.

**William Browne,** 1591—*c.* 1643, pastoral poet. Born at Tavistock, Devonshire. Educated at Exeter College, Oxford (1604). Entered the Inner Temple (1611). Admirer and imitator of Spenser. Occasionally melodic lyrics; at his ripest reveals sweetness, grace, and a sensitive affection for Devonshire country life. Of his prettified songs the most happy is *The Complete Lover* ("For her gait, if she be walking"). Combines an Arcadian with a Donne-like style. Influenced Milton and Keats.

***Britannia's Pastorals*** (I, 1613; II, 1616; III, 1852). Fluent, discursive, mediocre pastoral allegory, threaded by the meandering love-tale of Marina and Celandine. Couplets, often epigrammatically turned, interspersed with lyrics: happy realistic descriptions of its epic similes. Influenced more by Sidney's *Arcadia* than by Spenser's *Shepheardes Calender.* Love poems: "Marma's gone, and now sit I"; "Shall I tell you whom I love?"

***Upon the Countess Dowager of Pembroke*** (*c.* 1613). Famous epitaph on Sidney's sister (previously assigned to Jonson). See p. 232.

***Shepherd's Pipe*** (1614). Pastoral in a set of seven Spenserian eclogues, written with Wither and others. Of biographical interest. Elegy on Philarete (Thomas Manwood) in fourth eclogue resembles Milton's *Lycidas* (p. 279).

***The Inner Temple Masque*** (1615). Dramatic tale of Ulysses and Circe. (*Odyssey,* X; *Metamorphoses,* XIV.)

**George Wither,** 1588—1667, poet, satirist. Educated at Magdalen College, Oxford. Captain of horse (1639) under Charles I. At least "thrice" imprisoned[2] for three works (1613, 1621, 1661), according to the conclusion of *Britain's Remembrancer.* (Often called himself the "Remembrancer.") Generally prosy; only seldom reveals a grace and noble exaltation. Notable: "Sleep, baby, sleep, what ails my dear"; "I loved a lass, a fair one."

---

1 See Cory, H. E., "Spenser, the School of the Fletchers, and Milton," *University of California Publications in Modern Philology,* II, No. 5 (1912) p. 330 *f.* (pp. 311-373); *Venus & Anchises* (*Brittain's Ida*), edited by Seaton, Ethel (1926).

2 French. J. M., "George Wither in Prison," *Publications of the Modern Language Association of America,* XLIV (1930), pp. 959-966.

***Abuses Stript and Whipt*** (1613). Twenty satires levelled against Gluttony, Revenge, Ambition, Avarice, Lust, and other vices of the Court. Sent to prison for a satire believed to be upon the Lord Chancellor.

***The Shepherd's Hunting*** (1614). Five pastorals written while imprisoned in the Marshalsey. William Browne (p. 253) and Wither figure as "Roget" and "Philarete."

***Fidelia*** (1615). One-toned love elegy in which a faithful nymph writes to her sweetheart. Lyric (included in edition of 1619): "Shall I, wasting in despair." Passionate reserve, exalted sincerity.

***Wither's Motto*** (1621). Invective's motto: *Nec habeo, nec careo, nec curo.* Second imprisonment.

***Fair-Virtue, or The Mistress of Phil'Arete*** (1622). Panegyric on his mistress. Characteristically long (almost 5,000 lines). Tendency to sermonize; but some good lyrics.

***Juvenilia*** (1622). Miscellaneous collection includes some of his best work; *e. g.*, the sonnet-sequence lament on Prince Henry. Sweet lyrics, skilled metres.

***Hymns and Songs of the Church*** (1623). Has been declared "worthy and profitable to be inserted, in convenient manner and due place, into every English Psalm-book to meter." According to R. D. Havens, Wither is perhaps our first important hymn writer.

***The History of the Pestilence*** (written 1625; published 1932).[1] Weak construction; but sincere accents.

***Britain's Remembrancer*** (1628). Over-long poem inspired by the London plague of 1625.

***Collection of Emblems, Ancient and Modern*** (1635). Written-to-order verses for the allegorical plates of Crispin van Passe.

***Hallelujah, or Britain's Second Remembrances*** (1641). Religious hymns and some beautiful songs capture again the felicity of his earlier work. (Some repeated from his volume of 1623.)

## *THE METAPHYSICAL SCHOOL*[2]

**John Donne** (pronounced "Dun"), *c.* 1572[3]—1631, poet, theologian, lawyer, greatest pulpit orator of his day. Father was Warden of the Ironmongers' Company (1574). Trinity College, Cambridge

---

1 *The History of the Pestilence,* edited by French, J. M. (1932).

2 Nethercot, A. H., "The Term 'Metaphysical Poets' before Johnson," *Modern Language Notes,* XXXVII (1922), pp. 11-17.

3 Izaak Walton's date of birth for Donne (1573), followed by most encyclopedias, is probably an error. See Wilson, F. P., "Notes on the Early Life of John Donne," *The Review of English Studies,* III (1927), pp. 276-278 (pp. 272-279).

(1587—1589), where he probably met Christopher Brooke. Lincoln's Inn (1592). Entered the Anglican Communion (1593, according to Izaak Walton; 1603, according to Sir Edmund Gosse). Travelled in foreign countries (*c.* 1595—1596).[1]

With Ralegh and the Earl of Essex on expedition to Cadiz (1596). With the Earl of Essex on naval expedition to the Azores ("The Islands Voyage," 1597). Appointed Secretary to Sir Thomas Egerton, keeper of the Great Seal from 1596 to 1601 (1598—1602). Alienated Sir Thomas's favor by clandestinely marrying (1601) sixteen-year-old Anne More, the Lord Keeper's niece by marriage (to his second wife, Lady Ellesmere). For this civil offense against the Common Law, and for the offense against the Canon Law (because of marrying a girl without her father's consent), Sir George More, Chancellor of the Garter and Lieutenant of the Tower, had his son-in-law imprisoned for a short time in the Fleet (1602). Famous letter to wife was signed: "John Donne, Anne Donne, Un-done." For many of the following years Donne was dependent upon patrons (1601—1615). Found asylum with Sir Francis Wooley, Mrs. Donne's cousin, at Pyrford (1602—1604). After a short period at Camberwell (1605), he resided at Mitcham (1605—1609). Employed by Thomas Morton (*c.* 1605—1607), who probably was assisted by Donne in the pamphlet-war with the Jesuits, and who urged Donne to take orders in the Church. Became reconciled with his father-in-law (1608). M. A., Oxford (1610). Resided at the Drury House (1610). Eulogy on the death of the fifteen-year-old Elizabeth Drury (1610), whom John Donne had never known, earned Sir Robert Drury's favor (1610). Travelled with the latter on the Continent (1611—1612). To obtain the aid of Robert Carr, then Viscount Rochester and afterwards the Earl of Somerset, in securing ordination, John Donne used his knowledge of law to support the suit of nullity brought by the infamous Countess of Essex against her first husband (1613).[2]

In honor of the marriage of Rochester and the Countess, he composed an epithalamion (1613). Ordained priest (1615). Doctor of Divinity, Cambridge (1615). Presented to the livings of Keyston in Huntingdonshire and of Sevenoaks in Kent. Reader in Divinity to the Benchers of Lincoln's Inn (1616—1622). Death of wife in childbirth (1617), who left him with seven children after having borne him twelve. Chaplain of Viscount Doncaster's embassy to Bohemia (1619—

---

1 There is no certainty about this date. According to Wilson, F. P., "Notes on the Early Life of John Donne," *The Review of English Studies,* III (1927), p. 279 (pp. 272-279), it is not known whether Donne started on his travels in 1588 or in 1594.

2 That Donne took an active part in the divorce proceedings is a traditional interpretation opposed by Simpson, E. M., *A Study of the Prose Writings of John Donne* (1924), p. 30 *f.*

1620). Dean of St. Paul's (1621). Prolocutor of the Lower House of Convocations (1624). Held the living of St. Dunstan's in the West (1624—1631).

**Prose**

***Juvenilia, or Paradoxes and Problemes*** (1597—1607; published 1633).[1] Slight essays, laboredly ingenious (even to the point of obscurity) if frequently clever, cynically amusing if frequently scurrilous. Woman, Death, God, and Suicide—are characteristically the basic subjects. Among the dozen paradoxes: "That a Wise Man is Known by much laughing"; "That the Gifts of the Body are Better than those of the Mind"; "That Virginity is a Virtue"; and "A Defense of Womens Inconstancy," wherein he declares that the "name of *Inconstancy*, . . . . ought to be changed to *variety*," for it is that which makes a woman "the most delightful thing in the world." Included with the score of problems: "Why hath the Common Opinion Afforded Women Souls?"; "Why are the Fairest Falsest?"; and "Why Puritans make long Sermons," in which he thinks that they "doe it out of a *zealous* imagination, that, *It is their duty to preach on till their Auditory wake*." (In 1652 the authorized edition added the probably spurious *A Sheaf of Miscellany Epigrams*, and the authentic two "characters": "The Character of a Scot at the first fight" and "The true Character of a Dunce.")

***Catalogus Librorum Aulicorum*** (*c.* 1600—*c.* 1607; printed 1650).[2] Latin-prose catalogue of books satirizes many authors. Examples: "3. The Art of copying out within the compass of a Penny all the truthful statements made to that end by John Foxe, by Peter Bale"; "10. John Harrington's *Hercules, or the method of purging Noah's Ark of excrement*"; "27. *The Brazen Head of Francis Bacon*: *concerning Robert the First, King of England*." (See pp. 117, 154, 268.)

***Biathanatos*** (*c.* 1608; printed 1646). Casuistical essay-defense of suicide. Vigorous special pleading reveals his obsession with death.

***Pseudo-Martyr*** (*c.* 1610). Erudition as obsolete and logic as careful as those in *Biathanatos*, but duller if more personal. Attacks the Roman Catholic recusants.

***Conclave Ignati*** or ***Ignatius his Conclave*** (1611). Forceful satire upon the Jesuits, with emphasis on St. Ignatius.

***Essays in Divinity*** (*c.* 1615; published 1651). Possibly written deliberately for the Archbishop to prove Donne's orthodoxy and erudition.

---

1 The series of essays may belong to 1603-1610: Simpson, E. M., "Two Manuscripts of Donne's *Paradoxes and Problems*," *The Review of English Studies*, III (1927), pp. 129-145.

2 *The Courtier's Library, or Catalogus Librorum Aulicorum*, edited by Simpson, E. M. (1930).

***Devotions Upon Emergent Occasions*** (1623—1624). Introspective meditations and prayers.

***Three Sermons*** (1623); ***Four Sermons*** (1625); ***Five Sermons*** (1626); ***LXXX Sermons*** (1640); ***Fifty Sermons*** (1649); ***XXVI Sermons***† (1660). Long paragraphs expose his individualistic imagery blended with sepulchral meditations, his sheer eloquence with his characteristic frankness, his sensual thoughts with his self-analytical subtlety.

***Letters to Several Persons of Honour*** (1651). First edition of about 130 letters successively increased to some 180 letters. Their primarily biographical value enhanced by their style—Donne's closest approximation to conversational writing.

**Poetry†**

Donne's poetry of mental contacts and worldly experiences sets itself in opposition to the Petrarchan (or orthodox) love-doctrine of his time. From among his songs and sonnets, divine poems, epigrams, elegies, an heroical epistle, epithalamions, satires, verse-letters, epicedes and obsequies, Latin poems and translations, and the like, different critics have singled out the following:

(1) *The Good-Morrow,* memorable for its first two lines;

(2) *The Autumnal,* beautiful elegy;

(3) *Twicknam Garden,* sonorous and thoughtful lyric;

(4) *A Nocturnall upon S. Lucies Day,* as subtle and as sincere as *Twicknam Garden;*

(5) *The Dreame,* differentiated from Donne's type by not being in couplets;

(6) *A Funerall Elegie,* and

(7) *An Anatomie of the World,* both resplendent in their insincere eulogy of Elizabeth Drury;

(8) *Second Anniversary,* a great epicede despite its faults;

(9) *The Progresse of the Soule,* an achievement in ugliness and splenetic scepticism, influenced, in the words of one critic, by a Pythagorean theory of metempsychosis;

(10) *The Canonization,* a piece of lyrical beauty whether interpreted in a Platonic sense or as a poem to Anne More;

(11) *Elegie on Mistris Boulstred,* possibly the best among his epicedes and obsequies;

(12) *The Litanie,* a divine poem academic rather than religious in its fervor;

(13) *A Hymne to Christ, at the Authors Last Going into Germany,* and

(14) *A Hymne to God the Father,* two of his best divine poems.

---

† * Explanation of symbols immediately precedes page one.

For Mrs. Donne, who, so the story goes, objected to his contemplated tour (1611—1612), he wrote at least two poems: *Song*: "Sweetest love, I do not goe," and *A Valediction: Forbidding Mourning,* deeply tender and movingly suggestive. *The Storme* and *The Calme,* verse-epistles to Christopher Brooke commemorating incidents of "The Islands Voyage," have a realism so vivid that Donne has been described as the "father of the poetry of reason."

His cynical point of view about woman is observable in *The Blossome*; his delightful disparagement of her, in "Goe, and catche a falling starre"; his inconstancy in love, in *The Indifferent,* a beautifully-executed quip. His perverse, tormented wit is, by common consent, best exemplified by *The Flea.* Amoral or anti-moral considerations have probably excluded *The Apparition* and *The Extasie* from anthologies, as must be particularly true of the "much 'fie-fied' *To his Mistress going to Bed,* a piece of frank naturalism redeemed from coarseness by passion and poetic completeness."[1]

Further Suggested Reading: *An Epithalamion, or Marriage Song on the Lady Elizabeth; Jealosie, The Perfume, The Comparison, His Parting from Her* (elegies); *The Blossome, The Primrose, The Relique, Farewell to Love, Loves Deitie, The Legacie, The Funerall, The Prohibition* (songs and sonnets).

*Estimate.* John Donne is becoming less of a problematic character, and his genius is being recognized as having taken a curiously modern direction. The verse-letters glow by reason of a thinking imagination, the letters are gay and wise despite an undercurrent of melancholy, the devotions are characterized by his tormented passion and wit, the sermons are swathed in a gorgeous prose and intensified by an almost subtle eloquence, the elegies are frequently voluptuous in their frank sensuality, the divine sonnets are sonorous. His oblique art makes large parts of his work unequal, tedious, even wire-drawn in their logic, while his lack of any apparent appreciation of beauty leads him into the use of cross-grained and mathematical imagery. It has been noted that the analogies and comparisons of his poetry are as unconventional as its dress: the images are drawn frequently from circles, maps, engravings, elephants, fleas, whales, new discoveries, and the like, his expanded or telescoped conceits bestowing upon his ideas significant metaphysical meaning. "Knowledge of the material from which the ideas are evolved aids in the intellectual effort of distinguishing in a poem the many ideas from which the single idea and emotion are compacted." On the whole, his verse, while occasionally achieving an impeccable rhythm, lacks smoothness, his expression lacks dignity and completeness, and is not infrequently coarse, and his construction lacks strength in longer endeavors. A metrical originality, a compact imagina-

1 Saintsbury, George, *Prefaces and Essays* (1933), p. 285 (pp. 273-291).

tion, a Browning-like dramatic quality and realism, a modern introspection, and a sensuous intensity of intellectuality are some of his characteristics. Bitter and even arrogant is his scepticism, very much in the vein of Montaigne; while his morbidity (see, for example, his divine poems, dominated by a preoccupation with Death) has been likened to that of Huysmans and of Baudelaire. If his lines do not achieve perfect fusion of ratiocination and feeling, they are impregnated with the reality of thought and the sinewy passion of meaning. To human experiences that are basically poetical, he gives vehement expression. While chiefly appealing to the intellect as the outstanding poet of revolt against conventional love, Donne is essentially a romantic by reason of an intense individuality.[1] One may think of him always as Dr. John Donne the Divine and John Donne the Pagan. (Compare him with Jonathan Swift, 1667—1745.)

**George Herbert,** 1593—1633, poet whose tercentenary fell in the Spring of 1933. Educated at Westminster and at Trinity College, Cambidge (1609—1616); at the latter was University orator (1619). B. A., 1609; M. A., 1615. Took holy orders. A year after his marriage in 1629 to Jane Danvers, Lord Danby's kinswoman, he became rector of Fuggleston St. Peter's at Bemerton, near Salisbury, where his life of saintly piety was immortalized by Walton (p. 275). Without Donne's cultivated obscurity, brutal cynicism, concentrated passion, or morbidness; without Crashaw's ardor and melody. Sane didacticism and devotional spirit; humor; theme is the love and glorification of God. Generally considered a poet of the Metaphysical School, but need not be. Note that all his English poems were published posthumously.

***The Temple: Sacred Poems and Private Ejaculations*† (1633).** Preceded by an induction called "The Church Porch": quaint or poetical religious maxims and new instances on the practical relationships of life. Of the 160 poems that follow, revelatory of his spiritual history, among the best are "Vertue," "The Pulley," and "The World." Occasionally inverted imagery, fanciful simile, and stylistic tricks unable to muffle the ring of true metal in poems. Smooth, musical verse; dominant personal note; concrete imagery. Zealous piety, ascetic spirit, intense religious feeling. Most popular, but not his best poem, is "Vertue." Representative conceits: "The Church-Floore" has stones of Patience and Humility cemented by Charity; "The Collar" is the yoke of God from which the poet can not extricate himself: but it is more important as one of the early instances of *vers libre,* and most important for its revolt against servitude, its acceptance of epicurean pleasures—until the astonishing last quatrain calms his rebellious soul.

---

1 T. S. Eliot has pointed out that Donne introduced the metrical or conversational style into the lyric. (The former is numbered among the many recent poets upon whom Donne has had considerable influence.)

† * Explanation of symbols immediately precedes page one.

***A Priest to the Temple*** (1652). Humorous, gnomic, pious prose-manual that lays down practical rules for the guidance of the ideal country parson. Counterpart to *The Temple.*

**Richard Crashaw.** *c.* 1612—1649, devotional poet. Son of a strongly anti-papistical preacher. Educated at Charterhouse and Pembroke Hall, Cambridge. Fellow at Peterhouse, Cambridge (*c.* 1635). Ejected for refusal to subscribe to the Puritan's Covenant (1644). Proceeded to Paris where he adopted the Roman Catholic faith. Some years of great pecuniary distress. Secretary to Cardinal Palotto of Rome (1649). Sub-canon of Our Lady of Loretto (1649).

***Epigrammatum Sacrorum Liber*** (1634). While generally clever, some of the 185 Latin verse epigrams are of questionable taste. Famous line in the epigram on the marriage-feast at Cana: "Nympha pudica Deum vidit, et erubuit." ("The modest water saw its Lord, and blushed": has many parallels.)

***Steps to the Temple*** (1646). Ecstatic sacred poems. Includes *Sospetto d'Herode,* a translation of Giambattista Marini's religious epic, *La Strage degl'Innocenti* (*c.* 1610). Shows general influence of the Spanish Mystics. Indebted to Herbert on the spiritual side. Included also a profane or secular section, *The Delights of the Muses,* pretty if threadbare in content.

**Individual Poems†**

***The Flaming Heart.*** A hymn to Teresa de Cepeda, the charming, witty, and wise Spanish saint. Its general inertness startled by electrical fervor at the end: "O thou undaunted daughter of desires!" Anticipates *The Hound of Heaven* by Francis Thompson (1859—1907).

***Hymn to St. Teresa.*** Even better than *The Flaming Heart.*[1]

***Wishes to his (supposed) Mistress.*** Best secular poem. "Who'er she be."

***The Weeper.*** Its defects became more frequent as its 23 stanzas grew, between 1646 and 1652, to 31 stanzas. Pathos. Somewhat frigid litany despite the Magdalen's tears. Possibly influenced by Marini, and by *Francisci Redmondi Societatis Iesu Epigrammata et Elegiae . . . . Antverpiae . . . . M. DCVI.*

***Music's Duel.*** Contention between the lute-player and the nightingale. Paraphrase of the Latin of the Jesuit, Famianus Strada (1572—1649). Praised by Swinburne.

---

1 Bernardin, (*Brother*), "Richard Crashaw: A Catholic Poet," *The Irish Ecclesiastical Record,* XXXIV (1929), p. 168 *f.* (pp. 164-172).

† * Explanation of symbols immediately precedes page one.

*General Estimate.* Mingling of good, bad, and indifferent work makes synthesis difficult. At inspired moments, lyrical sweetness, unearthly and almost "electrical" fervor, delicate sentiment, subtlety of thought, wildly metaphorical but effective expression. Rises at times to ecstatic grandeur, as in *The Flaming Heart.* Greater than Herbert and Vaughan: his verse has been characterized as being "studded with fiery beauties and sudden felicities of language, unsurpassed by any lyrist between his own time and Shelley's." However, many *concetti* and symbolical obscurities, even in his better work. "Crashaw is primarily a European . . . . Indeed Mr. Mario Praz . . . . puts Crashaw above Marino, Góngora, and everybody else, merely as the *representative* of the baroque spirit in literature."[1]

**Henry Vaughan,** *c.* 1622—1695, poet, mystic. Known as "The Silurist" because he was born in Breconshire (Brecknockshire, Wales), a county included in the Roman district of Silures. Educated with his twin-brother Thomas[2] probably at Jesus College, Oxford (1638). Became a physician (*c.* 1645). At the death of his wife, probably married her sister. Last line of epitaph on tombstone: *Gloria! miserere!* ("Glory to God! Have mercy upon me!") Felicitous phrases, planned technique, effective organization; deep feeling, expectant yet hushed wonder, mystical yet close observation of nature.[3]

*Silex Scintillans: or Sacred Poems and Pious Ejaculations*† (1650). "Sparkling Flint" or "Sparks from the Flint" is a body of religious poems. Revelatory, now and then, of delicate feeling for nature and of spiritual moods ranging from ecstasy to sorrow; often, of dullness, frigidity, and banality. While influenced by Herbert, frequently surpasses the latter in depth of thought, intensity of expression, unearthliness of music; fundamentally more spiritual.[4] "The Retreate" anticipates not merely the "vocabulary and general use of language"[5] but essentially the central theme of Wordsworth's *Ode on the Intimations Of Immortality* (1807). Other poems are "The World" ("I saw Eternity the other night"), "Departed Friends" ("They are all gone into the

1 Eliot, T. S., *For Lancelot Andrewes* (1928), Chap. VII, "A Note on Richard Crashaw," p. 125 (pp. 117-125).

2 For Thomas Vaughan's influence upon Henry Vaughan, see Judson, A. C., "The Source of Henry Vaughan's Ideas concerning God in Nature," *Studies in Philology,* XXIV (1927), pp. 592-606; Smith, A. J. M., "Some Relations between Henry Vaughan and Thomas Vaughan," *Papers of the Michigan Academy of Science, Arts, and Letters,* XVIII (1933), pp. 551-561; Clough, W. O., "Henry Vaughan and the Hermetic Philosophy," *Publications of the Modern Language Association of America,* XLVIII (1933), pp. 1108-1130.

3 Judson, A. C., "Henry Vaughan as a Nature Poet," *Publications of the Modern Language Association of America,* XLII (1927), pp. 146-156; Holmes, Elizabeth, *Henry Vaughan and the Hermetic Philosophy* (1932).

4 Hartley, L. C., "Henry Vaughan," *The Manchester Quarterly,* XL (1921), pp. 170-177 (pp. 153-177).

5 Blunden, Edmund, "On the Poems of Henry Vaughan," *The London Mercury,* XV (1926-1927), p. 74 *f.* (pp. 59-75).

† * Explanation of symbols immediately precedes page one.

world of light"), "Beyond the Veil," "The Lampe," "Peace," "The Night," and (the original conclusion of) "The Shepherds." Most of the selections of Vaughan in anthologies are likely to be truncated.

***Olor Iscanus*** (1651). Secular verse, the title of which is derived from opening lines addressed to the Isca ("The Swan of Usk": by which he had already become known). "To Amoret, of the Difference 'twixt him, and other Lovers, and what true Love is" reveals plagiarisms from Donne (p. 254).

***The Mount of Olives*** (1652). Life of Paulinus. Partly translation, partly original. (Also has a poem in *Silex Scintillans* called "Mount of Olives.")

## THE CAVALIER POETS

**Thomas Carew** (pronounced "Carey"), *c.* 1595—*c.* 1639, poet. Son of Sir Matthew Carey. Obtained degree at Oxford (1611). Travelled to Italy with Ambassador Carleton, whose secretary he later became. Went to France as one of Lord Herbert's train (1619). Gentleman of the privy chamber (1628). Taster-in-ordinary to the King (1630). Friend of Suckling. Brilliant wit, lover of women and rime. Skilfully polished verse, neat and tuneful phrase, mastery of the overlapped heroic couplet. Second only to Herrick, lacking the latter's warmth and love of nature, but possessing a sensuous fancy and a becoming virility.

***Coelum Britannicum*** (1634). Sublime masque.

***Elegy upon the Death of Dr. Dunne.*** Sound estimate of Donne's place in poetry.

***Poems***† (1640). Reveals the two-sided influence of Jonson and Donne. Best in his shorter lyrics: "Ask me no more where Jove bestows"; "To my Inconstant Mistress" ("When thou, poor Excommunicate"); "Mediocrity in Love Rejected" ("Give me more love"); "Disdain Returned" ("He that loves a rosy cheek"). Best of his longer poems is "A Rapture," audaciously amatory and "marred" by unreticent passionate "impurity," emphasizing the physical (and to some the "perverted") side of love much in the way of Aretino and Donne. In the latter poem his expressions, metaphysical either through volition or constraint, are not inappropriately imaginative; *e. g.*, "And we will coyne young *Cupids,*" and taste "The warme firme Apple, tipt with corall berry." Two of his most common stanzaic structures are *ababcc* and *ababb.*[1]

---

1 Sembower, C. J., "A Note on the Verse Structure of Carew," in *Studies in Language and Literature in celebration of the Seventieth Birthday of James Morgan Hart* (Henry Holt and Company, 1910), pp. 456-466.

† * Explanation of symbols immediately precedes page one.

**Sir John Suckling,** 1609—1642, poet, soldier, inventor of cribbage. Educated at Trinity College, Cambridge (1623). Entered at Gray's Inn (1627). Travelled in France and Italy. Implicated in the abortive army plot to rescue Strafford from the Tower (1641), he fled to France and finally to Spain, where he was imprisoned by the Spanish Inquisition for a time. Died by taking poison. As a lyricist, light and tuneful, never involved; mercurial humor, strutting insolence, adamant cynicism, careless technique.

***Aglaura*** (*c.* 1638). Elaborately-mounted masque. Complicated plot. Famous for having two fifth acts, one tragic, the other not. Allusions to contemporaneous affectations and politics. Rememberable, as are his other plays, for his lyrics. Most famous: "Why so pale and wan, fond lover?"

***The Goblins*** (1638). Possibly an exaggeration to describe it, conventionally, as a sprightly comedy. Thieves disguise themselves as devils.

***Brennoralt*** (1639). Tragedy. An attack upon the Scotch. (Originally, *The Discontented Colonel.*)

***Fragmenta Aurea*** (1646). Contains letters, parodies, and three plays; and *An Account of Religion by Reason,* a limpid prose tract against Socinianism. His poems include the ironical "Out upon it, I have loved"; his best poem, "When, dearest, I but think of thee"; and the racy, delightful (and most popular) "A Ballade upon a Wedding," an unconventional epithalamium upon Roger Boyle, First Earl of Orrery, and Lady Margaret Howard. (Original title of the last-named poem was "A Ballade: A Discourse between two Countrey-men.")

***A Sessions of the Poets*** (1637; in *Fragmenta Aurea*). Aptly-phrased if unpoetical satire in which the day's versifiers meet with Apollo as Chairman to choose the wearer of the laurel wreath or crown, which goes to neither Jonson nor Carew but to an alderman.

**Richard Lovelace,** 1618—1658, poet. Educated at Charterhouse and at Gloucester Hall, Oxford. Heir to great Kentish estates. Imprisoned for seven weeks for petitioning the Commons in the King's favor (1642). Took part in the siege of Dunkirk (1646). Again imprisoned (1648). Spent his estate, and died in hopeless poverty. Because of his striking beauty, irregular life, and romantic career, Samuel Richardson used his name for the hero of *Clarissa Harlowe* (1747—1748).

***Lucasta*** (1649). ***Lucasta: Posthume Poems***† (1659). In the main his poems are original but inferior—laboredly elaborate, elliptically metaphysical, pruriently cynical, boringly dull.[1] Immortalized, however, by "The Grassehopper" (his best long poem, even if it is fre-

1 But see *The Poems of Richard Lovelace,* edited by Wilkinson, C. H. (1930), pp. LXVI-LXXI.

† * Explanation of symbols immediately precedes page one.

quently harsh and obscure), "To Lucasta, Going beyond the Seas," and, above all, for two perfect as well as chivalric lyrics, "To Althea, From Prison"—

"Stone Walls doe not a Prison make,
Nor I'ron bars a Cage;"

and "To Lucasta, Going to the Warres," with its last couplet—

"I could not love thee (Deare) so much,
Lov'd I not Honour more."

The last three are traditionally considered as identical with, and inspired by, his betrothed, Lucy Sacheverell, who had married another when a false report of Lovelace's death had reached her. (*Lucasta,* his poetic name for Lucy, contracted from *Lux Casta.*)

**Robert Herrick,** 1591—1674, poet. Son of a goldsmith who in 1592 fell to his death from a window. After ten years as an apprentice to his uncle Sir William Herrick, a wealthy goldsmith, Robert entered Cambridge (1613). B. A. (1619); M. A. (1620). Vicar of Dean Prior, Devonshire (1629). A sturdy Royalist, he was ousted by the Long Parliament to make way for a Puritan (1647). Regained his living through Charles II (1662). Not only the greatest of Cavalier poets but also the first of pastoral lyrists. Foremost of Ben Jonson's "sons," adding to his master's precision and sense of form a liveliness and grace. Imitates Horace, Catullus, and Martial[1]; but of essential originality. Dominant in his poetry is the love-element. Several of his love-lyrics are among the best in the language.[2]

***Hesperides; or the Works both Human and Divine of Robert Herrick*†** (1648). Collection of about 1,130 short secular poems—epistles, epigrams, folk-songs, eclogues. Some 70 of these are addressed directly to "Julia." His epigrams have generally been described as ugly and improper; but by a modern reader they are, except in a few cases, not considered coarse. Personal charm, delicate lucidity, Arcadian glow, exquisite play of fancy, pagan mood, immoral sense, hedonistic zest, Horace-like realism toward life; yet frequently his poems are artificial. Direct expressions of his love of books and July flowers, of wakes and bridal cakes; his is the *carpe diem* theme. Apparent spontaneity and technical ease are the result of careful workmanship; faultless knack of finding the inevitable word; perfect master of melodic meter. "To the Virgins, To Make Much of Time" ("Gather ye Rose-buds while ye may"); "Cherrie-Ripe" ("Cherrie-Ripe, Ripe, Ripe, I cry"); "To Anthea,

1 For his indebtedness to classical writers and elegists, refer to Pollard, A. W., "Herrick Sources and Illustrations," *The Modern Quarterly of Language and Literature,* I (1898-1899), pp. 175-184; Aiken, Pauline, "The Influence of the Latin Elegists on English Lyric Poetry, 1600-1650," *University of Maine Studies, Second Series,* No. 22, XXXIV, No. 6 (1932).

2 *The Poetical Works of Robert Herrick* (The Cresset Press, 1928, Vol. I), preface by Wolfe, Humbert.

† * Explanation of symbols immediately precedes page one.

Who may Command Him Any Thing" ("Bid me to live, and I will live"); "Corinna's Going A Maying" ("Get up, get up for shame, the Blooming Morne"); "The Mad Maids Song" ("Good morrow to the Day so faire"); "To Daffadills" ("Faire Daffadills, we weep to see'); "The Night-Piece, to Julia" ("Her Eyes the Glow-worme lend thee"); "Upon Julia's Clothes" ("When as in silks my *Julia* goes"); and "The Hock-Cart, or Harvest Home: To the Right Honorable, Mildmay, Earle of Westmorland" ("Come Sons of Summer, by whose toile"). Two of his marriage hymns: "Connubii Flores, or the Well-Wishes at Weddings" ("From the Temple to your home"); "A Nuptiall Song, or Epithalamie, on Sir Clipseby Crew and His Lady" ("What's that we see from far? the spring of Day").

*Noble Numbers*† (1648). Published in the same volume with *Hesperides,* it is the "divine" section of the book. Separate title page within, following *Hesperides* and preceding *Noble Numbers,* is dated 1647. About 270 sacred poems include "His Litany to the Holy Spirit," "A Thanksgiving to God for his House," "Prayer for Absolution." Of note is "The Widowe's Tears or Dirge of Dorcas." Unreality and lack of profundity are counterbalanced by sincerity, simple piety, and occasional emotional intensity. Because of this section, is considered as belonging as rightfully to the group of *Religious Poets* (p. 259 *ff.*) as to that of the *Cavalier Poets* (p. 262 *ff.*).

## TRANSITIONAL POETS: THE CLASSICAL REACTION

**Abraham Cowley,** 1618—1667, poet, pioneer in the essay. Educated at Westminster and Trinity College, Cambridge. M. A. (1642). Expelled from his fellowship at Cambridge by the Parliamentarians (1643). Later went with Queen to Paris (1646). Returned from exile (1656). M. D. (1657). Escaped again to Paris (1658). Finally returned with Charles II upon the Restoration. Poetry, while readable, is as labored and metaphysical (*e. g.,* "Drinking") as his prose is in the main naturally direct, colloquially lively, and gracefully brilliant. Was once considered the equal of Chaucer and Spenser, and even superior to Milton.[1] Of great historical importance: while retaining decadently the characteristics of the Metaphysical School, particularly its abundant elaboration of metaphors, he foreshadows the beginnings of the prose-poetry of "reason and correctness"—*e. g.,* in his adaptation of the couplet to the exigencies of narrative verse.[2]

### Poems

*Poetical Blossoms* (1633). Collection of five precocious poems, published when he was fifteen years old. Superficial beauty, empty

1 Nethercot, A. H., "The Reputation of Abraham Cowley," *Publications of the Modern Language Association of America,* XXXVIII (1928), pp. 588-641.

2 Nethercot, A. H., *Abraham Cowley* (1931).

† * Explanation of symbols immediately precedes page one.

thought; some melodious lines. Epitaph: "Underneath this Marble Stone," in *Piramus and Thisbe,* an epical romance written, according to Cowley's claim, at the age of ten. Song: "To whom shall I my Sorrows show?" in *Constantia and Philetus,* written when he was twelve.

***The Mistress*** (1647). Cycle of love-poems, frigid, passionless, cleverly affected, ingenious, metaphysical. Frequent imitations of Donne in the pretty "The Spring." Famous is the fourth stanza of "The Waiting-Maid." Best is "The Wish"—with its pleasant personal note.

***Davideis*** (1656). Incomplete sacred epic on King David is the first religious epic in English. Digressive, sluggish, elaborate, dreary, "conceited." Parallel in Crashaw's *Sospetto D'Herode.* Of significance only for its use of rimed decasyllabic (heroic) couplets.

***Pindarique Odes*** (1656). In a colorful but direct style popularized, more or less effectively, the outward form of the Pindaric Ode[1]; but could not capture the spirit of Plato's "inspired man." Set a fashion followed by Dryden, Gray, Wordsworth, and Tennyson. "To the Royal Society," a tribute to Bacon (p. 268).

**Plays[2]**

***The Guardian*** (1641). Brisk, racy comedy levelled against the Puritans. Subsequently revised and reissued as *Cutter of Coleman-Street* (1663). Concerns the love of Cutter and Tabitha Barebottle.

***Love's Riddle*** (1638). Weak pastoral comedy.

**Prose†**

***The Advancement of Experimental Philosophy*** (1661). Influenced the founding of the Royal Society.

***Several Discourses by way of Essays, in Verse and Prose*** (1668).[3] Eleven graceful, balanced, personal and anecdotal, mellow, conversational discourses on ordinary subjects; *e. g.,* "Of Greatness," "Of Solitude," "Of Liberty." Interesting for its biographical detail is "Of My Self." Easy verse and colorful prose competently harmonized with a Gallicized Epicurean tone.

***Letters.***[4] Some excellent ones to Henry Bennet, later Earl of Arlington.

---

1 Not infrequently it is asserted that the *Pindarics* are an invention of Cowley. Consult, however, Nethercot, A. H., "The Relation of Cowley's 'Pindarics' to Pindar's Odes," *Modern Philology,* XIX (1921-1922), pp. 107-109.

2 Nethercot, A. H., "Abraham Cowley as Dramatist," *The Review of English Studies,* IV (1928), pp. 1-24.

3 Nethercot, A. H., "Abraham Cowley's Essays," *The Journal of English and Germanic Philology,* XXIX (1930), pp. 114-130.

4 Nethercot, A. H., "The Letters of Abraham Cowley," *Modern Language Notes,* XLIII (1928), pp. 369-375.

† * Explanation of symbols immediately precedes page one.

**Andrew Marvell,** 1621—1678, poet, satirist, pamphleteer. Educated at Trinity College, Cambridge. B. A. (1639). Travelled for four years on the Continent (*c.* 1642—*c.* 1646). Tutor to Mary, or "Moll," twelve-year-old daughter of Lord Fairfax at Nun Appleton, near York (1650). Resulted in the Appleton poems in praise of country life. Secretary for Foreign Tongues to Milton (1657). Politician that he was, he accepted with equal readiness Charles I, Cromwell, and Charles II. Member of Parliament (1659—1678). His satires and pamphlets have an historical significance. Not infrequently fresh and rich in imagery, sweet and virile in their notes; conceits are imaginative as well as intellectual. However, often bitter and abusive; singularly fanciful and unequal in his poetry; often indiscreet in his conceits, as in *Eyes and Tears, The Match.*

**Poems†**

***An Horatian Ode upon Cromwel's Return from Ireland*** (1650). Poem stately despite some inert figures and almost grating constructions; meter is Marvell's invention. Not merely encomiastic verses on the Lord Protector but also princely stanzas describing Charles I on the scaffold. James Russell Lowell has rated it "the most truly classic in our language."

***To his Coy Mistress.*** Slow movement gathers speed with every line: a Cavalier piece where the concentrated conceits are happily turned in quick succession and where the last four lines rise to a crescendo of fury, deftly catching up and relating the images to human existence.

***The Garden.*** Free, beautiful translation of his own Latin poem, *Hortus.*

***Upon the Hill and Grove at Bill-borow.*** An Appleton poem Wordsworthian in its sweet strength.

***Upon Appleton House, to my Lord Fairfax.*** Like Wordsworth (1770—1850), chooses the song of the dove rather than that of the nightingale. Pleasant observation of nature, but long and tedious.

***Bermudas.*** Beautiful Puritan song in which a group of exiles offer praise to God on approaching those islands.

***On Mr. Milton's Paradise lost.*** Verses in praise of Milton.

***The Nymph complaining for the death of her Faun.*** Pretty artificiality; many *concetti.*

**Satires†**

***The last Instructions to a Painter*** (1667). Presents England without a fleet in contrast to the activity of the Dutch. Scurrilous. Like his other satires, political, timely, and biting in nature. Title derived from Waller's panegyric on the Duke of York's naval victory (1666).

† * Explanation of symbols immediately precedes page one.

*The Rehearsal Transprosed*† (1672). Chief prose work attacks the corruptions of the Restoration (1660—1700). Controversial wit. Part mocked Samuel Parker, the Anglican champion, afterwards Bishop of Oxford. Praised by Swift in preface to *The Tale of a Tub* (*c.* 1696). Second part (1673) defends Milton's *Paradise Lost.*

## *SCIENTIFIC PROSE*

**Francis Bacon,** 1561—1626, essayist, philosopher, statesman,[1] scientist, jurist; "Father of Inductive Philosophy." Younger son of Sir Nicholas Bacon by his second wife Anne, second daughter of Sir Anthony Cooke, Edward VI's tutor.[2] Father was Lord Keeper of the Great Seal in Queen Elizabeth's reign. Trinity College, Cambridge (1573—1575). Admitted to Gray's Inn (1576). To Paris in the suite of the British Ambassador, Sir Amyas Paulet (1577). Travelled in Italy and Spain as well as in France. Death of his father (1579). Returned to England. Utter barrister (1582). Member of Parliament for different constituencies (Malcombe Regis, 1584; Taunton, 1586; Liverpool, 1589; Middlesex, 1593). Reader (1588, 1590). Friend of Essex (1592), in whose prosecution (1601) he later assisted. Knighted (1603). Received a pension of £60 a year (1604). Married fourteen-year-old Alice Barnham (1606).[3] Solicitor-General (1607). Clerk of the Star Chamber (1608). Attorney-General (1613). Privy-Counsellor (1616). Lord Keeper (1617). Lord Chancellor (1618). Raised to the peerage as Baron Verulam (1618). Created Viscount St. Albans (1621). Usually if somewhat loosely styled "Lord Bacon." Charged with bribery (1621).[4] Practically admitted, in a letter to the Lords, that he had received money. It was ordered that he be fined £40,000 (partly remitted), that he be confined during the King's pleasure, and that he be disqualified from sitting in Parliament. Released after some four days in the Tower, he retired to his family residence at Gorhambury. Died of a chill, contracted from stuffing a hen with snow, in order to test the hypothesis that flesh might be preserved in snow.[5]

His works are in three divisions: (1) Philosophical—*The Advancement of Learning, Novum Organum, De Augmentis Scientiarum, Sylva*

1 "But for his wise counsels and far-seeing statesmanship, British Settlements in the New World might have passed away as a dream or a tale that is told, and English might not be the language now spoken on the American Continent," says Cockburn, Sir John, "Francis Bacon as an Empire Builder," *United Empire,* XIV; New Series (1923), p. 277 (pp. 272-280).

2 Was Bacon the illegitimate son of Elizabeth, the Virgin Queen, and Robert Dudley, and therefore the legal heir to the throne? See Willard Parker's preface to *Francis Bacon, Last of the Tudors* (1924), by Deventer Von Kunow, Amelie; *The Personal Poems of Francis Bacon,* edited by Dodd, Alfred (1931), pp. 14-23, p. 223 *f.*

3 Bunten, A. C., *Life of Alice Barnham* (1928).

4 Refer, however, to Theobald, B. G., (1) *Francis Bacon Concealed and Revealed* (1930), pp. 383-388; (2) *Enter Francis Bacon* (1932), pp. 1-4.

5 ". . . . on the strength of the bronchitis, which followed a cold caught when the candle of his life was burning low, Bacon has been claimed, quite unjustifiably, as a martyr to experimental science." See Sturt, Mary, *Francis Bacon* (1932), p. 208.

†* **Explanation of symbols immediately precedes page one.**

*Sylvarum;* (2) Literary—*Essays, The New Atlantis, The History of Henry the Seventh, Apophthegms New and Old* (1624; a kind of jest-book); (3) Professional—*Maxims of the Law* (1630; pleadings in law cases), *Reading on the Statute of Uses* (1642; speeches in Parliament). Possibly better to consider his English as separate from his Latin works.

**English Writings**

***Essays*†** (Ten essays, 1597; Thirty-eight, 1612; Fifty-eight, 1625). Three collections of "civil and moral" counsels. Sometimes commonplace in their protean reflections and generalizations, his three-score essays frequently reveal acuteness of observation, acumen of intellect, and breadth of worldly sense. The stenographic and acid style of his earlier essays was gradually elaborated into the rich discursiveness and warm color of his later ones. Counsels for the practical conduct of life are nucleated by three staple subjects: (1) Man in his relation to a Supreme Being, (2) Man in his relation to himself, and primarily (3) Man in his relation to Society and the World.[1] Weaknesses include a tendency to "conceited" writing and an absence of emotional depth. Essentially has a loose style, the unit of which is the short clause. Rememberable for frequent Biblical and classical quotations, apt illustrations, brilliant aphorisms, extreme conciseness, balanced structure; for extremely prosaic common sense, crisp suggestiveness, planned elaboration of contents, luminous wisdom, intellectual elevation, knowledge of human nature. Traditionally considered more or less influenced by Montaigne, with whom he is frequently compared.[2]

***The Advancement of Learning*** (1605).[3] Philosophic treatise reviews the state of knowledge in his own time. Design is to clear away the objections to learning, to estimate its true value, and to analyze the methods of advancing knowledge. Subordinates Rhetoric to Logic, Imagination to Reason. Rhetorically-enthusiastic prose, flexible English, vigorous thought. Contains the essence of some of his famous essays; *e. g.,* "On Studies," "On Seeming Wise."

***History of Henry the Seventh*** (1622). Philosophical history, probing in its impartial analysis of events and psychological understanding of personalities. Aphoristic lucidity and right balance give point to his essential intellectuality and historical perspective.

***The New Atlantis*†** (1622—1624; published 1626). Unfinished philosophical semi-romance in the form of a "fable" devised for the

1 *The Essayes or Counsels Civill and Morall, of Francis Bacon,* p. XLVII *ff.,* edited by Worrall, Walter (1900); introduction by Smeaton, Oliphant.

2 *The Essayes or Counsels Civill and Morall, of Francis Bacon, pp.* XLV-XLVII, edited by Worrall, Walter (1900); introduction by Smeaton, Oliphant; Zeitlin, Jacob, "The Development of Bacon's Essays—with Special Reference to the Question of Montaigne's Influence upon Them," *The Journal of English and Germanic Philology,* XXVII (1928), p. 519 (pp. 496-519).

3 Williams, Charles, *Bacon* (1933), Chap. V, pp. 138-150.

† * Explanation of symbols immediately precedes page one.

purpose of exhibiting "therein a Model or Description of a College, instituted for the Interpreting of Nature, and the producing of great and marvellous Works for the benefit of Men, under the name of Solomons House, or, The College of Six days Works" (W. Rawley). While suggested by More's *Utopia* (p. 114), Bacon's ideal commonwealth[1] is narrower in range and less intense in its dramatic progression. Indebted to Plato. Among the advances anticipated by Bacon's university of research are: refrigeration, vivisection, artificial mineral waters, the telephone, submarine, and aeroplane.

### Latin Writings

Largest division of his Latin works was to be part of a great undertaking, which he called *Instauratio Magna,*[2] consisting in its final, half-finished form of six divisions:

I. *Partitiones Scientiarum.* This division is represented by *De Augmentis Scientiarum* (1623), a summary of existing human knowledge, and really an expansion into Latin of his *Advancement of Learning* (p. 269).

II. *Interpretatio Naturae.* The principles of the new art of interpreting nature are represented by the *Novum Organum*[3] (1620). Philosophical treatise. This "New Instrument" (for Man's interpretation of Nature and thereby his sovereignty over Her operations) describes the method to be used in order to universalize knowledge. The word "organon" was applied to the logical treatises of Aristotle: title of Bacon's work is a key to his main object, which is to replace blind submission to Authority and Scholasticism by Experience and Reason, to substitute for Aristotle's deductive method the inductive one. (While he did not invent the inductive method, he did demonstrate its potentialities.) Describes four idols (fallacies or phantoms) by which the mind is particularly prepossessed: (1) *Idola tribus* ("Idols of the Tribe"), (2) *Idola specus* ("Idols of the Cave"), (3) *Idola fori* ("Idols of the Forum" or of the Market-place), (4) *Idola theatri* ("Idols of the Theatre" or of the School).

III. *Historia Naturalis et Experimentalis.* Purpose is to collect data specially arranged according to the empirical principles laid down in Part II. Represented by *Sylva Sylvarum* (1627), miscellaneous observations primarily collected from books.

IV. *Scala Intellectus.* "The Ladder of the Intellect" was to consist of examples worked out according to his method. Only a short preface is left.

V. *Prodromi.* "The Forerunners, or Anticipations, of the New Philosophy" was to contain generalizations arrived at without using his special method. A preface is extant.

VI. *Philosophia Secunda.* "The New Philosophy" was to consist of the complete science of Nature formed through the facts of Part III and the methods of Part II.

---

1 Blodgett, E. D., "Bacon's *New Atlantis* and Campanella's *Civitas Solis*: A Study in Relationships," *Publications of the Modern Language Association of America,* XLVI (1931), pp. 763-780.

2 Steegmüller, Francis (Steel, Byron, *pseud.*), *Sir Francis Bacon* (1930), pp. 193-197.

3 Williams, Charles, *Bacon* (1933), Chap. VIII, pp. 241-254.

*Estimate.* Bacon's fundamental purpose was to extend and organize human knowledge brought to a common center by systematic observation and experiment. Neither the speculative idealism of the Neo-Platonists nor the barren subtleties of the Aristotelians held him. Not knowledge itself was his object but a practical science conducing to the ultimate establishment of man's sovereignty over Nature. He exemplifies best an intellectual activity found, for example, in the work of Giordano Bruno; he gave body to the later foundation of the Royal Society; he influenced the Lockian school and fathered "English psychological speculation" and "the empirical method in the department of ethics." His inductive method is opposed to the *a priori* method of Scholasticism. But caution must be taken against considering Bacon, the propagandist of induction, as a great scientist from whom modern science derives its general outlook, even if modern research implicitly uses his principles of inductive proof.[1] (For the *Baconian Theory,* see p. 170, note 1.)[2]

**Robert Burton,** 1577—1640, visionary savant, essayist, mathematician, bibliophile, astrologer, and divine. Educated at Nuneaton, and Sutton Coldfield, both in Warwickshire. Entered Brasenose College (1593). Student at Christ Church, Oxford (1599—1602). M. A. (1605). B. D. (1614). Vicar of St. Thomas Church, Oxford (1616). Rector of Walesby, Lincolnshire (1624—1631). Called himself "Democritus Junior." Influenced Ford's *The Lover's Melancholy* (p. 246); Milton's *L'Allegro* and *Il Penseroso* (p. 278); Keats's *Lamia* (1819) and possibly his *Eve of St. Agnes* (1819); Thackeray's *The Virginians* (1857—1859). Sterne plagiarized from him, in *Tristram Shandy* (1759—1767). Important influence on Lamb (1775—1834).[3]

***Philosophaster***[4] (written 1606; acted 1617; printed 1862). Latin comedy exposing charlatanism. Lack of construction; but entertaining in its humor and satire. Similar to Jonson's *Alchemist* (p. 229). Influenced particularly by the *Colloquies of Erasmus,* as well as by Plautus, Terence, Ovid, Cicero, Seneca, Virgil.

---

1 Levine, Israel, *Francis Bacon* (1925); Broad, C. D., *The Philosophy of Bacon* (1926).

2 Bacon's wide learning and universal experience have made him one of the contemporaries of Shakespeare to be credited with the Shakespearean plays in the so-called Bacon-Shakespeare Controversy. Among the most conclusive arguments against Bacon's authorship of the great English plays are the unpoetical quality of mind and essentially uninspired prose of his pen. See Selby, F. G., "Bacon and Montaigne," *The Criterion,* III (1924-1925), p. 263 (pp. 258-277); Bundy, M. W., "Bacon's True Opinion of Poetry," *Studies in Philology,* XXVII (1930), pp. 244-264. For a short, useful bibliography concerning the *Bacon-Shakespeare Controversy,* see Steegmüller, Francis (Steel, Byron, *pseud.*), *Sir Francis Bacon* (1930), pp. 198-208; also see Theobald, B. G., *Enter Francis Bacon* (1932), p. 14 *f.* Refer, also, to p. 170, footnote 1.

3 Lake, Bernard, *A General Introduction to Charles Lamb* (1903), pp. 61-91.

4 *Robert Burton's Philosophaster,* done into English for the first time by Jordan-Smith, Paul (1931).

***The Anatomy of Melancholy*** † (1621).[1] After a long preface, which includes practical suggestions (*e. g.*, on old-age pensions), he carefully dissects and analyzes the causes and symptoms of melancholia (I), and the cure (II); treats in a romantic-idealistic fashion of love-melancholy and religious melancholy (III).[2] New material added to each of the succeeding editions (1624, 1628, 1632, 1638, 1651—1652); its some 465,000 words are all readable. Endless Biblical, Latin, Greek, and French quotations, generally paraphrased, and apposite allusions pillaged from innumerable raids upon innumerable books.[3] Discursive essay style, with its winding, often disconnected sentences and euphuistic antitheses. Whimsical, learned, profound irony (rather than humor); strange charm, romantic earnestness, sensibility, and pathos; religious tolerance. To Dr. Johnson, it is "the only book that took him out of bed two hours sooner than he wished to rise"; to Sir William Osler, "the greatest medical treatise written by a layman"; to Arthur Machen, "a great refuge, . . . . a world of literature in itself."

**Sir Thomas Browne,** 1605—1682, classical scholar, antiquary, mystical philosopher; (according to Symons) the man-of-letters' prosaist. Born in Cheapside. Educated at Winchester and Pembroke College, Oxford. Travelled in Ireland, France, and Italy (1630—1633); continued his Oxfordian studies of medicine at Montpelier and Padua; obtained an M. D. at Leyden (1633). Began practise at Shipden Hall, near Halifax (*c.* 1634); later removed to Halifax (1637). Married Dorothy Mileham, sixteen years his junior; she bore him a dozen children. Knighted by Charles II (1671). Lordly if hyperlatinated eloquence, and overpowering if chaotic imagination influenced Johnson, Coleridge, Lamb, De Quincey, Stevenson, and other writers.[4]

***Religio Medici*** † (written *c.* 1634; authentic edition, 1643). "The Religion of a Physician" is an erudite prose-confession of Christian faith, qualified by a mind at once religious and scientific. While at first he was claimed by Roman Catholics, Protestants, and Quakers, he was soon placed (1646) and is still listed on the *Index Librorum Prohibitorum*,[5] despite a gentle Anglicanism that makes him suspected of being a Catholic. Plea for the formalism of the Established Church, yet tolerant of other points of view. Some indelicacies; quaint expression, ingenious epigrams; a generous, if not over-parading, egotism;

---

1 An analysis of the work is presented by Osler, Sir William, "Burton's Anatomy of Melancholy," *Yale Review*, New Series, III (1913-1914), pp. 251-271; Osler, Sir William, "Robert Burton and the Anatomy of Melancholy," *Oxford Bibliographical Society Proceedings and Papers*, I, Part 3 (1925), (1922-1926; published 1927).

2 Reed, A. L., *The Background of Gray's Elegy* (1924). Depends rather completely upon Burton for a definition of "melancholy": Chap. I, pp. 1-26.

3 Jordan-Smith, Paul, *Bibliographia Burtonia* (1931), Chap. II, "The Theme and Principal Sources of *The Anatomy*," pp. 19-62.

4 Gosse, Edmund, *Sir Thomas Browne* (1905); Strachey, Lytton, *Books and Characters* (1922), "Sir Thomas Browne," pp. 31-44.

5 His writings "reveal the temperament of a good and pious man, 'of settled years and Christian constitution,'" says Tuell, A. K., "Sir Thomas Browne Again," *The Catholic World*, CXXXIII (1931), p. 189 (pp. 186-190).

† * Explanation of symbols immediately precedes page one.

restrained imaginative fervor, subtle irony, grave humor, quiet piety, unrivaled rhythm, sustained eloquence, complete faith. Cadenced style and sonorous vocabulary are its distinctions, although sometimes over-latinized and confusing.

***Pseudodoxia Epidemica, or Vulgar Errors***† (1646).[1] Longest work is an encyclopedic inquiry into the causes of mistaken popular beliefs; but while quaintly and pleasantly exploding popular superstitions, he accepts others as true, he himself believing in witchcraft, astrology, and alchemy.[2] Less gorgeous in style than preceding book. Accurate observation, quiet fun, recondite lore. Has had many forerunners and imitators. Some quaint and curious ideas discussed: "that Crystal is nothing else but Ice or Snow concreted, and by duration of time, congealed beyond liquidation"; "That a Diamond, which is the hardest of stones, not yielding unto Steel, Emery, or any thing but its own powder, is yet made soft, or broke by the blood of a Goat"; "That a Bever to escape the Hunter, bites off his testicles or stones"; "That Storks are to be found, and will only live, in Republikes or free States"; "That a Man hath one Rib less than a Woman."[3]

***Hydriotaphia or Urn-Burial; or, a Discourse of the Sepulchral Urns lately found in Norfolk***† (1658). Ostensibly comments upon the various forms of burial, and upon cinerary urns and their contents. In reality, a series of picturesque reflections on the mutability of mocking time and the futility of earthly immortality. Imagination fires the curious descriptions of burial modes; richly-embroidered diction harmonizes with learnedly elevated and elfinly mystical thoughts. Latinized monody unable to throw out of time its musical qualities. Vast sweeps of thought; *teste*: the concluding chapter that climaxes the thought: the perishable quality of all earthly memorials, from urn to pyramid, in perpetuating the memory of man.

***The Garden of Cyrus*** (1658). Quaintly-learned, discursive treatise in tasseled prose on the mystic qualities of the quincunx, or the figure of five geometrically arranged as in a die or domino ( ⁙ ) Elaborately wrought conceit. Points out how the quincunx is reproduced everywhere in nature and in art; *e.g.*, in the Gardens of Antiquity, including that of Cyrus. Coleridge has described him as finding "Quincunxes in heaven above, quincunxes in earth below, quincunxes in tones, in optic nerves, in roots of trees, in leaves, in everything!" (In same volume with *Hydriotaphia*.)

---

1 His *Pseudodoxia Epidemica* as well as his *Religio Medici* has had either forerunners or imitators, or both. Consult Keynes, Geoffrey, *A Bibliography of Sir Thomas Browne* (1924) pp. 186-208, 209-220.

2 For a discussion of Sir Thomas Browne's public view concerning witchcraft, in the case of Amy Duny and Rose Cullender, in 1664, see Lloyd, J. H., "Sir Thomas Browne and the Witches," *Annals of Medical History,* x (1928), pp. 133-137.

3 *The Works of Sir Thomas Browne,* (1928), edited by Keynes, Geoffrey. See Vol. II, pp. 87-99, 139 *f.*, 190-194, 293; Vol. III, pp. 265-267.

† * Explanation of symbols immediately precedes page one.

***A Letter to a Friend*** (written *c.* 1672; printed 1690). Written to one whose friend had died of phthisis. Introductory, in a way, to *Christian Morals*: concluding paragraphs of the former incorporated in the latter.

***Christian Morals*** (1716). Bundle of maxims lauding goodness, virtue, and truth. If intended as a continuation of *Religio Medici,* it is poorly executed, particularly in point of style.

## *THEOLOGICAL WRITERS*

**Thomas Fuller,** 1608—1661, divine, historian, antiquary. Educated at Queens' College, Cambridge (1621). B. A. (1625). M. A. (1628). Prebendary of Salisbury (1630). Rector of Broadwindsor, Dorsetshire (1634—1641). Married twice (1637; 1651). Chaplain-in-extraordinary to Charles II. Died from typhus fever. Tolerant Royalist and unfanatic radical. Sharp wit, notable memory, remarkable common sense; original, humorous, vivacious; erudite but not pedantic. Garrulous yet axiomatic style, gentle but quaint humor, grave attitude subverted by sallying conceits and verbal somersaults. A supreme punster.

***The Historie of the Holy Warre*** (1639). Vivacious account of the Crusades.

***The Holy and Profane State*** (1642). Sensible, personal, genial descriptions of some good and evil characters; *e.g.,* "The Good Merchant," "The Liar." Divided into five books. Other varied subject-essays indicate rules of conduct. Quotation: "The pyramids themselves, doting with age, have forgotten the names of their fathers."

***Good Thoughts in Bad Times*** (1645). ***Good Thoughts in Worse Times*** (1647). ***Mixt Contemplations in Better Times*** (1660). Series of wholesome devotional and moral reflections on himself, current events, passages of scripture. Bright, whimsical, honest, imaginative, sometimes fantastic, frequently wise.

***A Pisgah-sight of Palestine*** (1650). History-geography of the Holy Land.

***Abel Redevivus*** (1651). Only seven of the 107 biographies are by Fuller.

***The Church-History of Britain*** (1655). From the birth of Christ to 1648. Apposite, entertaining, sententious, erudite.

***The History of the Worthies in England*** (1662). Cyclopedia of heterogeneous, curious facts, valuable for information on provincial history and manners. Describes and comments quaintly and humorously on the manufactures of different countries; lists the sheriffs. Note its short biographies or "characters"; *e.g.,* one each on Archbishop Laud and on Sir Walter Ralegh.

**Jeremy Taylor,** 1613—1667, author, schoolmaster, greatest preacher of his day. Son of a barber. Educated at Gonville and Caius College, Cambridge. Nominated by Archbishop Laud, who had befriended him before, to a fellowship at All Souls College, Oxford. Chaplain to Laud and Chaplin-in-ordinary to Charles I. Rector of Uppingham, Rutlandshire (1638). Rector of Overstone, Northamptonshire (1643). After his capture in the Royalist defeat at Cardigan Castle (1645), he found refuge in Golden Grove, Carmarthenshire, where he produced much of his best work. Three times imprisoned(1654—1655, 1655, 1657—1658). After the Restoration he became Bishop of Down and Connor in Ulster, Ireland. Friend of John Evelyn (1620—1706). Often dry, impersonal, grotesque; but survives in English literature for his brocaded, sometimes florid, rhetoric and colorful imagery, Miltonic majesty of prose, and for his tolerant spirit.[1] Has been called the Shakespeare of the pulpit.

***A Discourse of the Liberty of Prophesying*** (1647). Most popular reply to the order for conformity to the Presbyterian service, and a strong defense of Episcopacy. Notable as a deliberate plea for universal religious toleration and charity of thought amid the conflicts of religious opinions; based less, however, upon the inalienable rights than upon the weaknesses of human beings.

***The Rule and Exercises of Holy Living***† (1650). Ripe wisdom on the duties and conduct of a Christian in this life. Probably influenced by St. Francois de Sales's *Introduction à la vie dévote.*

***The Rule and Exercises of Holy Dying*** (1651). His masterpiece points out the shortness and uncertainty of this life, and persuasively exorts men to prepare for the world to come. Platitudinous at times; arrangement not always coherent.

***A Course of Sermons for all the Sundays of the Year*** (1651, 1653). Includes his *Twenty-Seven Sermons* (1651) and the *Twenty-five* (1653). Real piety, charitable spirit, rhetorical beauties of prose, melodious majesty of sentences, magnificent rhetoric alternated with direct simplicity, lack of profundity but range and aptness of illustration—point to him as the English Chrysostom. (Surname "Chrysostom" means "golden-mouthed.")

***The Golden Grove; or a Manuall of daily prayers and letanies*** .... (1655). His great manual of devotions.

## *PASTORAL PROSE*

**Izaak Walton,** 1593—1683, idyllist, essayist, poet. Ironmonger. Retired to a country life. Married Rachel Floud (1626), who bore him six children before her death in 1640; married Anne Ken (1646), who

1 For an appreciation of Taylor's style and thought, see *The Golden Grove,* edited by Smith, L. P., (1930), pp. XXVII-LXIII.

† * Explanation of symbols immediately precedes page one.

bore him three before her death in 1662. Wrote elegies, epitaphs, occasional verses, letters. Favorite motto: "Study to be quiet." A careful artist whose apparently natural style enhances the charm of his personality.

***The Compleat Angler, or the Contemplative Man's Recreation***† (1653). Written in the form of a dialogue between Piscator (Fisherman) and Venator (Hunter: the first edition calls him Viator or "Traveller") who meet by chance on a fresh May morning. Each commends to the other his favorite pastime, but Piscator does most of the talking. Second edition introduces Auceps (Falconer). Further revisions permitted Walton to make material contributions consisting of technical details, poems, anecdotes, characters. Plagiarized, borrowed, adapted. Includes verse; *e. g.*, "Come live with me and be my love," and the milkmaid's mother's answer, "If all the world and love were young." Influenced by Dame Berners (p. 99), Gervase Markham's *The Art of Angling* (1614), Thomas Barker's *Barker's Delight, or the Art of Angling* (1651); and also by *A Treatise of the Nature of God* (1599).

Fisherman's classic reflects the author's philosophic personality. Prose pastoral, occasionally tedious to a modern reader, yet generally presents characters who walk, talk, and eat humanly. Interspersed verses and songs, quaint style, mellow kindliness, quiet humor, placid thought, "golden simplicity," unadorned rural descriptions, companionable garrulity, charitable spirit. (A continuation supplied by Charles Cotton, 1630—1687, in the fifth or 1676 edition is in the main a supplementary dialogue between Piscator Junior and Viator upon fly-fishing.)

***Lives*** (1640—1678). Delightful biographies in miniature of Dr. John Donne (1640), Sir Henry Wotton (1651), Richard Hooker (1665, separate volume), George Herbert (1670), and Bishop Robert Sanderson (1678). Knew most of these men personally. Excellent but one-sided analysis of Donne.

***Love and Truth*** (1680). Two serious letters probably by Walton.

---

† * Explanation of symbols immediately precedes page one.

## Chapter XIV

# THE AGE OF MILTON: JOHN MILTON

**John Milton,** 1608—1674, epic poet, sonnet writer, greatest pamphleteer of his day. Born in London, December 9, 1608. Son of a refined mother, Sarah Jeffrey, and a broad-minded Puritan banker-lawyer of the humbler sort, named John Milton. Educated at St. Paul's School (1620) and at Christ's College, Cambridge (1625—1632), where he was unpopularly known as "The Lady" or "The Lady of Christ's" (Christ's College), probably because of the almost feminine beauty of his features, slender build, chasteness of manners, and haughty seriousness.[1] B. A., 1629; M. A., 1632. Being out of sympathy with the High Church or Anglican hierarchy, Milton revoked his intention of taking holy orders, and resolved to devote himself to literature. The next six years he spent studying and writing, at his father's country home at Horton in Buckinghamshire (1632—1638). In the spring of 1638 he set out on a journey to the Continent, spending most of his time in Italy in the company of the choicest scholars, who appreciated Milton's art. When in the summer of 1639 disquieting rumors reached him of the impending break at home between the King and the Parliament, he started to return to England. He thought it base, he explained later, to be traveling at his ease in intellectual pursuits while his fellow-countrymen were fighting at home for liberty. (Thus ended his first period, that of his Formal Education and Early Poems.)

For ten years he settled down as a writer and a private tutor. Marriage (1642)[2] to Mary Powell, seventeen-year-old daughter of Royalist parents, resulted in much friction[3]; only a few weeks passed before she fled to her family, and not until 1645, when the Cavalier cause was ruined, did she seek and accomplish a reconciliation with her husband. (She bore Milton four children.) Meanwhile Milton published numerous tracts on political, social, and religious subjects.

---

1 Milton was an albino, says Mutschmann, Heinrich, *The Secret of John Milton* (1925). This charge has of course been attacked. Consult references to Milton's blindness, Note 1 on page 278. Professor T. O. Mabbott, in a letter, states that "the portrait now reproduced in the Columbia University edition (Volume I) in colors, combats this theory completely. Milton's eyes are *dark*. All blondes are sensitive to light."

2 Martin, Burns, "The Date of Milton's Marriage," *Studies in Philology,* XXV (1928), pp. 457-461; Wright, B. A., (1) "Milton's First Marriage," *The Modern Language Review,* XXVI (1931), pp. 383-400; (2) *The Modern Language Review,* XXVII (1932), pp. 6-23.

3 That the marriage may not have been consummated is a theory advanced by some commentators. See Pattison, Mark, *Milton* (1900), p. 58; Saurat, Denis, *Milton, Man and Thinker* (1925), p. 55. His attitude toward women is revealed in *Paradise Lost; e.g.,* see Guthrie, A.M.B., *Wordsworth and Tolstoi and Other Papers* (1922), "Milton and Shakespeare as Lovers," pp. 37-73.

In 1647 he gave up teaching, for the death of his father in the preceding year had made circumstances easier. Foreign Secretary under the Commonwealth government (March, 1649). Became totally blind (*c.* 1652).[1] Wife died (1652), leaving him with three young daughters. Married Catharine Woodcock (1656), who died in 1658. The *Restoration* (1660) changed his fortunes once again. (Thus ended his second period, that of his Political Activity.)

With the *Restoration* (1660), Milton was arrested, fined, and imprisoned for a short time. Married Elizabeth Minshull (1663), a girl in her early twenties, who survived him. Until his death on November 8, 1674, he lived in literary seclusion.[2] (Thus ended his third period, that of his Culminating Powers.)

## *FIRST PERIOD: POETRY TO 1640*

### Major Poems

***On the Morning of Christ's Nativity*** (1629). Ode on the common theme of the victory of the newly-born child over the pagan deities. Influenced by Spenser, and by contemporaneous pastoral poets; yet foreshadows *Paradise Lost.* Its too many far-fetched, almost baroque ideas ("conceits," said Warton) go, however, beyond mere intellectual gymnastics into a poetic mould ("perhaps the most beautiful ode in the language," said Hallam). Skilled construction, different meters, sure if elaborate expression, humanistic tone, grand conception.

***L'Allegro*** and ***Il Penseroso***† (*c.* 1632—1634).[3] Twin idealized visions contrasting the cheerful with the contemplative man—the invocation to "heart-easing" Mirth with that to "sage and holy" Melancholy: Milton's momentary gayety vies with his characteristic pensive meditation. Sensuous appeals and consummate perfection of melodic expression. Octosyllabic couplet handled with ease and variety: except for the first ten lines of each poem in iambic trimeter alternating with pentameter, both are prevailingly in iambic tetrameter lines arranged in couplets. Influenced by Burton's *Anatomy of Melancholy* (p. 272), Beaumont and Fletcher's *Nice Valour,* and one of Nicholas Breton's lyrics.

***Arcades*** (*c.* 1630—1632). Slight, imaginative, and serene masque presented to the Countess-Dowager of Derby. Fragment consists of three songs (notably, "O'er the smooth enamelled green") and a recita-

1 Sorsby, Arnold, "On the Nature of Milton's Blindness," *British Journal of Ophthalmology* (1930), pp. 339-354; Wilmer, W. H., "The Blindness of Milton," *The Journal of English and Germanic Philology,* XXXII (1933), pp. 301-315; Brown, E. G., *Milton's Blindness* (1934).

2 Was Milton's body disinterred and despoiled by souvenir hunters in 1790? Question discussed by Reed, A. W., "The Disinterment of Milton's Remains," *Publications of the Modern Language Association of America,* XLV (1930) pp. 1050-1068.

3 Possibly 1631, according to Tillyard, E. M. W., *Milton: L'Allegro and Il Penseroso* (1932), p. 18; Parker, W. R., "Some Problems in the Chronology of Milton's Early Poems," *The Review of English Studies,* XI (1935), pp. 276-283.

† * **Explanation of symbols immediately precedes page one.**

tion in pentameter couplets. Henry Lawes, at whose request *Arcades* was composed, probably acted the Genius of the Wood who, in decasyllabic couplets, addresses the Countess.

***A Mask Presented at Ludlow-Castle*†;** known as **Comus** (1634). Masque-pageant presented on Michaelmas Night (September 29), 1634, in honor of John Egerton, second Viscount Brackley and first Earl of Bridgewater, whose entry upon the Presidency of Wales came two years after his appointment in 1631 as Lord President of Wales and of the Marches. With the assistance of Thyrsis (the Attendant Spirit), two brothers in search of their sister astray in a forest at last find her; but she has been saved from her imprisoner Comus, the personification of Revelry, by her unassailable virtue. The Attendant Spirit (acted by Henry Lawes) closes the performance by urging the audience to "Love Virtue; she alone is free." Puritan allegory on the triumph of Chastity over the god of Revelry and his crew is a protest against the carnality of the day. Somewhat stiff approach and poor dialogue redeemed by exquisite poetical elaboration and sublime uninterrupted passages; while the verse, generally more graceful than Milton's later manner, only occasionally anticipates his characteristic grandeur by "the introduction of certain unusually heavy feet."[1] Lyric: "Sweet Echo, sweetest nymph that liv'st unseen."

Fictional source derived primarily from Peele's *Old Wives' Tale* (p. 155), with suggestions from *The Faerie Queene* (III, 12), *The Faithful Shepherdess* (p. 241), Erycius Puteanus's *Comus,* a Latin play, and Jonson's *Pleasure reconciled to Vertue* (p. 231). For the first presentation Henry Lawes set the songs to music.

***Lycidas*†** (1637). Supreme monody in memory of a college acquaintance, Edward King, who had been drowned by shipwreck in the Irish Sea on August 10, 1637. King, however, is only the nominal subject,[2] merely an excuse for a pastoral elegy. Adopts the classical convention or pastoral form of Theocritus, Virgil, and Bion. In the midst of the threnody nobly expressing his thoughts on true fame, Milton suddenly breaks out into passionate denunciation of the corruption of his times, especially of the recreant leaders of the English Church, and their neglect of moral literature, thereby sounding a few premonitory notes of the polemics of his middle period. Somewhat incongruously mingles pagan myths, Christian elements, and contemporaneous political and ecclesiastical problems.[3] Samuel Johnson, who found the diction harsh, disliked the rimes for their uncertainty; but

1 Hamer, Enid, *Metres of English Poetry* (1930), p. 86.

2 Stevens, D. H., *Milton Papers* (1927), "The Will of Edward King," p. 37 *f.* (pp. 35-38).

3 For his sources, consult Friedland, L. S., "Milton's *Lycidas* and Spenser's *Ruines of Time,*" *Modern Language Notes,* XXVII (1912), pp. 246-250; Sandys, J. E., "The Literary Sources of Milton's 'Lycidas,'" *Transactions of the Royal Society of Literature,* Second Series, XXXII (1914), pp. 233-264.

† * Explanation of symbols immediately precedes page one.

this subtle irregularity is the very thing that gives the poem distinction. Spenserian color and music, ornamental and allusive style; meter is iambic pentameter, with an occasional trimeter. Influenced by *The Shepheardes Calender* (November eclogue) and possibly by Castiglione's *Alcon,* a Latin elegy.

***Sonnets.*** See page 285.

**Minor Poems**

***On the Death of a fair Infant dying of a Cough*** (1625—1626). Refers to the daughter of his eldest sister Ann and Edward Phillips. Labored images can not muffle sincere tone. Fifth stanza best. Spenserian style; rimes *ababbcc* with a final Alexandrine. Stately line: "Yet art thou not inglorious in thy fate."

***At a Vacation Exercise in the College*** (*c.* 1628). First poem to express his ambition to compose an epic in English. Heroic couplet. Anticipatory of his sublime rhythm. Part of speech delivered at a holiday celebration. In Latin and in English. Originally formed a part of the *Sixth Prolusion* (p. 289).

***The Passion*** (1630). Uninspired fragment, full of commonplace conceits.

***Song. On May Morning*** (*c.* 1630). Freedom from metaphysical conceits. Pretty touch shows Jonsonian influence. Uses the rimed eight-syllable lines of *L'Allegro* and *Il Penseroso.*

***On Shakespear.*** (1630). Metaphysical poem in heroic couplets printed in second folio edition of Shakespeare. Jonsonian influence. Concluding couplet:

> "And so sepulchered in such pomp dost lie
> That kings for such a tomb would wish to die."

***On the University Carrier*** (1631). Light touch. Inspired by the death of Hobson, the carrier "who sick'n'd in the time of his Vacancy, being forced to go to London, by reason of the Plague."

***An Epitaph on the Marchioness of Winchester*** (1631). On Jane, John Paulet's wife, who at the age of twenty-three had died in childbirth. Tenderness and sweet purity marred possibly by its artificial and false ending, "No Marchioness, but now a Queen."

***On Time*** (1632—1633). Skilfully-sustained ode.

***Upon the Circumcision.*** (1632—1633). Ode in Milton's grand way.

***At a Solemn Musick*** (1632—1633). Inspired ode even more sustained in its rhythm than *On Time.*

***Sonnets.*** Nos. I—VII. See page 285.

**Miscellaneous Shorter English Poems**

These include *A Paraphrase on Psalm 114, The Fifth Ode of Horace, On the new Forcers of Conscience,* Psalms I, II, XXXIV, LVI, LVII, LVIII, LXXX—LXXXVIII.

## SECOND PERIOD: 1640—1660

## I. PROSE

### A. Anti-Prelatical Tracts

***Of Reformation Touching Church-Discipline in England*** (1641).[1] First controversial work, anonymously issued, points out that the progress of the Reformation has been obstructed by three groups —the Antiquarians, the Libertines, and the Politicians. Argues against the principle of episcopacy and urges synodical government. Poetical prose-parts.

***Of Prelaticall Episcopacy*** (1641). Second defence of the Smectymnuan side is an anonymous refutation of the patristic philosophy; *i. e.,* that episcopacy can be deduced from apostolic times. Answers particularly Archbishop Ussher's tract, *The Apostolical Institution of Episcopacy.*

***Animadversions upon the Remonstrants Defence, against Smectymnuus*** (1641). Anonymous, but not impersonal answer to Bishop Joseph Hall's *Defence of the Humble Remonstrance against the frivolous and false exceptions of Smectymnuus.* In dialogue-form between the Remonstrant and the Puritans. Frequently heavy and tedious; bitter, brutal humor. (Combining their initials, Stephen Marshal, Edward Calamy, Thomas Young, Matthew Newcomen, and William Spurstow had published a pamphlet attacking episcopacy, which was answered by Bishop Hall and defended by Milton.)

***The Reason of Church-government urg'd against Prelaty***† (1642). Chief interest, in his weightiest argument for the presbyterian as against the episcopal system, is the autobiographical elements: *e. g.,* his declared belief in "the honest liberty of a free speech" and his strict opposition to any imposed uniformity of belief. He also mentions, as he did in *At a Vacation Exercise in the College* and in *Epitaphium Damonis,* his intention to write an epic poem.

***An Apology against a Pamphlet call'd A Modest Confutation of the Animadversions of the Remonstrant against Smectymnuus***† (1642). Subverts the gross personal arguments against his moral life as made by Bishop Hall and his son by a great autobiographical passage on Milton's early studies and serious habits of life.

---

1 *Of Reformation Touching Church-Discipline in England,* edited by Hale, W. T., (1916).

† * Explanation of symbols immediately precedes page one.

### B. Divorce Tracts[1]

***The Doctrine and Discipline of Divorce*†** (1643). Main plea is that incompatibility of temper—"contrariety of mind"—is a just ground for divorce. Proclaimed "the supremacy of the substance of marriage over the form of it"; "the doctrine that marriage is a private matter, and that, therefore, it should be freely dissoluble by mutual consent, or even at the desire of one of the parties."[2] (See his sonnets, XI and XII, p. 286.)

***The Judgment of Martin Bucer, concerning Divorce*** (1644). Utilizes the pertinent chapters of *De Regno Christi ad Edw. VI* by Martin Bucer, German Protestant divine invited by Edward VI in 1549 to Cambridge as Professor of Divinity, in which book Bucer had argued that incompatibility is a ground for a marriage-annulment.

***Tetrachordon*** (1645). Takes its name from dealing with "the four chief places in Scripture which treat of Marriage, or Nullities in Marriage": Genesis, Deuteronomy, the Gospel of St. Matthew, and the First Epistle to the Corinthians. Less personal than usual.

***Colasterion*** (1645). Drearily refutes his opponents, including Herbert Palmer, William Prynne, and Daniel Featley.

### C. Educational Pamphlets

***Of Education*†** (1644). Statement issued as a letter to Samuel Hartlib, who had requested Milton's views on education. Purely ideal, in thorough harmony with conceptions advocated by humanistic realists.[3] Opposed empty scholastic exercises, urged that actual should supplement vicarious experience (useful information, however, to be drawn almost entirely from the books of the ancients), and outlined a course of study enormous in scope. Influenced by predecessors and contemporaries, particularly by Juan Luis Vives's *De Tradendis Disciplina,* a great (if not the greatest) Renaissance book on pedagogy.

***Areopagitica; for the Liberty of Unlicenc'd Printing*†** (1644).[4] Eloquent and noble classical oration for the freedom of the press and against the licensing system is as much a plea for free thought as it is a protest against censorship.[5] Act of Parliament on June 14, 1643,

---

1 His four divorce tracts are traditionally considered as resulting from his own matrimonial difficulties with Mary Powell. These pamphlets were addressed to the Parliament; and were attacked before it by Mr. Herbert Palmer.

2 Ellis, Havelock, *Studies in the Psychology of Sex* (1927), VI, p. 443 *f.*

3 Webb, W. A., "Milton's Views on Education, Their Present Significance and Value," *Educational Review,* LV (1918) pp. 136-148; Bundy, M. W., "Milton's Views of Education in *Paradise Lost,*" *The Journal of English and Germanic Philology,* XXI (1922), pp. 127-152; Ainsworth, O. M., *Milton on Education* (1928).

4 For a summary, see Jebb, R. C., *Areopagitica* (1918), pp. XXXI-XL.

5 Does Milton deserve the traditional credit for having "enunciated" an "ideal of freedom as an end in itself"? Consult Haller, William, "Before *Areopagitica,*" *Publications of the Modern Language Association of America,* XLII (1927), pp. 875-900.

† * **Explanation of symbols immediately precedes page one.**

had required the licensing of all books before publication; and a suit had been begun against Milton for publication of his divorce pamphlets. Give me, says Milton, "the liberty to know, to utter, and to argue freely according to conscience."[1] Ape not the practice of the Papacy and the Inquisition; fly not in the face of Moses, Daniel, and the Fathers. Abundance of classical and historical allusions; effective sarcasm. Title derived from a written speech of Isocrates addressed to the Athenian Court of the Areopagus. Memorable: "Though all the winds of doctrine were let loose to play upon the earth, so Truth be in the field"; "he who destroys a good book, kills reason itself"; "a good book is the precious life-blood of a master-spirit, embalmed and treasured up on purpose to a life beyond life."

### D. Political Controversial Works

#### 1. Tyrannicidal Tracts

*The Tenure of Kings and Magistrates*† (1649).[2] Endorsement of tyrannicide probably brought him the appointment in March, 1649, to the office of Secretary for Foreign Tongues. Clear argument in unruffled style maintains that men are by nature free, that their voluntary contract with a ruler may be terminated at will, that theirs is the right to bring a tyrant (Charles I?) to trial, to depose him, and even to put him to death.

***Eikonoklastes*** (1649). Political attempt to refute, section by section, the twenty-eight parts of the *Eikon Basilike, the Pourtraicture of His Sacred Maiestie in His Solitudes and Sufferings,* the putative autobiography of Charles I that was stirring up sympathy by supposedly revealing the pious character of the deceased King, almost certainly the work of Dr. John Gauden, afterwards Bishop of Exeter. Most interesting part of this tedious paragraph-by-paragraph answer is the introduction. Sources include *Eikon Alethine* . . . . (1649) and Thomas May's *The History of the Long Parliament* (1647).[3] (*Eikon Basilike* means "royal image," *i. e.,* the *King's Book; Eikonoklastes* means "image-breaker.")

#### 2. Tracts Answering Salmasius and Morus

***Joannis Miltoni Angli Pro Populo Anglicano Defensio*† (1651).** "Defence of John Milton, Englishman, for the People of England" is a chapter-by-chapter answer in 244 pages to the 468 pages of *Defensio Regia pro Carolo I* (1649), by Claudius Salmasius, Latinized name of a

1 Mack, J. F., "The Evolution of Milton's Political Thinking," *The Sewanee Review,* xxx (1922), pp. 189-205; Buck, P. M., "Milton on Liberty," *University Studies* (University of Nebraska), xxv, No. 1 (1925).

2 *The Tenure of Kings and Magistres* (1911), edited by Allison, W. T.

3 Lowenhaupt, W. H., "The Writing of Milton's *Eikonoklastes," Studies in Philology,* xx (1923), pp. 29-51; Whiting, G. H., "The Sources of Milton's *Eikonoklastes*: A Resurvey," *Studies in Philology,* xxxii (1935), pp. 74-102.

† * Explanation of symbols immediately precedes page one.

French scholar, Claude de Saumaise, who had been commissioned by the exiled Charles II to defend the latter's father and to indict the regicide government. Milton's answer, elaborated from his *Tenure of Kings and Magistrates* and *Eikonoklastes,* ridiculed Salmasius out of the court of Queen Christina. Erudition and excellent Latin style unable to leash Milton's vigorous attack. (Close work on this so-called *Defence of the English People against Salmasius* ruined Milton's eyesight.)

***Joannis Miltoni Angli Pro Populo Anglicano Defensio Secunda***† (1654). "Second Defence of John Milton, Englishman, for the People of England" is a reply to the anonymous *Regii Sanguinis Clamor ad Coelum adversus Parricas Anglicanos* ("The Cry of the Royal Blood to Heaven, Against the English Parricides"), published in 1652. Author was a certain Peter du Moulin; but Milton, attributing the "Cry" to Alexander Morus or More, a Scottish-French scholar intimate with Salmasius, levelled an interesting but crudely-toned and personal attack upon Morus, who had written the preface. Of autobiographical value; *e. g.,* he classifies his own prose works. To Tillyard, it is "the greatest of Milton's prose works, and one of the greatest of the world's rhetorical writings."

***Joannis Miltoni Angli Pro Se Defensio contra Alexandrum Morum Ecclesiasten*** (1655). "John Milton, an Englishman's Defense of Himself, an answer to Alexander More," places full responsibility for the *Regii Sanguinis Clamor* upon More, whose *Fides Publica* (1654) had disclaimed authorsip of the "Cry." Gross charges.

## 3. English Political Tracts

Includes *A Letter to a Friend, Concerning the Ruptures of the Commonwealth* (1659)[1]; *The Present Means, and brief Delineation of a Free Commonwealth .... In a Letter to General Monk* (1660); *Brief Notes upon a late Sermon, Titl'd, The Fear of God and the King, &c.* (1660); *A Declaration of Letters Patents of the Election of this Present King of Poland;* and—

***Articles of Peace .... Observations*** (1649). Dull political attack upon the agreement (1649) releasing Ireland from fealty to England—an agreement made by James Butler Ormonde, representative of Charles I.

***A Treatise of Civil Power in Ecclesiastical causes*** (1659). Argues for the complete separation of Church and State, and in favor of universal toleration (excepting toleration of Papism because its political representations are subversive of the State).

---

1 *A Letter Written To a Gentleman in the Country, touching the Dissolution of the ... late Parliament, And The Reasons thereof ....* (1653) is probably by John Hall. See Havens, P. S., "A Tract Long Attributed to Milton," *The Huntington Library Bulletin,* No. 6 (1934), pp. 109-114.

† * Explanation of symbols immediately precedes page one.

***Considerations touching the likeliest means to remove Hirelings out of the church*** (1659). Advocates withdrawal of State support from the Established Church.

***The Readie & Easy Way to Establish a Free Commonwealth*** (1659).[1] Desperate argument against the restoration of Charles II proposes that sovereignty be vested in a Grand Council sitting in perpetuity. Influenced by the ideal commonwealth of Plato. Attacked by press and pulpit.

***Of True Religion, Haeresie, Schism, Toleration*** (1673). Urges upon the Protestant sects mutual tolerance of minor doctrinal differences.

## *II. POETRY*

**Sonnets†**

Not one of his sonnets is strictly a love-poem, save possibly No. I and No. XXIII. While adhering in his English sonnets to the Petrarchan arrangement of the octave, he almost invariably dispenses with the division between the octave and the sestet—only once, in the sonnet on Cromwell, closing with a couplet. Sestet commonly rimes *cdcdcd* and *cdecde;* note the rarity of his end-stopped lines. Best are No. I, flawless in structure, felicitous if unoriginal; No. VII, the "best short expression in literature of the dedication of one's life and powers to God"; No. VIII; No. IX, interesting for its Biblical imagery; Nos. XI and XII; No. XV, the sestet of which is applicable to-day; No. XVI; No. XVIII, elevated, and sometimes recognized as the mightiest sonnet in any language; No. XIX; No. XXI; No. XXII; No. XXIII, a tribute to his second wife, who died in childbirth. Note the five fluent Italian sonnets, with canzone, addressed to a young lady of Bologna (II—VI). The sonnets are:

I. "O Nightingale, that on yon bloomy Spray " (*c.* 1630)
II. "Donna leggiadra il cui bel nome honora" (*c.* 1630)
III. "Qual in colle aspro, al imbrunir di sera" (*c.* 1630)
IV. "Diodati, e te'l diro con maraviglia" (*c.* 1630)
V. "Por certo i bei vostr'occhi, Donna mia" (*c.* 1630)
VI. "Giovane piano, e semplicetto amante" (*c.* 1630)
VII. "How soon hath time the suttle theef of youth," (1631)
VIII. "Captain or Colonel, or Knight in Arms," (1642)
IX. "Lady that in the prime of earliest youth" (1642—1645)
X. "Daughter to that good Earl, once President"(1644—1645)

---

1 *The Ready and Easy Way to Establish a Free Commonwealth,* edited by Clark, E. M. (1915).

† * Explanation of symbols immediately precedes page one.

XI. "A Book was writ of late call'd *Tetrachordon;*" (1645—1646)
XII. "I did but prompt the age to quit their cloggs" (1645—1646)
XIII. "*Harry* whose tuneful and well-measur'd Song" (1646)
XIV. "When Faith and Love which parted from thee never," (1646)
XV. "Fairfax, whose name in armes through Europe rings" (1648)
XVI. "Cromwell, our cheif of men, who through a cloud" (1652)
XVII. "Vane, young in yeares, but in sage counsell old," (1652)
XVIII. "*On the late Massacher in Piemont*":
"Avenge O Lord thy slaughter'd Saints, whose bones" (1655)
XIX. "When I consider how my light is spent," (*c.* 1652—1655)
XX. "*Lawrence* of vertuous Father vertuous Son," (*c.* 1656)
XXI. "*Cyriack,* whose Grandsire on the Royal Bench" (*c.* 1655)
XXII. "*Cyriack,* this three years day these eys, though clear" (*c.* 1655)
XXIII. "Methought I saw my late espoused Saint" (1658)

## *THIRD PERIOD: 1660—1674*

**Major Poems**

***Paradise Lost***† (written 1658—1665; printed 1667 in ten books; 1674, in twelve books, Bks. VII and X being divided into two books each).

Milton often had expressed an ambition to produce an epic poem in English (see his *Vacation Exercise, Epitaphium Damonis, Lycidas*). From some five-score possible subjects that he himself had listed, Milton, first choosing and quickly abandoning the plan of writing an epic nucleated by King Arthur, who was not a universal hero, selected instead the immortal theme of the Fall of Man. Milton himself announced the theme as one to "justify the ways of God to men" (I, 26). His preface, boldly defying the use of the popular heroic couplet, chose the pentameter blank verse of Surrey, Marlowe, and other poets.

POSSIBLE LITERARY SOURCES. His chief sources probably included (1) Scriptural and Talmudic writings,[1] (2) the *Iliad, Odyssey,* and

1 Fletcher, H. F., (1) *Milton's Semitic Studies* (1926); (2) "The Use of the Bible in Milton's Prose," *University of Illinois Studies in Language and Literature,* XIV, No. 3 (1929); (3) *Milton's Rabbinical Readings* (1930). Consult also Baldwin, E. C., "Some Extra-Biblical Semitic Influences upon Milton's Story of the Fall of Man," *The Journal of English and Germanic Philology,* XXVIII (1929), pp. 366-401. For the influence of the *Kabbalah,* refer to Saurat, Denis, *Milton, Man and Thinker* (1925), pp. 281-300.

† * Explanation of symbols immediately precedes page one.

*Aeneid*,[1] (3) St. Augustine's *Civitas Dei*, (4) Claudian's *De Raptu Proserpine*, (5) St. Avitus's *De Mosaicae Historiae Gestis*, (6) Du Bartas's *La Première Semaine* and *La Seconde Semaine*,[2] (7) Hugo Grotius's *Adamus Exul*, (8) G. B. Andreini's *L'Adamo*, (9) Vondel's *Lucifer*, (10) Caedmon (p. 12 *f*.), Marlowe (p. 156), Shakespeare (p. 160), Giles Fletcher (p. 251), and Phineas Fletcher (p. 252).

DOCTRINAL CONTENT. (1) God did not create the world out of nothing. (2) Christ is the son of God, but his inferior. (3) Absolute freedom of the human will. (4) In epitome, a belief in Reformed Catholicism, in Calvinism.[3]

COSMOGRAPHY. The Copernican system was known to Milton; but in his poem he chose to represent the universe by the older Ptolemaic system, essentially the geocentric view as found in Plato, Aquinas, and Dante.[4] Milton made this choice out of his belief that the Ptolemaic system was not only established in poetic and theological tradition, but also would be better adapted to his contemplated poetic representations.

METER. Milton chose pentameter blank verse. He stated: "The measure is English Heroic Verse without Rime,[5] as that of Homer in Greek, and of Virgil in Latin; Rime being no necessary Adjunct or true Ornament of Poem or good Verse, in longer Works especially, but the Invention of a barbarous Age, . . . ."

ARGUMENT. (I) The fall of Satan and his angels; the burning lake of Hell; the palace of Pandemonium. (II) The consultation in Hell and the decision to investigate the new world; Satan departs for it alone, passing through Hellgates, guarded by Sin and Death, and upward through the realm of Chaos. (The first two books are superb.) (III) God foretells Satan's success, and Man's fall and punishment; the Son of God is accepted and exalted; Satan, guided by Uriel to the Earth, alights on Mount Niphates. (IV) Satan's arrival at the Garden of Eden; Adam and Eve discourse on the Forbidden Tree; Satan's ejection by Gabriel and Ithuriel. (V) "To render Man inexcusable," Raphael is sent by God to Paradise to warn Adam of the Tempter's presence; also relates how and why Satan incited the revolt, and describes the creation of

1 Riley, E. H., "Milton's Tribute to Virgil," *Studies in Philology*, XXVI (1929), pp. 155-165.

2 Taylor, G. C., *Milton's Use of Du Bartas* (1934). Discusses the indebtedness of *Paradise Lost* to the translation of *La Sepmaine ov Creation*, entitled *Du Bartas His Divine Weekes and Workes.*

3 Milton is frequently recognized as one of the two great English writers distinguished by a marked hostility to the teachings of the Catholic Church. For a strengthening of the theory that he is a non-Catholic poet, consult Gertrude, Mary Rose (*Sister*), *Renouncement in Dante* (1929), Chap. v, pp. 93-114.

4 Orchard, T. N., *Milton's Astronomy* (1913); Warren, W. F., *The Universe as Pictured in Milton's Paradise Lost* (1915). For a fresh critical understanding of Milton's conception of interstellar space, see Nicolson, Marjorie, "Milton and the Telescope," *ELH: A Journal of English Literary History*, II (1935), pp. 1-32.

5 But see Diekhoff, J. S., "Rhyme in *Paradise Lost*," *Publications of the Modern Language Association of America*, XLIX (1934) pp. 539-543.

the world. (VI) Raphael narrates how, after Michael and Gabriel had fought against Satan, the Son of God himself had alone forced the hosts of Satan to leap from the edge of Heaven down into the deep. (VII) Raphael tells the story of Creation. (VIII) Raphael and Adam discuss the Cosmogony; Adam relates what he remembers since his own creation; Raphael departs after warning Adam against the coming catastrophe. (IX) The temptation and fall of Eve; Adam, out of love for her, also eats of the fruit: they are ashamed of their nakedness. (X) The judgment of God; Sin and Death build a causeway from Hell to the World; Satan returns to Hell; Adam and Eve supplicate the Son of God. (XI) The Son of God intercedes for Adam and Eve; Michael, sent by God to expel them from Paradise, prophecies the history of Man till the Flood. (XII) Michael continues the narrative: of the coming of the Messiah, his incarnation, death, resurrection, and ascension, and the history of Man to the second Advent; Adam and Eve expelled from Paradise.

***Paradise Regain'd***† (written 1665—1667; printed 1671). Traditionally said to have been composed at the suggestion of his friend, Thomas Ellwood. Four books relate the baptism of Christ, the proclamation that he is the son of God, his temptation in various ways by Satan, and his final victory over Satan: thus follows the temptations of Christ as given in Luke IV: 1—12. Finest passages in III and IV. Considered by Milton himself, Coleridge, and Wordsworth to be his masterpiece. Inferior to *Paradise Lost* in poised imagination and dramatic theme; but not in harmonious workmanship. Influenced by Giles Fletcher's *Christ's Victorie, and Triumph* (p. 252).

***Samson Agonistes***†(written 1668—1670; published 1671). Tragedy in blank verse and irregular meters. "Samson the Athlete or Wrestler" or "Samson in His Death Struggle" is limited to the final episode in the life of Samson as told in the Book of Judges (XIII—XVI). Cast in the form of a Greek tragedy, it strictly observes the unities of time and place, and employs the chorus and the messenger. Parallels in the lives of Samson and of Milton accentuate the interest: "He too was blind and 'fallen on evil days' living among the triumphant enemies of the cause to which he had devoted the best years of his life; he too had wedded a wife from among the Philistines and she had betrayed his fondest hopes; he too had driven from the field of battle a boasting Harapha in the person of the great French scholar Salmasius."[1] Lacks

---

1 Grierson, H. J. C., "A Note upon 'Samson Agonistes' of John Milton and 'Samson of Heilige Wraeck' by Joost van der Vondel," *Mélanges D'Histoire Littéraire Genérale et Comparée* (Offerts A Fernand Baldensperger A L'Occasion De La Trentième Année De Son Enseignement Des Littératures Comparées: Ses Collègues Ses Disciples Ses Amis), I (1930), p. 338 (pp. 332-339).

See also Hanford, J. H., "*Samson Agonistes* and Milton in Old Age," ***Studies in Shakespeare, Milton and Donne***, pp. 165-189, edited by ***Members of the English Department of the University of Michigan*** (The Macmillan Company, 1925).

† * Explanation of symbols immediately precedes page one.

warmth, color, and action; has no middle—but is memorable for its severe dignity, Job-like if rather bitter tone, the emotional efficacy of the chorus, and profound spiritual energy. Note the allegorical application of the life of Samson to English national affairs.

### Miscellaneous and Posthumous Works

***Accedence Commenc't Grammar*** (1669). A Latin grammar in English.

***Artis Logicae Plenior Institutio*** (1670). "A Latin digest of Ramist logic."

***The History of Britain*** (1670). Popular prose compilation covers period from prehistoric origins to the Norman Conquest. Based on Tacitus, Caesar, and Anglo-Saxon chroniclers. Interesting for personal views.

***Prolusiones Oratoriae*** or ***Prolusions*** (1674).[1] "Academic Exercises" in Latin, written at Cambridge in fulfillment of requirements for his degree. Public-pleading interesting for sidelights on Milton.

***Familiarum Epistolarum*** (1625—1666; published 1674).[2] "Familiar Epistles" to rich men such as Charles Diodati, to the Florentine grammarian Buommatei, to Lucas Holstenius.

***The Private Letters of John Milton*** (1674). Serious Latin letters, the longer ones better than the shorter. Urbane if rhetorical. See Letter XII: "To the renowned Leonard Philaras, of Athens, Ambassador of the Duke of Parma to the King of France."

***A Brief History of Moscovia*** (*c.* 1630—1635; published 1682). Latinistic prose-compilation from other sources, such as, according to Milton, the works of "Sir High Willowby," "Richard Chancelor," "Richard Johnson," and others.

***De Doctrina Christiana***† (1655—1660; discovered 1823; published 1825).[3] Logical insistence in Latin on man's free will and an unimpassioned denial of the Calvinistic theory of predestination. Reveals himself as an Arminian, an Arian, a Theoretic Polygynist, an Anti-Sabbatarian. Prefers reasons drawn from the Bible rather than interpretations made by man. Maintains that polygamy is lawful, pleads against the Incarnation, questions the immortality of the soul. Without his characteristic unbridled epithets.

***Milton-Ovid Script*** (*c.* 1623; discovered 1921; printed 1922—1924).[4] Series of 166 stanzas, asserted (doubtfully) to be an early work by Milton. Modern scholars generally discredit this supposition.

---

1 First translated by Tillyard, P. B., *Milton: Private Correspondence and Academic Exercises* (1932).
2 Professor T. O. Mabbott states that Milton's *Familiarum Epistolarum Liber* and *Private Letters* are all one work.
3 Lawson, Evangeline, "Milton's Theology," *The Open Court,* XLII (1928), pp. 407-413.
4 Candy, H. C. H., *Some Newly Discovered Stanzas written by John Milton on Engraved Scenes illustrating Ovid's Metamorphoses* (1924).

† * Explanation of symbols immediately precedes page one.

**Miscellaneous Poetry**

***Latin and Greek Poems.***[1] Includes seven elegies forming an "Elegiarum Liber Primus," ten poems in various meters on various subjects forming a "Sylvarum Liber," and eleven epigrams. Reveal Milton's excellent style and erudition. Most interesting are: the three Latin epigrams *Ad Leonoram Romae Canentem* (1638—1639), the hexameter poem *In quintum Novembris* (1626), the piece *Naturum non pati senium,* the Latin scazons *Ad Salsillum poetam Romanum* (1638—1639), the Latin hexameters addressed to the Marquis of Manso under the title of *Mansus* (1639). Most significant are: (a) *Elegie prima* (1625—1626), addressed to his close friend Charles Diodati, reveals his susceptibility to the beauty of young ladies; (b) *Elegie sexta* (1629), also addressed to Diodati, states his noble poetic creed; (c) *Ad Patrem* (1635—1637), avows his indebtedness to his father for encouraging support; and (d) *Epitaphium Damonis* (1639). In the last-named beautiful elegy, possibly his noblest Latin poem, composed in memory of Diodati, who had died in 1638, Milton announced his intention to write his succeeding poetry in English. It is the Latin counterpart of *Lycidas,* and superior to the latter in sincerity and purpose.

## MAIN CHARACTERISTICS[2]

***Prose.*** Milton's prose writing is principally of a controversial nature. He is frequently involved and cumbrous, pugnaciously scurrilous and abusive—even careless of euphony.[3] However, he has many passages of a swelling cadence, and has been called "the great architect of the paragraph." Throughout his unbridled personal invective you recognize the sincere utterance of a powerful mind.[4]

***Poetry.*** Standing between two ages, he nobly weds the Puritan spirit[5] with that of the Renaissance.[6] Matthew Arnold has declared him the only English poet who sustains the so-called "grand style"; but this statement may admit qualification, for there are not a few passages in *Paradise Lost* and *Paradise Regained* wherein Milton descends from the grand style.[7]

---

1 MacKellar, Walter, *The Latin Poems of John Milton* (1930).

2 See Havens, R. D., *The Influence of Milton on English Poetry* (1922), particularly pp. 637-684.

3 Thompson, E. N. S., "Milton's Prose Style," *Philological Quarterly,* XIV (1935), pp. 1-15.

4 For his political and social philosophy, see Raymond, D. N., *Oliver's Secretary* (1932).

5 But see Larson, M. A., "Milton and Puritanism—clarified," *Philological Quarterly,* IX (1930), pp. 308-311.

6 Among those who regard him as a man of the Renaissance are A. H. Gilbert, J. H. Hanford, and R. D. Havens. For an interpretation of Milton as an anticipator of the Romantic movement, consult Stoll, E. E., "Milton a Romantic," *The Review of English Studies,* VIII (1932), pp. 425-436.

7 Raleigh, Sir Walter, *Milton* (1913), Chaps. VI-VII, pp. 170-255; Langdon, Ida, *Milton's Theory of Poetry and Fine Art* (1924); Larson, M. A., *The Modernity of Milton* (1927), pp. 260-267.

**SUGGESTED MERITS**

1. Cosmic sweep of theme and sublimity of execution.
2. Sharp concreteness yet sustained massiveness of imagination.
3. Intensity of religious idealism and austere sublimity.
4. Profound scholarship, pregnant with classical allusions to literature and history and rich with classic idiom.
5. Organ-roll of linked vowel-sounds, prolonged periods, and solemn music.
6. Consummate master of English blank verse[1]—gifted in its varied movement and the placing of phrases, majestic in its flowing cadence, stern in its beauty, lofty in its tone, incomparable in its dignity.
7. Power of delineating character. Satan is his greatest creation.
8. Vivid, accurate description and presentation of nature.
9. Simple, sensuous, and passionate —thus following his own rule of poetry.[2]
10. Adaptation of sound and movement of verse to the meaning of the passage; unit of composition is not the line but the verse-paragraph.

**SUGGESTED DEFECTS**

1. Narrowness of sympathy; keeps aloof from the "rabble."
2. Puritanical zeal for holiness mars even **Paradise Lost.**
3. Occasional disfigurement by over-bookishness.
4. Egoism.
5. At times a deficiency in the dramatic spirit.
6. Little (if any) sense of humor.
7. Lack of action in some books.
8. Certain incongruities and contradictions.

---

1 *"Paradise Lost,"* writes Professor R. D. Havens in a letter, "is the fountain-head of English non-dramatic blank-verse."

2 Ker, W. P., *Form and Style in Poetry* (1928), pp. 175-184.

## APPENDIX A

# SUPPLEMENTARY LIST OF WRITERS[1]

À Beckett, Gilbert Abbott, 1811—1856.
Acton, Sir John Emerich Edward Dalberg, *first Baron Acton,* 1834—1902.
Adams, Sarah Flower, 1805—1848.
Adamson, Robert, 1852—1902.
Ainger, Alfred, 1837—1904.
Ainsworth, William Harrison, 1805—1882.
Akenside, Mark, 1721—1770.
Alexander, Sir William, *Earl of Stirling, c.* 1567—1640.
Alison, Sir Archibald, 1792—1867.
Alken, Henry, *fl.* 1816—1831.
Allen, Grant, 1848—1899.
Allen, Ralph, 1694—1764.
Allingham, William, 1824—1889.
Amory, Thomas, *c.* 1691—1788.
Andrewes, Lancelot, 1555—1626.
Angelo, Henry, 1760—*c.* 1839.
Anson, George, *Baron Anson,* 1697—1762.
Anson, Sir William Reynell, 1843—1914.
Anstey, Christopher, 1724—1805.
Arbuthnot, John, 1667—1735.
Armstrong, John, 1709—1779.
Arnold, Sir Edwin, 1832—1904.
Arnold, Thomas, 1795—1842.
Arnold, Sir Thomas Walker, 1864—1930.
Ashe, Thomas, 1836—1889.
Ashmole, Elias, 1617—1692.
Astley, Sir Jacob, *Baron Astley.* 1579—1652.
Atterbury, Francis, 1662—1732.
Aubrey, John, 1626—1697.
Auden, W. H., 1907— .
Austin, Alfred, 1835—1913.
Austin, John, 1790—1859.
Austin, Sarah, 1793—1867.
Aytoun or Ayton, Sir Robert, 1570—1638.
Aytoun, William Edmondstoune, 1813—1865.

Baffin, William, *d.* 1622.
Bage, Robert, 1728—1801.
Bagehot, Walter, 1826—1877.
Bailey, Nathan or Nathaniel, *d.* 1742.
Bailey, Philip James, 1816—1902.
Baillee, Robert, 1599—1662.
Baillie, Joanna, 1762—1851.
Baker, Sir Samuel White, 1821—1893.
Balfour, Arthur James, *Earl of,* 1848—1930.
Ballantyne, Robert Michael, 1825—1894.
Banim, John, 1796—1874.
Banks, Sir Joseph, 1743—1820.
Barbauld, Mrs. Anne Letitia, 1743—1825.
Barclay, John, 1582—1621.
Barham, Richard Harris, 1788—1845.
Baring-Gould, Sabine, 1834—1924.
Barker, Harley Granville, 1877— .
Barnes, Barnabe, *c.* 1569—1609.
Barnes, William, 1801—1886.
Barnfield, Richard, 1574—1627.
Barrow, Isaac, 1630—1677.
Barrow, Sir John, 1764—1848.
Bates, Henry Walter, 1825—1892.
Baxter, Richard, 1615—1691.
Bayly, Thomas Haynes, 1797—1839.
Beardsley, Aubrey Vincent, 1872—1898.
Beattie, James, 1735—1803.
Beaumont, Sir John, 1582—1627.

1 To facilitate reference, the arrangement of the authors is alphabetical. It is suggested that some information be compiled about each author in the list, possibly in the manner exemplified by the Charts in the *Survey-History* (pp. 21, 33-38, 61, 99). Note, however, that this supplementary list does not include the major writers treated in *Volume II—Since Milton.*

Beckford, Peter, 1740—1811.
Beckford, William, *c.* 1760—1844.
Beddoes, Thomas Lovell, 1803—1849.
Bellenden, John, *c.* 1495—*c.* 1550.
Benson, Edward Frederic, 1867— .
Bentham, Jeremy, 1748—1832.
Bentley, Phyllis (Eleanor), 1894— .
Bentley, Richard, 1662—1742.
Beresford, John Davys, 1873— .
Berkeley, George, 1685—1753.
Bertram, Charles, 1723—1765.
Besant, Sir Walter, 1836—1901.
Besier, Rudolf, 1818— .
Bickerstaffe, Isaac, *d. c.* 1812.
Birrell, Augustine, 1850—1933.
Black, William, 1841—1898.
Blackmore, Sir Richard, *d.* 1729.
Blackmore, Richard Doddridge, 1825—1900.
Blackstone, Sir William, 1723—1780.
Blair, Robert, 1699—1746.
Blakman, John, *fl.* 1436—1448.
Blessington, Marguerite Power, *Countess of,* 1789—1849.
Bloomfield, Robert, 1766—1823.
Bohn, Henry George, 1796—1884.
Bolingbroke, Henry St. John, *first Viscount,* 1678—1751.
Borrow, George, 1803—1881.
Bowdler, Thomas, 1754—1825.
Bowen, Elizabeth D. C., 1899— .
Bowles, William Lisle, 1762—1850.
Boyer, Abel, 1667—1729.
Boyle, Roger, *first earl of Orrery,* 1621—1679.
Bracton, Henry de, *d.* 1268.
Braddon, Mary Elizabeth (Mrs. Maxwell), 1837—1915.
Bradlaugh, Charles, 1833—1891.
Bradley, Andrew Cecil, 1851— .
Bradley, Edward, 1827—1889.
Bradley, Francis Herbert, 1846—1924.
Bradley, Dr. Henry, 1845—1923.
Bradshaw, Henry, 1831—1886.
Breton, Nicholas, *c.* 1545—*c.* 1626.
Brighouse, Harold, 1882— .
Brooke, Henry, 1703—1783.
Brome, Richard, *d. c.* 1652.
Brooke or Broke, Arthur, *d.* 1563.
Brougham, Henry Peter, (Baron Brougham and Vaux), 1778—1868.
Broughton, Rhoda, 1840—1920.
Brown, G. D., 1869—1902.
Brown, Dr. John, 1810—1882.
Brown, Thomas, 1663—1704.
Brown, Thomas Edward, 1830—1897.
Browne, Isaac Hawkins, 1705—1760.
Browne, Thomas Alexander, 1826—1915.
Bruce, James, 1730—1794.
Bryce, James, 1838—1922.
Brydges, Sir Samuel Egerton, 1762—1837.
Buchan, John, 1875— .
Buchanan, George, 1506—1582.
Buchanan, Robert Williams, 1841—1901.
Buck, Sir George, *d.* 1623.
Buckingham, George Villiers, *second duke of,* 1628—1687.
Buckland, Francis Trevelyan, 1826—1880.
Buckle, Henry Thomas, 1821—1862.
Budgell, Eustace, 1686—1737.
Bullett, Gerald W., 1893— .
Bunbury, Henry William, 1750—1811.
Burdett, Osbert, 1885— .
Burgoyne, Sir John, 1722—1792.
Burke, Thomas, 1887— .
Burnaby, Frederick Gustavus, 1842—1885.
Burnand, Sir Francis Cowley, 1836—1917.
Burnet, Gilbert, 1643—1715.
Burnet, Thomas, *c.* 1635—1715.
Burton, John Hill, 1809—1881.
Burton, Sir Richard Francis, 1821—1890.
Butler, Alban, 1711—1773.
Butler, Joseph, 1692—1752.
Byrom, John, 1692—1763.
Byron, Henry James, 1834—1884.
Byron, John, 1723—1786.
Bywater, Ingram, 1840—1914.

Caine, Sir Thomas Henry Hall, 1853—1931.
Caird, Edward, 1835—1908.
Caird, John, 1820—1898.
Calverley, Charles Stuart, 1831—1884.
Camden, William, 1551—1623.
Campbell, Roy D., 1902— .
Campbell, Thomas, 1777—1844.
Cannan, Gilbert, 1884— .
Canning, George, 1770—1827.
Carey, Henry, *d.* 1743.
Carleton, William, 1794—1869.
Carlisle, Frederick Howard, *fifth earl of,* 1748—1825.
Carlyle, Alexander, 1722—1805.
Carpenter, John, *c.* 1370—*c.* 1441.
Carter, Elizabeth, 1717—1806.
Carton, Richard Claude, 1856—1928.

CARY, HENRY FRANCIS, 1772—1844.
CARYLL, JOHN, 1625—1711.
CAVENDISH, GEORGE, 1500—*c.* 1561.
CECIL, LORD (EDWARD CHRISTIAN) DAVID, 1902— .
CENTLIVRE, SUSANNAH, *c.* 1667—1723.
CHALMERS, THOMAS, 1780—1847.
CHAMBERLAYNE, EDWARD, 1616—1703.
CHAMBERLAYNE, WILLIAM, 1619—1689.
CHAMBERS, SIR EDMUND KERCHEVER, 1866— .
CHAMBERS, EPHRAIM, *d.* 1740.
CHAMBERS, ROBERT, 1802—1871.
CHAPONE, HESTER, 1727—1801.
CHEKE, SIR JOHN, 1514—1557.
CHETTLE, HENRY, *d.* 1607.
CHESNEY, SIR GEORGE TOMKYNS, 1830—1895.
CHILLINGWORTH, WILLIAM, 1602—1644.
CHRISTOPHER NORTH, a pseudonym used by J. Wilson, 1785—1854, *q.v.*
CHURCH, RICHARD WILLIAM, 1815—1890.
CHURCHILL, CHARLES, 1731—1764.
CHURCHILL, RT. HON. WINSTON (LEONARD SPENCER), 1874— .
CHURCHYARD, THOMAS, *c.* 1520—1604.
CIBBER, COLLEY, 1671—1757.
CIRCENSTER, RICHARD of, *d. c.* 1401.
CLARE, JOHN, 1793—1864.
CLARENDON, EDWARD HYDE, *First Earl of*, 1609—1674.
CLARK, CHARLES COWDEN, 1787—1877.
CLARK, JOHN WILLIS, 1833—1910.
CLARKE, MARCUS ANDREW HISLOP, 1846—1881.
CLARKE, MARY VICTORIA COWDEN, 1809—1898.
CLARKE, SAMUEL, 1675—1729.
CLARKHILL, JOHN, *fl.* 1600.
CLERK-MAXWELL, JAMES, 1831—1879.
CLEVELAND, JOHN, 1613—1658.
CLIFFORD, SOPHIA LUCY, *d.* 1920.
CLIFFORD, WILLIAM KINGDON, 1845—1879.
CLIVE, MRS. CAROLINE ARCHER, 1801—1873.
CLOUGH, ARTHUR HUGH, 1819—1861.
COBBE, FRANCES POWER, 1822—1904.
COBBETT, WILLIAM, 1762—1835.
COCKER, EDWARD, 1631—1675.
COKE, SIR EDWARD, 1552—1634.
COLE, G. D. H., 1889— .
COLENSO, JOHN WILLIAM, 1814—1883.
COLERIDGE, HARTLEY, 1796—1849.
COLERIDGE, MARY ELIZABETH, 1861—1907.
COLERIDGE, SARA, 1802—1852.
COLLINS, ANTHONY, 1676—1729.
COLLINS, JOHN CHURTON, 1848—1908.
COLLINS, WILLIAM WILKIE, 1824—1889.
COLMAN, GEORGE, the elder, 1732—1794.
COLMAN, GEORGE, the younger, 1762—1836.
COLTON, CHARLES CALEB, *c.* 1780—1832.
COLVIN, SIR SIDNEY, 1845—1927.
COMBE, WILLIAM, 1741—1823.
CONINGTON, JOHN, 1825—1869.
CONSTABLE, HENRY, 1562—1613.
COOK, ELIZA, 1818—1889.
COOK, JAMES, 1728—1779.
CORBET, RICHARD, 1582—1635.
CORELLI, MARIE, 1864—1924.
CORY, WILLIAM JOHNSON, 1823—1892.
CORYATE, THOMAS, *c.* 1577—1617.
COTGRAVE, RANDLE, *d. c.* 1634.
COTTON, SIR ROBERT BRUCE, 1571—1631.
COUCH, SIR ARTHUR THOMAS QUILLER, 1863— .
COURTHOPE, WILLIAM JOHN, 1842—1917.
COVENTRY, FRANCIS, *d.c.* 1759.
COWLEY, MRS. HANNAH, 1743—1809.
CRAIK, DINAH MARIA, 1826—1887.
CREEVEY, THOMAS, 1768—1838.
CREIGHTON, MANDELL, 1843—1901.
CRICHTON, JAMES, *The Admirable*, 1560—*c.* 1585.
CROCKETT, S. R., 1860—1914.
CROKER, JOHN WILSON, 1780—1857.
CROKER, THOMAS CROFTON, 1798—1854.
CROLY, GEORGE, 1780—1860
CROWNE, JOHN, 1640—*c.* 1703.
CRUDEN, ALEXANDER, 1701—1770.
CUDWORTH, RALPH, 1617—1688.
CULVERWEL, NATHANAEL, *d.* 1651.
CUMBERLAND, RICHARD, 1732—1811.
CUNNINGHAM, ALLAN, 1784—1842.
CUNNINGHAM, JOHN, 1729—1773.
CURLL, EDMUND, 1675—1747.
CURZON, ROBERT, *fourteenth Baron Zouche*, 1810—1873.
CURZON OF KEDLESTON, GEORGE NATHANIEL, *first Marquess*, 1859—1925.
DAMPIER, WILLIAM, 1652—1715.
DANETT, THOMAS, *fl.* 1566—1601.
DARLEY, GEORGE, 1795—1846.
DARWIN, CHARLES ROBERT, 1809—1882.
DARWIN, ERASMUS, 1731—1802.
DASENT, SIR GEORGE WEBBE, 1817—1896.

D'AVENANT, SIR WILLIAM, 1606—1668.
DAVENPORT, ROBERT, *fl.* 1623.
DAVIES, JOHN, *of Hereford*, *c.* 1565—1618.
DAVISON, FRANCIS, *fl.* 1602.
DAVY, SIR HUMPHREY, 1778—1829.
DAY, JOHN, 1574—*c.* 1640.
DAY, THOMAS, 1748—1789.
DEE, JOHN, 1527—1608.
DELAFIELD, E. M., 1890— .
DELANY, MRS. MARY, 1700—1788.
DE LA RAMEE, LOUISE "OUIDA," 1839—1908.
DE LA ROCHE, MAZO, 1885— .
DELONEY, THOMAS, *c.* 1543—*c.* 1600.
DEMORGAN, WILLIAM FREND, 1839—1917.
DENHAM, SIR JOHN, 1615—1669.
DENNIS, JOHN, 1657—1734.
DE SELINCOURT, HUGH, 1878— .
DE TABLEY, LORD, 1835—1895.
DIBDIN, CHARLES, 1745—1814.
DIBDIN, THOMAS FROGNALL, 1776—1847.
DICEY, ALBERT VENN, 1835—1922.
DIGBY, SIR KENELM, 1603—1665.
DIGBY, KENELM HENRY, 1800—1880.
DILKE, SIR CHARLES WENTWORTH, 1843—1911.
D'ISRAELI, ISAAC, 1766—1848.
DIXON, RICHARD WATSON, 1833—1900.
DOBELL, SYDNEY THOMPSON, 1824—1874.
DOBREE, BONAMY, 1891— .
DODD, WILLIAM, 1729—1777.
DODDRIDGE, PHILIP, 1702—1751.
DODGSON, CHARLES LUTWIDGE, 1832—1898.
DODINGTON, GEORGE BUBB, 1691—1762.
DODSLEY, ROBERT, 1703—1764.
DOLBEN, DIGBY MACKWORTH, 1848—1867.
DOMETT, ALFRED, 1811—1887.
DOWLAND, JOHN, *c.* 1563—*c.* 1626.
DOYLE, SIR ARTHUR CONAN, 1859—1930.
DOYLE, SIR FRANCIS HASTINGS CHARLES, 1810—1888.
DRUMMOND, HENRY, 1851—1897.
DRUMMOND, WILLIAM, *of Hawthornden*, 1585—1649.
DRUMMOND, WILLIAM HENRY, 1854—1907.
DUFFY, SIR CHARLES GAVAN, 1816—1903.
DUGDALE, SIR WILLIAM, 1605—1686.
DU MAURIER, GEORGE LOUIS PALMELLA BUSSON, 1834—1896.
DUNTON, JOHN, 1659—1733.
D'URFEY, THOMAS, 1653—1723.
DYER, SIR EDWARD, *d.* 1607.
DYLER, JOHN, *c.* 1700—1758.

EARLE, JOHN, *c.* 1601—1665.
EDDINGTON, SIR ARTHUR STANLEY, 1882— .
EDEN, EMILY, 1797—1869.
EDGEWORTH, MARIA, 1767—1849.
EGAN, PIERCE, the elder, 1772—1849.
EGAN, PIERCE, the younger, 1814—1880.
ELIOT, SIR CHARLES, 1863—1931.
ELLIOT, JANE, 1727—1805.
ELLIOTT, EBENEZER, 1781—1849.
ELLIS, GEORGE, 1753—1815.
ELPHINSTONE, MOUNTSTUART, 1779—1859.
ELTON, OLIVER, 1861— .
ESMOND, HENRY VERNON, 1869—1922.
EUSDEN, LAURENCE, 1688—1730.
EVANS, SIR ARTHUR JOHN, 1851— .
EVANS, SEBASTIAN, 1830—1909.
EWING, MRS. JULIANA HORATIA, 1841—1885.

FABER, FREDERICK WILLIAM, 1814—1863.
FAIRFAX, EDWARD, *d.* 1635.
FALCONER, WILLIAM, 1732—1769.
FANSHAWE, ANNE, LADY, 1625—1680.
FANSHAWE, CATHERINE MARIA, 1765—1834.
FANSHAWE, SIR RICHARD, 1608—1666.
FARADAY, MICHAEL, 1791—1867.
FAUSSET, HUGH I'ANSON, 1895— .
FELL, DR. JOHN, 1625—1686.
FELLTHAM, OWEN, 1602—1668.
FENTON, GEOFFREY, *c.* 1539—1608.
FERGUSON, SIR SAMUEL, 1810—1886.
FERGUSSON, ROBERT, 1750—1774
FERRIER, JAMES FREDERICK, 1808—1864.
FERRIER, SUSAN EDMONSTONE, 1782—1854.
FIELD, NATHAN, 1587—1620.
FIELDING, SARAH, 1710—1768.
FINCH, ANNE, Winchilsea, Countess of, *d.* 1720.
FINLAY, GEORGE, 1799—1875.
"FIONA MACLEOD," pseudonym of SHARP, WILLIAM, 1855—1905.
FIRTH, SIR CHARLES HARDING, 1857— .
FISHER, JOHN, 1459—1535.
FITZGERALD, EDWARD, 1809—1883.
FITZRALPH, RICHARD, *d.* 1360.
FITZROY, VICE-ADMIRAL ROBERT, 1805—1865.

Fitz Stephen, William, *d. c.* 1190.
Flatman, Thomas, 1637—1688.
Flecker, Herman James Elroy, 1884—1915.
Flecknoe, Richard, *d.c.* 1678.
Fleming, Margaret, 1803—1811.
Fletcher, Giles (the Elder), *c.* 1549—1611.
Flint, F. S., 1885— .
Florio, John, *c.* 1553—1625.
Fludd, Robert, 1574—1637.
Foote, Samuel, 1720—1777.
Ford, Richard, 1796—1858.
Forster, John, 1812—1876.
Fortescue, Hon. Sir John, 1859— .
Fox, George, 1624—1691.
Francis, Sir Philip, 1740—1818.
Franklin, Sir John, 1786—1847.
Fraser, Alexander Campbell, 1819—1914.
Fraunce, Abraham, *fl.* 1587—1633.
Frazer, Sir James George, 1854— .
Freeman, Edward Augustus, 1823—1892.
Frere, John Hookman, 1769—1846.
Froude, James Anthony, 1818—1894.
Froude, Richard Hurrell, 1803—1836.
Furnivall, Frederick James, 1825—1910.

Gairdner, James, 1828—1912.
Gale, Norman Rowland, 1862— .
Galt, John, 1779—1839.
Gardiner, Samuel Rawson, 1829—1902.
Garnett, Edward William, 1868— .
Garnett, Richard, 1835—1906.
Garrick, David, 1717—1779.
Garth, Sir Samuel, 1661—1719.
Garvice, Charles, *d.* 1920.
Gauden, John, 1605—1662.
Genest, John, 1764—1839.
Gerard, John, 1545—1612.
Gerhardi, William Alexander, 1895— .
Gifford, William, 1756—1826.
Gilbert, Sir Humphrey, *c.* 1539—1583.
Gilbert, William, 1540—1603.
Gilchrist, Alexander, 1828—1861.
Gilpin, William, 1724—1804.
Gissing, George Robert, 1857—1903.
Gladstone, William Ewart, 1809—1898.
Glanvill, Joseph, 1636—1680.
Glanville, Ranulf de, 1130—1190.
Glapthorne, Henry, *fl.* 1635—1643.
Glasse, Hannah, *fl.* 1747.
Glover, Richard, 1712—1785.
Godley, Alfred Denis, 1856—1925.
Godwin, Mrs. Mary Wollstonecraft, 1759—1797.
Golding, Arthur, *c.* 1536—*c.* 1605.
Googe, Barnabe, 1540—1594.
Gordon, Adam Lindsay, 1833—1870.
Gordon, Charles George, 1833—1885.
Gore, Mrs. Catherine Grace Frances, 1799—1861.
Gore, Charles, 1853—1932.
Gould, Gerald, 1885— .
Gould, Nathaniel, 1857—1919.
Grafton, Richard, *d. c.* 1572.
Grahame, Kenneth, 1859—1932.
Grainger, James, 1721—1766.
Grand, Sarah (pseudonym of Mrs. David C. M'Fall, *née* Frances Elizabeth Clarke), 1862— .
Grant, James, 1822—1887.
Graves, Alfred Perceval, 1846—1931.
Graves, Richard, 1715—1804.
Gray, David, 1838—1861.
Green, John Richard, 1837—1883.
Green, Mrs. Mary Anne Everett, 1818—1895.
Green, Matthew, 1696—1737.
Green, Thomas Hill, 1836—1882.
Greenaway, Kate, 1846—1901.
Greg, Walter Wilson, 1875— .
Greville, Charles Cavendish Fulke, 1794—1865.
Greville, Sir Fulke, *Baron Brooke*, 1554—1628.
Grey of Fall'odon, Edward Grey, *Viscount*, 1862—1933.
Griffin, Gerald, 1803—1840.
Grimald, Grimalde, or Grimvald, Nicholas, 1519—1562.
Grosart, Alexander Balloch, 1827—1899.
Grose, Francis, *c.* 1731—1791.
Grosseteste, Robert, *d.* 1253.
Grote, George, 1794—1871.
Grove, Sir George, 1820—1900.
Guedalla, Philip, 1889— .
Gunning, Mrs. Susannah, c. 1740—1800.
Gurney, Thomas, 1705—1770.

Habington, William, 1605—1654.
Haggard, Sir Henry Rider, 1856—1925.
Hake, Thomas Gordon, 1809—1895.
Haldane, Richard Burdon, *Viscount*, 1856—1928.
Hale, Sir Matthew, 1609—1676.
Hales, John, 1584—1656.

Haliburton, Thomas Chandler, 1796—1865.
Hall, Edward, *d.* 1547.
Hall, Joseph, 1574—1656.
Hallam, Arthur Henry, 1811—1833.
Hallam, Henry, 1777—1859.
Halliwell, afterwards Halliwell-Phillipps, James Orchard, 1820—1889.
Hamilton, William, of Bangour, 1704—1754.
Hamilton, Sir William, 1788—1856.
Hamilton, Sir William Rowan, 1805—1865.
Hannay, J. O., 1865— .
Hare, Julius Charles, 1795—1855.
Harington or Harrington, James, 1611—1677.
Harington, Sir John, 1561—1612.
Harpur, Charles, 1817—1868.
Harrison, Frederic, 1831—1923.
Harrison, William, 1534—1593.
Hartley, David, 1705—1757.
Harvey, Gabriel, *c.* 1545—1630.
Harvey, William, 1578—1657.
Hawker, Robert Stephen, 1803—1875.
Hawkins, Anthony Hope, 1863—1933.
Hayward, Sir John, *c.* 1564—1627.
Haydon, Benjamin Robert, 1786—1846.
Hayley, William, 1745—1820.
Hayward, Abraham, 1801—1884.
Haywood, Mrs. Eliza, *c.* 1693—1756.
Hearne, Thomas, 1678—1735.
Heber, Reginald, 1783—1826.
Heber, Richard, 1773—1833.
Helps, Sir Arthur, 1813—1875.
Hemans, Mrs. Felicia Dorothea, 1793—1835.
Henley, John, 1692—1756.
Henslowe, Philip, *d.* 1616.
Henty, George Alfred, 1832—1902.
Herbert, A. P., 1890— .
Herbert, Edward, *first Baron Herbert of Cherbury,* 1553—1648.
Hervey, James, 1714—1758.
Hervey, John, *Baron Hervey of Ickworth,* 1696—1743.
Heylyn, Peter, 1600—1662.
Hichens, R. S. (Robert Smythe), 1864— .
Higgins, Matthew James, 1810—1868.
Hill, Aaron, 1685—1750.
Hill, George Birkbeck Norman, 1835—1903.
Hoadly, Benjamin, 1676—1761.
Hoadly, Dr. Benjamin, 1706—1757.
Hobbes, John Oliver, pseudonym of Mrs. P. M. T. Craigie, 1867—1906.
Hoby, Sir Thomas, 1530—1566.
Hodgson, Shadworth Hollway, 1832—1912.
Hogarth, David George, 1862—1927.
Hogarth, William, 1697—1764.
Hogg, James, 1770—1835.
Hogg, Thomas Jefferson, 1792—1862.
Holcroft, Thomas, 1745—1809.
Hole, Samuel Reynolds, 1819—1904.
Holland, Philemon, 1552—1637.
Home, Daniel Dunglas, 1833—1886.
Home, Henry, Lord Kames, 1696—1782.
Home, John, 1722—1808.
Hone, William, 1780—1842.
Hood, Thomas, 1799—1845.
Hook, Theodore Edward, 1788—1841.
"Hope, Anthony," pseudonym of Sir Anthony Hope Hawkins, 1863—1933.
Hope, Thomas, *c.* 1770—1831.
Hopkins, Gerard Manley, 1844—1889.
Hopkins, Matthew, *d.* 1647.
Horman, William, *d.* 1535.
Horne, Richard Henry or Hengist, 1803—1884.
Hort, Fenton John Anthony, 1828—1892.
Houghton, William Stanley, 1881—1913.
Hovedon or Howden, Roger of, *d. c.* 1201.
Howell, James, *c.* 1594—1666.
Hoyle, Edmond, 1672—1769.
Huchown or Huchoun, *fl.* 14th century.
Hughes, Thomas, 1822—1896.
Hume, David, 1711—1776.
Hunter, John, 1728—1793.
Hunter, Sir William Wilson, 1840—1900.
Hurd, Richard, 1720—1808.
Hutcheson, Francis, 1694—1746.
Hutchinson, Mrs. Lucy, *b.* 1620.
Huth, Henry, 1815—1878.
Hutton, Richard Holt, 1826—1897.
Huxley, Thomas Henry, 1825—1895.

Inchbald, Mrs. Elizabeth, 1753—1821.
Inge, William Ralph, 1860— .
Ingelow, Jean, 1820—1897.
Ireland, William Henry, 1777—1835.

JACKSON, HOLBROOK, 1874— .
JAGO, RICHARD, 1715—1781.
JAMES I (JAMES VI of Scotland), King of England, 1566—1625 (1603—1625).
JAMES, GEORGE PAYNE RAINSFORD, 1799—1860.
JAMES, HENRY, 1843—1916.
JAMESON, ANNA BROWNELL, 1794—1860.
JAMESON, (MARGARET) STORM, 1897— .
JAMIESON, JOHN, 1759—1838.
JEBB, SIR RICHARD CLAVERHOUSE, 1841—1905.
JEFFERIES, RICHARD, 1848—1887.
JEFFREY, FRANCIS, *Lord Jeffrey*, 1773—1850.
JENNER, EDWARD, 1749—1823.
JENYNS, SOAME, 1704—1787.
JERROLD, DOUGLAS WILLIAM, 1803—1857.
JEWSBURY, GERALDINE ENDSOR, 1812—1880.
JOHNSON, LIONEL PIGOT, 1867—1902.
JOHNSON, RICHARD, 1573—*c.* 1659.
JOHNSTONE, CHARLES, *c.* 1719—1800.
JONES, SIR WILLIAM, 1746—1794.
JOWETT, BENJAMIN, 1817—1893.
JOYCE, PATRICK WESTON, 1827—1914.
JULIANA (of Norwich), 1343—1443.
"JUNIUS," (FRANCIS, SIR PHILIP), *c.* 1740—*c.* 1818.

KAMES, LORD. *See* Home, Henry.
KAVANAGH, JULIA, 1824—1877.
KEBLE, JOHN, 1792—1866.
KELLY, HUGH, 1739—1777.
KEMBLE, FRANCES ANNE, afterwards MRS. BUTLER, generally known as FANNY KEMBLE, 1809—1893.
KEN, THOMAS, 1637—1711.
KENDALL, HENRY CLARENCE, 1841—1882.
KER, WILLIAM PATON, 1855—1923.
KEYNES, JOHN MAYNARD, 1883— .
KILLIGREW, HENRY, 1613—1700.
KILLIGREW, THOMAS, the elder, 1612—1683.
KILLIGREW, THOMAS, the younger, 1657—1719.
KILLIGREW, SIR WILLIAM, 1601—1695.
KING, HENRY, 1592—1669.
KING, WILLIAM, 1650—1729.
KING, WILLIAM, 1663—1712.
KINGLAKE, ALEXANDER WILLIAM, 1809—1891.
KINGSLEY, HENRY, 1830—1876.
KINGSTON, WILLIAM HENRY GILES, 1814—1880.
KNIGHT, CHARLES, 1791—1873.
KIRKE, JOHN, *fl.* 1638.
KNOWLES, JAMES SHERIDAN, 1784—1862.
KNOLLES, RICHARD, *c.* 1550—1610.
KNOX, JOHN, 1505—1572.
KNYNVETT, THOMAS (of Ashwellthorpe), 1596—1658.
KNYVETT, SIR HENRY, *fl.* 1596.

LAMB, LADY CAROLINE, 1785—1828.
LAMB, MARY ANN, 1764—1874.
LAMPMAN, ARCHIBALD, 1861—1899.
LANCASTER, JOSEPH, 1778—1838.
LANDON, LETITIA ELIZABETH, 1802—1838.
LANDOR, ROBERT EYRES, 1781—1869.
LANE, EDWARD WILLIAM, 1801—1876.
LATHAM, SYMON, *fl.* 1618—1633.
LAUD, WILLIAM, 1573—1645.
LAUDER, WILLIAM, *d.* 1771.
LAW, WILLIAM, 1686—1761.
LAWLESS, EMILY, 1845—1913.
LAWRENCE, GEORGE ALFRED, 1827—1876.
LAYARD, SIR AUSTEN HENRY, 1817—1894.
LEAR, EDWARD, 1812—1888.
LEAVIS, FRANK RAYMOND, 1895— .
LECKY, WILLIAM EDWARD HARTPOLE, 1838—1903.
LEE, HARRIET, 1757—1851.
LEE, SIR SIDNEY, 1859—1926.
LEE, SOPHIA, 1750—1824.
LE FANU, JOSEPH SHERIDAN, 1814—1873.
LEFROY, EDWARD CRACROFT, 1855—1891.
LELAND, JOHN, *c.* 1506—1552.
LEMON, MARK, 1809—1870.
LEMPRIERE, JOHN, *c.* 1765—1824.
LENNOX, CHARLOTTE, 1720—1804.
LESLIE, JOHN, 1527—1596.
LESLIE, JOHN RANDOLPH SHANE, 1885— .
L'ESTRANGE, SIR ROGER, 1616—1704.
LEVER, CHARLES JAMES, 1806—1872.
LEWES, GEORGE HENRY, 1817—1878.
LEWIS, SIR GEORGE CORNEWALL, 1806—1863.
LEWIS, MATTHEW GREGORY, 1775—1818.
LEYDEN, JOHN, 1775—1811.
LIDDELL, HENRY GEORGE, 1811—1898.
LIDDON, HENRY PARRY, 1829—1890.
LIGHTFOOT, JOSEPH BARBER, 1828—1889.
LILLO, GEORGE, 1693—1739.
LILLY, WILLIAM, 1602—1681.
LILY, WILLIAM, *c.* 1468—1522.
LINACRE, THOMAS, *c.* 1460—1524.

Lindsay, Lady Anne, 1750—1825.
Lindsay, Robert, *fl.* 1565.
Lingard, John, 1771—1851.
Lithgow, William, 1582—*c.* 1645.
Littleton, Sir Thomas, 1422—1481.
Livingstone, David, 1813—1873.
Locke, William John, 1863—1930.
Locker-Lampon, Frederick, 1821—1895.
Lockhart, John Gibson, 1794—1854.
Lodge, Sir Oliver Joseph, 1851—
Logan, John, 1748—1788.
Lover, Samuel, 1797—1868.
Lowndes, William Thomas, *d.* 1843.
Lubbock, Sir John, *first Baron Avebury,* 1834—1913.
Lubbock, Percy, 1879— .
Ludlow, Edmund, *c.* 1617—1692.
Luttrell, Henry, *c.* 1765—1851.
Luttrell, Narcissus, 1657—1732.
Lyall, Sir Alfred Comyn, 1835—1911.
Lyell, Sir Charles, 1797—1875.
Lynd, Robert, 1879— .
Lyttelton, George, *first Baron Lyttelton,* 1709—1773.
Mabbe, James, 1572—*c.* 1642.
M'Carthy, Justin, 1830—1912.
Macdonald, George, 1824—1905.
Machen, Arthur, 1863— .
McKerrow, Ronald Brunlees, 1872— .
Mackintosh, Sir James, 1765—1832.
Macklin, Charles, *c.* 1697—1797.
Madden, Dodgson Hamilton, 1840—1928.
Maginn, William, 1793—1842.
Mahony, Francis Sylvester, 1804—1866.
Maine, Sir Henry James Sumner, 1822—1888.
Maitland, Frederic William, 1850—1906.
Maitland, Sir Richard, 1496—1586.
Major, John, 1496—1550.
Mallet, (or Malloch) David, *c.* 1705—1765.
Mallock, William Hurrell, 1849—1923.
Malone, Edmond, 1741—1812.
Malthus, Thomas Robert, 1766—1834.
Mandeville, Bernard De, *c.* 1670—1733.
Mangan, James Clarence, 1803—1849.
Manley, Mrs. Mary De La Riviere, 1663—1724.
Manning, Henry Edward, 1808—1892.
Mansel, Henry Longueville, 1820—1871.
Markham, Gervase, *c.* 1568—1637.
Markham, Mrs., pseudonym of Mrs. Elizabeth Penrose, 1780—1837.
Marmion, Shackerley, 1603—1639.
Marryat, Frederick, 1792—1848.
Marshall, Archibald, 1866—1934.
Marston, John Westland, 1819—1890.
Marston, Philip Bourke, 1850—1887.
Martineau, Harriet, 1802—1876.
Martineau, James, 1805—1900.
Martyn, Edward, 1859—1924.
Mason, Alfred Edward Woodley, 1865— .
Mason, William, 1724—1797.
Masson, David, 1822—1907.
Mathias, Thomas James, *c.* 1754—1835.
Maturin, Charles Robert, 1782—1824.
Maurice, John Frederick Denison, 1805—1872.
Maxwell, William Babington, 1876— .
May, Thomas, 1595—1650.
May, Sir Thomas Erskine, *first Baron Farnborough,* 1815—1886.
Mayne, Jasper, 1604—1672.
Meres, Francis, 1565—1647.
Merivale, Charles, 1808—1893.
Merivale, Herman, 1806—1874.
Merrick, Leonard, 1864— .
Merriman, Henry Seton, pseudonym of Hugh Stowell Scott, 1862—1903.
Mickle, William Julius, 1735—1788.
Middleton, Conyers, 1683—1750.
Mill, James, 1773—1836.
Mill, John Stuart, 1806—1873.
Miller, Hugh, 1802—1856.
Milman, Henry Hart, 1791—1868.
Milnes, Richard Monckton, *first Baron Houghton,* 1809—1885.
Milward, Richard, 1609—1680.
Mitchel, John, 1818—1875.
Mitford, Mary Russell, 1878—1855.
Mitford, William, 1744—1827.
Moir, David Macbeth, 1798—1851.
Monboddo, James Burnett, Lord, 1714—1799.
Montagu, Basil, 1770—1851.
Montagu, Mrs. Elizabeth, 1720—1800.
Montagu, Lady Mary Wortley, 1689—1762.
Montgomerie, Alexander, *c.* 1556—*c.* 1610.
Montgomery, James, 1771—1854.

MONTGOMERY, ROBERT, 1807—1855.
MOORE, EDWARD, 1712—1757.
MOORE, DR. JOHN, 1729—1802.
MOORE, THOMAS, 1779—1852.
MORE, HANNAH, 1745—1833.
MORE, HENRY, 1614—1687.
MORGAN, SYDNEY, LADY, *c.* 1783—1859.
MORGANN, MAURICE, 1726—1802.
MORIOR, JAMES JUSTINIAN, *c.* 1780—1849.
MORLEY, JOHN, *first Viscount Morley of Blackburn*, 1838—1923.
MORRIS, SIR LEWIS, 1833—1907.
MORRISON, ARTHUR, 1863— .
MORTON, JOHN MADDISON, 1811—1891.
MORTON, THOMAS, *c.* 1764—1838.
MOTHERWELL, WILLIAM, 1797—1835.
MOTTEUX, PETER ANTHONY, 1660—1718.
MOTTLEY, JOHN, 1692—1750.
MOTTRAM, RALPH HALE, 1883—
MOXON, EDWARD, 1801—1858.
MUIR, EDWIN, 1887— .
MULCASTER, RICHARD, *c.* 1530—1611.
MUNDAY, ANTHONY, 1553—1633.
MUNRO, CHARLES KILPATRICK, 1889— .
MUNRO, HECTOR HUGH, 1870—1916
MUNRO, HUGH ANDREW JOHNSTONE, 1819—1885.
MURPHY, ARTHUR, 1727—1805.
MURRAY, GEORGE GILBERT AIME, 1866— .
MURRAY, SIR JAMES AUGUSTUS HENRY, 1837—1915.
MURRAY, LINDLEY, 1745—1826.
MYERS, FREDERIC WILLIAM HENRY, 1843—1901.

NABBES, THOMAS, *fl.* 1638.
NAIRNE, CAROLINA, BARONESS, *née* OLIPHANT, 1766—1845.
NAPIER or NEPER, JOHN, 1550—1617.
NAPIER, SIR WILLIAM FRANCIS PATRICK, 1785—1860.
NEALE, JOHN MASON, 1818—1866.
NEWMAN, FRANCIS WILLIAM, 1805—1897.
NICHOLS, JOHN, 1745—1826.
NICHOLS, ROBERT, M. B., 1893— .
NICOLSON, HAROLD G., 1886— .
NOEL, RODEN BERKELEY WRIOTHESLEY, 1834—1894.
NORRIS, JOHN, 1657—1711.
NORTH, ROGER, 1653—1734.
NORTHCLIFFE, ALFRED CHARLES WILLIAM HARMSWORTH, VISCOUNT, 1865—1922.
NYREN, JOHN, 1764—1837.

OGILBY, JOHN, 1600—1676.
O'KEEFFE, JOHN, 1747—1833.
OLD MOORE, FRANCIS MOORE, 1657—*c.* 1715.
OLDHAM, JOHN, 1653—1683.
OLDMIXON, JOHN, 1673—1742.
OLDYS, WILLIAM, 1696—1761.
OLIPHANT, LAURENCE, 1829—1888.
OLIPHANT, MARGARET OLIPHANT, 1828—1897.
OLIVER, GEORGE, "OLIVER ONIONS," 1873— .
OMAN, CAROLA M. A., 1897— .
OPIE, MRS. AMELIA, 1769—1853.
ORAGE, ALFRED RICHARD, 1873—1934.
O'RIORDAN, CONAL, 1874— .
ORATOR HUNT, HENRY HUNT, 1773—1835.
ORME, ROBERT, 1728—1801.
OSBORNE, DOROTHY, 1627—1695.
O'SHAUGHNESSY, ARTHUR WILLIAM EDGAR, 1844—1881.
OSLER, SIR WILLIAM, 1849—1919.
OUIDA (MARIE LOUISE DE LA RAMEE), 1839—1908.
OWEN, JOHN, *c.* 1560—1622.
OWEN, SIR RICHARD, 1804—1892.
OWEN, ROBERT, 1771—1858.

PAGAN, ISOBEL (TIBBY), *d.* 1821.
PAIN, BARRY ERICODELL, 1864—1928.
PAINE, THOMAS, 1737—1809.
PAINTER, WILLIAM, *c.* 1540—1594.
PALEY, WILLIAM, 1743—1805.
PALGRAVE, SIR FRANCIS, 1788—1861.
PALGRAVE, FRANCIS TURNER, 1824—1897.
PALGRAVE, WILLIAM GIFFORD, 1826—1888.
PALTOCK, ROBERT, 1697—1767.
PARK, MUNGO, 1771—1806.
PARKER, SIR GILBERT, 1862—1932.
PARKER, MATTHEW, 1504—1575.
PARKINSON, JOHN, 1567—1650.
PARNELL, CHARLES STEWART, 1846—1891.
PARNELL, THOMAS, 1679—1718.
PARR, SAMUEL, 1747—1825.
PARRY, SIR WILLIAM EDWARD, 1790—1855.
PATMORE, COVENTRY KERSEY DIGHTON, 1823—1896.
PATTISON, MARK, 1813—1884.
PAYN, JAMES, 1830—1898.
PEACHAM, HENRY, *c.* 1576—*c.* 1643.
PEACOCK, THOMAS LOVE, 1785—1866.
PEARSON, JOHN, 1613—1686.
PENN, WILLIAM, 1644—1718.
PENNANT, THOMAS, 1726—1798.
PETTY, SIR WILLIAM, 1623—1687.
PHAER, THOMAS, *c.* 1510—1560.

Philips, Ambrose, *c.* 1675—1749.
Philips, John, 1676—1709.
Philips, Katherine, 1631—1664.
Phillips, John, 1631—1706.
Phillpotts, Eden, 1862— .
Pickthall, Marjorie L. C., 1883—1922.
Pickthall, Marmaduke William, 1875— .
Piozzi, Hester Lynch, 1741—1821.
Pitman, Sir Isaac, 1813—1897.
Planche, James Robinson, 1796—1880.
Pollard, Alfred William, 1859— .
Pollock, Sir Frederick, 1845— .
Pomfret, John, 1667—1702.
Poole, John, *c.* 1786—1872.
Pordage, Samuel, 1633—*c.* 1691.
Porson, Richard, 1759—1808.
Porter, Anna Maria, 1780—1832.
Porter, Jane, 1776—1850.
Porter, Henry, *fl.* 1599.
Praed, Winthrop Mackworth, 1802—1839.
Preston, Thomas, 1537—1598.
Price, Richard, 1723—1791.
Priestley, John Boynton, 1894— .
Priestley, Joseph, 1733—1804.
Pringle, Thomas, 1789—1834.
Prior, Matthew, 1664—1721.
Proctor, Adelaide Anne, 1825—1864.
Proctor, Bryan Waller, 1787—1874.
Prynne, William, 1600—1669.
Psalmanazar, George, *c.* 1679—1763.
Purcell, Henry, 1658—1695.
Purchas, Samuel, *c.* 1575—1626.
Pusey, Edward Bouverie, 1800—1882.
Pye, Henry James, 1745—1813.

Quaritch, Bernard, 1819—1899.
Quarles, Francis, 1592—1644.
Quennell, Peter Courtney, 1905— .

Ramsay, Allan, 1686—1758.
Randolph, Thomas, 1605—1635.
Rashdall, Hastings, 1858—1924.
Raspe, Rudolf Erich, 1737—1794.
Rawlinson, George, 1812—1902.
Rawlinson, Sir Henry Creswicke, 1810—1895.
Rawlinson, Thomas, 1681—1725.
Reeve, Clara, 1729—1807.
Reid, Thomas, 1710—1796.
Reid, Thomas Mayne, 1818—1883.
Reresby, Sir John, 1634—1689.
Reynolds, Sir Joshua, 1723—1792.
Ricardo, David, 1772—1823.
Rice, James, 1843—1882.
Rich, Barnabe, *c.* 1540—1617.
Rich, John, *c.* 1682—1761.
Ridge, W. P., *c.* 1860—1930.
Ridley, Nicholas, *c.* 1500—1555.
Ritchie, Anne Isabella Thackeray, *Lady, c.* 1838—1919.
Ritson, Joseph, 1752—1803.
Roberts, Charles George Douglas, 1860— .
Roberts, Morley, 1857— .
Robertson, Frederick William, 1816—1853.
Robertson, Thomas William, 1829—1871.
Robertson, William, 1721—1793.
Robinson, Henry Crabb, 1775—1867.
Rogers, James Edwin Thorold, 1823—1890.
Rogers, Samuel, 1763—1855.
Rogers, Woodes, *d.* 1732.
Roper, William, 1496—1578.
Roscoe, William, 1753—1831.
Roseberry, Archibald Philip Primrose, *fifth earl of,* 1847—1929.
Ross, Alexander, 1699—1784.
Ross, Sir James Clark, 1800—1862.
Ross, Sir John, 1777—1856.
Rossetti, William Michael, 1829—1919.
Routh, Martin Joseph, 1755—1854.
Rowlands, Samuel, *c.* 1570—*c.* 1630.
Rowley, Samuel, *d. c.* 1633.
Rowley, William, *c.* 1585—*c.* 1642.
Russell, George William, 1867— .
Russell, Lord John, *first Earl Russell.* 1792—1878.
Russell, William Clark, 1844—1911.
Russell, Sir William Howard, 1820—1907.

Saint-Evremond, Charles De Marguetel De Saint-Denis De, *c.* 1613—1703.
Sandys, Edwin, *c.* 1516—1588.
Sandys, Sir Edwin, 1561—1629.
Sandys, George, 1578—1644.
Savage, Richard, *d.* 1743.
Savile, Sir Henry, 1594—1622.
Schreiner, Olive Eilie Albertina, 1855—1920.
Scott, Alexander, *c.* 1525—*c.* 1584.
Scott, Michael, *c.* 1175—*c.* 1234.
Scott, Michael, 1789—1835.
Scott or Scot, Reginald, 1538—1599
Scott, Robert Falcon, 1868—1912.

SCOTT, WILLIAM BELL, 1811—1890.
SEAMAN, OWEN, 1861— .
SEELEY, SIR JOHN ROBERT, 1834—1895.
SELDEN, JOHN, 1584—1654.
SENIOR, NASSAU WILLIAM, 1790—1864.
SEMPILL, ROBERT, *c.* 1530—1595.
SETTLE, ELKANAH, 1648—1724.
SEWARD, ANNA, 1747—1809.
SEWELL, ANNA, 1820—1878.
SHADWELL, THOMAS, *c.* 1642—1692.
SHAFTESBURY, ANTHONY ASHLEY COOPER, *first Baron Ashley and first earl of Shaftesbury*, 1621—1683.
SHAFTESBURY, ANTHONY ASHLEY COOPER, *third earl of*, 1671—1713.
SHARP, WILLIAM, ("FIONA MACLEOD") 1855—1905.
SHARPHAM, EDWARD, 1576—1608.
SHELLEY, MARY WOLLSTONECRAFT, 1797—1851.
SHENSTONE, WILLIAM, 1714—1763.
SHERATON, THOMAS, 1751—1806.
SHERIDAN, MRS. FRANCES, 1724—1766.
SHERLOCK, THOMAS, 1678—1761.
SHERLOCK, WILLIAM, *c.* 1641—1707.
SHERWOOD, MRS. MARY MARTHA, 1775—1851.
SHORTHOUSE, JOSEPH HENRY, 1824—1903.
SIDGWICK, HENRY, 1838—1900.
SIDNEY, or SYDNEY, ALGERNON, 1622—1683.
SINCLAIR, CATHERINE, 1800—1864.
SKEAT, WALTER WILLIAM, 1835—1912.
SKEFFINGTON, SIR LUMLEY ST. GEORGE, 1771—1850.
SKINNER, JOHN, 1721—1807.
SLOANE, SIR HANS, 1660—1753.
SMART, CHRISTOPHER, 1722—1771.
SMEDLEY, FRANCIS EDWARD, 1818—1864.
SMILES, SAMUEL, 1812—1904.
SMITH, ADAM, 1723—1790.
SMITH, ALEXANDER, 1830—1867.
SMITH, GEORGE, 1824—1901.
SMITH, SIR GEORGE ADAM, 1856— .
SMITH, GOLDWIN, 1823—1910.
SMITH, HORATIO (HORACE), 1779—1849.
SMITH, JAMES, 1775—1839.
SMITH, JOHN (of Cambridge), 1618—1652.
SMITH, JOHN THOMAS, 1766—1833.
SMITH, ROBERT PERCY, *'Bobus Smith,'* 1770—1845.
SMITH, SYDNEY, 1771—1845.
SMITH, THOMAS, *b.* 1790.
SMITH, SIR THOMAS, 1513—1577.
SMITH, SIR WILLIAM, 1813—1893.
SMITH, WILLIAM ROBERTSON, 1846—1894.
SOMERVILLE, WILLIAM, 1675—1742.
SOUTH, ROBERT, 1634—1716.
SOUTHERNE or SATHERN, THOMAS, 1660—1746.
SOUTHWELL, ROBERT, *c.* 1561—1595.
SPEDDING, JAMES, 1808—1881.
SPEED, JOHN, *c.* 1552—1629.
SPEKE, JOHN HANNING, 1827—1864.
SPENCER, HERBERT, 1820—1903.
SPURGEON, CHARLES HADDON, 1834—1892.
SQUIRE, SIR JOHN COLLINGS, 1884— .
STANHOPE, PHILIP HENRY, *fifth earl*, 1805—1875.
STANLEY, ARTHUR PENRHYN, 1815—1881.
STANLEY, SIR HENRY MORTON, 1841—1904.
STANLEY, THOMAS, 1625—1678.
STANYHURST, RICHARD, 1547—1618.
STEAD, WILLIAM THOMAS, 1849—1912.
STEEL, FLORA ANNIE, 1847—1929.
STEEVENS, GEORGE, 1736—1800.
STEPHEN, SIR JAMES, 1789—1859.
STEPHEN, SIR JAMES FITZJAMES, 1829—1894.
STEPHEN, JAMES KENNETH, 1859—1892.
STEPHENS, JOHN, *fl.* 1615.
STERLING, JOHN, 1806—1844.
STEUART, SIR JAMES, 1712—1780, who assumed the name of DENHAM.
STEVENSON, JOHN HALL, 1718—1785.
STEWART, DUGALD, 1753—1828.
STEWART, JOHN, 1749—1822.
STILL, JOHN, 1543—1608.
STILLINGFLEET, EDWARD, 1635—1699.
STIRLING, JAMES HUTCHISON, 1820—1909.
STOW, JOHN, *c.* 1525—1605.
STRANGFORD, PERCY CLINTON SYDNEY SMYTH, *sixth visc.*, 1780—1855.
STRICKLAND, AGNES, 1796—1874.
STRONG, L. A. G., 1896— .
STRUTT, JOSEPH, 1749—1802.
STRYPE, JOHN, 1643—1737.
STUART, DANIEL, 1766—1846.
STUART, FRANCIS, 1902— .
STUBBS or STUBBES, PHILIP, *fl.* 1581—1593.
STUBBS, WILLIAM, 1825—1901.
STUKELEY, WILLIAM, 1687—1765.
SURTEES, ROBERT, 1779—1834.
SURTEES, ROBERT SMITH, 1803—1864.
SUTRO, ALFRED, 1863—1933.

SYLVESTER, JOSHUA, 1563—1618.
SYMONDS, JOHN ADDINGTON, 1840—1893.

TALFOURD, SIR THOMAS NOON, 1795—1854.
TANNAHILL, ROBERT, 1774—1810.
TATE, NAHUM, 1652—1715.
TAYLOR, ANN, 1782—1866.
TAYLOR, SIR HENRY, 1800—1886.
TAYLOR, JANE, 1783—1824.
TAYLOR, JOHN, 1580—1653.
TAYLOR, JOHN, 1703—1772.
TAYLOR, PHILIP MEADOWS, 1808—1876
TAYLOR, THOMAS, 1758—1835.
TAYLOR, TOM, 1817—1880.
TELFORD, THOMAS, 1757—1834.
TENNANT, WILLIAM, 1784—1848.
TENNIEL, SIR JOHN, 1820—1914.
TENNYSON, FREDERICK, 1807—1898.
TENNYSON TURNER, CHARLES, 1808—1879.
THEOBALD, LEWIS, 1688—1744.
THIRLWALL, CONNOP, 1797—1875.
THOMAS, of Erceldoune, called the Rhymer, *c.* 1220—*c.* 1297.
THOMPSON, SYLVIA ELIZABETH, 1902— .
THOMS, WILLIAM JOHN, 1803—1885.
THOMSON, SIR WILLIAM, *first Baron Kelvin,* 1824—1907.
THRALE, HESTER LYNCH, MRS., 1741—1821.
TICKELL, THOMAS, 1686—1740.
TOLAND, JOHN, 1670—1722.
TOMKIS, THOMAS, *fl.* 1604—1615.
TOOKE, JOHN HORNE, 1736—1812.
TOPLADY, AUGUSTUS MONTAGUE, 1740—1778.
TORRENS, WILLIAM MCCULLAGH, 1813—1894.
TOURNEUR, CYRIL, *c.* 1575—1626.
TRADESCANT, JOHN, 1608—1662.
TRAILL, HENRY DUFF, 1842—1900.
TRELAWNEY, EDWARD JOHN, 1792—1881.
TRENCH, RICHARD CHENEVIX, 1807—1886.
TREVELYAN, GEORGE MACAULAY, 1876— .
TREVELYAN, SIR GEORGE OTTO, 1838—1928.
TRIMMER, MRS. SARAH, 1741—1810.
TROLLOPE, FRANCES, 1780—1863.
TROLLOPE, THOMAS ADOLPHUS, 1810—1892.
TUCKER, ABRAHAM, 1705—1774.
TUPPER, MARTIN FARQUHAR, 1810—1889.
TURBERVILLE, GEORGE, *c.* 1540—*c.* 1610.
TURNER, SHARON, 1768—1847.
TURNER, W. J. R., 1889— .
TUSSER, THOMAS, *c.* 1524—1580.
TYNDALL, JOHN, 1820—1893.
TYRRELL, GEORGE, 1861—1909.
TYRWHITT, THOMAS, 1730—1786.
TYTLER, PATRICK FRASER, 1791—1849.

UNDERHILL, EVELYN, 1875— .
URQUHART, SIR THOMAS, 1611—1660.
USSHER, JAMES, 1581—1656.

VANCOUVER, GEORGE, 1758—1798.
VAUGHAN, HENRY, 1622—1695.
VAUGHAN, THOMAS, 1626—1666.
VAUX, THOMAS, 1510—1556.
VERGIL, POLYDORE, *c.* 1470—*c.* 1555.
VINER, CHARLES, 1678—1756.
VOYNICH, E. L. B., 1864— .

WAINEWRIGHT, THOMAS GRIFFITHS, 1794—1852.
WAKEFIELD, EDWARD GIBBON, 1796—1862.
WAKEFIELD, GILBERT, 1756—1801.
WALKER, THOMAS, 1784—1836.
WALLACE, ALFRED RUSSEL, 1823—1913.
WALLACE, EDGAR, 1875—1932.
WALLACE, WILLIAM, 1844—1897.
WALLIS, JOHN, 1616—1703.
WALPOLE, SIR SPENCER, 1839—1907.
WANLEY, HUMFREY, 1672—1726.
WANLEY, NATHANIEL, 1634—1680.
WARBURTON, ROWLAND EYLES EGERTON, 1804—1891.
WARBURTON, WILLIAM, 1698—1779.
WARD, EDWARD, ("Ned"), 1667—1731.
WARD, WILLIAM GEORGE, 1812—1882.
WARNER, WILLIAM, *c.* 1558—1609.
WARREN, JOHN BYRNE LEICESTER, *Baron de Tabley,* 1835—1895.
WARREN, SAMUEL, 1807—1877.
WARTON, JOSEPH, 1722—1800.
WARTON, THOMAS, 1728—1790.
WATERTON, CHARLES, 1782—1865.
WATSON, RICHARD, 1737—1816.
WATSON, THOMAS, *c.* 1557—1592.
WATT, ROBERT, 1774—1819.
WATTS, ISAAC, 1674—1748.
WATTS-DUNTON, WALTER THEODORE, 1832—1914.
WAUGH, ALEC, 1898— .
WAUGH, EVELYN, 1903— .
WEBB, MARY, 1881—1927.
WEBBE, WILLIAM, *c.* 1552—*c.* 1600.

Wells, Charles Jeremiah, *c.* 1800—1879.

Wesley, Charles, 1707—1788.

Wesley, John, 1703—1791.

Westcott, Brooke Foss, 1825—1901.

Weyman, Stanley J., 1855—1928.

Whately, Richard, 1787—1863.

Whetstone, George, *c.* 1554—*c.* 1587.

Whewell, William, 1794—1866.

White, Gilbert, 1720—1793.

White, Henry Kirke, 1785—1806.

White, Joseph Blanco, 1775—1841.

White, William Hale, pseudonym of Mark Rutherford, 1831—1913.

Whitefield, George, 1714—1770.

Whitehead, Alfred North, 1861— .

Whitehead, Charles, 1804—1862.

Whitehead, William, 1715—1785.

Whitelocke, Bulstrode, 1605—1675.

Whymper, Edward, 1840—1911.

Whyte-Melville, George John, 1821—1878.

Wilberforce, William, 1759—1833.

Wilkes, John, 1727—1797.

Wilkins, John, 1614—1672.

Wilkinson, Sir John Gardner. 1797—1875.

Williams, Helen Maria, 1762—1827.

Williams, Isaac, 1802—1865.

Williamson. Henry, 1897— .

Willoughby De Broke, Richard Grevill Verney, *nineteenth Baron,* 1869—1923.

Wills, William Gorman, 1828—1891.

Wilmot, Robert, *fl.* 1568—1608.

Wilson, Sir Arnold Talbot, 1884— .

Wilson, Sir Daniel, 1816—1892.

Wilson, John, *c.* 1627—1696.

Wilson, John, 1785—1854.

Wilson, Romer, pseudonym of Florence Muir Wilson, 1891—1930.

Winchilsea, Anne Finch, *Countess of,* 1661—1720.

Winzet, Ninian, 1518—1592.

Wodehouse, Pelham Grenville, 1881— .

Wodrow, Robert, 1679—1734.

Wolcot, John, 1738—1819.

Wolfe, Charles, 1791—1823.

Wood, Anthony, or as he latterly called himself, Anthony À Wood, 1632—1695.

Wood, Ellen, better known as Mrs. Henry Wood, 1814—1887.

Woodforde, James, 1740—1803.

Woolf, Leonard Sidney, 1880— .

Woolner, Thomas, 1825—1892.

Wordsworth, Dorothy, 1804—1847.

Wotton, Sir Henry, 1568—1639.

Wren, Sir Christopher, 1632—1723.

Wright, Thomas, 1810—1877.

Yarrell, William, 1784—1856.

Yonge, Charlotte Mary, 1823—1901

Young, Arthur, 1741—1820.

Young, Emily Hilda, 1880— .

Young, Francis Eric Brett, 1884— .

Zangwill, Israel, 1864—1926.

## APPENDIX B

# ALPHABETICAL GUIDE TO MISCELLANEOUS INFORMATION

***Alchemist, The*** (p. 229). Subtle, the quack, aided by Dol Common, his consort, and Captain Face, Lovewit's house-servant, dupes Drugger, a tobacco man, Dapper, a clerk, and particularly the purse-proud Sir Epicure Mammon into supplying funds for the purpose of discovering the philosopher's stone and the elixir of life. The *exposé* is brought about through the unexpected return of Lovewit.

***Alexander and Campaspe*** (p. 151). After a stratagem has made Apelles reveal his love for Campaspe, Alexander the Great magnanimously relinquishes his Theban concubine to the portrait-painter.

***All Fools*** (p. 234). Gostanzo, gulled by Rinaldo into believing that Fortunio, elder son of Marc Antonio, and Gratiana are secretly married, comes upon his son Valerio embracing Gratiana. Unaware that the latter two are man and wife, and unaware that Fortunio is in love with Bellonora, (Gostanzo's own daughter), he is again mislead by Rinaldo into banishing his son Valerio under the pretense (so he thinks) that Valerio and Gratiana are already married. Eventually the tables are turned upon Rinaldo.

***Amis and Amiloun*** (p. 40). Amiloun, perjuring himself by taking the place of his foster-brother Amis in an ordeal by battle, becomes lepered and poverty-stricken. Amis cuts the throats of his two children upon being advised that only by bathing his friend with their blood can the leprosy be cured. But the children are found miraculously alive and well.

***Andreas*** (p. 14). In a dream St. Andrew is commanded by the Lord to rescue St. Matthew from the cannibal Mermedonians. Unknown to St. Andrew the boat is piloted across the tempestuous sea by Christ and two angels, disguised as helmsman and sailors. St. Matthew is released, but, later, St. Andrew himself is imprisoned and tortured. By working a miracle (ordering a marble pillar to let loose torrents of water upon the town) he secures his freedom and converts a savage tribe.

***Anelida and Arcite*** (p. 69). Upon beholding another lady, Arcite "falsed fair Anelida the quene." She breaks out into a complaint about her knight-lover's faithlessness. (The poem was left unfinished.)

***Ane Pleasant Satyre of the Thrie Estaitis, in Commendatioun of Vertew and Vituperatioun of Vyce*** (p. 91). Describes, first, the seduction of Rex Humanitas by the Lady Sensuality, and the rescue by Correction; then, the adventurous interludes of Chastity before being put in the stocks, and the ecclesiastical abuses undergone by a farmer; and, finally, the King's summoning of the Three Estates (Spiritualitie or the Clergy, Temporalitie or the Landholders. Burgesses or the Merchants), and their indictment by John the Commonweal (Scotland).

***Arden of Feversham***(p. 153). For the love she bears Mosbie, the lying and brazenly hypocritical Mistress Arden hires two ruffians, Black Bill and Shakbag, to murder her husband.

***Arraignment of Paris, The*** (p. 155). Juno and Pallas, disappointed contestants for the golden apple awarded to Venus as the most beautiful divinity, arraign Paris before a council of gods for his erroneous judgment. Diana re-awards the apple, but to none of the three original contestants.

***Arthurian Framework*** (p. 43). Arthur, the natural son of King Uther and the Duke of Cornwall's wife Igerna, becomes the fifteen-year-old King of Britain. Assisted by a magic sword Caliburn (Excalibur), a spear Ron, and a shield Pridwen on which is painted the image of the Virgin Mary, he subdues the twelve rebellious princes and, later, repulses the Saxon invaders. He marries Guanhamara (Guinevere), a noble Roman lady. Beginning warfare anew, after twelve years of peace, Arthur reduces to submission such countries as Norway, Gaul, and Dacia. When the procurator Lucius Hiberius of Rome demands tribute, Arthur, declaring war, subjugates many lands on the Continent. He is about to pass the Alps in order to invade Rome when word is brought that his nephew Modred has illicitly married the Queen and usurped the throne. Returning immediately, at the end of a campaign he gives desperate battle with Modred. The latter is slain; and Arthur himself is borne off to the Isle of Avalon for the healing of his wounds. The Queen betakes herself to a nunnery, and the crown passes to Constantine. (In the popular belief Arthur still dwells in Avalon, whence he will some day return to restore the British people to supreme power.)

***Babylon; or the Bonnie Banks o Fordie*** (p. 101). Two of three sisters accept death rather than the marriage-proposal of an outlaw; but the third threatens the robber with the vengeance of her brother, Baby Lon. At that the outlaw, made aware that he has murdered his own sisters, "twyned (deprived) himself o his ain sweet life."

***Bartholomew Fayre*** (p. 229). At the bustling Fair all are victimized—Bartholemew Cokes, an esquire of Harrow, Humphrey Wasp, his man, Zeal-of-the-Land Busy, a Banbury puritan, and Adam Overdo, a justice of the peace. Splendid Hogarthian portraits of Edgeworth, a cutpurse, Knockhum, a horse-courser or horse-trader, and Punk Alice, whose very name means "prostitute," just as "Cokes" means "simpleton."

***The Battle of Otterbourne*** (p. 101). Earl Douglas, the commander of the Scots, is killed, and Lord Percy, of the English forces, is taken prisoner.

***Bedwyr*** (p. 42). Bedwyr (Bedivere) is described in *Kilhwch and Olwen* (p. 42) as one-handed, unequaled in swiftness, and as one whose lance could produce a wound "equal to those of nine opposing lances."

***Beowulf*** (p. 6).

I

(a) Hrothgar, Lord of the Scyldings or Danes, has built a bright mead-hall called Heorot. Every night the monster Grendel—half-man, half-beast—comes from the fens and ravages the beer-hall, carrying off to his subterranean dwelling a number of the King's thanes. For twelve years this continues, when, hearing of it, Beowulf, a prince among the Geats (of South Sweden), crosses the sea with fourteen companions to rid Hrothgar of the cannibal-ogre. The small band is feasted; the Danes withdraw. Grendel enters and kills one of Beowulf's comrades. In a mighty hand-to-hand struggle Grendel, after having an arm wrenched from the socket by Beowulf, flees, howling, to the fens to die.

(b) The next night, while Beowulf and his companions are lodged elsewhere, Grendel's dam (mother), descends upon Heorot to avenge her son and bears away Aeschere, Hrothgar's dearest friend. In the morning Beowulf pursues the bog-monster. He descends to her lair in the caves of the sea and slays the water demon with a sword wrought by the giants. Finding the corpse of Grendel, he cuts off its head and to the surface brings it back in triumph.

II

(a) Loaded down with treasures, Beowulf returns in glory to his uncle, King Hygelac. During the reigns of Hygelac and his son Heardred, Beowulf is the mightiest man in the kingdom. When Heardred is slain in battle, Beowulf succeeds him as King.

(b) After Beowulf has reigned prosperously for fifty years, a fire-spewing dragon, robbed of a cup from an immense gold hoard that he had guarded for 300 years, becomes enraged and begins to devastate the land. The aged King with eleven chosen thanes journeys to the fiery dragon's barrow. All except his shield-bearer Wiglaf, son of Weohstan, seek safety in flight. With the aid of this kinsman Beowulf succeeds in dispatching the fire-drake. But, severely wounded, he dies after viewing the treasures and naming Wiglaf his successor. His body and the treasures are placed on a funeral pile. Twelve warriors ride around the great mound, celebrating the deeds of the bravest, gentlest, and most generous of Kings.

***Bevis of Hampton, Sir*** (p. 49). After instigating the murder of Guy, Earl of Hampton (Southampton), the widow marries the slayer. Her rebelling son Bevis, sold into slavery, reaches the court of King Hermin of Armenia. With the aid of a magic sword Morglay and a wonderful steed Arundel, both given to him by the princess Josian, afterward Bevis's wife, the hero performs such exploits as the slaying of a huge boar and a terrible dragon, the defeat of Josian's suitor Brademond of Damascus, the subduing of the thirty-foot giant Ascapart, the slaying of Yvor, King of Mombrant, to whom Josian was (in name only) first married, and the final vengeance on his stepfather. Much later Bevis and Josian die in each other's arms.

***Bonnie George Campbell*** (p. 101). Tells how he rides forth to battle never to return.

***Book of the Duchess, The*** (p. 64). The story of Ceyx and Alcyone has such an effect upon Chaucer that he falls asleep. In a dream he finds himself in a chamber painted in illustration of the tale of Troy, and of the *Romaunt of the Rose*. Investigating the noise of horses and hounds, he discovers and joins a hunting party of the Emperor Octavian. A fawning whelp entices the poet into a forest, where he comes upon a knight in black who is lamenting the death of his lady. The knight explains the extent of his sorrow, telling of the innumerable perfections of his lady, and of their courtship. In answer to the dreamer's direct question, the knight declares that his lady is dead. The poet, awakened by a bell striking twelve, finds the story of Ceyx and Alcyone still in his hand.

***Broken Heart, The*** (p. 246). While presiding over a feast, "one news straight came huddling on another" to Calantha, the King of Laconia's daughter: the death of her father, the death of Penthea, sister to Ithocles, and the murder of Ithocles, her "contracted lord." She continues dancing, to all outward appearances unmoved. In the next (and last) scene she puts her mother's wedding ring on the lifeless fingers of Ithocles, and, broken-hearted, dies.

***Bussy D'Ambois*** (p. 234). Unaware that his assignations with Tamyra, Countess of Montsurry, have been revealed, or that his clandestine mistress has even been stabbed twice in order to force her to send for him, Bussy d'Ambois responds to her summons. He is set upon by the Count, and slain by the hirelings of Monsieur and the Duc de Guise.

***Canon's Yeoman's Tale, The*** (p. 76). A priest, convinced by a trick that a canon has the formula for converting rubbish into gold, pays a large sum of money to the alchemist for the secret.

***Cardinall, The*** (p. 248). On the marriage-night of the Duchess Rosaura and the Count d'Alvarez, Columbo, the Cardinal's nephew, murders the bridegroom. In turn, the bluff Hernando, instigated by the Duchess, kills Columbo. The

Cardinal plans to administer a poison to the Duchess after he "had enjoy'd her." Although Hernando has, in his own words, "preserv'd the duchess from a rape," the Cardinal nevertheless succeeds in poisoning the Duchess by means of a bowl of wine containing, so she is made to believe, a "great magistral medicine" or antidote. Hernando as well as the Cardinal dies.

***Changeling, The*** (p. 237). Beatrice-Joanna, daughter of Vermandero, Governor of Alicant, hires the unscrupulous De Flores to murder Alonzo de Piracquo, an unwelcome suitor favored by her father. As the price for his silence the hired assassin will be satisfied with nothing but the surrender of her virtue. In order to keep secret this unexpected turn of events, Beatrice-Joanna, on her wedding-night to Alsemero, the suitor of her choice, substitutes her waiting-woman Diaphanta, who is then murdered by De Flores in order to seal her lips. Their guilt is discovered, and they commit suicide.

***Chevy Chase*** (p. 101). In a border skirmish Percy, the Englishman, and Douglas, the Scotchman, meet their death.

***Childe Waters*** (p. 101). The pearl of English ballads describes the cruelty of Childe Waters to his page Ellen, and how her constancy in love is finally rewarded.

***Clerk's Tale, The*** (p. 75). Walter, the Marquis of Saluces, weds Griselda, the daughter of a very poor charcoal-burner. With fortitude the heroine bears every test to which her husband puts her: from her, at different times, he takes away both children, saying that they have been murdered; and he even sends forged documents of divorce to her, explaining that he wishes to wed another. Through it all Griselda keeps her marriage vow never in deed or thought to disobey her husband. Finally, the Marquis introduces the new bride-to-be to Griselda, who is overjoyed to find that the pretended future wife is no other than her own daughter. To Griselda he also restores the boy-child previously taken away. Happiness for all follows.

***Confessio Amantis*** (p. 54). On a May day in a woods a lamenting lover, wishing for death, appeals to Venus for grace. Cupid transfixes him with a dart, thus increasing his suffering; but Venus compassionately bids him make full confession to her priest, Genius. After a lengthy interlude in which the latter, through illustrative stories, instructs the lover concerning love and its connection with the Seven Deadly Sins and their individual remedies, the poet is counseled by Genius to renounce Love, and to follow the law of Reason. While the despairing lover's petition is being carried to Venus and Cupid, the Goddess of Love, reappearing, shows him his hoary locks in a mirror as proof of his ineligibility to be a lover. The poet swoons; and before him pass folk who were once famous lovers, such as Tristram and Belle Isolde, Jason and Creusa. Then Cupid draws out the fiery dart which pierces the lover's heart, and Venus bathes and anoints the wound. Reason returns to the lover; Genius shrives him; and Venus presents him with a pair of black beads. With the beads in his hands the poet slowly goes home.

***Cook's Tale, The*** (p. 72). The tale breaks off before it has told much about a dissolute apprentice, his dismissal from his master's service, and his friendship with a man and wife, both as licentious as he is. (Some manuscripts, however, have inserted after *The Cook's Tale* what is probably the spurious *Tale of Gamelyn.**)

***Cruel Brother, The*** (p. 101). On her wedding-day a brother stabs his sister because her suitor has neglected to ask the brother's consent to the marriage.

***Debate of the Body and the Soul*** (p. 31). The poet dreams how the Body and the Soul (the Flesh and the Spirit) upbraid each other for causing the moral downfall of the knight stretched dead on a bier. Finally the Soul is claimed by a pack of misshapen creatures who hustle it off to Hell. The dreamer awakes.

***Dialogue Concerning Witty and Witless, A*** (p. 122). Theme: Who has the happier existence, the fool or the wise man?

***Doctor Faustus, The Tragical History of*** (p. 157). In return for twenty-four years of magical power and knowledge, during which Mephistophilis will do his every bidding, Faustus trades his soul to the Devil.

***Douglas Tragedy, The*** (p. 101). Lord William, while carrying off Lady Margaret Douglas, is pursued by her father and seven brothers, all of whom, pursuers and pursued, die in the fight or soon after.

***Dream of the Rood, The*** (p. 14). The poet has a vision of the Rood (Cross), adorned with dazzling gems, daubed with running blood, and wreathed with radiant light. The Tree of Victory speaks, telling of its sufferings as it bore Christ crucified, their burial together, the discovery of the cross later, and the veneration paid it. The dreamer confesses his wretched sins, and speaks of the redeeming power of the Cross.

***Duchess of Malfi, The*** (p. 245). Because she has married beneath her rank, and because they desire to be her inheritors, Ferdinand, Duke of Calabria, and the Cardinal torture their sister, the Duchess, with a procession of dancing madmen and with the murder of her children. Daniel de Bosola, the gentleman-of-the-horse hired by the brothers to spy upon the Duchess and Antonio Bologna, her steward-husband, repents his part, accidentally murders Antonio, and deliberately murders the Cardinal. Bosola himself meets death at the hands of the crazed Ferdinand, who in turn has received a fatal wound.

***Edward*** (p. 101). Edward finally admits that he has killed not his red-roan steed but his father.

***Edward II*** (p. 157). The plot is woven of historical facts, including Edward II's relation with Pierce de Gaveston, Hugh Spencer, Earl Lancaster, the elder and younger Mortimer, and Queen Isabella, from whom the King is estranged. It ends with Edward II's resignation of the Crown, and his assassination in Berkeley Castle.

***Elene*** (p. 14). Elene, or Helena, the mother of Constantine, Emperor of Rome, journeys to Jerusalem in search of the Cross on which the Master of Men was crucified. Judas, the son of Simon, is starved into submission; and on each of the three crosses he finds, Elene places, in turn, a dead child. The true Cross reveals itself by restoring the child to life.

***Epicoene, or the Silent Woman*** (p. 229). Morose, a miser who hates every kind of noise, is glad to marry one who is passed off as a silent woman, but who is in reality a boy in disguise hired by Sir Dauphine, Morose's nephew. The boy-wife, immediately after the marriage, acts the part of a loud-mouthed chatter-box, until Morose promises to grant Sir Dauphine £500 a year and a special inheritance.

***Euphues, or the Anatomy of Wit; Euphues and his England*** (p. 150).

I

After striking up a friendship with Philautus in Naples, Euphues the Athenian proceeds to oust the Italian from the affections of the fickle Lucilla, the governor's daughter, who, however, unexpectedly marries Curio. The Athenian and the Italian become friends again. (The rest of the book consists of letters to friends, particularly an epistle entitled "Euphues and his Ephoebus," a rather full essay on education based on Plutarch.)

II

After visiting the home of Fidus, in Canterbury, England, both go to London. Philautus marries. Euphues returns to Greece, and from Athens addresses a letter to the ladies of Italy in which he describes England. An epistle to his friend Philautus ends the story.

***Every Man in his Humour*** (p. 227). Each character's temperament is the result of a preponderant or excessive "humour": Kitely is jealous of his young Dame; Stephen is a country gull, and Matthew is a town gull; Knowell is worried about the morals of his son Edward; Captain Bobadil is a Paul's man (*i.e.,* a loafer) and a *miles gloriosus.* Brainworm, Knowell's familiar, is the contriver of the intrigues, and the old, merry Justice Clement is the resolver of them.

***Finnesburh*** (p. 8). Finn, King of the North Frisians, has married the Danish princess Hildeburh, whose brother Hnaef is invited for a visit. When the guest and his three-score followers are lodged in a great hall, the treacherous Finn attacks with overwhelming forces. Hnaef is slain. In a subsequent counterpart Finn falls at the hands of Hnaef's men, and Hildeburh is brought back to Denmark.

***Four P's, The*** (p. 122). A Palmer, a Pardoner, and a Poticary (apothecary) compete in telling the greatest lie. The Poticary tells of a miraculous cure, and the Pardoner of a woman freely released by the Devil because she was a plague in Hell. The Peddlar, however, acting as referee, awards the decision to the Palmer upon the assertion that out of the thousands of women known to him he never saw one out of patience (*i.e.,* out of temper).

***Franklin's Tale, The*** (p. 75). Only when he has removed the rocks round the coast of Brittany will Dorigen, the wife of Arveragus, consent to listen to the overtures of Squire Aurelius. This seemingly impossible task the Squire achieves two years later with the aid of a magician. Hearing how Arveragus had insisted that she keep her rash word, Aurelius graciously releases Dorigen from her promise.

***Friar Bacon and Friar Bungay*** (p. 154). One plot is concerned with the romance of Lacy, Earl of Lincoln, who in disguise woos Margaret, the daughter of the Keeper of Fressingfield, for Edward, Prince of Wales—a John Alden-Miles Standish courtship in which Prince Edward surrenders the maiden to the Earl. Another plot deals with the fabled Brazen Head. Miles, the servant of Bacon, is left to watch the head of brass constructed by his master and Friar Bungay. The Brazen Head successively says: "Time is," "Time was," and finally "Time is past," when it falls down and is shivered into pieces—awakening Bacon too late. (For an entertaining scene, read that in which Friar Bacon, Friar Bungay, and Jacques Vandermast, a German, perform before Frederick II, King of Germany, Ferdinand III, King of Castile, and the English King.)

***Friar's Tale, The*** (p. 74). A Summoner meets the Devil dressed as a yeoman, and they agree to share whatever they may get. When the Summoner attempts to extort twelve pence out of a poor old widow for an uncommitted sin, and when she insistently consigns his body and brain-pan to the devil, the disguised fiend carries the Summoner off to hell.

***Gamelyn, Tale of, The*** (p. 38). Gamelyn, a younger son of Sir John de Boundys, is deprived by his eldest brother of a rightful share in the father's estate. The hero rebels, downs the champion wrestler, becomes a leader of a band of outlaws in the forest, and finally obtains justice.

***Gammer Gurton's Needle*** (p. 121). Complications arise when Diccon the Bedlam (a *Vice* character) prompts Gammer Gurton into believing that the needle which she had lost while mending her servant Hodge's breeches is now in the possession of Dame Chat. To the spectator the *dénouement* is surprising; to Hodge, it is painful, for he becomes acutely aware of the missing needle sticking in the seat of his breeches.

***Gawayne and the Grene Knight, Sir*** (p. 60).

I

*Fytte the First: The Challenge.* A giant figure clad, like his horse, entirely in green and armed with a battle-axe, interrupts Arthur and his court revelling at Camelot in Christmas season. This enormous man challenges any knight to give him a buffet with the challenger's axe on condition that a return stroke be permitted a twelvemonth and a day hence at the Green Chapel. No knight dares accept; and when the King, rising in wrath, himself grasps the axe, Gawain, his nephew, taking up the challenge, beheads the Green Knight. The latter, however, picks up the rolling head by the hair, remounts his green steed, adjures Gawain to fulfill the compact, and takes his leave.

II

*Fytte the Second: The Compact.* On All-Hallow's Day Gawain sets out from Camelot upon his horse Gringolet for the rendezvous in North Wales. On Christmas Day, lost in a forest, his prayers for assistance are answered by the appearance on a hill of a great castle where he is entertained by the Lord and the Lady, as well as by an ancient, hideous dame. Since the Green Chapel is only a few miles away, Gawain's host arranges for three days of hunting, with the two agreeing to exchange at nightfall whatever each may get during the day.

III

*Fytte the Third: The Testing.* After the first day Gawain returns the unsought-for kiss bestowed by the Lady; after the second day, two kisses; but after the third day, while returning the three kisses, Gawain retains and conceals the green girdle which he had accepted from the chatelaine when told that the belt would make its wearer invulnerable.

IV

*Fytte the Fourth: The Counter-Buffet.* Proceeding to the Green Chapel on New Year's Day, Gawain there meets the Green Knight. Twice Arthur's nephew shrinks from the descending feints, but the third stroke gashes his neck. Then the Green Knight reveals that he, Bernlak (Bercilak) de Hautdesert by name, is the Lord of the Castle, and that the ancient dame is Morgan le Fay, the fairy-sister of Arthur, who, wishing to grieve Queen Guinevere, whom she hates, and to shame Arthur's court, has attempted to corrupt Gawain. A slight wound has been suffered only because Arthur's knight broke faith by not returning the green baldric.

Thereafter all the lords and ladies of the Court wear girdle-laces of green.

***Get Up and Bar the Door*** (p. 101). A goodman loses in the agreement with his goodwife that the first to speak is to bar the door.

***Glasgerion*** (p. 101). The substitution of a page for a prince at his clandestine appointment-place with his sweetheart, the princess, brings tragedy to all three.

***Goldyn Targe, The*** (p. 89). A May morning finds the poet on a flower-bed dreaming of a ship which disgorges Venus and her court of ladies. These surround the dreamer, but Reason with her golden targe or shield endeavors to deflect the arrows of Beauty and her warriors. The shield of Reason is beaten down, a powder is thrown into her eyes bereaving her of her powers, and the poet is captured. (Thus the allegory demonstrates how the golden targe of Reason is eventually made impotent by the gradual assaults of Love.)

***Gorboduc,*** or ***Ferrex and Porrex*** (p. 121). Gorboduc's division of his realm between his two sons stirs up jealousy. Porrex finally slays his brother Ferrex, who is the favorite son of their mother. In revenge Queen Videna murders Porrex.

***Guthlac*** (p. 14). It is the story of the historical Guthlac of the eighth century who forsook the world and lived the life of an anchorite—of his tormenting by demons, his triumph, and his death.

***Guy of Warwick*** (p. 48). Guy, the son of Siward of Wallingford, who is steward to Rohand, Earl of Warwick, is rejected by Felice, the Earl's daughter. From deeds of prowess performed in France, Germany, Italy, and Greece, he returns to England, slays a dragon, and marries Felice. He departs for further adventures to the Holy Land, where he slays the giant Amarant; but returns in time to deliver England from the Danes by defeating their champion, the giant Colbrand. He then becomes a hermit near Warwick, and only when on his death-bed does he reveal his identity, by sending Felice a ring that she recognizes. Felice dies soon after.

***Havelok the Dane*** (p. 48). The dying Aethelwold, King of England, leaves his daughter Goldborough to the guardianship of Earl Godrich of Cornwall. Almost simultaneously in Denmark, King Birkabeyn (Gunter) consigns his son Havelok and two daughters to the unprincipled Earl Godard. The latter kills the infant girls, but delivers the lad to the fisherman Grim to be drowned. When, during the night, a mystic light issuing from Havelok's mouth reveals the royal kinmark on Havelok's shoulder, Grim and his family escape with the boy to a place on the Humber, that part of England later called Grimsby.

As a kitchen-churl, known as Cuaran or Cuheran in Earl Godrich's household, the hero distinguishes himself by feats of strength. Impelled by the motive of making Goldborough forfeit her claim to the throne through marriage with a person of low rank, Godrich unites her to Havelok. Again, but this time to Goldborough, the mystic flame and an angel's voice disclose the identity of Havelok.

With Grim and his three sons, Havelok returns to Denmark, enlists the aid of Earl Ubbe, hangs Earl Godard, and is crowned king. With a Danish army Havelok invades England, burns Earl Godrich at the stake, and becomes also the King of England.

***Helen of Kirkconnell*** (p. 101). When a disappointed suitor shoots at Adam Fleming, Helen flings herself to death in front of her successful lover. Adam then kills the murderer. (Some versions do not name the lover.)

***Honest Whore, The*** (p. 236). Count Hippolito effects the regeneration of Bellafront, who gives up her harlotries and marries her seducer, Matheo. The Count, now the husband of Infelice, daughter of Gasparo Trebazzi, Duke of Milan, attempts to seduce the Magdalen he had formerly converted. Bellafront is saved by her father Orlando Friscobaldo, disguised as an old serving-man.

***House of Fame, The*** (p. 66). The poet dreams of being within the Glass Temple of Venus, the walls of which are graven with the whole story of the *Aeneid*. In particular does the betrayal of Dido by Aeneas conjure up other betrayers of women, among whom the author includes (lines 388—426) the falseness of Demophon to Phyllis, of Achilles to Briseis, of Paris to Oenone, of Jason to both Hypsipyle and Medea, of Hercules to Dejanira, of Theseus to Ariadne. (The legends of many of these are told also in *The Legend of Good Women,* page 68.) The ensuing two books describe how the poet is carried by a golden eagle to the heavens, with the eagle acting in the capacity of a guide to the House of Fame. When the dreamer has seen for himself the capriciousness of the Goddess, who now withholds fame from the deserving suitors, now grants fame to the pretending, he enters the sixty-miles-long House of Rumor, whither all false tidings fly. After describing how at all times the house is full of shipmen and pilgrims, with scripts brimful of lies, and also pardoners, couriers, and messengers, with boxes crammed full of lies as ever vessel was with lees, the poet at last sees a man whose name he knows not, but who seems to be "A man of gret auctorite." With these five words the fragment, in the middle of the sentence, breaks off. (The "man of great authority" has been interpreted as referring to either Richard II or to John of Gaunt.)

***Hyde Park*** (p. 247). One plot relates how Bonavent, supposedly lost at sea, recovers his own wife. Another is concerned with Mistress Carol, and how she soon finds herself unable to jeer at Fairfield, as she has already jeered at Rider and Venture. The third story tells how Trier, through his own misguided plan, loses Julietta Fairfield, his betrothed, to Lord Bonvile.

***Jew of Malta, The*** (p. 157). For the purpose of helping pay the tribute demanded by the Grand Seignior of Turkey, the Governor of Malta, Ferneze by name, orders the impounding of half of the Jew Barabas's wealth. Barabas himself brings about the death of his daughter Abigail and her lover, and succeeds in destroying the Governor of Malta and usurping the position. He meets his death by being hurled through the collapsible floor into that very cauldron of boiling water into which he had planned to throw the Turkish commander to whom he had previously betrayed the town.

***Juliana*** (p. 14). Juliana, a devout Christian maiden who lived in the days of the Roman emperor Maximian, refused to marry Heliseus, persecutor of the Christians. That heathen and her father Africanus torture and imprison her, hoping that she will thereby be coerced. She routs the demon Belial who appears in the guise of an angel. Summoned by the governor at daybreak, she suffers martyrdom by decapitation.

***Kai*** (p. 42). In *Kilhwch and Olwen,* Kai (Kay) is described as one whose breath lasted nine nights and nine days under water, and whose sword-wound no physician could heal.

***Kemp Owyne*** (p. 101). Three kisses of Kemp Owyne metamorphose Isabel to her human form.

***Kilhwch and Olwen, or the Twrch Trwyth*** (p. 42). Kilhwch succeeds in gaining the hand of Olwen, daughter of Yspaddaden Penkawr, King of the Giants; but achieves the thirteen well-nigh insurmountable tasks set by the giant-king only after being assisted by his cousin Arthur, who at first gives him a retinue of knights in attendance, and later joins personally in the quest. Arthur really is the central figure; and Yspaddaden himself, in yielding up his daughter, says to Kilhwch, "She is thine; but therefore needest thou not thank me, but Arthur, who hath accomplished this for thee."

***King Estmere*** (p. 101). In order to marry King Adland's daughter, Estmere, King of England, slays his rival Bremor, King of Spain.

***King Horn*** (p. 48). The invading Saracens kill King Murray of Suddene, while Queen Godhild escapes. Horn, their fifteen-year-old son, is set adrift with some boy-companions, among whom are Athulf and Fikenhild. Landing at Westernesse, Horn is well received by King Ailmar, who adopts him as his foster-child. Rymenhild the princess falls in love with Horn, and they secretly plight their troth. The scheming Fikenhild, by betraying the lovers to the King, succeeds in having the hero banished.

In Ireland, under the name of Cutberd, Horn slays the champion of the pillaging Saracens. Thereupon King Thurston offers his daughter's hand in marriage; but for seven years Horn postpones acceptance. When word is brought of Rymenhild's intended nuptials, Horn, returning garbed as a palmer, reveals his identity to her by means of a magic ring she had once given him; with the aid of Athulf, kills the would-be husband, King Modi; discloses his noble birth to King Ailmar; and then leaves to recover his father's kingdom of Suddene. Warned in a dream of Rymenhild's danger and possible marriage, Horn returns in time to save his love by killing the traitor Fikenhild. Then comes the "wedding bell" ending.

***Kingis Quair, The*** (p. 88). From the prison window of the English Castle the prince sees the Lady Jane walking in the garden below. For him it is love at first sight. In a dream at night the royal poet is carried up to the palace of Venus, where the Goddess sends Good Hope to guide the prince to Minerva, who promises to help him in his suit. Good Hope now leads him to the goddess of Fortune, who has James climb upon her ever-revolving wheel. Upon awakening, a message arrives from Venus promising him success in his wooing. When the royal poet has thanked all who have aided him, he pens an Envoy addressed to the works of Chaucer and Gower.

***Knight's Tale, The*** (p. 72). Palamon and Arcite, two young Theban knights, cousins, and sworn-brothers, are the prisoners of Theseus, Duke of Athens. A fatal passion for Emilia, sister of Queen Hippolyta, ruptures their friendship. To decide who should marry Emilia, the Duke's sister-in-law, a grand tournament is held. Arcite, who has prayed to Mars, wins,—but, thrown from his horse, loses the Lady in the very hour of his triumph. On the other hand. Palamon, who has prayed to Venus, loses in combat—but, after much sorrow, marries Emilia. (Practically the identical story is told in *The Two Noble Kinsmen,* p. 226, and in John Dryden's *Palamon and Arcite.*)

***Lanval*** (p. 46). Supreme in his happiness with a wondrous fairy maiden who appears whenever he summons her, Lanval rejects the advances made by the Queen and in violation of his pledge to the maiden, boasts of the secret love-affair. As a result, not only does the fay no longer heed his call, but the Queen brings him to trial for being insulting. Lanval is sentenced to death unless he can prove that his sweetheart is, as he had stated to the Queen, the paragon of women. At the very last moment the maiden, in all her confounding beauty and splendor, appears; and Lanval, thereupon released by Arthur, betakes himself with his beloved to the Isle of Avalon.

***Lord Thomas and Fair Annet*** (p. 101). A "nut-browne" maid kills Fair Annet, her rival, with a bodkin, and Lord Thomas in turn drives his dagger into his "nut-browne bride" and then turns it against himself.

***Luve Ron*** (p. 26). A nun entreats the Franciscan friar to write a love rune or letter from which she can learn how to choose a "soth lefmon" or true lover. Earthly love, the poet says, is inconstant and transient; and only the love of the Heavenly Bridegroom will bring eternal happiness.

***Maid's Tragedy, The*** (p. 243). Amintor, betrothed to Aspatia, daughter of the old humorous Calianax, is ordered by the King to marry Evadne. In the bridal-chamber she reveals to Amintor's unbelieving ears that she is the King's mistress, that not for a night or two but for ever will she forbear Amintor's bed, and that the marriage has been engineered by the King because Evadne must have a husband "to father children," so that her sin may be more honorable. Melantius, her soldier-brother, bullies her into slaying her royal seducer; but when Amintor still does not forgive her, Evadne kills herself. (The drama gets its name from the tragic death of Aspatia, "troth-plight wife to Amintor," who, disguised, is killed in a duel with Amintor.)

***Malcontent, The*** (p. 240). Disguised as Malevole the Malcontent, Giovanni Altofronto returns to Genoa, from which, as the Duke, he had been usurped by Pietro Jacomo. Mendoza, a minion to Aurelia, Jacoma's Duchess, and Mendoza's paramour, bribes Malevole to poison Pietro. When Mendoza attempts to force Maria, Altofronto's Duchess, into marriage, Malevole takes off his disguise and resumes the throne.

***Manciple's Tale, The*** (p. 76). Phebus shoots his wife through the heart with his bow, for his snow-white speaking crow has revealed to him that she is unfaithful. Then the god in anger pulls out every white feather of the crow, takes away the bird's power of song, deprives it of the ability to counterfeit the speech of man, flings it out of the door to the devil, "And for this caas been alle crowes blake." Moral—Tell no man how another has treated his wife; "Kepe wel they tonge, and thenk upon the crow."

***Man of Law's Tale, The*** (p. 72). The Sultan of Syria's mother has her converted son murdered; and Constance, the daughter of the Christian Emperor of Rome who had married the heathen prince on condition that he should turn

Christian, is set adrift on a raft with provisions for three years. Rescued by Elda and his wife Hermengyld, Constance converts both. Later, a felon knight, to whom the heroine has refused to yield herself, kills Hermengyld; and Constance, by a miracle proved innocent of the false accusation of murder, is thereupon married to King Aella of Northumberland. To them is born a son Maurice. Again a mother-in-law proves Constance's undoing; for Donegild, the King's mother, wroth with the Queen for having introduced Christianity, in the absence of the King forges letters in Aella's name so that as a result the Queen and her son are turned adrift on a raft. Upon returning from Scotland, the King, discovering the truth, slays his mother; then, conscience-stricken, sets out on a pilgrimage to Rome. There he is reunited with Constance and Maurice, both of whom, rescued from the sea by a senator of Rome, had been living in Rome for twelve years with a noble couple called Arsemius and Helen.

***Merchant's Tale, The*** (p. 75). The sixty-year-old Baron January becomes blind; and his young wife May and her lover Damyan take advantage of this in a tree. At that moment Pluto restores the old man's eyesight, and he sees what is occurring. But realizing that nothing can be done about it, the Baron accepts as true his wife's statement that his eyes have deceived him.

***Miller's Tale, The*** (p. 72). The poor scholar Nicholas and the young Alison, wife of the wealthy carpenter John, succeed in gulling the unsuspicious husband by predicting a second flood. (The important episode of the story is that of the sidetracked kiss, in which the parish clerk Absalom has the major part.)

***Monk's Tale, The*** (p. 73). First, the monk explains in the prologue that by tragedy is meant a story:

> "Of hym that stood in greet prosperitee,
> And is yfallen out of heigh degree
> Into myserie, and endeth wrecchedly."

Then, to illustrate his definition of tragedy, he gives a succession of seventeen short accounts of misfortunes of famous persons: Lucifer, Adam, Samson, Hercules, Nebuchadnezzar, Belshazzar, Zenobia, Pedro of Spain, King Pierre (de Lusigan) of Cyprus, Bernabò Visconti, Hugolin of Pisa (Ugolina), Nero, Holofernes, Antiochus, Alexander (the Great), Julius Caesar, and Croesus.

***Myrrdhin*** (p. 42). According to fable, Myrrdhin sprang from the union of a demon and a Welsh princess. There also seems to be some connection with the Merlin of the Arthurian tradition and the historical Myrrdhin (Merlin), a Welsh or British bard of the fifth century to whom a group of patriotic poems have been more or less doubtfully ascribed.

***New Way to Pay Old Debts, A*** (p. 245). Frank Wellborn, prodigal nephew of Sir Giles Overreach, persuades Lady Allworth to act in such a manner that his Uncle will be led to believe that Wellborn and the wealthy widow are soon to marry. On the strength of the attentions Lady Allworth pays his nephew, Sir Giles wipes out his relative's debts because of the expected ease with which he will cozen his nephew out of the wealthy dowager's property. At the same time Lord Lovell pretends to court Margaret, Overreach's daughter, but is really assisting Tom Allworth (Lord Lovell's page) and Margaret to see more of each other. In the end the knighted scamp finds himself thrice duped: Lord Lovell and Lady Allworth marry, Margaret and Tom become man and wife, and even the deeds of conveyance to the estate of his nephew Frank turn out to be blank papers.

***Nun's Priest's Tale, The*** (p. 74). Master Chaunticleer the cock, vainglorious among his many hens, tells his favorite, Dame Pertelote, of a dream in which he dies, his killer being a monster whose color was a cross between yellow and red, and whose tail and ears were black. In the interesting discussion that follows, his wife minimizes, while Chaunticleer emphasizes, the significance of dreams.

More than a month later Dan Russell the fox appears and flatters the cock on his singing. The latter, beguiled by the praise, shuts his eyes and begins to crow most lustily. Immediately seizing Chaunticleer by the throat, the fox makes off. In the woods the cock advises Dan Russell to make a meal of him quickly, for pursuers are fast approaching. When the fox opens his mouth to reply that he intends doing so at once, Master Chaunticleer escapes by flying into a tree. Moral: Beware of giving ear to flattery.

***Nut-Browne Maid, The*** (p. 98). To test the maid whom he has wooed and won, the knight declares himself to be an outlaw, and describes the humiliations and hardships that are the lot of a man with a price on his head. She still declares herself in love, and she is rewarded for her constancy when her lover reveals that he is an earl's son.

***Old Fortunatus*** (p. 235). When offered his pick among six things (Wisdom, Strength, Health, Beauty, Long Life, and Riches), Fortunatus, a native of Cyprus, chooses an inexhaustible purse. After world-wide travels he reaches Babylon, where he steals from his host the Soldan a magical wishing-cap that can transport its wearer to any part of the world. The goddess Fortune berates him for abusing her gift, and tells him that he is to die. His sons, Ampedo and Andelocia, inherit the wishing-cap and the bottomless purse, but because of their father's choice they also die.

***Old Wives' Tale, The*** (p. 155). Delia, a king's daughter, falls into the hands of the magician Sacrapant, who also makes captive the two brothers who search for her. Eumenides, a knight, and the Ghost (of Jack, befriended by Eumenides) rescue all three.

***Pardoner's Tale, The*** (p. 74). In the prologue the Pardoner describes his method of gulling the people by playing upon their superstitions; at the conclusion of his sermon-tale, the text of which is "The love of money is the root of all evil," the Pardoner has the effrontery to try the very same deceitful game upon his listeners.

The Pardoner's discourse on the evils of Gluttony, Drunkenness, and Swearing is illustrated by this story of three rioters who, setting out to find Death in order to slay him, find an old man who directs them in their search. Instead of meeting Death, they find under an oak a heap of golden florins. While the youngest is sent to fetch bread and wine to sustain them until nightfall, when they hope to carry the treasure to a safe place, the other two plot to increase their share by putting the third reveller to death upon his return. This is done; and then the murderers sit down to eat and drink. Two of the three bottles of wine, however, have been poisoned by the now-dead rioter, who had wished to obtain the whole treasure for himself; and so all three find Death under the oak to which the old man had sent them.

***Parliament of Fowls, The*** (p. 67). Lack of light compels Chaucer to betake himself to bed, just as he is summarizing the contents of *Tully on the Dream of Scipio* (Cicero's *De Re Publica,* Bk. VI, "Somnium Scipionis"), particularly that part where the elder Africanus, appearing to Scipio the younger in his sleep, shows him the Milky Way, and the nine spheres (the seven planets, that of the fixed stars, and the primum mobile).

In a dream Scipio's ancestor Africanus leads Chaucer to a garden to which, in full parliament, every fowl has come, as on every Saint Valentine's day, to choose a mate. Upon the hand of the goddess Nature, enthroned on a flowery hill, perches the most noble formel (female) eagle. This bird is claimed by the royal tercel eagle, who, being above all others in rank, has first choice. When two other tercels, of a lower rank, advance individual suits for the same formel eagle, a debate is precipitated in the parliament, each bird-folk being permitted by Nature to elect one representative to render the verdict for all.

It seems there must be battle is the first thought of the tercel-falcon, the representative of the birds of prey; but his second thought advocates the choice of the worthiest knight, he highest in degree and of the gentlest blood—

" 'And of these thre she wot hireself, I trowe,
Which that he be, for it is light to knowe.' "

Let the male eagle love elsewhere if she will not love him, counsels the goose, elected by the waterfowl; but this advice provokes the sparrow-hawk's insult, that the goose could have hidden her folly by restraining her wagging tongue, yet after all,

" 'A fool can not be stille.' "
(A fool can not be silent.)

As the aroused laughter dies down, the seed-eating fowl straightway choose the faithful ring-dove, whose statement that a lover should serve his lady until death, occasions further wrangling. In objecting to the ring-dove's point of view the duck asks,

"That men shulde loven alwey causeles,
Who can a resoun fynde or wit in that?"
(" 'That men should love forever, without cause,
Who can find a reason or wit there?' ")

So low and wretched is your nature that you can not see or guess what love is, is the noble falcon's reproof of the duck. When the cuckoo has declared that while she can have her mate it matters not how the three eagles fare, the merlin makes a vitriolic attack upon the cuckoo as one who so long as his paunch is well filled, thinks it should suffice for all.

Finally, Nature commands the bickering to cease, for no nearer are they to a conclusion. Her decision is that the formel eagle shall choose the mate she wishes, counseling the latter, however, that she should take the royal tercel, as the falcon said full wisely, for the tercel is noblest and most worthy. Timidly the formel eagle asks a boon, granted by Nature, that she choose her mate one year later. After all the other birds have selected their mates, a roundel is sung in honor of Nature. And with the shouting raised by the birds, Chaucer wakes.

***Parson's Tale, The*** (p. 76). The tale is a sermon in conventional style on Penitence, emphasizing the Seven Deadly Sins (Pride, Wrath, Envy, Accidia or Sloth, Avarice, Gluttony, Lechery) by describing each of them and immediately giving the proper remedy. Each sin has its branches and twigs; for example, some of the evils that come from Pride, the general root of all evils, are Disobedience, Hypocrisy, Swelling of Heart, Impatience, Vain Glory.

***Pearl, The*** (p. 59). The poet laments over the grave of a baby-girl (probably his daughter) who had died before she was two years old. In his sleep a vision reveals his Margaret (the word means *pearl* in Latin) on the opposite side of the bank, seated as a queen of heaven. Pearl, now a bride of the Lamb of God, and matured in wisdom, instructs him that her paradisiac state renders needless his great grief, and by the favor of the Lamb grants him a distant glimpse of the New Jerusalem. Rashly he desires to plunge into the stream to join her on the opposite side; but wakes to find himself beside her grave.

***Peredur*** (p. 42). In Welsh legend Peredur is the subject of a tale in *The Mabinogion* (p. 41). The knight is possibly identified with Perceval, the subject of a legend or folk-tale, with Sir Percival of the Round Table, and with Parzival of the German epic by Wolfram von Eschenbach.

***Perkin Warbeck, The Chronicle History of*** (p. 247). Warbeck, the false pretender to the throne of England, marries Lady Katherine Gordon at the request of James IV of Scotland and against the wishes of her father, the Earl of Huntley. Later, deserted by James IV in their joint expedition to England, Warbeck is captured and executed.

***Philaster, or Love lies a-Bleeding*** (p. 244). Philaster, heir to the crown of Sicily, loves Arethusa; but her father, the usurping King, favors her marriage to Pharamond, Prince of Spain The latter, however, is detected in an intrigue with Megra, an abandoned lady of the court who spitefully accuses Arethusa of misconduct with Bellario, Philaster's page. Even the rightful heir believes the aspersions, and wounds both his page and his sweetheart. But everything rights itself when it transpires that Bellario is no other than Lady Euphrasia, daughter of Dion, whose love of Philaster had led her to enter his service in disguise.

***Physician's Tale, The*** (p. 74). Before Virginius can prove that Virginia is his daughter, the wicked judge Appius awards the maiden to the villein Claudius, who has been suborned by the lustful magistrate to claim that Virginia is his long-stolen child-thrall. Advised by her father that her chastity will cost her either death or shame, the virtuous heroine, rather than be possessed by the decemvir, chooses decapitation at the hands of Virginius. When the judge in turn decrees that Virginius be hanged, the people revolt. Appius commits suicide in prison; and only by the grace of Virginius is the churl exiled instead of hanged.

***Play of Love, The*** (p. 122). Their own vicissitudes are discussed by "Neither Loving nor Loved," "Loving and Not Loved," "Loved and Not Loving," and "Both Loved and Loving."

***Play of the Wether, The*** (p. 122). Various petitioners request from Jupiter the specific kind of weather best for their individual occupations. Their opinions are so conflicting that Jupiter decides to continue providing changeable weather.

***Prioress's Tale, The*** (p. 73). A seven-year-old boy, on his way to and from school through the Jews' quarters, sings the *Alma redemptoris* (found in the Roman Breviary). One day some Jews cut the throat of the widow's child and cast his body into a pit. When searched for by his distracted mother, the "litel clergeon" discovers himself to her by miraculously singing the hymn. The Provost, when told, has the guilty Jews executed. Then the child, still singing *O Alma redemptoris mater,* is drawn up from the well. A monk, told that death can not overtake the boy until the grain placed on his tongue by "Christes mooder sweete" is taken off, does just that: the child gives "up the goost ful softely," and the body is buried in a marble tomb.

***Ralph Roister Doister*** (p. 120). Ralph, a good-natured if boasting simpleton, presumes to woo Dame Christian Custance, a wealthy widow, whose betrothed, Gavin Goodluck, is absent. Matthew Merrygreek, the go-between, provides much of the fun by deliberately misreading Ralph's letter to Custance. Goodluck, alienated from the widow by the reports that she is permitting other suitors to court her, finally learns of her constancy in love, and marries her.

***Reeve's Tale, The*** (p. 72). (The Miller had directed his tale at the Reeve, who had been a carpenter; and this story retaliates at the former's expense.) Cheated of part of their meal by Simon Simkin, the miller of Trompington, the two poor scholars John and Aleyn revenge themselves by having intimate relations with the miller's wife and his daughter.

***Rime of Sir Thopas*** (p. 73). Sir Thopas, a native of Poperyng in Flanders, is described as a fine hunter, archer, and wrestler. He sets out for Fairyland, for it is his avowed purpose to marry only an elf-queen; but, in order to give single battle to the giant Olifaunt met on the way, he returns for his armor. (The tale is cut short by Mine Host, and Chaucer attempts a second, that of Melibee.)

***Roaring Girl, The*** (p. 237). The notorious Moll Cutpurse helps Sebastian Wentgrave trick his father into sanctioning Sebastian's marriage to Mary Fitz-allard.

***Robin Hood and Guy of Gisborne*** (p. 101). Robin Hood slays Guy of Gisborne, and then, representing himself as Guy, tricks the Sheriff of Nottingham into releasing Little John.

***Romaunt of the Rose, The*** (p. 64). A young man of twenty (L'Amant, or the Lover) dreams that on a May morning his wanderings bring him to a high wall enclosing a garden. On the outside are graven the grim-visaged figures of Hate, Felonye, Vilanye, Coveitise, Avarice, Envye, Sorowe, Elde, Poope Holy (Hypocrisy), and Povert. Smiting upon a small wicket in the wall gains him admittance by the maiden-porter Ydelnesse, the friend of Myrthe, lord of the garden, who with his companions Curtesie, the God of Love, and Swete-Lokyng, is dancing merrily on the greensward of the park. Each of the two quivers that Swete-Lokyng is carrying contains a set of five arrows: the first, the golden arrows called Beaute, Symplesse, Fraunchise, Compaignye, and Fair-Semblaunt; the other, the black-as-hell ones designated as Pride, Vylanye, Shame, Wanhope, and Newe-Thought. The others in the dance include Beaute, Richesse, Largesse, Fraunchise, Curtesye, Fair Idleness, and Youthe. When the dance, in which the young man has participated upon the invitation of Curtesye, is over, he continues walking, and, aware of being followed by the God of Love, comes to a fountain on which appears the inscription: "Here starf the fayre Narcisus." (Here died the beautiful Narcissus.) In the spring, which mirrors the wonders of the garden, the lover sees among the hundreds of objects "A roser chargid full of rosis," and, particularly enamored of one more lovely than the rest, advances to pluck it. (End of Fragment A, line 1,705.)

While fearing to grasp the rose because of the surrounding thorns, the young man is shot at by the God of Love, the first arrow Beaute being followed by Symplesse, Curtesie (Fraunchise), Company, and Fair-Semblaunt. When the lover consents to yield hastily, the God of Love proceeds to give full instructions in the art of love, leaving behind with the youth the company of Swete-Thought, Swete-Thenkyng, and Swete-Lokyng.

Near the rose-tree lies hidden the churl Daunger, with Wykked-Tonge, Shame, born of Trespas and Resoun, and Chastite; and when the Lover attempts, with the assistance of Bialacoil (Fair Welcomyng) to pluck the Rose, Daunger awakes and drives away both Bialacoil and the young man. When Resoun urges the lover to relinquish his hope, for all love is folly, the lover, rejecting the advice, concludes with "Who that me chastisith, I hym hate." The lover attempts to appease Daunger, following the counsel of Freend to use flattery, and helped by Fraunchise and Pity. Finally, with the direct assistance of Bialacoil he succeeds in kissing the Rosebud; but Wykked-Tonge, awakening, arouses Jelousie, who imprisons Bialacoil, and confines the Rosebud in a tower, guarded by Daunger, Shame, and Drede. At the point where the lover is bemoaning his fate, this part comes to an end, (line 4,432 of the English translation). However, (this is the continuation of the story, forty years later, by Jean de Meun) with the aid of Venus, Nature, and Genius, the tower of Jealousy is forced, after a long siege, to capitulate and L'Amant finally gains possession of the Rosebud.

***Sapho and Phao*** (p. 151). Recounts the love of Phao for Queen Sapho whom jealous Venus has rendered impervious to love.

***Second Nun's Tale*** (p. 76): On her marriage night the maiden Cecilia tells her bridegroom Valerian that the angel who guards her continuously will slay the man who loves her ignobly. Before Valerian can acquire proof of his wife's statement, he must, she explains, be baptized. Through the offices of Saint Urban the bridegroom beholds the angel. Valerian asks a boon, that his brother Tiburtius should know the truth, and this is granted. The brothers are later arrested and decapitated, but not until they have converted their jailor Maximius, an officer of the prefect who is beaten to death with a whip of lead by order of the pagan lord Almachius. When Cecilia can not be burned to death by a bath of flames, she is given three strokes on the neck, and left to die (for the law did not permit a fourth stroke). After preaching the faith for three days, Cecilia passes away. The house in which she is buried is called Saint Cecilia's Church.

***Secunda Pastorum*** (p. 106). Upon discovering that the "new-born infant" in the cradle is really the stolen sheep for which they are searching, the three shepherds toss Mak the sheep-stealer in a blanket. After a night's sleep the shepherds are awakened by an angel who tells them that the Christ Child has been born and that they must hasten to Bethlehem.

***Shipman's Tale, The*** (p. 73). In return for the loan of a hundred francs, the wife of a merchant permits intimacies on the part of the monk John. The latter, however, had borrowed the same sum of money from the merchant, who, returning from a trip to Flanders, is told by the monk that the loan has been repaid to the wife. After a conversation with his spouse, the merchant realizes only too well what has happened.

***Shoemaker's Holiday, The*** (p. 235). Rowland Lacy loves Rose, daughter of Roger Oateley, Lord Mayor of London; but both Sir Hugh Lacy, Earl of Lincoln, and Rose's father disapprove of the affair. Rowland disguises himself as Hans the Dutch shoemaker and enters the service of Simon Eyre, master shoemaker to the Lord Mayor's household. By an elopement the lovers thwart the opposition of both families.

***Spanish Tragedy, The*** (p. 152). Aroused by the screams of Princess Bel-imperia, Hieronimo, Marshal of Spain, rushes with a torch into the arbor, only to find his son Horatio strung up to a tree. While nestling in an alcove with the Princess, Horatio had been killed in her very presence by Lorenzo, her brother, and Balthazar, the prisoner-son of the Viceroy of Portugal, whose suit for the hand of Bel-imperia is favored by her father and brother. The crazed Hieronimo arranges to have all the implicated characters act in a play before the court, in the course of which Balthazar and Lorenzo are killed, while the Princess and the Marshal of Spain commit suicide.

***Spens, Sir Patrick*** (p. 101). The Scotch hero with his ship's company is destroyed on the return voyage from a mission to Norway.

***Squire's Tale, The*** (p. 75). At Sarray, in the land of Tartary, lived King Cambiuskan with his wife Elpheta, his daughter Canacee, and his two sons, Algarsyf and Cambalus. At the King's birthday feast there appears a knight, bringing from the King of Arabia magic gifts. In the mirror one could forsee the future and, above all, a lady could tell if her lover were true or false. The ring gave to its wearer the power to understand and answer all birds, and also the knowledge of every grass that has root, and whom it would heal. While both the mirror and the ring are for Canacee, the sword is not. This third gift could cut through any armor, and only a stroke with the flat side of the blade would heal the wound. The next morning Canacee, while out on a walk, and wearing the ring, understands the story of a tercelet who had been abandoned by her lover. Taking the falcon home, the young maiden gives it tender care. Chaucer professes to be about to tell how the tercelet's lover is recovered through Cambalus; of Cambiuskan's conquests; of Algarsyf's winning of Theodora; of the brothers' fight with the lover of Canacee. At this point, however, the fragment breaks off.

***Summoner's Tale, The*** (p. 75). (The purpose of this tale is to discredit the Friar, just as the Friar has attempted in his tale to discredit the Summoner.) A greedy and hypocritical friar begs a benefaction from the invalid Thomas, whom he has just lectured. The largess which the goodman of the house bestows upon the Friar sends the religious man to seek satisfaction from the lord of the district. The squire Jenkin proposes an ingenious solution.

***Tale of Melibee*** (p. 73). While the wealthy young Melibeus is in the fields, three enemies beat up his wife Prudence, and, wounding his daughter Sophie in five places, leave her for dead. At his summons, true and false friends arrive, and contradict each other as to what he should do. When they are gone, his wife urges him to forgive his enemies, citing, among her various authorities for this counsel, Ovid's *The Remedy of Love.* Melibeus, thanking God for having sent him a wife of so great discretion and mercy, forgives his adversaries.

***Tamburlaine the Great*** (p. 156). Tamburlaine helps Cosroe take the kingdom of Persia from the latter's brother Mycetes, and then he himself usurps the throne. He tortures Bajazeth, Emperor of the Turks, and Zabina, the Empress, until they kill themselves; he compels conquered Kings to drag his chariot about. Zenocrate, the captured daughter of the Soldan of Egypt, alone brings out Tamburlaine's sympathy. Both she and Tamburlaine die.

***Tam Lin*** (p. 101). Tam Lin is rescued from the Queen of the fairies by his mortal sweetheart Janet.

***Testament of Cresseid, The*** (p. 88). Deserted by Diomede, Cresseid returns in shame to her father Calchas. For blaspheming Venus and Cupid, the gods spoil her beauty and smite her with leprosy. While Cresseid is begging by the roadside with other lepers, Troilus and his knights ride by. Because she is so changed, he does not recognize her; because her eyes have been affected by the disease, she does not recognize him. But something in her face conjures up the memory of his old love, and he casts a purse of pearls and jewels to her. Upon learning through another leper who her benefactor has been, Cresseid swoons away and dies. To Prince Troilus is brought the ruby he once had given her. He raises a tomb to her memory.

***Thomas Rymer*** (p. 101). Thomas loved a fairy who took him with her to Elfland:

> "And till seven years were past and gone,
> True Thomas on earth was never seen."

***'Tis Pity She's A Whore*** (p. 246). To give her child a name, Annabella marries Soranzo, a nobleman. Her husband, through the investigation of his servant Vasques, discovers that her brother Giovanni is the father of the new-born. To save his sister from vengeance, Giovanni stabs her; then he kills Soranzo at a banquet; but falls before Vasques.

***Trick to Catch the Old One, A*** (p. 237). Lucre, a usurer, is fleeced by his nephew Witgood who, so the Uncle is led to think, will soon come into a fortune by marrying the wealthy Widow Medler of Staffordshire.

***Troilus and Criseyde*** (p. 66). The poet announces that he will write of the double sorrows of Troilus's love for Criseyde, and how in the end she forsook him.

The priest Calchas, divining the doom of Troy, deserts to the Greeks, leaving behind his widow-daughter Criseyde. Troilus, a son of Priam, King of Troy, falls deeply in love with the soothsayer's daughter; and finally, with the assistance of her uncle Pandarus, who acts as the go-between, Criseyde capitulates to the prince. Both vow eternal fidelity. Meanwhile Calchas has arranged that Criseyde be exchanged for the Trojan Antenor recently captured by the Greeks. Not only does Criseyde find it impossible to return to Troilus within ten days, as she had promised him, but also finds it impossible to keep her vow to remain constant: she has finally succumbed to the overtures of Diomede the Greek.

One day Troilus notices a sort of tunic which in battle had been torn off Diomede. While observing its workmanship he suddenly sees on the collar a brooch which he had given Criseyde the morning she was compelled to leave Troy. After that, the disillusioned prince always seeks Diomede in battle, but, although they often meet, Fortune would not that either should die by the other's hand. Later, Troilus, who never meets Criseyde again, is killed by Achilles.

***Two Sisters, The*** (p. 101). An older sister drowns her younger sister, whose beauty had alienated the affections of the older sister's sweetheart.

***Voiage and Travail of Sir John Maundeville, Knight, The*** (p. 91). This popular book of travels, deviating from its professed purpose of being a sort of guide-book for pilgrims to the Holy City of Jerusalem and other consecrated places thereabout, is both a compendium of popular information about Turkey and Tartary, Persia and Egypt, Syria and Arabia, Chaldea and India, and a treasury of entertaining, quaint, and curious stories taken from romance, natural history, and geography. Among the wonders described are those of the Ypocras daughter who was transformed from a woman to a dragon, of the land where women dwell without company of men, of the roses and how they first came into the world, of a tribe of cannibals with the heads of hounds, of people of flat face, lacking nose and mouth, of the land of Prester John where precious stones are so large that they are used for dishes and cups, of women who slay by a look, of diamonds that can be made to grow, of headless men with eyes in their shoulders, of horned wild men who speak not, but grunt like pigs, of men whose enormous feet can be held over their heads as an umbrella warding off the rays of the sun, of pygmies and one-eyed men and two-headed wild geese. In some cases, however, later discoveries have confirmed such accounts as the burning of widows on the pyre of their husbands, and the statement, made at a time when the belief prevailed that the earth was flat, that it is of spheroidal form. Even in that day products were adulterated; for example, turpentine was adulterated to give the odor of balm and sold as balm.

***Volpone, or The Fox*** (p. 228). Volpone, a magnifico, assisted by his familiar servant Mosca, pretends that he is about to die, in order to cozen one would-be heir after another into making extreme offerings in return for an inheritance. Retribution falls upon the miser-sensualist and his knavish parasite, as well as upon Voltore, the shyster advocate, Corbaccio, who had disinherited his son Bonario, and Corvino, the shameless merchant who had even offered his wife to Volpone.

***Vox Clamantis*** (p. 54). In a dream-allegory the poet has different adventures, all symbolizing the Peasants' Rising of 1381, the terror of the wealthy, and the death of Wat Tyler. After vividly describing the insurrection in the first book, Gower, grieved at the moral decay of his England, proceeds to examine and indict all orders of society—which he classifies as being the clergy, the knights, and the laborers. After scolding roundly the corrupt clergy, (Bk. IV), the debased knights (Bk. V), and the knavish lawyers (Bk. VI), he reaches the seventh and the last book. In this, as in his *Mirrour de l'Omme,* Gower again dwells upon the Seven Sins, the evil condition of the land, and the need of repentance. His conclusion carries his appeal up to the throne itself, as the power from which all good must come. (Ruskin, in his *Fors Clavigera,* Letter XV, follows the classification, dividing the three great classes into the soldiers, "those who live by fighting, either by robbing wise peasants, or getting themselves paid by foolish ones"; the clergy, "those who live by teaching or exhibition of labor"; and the peasants, "the producers of food, out of land or water.")

***Waldere*** (p. 9). Other sources help complete the story of the heroic exploits of Walther (Waldere), the West Gothic hero of Aquitaine who when a child was given as a hostage to Attila, King of the Huns, and who grew up to be a great general in the wars against Attila. The first fragments give Hildegund's (Hildegyth's) heartening of her lover; the second, preserve the answering challenges of Gunther (Guthhere) and Walther.

***Wanderer, The*** (p. 10). A man's kinsmen and lord have been slain. Utterly friendless and weary of heart, he roams, nursing his grief. In his dreams he embraces his liege lord, and relives the joys of the past. When he awakes and sees nothing but the cold gray waves, the scurrying snow, the sharp hail, and the birds dipping their wings in the waves, he is moved to the reflection that the world is full of care, and that we are all in the hands of Fate. Then comes the Christian sentiment: happy is he who seeks comfort with his Father in heaven, with whom alone all things are enduring.

***White Divil, The, or Vittoria Corombona*** (p. 245). Francisco de' Medicis, Duke of Florence, assisted by Ludovico and Gaspara, disguised as Carlo and Pedro, avenges the death of his daughter Isabella by poisoning Brachiano, her husband-murderer, and by having Zanche, Flamineo, and Vittoria, the white devil, stabbed to death.

***Widsith*** (p. 9). Widsith, a scop, professes to tell how he fared forth over Europe and Asia, sojourning among the tribes, chanting in their mead-halls, and receiving rich gifts from the chieftains. Always, he says, the singer finds a princely welcome, for these Kings know that the scop's songs perpetuate fame. (The Kings and the places mentioned are partly historical, partly mythical, or unidentified.)

***Wife of Bath's Tale, The*** (p. 74). To stay his execution for violating a maid, a knight of King Arthur's court must, within the year, find the answer to the question, "What thyng is it that wommen most desiren?" Finally, to save his life, for the answer he pledges to grant anything within his power to a foul hag, who tells him that women like best to have their own way (thus exemplifying the Wife of Bath's theory of sovereignty over one's husband, as stated in the Prologue to her tale). Now that his execution is thereby stayed, the ugly dame requests that the knight marry her. He does so, somewhat reluctantly; but at his first kiss she is transformed into a young, beautiful maid.

***Wife of Usher's Well, The*** (p. 101). At daybreak vanish the ghosts of three sons who had appeared before their mother on the preceding night.

***Woman in the Moone, The*** (p. 151). In creating Pandora, Nature endows her with the respective qualities of the Seven Planets, such as the amorousness of Venus and the battling-spirit of Mars. Soon the shepherds of Utopia are avoiding a woman whose moods and actions vary so drastically, and finally Pandora makes her abode in the changeable moon.

***Woman Kilde with Kindnesse, A*** (p. 239). John Frankford finds his essentially virtuous but weak-willed wife Anne and his friend Wendoll "close in each other's arms, and fast asleep." He orders her to live in a manor seven miles away, and in no way ever to communicate with him and their two children. On her death-bed Frankford forgives his remorseful wife and with a kiss weds her once again. This epitaph goes on her tomb: *"Here lies she whom her husband's kindness kill'd."*

***Young Waters*** (p. 101). The Queen becomes enamored of Young Waters, and therefore the King has him killed.

# INDEX

The aim of this *Index* is to cover all *substantial* references to authors, works, events, periods, and the like. No attempt is made to direct the reader to every subject and to every proper name mentioned in the OUTLINE-HISTORY. Note, especially, the omission in this *Index* of the authors included in the *Supplementary List of Writers* (pages I-XIII) and the hundreds of titles in the final chapter (pages 581-600).



See Volume II for all references from page 292 on.

---

See Volume II for all references from page 292 on.

See Volume II for all references from page 292 on.

See Volume II for all references from page 292 on.

See Volume II for all references from page 292 on.

See Volume II for all references from page 292 on.

See Volume II for all references from page 292 on.

See Volume II for all references from page 292 on.

See Volume II for all references from page 292 on.

---

See Volume II for all references from page 292 on.

See Volume II for all references from page 292 on.

See Volume II for all references from page 292 on.

See Volume II for all references from page 292 on.

---

See Volume II for all references from page 292 on.

See Volume II for all references from page 292 on.

See Volume II for all references from page 292 on.

---

See Volume II for all references from page 292 on.

---

See Volume II for all references from page 292 on.

See Volume II for all references from page 292 on.

See Volume II for all references from page 292 on.

---

See Volume II for all references from page 292 on.

See Volume II for all references from page 292 on.

See Volume II for all references from page 292 on.

See Volume II for all references from page 292 on.

See Volume II for all references from page 292 on.

---

See Volume II for all references from page 292 on.

See Volume II for all references from page 292 on.

See Volume II for all references from page 292 on.